TH

Sicily

This ninth edition updated by

Ros Belford

ROUGH
GUIDES

roughguides.com

Contents

Introduction to
Sicily

To say that Sicily isn't Italy is trite but true – only 3km of water separate the island from the Italian mainland, but the historical and cultural gulf is far wider. The locals see themselves as Sicilians first and Italians a very firm second, a difference that is celebrated at every turn. On this strategically located island at the heart of the Mediterranean, some of the western world's greatest civilizations have left their indelible mark, from ancient temples to stunning mosaic-decorated churches. The distinct Sicilian language thrives, while many place names are derived from the Arabic that was once in wide use across the island, and markets brim with produce that speaks firmly of the south – oranges, lemons, olives, rice, almonds and peppers.

Moreover, the historic combination of island mentality and wild, lawless, mountainous interior has fostered an "us-and-them" attitude that still defines the relationship between modern-day Sicily and Italy. The island was probably the most reluctantly unified of all Italian regions back in the nineteenth century, with Sicilians unsurprisingly suspicious of the intentions of the latest in a long line of rulers – Phoenicians, Greeks, Romans, Arabs, Normans, Angevins and Spanish. For many Sicilians, their place in the modern Italian state is illustrated every time they look at a map to see the island being kicked – the perpetual football.

And Sicilians do have a point. Pockets of the island have been disfigured by bleak construction projects and unsightly industry, and despite Sicily's limited political autonomy, little has really been done to tackle the more deep-rooted problems: youth unemployment is at an all-time high, emigration of the brightest on the rise, poverty is seemingly endemic and there's an almost feudal attitude to business and commerce. Aid and investment pour in, but much is still siphoned off by the Mafia. Visitors, of course, see little of this. Mafia activity, for example – almost a byword for Sicilian life when viewed from abroad – is usually an in-house affair, with little or no consequence for travellers.

ABOVE RUINS AT SELINUNTE

FACT FILE

- Sicily is the largest island in the Mediterranean, with extensive areas of **mountains** in the north and east, the highest being Mount Etna (3323m) – Europe's biggest active volcano. Apart from Etna's sporadic eruptions, Sicily is also prone to seismic upheavals – massive **earthquakes** destroyed the southeast from Catania to Ragusa in 1693, Messina in 1908, and rocked the western part of the island in 1966.

- Sicily has a semi-autonomous status within the Italian republic, with its own **parliament** and **president**, and limited legislative powers in such areas as tourism, transport, industry and the environment. There is no **separatist movement** to speak of, though suspicion of central government runs deep.

- Compared to north Italy, the **economy** has remained relatively underdeveloped. Though there are pockets of industrial activity, Sicily is mainly **agricultural**. However, the sector has suffered considerable setbacks over recent years, while local fishermen struggle with quota restrictions and competition from international mega-boats that hoover up vast shoals of tuna. These days, **tourism** plays an increasingly crucial role in the Sicilian economy.

- One of the most densely populated islands in the Mediterranean, Sicily's **population** is something over five million, with settlement mainly concentrated in the two cities of Palermo and Catania, on the northern and eastern coasts.

- Disregard for **regulations** long accepted in the rest of Europe is rife in Sicily, and this anarchic approach to the law manifests in myriad ways. Thanks to the local distaste for wearing **seat belts**, most garages now stock a device designed to override car safety systems and save drivers the irritation of bleeping belt alerts.

What Sicily does offer is a remarkably fresh Mediterranean experience. Its main resorts and famous archeological sites have attracted visitors for many years, but budget airline routes have opened up lesser-known parts of this fascinating island, while boutique accommodation and sustainable tourism projects have mushroomed in recent years. The rewards are immediate, notably the dramatic landscapes that range from pin-prick outlying islands to the volcanic heights of Mount Etna. Much of the island is underpopulated, and outside the few tourist zones crowds are rare – which means plenty of opportunity to make your own personal discoveries: dazzling white- and black-sand beaches, sparkling coves, rolling wheat plains, upland wildflower meadows and precarious mountain passes. Sicily was an important powerbase during Greek and Roman times, and its excavated ancient cities and temples especially are superb, standing comparison with any ruins in Greece itself. There are stunning Arab and Norman palaces, churches and castles across the island, while the devastation wrought by the great earthquake of 1693 provided a blank slate for some of the most harmonious Baroque architecture to be seen in Europe.

Perhaps above all, there's a distinct way of day-to-day living that separates Sicily from the rest of Italy – an almost operatic exuberance that manifests itself in some extraordinarily vibrant festivals and celebrations. You're unlikely to forget the intensity of the Sicilian experience, whether you're shopping for swordfish in a raucous souk-like market, catching a concert in a dramatic open-air Greek theatre, bathing in a hidden hot spring or island-hopping by hydrofoil across azure seas.

CLOCKWISE FROM TOP PIAZZA XI APRILE, TAORMINA; NECROPOLIS, PANTALICA; PANAREA

Where to go

Set in a wide bay at the foot of a fertile valley, the capital, **Palermo**, is an essential part of any Sicilian visit, with a vibrant – almost Middle Eastern – flavour and featuring some of the island's finest churches, historic treasures, markets and restaurants. It gets hot and stuffy here in summer, though, which makes escapes out of the city all the more tempting, above all to the offshore island of **Ustica**, or to the extraordinary church mosaics at **Monreale**. An hour east of Palermo, meanwhile, lies one of Sicily's premier resorts, **Cefalù**, with its own fabulous church mosaics. Cefalù is also the jumping-off point for the **Madonie** natural park, whose mountains are the highest on the island after Etna.

Ferries and hydrofoils depart from Milazzo and Messina to the **Aeolians**, a stunning chain of seven volcanic islands – including the famed Stromboli – that attract

ICE CREAM

Eating a genuine Sicilian **ice cream** is one of the world's most voluptuous gastronomic experiences, a melt-in-the-mouth sensation that suffuses your tastebuds with the unadulterated essence of mandarin, almond, rose or whichever locally grown fruit, nut or flower the *gelataio* has decided is at its prime.

The art of ice cream making is around a thousand years old here – the Arabs brought with them the technique of making sherbet or *sharbat* by blending fruit syrups and flower essences with snow taken from Mount Etna and other mountains. It seems probable that it was a resourceful Sicilian who got the idea of making a good thing better, freezing a mixture of milk, sugar or honey. By the sixteenth century ices were all the rage at the trendsetting French court of Catherine de' Medici, who imported a Sicilian into her kitchen with the sole job of making ice creams, *granite* and sorbets.

By the eighteenth century ices were so popular that virtually the entire revenue of the Bishop of Catania came from selling the snow of Mount Etna. Years when snowfall was scant or nonexistent provoked civil unrest during the steamy summers: in 1777 a boat rumoured to be carrying snow was attacked and its precious cargo seized by Siracusans desperate for ice cream.

Ices and ice creams were loved by rich and poor alike: at a banquet in eighteenth-century Palermo, 5000kg of snow were needed to keep the 300 guests in constant supply of frozen refreshment, while at the other end of the scale, street vendors throughout the island ensured that ice cream could be enjoyed by all but the very poorest, selling it by the spoonful to those who could afford no more.

CATACOMBS, CAVES AND HOLES IN THE GROUND

Sicily is home to some of the world's creepiest tourist destinations, in the form of its **catacombs** and **caves**, used as burial places for thousands of years and accessible to anyone with a torch and a strong nerve. The oldest, the rock-cut tombs of the great necropolis at **Pantalica**, were first used in the thirteenth century BC. Another huge swathe of tombs is on view below the Greek temples at **Agrigento**, while catacombs riddle the ground in the city of **Siracusa**. But for sheer hands-in-the-air horror, there's no beating the infamous preserved bodies that line the catacombs of Palermo's **Convento dei Cappuccini**, or the smaller-scale show in the little village of **Savoca**, near Taormina. Bodies were placed here as late as the nineteenth century, and the locals used to pay daily visits, often standing in the adjacent niches to accustom themselves to the idea of the great ever-after.

sun-worshippers, celebrities and adventurous hikers alike. Otherwise, the northeastern tip of the island is marked by the bustling city of **Messina** – crossing-point to mainland Italy – with the fashionable resort of **Taormina** to the south, the latter perhaps the single most popular holiday destination in Sicily. Further south, halfway down the Ionian coast, dark, Baroque **Catania** is the island's second city, dominated entirely by the graceful cone of **Mount Etna**, Europe's largest and most active volcano.

The island's best concentration of historical and architectural sites is arguably in **Siracusa**, where classical ruins and stunning Baroque buildings decorate Sicily's most attractive city. In the southeast region beyond, beautiful towns like **Noto**, **Ragusa** and **Modica** were rebuilt along planned Baroque lines after the devastating 1693 earthquake, though the unique Neolithic cemeteries of **Pantalica** survived to provide one of Sicily's most atmospheric backwaters.

After the richness of the southeast towns, many find the isolated grandeur of the interior a welcome change. This is the most sparsely populated region, of rolling hills and craggy mountains, yet it hides gems like the historic stronghold of **Enna**, the well-preserved Roman mosaics at **Piazza Armerina**, the majestic Greek excavations of **Morgantina** and the Baroque ceramics town of **Caltagirone**. Away from these few interior towns, remote roads wind back and forth, towards Palermo or Catania, through little-visited destinations like **Corleone**, whose names chime with the popular image of Sicily as a nest of Mafia intrigue.

Along the south coast, only the spectacular ancient temples of **Agrigento** and the Greek city and beach at **Eraclea Minoa** attract visitors in any numbers. Further around the coast, the up-and-coming city of **Trapani** anchors the west of the island, a great base for anyone interested in delving into the very different character of this side of Sicily. The Arabic influence is stronger here than elsewhere, especially in **Marsala** and **Mazara del Vallo**, while **Selinunte** and **Segesta** hold the island's most romantic sets of ancient ruins. It's from ports on the south and west coasts, too, that Sicily's most absorbing outlying islands are reached. On **Lampedusa**, on the **Egadi Islands** and, above all, on distant **Pantelleria**, the sea is as clean as you'll find anywhere in the Mediterranean, and you truly feel you're on the edge of Europe.

When to go

Sicily can be an extremely uncomfortable place to visit at the height of summer, when the dusty *scirocco* winds blow in from North Africa. In **July** and **August**, you'll roast – and you'll be in the company of tens of thousands of other tourists all jostling for space on the beaches, in the restaurants and at the archeological sites. Hotel availability is much reduced and prices will often be higher. If you want the heat but not the crowds, go in May, June or September, while swimming is possible right into November.

Spring is really the optimum time to come to Sicily, and it arrives early: the almond blossom flowers in early February, and there are fresh strawberries in April. **Easter** is a major celebration, a good time to see traditional festivals like the events at Trapani, Erice, Scicli and Piana degli Albanesi, though again they'll all be over-subscribed with visitors.

Winter is mild by northern European standards and is a nice time to be here, at least on the coast, where the skies stay clear and life continues to be lived very much outdoors. On the other hand, the interior – especially around Enna – is very liable to get snowed under, providing skiing opportunities in the Monti Madonie or on Mount Etna, while anywhere else in the interior can be subject to blasts of wind and torrential downpours of rain.

AVERAGE DAYTIME TEMPERATURES

	Jan	Feb	Mar	Apr	May	Jun	Jul	Aug	Sep	Oct	Nov	Dec
PALERMO												
°C	10.3	10.4	13	16.2	18.7	23	25.3	25.1	23.2	19.9	16.8	12.6
TAORMINA												
°C	11	10.6	13.1	16.2	20.1	24.1	27.1	27.1	23.7	20	16	12.6

Author picks

Our authors have explored every corner of the island over several decades and here share some of their top tips, favourite sights, hidden gems and quintessential Sicilian experiences.

Unspoilt beaches Head for the wild sands of the nature reserves at Vendicari (p.240), Marinello (p.110) or Zingaro (p.317), or to the long dune-fringed strands at Sampieri (p.251) and Torre Salsa (p.293).

Ancient places When the Greeks ruled Sicily it was the most powerful centre in the Mediterranean. Outstanding among relics from this time are the Valley of the Temples at Agrigento (p.285), the temples of Segesta (p.318) and Selinunte (p.352), and the theatres of Siracusa (p.225), Palazzolo Acreide (p.234), Tindari (p.110) and Taormina (p.170).

Hot, hot, hot Sicily is crossed by a fault line, and has three active volcanoes – Etna (p.199), Stromboli (p.146) and Vulcano (p.129). As well as visible eruptions – most reliably and regularly on Stromboli – there are other vulcanological phenomena too, from the steaming mud baths of Vulcano to emissions of underwater gases off the island of Panarea (p.140).

Baroque and roll Sicilian Baroque reaches heights of exuberance not seen elsewhere in Italy, from the chiaroscuro exotica of Catania (p.182) and the palaces of Ortigia (p.215) to the flamboyant towns of Noto (p.235), Modica (p.243), Scicli (p.245) and Ragusa (p.247).

Away from it all Come to Sicily out of season – late autumn, winter or spring – and head to the Egadi (p.333), Aeolian (p.116) or Pelagie (p.300) islands for guaranteed solitude. Or find peace inland, exploring the Madonie (p.100) or Nébrodi mountains (p.107) or the Pantalica gorge (p.232).

> Our author recommendations don't end here. We've flagged up our favourite places – a perfectly sited hotel, an atmospheric café, a special restaurant – throughout the Guide, highlighted with the ★ symbol.

FROM TOP RISERVA NATURALE DELLO ZINGARO; PARCO REGIONALE DELLE MADONIE; STROMBOLI

18

things not to miss

It's not possible to see everything Sicily has to offer in one trip – and we don't suggest you try. What follows is a selective taste of the island's highlights – extravagant architecture, dramatic landscapes, idyllic islands and exciting outdoor adventures. All the highlights have a page reference to take you straight into the Guide, where you can find out more.

1

1 MOUNT ETNA
Page 199

Climbing Europe's greatest volcano – still very active – is the ultimate Sicilian adventure trip.

2 SIRACUSA
Page 212

As well as the ruins of a magnificent ancient Greek city, Siracusa has a Baroque centre with plenty of places to sit and relax.

3 SEGESTA
Page 318

Transport yourself back in time with a visit to the dramatic Greek temple at Segesta.

4 EGADI ISLANDS
Page 333

The three west-coast Egadi Islands retain a real air of adventure, offering boat tours, fishing trips and excursions.

15

16

17

18

Itineraries

These itineraries are designed to give you a taste of Sicily's many and varied attractions. Our Grand Tour takes in unmissable historic towns, ancient sites and natural attractions; we've also picked out the most outstanding gastronomic experiences and the best destinations for a taste of adventure.

THE GRAND TOUR

Follow in the footsteps of illustrious travellers such as D.H. Lawrence, Jules Verne and Goethe and make a two-week Grand Tour of the island's highlights.

❶ Palermo See the glories left behind by Sicily's Norman rulers, such as the vibrant mosaics of the Cappella Palatina, then visit the Galleria Regionale della Sicilia to marvel at the island's best collection of medieval art, and take a trip to Monreale to revel in the jewel-box hues of the mosaics in its Duomo. **See p.56, p.61 & p.77**

❷ Cefalù Feast your eyes on magnificent mosaics in the town's cathedral, then spend a lazy afternoon on one of Sicily's finest sandy beaches. **See p.90**

❸ The Aeolian Islands Climb Stromboli, Europe's most active volcano, then wind down on the island's picture-perfect village of sparkling-white cubic houses awash with bougainvillea. **See p.146 & p.143**

❹ Taormina Spoil yourself with a night in one of the town's many historic hotels, and take a day-trip by jeep up Mount Etna. **See p.172**

❺ Siracusa Spend a couple of days in historic Ortigia, taking in masterpieces by Caravaggio and Antonello da Messina, and an ancient Greek temple converted into a cathedral. Devote another day to the Archeological Museum and beautifully preserved Greek theatre. **See p.215**

❻ Piazza Armerina Stay overnight to linger over the extensive ruins of a Roman villa, decorated with splendid mosaics. **See p.266**

❼ Agrigento Set aside at least a day to explore the Valley of the Temples, and leave time enough to see the site museum's marvellous collection of Greek black-figure pottery. Fans of crime writer Andrea Camilleri should add an extra day to see the Porto Empedocle and Agrigento locations that inspired the Montalbano novels. **See p.283**

❽ Ragusa Ibla Spend a day or two admiring some of Sicily's finest Baroque architecture, then splash out on a gourmet dinner before flying home from the new airport at nearby Comiso. **See p.247**

FOODIES' SICILY

Eating in Sicily is a gastronomic trip through time – from the indigenous vegetables that have been eaten since dwarf mammoths roamed the island, to the exotic flavours of rose-petal and jasmine flowers, cinnamon and saffron brought by the Arabs.

❶ Palermo Graze on local street food such as soft rolls stuffed with chickpea-flour fritters, or sautéed offal with ricotta and caciocavallo cheese. **See p.73**

FROM LEFT BARRACUDA, USTICA; DUOMO, CEFALÙ; MODICA CHOCOLATE

❷ Aeolian Islands Head to the island of Salina to taste malvasia wine in local cantinas, discover myriad uses for the bud of the caper flower, and sample what may well be the best *granitas* in Sicily. **See p.132**

❸ Catania Drink a fizzy seltz, made with lemon and salt or sweet fruit syrup and sold from kiosks throughout the city centre, and visit the best fish market on the island. **See p.194 & p.187**

❹ Etna Tour Etna's vineyards and look out for stalls selling tiny apples and pears, hazelnuts, chestnuts and Sicily's famous tarrocco blood oranges, grown in the volcanic soil of the plains below. **See p.204**

❺ Bronte This town in the foothills of Etna produces the best pistachios on the island. **See p.207**

❻ Noto The two outstanding *gelaterias* here are famous throughout Italy – skip lunch and sample delectable cones of saffron and basil, dark chocolate and orange, or the classic jasmine or rose petal. **See p.238**

❼ Modica Made using a technique developed by the Aztecs and introduced to Sicily by the Spanish, Modica's chocolate is powerful, gritty-textured stuff, and comes in flavours ranging from chilli to vanilla. **See p.244**

SICILY OUTDOORS

With its extensive coastline, offshore islands, volcanoes and rugged mountains, Sicily offers plenty of scope for outdoor adventures.

❶ Ustica Dive the fabulous waters around the island of Ustica to see a submarine wonderland of plants, fish and fabulous rock formations. **See p.87**

❷ Aeolian Islands Climb the active volcanoes or dive over shipwrecks and bubbles made by emissions of volcanic gas. **See p.146 & p.140**

❸ Mount Etna See Mount Etna by quad bike in summer, or go cross-country or downhill skiing in the winter. **See p.199**

❹ Gole dell'Alcantara Wade up the river that gouges between the dramatic volcanic rocks of the Alcantara Gorge. **See p.178**

❺ Cava Grande Take a trek in this marvellous gorge to discover cave-habitations, rushing streams, swimmable pools and fabulous views. **See p.239**

❻ The Vendicari Nature Reserve Take a hike in spring or autumn, when the salt lakes attract migratory birds such as flamingos. **See p.240**

CAPPELLA PALATINA, PALERMO

Basics

Getting there

Budget airlines fly direct to Sicily from all over Europe and, outside peak holiday periods, the taxes often exceed the price of the ticket. The island has two main airports, at Palermo in the west and Catania in the east, though Ryanair and others also use Trapani airport in the far west. In September 2013, a new airport opened in the southeast at Comiso, served by Ryanair flights from Stansted, Rome Ciampino and Brussels Charleroi. There are also airports on the main outlying islands of Pantelleria and Lampedusa.

No direct flights go to Sicily from the US, Canada, Australia or New Zealand: the main points of entry to Italy are Rome and Milan, from where it's easy to pick up a connection to any of the Sicilian airports. If you want to see some of France or Italy en route, or are taking a vehicle, various overland combinations of **ferry**, **rail** and **road** are possible, though these will nearly always work out pricier than flying direct. European rail passes will save you some money, but most need to be purchased before you leave. Finally, **package holidays** and **tours** can be good value – from beach breaks to escorted historical tours – while airlines, travel agents and specialist operators can all also provide car rental, hotel bookings and other useful services.

Air fares are seasonal, at their highest at Easter (a big celebration in Sicily), Christmas and New Year (as Sicilian émigrés come home), and between June and August (when the weather is hottest and the island the busiest). The **cheapest flights** from the UK and Europe are usually with no-frills budget and certain charter airlines, especially if you're prepared to book several weeks in advance or chance a last-minute deal. Budget airline tickets are sold on a one-way basis, so you may find the outward or return leg of your journey significantly more expensive depending on demand. Cheap flights also tend to have fixed dates and are non-changeable and non-refundable. Major **scheduled** airlines are usually (though not always) more expensive, but tickets remain valid for three months and usually have a degree of flexibility should you need to change dates after booking.

Flights from the UK and Ireland

There are daily **direct flights to Sicily** (around 3hr) with easyJet (London Gatwick to Palermo and Catania), Ryanair (Stansted to Palermo and Comiso, Luton and Manchester to Trapani, Stansted, Luton and Liverpool to Trapani) and British Airways (Gatwick to Catania), while Thomsonfly has a weekly seasonal service (May to Oct) from either Gatwick or Manchester to Catania. **Prices** on all routes can range from as little as £7.99 plus taxes each way to over £600 return. **From Ireland**, Ryanair offers a direct flight from Dublin to Palermo.

The alternative from the UK or Ireland is to fly to one of the many airports on the **Italian mainland**, and travel onwards from there. Ryanair alone flies to around twelve Italian airports, and uses Trapani as its Sicilian hub, easyJet flies from Milan to Catania, while Alitalia and British Airways have decent connections from Rome, Milan and others to Palermo, Catania, Trapani, Lampedusa and Pantelleria. There are also flights to Sicily with the budget and holiday airlines of other countries (like Germany) with an established tourist connection. In the end, you'll have to weigh up the extra travelling time flying via mainland Italy, or elsewhere, with the savings you might make.

Flights from the US and Canada

There are **no direct flights** from the US and Canada to Sicily, so you'll have to fly first to Rome or Milan (9 hours from east coast US/Canada, 12 hours from Chicago, 15 hours from west coast US/Canada). For the connection to Sicily add on another hour and a half or so, plus any time spent waiting for the connection itself.

Alitalia flies direct every day between the US or Canada and Italy, and their great advantage is the ease of making the connecting flight to Sicily with

---

A BETTER KIND OF TRAVEL

At Rough Guides we are passionately committed to travel. We believe it helps us understand the world we live in and the people we share it with – and of course tourism is vital to many developing economies. But the scale of modern tourism has also damaged some places irreparably, and climate change is accelerated by most forms of transport, especially flying. All Rough Guides' flights are carbon-offset, and every year we donate money to a variety of environmental charities.

the same airline. But several other airlines – including Delta and Air Canada – fly to Rome or Milan, and can arrange an onward connection for you. Or you can fly to Italy with airlines like British Airways, Air France, Lufthansa and Iberia, which travel via their respective European hubs.

Generally, the cheapest round-trip **fare** from the US to Palermo or Catania, via Rome or Milan, starts at around US$600, rising to US$1500 during the summer. From Canada, low-season fares start at around Can$800, increasing to around Can$2300 in high season. The alternative option is to pick up a discounted flight to the UK, and then fly on to Sicily with one of the European budget airlines (see p.21). It depends on how soon in advance you book, and the season, as to whether this will be a realistic way to save money. The easiest way to research the best available deals are price-comparison sites such as Ⓦskyscanner.com, Ⓦkayak.com or Ⓦedreams.com.

Flights from Australia and New Zealand

Although there are **no direct flights** from Australia or New Zealand to Sicily, many airlines offer through-tickets with their partners via European or Asian hubs. Round-trip **fares** from the main cities in Australia start from around Aus$1700 in low season, going up to around Aus$2000 in high season; from New Zealand, fares cost from NZ$3000. Fares don't vary as much between airlines as you might think, and in the end you'll be basing your choice on things like flight timings, routes and possible stop-offs on the way. If you're seeing Sicily as part of a wider European trip, you might want to aim first for the UK in any case, since there's a wider choice of cheap options to Sicily once there.

Trains

It's a long journey **from the UK to Sicily** by **train** (2672km from London to Messina). The fastest **route** (via Paris, Rome and Naples) is scheduled to take around 30 hours, but delays on the Italian stretch – especially south of Rome – are not uncommon. **Tickets** include seat reservations, though for any degree of comfort it's also worth reserving a couchette or sleeping car for the overnight part of the journey. The easiest way is to take the **Eurostar** service from London to Paris (from £70 return), then the **overnight train from Paris to Rome** (from £95 return), followed by the direct Intercity express **from**

Rome to Sicily (calling at Messina, Taormina, Catania and Siracusa, or to Palermo, from around £70 return). There's also an overnight Rome-to-Sicily service. You can book tickets online with Rail Europe and with Italian Railways – the Italian Railways site has an English-language version and posts fares and full Italian train timetables.

The invaluable train travel website Ⓦseat61 .com tells you exactly how to book the entire journey, down to precise details about the various sleeper-train options. It also has a "Railpasses" section which will help you decide whether or not buying a rail pass is a good idea. InterRail and Eurail are the best known of these, giving unlimited rail travel throughout Europe, as well as providing discounts on Eurostar and cross-Channel ferry crossings.

Buses

It's difficult to make any case for travelling to Sicily by **bus**, especially as there's no direct service from the UK. **Eurolines** has a service from London Victoria to Naples, but that takes at least 35 hours depending on connections in Paris and Milan, and then you'll have to take a second overnight bus with Italian bus company SAIS on to Sicily (another 6 hours to Messina, 10 to Palermo). Even with book-in-advance promotional fares (up to thirty days in advance), buses cost far more than the average low-cost flight.

Car and ferry

Driving to Sicily from the UK, using the standard **cross-Channel services or Eurotunnel** (Ⓦeuro tunnel.com) through the Channel Tunnel, takes at least two full days. From the France/Italy border, it's possible, with a bit of luck, to reach the Straits of Messina in a long day if you keep on the autostradas. While not a cheap option (factoring in the cross-Channel trip, tolls, overnight stops and meals), it is a good way of seeing something of France and Italy on the way.

The shortest crossing from the Italian mainland, over the Straits of Messina, is from **Villa San Giovanni by ferry** (see p.162); or, fifteen minutes further south – at the end of the motorway – by hydrofoil or fast ferry from **Reggio di Calabria** (see p.162).

To cut the driving time in Italy, you could use one of the earlier ferry or hydrofoil crossings from the Italian mainland to Sicily, **from Genoa** (to Palermo, 20hr), **Salerno** (to Palermo, 12hr, or Messina, 8hr),

Civitavecchia (near Rome, to Palermo, 12hr and Termini Imerese, 13hr) or **Naples** (to Palermo 11hr, or Aeolian Islands from 10 hours by ferry (year-round), 4–6hr by hydrofoil in summer). Non-drivers could even combine a cheap flight (say Ryanair to Genoa) with one of these ferry crossings. You can also approach Sicily by travelling **via Corsica or Sardinia**, though obviously this is a somewhat complicated route involving two lengthy crossings – it's not recommended for a short trip to Sicily. The Genoa, Salerno and Naples crossing schedules are seasonal, and with several different operators, but there are daily sailings in summer and at least two or three per week throughout the year. The best places to check schedules and fares, and book tickets, are the exhaustive websites **W directferries .co.uk** and **W viamare.com**, which contain details about every Italian ferry service.

Airlines, agents and operators

AIRLINES

Air Canada W aircanada.com
Alitalia W alitalia.com
British Airways W ba.com
Delta W delta.com
easyJet W easyjet.com
Ryanair W ryanair.com
Thomsonfly W thomsonfly.com

DISCOUNT FLIGHT AGENTS

North South Travel UK T 01245 608 291, W northsouthtravel .co.uk. Friendly, competitive travel agency, offering discounted fares worldwide. Profits are used to support projects in the developing world, especially the promotion of sustainable tourism.
STA Travel UK T 0871 2300 040, US T 1800 781 4040, Australia T 134 782, New Zealand T 0800 474 400, South Africa T 0861 781 781, W statravel.com. Worldwide specialists in independent travel; also student IDs, travel insurance, car rental, rail passes, and more. Good discounts for students and under-26s.
Trailfinders UK T 0845 058 5858, Republic of Ireland T 01 677 7888, Australia T 1300 780 212, W trailfinders.com. One of the best-informed and most efficient agents for independent travellers.

TOUR OPERATORS

ART AND CULTURE

Martin Randall Travel UK T 0208 742 3355, W martinrandall .com. Small-group cultural tours, led by experts on art, history, archeology and music, to the classic sites of Sicily. Tours depart two or three times a year, costing from £3780 for twelve days, including flights, meals and transport.
Tabona and Walford UK T 0208 767 6789, W tabonaandwal ford.com. Tailor-made as well as itinerary-based cultural walking holidays in Erice and the Egadi Islands or the Madonie and Lipari, with

bike and market excursions, vineyard visits, cooking courses, language lessons and other activities. From around £900.

FOOD AND DRINK

Arblaster & Clarke UK T 01730 263 111, W arblasterandclarke .com. Deluxe seven-night wine cruises around Sicily and its offshore islands for £5250 including flights, meals and tastings, plus an expert guide.
The International Kitchen US T 1800 945 8606, W theinternationalkitchen.com. Six-night all-inclusive Sicilian culinary tours and cooking school holidays, from US$2750, with winery and market visits included. Bases include Palermo, Agrigento, Modica and Palermo.
Italian Connection Canada T 1800 462 7911, W italian -connection.com. The "Experience Sicily" walking and culinary tour (seven days, from US$4990) ranges across the island from east to west. More specialized tours and one-day walking and cooking excursions (from US$260) are all accompanied by local experts.

GENERAL

Citalia UK T 0800 232 1802, W citalia.com. Italian holiday specialist, offering short breaks, resort holidays, tailor-made island tours, villas and car rental.
CIT Holidays Australia T 1300 361 500, W cit.com.au. Italian travel specialists, offering Sicily tours, hotel reservations, car rental and rail passes.
Italiatours US T 1800 283 7262, W italiatours.com. Low-cost Italy specialist with a range of escorted bus-tour programmes, from three days to a week exploring the island highlights (from US$1161). Also hotel bookings, flights and transfers.

SAILING

Nautilus Yachting UK T 01732 867 445, W nautilus-yachting .co.uk. Yacht holidays, operating out of Sant'Agata di Militello and Portorosa (for the Aeolians) and Marsala (the Egadis). Prices start from £1150 for the boat for a week, though if you have no experience you can add the services of a skipper for €1000 per week.

WALKING

Adventure Center US T 1800 228 8747, W adventurecenter.com. The worldwide adventure and hiking specialist has an eight-day "Sicilian Volcano Hike" walking tour that ranges from Etna to the Aeolian Islands, from US$1490; a Mount Etna walking weekend for US$960; and a nine-day cycling tour of the west starting from Scopello for US$2249.
Alternative Travel Group UK T 01865 315 678, W atg-oxford .co.uk. Eight-day walking holidays (April–June & Sept/Oct) in the Monti Madonie, from Enna to Cefalù. Accommodation is mostly two- and three-star standard, and prices start at £2175 for a fully inclusive escorted programme.
Ramblers Worldwide Holidays UK T 01707 331 133, W ramblersholidays.co.uk. Eight-day walking holidays (including flights, accommodation and food) based in Francavilla (near Taormina) for seeing eastern Sicily (from around £665), or a twelve-day touring holiday of the island taking in Siracusa, Selinunte, Agrigento and Palermo (from around £1235). Weekly departures Feb, March–May, Sept, Oct & Dec.

RAIL CONTACTS

Eurostar UK ☎ 08432 186 186, outside the UK ☎ +44 (0)1233 617 575, ⓦ eurostar.com
Rail Europe UK ☎ 0844 848 4078, US ☎ 1800 622 8600, Canada ☎ 1800 361 7245, ⓦ raileurope.co.uk
Italian Railways ☎ 892021, ⓦ trenitalia.com

BUS CONTACTS

Eurolines UK ☎ 0871 781 8178, Textphone for UK customers who are deaf ☎ 0121 455 0086, ⓦ eurolines.com.
SAIS ☎ 091 617 1141, ⓦ saistrasporti.it

STAMP IT

All stations have yellow **validating machines** in which passengers must stamp their ticket before embarking on their journey. Look out for them as you come onto the platform: if you fail to **validate your ticket** you'll be given a hefty on-the-spot fine. Note that if your ticket is booked for a specific train, validation is not necessary – but if in doubt, ask.

Getting around

You don't have to rent a car to see Sicily's major towns and sights, but getting around by public transport is not always as easy as it should be. The rail system is slow, few buses run on Sundays and route information can be frustratingly difficult to extract, even from the bus and train stations themselves. On the positive side, public transport prices are reasonable.

The "Arrival and departure" sections in this book give the full picture on transport schedules and frequencies. Note that unless specified, these refer to regular working-day schedules, ie Monday to Saturday; services are much reduced, or even nonexistent, on Sundays. Note also that comments such as "every 30min" are approximations – on the railways in particular, there are occasional gaps in the schedule, typically occurring just after the morning rush hour, when the gap between trains may be twice as long as normal.

One thing to bear in mind is that travelling by train is not the best way to see all of the island. Some stations are located a fair distance from their towns – Enna and Taormina are two notable examples (though there are bus connections) – while much of the west and centre of Sicily is only accessible by bus or car.

By train

Italian State Railways, **Ferrovie dello Stato** (**FS**), operates the trains in Sicily though a private railway, the Ferrovia Circumetnea, operates a route around the base of Mount Etna (see p.200). The FS website ⓦ **trenitalia.com** has a useful English-language version, where you can view timetables and book tickets. Trains connect all the major Sicilian towns, but are more prevalent in the east of the island than the west. On the whole they do leave on time, with the notable exception of those on the Messina–Palermo and Messina–Catania/Siracusa routes that have come from the mainland. These latter can be delayed by up to three hours, though around an hour late is more normal.

Of the various types of train, the most expensive are the **Intercity** (**IC**) trains that link the main cities. **Diretto** and **Interregionale** trains are long-distance expresses, calling only at larger stations, while the **Regionale** services (also called **Locale**), which stop at every place with a population higher than zero, are usually ones to avoid. A **seat reservation** (*prenotazione*) is obligatory on Intercity services and advisable on other trains where possible, especially in summer when trains can get crowded. You can buy tickets and make reservations at any major train station, or buy online on the FS website (both regional and Intercity services) and print your own tickets. **Fares** are very reasonable – a typical journey, say Palermo to Catania, costs around €16. Children aged 4–12 pay half price, while the under-4s travel free provided they do not occupy a seat. If you jump on the train without a ticket you'll pay the full fare plus a fine to the conductor.

Information boards and **timetables** are displayed at stations. "Departures" are *Partenze*, "Arrivals" *Arrivi*, "Delayed" *In Ritardo*, while some services are seasonal (*periodico*) or only operate between certain dates (*Si effetua dal… al…*). *Feriale* is the word for the Monday-to-Saturday service, symbolized by two crossed hammers; *festivo* means that a train runs only on Sundays and holidays, with a cross as its symbol.

Unless you're visiting Sicily as part of a wider Italian or European tour, the major pan-European **rail passes** (InterRail and Eurail) are not worth considering. Both schemes do also have single-country Italy rail passes, but given the relative cheapness of local train tickets, and the restricted service in some parts of Sicily, buying one of these probably won't save you any money either.

By bus

Almost anywhere you want to go will have some kind of **regional bus** (*autobus* or *pullman*) service, usually quicker than the train (especially between the major towns and cities), but generally more expensive.

Between them, four main **companies** – SAIS Trasporti (W saistrasporti.it), SAIS Autolinee (W sais autolinee.it), AST (W aziendasicilianatrasporti.it) and Interbus (W interbus.it) – cover most of the island. Other companies stick to local routes. Many routes are linked to school/market requirements, which can mean a frighteningly early start, last departures in the early afternoon, and occasionally no services during school holidays, while nearly everywhere services are drastically reduced, or nonexistent, on Sundays.

The local **bus station** (*autostazione*) is often in a central piazza, or outside the train station, though in some towns different bus companies have different bus terminals. **Timetables** are available on the companies' websites, and also from company offices and bus stations. You usually buy tickets on the bus, and increasingly online, something worth doing for a longer route, such as Messina to Rome, for which tickets often sell out. On most routes, it's possible to flag a bus down if you want a ride. If you want to get off, ask "*posso scendere?*"; "the next stop" is "*la prossima fermata*".

City buses usually charge a flat **fare** of €1–€1.80, and the tickets are often valid for ninety minutes, allowing you to change services for free within that time. Invariably, you need a **ticket** before you get on. Buy them in *tabacchi*, or from the kiosks and vendors at bus stops, and then validate them in the machine in the bus. Checks are frequently made by inspectors who block both exits as they get on, though if you don't have a ticket you'll usually get off with an earful of Sicilian and be made to buy one; some inspectors might hold out for the spot fine. Several cities, including Agrigento and Palermo, now allow passengers to buy tickets on board at a slightly higher price.

By car, scooter and quad

Driving in Sicily is almost a competitive sport, and although the Sicilians aren't the world's worst drivers they don't win any safety prizes either. However, with a car you'll be able to see a lot of the island quickly, and reach the more isolated coastal and inland areas.

Most **main roads** are prefixed SS (Strada Statale) or SP (Strada Provinciale), and signposting is pretty good. On the whole they are two-lane roads with passing places on hills, though some stretches near towns and cities are dual carriageway. **Road maintenance**, however, is very patchy and even major routes can be badly potholed. In the interior, on long routes like the SS120, SS121 or SS189, you should expect road washouts, resurfacing work and other interruptions on any journey.

Some roads provide spectacular cross-country driving routes (see box below), as do the impressive Sicilian **motorways** (autostrada), which are carried on great piers spanning the island. These link Messina–Catania–Siracusa (A18), Catania–Palermo (A19), Palermo–Trapani/Mazara del Vallo (A29) and Messina–Palermo (A20), while work continues on extending the autostradas network towards Agrigento and Gela (it has so far reached Rosolini). The Messina–Catania–Siracusa and Messina–Palermo autostradas are **toll-roads** (*pedaggio*, toll; *autostrada a pedaggio*, toll-motorway). Take a ticket as you come on, and pay on exit; the amount due is flashed up on a screen.

Rules of the road are straightforward: drive on the right; at junctions, where there's any ambiguity, give precedence to vehicles coming from the right; observe the speed limits (50km/h in built-up areas, 110km/h on country roads, 130km/h on autostradas); and don't drink and drive. Speed cameras and traffic-calming humps are becoming more evident, but this doesn't seem to deter Sicilians from travelling at any speed they choose.

SICILY'S SIX BEST DRIVES

SS120, Nicosia to Polizzi Generosa Bare landscape punctuated by isolated hilltop villages, with Etna dominating the eastern horizon.

SS185, Tyrrhenian coast to Taormina Across the Peloritani mountains to Etna and the sea.

Avola to Cava Grande Winding up the mountainside to where eagles dare.

SP624 and SP5, Palermo to Piana degli Albanesi Past jagged fangs and towers of rock, with glimpses of lakes and lingering views over fertile valleys.

Trapani to Erice For the startling interplay of coast and mountain.

SS118, Agrigento to Corleone Remote western valleys and crags, rock tombs and Mafia towns.

THE SICILIAN DRIVING EXPERIENCE

If all you had to do was drive on Sicilian **motorways** – light traffic, fast travel, dramatic scenery – things would be fine. Unfortunately, you have to come off them sooner or later and drive into a town, and then all bets are off. The good news is that the swirling town **traffic** isn't as horrific as it first looks – the secret is to make it *very* clear what you're going to do, using your horn as much as your indicators and brakes. There are established **rules** of the road in force, though Sicilians, needless to say, ignore most, if not all, of them as a matter of principle. A character in Andrea Camilleri's Inspector Montalbano novels drives "like a dog on drugs", which is a pretty fair assessment of local driving skills, and if you go your entire holiday without being cut up on the inside, jumped at a junction or overtaken on a blind bend, you'll have done well.

You'll switch your satnav off the first time you encounter a Sicilian **one-way system** – installed by traffic engineers with a sense of humour – which lead you into old-town areas where the streets grow ever narrower until the point that you can't back out or turn round. It usually works out fine if you rigidly follow the one-way signs, though matters aren't helped by it being accepted local **parking** practice simply to drive your car up on the pavement, or stop where it's most convenient for the driver – this can include the middle of the street, or pausing for a chat with a mate at a major road junction. Out in the **countryside** it's generally less of a hassle, though you do have to allow for shepherds and their sheep (and there aren't many places in Europe you can still say that about) idling around the next bend.

Pedestrians, meanwhile, deal with the general mayhem by taking a deep breath, staring straight at the drivers and strolling boldly across the road. If in doubt, follow someone old and infirm, or put out your hand policeman-like, but *never* assume that you're safe on a pedestrian crossing – they're regarded by most drivers as an invitation to play human skittles.

Italian **fuel prices** are roughly in line with those in the UK, with unleaded petrol (*senza piombo*) slightly cheaper than leaded (*super*). Blue lines in towns signify authorized **parking zones**, where you'll pay around €1 an hour, either in a meter or to an attendant hovering nearby. You can also often buy a *biglietto parcheggio*, a scratch card, from *tabacchi* or local bars, where you scratch off the date and time and leave it in the windscreen. However, if you've parked in a street that turns into a market by day, you'll be stuck until close of business, while if you park in a *zona di rimozione* (tow-away zone), your car will most likely not be there when you get back. Most cities also have official **car parks** and garages, charging between €10 and €15 a day. **Never leave anything visible in the car** when you leave it (hide away or remove MP3 players and satnavs), and always depress your aerial and tuck in the wing mirrors.

To drive in Sicily, you need a valid **driving licence** and, if you are a non-EU licence holder, an international driving permit. It's compulsory to carry your car documents and passport while you're driving, and you'll be required to present them if you're stopped by the police – not an uncommon occurrence. You are also required to carry a triangular danger sign, which will be provided with rental cars. Many car insurance policies cover taking your own car to Italy; check with your insurer when planning your trip (you'll need an international green card of

insurance). You'd also be advised to take out extra cover for motoring assistance in case you break down, and **motoring organizations** like the RAC (W rac.co.uk) or the AA (W theaa.co.uk) can help. Alternatively, by dialling ☎116 you can get 24-hour assistance from the Automobile Club d'Italia (W aci.it).

Car rental

Car rental in Sicily starts at around €200 per week for a three-door, a/c Fiat Punto, with unlimited mileage. It's usually cheaper arranged in advance through an online broker (though watch out for hidden extras), with your travel agent or tour operator, or through a large international chain such as Avis, Budget, Europcar, Hertz, Holiday Autos and Thrifty – check their websites for online-only deals and special offers. Otherwise, rental agencies – including local companies like Maggiore (W maggiore.it) – are found in the major cities and at Palermo, Catania, Trapani and Comiso airports.

It's essential to check that you have adequate **insurance cover** for a rental car. Going by the dents and scratches on almost every car on the road, you want to make sure that your liability is limited as far as possible. Ensure that all visible damage on a car is duly marked on the rental sheet. It's worth paying the extra charge to reduce the "excess" payment levied for any damage, and most rental companies these days offer a zero-excess option for an extra charge. You can also avoid excess charges by taking out an annual insurance policy (from £38.99) with ⓦinsurance4carhire.com, which also covers windscreen and tyre damage.

Scooters, quads and mokes

Virtually everyone in Sicily – kids to grandmas – rides a **moped or scooter**, although the smaller models are not suitable for any kind of long-distance travel. They're ideal for shooting around towns, and you can rent them in Taormina, Cefalù and other holiday centres – check the Guide for details. Crash helmets are compulsory, though you'll see many Sicilian youths just riding with one slung over one arm. Lampedusa and other minor islands also have **quad-bikes** and **mini-mokes** available for rent, which are great for bashing around local roads to beaches and beauty spots – just be aware that there's a high accident rate with machines like these.

Taxis

There are plenty of honest, reliable taxi drivers in Sicily, but as ever there are a few sharks; to be on the safe side, always establish a price before you set off. Although meters are supposed to be used by law, both passengers and drivers usually prefer to settle on a fee before setting out. **Fares** for long-distance journeys are published by each city – for example, the official rate from Siracusa to Catania airport is €70, though you may be able to negotiate. A day-tour by taxi, say taking in Siracusa, Piazza Armerina and the temples of Agrigento will cost around €250.

By ferry and hydrofoil

There are **ferries** (*traghetti*) and **hydrofoils** (*aliscafi*) to the Aeolians, the Egadi and Pelagie islands, and Pantelleria and Ustica, and there's also a summer hydrofoil service from Palermo to the Aeolians. The main **operators** are Siremar (ⓦsiremar.it), SNAV (ⓦsnav.it), NGI (ⓦngi-spa.it) and Ustica Lines (ⓦusticalines.it), and you'll find full details of services, schedules and fares in the relevant sections of the Guide. Timetables also available online, pinned up at the dockside or available from the ferry offices and tourist offices.

You can **island-hop** year-round in the Aeolians and Egadis. Services are busy in summer, making early booking advisable, though you should always be able to get on a ferry if you just turn up. Both passenger and **car-ferry** services operate, though non-resident vehicles are banned on several islands during the summer. In fact, it's debatable how much you'll need a car on any of the islands – only Lipari, Pantelleria and Lampedusa are of any size, and in any case you can rent a vehicle there if you need to.

By plane

If you're short on time, consider flying to **Lampedusa** or **Pantelleria** from Trapani, Palermo or Catania – otherwise, the alternative is an overnight ferry ride. Flights are with Darwin Airline (ⓦdarwinairline.com), and prices start at around €60 one-way – check the website for timetables and the latest offers.

Accommodation

On the whole, accommodation in Sicily is slightly cheaper than in the rest of Italy, starting at around €60 a night for a basic double or twin room (though prices can double in summer in the most popular resorts). The only accommodation cheaper than this comes in the form of the very few youth hostels and the many campsites across the island. Hotels run across the entire range, from crumbling townhouses to five-star palaces, and restored country villas to resort hotels. There's also a large number of "bed and breakfast" places and "*agriturismo*" rural properties, where the attraction is mixing with your hosts and experiencing something of Sicilian life.

All hotel accommodation is officially graded and the tariffs fixed by law. In tourist areas, there's often a low-season and high-season **price**, but whatever it costs, the rate should be posted on the door of the

---

ACCOMMODATION PRICES

The prices quoted in this book are for the establishment's **cheapest double room in high season** – there may well be other rooms that cost more. For much of the year, however, you can expect to pay a lot less, especially as internet booking becomes the norm (hence with prices based on availability rather than season).

Prices are for the room only, except where otherwise indicated; fancier places often include breakfast in the price – we indicate this in the listing, but check when booking.

ACCOMMODATION ALTERNATIVES

CouchSurfing ⓦcouchsurfing.org
Vacation Rentals by Owner ⓦvrbo.com
Airbnb ⓦairbnb.com
Crashpadder ⓦcrashpadder.com

room. In summer (usually in August) some places – especially in major resorts or on outlying islands – insist on half-board accommodation (*mezza pensione*, full-board *pensione completa*), when the price will also include lunch or dinner, and there may even be a three-night or longer minimum stay. Few single rooms are available anywhere and, in high season especially, lone travellers will often pay most of the price of a double. B&Bs are also regulated by law, but such is their proliferation that many – while offering a perfectly fine experience – operate outside the tax regime and may not be interested in seeing your passport or providing you with a receipt. **Breakfast** is usually included in the price in hotels (save perhaps in the very cheapest places), but not when you stay in *afittacamere* ("rooms") places or apartments – while, sometimes, in "bed and breakfast" places, you'll be given a voucher instead for breakfast at a nearby bar.

Hotels

Sicilian hotels are known by various titles (*pensione*, *albergo* – plural *alberghi* – or even simply "hotel") and are graded with one to five stars. Some cheaper hotels, especially in town centres, are located in old mansion buildings or palaces, which can be characterful places to stay. However, not all have been modernized, so plumbing, heating and decor might occasionally be on the primitive side, and they probably won't take credit cards either.

Official star ratings still exist, although with the rise in B&B accommodation, boutique hotels and *affitcamere*, they have become almost irrelevant, and are not by any means always displayed. Facilities in a one-star hotel tend to be minimal (there are exceptions), but once you're up to three-star level (€90–120) you can expect an en-suite room with satellite TV, air conditioning and, increasingly, internet and wi-fi. Four-star hotels, plus hotels in resorts and on islands, can charge pretty much what they like, especially in August when room prices can top €300, while the dozen or so five-star hotels on the island (notably in Palermo, Taormina, Siracusa and the Aeolian Islands) charge international rates. There are some bargains around out of the summer season, when even the classier hotels drop their room rates by as much as forty percent, and in cheaper places you might be able to negotiate a lower rate for a longer stay (ask "*Cè uno sconto per due/tre/quattro notti?*").

In the cheaper places especially, you can always **ask to see the room** before you take it ("*Posso vedere?*") – and check if it's en suite ("*La camera ha un bagno privato?*") or air conditioned ("*Cè aria condizionata?*"). It's worth noting that smaller, inexpensive places don't have much in the way of heating in the winter – you can freeze in some of the older *palazzi*.

Private rooms and B&Bs

Private rooms (*camere*, *affitacamere*) for rent are common in beach resorts and on the Aeolian and Egadi Islands. Facilities vary, but the best are clean and modern, with private bathroom and often with a kitchenette. Prices start at about €50, with variations depending on the season and location – in August in Taormina and on the Aeolians you might pay as much as €100 a night for a room. Breakfast isn't usually included, but is sometimes available for an extra charge.

Recent years have seen a huge growth in the number of "**bed and breakfasts**" (as they term themselves). Pretty much every Sicilian town now has some B&B choices, all liberally signposted as you tour around, and in many places they've taken over from the old-fashioned family-run pensions.

TOURIST TAX

The Sicilian authorities have introduced a new experimental **tourist tax** (of €1–1.50 per night) in recent years, levied in several cities, towns and even whole islands. It's not yet in place everywhere, but in cities such as Catania, it's charged to anyone spending a night in a hotel or B&B; and in the Aeolian Islands to anyone travelling in via hydrofoil or ferry, or even on a tour boat. We've noted all the places that levy the tax in the Guide, but it remains to be seen whether the effort and cost of collecting and administrating the tax will be deemed to make it worthwhile – however, don't be surprised if other major tourist destinations decide to introduce it as well.

UNUSUAL PLACES TO STAY

L'Atelier sul Mare, Castel di Tusa. Extraordinary "art hotel" on the northern coast. See p.105.

Dammuso houses, Pantelleria. Native domed cube-houses, available for rent. See p.362.

Eremo della Giubiliana, Ragusa. Medieval feudal estate and hermitage, now five-star country retreat with its own airstrip. See p.250.

Grand Hotel Villa Igiea, Acquasanta, near Palermo. Luxury Art Nouveau seaside villa. See p.71.

Azienda Agricola Silvia Sillitti, Caltanissetta. Stay on a working, organic olive, almond and wheat farm. See p.266.

Ostello del Borgo, Piazza Armerina. Ancient Benedictine convent, now backpackers' hostel and budget hotel. See p.268.

Palazzo Il Cavaliere, Modica. Stylishly restored Baroque B&B. See p.244.

La Salina Borgo di Mare, Salina. Aeolian Island chic in an old saltworks. See p.135.

Stenopus Greco, Porticello. Boutique rooms in a working fishing port near Palermo. See p.80.

Suite d'Autore, Piazza Armerina. Every artwork and piece of furniture is for sale in this outrageously quirky designer hotel. See p.268.

Tonnara di Bonagia, Bonagia, near Trapani. Fun, family lodgings in a converted tuna-fishing village. See p.331.

Many are actually little different from private rooms, with the owners either not living on the premises or not always available throughout the day – often, you have to call a mobile phone number to summon attendance. Prices start at around €30 per person per night, usually for an en-suite room in a nicely maintained building where you'll get a flavour of Sicilian home life. Some B&Bs are truly magnificent, based in remarkable Baroque *palazzi* or elegant country houses, and you can pay as much as €90 per person. The southeast particularly has lots of B&Bs, and tourist-friendly towns like Siracusa, Ragusa, Modica and Noto are awash with stylishly converted old homes. Check the very useful websites of **Bed and Breakfast Italia** (Ⓦ bbitalia.it and Ⓦ venere.it).

Self-catering villas and apartments

Private **holiday apartments** and villas are available in places like Taormina, Cefalù, Siracusa and the Aeolians, and are generally rented for anything from a couple of nights to a month. Although these can be very expensive in the peak summer season – when Italian families come on holiday – real bargains can be found in May or late September, and during the winter. Good websites are Ⓦ homelidays.it, Ⓦ casa.it, Ⓦ homeaway.it and Ⓦ casavacanze.it.

Tour operators and villa companies also have self-catering **villas**, **farmhouses** and **apartments** located right across the island, usually in beautiful locations, often with swimming pools. Rates vary wildly, from €600 a week (sleeping four) to thousands for a place suitable for a house party.

For an idea of what's available, contact companies like Think Sicily (Ⓦ thinksicily.com), Bridgewater (Ⓦ bridgewater-travel.co.uk), Travel Sicilia (Ⓦ travel sicilia.com), Italian Breaks (Ⓦ italianbreaks.com), Solo Sicily (Ⓦ solosicily.com) or Dolce Vita Villas (Ⓦ dolce vitavillas.com).

Rural accommodation

Rural tourism has expanded significantly in Sicily in recent years, and every region now holds a choice of interesting places to stay, from **working farms** and **wine estates** to **restored palaces** and **architect-designed homes**. Accommodation is in private rooms or apartments, and many establishments also offer activities such as cooking courses, horseriding, mountain-biking, walks and excursions. Hosts often speak English or French, and sometimes offer meals (or there might be a restaurant attached serving home-produced food, as is the case in many farmhouse-style places). We've recommended some of our favourites in the Guide, but many others fall within various umbrella schemes like Agriturist (Ⓦ agriturist.it) and Agriturismo (Ⓦ agriturismo.com), whose websites have sections on Sicily, with links to the properties. Rooms usually cost €80–120, depending on the establishment, and note that some places require a minimum stay of three nights.

Hostels, campsites and mountain huts

Hostels are rare in Sicily – there are only seven or eight on the whole island, though they're in useful tourist destinations like Palermo, Catania, Taormina,

Noto, Siracusa, Lipari and Piazza Armerina. Dorm beds cost €16–20 a night, depending on season, and all have some kind of self-catering facility available. Some are official IYHF hostels, others are independent backpackers' (ie no membership required), but the official ones at least are detailed on the Hostelling International website (**W** hihostels .com), and if you aren't already a member of your home hostelling organization you can join upon arrival at any hostel.

There are approximately ninety officially graded **campsites** dotted around the island's coasts, on the outlying islands, and around Mount Etna. Few are open year-round; indeed, campsites generally open or close whenever they want, depending on business, but there are more details on the comprehensive website **W** camping.it. Many of the sites are large, family-oriented affairs, often complete with pools, bars, shops and sports facilities. Charges are usually between €5 and €7 per person per day, plus the same again for a tent and vehicle. Many campsites also have bungalows, caravans or apartments for rent (often with self-catering facilities) – demand and prices are high in summer (when a week's minimum stay might be required), but out of season you can expect to pay €35–50 a night.

Staffed **mountain huts** (*rifugio*, plural *rifugi*) are available in certain magnificent locations, particularly in the Madonie and Nébrodi ranges and on Mount Etna. They're used mainly by hikers and outdoor enthusiasts, and operated by the Club Alpino Italiano (**W** cai.it) – non-members can use them for around €20 a night, but advance reservations are essential.

Food and drink

There's much to be said for coming to Sicily just for the eating and drinking. Often, even the most out-of-the-way village will boast somewhere you can get a good lunch, while places like

Catania, Palermo, Ragusa, Trapani and Siracusa can keep a serious eater happy for days. And it's not ruinously expensive either, certainly compared to prices in the rest of mainland Italy: a full meal with local wine generally costs around €30 a head, a pizza, drink and ice cream around half that.

Contemporary Sicilian cooking leans heavily on locally produced foodstuffs and whatever can be fished out of the sea, mixed with the Italian staples of pasta, tomato sauce and fresh vegetables. Red chillies, tuna, swordfish, sardines, olives, pine nuts and capers all figure heavily, while the mild winter climate and long summers mean that fruit and vegetables are less seasonal (and much more impressive) than in northern Europe: strawberries appear in April, for example, while oranges are available right through the winter. The **menu reader** (see p.397) covers all the basics, as well as including a full rundown of Sicilian specialities, some of which crop up in nearly every restaurant.

Breakfast, snacks and markets

For most Sicilians, **breakfast** (*prima colazione*) is an espresso or cappuccino, and the ubiquitous *cornetto* – a jam-, custard- or chocolate-filled croissant. Many bars and patisseries (a *pasticceria*) also offer things like an *iris* (a pastry ball stuffed with sweet ricotta cheese), a *romano* (deep-fried sugared turnover filled with sweet ricotta), and *cannoli* (pastry tubes with sweet ricotta cheese and candied fruit). The traditional summer breakfast is a *granite* (preferably almond or coffee) with a brioche. Look out also for almond milk in summer, and freshly squeezed red oranges in winter.

There are **sandwich** (*panini*) bars in the bigger towns, though alternatively, in most places, you can simply go into an *alimentari* (grocer's shop) and ask them to make you a sandwich from whatever they've got. Bakeries sometimes sell *panini* or *pane*

ICE CREAM

A cone (*un cono*) of famous Sicilian **ice cream** (*gelato*) – or perhaps a dollop in a brioche – is the indispensable accessory to the evening *passeggiata*. The best choice is at a **gelateria**, where the range is a tribute to the Italian imagination and flair for display. If they make their own on the premises, there'll be a sign saying "*produzione propria*"; sadly, however, this increasingly means they make the stuff from pre-packed commercial pastes and syrups. Anyhow, there's no trouble in locating the finest *gelateria* in town: it's the one that draws the crowds. And as it's hard to find decent ice cream in restaurants these days (it's mostly *confezionato*, ie mass-produced), many locals also head to the *gelateria* for dessert.

THE ORIGINAL FUSION FOOD

Historically, **Sicilian cuisine** has been held in high regard: one of the earliest of cookbooks, the *Art of Cooking* by Mithaecus, derived from fifth-century BC Siracusa, while in medieval times Sicilian chefs were much sought after in foreign courts. As the centuries passed, the intermittent waves of immigration left their mark, from the use of prickly pears (originally imported from Mexico by the Spanish) to the North African influence evident in the western Sicilian version of couscous or in orange salads. The **Arab influence** is also apparent in the profusion of sweets – marzipan is used extensively, while *cassata*, the most Sicilian of desserts, derives from the Arabic word *quas-at*, referring to the round bowl in which it was traditionally prepared. Indeed, virtually every dish – though apparently common-or-garden Italian/Sicilian – calls upon 2500 years of cross-cultural influences, from the Greeks and Romans to the Arabs, Normans and Spanish.

cunzati, crusty bread rolls filled with pungent combinations such as tuna, tomato, anchovy and capers. *Tramezzini* are ready-made sliced white-bread sandwiches with mixed fillings, while toasted sandwiches (*toste*) tend to be a variation on cheese with ham or tomato. Look out also for *impanata* or *scacce*, bread turnovers filled with combinations of potato, onion, fennel-seed and chilli sausage, broccoli and wild greens.

You'll get most of the things already mentioned, plus small pizzas, ready prepared pasta and deep-fried, breadcrumbed balls of rice known as *arancini* (usually either *ragù*, with Bolognese sauce, peas and cheese, or *al burro*, with cheese and ham) and full hot meals in a **tavola calda** (literally, "hot table"), a sort of stand-up snack bar. In the larger cities, you'll occasionally come across an old-fashioned **focac-ceria** – takeaway establishments selling *focaccia* (an oven-baked flatbread, with a topping or filling) and other bread-based snacks. Or there's the ubiquitous **rosticceria** in every Sicilian town, a takeaway grill-house where the speciality is spit-roast chicken (*pollo allo spiedo*).

Grocers' shops (*alimentari*) and **markets** are the best places for fruit, veg and picnic food, and you'll usually be able to jazz up your picnic lunch with sweet peppers, olives, seafood salad and pickled vegetables. Some markets also sell **traditional takeaway food**, loved by Sicilians, though perhaps a challenge for some visitors – usually things like boiled artichokes, cooked octopus, raw sea urchins and mussels, and fried offal sandwiches.

Pizza

Outside its home of Naples, Sicily is the best place to eat **pizza** in Italy. It comes flat, not deep-pan, and there are some fairly distinctively Sicilian combinations – using pecorino cheese instead of mozzarella, oregano instead of basil, and lots of anchovies,

capers and hot peppers. It's also easy to find pizzas cooked in the traditional way, in **wood-fired ovens** (*forno a legna*), so that they arrive blasted and bubbling on the surface, with a distinctive charcoal taste. Unfortunately, because of the time it takes to set up and light the ovens, *forno a legna* pizzas are usually only served at night, except on Sundays and in some resorts in summer.

Restaurant meals

For a full meal, rather than just a pizza, you'll have to go either to a **trattoria** or a **ristorante**. A trattoria is usually the cheaper, more basic choice, offering good home cooking (*cucina casalinga*), while a *ristorante* is often more upmarket (tablecloths, printed menu and uniformed waiters). In small towns and villages, the local trattoria is often only open at lunchtime, there may not be a menu and the waiter will simply reel off a list of what's available. In tourist resorts and larger towns you'll come across hybrid establishments (a *trattoria-ristorante*, say, or *ristorante-pizzeria*) that cater to all tastes, while there are also more youthful pasta-oriented restaurant-bars called *spaghetterias*. Signs or blackboards announcing "*pranzo turistico*" or "*pranzo completo*" are advertising a limited-choice **set menu** which can be pretty good value at €15–30.

Traditionally, lunch (*pranzo*) or dinner (*cena*) starts with an **antipasto** (literally "before the meal"), at its best when you circle around a table and help yourself to a cold buffet selection. If you're moving on to pasta and the main course you'll need quite an appetite to tackle the *antipasti* as well. Otherwise, the menu starts with soup or pasta, **il primo**, and moves on to **il secondo**, the meat or fish dish. Note that fish will either be served whole (like bream or trout) or by weight (usually per 100g, *all'etto*, like swordfish and tuna), so ask to see what you're going to eat and check the price first. The

---

SICILIAN TIME

Sicily is a part of Europe where time is still a fluid concept, so giving accurate **opening hours** for bars, cafés and restaurants is difficult. In general, daytime **bars** and **cafés** open around 7.30am for breakfast and close at 8.30–9.30pm, depending on how busy they are. **Restaurants** will usually be able to feed you if you turn up at noon, but expect to be eating alone – traditional lunchtime is 1–3pm here. In the evening, most restaurants open around 8pm, and are at their busiest at around 9–9.30pm. In winter most restaurants continue serving until at least 10pm, but in summer – especially in holiday places – they will carry on for as long a there are people turning up to eat.

---

second course is generally served unadorned, except for a wedge of lemon or tomato – **contorni** (vegetables and salads) are ordered and served separately, and often there won't be much choice beyond chips and salad. If there's no menu, the verbal list of what's available can sometimes be a bit bewildering, but if you don't hear anything you recognize just ask for what you want: everywhere should have pasta with tomato or meat sauce. Dessert (**dolci**) is almost always fresh fruit, fruit salad or ice cream, though restaurants may also have a choice of cakes, tarts and puddings – unfortunately, though, many of these are mass-produced (by such brands as Ranieri), and a restaurant *tiramisù* or *cassata*, say, can be a poor substitute for the real thing.

Although Sicily has hardly any specifically **vegetarian** restaurants, most pasta sauces are based on tomatoes or dairy products, and it's easy to pick a pizza that is meat- (and fish-) free. Pizzas are also available without cheese, though soups are usually made with a fish or meat broth.

In many places, the **bill** (*il conto*) doesn't amount to much more than an illegible scrap of paper so, if you want to be sure you're not being ripped off, ask for a receipt (*una ricevuta*). Nearly everywhere, you'll pay a small **cover charge** per person for the bread (*pane e coperto*); **service** (*servizio*) will be added as well in many restaurants – it's usually ten percent, though fifteen or even twenty percent isn't unheard of. If service isn't charged, leaving ten percent would do, though most pizzerias and trattorias won't expect it.

Coffee, tea and soft drinks

One of the most distinctive smells in a Sicilian street is that of fresh **coffee**. The basic choice is either an espresso (or just *caffè*) or a cappuccino. The latter is primarily a breakfast drink – no Italian would order a cappuccino after a meal. A watered-down espresso is a *caffè lungo*, with a drop of milk it's *caffè macchiato* ("stained"), while coffee with a shot of alcohol is *caffè corretto*. In summer you might want

your coffee cold (*caffè freddo*), or try a *granita di caffè* – cold coffee with crushed ice that's usually topped with whipped cream (*senza panna*, without cream). **Tea**, too, can be drunk iced (*tè freddo*), usually mixed with lemon. Hot tea (*tè caldo*) comes with lemon (*con limone*) unless you ask for milk (*con latte*).

For a fresh **fruit juice** (usually orange, lemon or grapefruit), squeezed at the bar, ask for a *spremuta*. Fruit juice mixed with crushed ice is that Sicilian speciality, *granita*; a *frullato* is a fresh fruit shake, while a *succo di frutta* is a bottled fruit juice. As an alternative to Coke try the home-grown Chinotto (Coke-like, but not so sweet, with a tamarind flavour). Tap water (*acqua normale*) is drinkable almost everywhere, and you won't pay for it in a bar, but **mineral water** (*acqua minerale*) is the usual choice, either still (*senza gas* or *naturale*) or fizzy (*con gas*, *gassata* or *frizzante*).

Beer, wine and spirits

Beer (*birra*) – generally lager in Sicily – usually comes in 33cl (*piccolo*) or 66cl (*grande*) bottles. The Sicilian brand Messina, and the Italian Peroni and Dreher, are widely available – ask for *birra nazionale*, otherwise you'll be given a more expensive imported beer, and note that draught beer (*birra alla spina*) is usually more expensive than the bottled variety. So-called "dark beers" (*birra nera*, *birra rossa* or *birra scura*) are also available, which have a slightly maltier taste, and in appearance resemble stout or bitter.

Local **wine** (*vino locale*) is often served straight from the barrel in jugs or old bottles, and costs as little as €2 a litre. You may be flummoxed by the *vino locale* not being the colour you've ordered, but you'll get whatever they make – in the west, for example, it's often a tart but refreshing rosé, in Marsala it's amber. Bottled wine is more expensive, though can still be good value, usually from €8–10 in a restaurant (though often much higher in tourist resorts).

The most famous Sicilian **dessert wine** is *marsala*, made in the western town of the same name (see box, p.344). If you're heading to the offshore islands, watch out for *malvasia* (from the

Aeolians) and *moscato* (from Pantelleria), while around Taormina the local speciality is *vino alla mándorla*, almond wine served ice-cold. **Spirits** are known mostly by their generic names, except brandy which you should call *cognac* or ask for by name – again, for cheaper Italian brands, ask for *nazionale*. At some stage you should also try an **amaro** (literally "bitter"), a remarkably medicinal after-dinner drink supposed to aid digestion. The favourite brand is Averna (from Caltanissetta) but there are dozens of different kinds. Look out, too, for artisan or home-made **rosolio**, alcohol infused with herbs or spices such as bay leaves, wild fennel, rose petal or cinnamon.

Where to drink

In most town and village **bars**, it's cheapest to drink standing up at the counter (there's often nowhere to sit anyway), in which case you pay first at the cash desk (*la cassa*), present your receipt (*scontrino*) to the bar person and give your order. There's always a list of prices (the *listino prezzi*) on display, and when you present your receipt it's customary to leave a small tip on the counter – though no one will object if you don't. It's more expensive to sit down inside than stand up (the difference in price is shown on the price list as *tavola*) and it costs up to twice the basic price if you sit at tables outside (*terrazza*).

Although bars have no set **licensing hours**, outside the cities it's often difficult to find a bar open much after 9pm. Children are allowed in and bars, like restaurants, are smoke-free (strictly enforced), though if you're drinking or eating outside it's fine to smoke. Tourist bars and cafés are open later, but they're more expensive than the typical chrome-counter-and-Gaggia-machine local joints.

Most Sicilians tend to drink when they eat, and young people especially don't make a night out of

getting wasted. In recent years the **aperitivo** scene has taken Sicily (and the rest of Italy) by storm. Bars advertising aperitivo (usually between 6.30pm or 7pm and 8.30pm or 9pm) will provide a buffet or table-served nibbles which can range from simple pizza, bruschetta, miniature *arancini*, and rice, pasta or couscous salad to delectable morsels of fish, cured hams and salamis, baked aubergines, courgette fritters, fresh ricotta or other local cheeses.

When young Sicilians do go out on the town, it's to a **birreria** (literally "beer shop") or something calling itself a "pub", which is actually a bar open at night. Needless to say, they're not much like English pubs, though in the various "Irish" **pubs** that are springing up in the cities and resorts, you'll be able to get a pint of Guinness and watch the big game.

The media

Many Sicilians prefer to read local newspapers rather than the national ones, even though these have local supplements. Sicilian TV is popular, too, playing to the insatiable appetite for local gossip and celebrity – you might find yourself turning to foreign TV channels or papers if you want an international outlook on events. For Italian news in English, go to ⓦlifeinitaly.com.

Newspapers and magazines

The two most widely read national **newspapers** are the centre-left *La Repubblica* and authoritative and rather right-wing *Il Corriere della Sera*, both published with local Sicilian supplements. If you have a smattering of Italian, you'll get far more of a flavour of Sicily by reading one of the **regional papers**, full

---

SICILIAN WINE

Over the past few years **Sicilian wines** have built an increasingly prestigious reputation. There's no shortage of the stuff either – the island often produces more wine in a year than any other Italian region, and as much as the whole of Australia. Typical of the wines making waves are those made from the local **Nero d'Ávola** grape variety (a hearty red, similar to a Syrah/Shiraz), which is well suited to the dry climate. Other Sicilian regions produce very distinct tastes, too, like the dry reds and whites made from grapes grown on the volcanic slopes of **Etna**; **Cerasuolo di Vittoria** (red and white) from vines in the area around Ragusa; and the famous **Malvasia** grapes of the Aeolian Islands. Boutique wineries are springing up all over Sicily – Etna and the Ragusa area are good destinations for a cantina-crawl – though the major **brands**, with decent mid-price wines that you'll see everywhere, include Corvo, Nicosia, Planeta, Donnafugata and Regaleali. Settesoli is a reliable budget brand sold at most supermarkets, while many market stalls and *alimentari* sell local wine in unlabelled plastic bottles for around €2 a litre.

of news on the latest Mafioso misdemeanours and arrests, political bickering, local gossip, transport schedules, reviews, film listings and suchlike. In Palermo, the most popular is *Il Giornale di Sicilia*; in Catania, *La Sicilia*; in Messina, *La Gazzetta del Sud*. **English-language newspapers** can be found in Palermo, Catania, Messina, Siracusa, Taormina and Cefalū, usually a day late, and for three times the UK cover price, so reading newspapers online is usually a more economic option.

TV

Italian **TV** is appalling, with mindless quiz shows, variety programmes and chat shows squeezed in between countless advertisements. There are three state-owned **channels** (Rai 1, 2 and 3) along with the dozen or so channels of Berlusconi's Mediaset empire. You'll also come across all kinds of tiny local channels busying themselves with the minutiae of local life, and running non-stop silent footage of scenic landscapes when budgets are tight.

Satellite television is fairly widely distributed, and three-star hotels and above usually offer a mix of BBC World, CNN and French-, German- and Spanish-language news channels, as well as MTV and Eurosport.

Radio

As for **radio**, the most serious RAI channel is RAI 3, while the most listened-to pop radio stations are RTL (102.5 FM) and Radio Deejay (frequency depends on where you are – check ⓦ radiodeejay .it). There are several free apps such as iRadio UK Free that allow you to listen to radio stations from home – great for when you have wi-fi on tap.

Festivals

There's nothing to beat arriving in a Sicilian town or village to discover that it's festival time. Many annual feast days have remained unchanged for decades, if not centuries, celebrating the life of a patron saint or some notable event lost in the mists of time. But whatever the reason for the party, you are guaranteed the time-honoured ingredients for a Sicilian knees-up – old songs and dances, a costumed procession, perhaps a traditional puppet show, special food and sweets, and noisy fireworks to finish.

Food-inspired *sagras* are lower-key, but no less enjoyable affairs, usually celebrating the local speciality of a town or village (with lots of free nibbles, copious wine and the usual music and dancing). There are literally hundreds of these food festivals, and driving around Sicily, you will come across posters advertising sagre of wild mushrooms, ricotta, pistachios, strawberries, capers or any local produce an area is famous for.

For online information on most Sicilain festivals, visit ⓦ siciliainfesta.com.

Carnevale

Carnevale (Carnival, or Mardi Gras) is celebrated in the five days immediately before the start of Lent (in practice, some time between the end of February and the end of March). Traditionally, its significance is as the last bout of indulgence before the abstinence of Lent, which lasts for forty days and ends with Easter. Sicily's best carnival is generally judged to be at **Acireale** on the Catania coast, where flower-filled floats, parades and concerts keep the townspeople occupied for days. Most towns and villages, however, manage to put on a little bit of a show, with kids walking around in costume, and street vendors selling local carnival food – inevitably a local variation of sweetened fried bread dough.

Easter

All over the island, **Easter** week is celebrated with slow-moving processions and ostentatious displays of penitence and mourning. Particularly dramatic events take place at **Erice**, **Marsala** and **Taormina**, while at **Enna** in the interior, thousands march in silent procession behind holy statues and processional carts. It's in **Trapani**, however, that the procession of statues is raised to an art form. Just as they have been every year since the seventeenth century, the city's "Misteri" figures, portraying life-sized scenes from the Passion, are paraded through the streets on Good Friday (see box, p.322). There are more curious events at **Adrano**, where the *Diavolata* is a symbolic display showing the Archangel Michael defeating the Devil; while in **Modica**, the Easter Sunday celebration known as Vasa Vasa sees a statue of the Madonna in mourning carried through the Baroque streets as if searching for her lost Son; when she meets the resurrected Christ she kisses him ("vasa" means kiss in Sicilian) and sheds her black veil). Meanwhile, at the Albanian village of **Piana degli Albanesi**, near Palermo, the villagers retain their ancient Orthodox traditions and costumes. Other, less conventional, parades take place at **Prizzi** in the western interior, and at **San Fratello** above the Tyrrhenian coast, where masked and hooded devils taunt the processions.

Ferragosto

The biggest island-wide celebration, bar none, is high summer's **ferragosto**, the Feast of the Assumption of the Virgin Mary. The day is actually August 15, but anywhere with a celebration of any size makes a meal of it, perhaps starting with services and parties a few days earlier before culminating, like all *ferragosto* celebrations, with spectacular fireworks on the night of the 15th. This is a particularly good time to be in **Messina**, where the procession of the city's enormous patron giants is followed by a mad scramble when the elaborate carriage on iron skis, known as the Vara, is pulled by the faithful through the streets, with water thrown down before it to ease the way. As the night wears on, flowers are thrown to the crowds before fireworks light up the Straits of Messina late at night (see box, p.164).

A festival calendar

JANUARY

New Year celebrations Taormina (from Jan 1). Puppet shows, folk-singing and concerts, ending on Epiphany (January 6).

Epiphany (Jan 6). Orthodox procession at Piana degli Albanesi; traditional costumes and the distribution of oranges. Elsewhere the Epiphany witch Befana gives stockings of sweets to children who've been good, and coal (made of black sugar honeycomb) to those who haven't.

FEBRUARY

Sagra del Mandorlo Fiore (first/second week). The almond-blossom festival sees elaborately costumed dancers and musicians from around the world perform in the Valle dei Templi and in Agrigento town.

Festa di Sant'Agata Catania (Feb 3–5). Boisterous street events, fireworks and food stalls, and a procession of the saint's relics.

Carnevale (weekend before Lent). Carnival festivities in Palazzolo Acreide, Cefalù, Taormina, Giardini Naxos and Acireale with processions, floats, fireworks and music. See opposite.

MARCH

San Giuseppe (March 19). On the Saturday closest to San Giuseppe, horses, astonishingly decorated with flowers, follow the Holy Family through town in a candlelit procession at Scicli. On March 19 at Malfa, Salina, participants feast on pasta and *ceci* (chickpeas) cooked in huge cauldrons, along with antipasti and puddings made by local people, presided over by locals dressed as Mary, Joseph and Jesus. Repeated in April at Lingua, and on May 1 in Leni.

Easter (dates vary). Celebrations islandwide (see opposite).

APRIL

St George's Day. There's a costumed procession and statues paraded through the streets at Ragusa Ibla (Last Sun), and another procession on the 23rd at Piana degli Albanesi.

MAY

Madonna delle Milizie Scicli (last Sat). Re-enactment of a battle between the Normans and Saracens, won by the Normans after they invoked the help of the Madonna.

Sagra del Lago Lago di Pergusa. Held throughout May, with folk events, fireworks, singing competitions and games.

THE WEIRD AND WONDERFUL

Sicily can boast some of the Mediterranean's most idiosyncratic festivals. The conquest by the Normans is echoed in August's **Palio dei Normanni** in Piazza Armerina, a medieval-costumed procession with jousting knights, while the similar **La Castellana** throngs the streets of Caccamo in September. The island's fishermen have their own rituals, such as the festive boat parade and fish-fry of **Sagra del Mare** at Sciacca. During May's **Pesce a Mare** festa at Aci Trezza, on the Catania coast, as the local tourist brochure puts it, "a fisherman pretends to be a fish and excitedly the local fishermen catch him". Unmissable, for different reasons, is the **pilgrimage** every May in the Etna foothills, when the pious run, barefoot and shirtless, up to the sanctuary at Trecastagni.

TRADITIONAL ENTERTAINMENT

Puppet theatre (*teatro dei pupi*) has been popular in Sicily since the fourteenth century. The shows are always the same, and all Sicilians know the stories, which centre on the clash between **Christianity** and **Islam**. As each strutting, stiff-legged knight, such as Orlando (Roland) and Rinaldo, is introduced, the puppeteer lists his exploits. There may be a love interest, perhaps a jousting tournament to win the hand of Charlemagne's daughter, before the main business of staged battles between the Christians and the Saracen invaders. Between bouts, Orlando may fight a crocodile, or confront monsters and magicians. Things climax with some great historical battle, like Roncesvalles, culminating in betrayal and treachery as the boys face an untimely and drawn-out death. The whole story plays out regularly in theatre shows in Acireale, and also tourist centres like Siracusa and Taormina, though it's Palermo where you can best explore the tradition (see p.59).

International Museum Day (mid-May). Sicily's museums put on events and stay open all night to celebrate the international initiative.

Greek Drama festival Siracusa (mid-May to mid-June). Classic plays performed by international companies in the spectacular ruins of the ancient Greek theatre.

Cantine Aperte (last Sun). Wine estates all over Italy open their cellars to the public.

Festa di Sant'Alfio Trecastagni (May 9–10). Traditional high jinks including a barefoot and shirtless pilgrimage by athletic souls who run the main road linking Catania to the sanctuary at Trecastagni.

Annual World Windsurfing Festival Mondello (last week). Races, food, drink and entertainment.

JUNE

Sagra di Fragola Maletto (dates vary). This little town is famous for its strawberries, considered to be the sweetest and most intense in Sicily, and the strawberry festival here sees a weekend of processions through the streets in traditional hand-painted Sicilian carts.

International Film Festival Taormina (second/third week in June). Screenings in the Teatro Greco.

Sagra del Mare Sciacca (June 27–29). A statue of St Peter is paraded on a boat at sea; there's a big fish-fry and maritime-themed games at the port.

JULY

Festival of St Rosalia Palermo (July 11–15). A procession of the saint's relics, fireworks and general mayhem.

Festival of Santa Marina Santa Marina Salina, Salina (July 17). A religious procession, market, music and fireworks.

Festival of Santa Maria di Terzito Salina (July 23). Music, market and more fireworks at the sanctuary of Madonna del Terzito.

Tindari festival Tyndaris. Theatre and concerts in the ancient theatre, from the last week in July until late August.

Castroreale Jazz Castroreale (late July to early Aug). The mountain village of Castroreale attracts international musicians for a series of open-air concerts.

Estate Ennese Enna (July & Aug). A series of concerts and opera in the open-air theatre at Enna's castle. Runs until end of Aug.

AUGUST

Il Palio dei Normanni Piazza Armerina (Aug 12–14). The largest of several similar events in surrounding towns, Piazza's medieval pageant commemorates Count Roger's taking of the town in the eleventh century with a processional entry into town on the 12th and a ceremonial joust on the 14th, along with costumed parades and other festivities.

Palio Ortigia island, Siracusa (first Sun in Aug). A boat race round the island, in which the five traditional quarters of the city compete with raucous enthusiasm.

Ferragosto (Aug 12–15). Processions and fireworks throughout Sicily (see p.35); Messina has perhaps the best event.

OCTOBER

Monreale concerts A week of ecclesiastical music concerts, staged at the cathedral from the last week in October to the first week in November.

DECEMBER

Christmas week Display of eighteenth-century cribs in Acireale.

Santa Lucia Siracusa (Dec 13). Festival of St Lucy: a procession to the church of Santa Lucia.

Nativity procession Salemi (Dec 24). Procession of locals dressed as characters from the Nativity story.

Sports and outdoor activities

As a Mediterranean island, Sicily is well set up for water sports of all kinds, from scuba-diving to windsurfing, while many come in the cooler months either side of summer (April, May, September and October) for the hiking. The volcanoes of Etna and Stromboli offer more adventurous excursions – probably the most emblematic Sicilian outdoor activity is the climb up Stromboli to see the nightly volcanic light show.

Watersports

The best places for **snorkelling** and **scuba-diving** are the limpid waters of the offshore islands, principally Ustica, the Aeolians, Lampedusa and Pantelleria. Diving schools on each of these offer day-trips and courses for beginners and experienced divers alike. Other areas are protected as marine and natural reserves, so even at far more touristed resorts like Mazzarò (Taormina) the water is often remarkably clear. **Windsurfing** gear is available for rent at most of the major resort beaches and lidos, and **kitesurfing** is increasingly popular at places like Mozia on the west coast.

Hiking

Hiking is growing in popularity, though it's nowhere near as established as in alpine Italy. If you're keen to do a lot of walking in a short time, your best bet is to join a **walking holiday** – several tour operators now offer this as an option (see p.23) and the routes used have all been thoroughly tried and tested. The best walking areas are in the interior, around **Etna** in the east, and in the mountain regions of the **Monti Madonie** and **Monti Nébrodi** (between Etna and the Tyrrhenian coast), where a few marked trails have been laid out, making use of existing paths.

On the whole, though, given the paucity of information and services, unsupported hiking in interior Sicily is more for the experienced and well-equipped walker. You'd do well to get hold of *Walking in Sicily* by Gillian Price, which details 42 walks across the whole island. However, if all you're looking for is a half-day stroll or short hike you're better off sticking to the coast or outlying islands. The Aeolians and Egadis in particular offer some lovely walking, while the protected coast between Scopello and San Vito Lo Capo (north of Trapani) has an excellent network of well-maintained paths.

Outdoor pursuits

The dramatic volcanic terrain around **Mount Etna** supports a whole **outdoor activities** industry, from guided summit hikes to 4WD safaris. Local tourist offices and travel agents as far away as Siracusa and Taormina are geared up to book visitors onto trips. The small mountain towns of Nicolosi and Linguaglossa are the centres for Etna's surviving **skiing** (ski lifts keep being destroyed by eruptions), and winter sports are also available in the Monti Madonie

around Piano Battaglia, where you can rent ski gear. Really, though, no one comes to Sicily just to ski. Volcanoes are a different matter, though, as few in the world are as active as Etna and **Stromboli** – the latter (the furthest flung of the Aeolian Islands) is another great base for guided crater treks (day and night), volcano-watching cruises and the like.

Finally, **horseriding and pony-trekking** are available in some areas – sometimes offered by *agriturismo* (rural tourism) properties.

Culture and etiquette

Sicilian society remains deeply conservative, though values are shifting in the big cities and in places that attract a lot of tourists. Urban Sicilians tend to dress far more smartly than their Northern European counterparts, and even in the most remote village, folk will put on their finery of an evening or for Sunday Mass. And even in holiday resorts, Sicilians would never go out for an evening drink straight from the beach, but go home to shower, and dress up first. Sicilians would rarely sport outright beachwear in a city, but in summer shorts and strappy tops for women, and shorts (of a certain length) for men are quite normal. However, the same clothes worn on a hot day in April or October will win you stares.

Gay and lesbian Sicily

Homosexuality is not illegal in Italy, and the age of consent is 16. That said, attitudes towards homosexuality are much less tolerant in Sicily than in Rome or the industrial north. Taormina is the only place in Sicily where there is any kind of gay scene, and even this is very low-key. Even so, physical contact between men is fairly common in Sicily, on the level of linking arms and kissing cheeks at greetings and farewells – though an overt display of anything remotely ambiguous is likely to be met with hostility. The main national gay organization, **ArciGay** (Warcigay.it), has branches all over the country, including Sicily, and its English-language website is a good place to look for information. The Wgay.it website also has a wealth of information for gays and lesbians in Italy.

VISITING CHURCHES, MUSEUMS AND RUINS

To visit churches and religious buildings you should **dress modestly** (which means no shorts, not even Bermuda-length ones, and covered shoulders for women), and avoid wandering around during a service. At otherwise free **chapels, museums and archeological sites**, if you're shown around by a custodian or caretaker it's customary to give a small tip – say €1 each.

Women travellers

Although Italy has a reputation for **sexual harassment** of women that is well known and well founded, there's no reason to presume unwarranted intrusion at every turn. A woman travelling alone, or with another woman, can expect a certain amount of attention, including staring, horn-tooting and whistling, though bear in mind that local custom dictates that every friend and acquaintance is greeted with a toot, and that staring openly at strangers is seen as perfectly acceptable. If you follow common-sense rules, the most that should worry you is the occasional try-on.

Travelling with children

Children are revered in Sicily and will be made a fuss of in the street, and welcomed and catered for in bars and restaurants. It's perfectly normal for Sicilian children to stay up until they drop, and in summer it's not unusual to see youngsters out at midnight, and not looking much the worse for it.

Pharmacies and supermarkets carry most **baby requirements**, from nappies to formula food. However, you may not see the brands you are used to at home, and don't expect there to be a full range of (or indeed any) organic food products, especially in smaller towns. Otherwise, **food** is unlikely to be a problem as long as your children eat pasta and pizza, and while specific children's menus are extremely rare, many restaurants are happy to provide a smaller version of an adult meal.

Hotels normally charge around thirty percent extra to put an additional bed or cot in the room. However, self-catering apartments, or rooms or B&Bs with the use of a kitchen, are quite common and most Sicilian resorts offer such options. Generous **discounts** apply for children at most sights and attractions, and also when travelling on trains.

Shopping

Sicilian street markets provide some of the best experiences on the island – the Ballarò and Capo in Palermo and Catania's fish market, for example, are sights in themselves, while any market can provide inexpensive souvenirs and gifts like stove-top coffee pots or espresso cups. You'll be taken for an imbecile if you don't haggle for everything except food – ask for "uno sconto" (a discount).

Other day-to-day items, toiletries and basic supplies can be bought in local supermarkets. Food and drink **souvenirs** are almost endless: a bag of dried wild oregano or salted capers from the Aeolians or Pantelliera; pistachios from Bronte; almonds from the Agrigento area; *frutta di martorana* from Palermo; or marsala wine from Marsala.

Clothes

Taormina and Ortigia, and islands such as Panarea and Salina, have excellent **boutiques**, with clothes and shoes often sourced from the many small Italian designers who work for big names such as Martin Margiela. All the main Italian labels and brands have outlets in Palermo, Catania and Messina, and over the last few years international high-street chains such as H&M, Zara and Mango are becoming more common; look out also for quality everyday clothes at the Italian chain Oviesse.

Souvenirs

Sicily has a reputation for its **ceramics**, widely available in tourist shops in the major resorts but best sourced at the production centres, like Santo Stéfano di Camastra (Tyrrhenian coast), Sciacca (south coast) and especially Caltagirone (southern interior).

You'll also see **lace and embroidery** in gift shops in places like Palermo, Taormina and Cefalù, and the quality isn't too bad. But keep an eye out, especially as you travel through small villages in the interior or on the islands, where you may find women and girls at work outside their homes – most will be only too happy to make an unexpected sale.

Recently, small Sicilian companies such as Siculamente have begun to apply a graphic eye to Sicilian tradition, producing witty clothes and accessories that make a change from the ubiquitous Godfather T-shirts. There has also been an explosion in stylishly packaged local oils, pestos, conserves and liqueurs, ideal for presents – though if you care more about contents than packaging, you'll do far better buying capers, wild oregano, olive oil and the like direct from small producers or markets.

Tourist tat outlets usually sell gift versions of traditional Sicilian **theatre puppets** and **hand-painted carts**, along with a vast array of souvenir fridge magnets. Anywhere near Etna, you're also guaranteed to find things in shops fashioned from **lava** – paperweights and jewellery to sculptures.

Travel essentials

Beaches

You'll have to pay for access to many of the island's better beaches (known as *lido*), with lounger, parasol and use of the showers often included in the price (usually €7–10 a day). Many lidos also have other facilities like pedalo- and windsurf-hire, bars and restaurants, and thus make a good bet for families. Elsewhere, beaches are free though not always clean – during the winter most look like dumps, as it's not worth anyone's while to clean them until the season starts at Easter.

Costs

Sicily isn't particularly cheap compared to other Mediterranean holiday spots, though it is usually better value than the popular tourist parts of mainland Italy. The single biggest cost is generally **accommodation**, with simple one-star hotels, private rooms and bed and breakfasts all starting at around €60 a night. A decent three-star hotel, on the other hand, will set you back up to €120. Of course, you'll pay a lot more in summer in the big tourist spots – Erice, Cefalù, Siracusa and Taormina – and more all year round on most of the offshore islands, particularly the Aeolians and Pantelleria.

Most other items are fairly inexpensive. The Sicilian staple, a pizza and a beer, costs around €10 just about everywhere, while a full **restaurant meal** can cost as little as €20 a head. Of course, there are some excellent Sicilian restaurants where the bill comes in much higher, up to say €50 or €60 a head, but even these are remarkably good value for the quality on offer. A litre of local house wine rarely comes to more than €10, a bottle €10–12, and the same wine in a supermarket might cost a third of that. Other snacks and drinks soon add up, especially in fancy resorts, and you should note that

if you sit down in a café (rather than stand at the counter) it'll cost twice as much. **Public transport**, on the other hand, is very cheap, while even the island's showpiece museums, archeological ruins and attractions rarely cost more than €8 – and under-18s and over-65s usually get in for free.

Overall, apart from accommodation, you could reasonably expect to spend €50 a day – taking the train, eating picnics, cheap meals and pizzas, seeing the sights and so on. For a more comfortable daily experience (meals in better restaurants, plus taxis, evening drinks, concerts and the like) you're looking at €80 and upwards.

Crime and personal safety

Although Sicily is synonymous with the **Mafia**, you'll forget the association as soon as you set foot on the island. Cosa Nostra is as invisible to the average tourist as it is ingrained for the islanders, and the violence that sporadically erupts is almost always an "in-house" affair. Of more immediate concern is **petty crime**, mainly in crowded streets or markets, where gangs of *scippatori*, or bag-snatchers, strike on foot or on scooters, disappearing before you've had time to react. As well as handbags, they whip wallets, tear off visible jewellery and, if they're really adroit, unstrap watches. Carry shoulder bags, as you'll see many Sicilian women do, slung across your body. It's a good idea, too, to entrust most of your money and valuables to hotel safes or management. The vast majority of petty crimes occur in Catania and Palermo, and at or on the way to and from the airports. On the whole it's common sense to avoid badly lit areas at night, and run-down inner-city areas at all times.

If the worst happens, you'll be forced to have some dealings with the police. Most conspicuous are the **Carabinieri** – the ones with the blue uniforms – who are a branch of the armed forces and organized along military lines, dealing with general crime and public disorder. They are also the butt of most of the jokes about the police, usually on the "How many Carabinieri does it take to…?"

EMERGENCY PHONE NUMBERS

Police (Carabinieri) ☎112
Emergency services (Soccorso Pubblico di Emergenze) ☎113
Fire brigade (Vigili del Fuoco) ☎115
Road assistance (Soccorso Stradale) ☎116

level. They share a fierce turf rivalry with the **Polizia Statale**, or state police, to whom you're supposed to report any theft at their local HQ, the Questura. The **Polizia Urbana**, or town police, are mainly concerned with directing the traffic and punishing parking offenders. The **Guardia di Finanza**, often heavily armed and screaming ostentatiously through the cities, are responsible for investigating smuggling, tax evasion and other similar crimes, and the **Polizia Stradale** patrol the autostrada.

Electricity

The **supply** is 220V, though anything requiring 240V will work. **Plugs** have two or three round pins (and some sockets have larger holes than others); a travel adaptor plug is very useful.

Entry requirements

British, Irish and other EU citizens can enter Sicily and stay as long as they like on production of a valid **passport**. Citizens of the United States, Canada, Australia and New Zealand don't need a visa, but are limited to stays of three months. Most other nationals will have to apply for a visa from an Italian embassy or consulate.

Legally, you're required to register with the police within three days of entering Italy, though if you're staying at a hotel this will be done for you. Although the police in some towns have become more punctilious about this, most would still be amazed at any attempt to register yourself down at the local police station while on holiday.

ITALIAN EMBASSIES ABROAD

Australia ☎ 02 6273 3333, 🅦 ambcanberra.esteri.it
Canada ☎ 613 232 2401, 🅦 ambottawa.esteri.it
Republic of Ireland ☎ 01 660 1744, 🅦 www.ambdublino.esteri.it
New Zealand ☎ 04 473 5339, 🅦 ambwellington.esteri.it
UK ☎ 020 7312 2200, 🅦 amblondra.esteri.it
USA ☎ 202 612 4400, 🅦 ambwashingtondc.esteri.it

Health

Sicily poses few **health problems** for visitors; the worst that's likely to happen is that you suffer from the extreme heat in summer or from an upset stomach. **Vaccinations** are not required, but you should take insect repellent and strong sun protection. The **water** is perfectly safe to drink (though bottled water tastes better). You'll find public drinking fountains in squares and city streets everywhere, though look out for "*acqua non potabile*" signs, indicating the water is not safe to drink.

An Italian **pharmacist** (*farmacia*) is well qualified to give you advice on minor ailments, and to dispense prescriptions. There's generally one pharmacy open all night in the bigger towns and cities. A rota system is used, and you should find the address of the one currently open late/all night on any *farmacia* door or listed in the local paper.

Every town and village has a **doctor** (*médico*). To find one, ask at a pharmacy, or consult the local yellow pages (*Pagine Gialle*) under "Azienda Unità Sanitaria Locale" or "Unità Sanitaria Locale Pronto Soccorso". Out of hours (ie weekends, holidays and night-time), the local **Guardia Médica** first-aid clinic is available in most towns and, though sometimes minimally equipped, will be able to treat stings, bites, fevers and minor accidents.

In an **emergency**, dial ☎113 and ask for "*ospedale*" or "*ambulanza*". The nearest hospital will have a **Pronto Soccorso** (casualty) section, while on smaller islands, or places with no hospital, there is usually a Guardia Medica clinic.

Insurance

It's essential to take out a **travel insurance** policy to cover against theft, loss, illness or injury during your travels. A typical policy will provide cover for the loss of baggage, tickets and – up to a certain limit – cash, as well as cancellation or curtailment of your journey. Most policies exclude so-called dangerous

ROUGH GUIDES TRAVEL INSURANCE

Rough Guides has teamed up with WorldNomads.com to offer great travel insurance deals. Policies are available to residents of over 150 countries, with cover for a wide range of adventure sports, 24hr emergency assistance, high levels of medical and evacuation cover and a stream of travel safety information. Roughguides.com users can take advantage of their policies online 24/7, from anywhere in the world – even if you're already travelling. And since plans often change when you're on the road, you can extend your policy and even claim online. Roughguides.com users who buy travel insurance with WorldNomads.com can also leave a positive footprint and donate to a community development project. For more information, go to 🅦 roughguides.com/shop.

sports, unless an extra premium is paid: in Sicily this can mean things like scuba-diving, windsurfing and volcano trekking. If you need to make a claim, you should keep receipts for medicines and medical treatment, and in the event you have anything stolen, you must obtain an **official statement from the police**. This is sometimes easier said than done in Sicily, but persevere; without it, you'll not be able to claim your money back.

Internet

There are **internet** places all over Sicily, with access costing up to €5 an hour. However, free **wi-fi** access is increasingly available in B&Bs, hotels and bars, and there are wireless hotspots in many public spaces (though you might need to sign up and pay for an hour's or day's use for these).

Laundry

Coin-operated laundries are very rare. More common is a *lavanderia*, a service-wash laundry, where you'll be able to get your washing done for €10 or so. Many B&Bs offer a laundry service as well. Although you can usually get away with it, washing clothes in your room can be problematic – simply because the ancient plumbing often can't cope with all the water. It's better to ask if there's somewhere you can wash your clothes.

Living and working in Sicily

Unemployment in Sicily is at a distressingly high level, so it is extremely unlikely that you will find a job that does not depend on your ability to speak English. All EU citizens are eligible to work and study in Italy. Work permits are pretty impossible for non-EU citizens to obtain: you must have the firm promise of a job that no Italian could do before you can even apply to the Italian embassy in your home country.

Red tape

The main bureaucratic requirements to stay legally in Italy are a *Permesso di Soggiorno* and a *codice fiscale*, respectively a piece of paper proving your right to be in the country and a tax number. Available from the *questura* (police station), a **Permesso di Soggiorno** requires you to produce a letter from your employer or place of study, or prove you have funds to maintain yourself. In reality, EU citizens can simply apply on the grounds of looking for work (*attesa di lavoro*), for which you'll need your passport and a copy of it, four passport photos, and

a lot of patience. A **codice fiscale** is essential for most things in Italy including buying a transport season pass, a SIM card, opening a bank account or renting a flat. It can be obtained from the local Ufficio delle Entrate, although you can start the process online at ⓦ www.agenziaentrate.gov.it.

Work options

One obvious option is to **teach English**, for which the demand has expanded enormously in recent years. You can do this in two ways: freelance private lessons, or through a language school. For the less reputable schools, you can get away without any qualifications, but you'll need to show a TEFL (Teaching of English as a Foreign Language) certificate for the more professional – and better-paid – establishments. For the main language schools, it's best to apply in writing before you leave (look for the ads in British newspapers), preferably before the summer. If you're looking on the spot, sift through the local English-language press and phone books and do the rounds on foot, but don't bother to try in August when everything is closed. Italian high schools are also required by law to have mother-tongue language assistants – another good source of work, though the best teaching jobs of all are with a university as a *lettore*, a job requiring fewer hours than the language schools and generally providing a fatter pay-packet. Universities require English-language teachers in most faculties; write directly to enquire about positions. Strictly speaking, you could get by without any knowledge of Italian while teaching, though it obviously helps, especially when setting up private classes.

Au pairing is another option: again sift through the ads in locally produced English-language publications in Sicily's big cities to find openings.

Study

The only academic institution offering **study abroad programmes** in Sicily is run by Arcadia University at MCAS, the Mediterranean Centre for Arts and Sciences. Based in Ortigia, Siracusa, it's a liberal arts faculty (part of Arcadia University) offering accredited courses to American students. Courses include archeology, marine biology and the Mediterranean diet.

Mail

Post office opening hours are usually Monday to Saturday 8.30am to 6.30pm; offices in smaller towns close on a Saturday, and everywhere else post offices close at noon on the last Saturday of the month. You can also buy **stamps** (*francobolli*) in some gift shops in tourist resorts, and in shops called *tabacchi*, recognizable by a sign displaying a white "T" on a black or blue background (these also sell cigarettes, sweets and stationery). The Italian **postal service** is among the slowest in Europe – if your letter is urgent, consider paying extra for the express service, or *posta prioritaria*.

Maps

The best large-scale **road map** of Sicily is published by the Touring Club Italiano (*Sicilia*, 1:200,000), available from map and travel bookshops or online retailers. Otherwise, the Automobile Club d'Italia issues a good, free 1:275,000 road map, available from the State Tourist Offices, while local tourist offices in Sicily often have free road maps of varying quality. Local tourist offices also hand out reasonable town plans and regional maps.

Hiking maps (scale 1:25,000 and 1:50,000) for the Monti Madonie and other areas can be ordered from the Istituto Geografico Militare (Wigmi.org), or check what's available at the Palermo stationer's shop Cartoleria de Magistris, Via A. Gagini 23 (T091 589 233). Note, however, that most of these maps were drawn up in the 1970s, and, particularly at altitudes above 1500m, many of the paths shown on them no longer exist. The Club Alpino Siciliano, Via A. Paternostro 43, Palermo (Wclubalpinosiciliano.it), or – sometimes – tourist and regional park offices in Palermo or Cefalù can supply you with 1:50,000 maps of the Monti Madonie, but again, these should be treated with caution. However, all national parks and nature reserves (Madonie, Nébrodi, Pellegrino, etc; see Wparks.it) have walking itineraries on their websites, while the various park offices listed in the Guide can supply rudimentary hiking maps and, occasionally, English-language route guides.

Money

Italy's currency is the **euro** (€); notes are issued in denominations of 5, 10, 20, 50, 100, 200 and 500 euros, and coins in denominations of 1, 2, 5, 10, 20 and 50 cents and 1 and 2 euros. At the time of writing the exchange rate was approximately €1 to £0.84 and €1 to US$1.35. Up-to-the-minute currency **exchange rates** are displayed at Wxe.com.

By far the easiest way to get money is to use your bank debit card to withdraw cash from an **ATM** (known as *bancomat* in Italy). These are found even in the smallest towns and on some of the more remote islands, as well as on arrival at the three main airports. Make sure that you have a PIN that's designed to work overseas, and check with your bank whether you can use your debit card directly in shops and petrol stations etc, as not all systems are available in Sicily.

Credit cards can also be used for cash advances over the counter in banks and for payment in most hotels, restaurants, petrol stations and some shops. MasterCard and Visa are the most widely accepted cards.

Banking hours vary slightly from town to town, but are generally Monday to Friday 8.30am to 1.20pm and 3pm to 4pm. Outside these times you can change foreign currency at large hotels, the airports at Palermo and Catania, and some main train stations.

Opening hours and public holidays

Basic opening hours for most **shops and businesses** are Monday to Saturday from 8am or 9am to around 1pm, and from around 4pm to 7pm or 8pm, though some offices work to a more standard European 9am to 5pm day. Everything, except bars and restaurants, closes on Sunday, though you might find cake shops, and fish shops in some coastal towns, open until lunchtime. Local religious holidays and festivals don't generally close down shops and businesses, but everything except bars and restaurants will be closed on the public holidays (see p.34).

Most **churches** open in the early morning (around 7am or 8am) for Mass and close around noon, opening up again at 4pm or 5pm, and closing at 7pm. More obscure ones will only open for early morning and evening services; some only open on Sunday and on religious holidays. One problem you'll face all over Sicily is that lots of churches, monasteries, convents and oratories are **closed for restoration** (*chiuso per restauro*). We've indicated the more long-term closures in the text, but even if there's scaffolding up you might be able to persuade a workman or priest/curator to show you around.

Museums are generally open daily from 9am to 1pm, and again for a couple of hours in the afternoon on certain days; likely closing day is Monday, while they close slightly earlier on Sunday, around 12.30pm. **Archeological sites** are usually open from 9am until an hour before sunset (in practice until around 4pm from November to March, 7pm from April to October, though never bet against a custodian bunking off early on a slow day). Sites are also sometimes closed on Mondays.

Phones

Dialling ☎ 170 or 176 will get you through to an English-speaking operator. You can **find numbers online** with the Italian Yellow Pages (W paginegialle .it) or White Pages (W paginebianche.it). To **call Sicily from abroad**, dial your international access number + 39 (Italy country code) + number.

Most **cellphones** bought in the UK and Ireland, Australia and New Zealand, will work in Sicily, though a mobile phone bought for use in the US might not work here unless it is triband or supporting GSM. To make sure, check to see if your phone supports GSM 900 and GSM 1800 frequencies. Prices are coming down, but it remains expensive to use your cellphone exclusively to make national and international calls in Sicily. You might simply be able to buy a replacement SIM card for your own phone, though this depends on the model, contract and service provider. Or, if you're coming for more than a couple of weeks, you could even buy a mobile in Sicily – basic models cost as little as €39. A mobile phone is *un cellulare* or *telefonino*, a recharger is *un ricaricatore*, and a text message is *un messaggio SMS*.

Time

Sicily (and Italy) is always one hour ahead of GMT. Italy is seven hours ahead of Eastern Standard Time and ten hours ahead of Pacific Time.

Tourist information

The **Italian Government Tourist Board** (W enit.it) has a useful website for general information, or you can contact the state tourist office organization in your own country. In Sicily, most towns, main train stations and the two principal airports have a **tourist office** (*ufficio di turismo*) or a **Pro Loco** office, usually funded by the *Comune*, overseeing cultural events and providing tourist information. Other than in the main tourist areas staff aren't likely to speak English, but you should at least be able to get a free town plan and a local listings booklet in Italian, and some offices will reserve you a room and sell places on guided tours.

Likely summer (April–Oct) tourist office **opening hours** are Monday to Friday 9am to 1pm and 4pm to 7pm, Saturday 9am to 1pm, though some offices in tourist areas open for longer. From November to March hours may be reduced. If the tourist office isn't open and all else fails, the local Sicilian telephone office and most bars with phones carry a copy of the local *Tuttocittà* (W tuttocitta.it), a listings

and information magazine which details addresses and numbers of most of the organizations you're likely to want to know about. It also has indexed street maps for local towns and adverts for restaurants and shops. The Palermo version (with an interactive map) is available online.

TOURISM WEBSITES

W **bestofsicily.com** Informative site detailing history, the arts, books, food and wine, sights and travel.
W **siciliaonline.it** Some information in English, with details on everything from folklore and the weather to transport and festivals.
W **press.sicilia.it** Mostly Italian, with extracts from all sorts of articles about Sicily, plus news and reviews.

ITALIAN STATE TOURIST OFFICES

Australia & New Zealand ☎ 02 9262 1666, W italiantourism .com.au
Canada ☎ 416 925 4882, W italiantourism.com
UK ☎ 020 7408 1254, W italiantouristboard.co.uk
USA ☎ 212 245 5095, W italiantourism.com

Travellers with disabilities

Although most Sicilians are helpful enough if presented with a specific problem, the island is hardly geared towards accommodating travellers with disabilities. In the medieval city centres and old villages, few budget hotels have elevators, let alone ones capable of taking a wheelchair, and rooms have rarely been adapted for use by disabled visitors. Narrow, cobbled streets, steep inclines, chaotic driving and parking are hardly conducive to a stress-free holiday either. Crossing the street in Palermo is a major undertaking even if you're fully mobile, while Taormina, the most popular resort, poses great **accessibility challenges** for anyone in a wheelchair.

If the thought of negotiating your own way around the island proves too daunting, an **organized tour** may be the way to go. While that will cost more than planning your own trip, you can request accommodation in higher-category hotels that should at least have some facilities for disabled travellers, and you'll also have someone on hand who speaks Italian to help smooth the way. Accessible Italy (W accessible italy.com) is an Italian organization offering tours and advice to foreigners, and though it's mainly useful for mainland Italy, you can ask for advice on travelling in Sicily. You can also contact one of the organizations in your own country dedicated to people with disabilities. Tourism For All (W tourismforall.org.uk), for example, publishes an information pack about holidaying in Italy for disabled travellers.

Palermo
and around

PALERMO CATTEDRALE

1

Palermo and around

Unmistakably the capital of Sicily, Palermo is fast, brash, loud and exciting. Hub of the island since the ninth century AD, it borrows heavily from the past for its present-day look, showing a typically Sicilian fusion of foreign art, architecture, culture and lifestyle. In the narrow streets of Palermo's old town, elegant Baroque and Norman monuments exist cheek by jowl with Arabic cupolas, while Byzantine street markets swamp the medieval warrens, and the latest Milanese fashions sit in shops squeezed between Renaissance churches and Spanish *palazzi*. And, ricocheting off every wall, the endless roar of traffic and wail of police sirens add to the confusion. Palermo is probably the noisiest city in Italy, which – coupled with the oppressive summer climate and frenetic street scenes – conjures up visions of North Africa. Indeed, there's little that's strictly European about Palermo, and its geographical isolation has forced this vibrant city of 700,000 to forge its own distinct identity.

You'll need at least three or four days to fully explore Palermo's historic sights, fascinating medieval quarters and chaotic markets, as well as enjoy its great restaurants and street-food offerings; and you could easily stay here for a week if you plan to use the city as a base for day-trips. The most essential of these is to the medieval cathedral of **Monreale** and its celebrated mosaics, which is a hugely popular (ie, tourist-thronged) destination – spending the night allows you to beat the crowds and see Monreale at a more leisurely pace.

Fewer visitors head east along the coast, which means you can spend an unhurried day at **Bagheria** and its Baroque *palazzi*, before taking in the fishing port of **Porticello** and the fascinating Roman site at nearby **Solunto**.

West of the city, a series of small family resorts lines the **Golfo di Carini**, while south of Palermo an enticing route heads to **Piana degli Albanesi**, a surviving Albanian Orthodox enclave in a stridently Catholic island, and then further into the mountains to the royal hunting lodge at **Ficuzza** and the notorious Mafia town of **Corleone**. For a real change of air, though, jump on a ferry or hydrofoil to the island of **Ustica**, as little as an hour and a quarter from the city. With its good, clean swimming and lazy feel, you may end up staying longer than planned.

MUSEO DELLE MARIONETTE

Highlights

❶ Cappella Palatina in the Palazzo dei Normanni The artistic gem of Palermo, this jewel-like chapel is entirely covered with outstanding Byzantine mosaics. **See p.56**

❷ Museo delle Marionette Catch a performance and admire the swashbuckling wooden Sicilian puppets in all their finery. **See p.59**

❸ Galleria Regionale della Sicilia If you only visit one Palermo museum, make it the island's finest collection of medieval art. **See p.61**

❹ The Duomo at Monreale The magnificently mosaiced cathedral is a stunning testament to Sicily's eclectic Arab, Norman and Byzantine heritage. **See p.76**

❺ Bagheria and Porticello Over-the-top Baroque villas, boutique lodgings and harbourside fish restaurants make for a great side-trip from the city. **See p.78 & p.80**

❻ A trip to Ustica Take the ferry or hydrofoil out to the relaxed island of Ustica for a spot of hiking, diving and snorkelling. **See p.84**

HIGHLIGHTS ARE MARKED ON THE MAP ON P.48

1

Palermo

In its own wide bay underneath the limestone bulk of Monte Pellegrino, and fronting the broad and fertile Conca d'Oro (Golden Shell) valley, **PALERMO** is stupendously sited. Originally a Phoenician colony, it was taken by the Carthaginians in the fifth century BC and became an important Punic bulwark against the Greek influence elsewhere on the island. It was named Panormus (All Harbour) after its obvious mercantile attractions, and it remained in Carthaginian hands until 254 BC, when the city fell to the Romans. Yet Palermo's most glorious days were still to come. In 831 AD the city was captured by the **Arabs**, under whose rule it thrived as an Islamic cultural and intellectual centre – the River Papineto that now flows beneath the city was said to speak with the Nile and abide by its tides. Two centuries later under the Normans, the settlement continued to flower as

PALERMO AND AROUND

HIGHLIGHTS

1 Cappella Palatina in the Palazzo dei Normanni
2 Museo delle Marionette
3 Galleria Regionale della Sicilia
4 The Duomo at Monreale
5 Bagheria and Porticello
6 A trip to Ustica

THE MAFIA IN PALERMO

The most glaring symptom of decay in Palermo, the **Mafia problem**, is intimately connected with the welfare of the city. For years it has been openly acknowledged that a large part of the funds pouring in from Rome and the EU, ostensibly to redevelop the city centre, are unaccounted for – channelled to dubious businessmen, or simply raked off by Mafia leaders. The subtle control exerted by the Mafia is traditionally referred to only obliquely, though it periodically erupts into the news.

The problem is deeply rooted and unlikely to disappear completely any time soon, despite the courageous efforts of various individuals. Prominent among these is **Leoluca Orlando**, currently serving his fourth term as mayor of Palermo, who attempts to combat corruption at municipal level by removing companies suspected of links with organized crime from the tenders list for new contracts. Resistance to Mafia corruption has also emerged at street level, notably with many owners of shops and businesses in Palermo banding together and refusing to pay *pizzo*, the protection money traditionally demanded by local crime gangs. A thriving organization, **Addiopizzo** (Ⓦ addiopizzo.org), coordinates the local resistance – their *consumo critico* (critical shopping) list publicizes the hundreds of enterprises now offering a *pizzo*-free Palermo experience (look for the stickers), including restaurants, bars and B&Bs.

Europe's greatest metropolis – famed for the wealth of its court, and unrivalled as a nexus of learning.

Palermo's later fortunes fluctuated with a succession of other foreign rulers, but the city always retained its pre-eminence on the island. However, Allied **bombs** during World War II destroyed much of the port area and turned large parts of the medieval town into a ramshackle demolition site – a state of affairs that is only now gradually being resolved. **Regeneration** has been aided by funds from the European Union – when not siphoned off by illicit means – (see box above), and nowadays although decay and deprivation are still apparent in Palermo, a more positive spirit animates the city, typified by a burgeoning number of boutique B&Bs sited in the old-town areas. Although there are notable relics from the ninth to the twelfth centuries – Palermo in its prime – it's the rebuilding of the sixteenth and seventeenth centuries that shaped the city as it appears today. Traditionally, Palermo has been a city of rich **palazzi** and **churches**, endowed by the island's ruling families and wealthy monastic orders, from the mighty Cattedrale to the nearby mosaic-decorated Cappella Palatina, tucked inside the Palazzo dei Normanni. Each old quarter features countless other fascinating churches and chapels, while enthusiasts can trace the city's Norman and Baroque heritage in a series of landmark buildings and sights. But just to see Palermo in terms of an architectural tour would be to ignore much of what makes it unique, from its rollicking **markets** and traditional **street food** to the backstreet **puppet theatres** and creepy **catacombs**. There's certainly never a dull moment in Sicily's feistiest city.

The Quattro Canti

The **Quattro Canti** or "Four Corners" is the centre (if anywhere is) of the medieval town. Erected in 1611, this is not so much a piazza as a set of Baroque crossroads that divides central Palermo into quadrants. In each concave "corner" are tiers of statues – respectively a season, a king of Sicily and a patron of the city – where, in previous centuries, the heads of convicted rebels were hung from poles. Only a few steps from here lie some of Palermo's most opulent piazzas and buildings, including several of the city's most extraordinary churches.

1

San Giuseppe dei Teatini

Corso Vittorio Emanuele • April–Oct Mon–Sat 7.30–11am & 6–8pm, Sun 8.30am–12.30pm & 6–8pm; Nov–March Mon–Sat 7.30am–noon & 5.30–8pm

Early seventeenth-century **San Giuseppe dei Teatini** is the most harmonious of the city's Baroque churches. The misleadingly simple facade conceals a wealth of detail inside, from tumbling angels holding the holy water on either side of the door to the lavish side chapels and ceiling encrusted with writhing putti. Next to the church, its

UNDERSTANDING PALERMO

Palermo is essentially a straightforward street-grid confused by the memory of an Eastern past and gouged by war damage. Historical, the city sits compactly around a central crossroads, the **Quattro Canti**, which is the intersection of Corso Vittorio Emanuele and Via Maqueda, two streets that date from the city's reconstruction in the sixteenth century. Parallel to Via Maqueda, and running north from Stazione Centrale, **Via Roma** was a much later addition, linking the old centre with the **modern city**. At the heart of this nineteenth-century grid of shops, apartments and office blocks are the double squares of Piazza Castelnuovo and Piazza Ruggero Séttimo – together known to Palermitans as **Piazza Politeama** – a lengthy 25- to 30-minute walk from the train station (or a quicker bus ride).

Four distinct medieval quarters lie around Quattro Canti: the **Albergheria** and **Capo** districts lie roughly west of Via Maqueda, **Vucciria** and **La Kalsa** to the east, closest to the water. In the past, the inhabitants of these quarters had their own dialects, trades, palaces and markets – even intermarriage was frowned upon. Today, the areas hold most of Palermo's most interesting sights and buildings, concealed within a tight, undisciplined web of alleys and piazzas. Often, you'll come across tranquil gardens or chapels containing outstanding works of art, or even stabling for a goat – a world away from the din of the urban assault course outside. Beyond the old centre, on the outskirts of the modern city, are other attractions, from Palermo's best park, the **Parco della Favorita**, to the ghoulish **Cappuccini monastery**, while the other quick retreat is to **Monte Pellegrino**, the mountain that looms beyond the city to the north.

Given that cars, let alone buses, can't get down many of the narrow streets in the old city centre, you'll have to **walk** around much of what is detailed in this chapter – although for certain specific sights, don't hesitate to jump on a bus, as it's no fun at all slogging up and down the long thoroughfares of the modern city.

former convent is now the main building of the **Università**. There are generally plenty of students around here, and a couple of good bars in the little piazza across from the entrance.

Museo d'Arte Contemporanea della Sicilia

Corso Vittorio Emanuele 365 • Tues–Sun 10am–7.30pm • €6 • ☎ 091 587 717, ⓦ palazzoriso.it

The restored eighteenth-century Palazzo Riso is now home to the **Museo d'Arte Contemporanea della Sicilia**, with a permanent collection of Sicilian art dating back to the 1950s, as well as a programme of temporary exhibitions. Whether you want to see the collection or not, the palazzo is a marvellous place to escape from the hubbub of the city, with a cool bar (see p.72), courtyard and arty book and gift shop.

Piazza Pretoria

Step into **Piazza Pretoria** and you're confronted by the gleaming-white nude figures of a racy sixteenth-century Florentine fountain, protected by railings to ward off excitable vandals. The piazza also holds the plaque-studded and pristine **Municipio** and, towering above both square and fountain, the massive late sixteenth-century flank of the church of **Santa Caterina**, its entrance around the corner on Piazza Bellini.

Piazza Bellini

Just around the corner from the Pretoria fountain, **Piazza Bellini** is largely a car park by day, with vehicles jammed together next to part of the city's old Roman wall. It's also home to three of Palermo's most distinct churches, **Santa Caterina**, **San Cataldo** and **La Martorana**. The first is Baroque, the latter two medieval, and you could do far worse than to spend your first hour in the city succumbing to their charms.

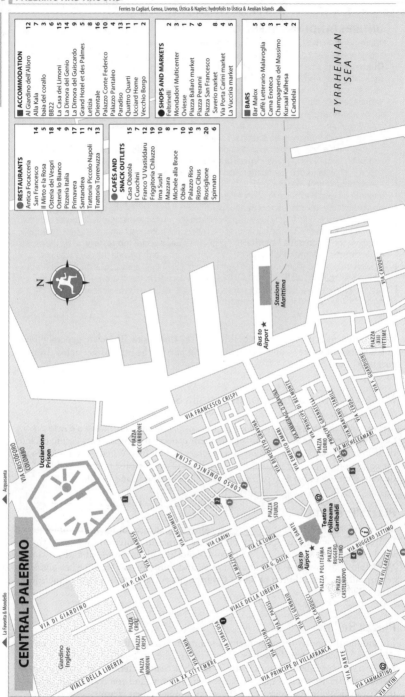

CENTRAL PALERMO

Ferries to Cagliari, Genoa, Livorno, Ústica & Naples; hydrofoils to Ústica & Aeolian Islands

ACCOMMODATION

Al Giardino dell'Alloro	12
Alla Kala	7
baia del corallo	3
BB22	6
La Casa dei Limoni	15
Osteria lo Bianco	14
La Dimora del Genio	9
La Dimora del Guiscardo	9
Grand Hotel et des Palmes	5
Letizia	8
Orientale	16
Palazzo Conte Federico	10
Palazzo Pantaleo	4
Paradiso	13
Quattro Quarti	11
Ucciard Home	1
Vecchio Borgo	2

SHOPS AND MARKETS

Feltrinelli	2
Mondadori Multicenter	3
Oviesse	1
Piazza Ballarò market	7
Piazza Peranni	6
Piazza San Francesco	8
Saverio market	4
Via Porta Carini market	4
La Vuccíria market	5

BARS

Bar Malox	5
Caffè Letterario Malavoglia	6
Cama Enoteca	3
Champagneria del Massimo	1
Kursaal Kalhesa	4
I Candelai	2

RESTAURANTS

Antica Focacceria San Francesco	14
Il Mirto e la Rosa	5
Osteria dei Vespri	18
Osteria lo Bianco	4
Pizzeria Italia	9
Primavera	17
Santandrea	11
Trattoria Piccolo Napoli	2
Trattoria Torrenuzza	13

CAFÉS AND SNACK OUTLETS

Casa Obatola	15
I Cuochini	7
Franco 'U Vastiddaru	12
Friggitoria Chiluzzo	19
Ima Sushi	10
Mazzara	8
Michele alla Brace	1
Obika	16
Palazzo Riso	3
Risto Cibus	20
Rosciglione	6
Spinnato	6

Stazione Marittima

Bus to Airport ★

TYRRHENIAN SEA

Ucciardone Prison

VIA CRISTOFORO COLOMBO

VIA FRANCESCO CRISPI

PIAZZA UCCIARDONE

CORSO DOMENICO SCINA

VIA PRINCIPE DI BELMONTE

VIA ENRICO AMARI

PIAZZA FLORIO

VIA PRINCIPE GRANATELLI

VIA MARIANO STABILE

VIA E. CAVOUR

VIA CANDIDO

VIA E. GUARDIONE

PIAZZA XIII VITTIME

VIA MICHELE AMARI

VIA ARCHIMEDE

VIA E. ALBANESE

VIA CARINI

VIA LA LUMIA

VIA G. DAITA

Bus to Airport

PIAZZA STURZO

Teatro Politeama Garibaldi

VIA DANTE

VIA RUGGERO SETTIMO

PIAZZA POLITEAMA

PIAZZA RUGGERO SETTIMO

PIAZZA CASTELNUOVO

VIA VILLAREALE

VIA P. CALVI

VIA MAZZINI

VIA DI GIARDINO

PIAZZA CROCI

PIAZZA CRISPI

VIALE DELLA LIBERTÀ

VIA XX SETTEMBRE

VIA SIRACUSA

VIA CATANIA

VIA MESSINA

VIA E. PARISI

VIA U. GENNAIO

VIA CARDUCCI

VIA DANTE

PIAZZA MORDINI

Giardino Inglese

VIALE DELLA LIBERTÀ

VIA PRINCIPE DI VILLAFRANCA

VIA SAMMARTINO

VIA LATINI

N

La Favorita & Mondello ▲

Acquasanta ▲

Museo Momimo ▼

Airport & Sferracavallo Campsites ▼

1

Santa Caterina

Piazza Bellini • April–Oct Mon–Sat 9.30am–1.30pm & 3–7pm, Sun 9.30am–1.30pm; Nov–March Mon–Sat 9.30am–1pm & 3–5.30pm, Sun 9.30am–1pm • Free

Founded in 1566, when Palermo was still under Spanish rule, the exterior of **Santa Caterina** has a certain gravitas, while the interior demonstrates Sicilian Baroque at its most daftly exuberant, as subtle as a multi-coloured wedding cake, with every centimetre of the enormous interior larded with pustular relief work, deep reds and yellows filling in between sculpted cherubs, Madonnas, lions and eagles. One marble panel (in the first chapel on the right) depicts Jonah about to be devoured by a rubbery-lipped whale, with a Spanish galleon above constructed from wire with string rigging.

San Cataldo

Piazza Bellini • April–Oct Mon–Sat 9am–2pm & 3.30–7pm, Sun 9am–2pm; Nov–March daily 9am–2pm • €2.50

The little Saracenic red golf-ball domes above Piazza Bellini belong to **San Cataldo**, a squat twelfth-century chapel on a palm-planted bank above the square. Other than the crenellations around the roof it was never decorated, and in the eighteenth century the chapel was even used as a post office. It still retains a good mosaic pavement in an otherwise bare and peaceful interior.

La Martorana

Piazza Bellini • Mon–Sat 9.30am–1pm & 3.30–5.30pm, till 6.30pm in summer, Sun 8.30–9.45am & noon–1pm

La Martorana is one of the finest surviving buildings of the medieval city. It was paid for in 1143 by George of Antioch, King Roger's admiral, from whom it received its original name, Santa Maria dell'Ammiraglio. After the Sicilian Vespers, the island's nobility met here to offer the Crown to Peter of Aragon, and under the Spanish the church was passed to a convent founded by Eloisa Martorana – hence its popular name. It received a Baroque going-over and its curving northern facade in 1588, but happily this doesn't detract from the great power of the **interior**; enter through the twelfth-century campanile, an original structure that retains its ribbed arches and slender columns. The church is a popular location for Palermitan weddings, spectacular events that often culminate in the newlyweds releasing a dozen white doves from the steps of the church.

The mosaics

A series of spectacular **mosaics** is laid on and around the columns supporting La Martorana's main cupola – animated twelfth-century Greek works, commissioned by the admiral himself, who was of Greek descent. A gentle Christ dominates the dome, surrounded by angels, with the Apostles and the Madonna to the sides. The colours are still strong, a golden background enlivened by azure, grape-red, light-green and white, and, in the morning especially, light streams in through the high windows, picking out the admirable craftsmanship. On both sides of the steps by the entrance, two more original mosaic panels (from the destroyed Norman portico) have been set in frames on the walls: a kneeling George of Antioch dedicating the church to the Virgin, and King Roger being crowned by Christ – the diamond-studded monarch contrasted with a larger, more simple and dignified Christ.

FRUTTA DI MARTORANA

When Palermo's religious houses were at their late medieval height, many supported themselves by turning out remarkable sculpted **confectionery** – fruit and vegetables made out of coloured almond paste. La Martorana was once famous for the quality of its almond "fruits", which were sold at the church doors, and today most Sicilian *pasticcerie* continue the tradition. In Palermo these creations are known as **frutta di Martorana**, and cake-shop windows usually display not only fruit but also fish and shellfish made out of the same sickly almond mixture. The best time to see the displays is in October, before the festival of Ognissanti (All Saints).

The Albergheria

The district bounded by Via Maqueda and Corso Vittorio Emanuele, just northwest of Stazione Centrale – the **Albergheria** – can't have changed substantially for several hundred years. Although there are proud *palazzi* on Via Maqueda itself, the real heart of the quarter is in the sprawling warren of tiny streets away from the main roads. The central core is taken up by the Ballarò, one of Palermo's liveliest **street markets**, and there are several fine **churches** interspersed among the tall, blackened and leaning buildings.

Il Gesù

Via Ponticello • Daily 7am–noon & 4–6.30pm

The most spectacular of the Albergheria's churches is **Il Gesù**, or **Casa Professa**, topped by a green-and-white-patterned dome. The first Jesuit foundation in Sicily, it was begun in the mid-sixteenth century and took over a hundred years to complete. It was later almost entirely rebuilt following bomb damage in World War II, and there are still signs of the devastation in the surrounding streets. The reconstruction has been impressively thorough, and the church's awesome interior, a glorious Baroque swirl of inlaid marble, majolica, intricate relief work and gaudily painted ceiling, takes some time to absorb.

Piazza Ballarò market

Market Mon–Sat, usually from 5am until around 1pm

Piazza Ballarò is the focus of a raucous daily fruit and vegetable **market** that starts early in the morning. Gleaming fish curl their heads and tails in the air, squashes come as long as baseball bats, and vine leaves trail decoratively down from stalls. There are some very cheap snack bars here, too, where you can sidle in among the locals and sample sliced-open sea urchins, fried artichokes and beer, along with unmarked drinking dens and gutsy snack stalls selling *pane e milza* and *pane e panelle*. Don't leave the area without visiting *Rosciglione* (see p.72), creators of the best *cannoli* in town.

At the southern end of Piazza Ballarò, the bright majolica-tiled dome of the seventeenth-century church of **Santa Maria del Carmine** looms above Piazza del Carmine, a singular landmark amid the market stalls and rubbish-strewn alleys.

San Nicolò

Via Nasi • Usually open Tues & Sat 10.30am–12.30pm • Donation expected

The **Torre di San Niccolò** started life as a watchtower in thirteenth-century Palermo, but in 1518 it was co-opted by the adjacent church as a campanile. These days you can climb the 84 steps to the top for an unsurpassed birds'-eye view of the market, teeming humanity and the city, while guides will help you identify surrounding landmarks.

San Giovanni degli Eremiti

Via dei Benedettini • Daily 9am–5pm, summer until 6.30pm • €6

Built in 1132, the deconsecrated church of **San Giovanni degli Eremiti** – St John of the Hermits – is the most obviously Arabic of the city's Norman relics, its five ochre domes topping a small church that was built upon the remains of an earlier mosque (part of which, an adjacent empty hall, is still visible). It was especially favoured by its founder, Roger II, who granted the monks of San Giovanni 21 barrels of tuna a year, a prized commodity controlled by the Crown. A path leads up through citrus trees to the church, behind which lie some celebrated late thirteenth-century cloisters – perfect twin columns with slightly pointed arches surrounding a wilted garden.

1

Palazzo dei Normanni

Royal Apartments Mon, Fri & Sat 8.15am–5.40pm, last entry at 5pm, Sun & hols 8.15am–1pm, last entry at 12.15pm • **Cappella Palatina** Mon–Sat 8.15am–5.40pm, last entry at 5pm, Sun & hols 8.15am–9.45am & 11.15am–1pm, last entry at 12.15pm • Check the website before visiting, as parliamentary sessions often disrupt the usual opening hours • Royal Apartments and Cappella Palatina €8.50, Cappella Palatina only €7 • Ⓦ federicosecondo.org

A royal palace has always occupied the high ground above medieval Palermo, and the vast length of the **Palazzo dei Normanni**, or Palazzo Reale, still dominates the western edge of the old town. Originally built by the Saracens in the ninth century, the palace was enlarged considerably by the Normans, under whom it housed the most magnificent of medieval European courts. The long front was added by the Spanish in the seventeenth century, and most of the interior is now taken up by the Sicilian regional parliament (hence the security guards and limited access).

Visitors can tour the **Royal Apartments**, whose showpiece is the **Sala di Ruggero**, one of the earliest parts of the palace and richly covered with twelfth-century mosaics of hunting scenes. Other rooms, such as the **Sala del Duca di Montalto**, are used for occasional exhibitions. The highlight of the entire palace, however – and the undisputed artistic gem of central Palermo – is the beautiful **Cappella Palatina**, the private royal chapel of Roger II, built between 1132 and 1143. Its intimate interior is immediately overwhelming, with cupola, three apses and nave entirely covered in **mosaics** of outstanding quality. The oldest are those in the cupola and apses, probably completed in 1150 by Byzantine artists; those in the nave are from the hands of local craftsmen, finished twenty-odd years later and depicting Old and New Testament scenes. The colours are vivid and, as at Monreale and Cefalù, it's the powerful representation of Christ as Pantocrator that dominates the senses, bolstered here by other secondary images – Christ blessing, open book in hand, and Christ enthroned, between Peter (to whom the chapel is dedicated) and Paul. The chapel also has a delightful Arabic ceiling with richly carved wooden stalactites, a patterned marble floor and an impressive marble Norman candlestick (by the pulpit), 4m high and contorted by manic carvings.

The Cattedrale

Piazza Cattedrale • **Cattedrale** Mon–Sat 7am–7pm, Sun 8am–1pm & 4–7pm; closed during services • **Area Monumentale** Mon–Sat: March–Oct 9am–5.30pm; Nov–Feb 9am–1.30pm • €3, or €7 including roof tour • **Roof** Mon–Sat: March–Oct 9am–5.30pm • €5 • ☎ 091 334 373, Ⓦ cattedrale.palermo.it

Walking down Corso Vittorio Emanuele from the Quattro Canti, there's no preparation for the sudden, huge bulk of the **Cattedrale**, an even more substantial Norman relic than the royal palace. Founded in 1185 by Palermo's English archbishop Gualtiero Offamiglio (Walter of the Mill), the cathedral was intended to be his power base in the city. Yet it wasn't finished for centuries, and in any case was quickly superseded by the glories of William II's foundation at Monreale. Less-than-subtle late eighteenth-century alterations added a dome – completely out of character – and spoiled the fine lines of the tawny stone. Still, the triple-apsed eastern end (seen from a side road off the Corso) and the lovely matching towers are all twelfth-century originals and, despite the fussy Catalan-Gothic facade, there's enough Norman carving and detail to give the exterior more than mere curiosity value. The same is not true, however, of the overblown interior, which was modernized by Fuga, the Neapolitan architect responsible for the dome. Instead, the main interest inside resides in the **Area Monumentale**, where you can view the **royal tombs**, Palermo's pantheon of kings and emperors. Gathered together in two crowded chapels are the mortal remains of some of Sicily's most famous monarchs, notably Frederick II (left front) and his wife Constance (far right), Henry VI (right front) and Roger II (rear left). In a reliquary chapel to the right of the choir

1

the remains of city patron, Santa Rosalia, are housed in a silver casket, while in the **treasury**, or *tesoro*, is a rare twelfth-century jewel- and pearl-encrusted skullcap and three simple, precious rings removed from the tomb of Constance of Aragon in the eighteenth century. The **crypt** is home to 23 impressive marble tombs, many of which are actually ancient sarcophagi with interesting decoration – no. 12 is a Greek sarcophagus boasting an imposing effigy by Antonello Gagini, one of a prolific dynasty of talented medieval sculptors who covered Sicily with their creations.

In summer, you can take a tour of the cathedral **roof**, reached via a spiral staircase in one of the towers, for breathtaking views of Palermo and a chance to appreciate the intricacy of the Arab-Norman architecture below.

Museo Diocesano
Tues–Fri 9.30am–1.30pm, Sat 10am–6pm, Sun 9am–1.30pm • €4.50 • ☎ 091 334 373

At the western end of the cathedral, over the road, stands the **Palazzo Arcivescovile**, the one-time archbishop's palace, entered through a fifteenth-century gateway. One wing of it holds the **Museo Diocesano**, which brings together religious art from the cathedral and from city churches destroyed during World War II. There's some marvellous work here from the medieval and Renaissance periods, including a twelfth-century mosaic of the Madonna, a startling flagellation of Christ by Antonio Veneziano (1388), and a couple of lovely fifteenth-century triptychs, both showing the *Coronation of the Virgin* (one with angels blasting on trumpets).

Porta Nuova
Corso Calatafimi

Alongside the Royal Palace, **Porta Nuovo** was Palermo's most important city gate. Erected in 1535, at the beginning of the road to Monreale, it commemorates Charles V's Turkish exploits, with suitably grim, turbaned and moustachioed Moorish prisoners appearing as telamons along the western side.

Il Capo

Around the back of the Cattedrale lies the **Capo** quarter, one of the oldest areas of Palermo and another labyrinthine web of run-down streets. The only touch of grace is in the tree-planted **Piazza del Monte**, while former grandeur is indicated by a few surviving sculpted portals in the decaying palaces. One alley, Via Porta Carini, climbs past shambolic buildings and locked, battered churches to reach the decrepit **Porta Carini** itself, one of the city's medieval gates.

These days Via Porta Carini holds one of the city's best **markets**, and the entire area is reminiscent at times of an Arab souk, though with a decidedly Sicilian choice of wares. The market extends on either side of Via Porta Carini, west to the edge of the Capo district and east, along **Via Sant'Agostino** – the closer you get to Via Maqueda, the more it's devoted to clothes and shoes rather than food.

Sant'Agostino
Via Sant'Agostino • Mon–Sat 7am–noon & 4–6pm, Sun 7am–noon

Sant'Agostino was founded by the Chiaramonte and Sclafani families in the thirteenth century. Above the main door (on Via Raimondo) there's a gorgeous latticework rose window and, inside through the adjacent side-door, some fine seventeenth-century stuccoes by Giacomo Serpotta. Another door leads to a quadrangle of calm sixteenth-century cloisters. Otherwise, turn the corner, and along Via Sant'Agostino, behind the market stalls, the church sports a badly chipped, sculpted fifteenth-century doorway attributed to Domenico Gagini.

1

SICILIAN PUPPET THEATRE

Sicily's most vibrant traditional entertainment is its puppet theatre, and in the engaging **Museo delle Marionette** (Mon–Sat 9am–1pm & 2.30–6.30pm, Sun 10am–1pm, closed Sun June, July & Aug; €5; ☎091 328 060, ⊕museomarionettepalermo.it) you'll find the country's definitive collection of puppets and painted scenery; the museum is just down Via Butera at Piazzetta Antonio Pasqualino. The fairly wide-ranging collection also encompasses puppet figures from Rajasthan, glittering dragons from Rangoon and the British Punch and Judy in their traditional booth, but it's the Sicilian puppets that steal the show. Best of all is to see one of the theatrical performances staged at the museum – enjoyably rowdy affairs of battles, chivalry, betrayal and shouted dialect, based around French and Sicilian history and specifically the exploits of the hero Orlando (Roland). Other backstreet **puppet theatres**, run by the same families for generations, include Figli d'Arte Cuticchio, at Via Bara all'Olivella 95, near Teatro Massimo (☎091 323 400, ⊕figlidartecuticchio.com); Teatro Argento, at Via Pietro Novelli 1, off Corso Vittorio Emanuele and opposite the Cattedrale (☎091 611 3680); and Teatro Ippogrifo, at Vicolo Ragusi 6, near Quattro Canti and off Corso Vittorio Emanuele (☎091 329 194).

Via Roma and Via Garibaldi

Starting out from Stazione Centrale, there doesn't seem too much along modern **Via Roma** to get excited about, but many of the side streets are traditionally devoted to particular trades and commerce. Ironmongery, wedding dresses, baby clothes and ceramics all have their separate enclaves, while the pavements of narrow Via Divisi are chock-full of stacked bikes from a series of cycle shops. Via Divisi itself runs to **Piazza della Rivoluzione**, from where the 1848 uprising began, marked by an oddly elaborate fountain. From here, **Via Garibaldi** marks the route that Garibaldi took in May 1860 when he entered the city; at Via Garibaldi 23, the immense, battered fifteenth-century **Palazzo Aiutamicristo** keeps bits of its original Catalan-Gothic structure.

Piazza Croce dei Vespri

North of Piazza della Rivoluzione, Via Aragona leads to Piazza Aragona, the first of a confusing jumble of squares. **Piazza Croce dei Vespri** is named for a cross erected in memory of the French who died in the 1282 Sicilian Vespers rebellion (see p.373). Dominating is the imposing entrance to the **Palazzo Valguarnera Gangi**, where Visconti filmed the ballroom scene in *The Leopard*; you may be able to get a glimpse of the interior by smooth-talking the porter.

San Francesco d'Assisi

Corso Vittorio Emanuele • Daily 8am–noon & 4–6pm • Free

From Corso Vittorio Emanuele, Via A. Paternostro swings right to the thirteenth-century church of **San Francesco d'Assisi**, whose well-preserved portal, picked out with a zigzag decoration, is topped by a wonderful rose window – a harmonious design that is, for once, continued inside. All the Baroque trappings have been stripped away to reveal a pleasing stone interior, the later side chapels showing beautifully crafted arches – the fourth on the left is one of the earliest Renaissance works on the island, sculpted by Francesco Laurana in 1468.

Oratorio di San Lorenzo

Via Immacolatella 5 • Mon–Sat 9am–5pm • €2

To the side of San Francesco d'Assisi, the renowned **Oratorio di San Lorenzo** contains another of Giácomo Serpotta's stuccoed masterpieces, namely intricately fashioned scenes from the lives of St Lawrence and St Francis. However the Oratorio is best

1

known for one of **Caravaggio**'s most dynamic and perfectly preserved canvases, *Nativity with Saints Francis and Lawrence*, stolen in 1969 and never recovered. There have been several attempts to establish the whereabouts of the painting, though in 2009, Mafia *pentito* Gaspare Spatuzza claimed that in the 1980s it had been given to one of Palermo's leading Mafia families, who then hid it in a stable, where it was nibbled to shreds by rats and pigs, then burned.

The waterfront

From the Quattro Canti, **Corso Vittorio Emanuele** stretches east towards the waterfront, where the old city harbour of **La Cala** is on the left. This thumb-shaped inlet was once the main port of Palermo, stretching as far inland as Via Roma, but the harbour was in decline from the sixteenth century, when silting caused the water to recede to its current position. With all the heavy work transferred to new docks to the northwest, La Cala's surviving small fishing fleet now plays second fiddle to the yachts of Palermo's well-heeled. The little harbour is overlooked on one side by the church of **Santa Maria della Catena**, named after the chain that used to close the harbour in the late fifteenth century. The Corso, meanwhile, ends at the Baroque **Porta Felice** gate, begun in 1582 as a counterbalance to the Porta Nuova, visible way to the southwest. From here, you can judge the extent of the late medieval city, which lay between the two gates.

The whole area beyond the Porta Felice was flattened in 1943, and has since been rebuilt as the **Foro Italico** promenade (also known as Foro Umberto I), complete with small amusement park, from where you can look back over the harbour to Monte Pellegrino. This is one of the liveliest places in the city on summer evenings, when the locals take to the street armed to the teeth with cellphones and ice creams. A street back, on Via Butera, the seventeenth-century facade of the **Palazzo Butera** faces out over the Foro Italico. Once the home of the Branciforte family, at one time the wealthiest family in Sicily, it was gradually partitioned and sold off, and is now only open for conferences or groups of visitors, but numerous films have been shot here, including *The Talented Mr Ripley* and *The Godfather Part III*.

Piazza Marina

The large square of **Piazza Marina** encloses the tropical **Giardino Garibaldi**, famed for its enormous banyan trees. It's a popular venue for the city's elderly card-players, who gather around green baize tables at lunchtime for a game. The square itself was reclaimed from the sea in the tenth century, subsequently used for jousting tournaments and executions, and is now overlooked by the lovely Renaissance facade of Santa Maria dei Miracoli, and surrounded by pavement restaurants and *palazzi*, including the second largest of Palermo's palaces, the **Palazzo Chiaramonte**, flanking the east side of the square. Dating from the fourteenth century, the palace was the home of the Inquisition from 1685 to 1782, before becoming the city's law courts (until 1972). Today, it is the administrative centre of the university and is only open to the public for occasional art exhibitions.

Palazzo Mirto

Via Merlo 2 • Tues–Fri 9am–6pm, Sat & Sun 9am–1pm • €4, or €10 with Galleria Regionale della Sicilia

Palazzo Mirto is a late eighteenth-century building that's one of the few in the city to retain its original furnishings, thus giving a rare insight into *palazzo* life. The exquisite ceilings, intimate Chinese Room, imposing *baldacchino*, vibrantly coloured tapestries and overblown Baroque fountain are perhaps all to be expected, but the family's more modest living quarters have also been preserved, while visits also take in the servants' kitchen and the carriages in the stables.

Galleria d'Arte Moderna

Via Sant'Anna 21 • Tues–Sun 9.30am–6.30pm • €7 • ☎ 091 843 1605, ⓦ galleriadartemodernapalermo.it

At the far end of Via Alloro, Piazza Sant'Anna is home to the Convento di Sant'Anna, which has been stunningly restored and opened as the seat of the **Galleria d'Arte Moderna**. The collection of nineteenth- and twentieth-century Sicilian works here is displayed thematically (portraits, nudes, mythology, seascapes, landscapes etc) to great effect. Its **café**, spilling into the courtyard in summer, is one of the loveliest places in the city for lunch or an aperitif. Prestigious international touring exhibitions often visit, too.

Galleria Regionale della Sicilia

Via Alloro 4 • Tues–Fri 9am–6pm, Sat & Sun 9am–1pm • €8, €10 with Palazzo Mirto • ☎ 091 623 0011, ⓦ regione.sicilia.it/beniculturali/palazzoabatellis

Sicily's finest medieval art collection is displayed in the **Galleria Regionale della Sicilia**, which occupies the princely Palazzo Abatellis, a fifteenth-century building that still retains elements of its Catalan-Gothic and Renaissance origins. There are some wonderful works here, by all the major names encountered on any tour of the island, starting with the fifteenth-century sculptor **Francesco Laurana**, whose white marble bust of *Eleonora d'Aragona* is a calm, perfectly studied portrait. Another room is devoted to the work of the **Gagini** clan, mostly statues of the Madonna, though Antonello Gagini is responsible for a rather strident *Archangel Michael*, with a distinct military manner. Highlight of the ground floor, though, is a magnificent fifteenth-century **fresco**, the *Triumph of Death*, by an unknown (possibly Flemish) painter. It's a chilling study, with Death cast as a skeletal archer astride a galloping, spindly horse, trampling bodies slain by his arrows. He rides towards a group of smug and wealthy citizens, apparently unconcerned at his approach; meanwhile, to the left, the sick and the old plead hopelessly for oblivion.

The first floor

There are three further frescoes (thirteenth- and fourteenth-century Sicilian, and rather crude) above the steps up to the **first floor**, which is devoted to painting. The earliest works (thirteenth- to fourteenth-century) are fascinating, displaying marked Byzantine characteristics, like the fourteenth-century mosaic of the *Madonna and Child*, eyes and hands remarkably self-assured. For sheer accomplishment, though, look no further than the collection of works by the fifteenth-century Sicilian artist **Antonello da Messina**: three small, clever portraits of saints Gregory, Jerome and Augustine (with a rakish red hat), followed by an indisputably powerful *Annunciation*, a placid depiction of Mary, head and shoulders covered, right hand slightly raised in acknowledgement of the (off-picture) Archangel Gabriel.

La Kalsa

La Gancia Mon–Sat 9.30am–noon & 3–6pm, Sun 10am–12.30pm • Orto Botanico Daily 9am–dusk • €5

The Galleria Regionale stands at the edge of the neighbourhood of **La Kalsa** (from the Arabic *khalisa*, meaning "pure"), one of the oldest quarters in Palermo, originally laid out by the Saracens and heavily bombed during World War II. It's still a little on the rough side, with some unkempt squares and alleys, although the area is showing some signs of gradual gentrification, with the opening of new bars, restaurants and some chic B&Bs.

There's more work by the Gagini family (sculpted fragments and reliefs) in the fifteenth-century church of **La Gancia** – or Santa Maria degli Angeli – next door to the gallery on Via Alloro. To escape La Kalsa and the city noise, walk a few minutes along Via Lincoln to the eighteenth-century gardens of **Villa Giulia**. There's a children's train

1

ride, plus bandstand, deer and ducks, while the **Orto Botanico**, next to the park, dates from 1795 and features tropical plants from all over the world.

Santa Maria dello Spasimo
Piazza Kalsa • Mon–Wed & Fri–Sun 8am–1pm & 4.30–6pm • ☎ 091 616 1486

The former church and convent of **Santa Maria dello Spasimo** is semi-ruined and roofless – and all the more romantic for it. None other than Raphael painted *Lo Spasimo di Sicilia* for the church, installed here in 1520 (though now in the Prado in Madrid). Since then, the church has been variously used as a theatre, barracks, plague hospital and rubbish tip; recently it has served as one of the city's most popular and atmospheric concert venues, but is currently undergoing restoration (call for an update).

La Magione
Piazza Magione • Mon–Sat 9.30am–noon & 3–6.15pm • Donation requested

La Kalsa's main highlight is the lovely church of **La Magione**, standing in isolation on Piazza Magione and approached through a pretty palm-lined drive and garden. A fine example of Arab-Norman architecture, it was originally built in 1151 for the Cistercians, but given to the Teutonic knights as their headquarters by Henry VI in 1197. The **cloister** resembles that at Monreale, and houses a rare Judaic tombstone re-carved into a basin for holy water. In the room between the cloister and the chapel, there's a **fresco** of the crucifixion and – far more interesting and rare – a plaster preparation of the fresco, opposite. It's the only example of a **fresco model** in Sicily, and its near-mathematical sketch lines show the care and detailed planning that went into the creation of such works.

La Vucciria

North of Corso Vittorio Emanuele and east of Via Roma, one of Palermo's oldest markets, **La Vucciria**, is said to be named after the French *boucherie*, for butcher's shop. Once the most renowned **market** in Palermo – and subject of one of Renato Guttuso's most famous paintings – it is now a shadow of its former self, though it still has several

---

SHOPPING IN PALERMO

Palermo's old quarter sometimes seems like one big market. Apart from the stalls of Il Capo, Vucciria and Ballarò, where a range of household items is on offer alongside the fruit and veg, the city has several **flea markets** (*mercati delle pulci*) – with the occasional antique lurking amid the knick-knacks and curios – notably on Piazza Peranni near the cathedral, displaying chandeliers galore, and the Albergheria's Piazza San Francesco Saverio off Corso Tukory (this last on Sunday). You're more likely to find jewellery, watches – often convincing copies of branded products – and "designer" clothing on Via Sant'Agostino and the backstreets of the Capo quarter. More upmarket **boutiques** are scattered along Via Roma and Via Ruggero Séttimo, and on and around Viale della Libertà.

Sicilian **puppets and ceramics** of varying quality are sold along Corso Vittorio Emanuele, Via Divisi and around Piazza Marina, or in the new city around Piazza Castelnuovo and along Viale della Libertà. You'll also find model **Sicilian carts** in abundance in all these areas – a typical, if rather corny, souvenir. For **frutta di Martorana** look in any decent *pasticceria* – these are sold by weight, and do not need to be kept chilled.

One of the best **supermarket** chains is Oviesse, which has a branch at Viale della Libertà, on the corner with Via Siracusa (Mon–Sat 9am–8pm, Sun 10am–1pm & 4–8pm). The ubiquitous SISA, CRAI and GS supermarkets are also perfectly adequate, though prices are much higher than at the street markets.

There's a large selection of English **books** at Mondadori Multicenter, Via Ruggero Séttimo 18 (daily 9.30am–8.30pm; ☎091 769 061); and Feltrinelli, Via Cavour 139 (Mon–Fri 9am–8.30pm, Sat 9am–9pm, Sun 10am–1.30pm & 4–8.30pm; ☎091 781 291).

basic bars and fish trattorias. There are a couple of excellent little trattorias tucked away in the alleys (best at lunchtime), and some very basic bars where the wine comes straight from the barrel.

San Domenico

Piazza San Domenico • Tues–Sun 8.15am–noon, Sat & Sun also 5–7pm

The northern limit of La Vucciria market is marked by the church of **San Domenico**, whose fine eighteenth-century facade, with its double pillars and slim towers, is lit at night to great effect. Inside, a series of tombs contains a horde of famous Sicilians – parliamentarians, poets and painters – of little interest to foreigners except to shed some light on Palermitan street-naming.

Oratorio del Rosario di San Domenico

Via dei Bambinai • Mon–Sat 9am–1pm • Donation requested

Behind San Domenico is a greater treat, the sixteenth-century **Oratorio del Rosario di San Domenico**, built and still maintained by the Knights of Malta, and adorned by the acknowledged master of the art of stucco sculpture, **Giacomo Serpotta**. Born in Palermo in 1656, Serpotta devoted his entire life to decorating oratories like this – here, the figures of *Justice, Strength* and suchlike (resembling fashionable society ladies, who often served as models) are crowned by an accomplished Van Dyck altarpiece.

Oratorio del Rosario di Santa Zita

Entrance on Via Valverde • Mon–Fri 9am–1pm, ring the bell if closed, or ask in the church • €2.50

Stucco-seekers will find splendour aplenty behind the late sixteenth-century church of Santa Zita (or Santa Cita) on quiet Via Squarcialupo. The marvellous **Oratorio del Rosario di Santa Zita** contains some of the wildest flights of Serpotta's rococo imagination – a dazzling confusion of allegorical figures, bare-breasted women, scenes from the New Testament, putti galore, and, at the centre of it all, a rendering of the Battle of Lepanto. It's a tumultuous work, depicted with loving care – notice the old men and women, or the melancholy boys perched on the ledge, and look for Serpotta's symbol on the left wall, the golden snake.

Piazza XIII Vittime

Piazza XIII Vittime is named for the five tall V-shaped steel plates that splinter out of the ground, commemorating the officials who have lost their lives in Palermo's enduring struggle with the Mafia. The installation replaces a monument commemorating thirteen citizens shot by the Bourbons in the 1860 revolt, which now stands along Via Cavour.

Museo Archeologico Regionale

Piazza Olivella 24 • Closed for restoration • ☎ 091 611 6806

The cloisters and surviving buildings of a sixteenth-century convent – once the property of the Sant'Ignazio all'Olivella church – now house Palermo's **Museo Archeologico Regionale**. Its magnificent collection gathers together artefacts found at all western Sicily's major Neolithic, Carthaginian, Greek and Roman settlements, but unfortunately the museum has been closed since 2009 for long-overdue renovations. These should improve the frankly old-fashioned displays, but you may have to take the projected re-opening date of 2014 with a pinch of salt. The new layout was undecided at the time of writing, but the highlights of the collection are described below.

1

In particular, the museum is the repository of the extraordinary finds from the Greek site of **Selinunte** on the southwest coast, gathering together the rich stone carvings that adorned the various temples (known only as Temples A–G). The oldest are single panels from the early sixth century BC, representing the gods of Delphi, the Sphinx, the rape of Europa, and Hercules and the Bull. Other reconstructed friezes are more vivid works from the fifth century BC, like Perseus beheading Medusa, while the most technically advanced tableaux are those from Temple E, portraying a lithe Hercules fighting an Amazon, the marriage of Zeus and Hera, Actaeon savaged by three ferocious dogs, and Athena and the Titan. Other Greek relics include the famous stone lion's-head water-spouts from the fifth-century BC Victory Temple at **Himera** – the fierce animal faces tempered by braided fur and a grooved tongue that channelled the water. Finds from the sites at Términi Imerese and Solunto are also here, as well as rich bronze sculptures like the naturalistic figure of an alert and genial ram (third century BC) from **Siracusa**, once one of a pair (the other was destroyed in the 1848 revolution). There's **Etruscan** funerary art, a wide range of **Neolithic** finds (including casts of the incised drawings from Addaura, on Monte Pellegrino, and Lévanzo), and a series of beautifully preserved **Roman mosaics** – the largest of which measures nearly 10m in length – excavated from Piazza della Vittoria in Palermo.

The modern city

Via Maqueda assumes an increasingly modern aspect as it progresses north from Quattro Canti. Barring the bustle of activity around **Via Candelai** – a busy shopping street by day, a hubbub of cafés at night – the interesting medieval alleys are gradually replaced by the wider and more nondescript streets around Piazza Verdi.

Beyond the Teatro Massimo theatre Via Maqueda becomes Via Ruggero Séttimo, which cuts through gridded shopping streets on its way to the huge double square that characterizes modern Palermo. Known as **Piazza Politeama**, it's made up of Piazza Castelnuovo to the west and Piazza Ruggero Séttimo to the east. Dominating the whole lot is Palermo's other massive theatre, the late nineteenth-century **Politeama Garibaldi**, built in overblown Pompeiian style and topped by a bronze chariot pulled by four horses. From here, broad boulevards shoot up to the shady nineteenth-century gardens of the Giardino Inglese.

Teatro Massimo

Piazza Verdi • Tours every 30min Tues–Sun 9.30am–5pm; last tour at 4.30pm, 4pm if there's a show starting at 5.30pm, and there are no tours during rehearsal times • €8 • ☎ 091 605 3267, ⓦ teatromassimo.it

Said to be the largest theatre in Italy, built on a scale to rival Europe's great opera houses, the nineteenth-century Teatro Massimo was constructed by Giovanni Battista

---

THE UCCIARDONE – NO NEED TO ESCAPE

A couple of blocks east of the Giardino Inglese is Palermo's notorious **Ucciardone prison**, connected by an underground passageway to the maximum-security bunker where the much-publicized *maxi processi* (maxi-trials) of Mafia suspects were held in the 1980s. At the time, the gloomy Bourbon prison was dubbed "the best-informed centre in Italy for gossip and intelligence about the operations of organized crime throughout the world", not least because it was home to a good percentage of the biggest names in the Italian underworld. Mafia affairs were conducted here almost undisturbed, by bosses whose food was brought in from Palermo's best restaurants and who collaborated with the warders to ensure that escapes didn't happen – something that might increase security arrangements and hamper their activities. However, following the murders of Mafia investigators Falcone and Borsellino in 1992, many of the highest-risk inmates were transferred to more isolated prisons in different parts of the country.

LA FESTA DI SANTA ROSALIA

Next to nothing is known for sure about **Rosalia**, who was probably a member of the Norman court in the twelfth century, except that at some point she rejected her wealthy background and lived as a hermit on Monte Pellegrino. Nothing more was heard of her until the early seventeenth century, when a vision led to the discovery of her bones in a mountain cave. Pronounced sacred relics, these were carried around Palermo in procession in both 1624 and 1625, thus staying the ravages of a terrible plague. It's a ceremony that is now re-enacted every July 15 (and also Sept 4), with a torchlight procession to the saint's sanctuary that forms part of Palermo's annual jamboree, **La Festa di Santa Rosalia** – "**U Fistinu**" in dialect. An ebullient blend of devotion and revelry, U Fistinu is the central event of the year for locals, while for tourists it's an uproarious party, perhaps the most exhilarating you'll see anywhere in Italy. The annual ritual includes both solemn processions and gaudy entertainment, with the passionate and vociferous participation of hundreds of thousands of Palermitani. The central event is a long parade through the centre of town, from the Palazzo dei Normanni along Corso Vittorio Emanuele to the seafront, headed by a candle-lit statue of the saint borne aloft on the "Carro Trionfale". There are puppet re-enactments of the saint's miracles, concerts, exhibitions, and a gastronomic feast on Foro Italico, where heaps of food are consumed – most famously, snails, nuts, watermelons and *dolci*. The celebrations culminate in a spectacular display of fireworks over the harbour.

Basile, whose Neoclassical design was possibly influenced by Charles Garnier's contemporary plans for the Paris Opéra. **Tours** with an English-speaking guide show you the rich, gilded, marble **Sala Pompeiana**, where the nobility once gathered, and the domed ceiling in the six-tiered **auditorium**, constructed in the shape of a flower head, its centre and petals adorned with an allegorical portrayal of the triumph of music. Francis Ford Coppola shot the long climactic opera scene of *The Godfather Part III* here, using the theatre's sweep of steps to great effect.

Museo Mormino

Viale della Libertà 52 • Mon–Fri 9am–1pm & 3–5pm, Sat 9am–1pm • €4 • ⓦ museo.fondazionebancodisicilia.it

Near the Giardino Inglese gardens, the **Museo Mormino** houses a beautifully presented collection of artefacts and paintings in the sumptuous Banco di Sicilia building. There's a wide selection of Italian majolica from the fifteenth to the eighteenth centuries, and an extensive collection of Greek vases, Etruscan finds, old maps and ancient coins, while nineteenth-century paintings on show include the seascapes and tuna-fishing scenes of Antonino Leto.

Out from the centre

It's well worth taking time to explore the Palermo that lies beyond the city centre. The highlights are the fine Arab Norman palace of **La Zisa** and the ghoulish mummies of the **Catacombe dei Cappuccini**. A one-time royal Bourbon hunting ground, **Parco della Favorita** is now a public park, its charms somewhat compromised by the fact that it's crisscrossed by roads – anyone wanting to escape the city for a few hours would be better advised to head for the nature reserve of **Monte Pellegrino**.

Parco della Favorita

3km north of Piazza Politeama • **Park** No set hours • Free • **Palazzina Cinese** Tues–Sat 9am–5pm, Sun 9am–1pm • Free • ⓦ parcodella favorita.it • Take bus #101 from Stazione Centrale to Piazza Giovanni Paolo II, then change to the #645 and ask to be dropped at the park

North of the centre lies the **Parco della Favorita**, a long, wooded expanse at the foot of Monte Pellegrino, with sports grounds and stadiums at one end, and formal gardens laid out a couple of kilometres beyond. The grounds were originally acquired in 1799 by the Bourbon king Ferdinand during his exile from Naples, and for three years he lived here in the **Palazzina Cinese**, a small but exquisite Chinese-style pavilion. There are plans afoot to close the entire park area to traffic.

1

Monte Pellegrino

Sanctuaries di Santa Rosalia Daily 7am–12.15pm & 2–6pm • ⓦ www.riservamontepellegrino.palermo.it • Bus #812 from Piazza Sturzo or Teatro Politeama

North of the city, and clearly visible from the port area, the massive bulk of **Monte Pellegrino** separates Palermo from the bay at Mondello. The mountain is a nature reserve, and there are marked paths across it, though for most locals Monte Pellegrino is primarily a venue for Sunday picnics and strolls. It's also a significant place of pilgrimage, the site of the shrine of the city's patron saint, St Rosalia.

The half-hour ride up the mountain provides wide views over Palermo and its plain. At the very end of the road stands the **Santuario di Santa Rosalia**, part of a ramshackle collection of huts and stalls, entered through a small chapel erected over a deep cave in the hillside where the saint's bones were discovered in 1624. Inside, a bier contains a reclining golden statue of the saint, thought by Goethe to be "so natural and pleasing, that one can hardly help expecting to see the saint breathe and move". The water trickling down the walls is supposedly miraculous.

A small road to the left of the chapel leads to the cliff-top promontory – a half-hour's walk – where a more restrained statue of Santa Rosalia stares over the sprawling city. Another path, leading up from the sanctuary to the right, takes you to the top of the mountain – 600m high, and around a forty-minute walk. Elsewhere, the trails that cover Monte Pellegrino are dotted with families picnicking, while kids play on rope swings tied to the trees.

La Zisa

Piazza Guglielmo II Buono • Mon & Sun 9am–1pm, Tues–Sat 9am–6.30pm • €6 • ⓣ 091 652 0269 • Bus #124 from Piazza Sturzo and Piazza Politeama stops at La Zisa

The palatial king's retreat of **La Zisa** – from the Arabic *al-aziz* or "magnificent" – was begun by William I in 1160, and later finished by his son William II. At one time its beautiful grounds were stocked with rare and exotic beasts, though a raid on the palace by disaffected locals in 1161 released some of the wild animals, which probably came as a bit of a shock to William's neighbours. It's now besieged by modern apartment blocks, but has been thoughtfully restored to something approaching its former glory. The centrepiece is the **Sala della Fontana**, comprising an elaborate fountain in a marble-sided chamber with glittering mosaic decoration. These are appropriate surroundings for a modest collection of Islamic art and artefacts, mostly inscribed copper bowls from periods much later than when La Zisa was constructed, and from different parts of the Mediterranean. The latticed windows afford impressive **views** over the surrounding greenery.

Catacombe dei Cappuccini

Piazza Cappuccini • April–Oct daily 9am–noon & 3–6pm; Nov–March daily 9am–12.30pm & 3–5.30pm • €3 • ⓣ 091 652 4156 • Take bus #327 from Piazza Indipendenza southwest along Via dei Cappuccini as far as Via Pindemonte, and then follow the signposts for a couple of hundred metres

Of all the attractions on the edge of Palermo, it's the **Catacombe dei Cappuccini** that generates the most interest among visitors. For several hundred years the Cappuccini placed its dead brothers in catacombs under the church and later, up until 1881, rich laymen and others were interred here too. Some 8000 bodies in all were preserved by various chemical and drying processes – including dehydration, the use of vinegar and arsenic baths, and treatment with quicklime – and then placed in niches along rough-cut subterranean corridors, dressed in a suit of clothes that they had previously provided for the purpose. In different caverns reserved for men, women, the clergy, doctors, lawyers and surgeons, the bodies are pinned with an identifying tag, some decomposed beyond recognition, others complete with skin, hair and eyes, fixing you with a steely stare. Those that aren't arranged along the walls lie in stacked glass coffins, and, to say the least, it's an unnerving experience to walk among them.

Times change, though, as Patrick Brydone noted in his late eighteenth-century *A Tour Through Sicily and Malta*:

Here the people of Palermo pay daily visits to their deceased friends … here they familiarize themselves with their future state, and chuse the company they would wish to keep in the other world. It is a common thing to make choice of their nich, and to try if their body fits it … and sometimes, by way of a voluntary penance, they accustom themselves to stand for hours in these niches …

Of all the skeletal bodies, saddest are the many remains of babies and young children, nothing more than spindly puppets. Follow the signs for the sealed-off cave that contains the coffin of two-year-old Rosalia Lombardo, who died in 1920. A new process, a series of injections, preserved her to the extent that she looks as though she's asleep. Perhaps fortunately, the doctor who invented the technique died before he could tell anyone how it was done.

ARRIVAL AND DEPARTURE
PALERMO

BY PLANE
Falcone Borsellino airport, also known simply as Punta Raisi (☎ 800 541 880, ⊛ gesap.it), is at Punta Raisi, 31km west of the city. **Buses** (Prestia & Comandè, ☎ 091 580 457, ⊛ prestiaecomande.it) run into Palermo (every 30min; 5am–midnight; 45min), and stop outside Politeama theatre, Stazione Marittima and at Stazione Centrale; tickets are €6.10 on board, or €11 return via the website. For the return, departures are at 4am, 5am and then every 30min until 11pm. **Trains** (€5.80) run from the airport to Stazione Centrale at 5.54am, 7.20am, and then on the hour and at 20min past the hour until 9.20pm, with the final departure at 10.05pm. From Stazione Centrale they leave at 4.45am, 5.09am, 6.07am and then every 30min between 7.09am and 8.09pm. The airport ticket office number is ☎ 091 704 4007.

BY TRAIN
All trains arrive at the Stazione Centrale at the southern end of Via Roma. Bus #101 runs from the station along Via

Roma to Via della Libertà. It has its own priority lane, so is much faster than most of the city's other services. Even the *linea gialla* and *linea rossa*, little buses that run through the *centro storico*, passing by the station, get terribly snarled up in the traffic.

Destinations Agrigento (10 daily Mon–Sat, 7 daily Sun; 2hr 15min); Bagheria (2–3 hourly; 10min); Capaci (hourly; 40min); Carini (hourly; 45min); Castellammare del Golfo (hourly; 1hr 30min); Castelvetrano via Alcamo (5–6 daily; 2hr 25min); Cefalù (hourly; 45min–1hr); Isola delle Fémmine (hourly; 30–45min); Mazara del Vallo via Alcamo (6 daily; 3hr); Milazzo (13 daily; 2hr 30min–3hr); Messina (13 daily; 3–4hr); Solunto (1–2 hourly; 15min); Términi Imerese (2–3 hourly; 25–40min); Trapani (5 daily; 2hr 15min–3hr 45min).

BY BUS
The majority of country- and island-wide buses operate from the recently opened Piazza Cairoli bus station alongside the train station.

BUS COMPANIES

AST Via Paolo Balsamo ☎ 091 680 0038, ⊛ aziendasicilianatrasporti.it. For Bagheria, Castelbuono, Corleone and Montelepre.
AST Piazzale John Lennon, near Viale Regione Siciliana ☎ 091 685 8015, ⊛ aziendasiciliana trasporti.it. For Capaci, Carini and Partinico.
Cuffaro Via Paolo Balsamo ☎ 091 616 1510, ⊛ cuffaro.info. For Agrigento.
Interbus Via Paolo Balsamo ☎ 091 616 7919, ⊛ interbus.it. For Catania and Siracusa.
Prestia & Comandè Stazione Centrale ☎ 091 586 351, ⊛ prestiaecomande.it. For the airport and Piana degli Albanesi.
Randazzo Via Paolo Balsamo ☎ 091 814 8235,

⊛ autobusrandazzo.altervista.org. For Caccamo and Términi Imerese.
Russo Piazza Marina ☎ 092 431 364, ⊛ russo autoservizi.it. For Castellammare del Golfo and San Vito Lo Capo.
SAIS Via Paolo Balsamo ☎ 091 616 6028, ⊛ saisautolinee.it. For Caltagirone, Catania, Cefalù, Enna, Gela, Messina and Piazza Armerina.
Segesta Via Paolo Balsamo ☎ 091 616 919, ⊛ segesta.it. For Alcamo, Messina, Partinico and Trapani.
Salemi Via Rosario Gregorio ☎ 092 398 1120, ⊛ autoservizisalemi.it. For Castelvetrano, Marsala and Mazara del Vallo.

1

Destinations Agrigento (5 daily; 2hr 30min); Bagheria (1–2 hourly Mon–Sat; 1hr 15min); Caccamo (4 daily Mon–Sat; 1hr); Caltagirone (1 daily except Sat; 3hr); Caltanissetta (7–10 daily Mon–Sat, 5 daily Sun; 1hr 40min); Capaci (Mon–Sat 1–2 hourly; 1hr); Carini (Mon–Sat 1–2 hourly; 1hr–1hr 30min); Castelbuono (5 daily Mon–Sat, 1 daily Sun; 1hr 40min–2hr 30min); Castellammare del Golfo (6 daily Mon–Sat, 1–3 daily Sun; 50min); Catania (hourly; 2hr 40min); Cefalù (5 daily; 1hr); Corleone (hourly Mon–Sat; 1hr 30min); Enna (5–7 daily; 1hr 35min–1hr 50min); Gela (3–4 daily; 2hr 45min–3hr); Marsala (hourly; 2hr 30min); Messina (5 daily Mon–Sat; 2hr 40min); Piana degli Albanesi (6 daily Mon–Sat; 1hr); Piazza Armerina (hourly; 2hr 15min); San Martino delle Scale (2 daily Mon–Sat; 30min); San Vito Lo Capo (2–4 daily Mon–Sat, 1–3 daily Sun; 2–3hr); Siracusa (3 daily; 3hr 15min); Términi Imerese (6 daily Mon–Sat; 40min); Trapani (Segesta; 1–2 hourly; 2hr).

BY FERRY OR HYDROFOIL

Stazione Marittima All ferry and hydrofoil services dock at the Stazione Marittima, just off Via Francesco Crispi. A free *navetta* bus shuttles constantly between the Stazione Marittima and the port entrance (though it is only a 5min walk), from where it's a 10min walk up Via E. Amari to Piazza Castelnuovo. There is a left luggage office at the port (€2.50 per piece of luggage); it's officially open daily 7am–8pm, but they may ask you what time you want to pick up your luggage, and close for a while if things are quiet.

City transport from the port Bus #139 connects the port with Stazione Centrale, though it is rather infrequent, so it is better to walk up Via E. Amari to Piazza Politeama from where buses #101 or #102, and the *linea rossa*, run regularly to the train station.

Schedules The ferry and hydrofoil services detailed here refer to the period from June to Sept; expect frequencies to be greatly reduced or suspended outside these months. Ferry details are available on ⊚ aferry.it, while all hydrofoils are run by Ustica Lines (⊚ usticalines.it).

Ferry destinations Cagliari (1 or less weekly; 14hr 30min); Civitavecchia (up to 3 weekly; 17hr); Genoa (1 daily; 20hr); Naples (1–2 daily; 11hr); Tunis (1–2 weekly; 10hr); Ustica (1 daily; 2hr 20min).

Hydrofoil destinations Aeolian Islands (all 1 daily) – Alicudi (2hr), Filicudi (2hr 30min), Rinella (3hr 15min), Santa Marina Salina (3hr 30min), Lipari (4hr), Vulcano (4hr 25min), Panarea (4hr 40min), Stromboli (5hr 15min); Ustica (2 daily; 90min).

GETTING AROUND

BY BUS

AMAT buses City buses (AMAT; ☎ 091 350 111, infoline ☎ 848 800 817 or from a mobile ☎ 199 240 800, ⊚ amat .pa.it) cover every corner of Palermo as well as Monreale and Mondello.

Fares and tickets There's a flat fare of €1.30 valid for 90min, or you can buy an all-day ticket for €3.50, while tickets for the *linea gialla*, *linea rossa* and *linea verde*, and the *circolare* minibus services (which all weave in and out and over the *centro storico*), cost just €0.52 for a day's use. Buy them from AMAT booths outside Stazione Centrale, at the southern end of Viale della Libertà, in *tabacchi* and anywhere else you see the AMAT sign, or, if you forget, from the driver for a supplement of €0.40. Validate tickets in the machine at the back of the bus as you board – there has recently been a clampdown on people travelling without tickets, with spot checks carried out by plainclothes inspectors. The main city bus rank is outside Stazione Centrale and buses run until midnight (11.30pm on Sun).

BY CAR

City driving It's far better not to drive in Palermo – you won't need a car to get around, and can pick up a rental car on the day you leave. Driving into the city can be a bit traumatic, as directional signs are confusing and the traffic unforgiving of first-time visitors. Following signs for "Stazione Centrale" – or anything that reads "Centro" – should at least get you into the city, while Piazza Politeama is a convenient first place to get your bearings and leave your vehicle.

Parking Finding a parking space can be a real problem, though you'll find somewhere eventually if you drive around for long enough. Metered parking costs €1 an hour (maximum 3hr) – either feed the ticket machine or buy a parking scratch card (*biglietto parcheggio*) from a nearby shop. In some areas, you will be ushered into a parking space by an unofficial attendant, who will expect a tip of 50 cents to €1. It's much less hassle to use a garage, especially if you have to leave your car in Palermo's old quarter overnight: useful ones include L'Oasi Verde (Corso Tukory 207, southwest of Stazione Centrale), Central Garage (Piazza Giulio Césare 43, in front of Stazione Centrale), Via Guardione 81 (near Stazione Marittima, behind Via Francesco Crispi) and Via Sammartino 24 (town centre, off Via Dante). It costs €10–20 per day to garage-park, usually less when arranged through a hotel.

Leaving the city Take Via Oreto (behind Stazione Centrale) for the Palermo–Messina (A19) and Palermo–Catania (A20) autostradas; Corso Vittorio Emanuele (westbound) for Monreale; and Viale della Libertà (northbound) for the airport and Trapani.

Car rental Avis, Via Francesco Crispi 115 (☎ 091 586 940); Hertz, Via Messina 7/E (☎ 091 323 439); Maggiore, Stazione Notarbartolo 79 (☎ 091 681 0801); Sicily By Car, Via Mariano Stabile 6/A (☎ 091 581 045). All of these also have desks at the airport.

OPPOSITE QUATTRO CANTI (P.49) >

1

BY TAXI

Taxi companies and ranks Palermo's three taxi companies – Auto Radio Taxi (☎091 513 311, ⓦ www.autoradiotaxi.it), Radio Taxi Trinacria (☎255 or ☎091 6878, ⓦ radiotaxitrinacria.it) and Sicilia Uno (☎339 408 5713, ⓦ siciliaunotaxipalermo.com) – all charge the same rates. The minimum fare is €4.50; if the driver doesn't want to switch the meter on, agree a fare you are prepared to pay first – not a bad strategy if there is more than one taxi driver about, as they may well bid for custom. There are ranks at the airport, train and bus stations, piazzas Castelnuovo, Verdi and Matteotti and at Via Roma.

Drivers For a good reliable official taxi driver who charges less than most call Pino ☎328 374 5341, who will do the airport run for €40, and Stazione Centrale to the port for €10.

BY HORSE-DRAWN CARRIAGE OR APE

Taking a horse-drawn carriage, a *carrozza*, is a suitably kitsch way to see the city, or you could take a tour on a Piaggio Ape, a three-wheeler pick-up. Both tout for business alongside Piazza Pretoria, outside the port and by the cathedral, and should charge around €20 per person for a tour of the city.

BY BIKE OR SCOOTER

If you're adept on two wheels, biking is not a bad option: as long as you realize the rules of the road – he who hesitates is lost, and go for the gap – weaving your way in and out of the traffic can be an exhilarating way to save time and legwork. Rent Bike, Via Giardinaccio 66, off Via Maqueda (☎331 750 7886) offer bicycle and scooter rental.

INFORMATION AND TOURS

Tourist offices Palermo's helpful city-centre tourist office, at Via Principe di Belmonte 92, Mon–Fri 8.30am–2pm, 2.30–6pm, ☎091 585 172, ⓦ palermotourism.com), has maps and plenty of information about the city and province. Information kiosks run by the city council (all theoretically open Sat–Wed 9am–1pm & 3–7pm, Thurs & Fri 9am–1pm & 3–6pm, but hours may be reduced) are scattered through the city centre, in places like Piazza Politeama, Piazza Bellini and at the Stazione Centrale.

Listings information For a rundown of what's on, the free Agenda Turismo lists useful contact details, museum times, transport links and cultural events in and around the city. For a more detailed look at arts and entertainment, there's *Lapis* (ⓦ palermoweb.com/lapis), published fortnightly and widely available from cultural venues, bars and cafés. The local edition of the daily newspaper *Il Giornale di Sicilia* also details forthcoming events.

Tours The Parco Culturale del Gattopardo offer guided walking tours in Italian and English focusing on places associated with Giuseppe Tomasi di Lampedusa and his iconic book, *The Leopard* (☎327 684 4052, ⓦ parcotomasi.it).

ACCOMMODATION

Most of Palermo's traditional budget **hotels** lie on and around the southern ends of Via Maqueda and Via Roma, close to Stazione Centrale, but you'll get far more for your money in the city's **B&Bs**, many of which are charming and extremely well run. Prices tend to stay the same year-round (except out on the nearby coast, where usual summer rates apply), but advance reservations are recommended if you want to be sure of a room in a particular place (and also around the time of Palermo's annual festival, July 11–15). The two nearest **campsites**, as well as Palermo's **youth hostel**, are actually all at the beachside town of Sferracavallo, 16km northwest of the city or a good half an hour on the bus – convenient for beach or airport but not really for city sightseeing or nights on the town.

OLD TOWN

★ **Al Giardino dell'Alloro** Vicolo S. Carlo 8 ☎338 224 3541, ⓦ giardinodellalloro.it; map pp.52–53. Lovely B&B in the heart of La Kalsa with books for guests to borrow, a courtyard where breakfast is served, and a living room used as an exhibition space for contemporary Sicilian artists. The five rooms feature original works of art, and have kettles and mugs. There is a small kitchen for guests' use, and more rooms in the recently opened annexe. **€85**

Alla Kala Via Vittorio Emanuele 71 ☎091 743 4763, ⓦ allakala.it; map pp.52–53. An excellent, centrally located choice, this spick-and-span B&B has five stylish designer rooms and a suite with magnificent views of the sailing marina. It has a keen following among those in the know, so book in advance. **€120**

BB22 Palazzo Pantelleria, Largo Cavalieri di Malta 22 ☎091 611 6100 or ☎335 790 8733, ⓦ bb22.it; map pp.52–53. Faultless Milanese designer-chic (resinated cement floors, perspex chairs, walls painted in matt stone hues) blended with a feeling of being at home (free wi-fi, coffee and water) in a historic *palazzo* a few steps from the Vucciria market. Breakfast is served on a small roof terrace. The owners also organize food and wine tours, in both Palermo and further afield, and boat trips to the beach at Mondello. **€140**

La Casa dei Limoni Piazza Giulio Césare 9 ☎334 834 3888 or 338 967 8907, ⓦ lacasadeilimoni.it; map pp.52–53. A friendly B&B right opposite the train station that's great value for money, and the perfect place to stay if you arrive late or have to leave early. **€64**

1

La Dimora del Genio Via Garibaldi 58 ☎ 347 658 7664, ⓦ ladimoradelgenio.it; 5min walk from Stazione Centrale; map pp.52–53. Three cosy rooms in a centrally heated seventeenth-century *palazzetto*, furnished with a tasteful blend of antiques, modern furniture and original paintings by the owner's artist husband. The friendly owner is a talented cook, and offers cooking courses for guests, as well as a splendid Sunday dinner for €30 a head. **€90**

La Dimora del Guiscardo Via Vetriera 83–5 ☎ 328 662 6074, ⓦ ladimoradelguiscardo.it; map pp.52–53. Little B&B in the heart of La Kalsa, close to the area's bars and restaurants. Clean, simple rooms, and a sole shared bathroom. The owner offers free pick-up from the port, station or airport bus stop, and organizes wine tastings at the nearby *Enoteca Cama* (see p.74). **€60**

Grand Hotel et des Palmes Via Roma 398 ☎ 091 602 811, ⓦ grandhoteldespalmes.com; map pp.52–53. Although it may no longer have the cachet of the days when guests included Wagner, the *Des Palmes* remains an extremely comfortable four-star chain hotel conveniently located on the main Via Roma. What's more, discounts via the website can result in room rates that compete with those of many B&Bs. **€130**

Letizia Via dei Bottai 30 ☎ 091 589 110, ⓦ hotelletizia .com; map pp.52–53. Each room in this delightful hotel, just off Piazza Marina, has its own colour scheme and furnishings. There's an enclosed courtyard for breakfast, free wi-fi, and the loan of a mobile phone for the duration of your stay. **€115**

Palazzo Conte Federico Via dei Biscottari 4 ☎ 091 651 1881, ⓦ contefederico.com; map pp.52–53. A magnificent (if chilly) Arabic Norman palace built over the Punic city walls close to Ballarò market, retaining fourteenth-century frescoed ceilings and an impressive armoury. The aristocratic owners have several comfortable and practical one- and two-bedroom apartments for rent, plus a palatial suite, and can offer cooking lessons – followed by a torchlit dinner in the defensive tower. Apartments **€120**, suite **€360**

Quattro Quarti Palazzo Arone di Valentino, Via Vittorio Emanuele 376 ☎ 347 854 7209, ⓦ quattro quarti.it; map pp.52–53. A superior B&B with four smart, elegant rooms in part of a huge *palazzo* owned by the Arone di Valentino family. Guests are very well looked after, making this a great choice if you're a little nervous about finding your feet in Palermo. In the main part of the palace, there is a plush suite of rooms furnished with antiques. Rooms **€130**

MODERN CITY

★ **Palazzo Pantaleo** Via Ruggero Settimo 74/H ☎ 091 325 471 or ☎ 335 700 6091, ⓦ palazzopantaleo.it; map pp.52–53. This outstanding B&B has seven huge, light, airy rooms in an eighteenth-century *palazzo*, set on a quiet square close to Piazza Politeama. Great attention to the details that matter to business travellers – internet access in all rooms, adaptors for charging mobile phones in all sockets – plus respect for the privacy and independence of guests. There's a small kitchen where you can make drinks or snacks. **€100**

Ucciard Home Via Enrico Albanese 34–36 ☎ 091 348 426, ⓦ hotelucciardhome.com; map pp.52–53. Trendy designer hotel opposite the prison, with sixteen comfortable, stylish rooms and lovely, luxurious bathrooms. Staff are excellent, breakfasts good and deals via the website can be fantastic. **€154**

Vecchio Borgo Via Quintino Sella 1–7 ☎ 091 611 8330, ⓦ www.hotelvecchioborgo.eu; map pp.52–53. A smart and appealing hotel between the Piazza Politeama and one of Palermo's best weekend markets. Comfortable rooms with bold printed fabrics and all amenities (including internet points). Excellent breakfast, including home-made cakes. Garage €10 a night, outdoor car park free, but spaces are limited. Website deals can make it cheaper than many B&Bs. **€119**

OUT FROM THE CENTRE

Baia del Corallo Via Plauto 27, Sferracavallo ☎ 091 679 7807, ⓦ www.ostellopalermo.it; bus #101 from the train station to Piazza de Gaspari, and then bus #628 to Punta Matese; map p.50. Palermo's youth hostel is by the sea 12km northwest of the city – not the most convenient choice for sightseeing, but handy for the airport and a good cheap option for a first or last night. There's accommodation in double and family rooms as well as in dorms. Dorms **€18**; doubles/family rooms **€56**

★ **Grand Hotel Villa Igiea** Via Belmonte 43 ☎ 091 631 2111, ⓦ villaigiea.com; bus 731 or 721 from Piazza Croce, halfway along Via Liberta; map p.50. This classic Art Nouveau building, originally a villa of the Florio family (the people who pioneered tuna canning), was designed by Ernesto Basile in 1900, and stands outside the city centre above the Acquasanta marina. It has a swimming pool overlooking the port, shady gardens, a tennis court and sweeping terraces for the most stylish aperitif in town. Give up all notions of sightseeing in favour of long lazy days by the pool. Boat trips and food tours available. **€180**

EATING

You can eat well and cheaply in Palermo, either snacking in **bars** and at **market stalls** or sitting down in one of dozens of good-value **restaurants** throughout the old town serving *cucina casalinga*. Pizzas and pastries, in particular, are among the best in Sicily, while fish is another local highlight – a typical Palermo speciality is **pasta con le sarde**, macaroni with fresh sardines, fennel, raisins and pine kernels. Traditional **street food** is enjoying something of a renaissance, and in hole-in-the-wall outlets and fancy bars alike you can try the sort of earthy snacks and fritters the locals have eaten for

1

decades. The other prime glory is **ice cream** – Palermo's best *gelaterie* (ice-cream parlours) are famed all over Italy. Restaurants tend to **close early**, especially in the central old town, where if you turn up at 10pm the waiters are likely to be packing up around you. For the most popular places, go before 8pm or be prepared to wait in line.

CAFÉS AND SNACK OUTLETS

Casa Obatola Via Alloro 16 ☎091 982 4442; map pp.52–53. Relaxing little bar with seats outside on a *piazzetta* below Via Alloro, good for a rest before or after visiting the nearby Galleria Regionale. Delicious sandwiches (from €3) and salads, and good pastries. Mon–Sat 8am–9pm.

I Cuochini Via Ruggero Settimo 68 ☎091 581 158; map pp.52–53. Diminutive, spick-and-span *frigittoria* – all gleaming white tiles and zinc – founded in 1826, and concealed within an arched gateway (the only sign is a small ceramic plaque). *Panzerotti* (deep-fried pastries, stuffed with tomato, mozzarella and anchovy, or aubergine, courgette and cheese), *arancini* (with ragù, or with cheese and ham), *pasticcino* (a sweet pastry with minced meat), *timballini di pasta* (deep-fried pasta), *besciamelle fritte* (breadcrumbed and deep-fried bechemel) and the like – all at €0.70 a portion. Mon–Sat 8.30am–2.30pm.

Franco 'U Vastiddaru Piazza Marina (no phone); map pp.52–53. Palermitani street food such as *pane e panelli*, *arancini*, *crochè* and *pane con la milza* (*pane ca meusa* in Sicilian) – which you can eat at plastic tables on plastic plates with plastic knives and forks, on the busy corner of Piazza Marina and Via Vittorio Emanuele. Daily lunch & dinner.

Friggitoria Chiluzzo Piazza Kalsa (no phone); map pp.52–53. Stand under a canopy, drink beer from a bottle, and eat *pane* and *pannelle* from a paper wrapping. Daily from morning until late.

Ima Sushi Rinascente, Via Roma/Piazza San Domenico ☎091 610 7811, ⓦwww.rinascente.it; map pp.52–53. If you want to pretend you're not in Palermo for a while (and it happens), head up to this sushi bar on the fourth floor of the Rinascente department store. Colour-coded plates of sushi, California rolls and sashimi on the obligatory conveyor belt, priced at between €2.50 and €7.50. Daily 9am–midnight.

Mazzara Via Magliocco 15 (off Via Ruggero Settimo) ☎091 321 443; map pp.52–53. Long-established bar-*pasticceria* where Tomasi di Lampedusa is reputed to have penned some of *The Leopard*. These days it serves light brunch and lunches – try the rare roast beef with rocket and shaved parmesan – alongside a dangerous selection of pastries and ice creams. Tues–Sun 7am–9pm.

Michele alla Brace Piazza Borgo Vecchio (no phone); map pp.52–53. At the tiny market of Piazza Borgo Vecchio, you can't miss this huge grill with a couple of plastic tables and a steaming cauldron of vegetables. Buy your fish from one of the nearby stalls and bring it to Michele, who will grill it and provide you with veg, drinks and a table. Mon–Tues & Thurs–Sat lunch.

Obika Rinascente, Via Roma/Piazza S. Domenico ☎091 601 7861, ⓦobika.it; map pp.52–53. On the top floor of the Rinascente department store, this is the Palermo branch of an exclusive chain of bars specializing in meticulously sourced *mozzarella di bufala*, which appears in exquisitely presented salads and other light dishes. A great lunchtime escape from the heat and chaos of Palermo, and a good place for an aperitivo (daily 6.30–9pm), the drinks accompanied by a selection of mouthwatering mozzarella tasters. Daily 9am–midnight.

Palazzo Riso Via Vittorio Emanuele 365 ☎091 320 532, ⓦpalazzoriso.it; map pp.52–53. Cool, white, minimalist bar inside Palermo's new contemporary art museum. Hazelnut- and chocolate-flavoured coffees, tisanes, *cornetti* with forest fruits, light lunches and aperitivos. Eat in the bar, or outside in the shady courtyard. Free wi-fi and use of computers. Daily 10am–11pm.

Risto Cibus Via E. Amari 79 ☎091 323 062, ⓦgustidisicilia.com; map pp.52–53. High-class grocery store with a great deli counter, and a wood-fired oven that cooks up pizzas and other savoury pastries to eat in or take away. It's 5min walk from the port, so ideal for stocking up if you are sailing to Ustica or the Aeolian Islands. Daily 8am–11pm.

Rosciglione Via Gian Luca Barbieri 5 ☎091 651 2959; map pp.52–53. Watch *cannoli* being made as you eat them at this bakery (which exports worldwide) on the edge of the Ballarò market. Mon–Sat 7am–2pm & 1.30–6pm.

Spinnato Via Principe di Belmonte 107–115 ☎091 749 5104, ⓦspinnato.it; map pp.52–53. With tables outside on a pedestrianized street, this is the perfect place for breakfast, delicious cakes and ice creams, or an aperitivo served with an aesthetic cascade of roast almonds, shelled pistachios and crisps. Daily from breakfast until late.

RESTAURANTS

Antica Focacceria San Francesco Via A. Paternostro 58 ☎091 320 264, ⓦafsf.it; map pp.52–53. This old-fashioned place has been in the same family for five generations. Downstairs they serve traditional Palermitani street food, such as *focaccia schietta* (focaccia with offal and caciocavallo cheese), *sfincione* (pizza with onion, tomato, caciocavallo and breadcrumbs), *crochè* (potato croquettes) and *panelle* (chickpea-flour fritters). Upstairs you can eat full meals (try the *pasta con le sarde*, pasta with sardines). There are also several fixed-price menus: *pannelle*, *crochè*, an *arancina* or slice of pizza, *cannolo* and a drink for €7; or the same, with pasta instead of the *arancina* or pizza for €8.50. In summer you can eat outside. Mon & Wed–Sun lunch & dinner.

PALERMO'S STREET FOOD

Street food in Palermo is pretty distinctive – away from pizza slices and pastries there are plenty of things you may not have come across before (and a few you may not wish to encounter again). Many of the more **traditional snacks** are straight out of the market, and while chopped boiled octopus (*purpu* in Sicilian), cooked artichokes and charcoal-roast peppers and onions are at least familiar, you might be less inclined to hover at the stalls selling *pani cu' la meuza* – bread rolls filled with sautéed beef spleen or tripe, which either come unadorned (*schiettu*, meaning "nubile") or topped with fresh ricotta and caciocavallo cheese (*maritatu*, "married"). Meanwhile, any old-fashioned **friggittoria** (deep-fry takeaway) – and there are still plenty in Palermo – serves up *arancini* (savoury rice balls), *pane e pannelle* (chickpea-flour fritter served in a bread roll) and *crocchè* (potato croquettes with anchovy and caciocavallo cheese). *I Cuochini* (see opposite) wins our vote for street food, but **markets** too are a great place to sample all these kinds of street food, especially at Ballarò market (in Piazza del Carmine), at Vecchio Borgo and along Via Sant'Agostino. The Ballarò market, in particular, has a few very basic *hosterie* – wooden tables scattered around the market stalls – where you can accompany your snack with a beer or two.

Il Mirto e la Rosa Via Principe di Granitello 30 ☏091 324 353; map pp.52–53. One of the Palermo businesses that don't pay *pizzo* (see p.384), *Il Mirto* began life as a vegetarian restaurant, and the emphasis on vegetables remains alongside carefully sourced local fish and meat. Signature dishes include *caponata* with pistachio-spiked couscous, and home-made *tagliolini* with a sweet, sticky tomato sauce, grilled aubergine and cheese from the Nébrodi mountains. Finish up with a voluptuous dessert followed by home-made cinnamon liqueur. Eating à la carte, you'll spend around €25 for three courses without wine, €30 with dessert, but there are various deals (€10 for a *primo*, *secondo* and salad, €15 for antipasto, *primo*, *secondo*, salad and dessert). Mon–Sat lunch & dinner.

★ **Osteria dei Vespri** Piazza Croce dei Vespri ☏091 617 1631, ⌨osteriadeivespri.it; map pp.52–53. Palermo's best restaurant was opened as a hobby a decade ago and continues to be run with passion by brothers Andrea and Alberto Rizzo, who cook complex meals with a loyal and intelligent use of local Sicilian ingredients. Dishes might include rabbit terrine with pistachios from Bronte, black *tagliolini* served with red mullet, ginger, red onion and fresh fava beans, or quail stuffed with prunes served on a puree of cannellini beans and celeriac. À la carte you'll pay at least €20 per course, while there are *degustazione* menus at €60 and €85 per person, excluding wine. Mon–Sat lunch & dinner.

★ **Osteria lo Bianco** Via E. Amari 104 ☏091 251 4906; map pp.52–53. Decorated with Juventus souvenirs and religious bric-a-brac, this is one of the cheapest places to eat in town. Traditional Palermitano food, such as *pasta con sarde*, *polpette* (meatballs) in tomato sauce, *ricciola* in a spicy tomato sauce, or a stew of beef, peas and carrots. Two courses with wine and fruit for under €15. Mon–Sat lunch & dinner, Sun lunch only.

Osteria Paradiso Via Serradifalco 23 (no phone); map p.50. Typical family-run trattoria, to the north of La Zisa, open only at lunchtime and specializing in fish. There is no written menu – the owner just tells you what's available that day. Specialities include fish cooked in seawater, raw prawns dressed with olive oil and lemon juice, and deep-fried *cicirello*, a long skinny silver fish. Arrive early to get a table. Mon–Sat lunch only.

Pizzeria Italia Via Orologio 54 ☏091 589 885; map pp.52–53. Opposite Teatro Massimo and attracting large queues, this is the best place in town for light, oven-blistered pizzas (€4–10). Try the "Palermitana" with tomato, anchovies, onion, artichokes, *caciocavallo* cheese and breadcrumbs. Dinner only; closed Mon.

Primavera Piazza Bologni 4 ☏091 329 408; map pp.52–53. Not far from the cathedral – off Via Vittorio Emanuele and across from the Palazzo Riso – with outdoor seating in a lovely little piazza with a recently restored garden, this popular, reasonably priced trattoria serves home-style cooking such as *pasta con le sarde* and *bucatini con broccoli* (both €10). Bottles of good, inexpensive local wine as well. Tues–Sun lunch & dinner.

Trattoria Piccolo Napoli Piazzetta Mulino di Vento 4 ☏091 320 431; map pp.52–53. Lively trattoria off the Vecchio Borgo market, founded in 1951 and run by three generations of the same family. They have two boats at Terrasini: fish is brought in daily, and anything not eaten that day is sold on to the local market stalls. Try raw prawns (€60/kg), pasta with *neonati* (newborn fish) when it's in season (€12) or what may prove to be the best *caponata* you will ever taste (€4). Mon–Sat lunch only.

★ **Trattoria Torrenuzza** Via Torrenuzza 17 ☏091 252 5532; map pp.52–53. Bustling, no-frills trattoria where fish is grilled on an outside brazier. Eat at streetside tables in summer, inside in winter. Antipasti (mussel soup, seafood salad, etc) and *primi* (pasta with broccoli, with mussels and clams, or with swordfish and aubergine) are all priced at €5, except for a couple of special dishes such as

1

spaghetti with *ricci di mare* (sea urchin) which ring in at €10. Meat *secondi* (*involtini*, charcoal-grilled sausage and the like) are also €5, while fish dishes (mixed fried or grilled fish, grilled prawns, grilled sea bream or sea bass) cost from €7–10. Calamari and swordfish are frozen (but none the worse for it), the rest of the fish is fresh. Wine is a dangerous €3 a litre, so lunch here could well write off your afternoon. Daily lunch & dinner.

DRINKING AND NIGHTLIFE

After dark and over much of the city, Palermo's frenetic lifestyle stops, pedestrians flit quickly through the shadows, and the main roads are given over to speeding traffic and screaming police sirens. The only place for a civilized, fume-free *aperitivo al fresco* is the pedestrianized **Via Principe di Belmonte**, off the upper part of Via Roma, which has a glitzy selection of bars and *pasticcerie*. For a livelier scene, head to the clutch of bars in the streets **behind the Museo Archeologico** – Via Spinuzza, Via Bara all'Olivella and Piazza Olivella – while things are grungier in the student-filled bars along and around **Via Candelai**, not far from the Quattro Canti, off Via Maqueda. There's also a burgeoning bar scene down in La Kalsa, on and off Via Alloro.

BARS

Bar Malox Piazzetta della Canna; map pp.52–53. Hidden away off an old-town alley near the Quattro Canto, this convivial student bar has plenty of tables outside where the drinking continues till late. Tues–Sun evenings only; closed every other Sun.

★ **Caffè Letterario Malavoglia** Piazzetta Pietro Speciale; map pp.52–53. You could easily miss this small, backstreet "literary café" near Corso Vittorio Emanuele, but it's a good find, with sofas, books, occasional exhibitions and live music, cheap drinks from 6–9pm, and late hours. Daily 5.30pm–2am

★ **Cama Enoteca** Via Alloro 105; map pp.52–53. This cosy candle-lit wine bar has an excellent choice of wines and nibbles. The bar staff are welcoming and knowledgeable, and the variety of wines almost overwhelming. Sept–June Tues–Sun 7pm–2am.

Champagneria del Massimo Via Salvatore Spinuzza 59; map pp.52–53. Charming wine bar with outdoor seating near the Teatro Massimo; along with the neighbouring bars, it's a lively spot on summer nights, and stays open till the early hours. Closed Sun.

★ **Kursaal Kalhesa** Foro Italico 21 ☎091 616 2282, ⓦkursaalkalhesa.it; map pp.52–53. Set deep in the echoing stone vaults of the ancient fortifications of Arabic Palermo, this impressive café and wine bar is furnished with traditional Sicilian furniture, has a huge fire in winter and is a great place for a Sunday brunch. In summer, the Palermo address closes and the bar shifts to the seaside town of Vergine Maria. Tues–Sat noon–3pm & 7pm–1.30am, Sun noon–1.30am.

Il Kursaal Tonnara Tonnara di Bordonaro, Via Bordornaro 9, Vergine Maria ☎091 637 2267, ⓦkursaaltonnara.it; bus #731; map p.50. Evocative place set in an atmospheric former tuna-fishing station at the foot of Monte Pellegrino. There are indoor and outdoor bars, a jasmine-scented courtyard, a fancy sea-facing restaurant and frequent concerts. Daily, usually 7pm–late; closed winter.

CLUBS

Palermo's clubs are almost exclusively found in the northern part of the city, especially on and around Viale della Regione Siciliana, a bus- or taxi-ride from the centre. They're mostly expensive dance clubs, rarely worth the long journey – note also that you may have to pay to "join" the club before they'll let you in. In summer, the scene switches to the coastal resorts of Mondello and Isola delle Fémmine, while the beach at Capo Gallo, between Mondello and Sferracavallo (about 30min north of the city), is popular with students for ad hoc weekend parties until dawn.

Cafè 442 Piazza Don Bosco 1 ⓦcafe442.it; map p.50. Lounge bar near Viale Lazio and La Favorita, with nightly DJ sets and dancing, as well as rather too frequent karaoke. Tues–Sun usually 6pm–late.

I Candelai Via Candelai 65 ☎091 327 151, ⓦcandelai.org; map pp.52–53. Seat of a cultural association that organizes music events all over Sicily. Good student vibe, and very unpretentious; check the website for DJ sets and live music events. Moves to Sferracavallo in summer. Sept–June Tues–Sun evenings only.

Zsa Zsa Mon Amour Via Angelitti 32 ⓦzsazsamonamour.com; map p.50. Live rock, metal and funk bands, and the place to come if an Iron Maiden tribute is your kind of thing. It's west of Stazione Notarbartolo, off Piazza Campolo. Oct–June evenings only.

PALERMO'S FESTIVALS

Palermo's biggest traditional **festival** is La Festa di Santa Rosalia, in honour of the city's patron saint (see box, p.65). The city's most interesting arts festival is **Kals'Art**, a cultural extravaganza of live music, theatre and cinema that takes place at a number of venues in the old-town La Kalsa neighbourhood, usually between mid-July and mid-September. However, at the time of writing, its existence was threatened by a lack of funding.

MUSIC, CULTURE AND THE ARTS

There's always something going on in Palermo, and you can check the current cultural calendar at the tourist office, in the arts publication *Lapis* or the daily newspaper *Il Giornale di Sicilia*. Teatro Massimo is the first choice for **classical music**, but lots of other smaller theatres and concert halls have good music programmes too. Independent **arts centres** put on a really mixed bag of concerts and events, and although there's no major venue for **live bands** (top British and American artists rarely make it further south than Naples) the *Comune* regularly stages open-air gigs in the summer, usually in the Giardino Inglese and other city parks. Mainstream Italian-language **theatre** is less accessible to foreign visitors, but a couple of more offbeat venues are worth checking out, while **puppet theatre** is easily the best night out at the theatre in Palermo (see box, p.65). **Cinemas** show the latest films dubbed into Italian – it's rare to find films in their original language with subtitles – and the main central screens, *ABC* and *Imperia*, are right next to each other at Via Emerico Amari 160–166.

THEATRES AND LIVE MUSIC VENUES

★ **Agricantus** Via XX Settembre 82A ☎091 309 636, ⓦagricantus.org. Arts centre near the Giardino Inglese, owned by and named after Italy's most outstanding World Music band (check out the album *Tuareg* or the soundtrack to the film *Bagno Turco*). Regular live music and dance sessions, as well as theatre, readings, festivals and events, and a bar that's open until 1.30am. Tues–Sun evenings only.

★ **Nuovo Montevergini** Via Montevergini 8 ☎091 612 4314, ⓦnuovomontevergini.com. Alternative culture, Palermo-style, in a monumental deconsecrated convent that supports its own theatre, arts festivals and events programme, from dance and live music to poetry and film. Bar open daily until late.

Lo Spasimo Via dello Spasimo, La Kalsa ☎091 616 1486. The former church hosts an excellent series of concerts, classical and jazz, many of them free. Undergoing restoration at the time of writing, but may re-open soon.

Teatrino Ditirammu del Canto Popolare Via Torremuzza 6, La Kalsa ☎091 617 7865, ⓦteatrino ditirammu.it. An intimate venue for Sicilian folk music and traditional dance performances.

Teatro Libero Salita Partanna 4, Piazza Marina ☎091 617 4040, ⓦteatroliberopalermo.it. Palermo's long-standing avant-garde theatre, with an annual festival that incorporates theatre, dance, music and performance art.

Teatro Massimo Piazza Verdi ☎091 605 3580, ⓦteatromassimo.it. The concert and dance programme (classical music, opera and ballet) at Palermo's most prestigious venue runs from October to June, while in summer shows shift to the Teatro del Parco di Villa Castelnuovo for concerts and outdoor performances of ballet and operetta.

DIRECTORY

Consulates UK, Via Cavour 117 (☎091 326 412); USA, Via Vaccarini 1 (☎091 305 857); South Africa, Largo degli Abeti 16 (☎348 340 0219). Other major consulates are in Milan or Rome.

Hospitals Ospedale Cívico, Via Carmelo Lazzaro (☎091 666 1111); Policlinica, Via Carmelo Lazzaro (☎091 655 1111). For an ambulance call ☎118.

Left luggage Stazione Centrale by track 8 (daily 7am–11pm; €3.80 for the first 5hr, then cheaper); Stazione Maríttima (daily 7am–7.30pm; €3 for 12hr).

Newspapers Foreign newspapers and magazines are sold at kiosks at Stazione Centrale, Piazza Verdi and Piazza Castelnuovo, and at *Kursaal Kalhesa*, Foro Italico 21.

Pharmacies All-night service at Lo Cascio, Via Roma 1; Di Naro, Via Roma 207; and Farmacia Inglese, Via Marina Stabile 177. Other chemists operate a rota system, with the address of the nearest open chemist posted on the door.

Post offices Palazzo delle Poste, Via Roma 320 (Mon–Sat 8am–6.30pm).

Mondello

On a hot summer's day, when the city heat is oppressive, the most obvious escape from central Palermo is the 11km run to **MONDELLO**, a small seaside resort tucked under the northern bluff of Monte Pellegrino. A 2km-long sandy beach fronts the town, and there's also a tiny working harbour, a jetty from which you can try your luck fishing, and the remnants of a medieval tower. In July and August, like most Sicilian resorts, it's a bit of a zoo, featuring tacky souvenir stalls, hot-dog and burger vans, pumped-up pizza places and packed lidos. At night, there's a crush in the bars in the main square while the roads around are filled with cruising cars and preening youth. In winter it's more laidback and rarely busy, but many of the restaurants and snack stalls stay open and it's usually warm enough to swim until well past the end of the official season.

By bus To get to Mondello, take bus #806 or #833 from Piazza Politeama or Viale della Libertà – a thirty-minute ride. The last bus back to town leaves around midnight.

By car Driving to Mondello, exit at the Tommaso Natale junction from the main road.

By taxi A taxi from Palermo costs about €35.

EATING

There's a line of **trattorias** along the seafront at Mondello – some with outdoor terraces – though the quality is patchy (have a good look at the fish on display in the fridges before you decide where to eat).

Da Calogero Via Torre 22 ☎ 091 684 1333. Right on the seafront, this is the best traditional choice in Mondello. You stand up at the window and eat freshly caught and cooked

octopus (they do have chairs and tables these days, but standing is *de rigueur*). Daily lunch & dinner.

Monreale

The major excursion from the city – rated almost unmissable – is to **MONREALE**, a small hill-town 8km southwest of Palermo. It commands unsurpassed views down the Conca d'Oro valley, with the capital shimmering in the distant bay, and while the panorama from the "Royal Mountain" alone is worth making the trip for, the real draw is the mighty Norman cathedral and its celebrated **mosaics**. These form one of the most extraordinary and extensive areas of Christian medieval mosaic-work in the world, and are the apex of Sicilian-Norman art. Monreale is an easy day-trip from Palermo, but once the tourists leave in the late afternoon the prospect of a quiet night in town might appeal, and there are plenty of characterful B&Bs in the medieval alleys near the cathedral.

It's hard to look beyond the Duomo, but Monreale itself is a handsome small town with a dense latticework of streets and (mostly locked) Baroque churches. For the famous view down the valley, stroll into the courtyard of the new convent (built in 1747) behind the cathedral cloisters to the **belvedere** (the entrance is from the other corner of Piazza Guglielmo). Come *passeggiata* time the main **Via Roma** pulses with life, and you don't have to walk very far along here to swap touristy mosaic galleries and gift shops for butchers, grocers and hardware stores.

Brief history

Monreale's cathedral owes its existence to young **King William II**'s rivalry with his powerful Palermitan archbishop, the Englishman **Walter of the Mill**. Work had started on Walter's fine cathedral in the centre of the city in 1172. Determined to quickly break the influence of his former teacher, William endowed a new monastery in his royal grounds outside the city in 1174, and its **abbey church** – the Duomo at Monreale – was thrown up in a matter of years. Monreale was made an archbishopric in 1183, two years before Walter's cathedral was finished, and this unseemly haste had two consequences. As a highly personal project, Monreale's power lasted only as long as William did: although he wanted to create a royal pantheon, he was the last king to be buried here. But the speed with which the Duomo was built ensured the splendid uniformity of its interior art – a galaxy of mosaic pictures bathed in a golden background.

The Duomo

Piazza Guglielmo II • Mon–Sat 9am–12.45pm & 2.30–6pm, Sun 8am–10am & 2.30–5.30pm • Tower and terrace €1.50, combined ticket with treasury €2 • ⓦ cattedraledimonreale.it

Monreale's **Duomo** presides magisterially over the town centre, facing two open squares and flanked by alleys teeming with souvenir stalls and gift shops. A ticket desk provides access to the **tower and terrace** for some sweeping views, and there's a combined ticket to see the collection of reliquaries in the **treasury**. Before or after going inside, walk around the

1

exterior to wonder at the enormous triple **apse**, a polychromatic jumble of limestone and lava, supported by slender columns and patterned by a fine series of interlacing arches. To see it, go through the arched alley (Arco degli Angeli) to the left of the Duomo entrance.

Bear in mind that despite the continual influx of tourists, you may not be allowed in if dressed in skimpy beach clothes.

The mosaics

The gleaming **mosaics**, almost certainly executed by Greek and Byzantine craftsmen, are a magnificent achievement, thought to have been completed in just ten years. They were designed for worshippers to be able to read the Testaments straight from the walls, and eyes are drawn immediately to the all-embracing half-figure of Christ in benediction in the **central apse**. The head and shoulders alone stand almost 20m high, face full of compassion, curving arms with outstretched hands seemingly encompassing the whole beauty of the church. Underneath are an enthroned Virgin and Child, attendant angels and, below, the ranks of saints – each subtly coloured and identified by name. The two **side-apses** are dedicated to saints Peter (right) and Paul (left), the arches before each apse graphically displaying the martyrdom of each – respectively, an inverse crucifixion and a beheading. The **nave mosaics** then start with the Creation (above the pillars to the right of the altar) and run around the whole church, while the **aisle mosaics** depict the teachings of Jesus. Most scenes are instantly recognizable: Adam and Eve; Abraham on the point of sacrificing his son; positively jaunty Noah's-ark scenes showing the ship being built, recalcitrant animals being loaded aboard and Noah's family peering out of the hatches; the Feeding of the Five Thousand; and the Creation itself, a set of glorious, simplistic panels portraying God filling His world with animals, water, light … and Man.

Above the two **thrones** (royal and episcopal) are more mosaics: William receiving the crown from Christ, and the king offering the cathedral to the Virgin. Both William I and William II are buried here in side chapels, the latter resting in the white marble sarcophagus to the right of the apse.

Chiostro dei Benedettini

Enter from the corner of Piazza Gugliemo II, by the right-hand tower of the Duomo • Daily 9am–7pm, last entry 6.30pm • €6

The **Chiostro dei Benedettini**, or cloisters, is one of the indisputed highlights of the Duomo complex, an elegant arcaded quadrangle with 216 twin columns supporting slightly pointed arches – a legacy of the Arab influence in Sicilian art. No two of the carved capitals are the same: on one, armed hunters do battle with winged beasts; another has two men lifting high a casket of wine; while flowers, birds, snakes and geometric shapes dip and dance from column to column.

ARRIVAL AND DEPARTURE
MONREALE

By bus Bus #389 runs frequently from Palermo's Piazza dell'Indipendenza (outside the Porta Nuova, reached by bus #109 from Stazione Centrale) through the western suburbs and up the valley, and takes around twenty minutes.

By taxi A taxi from Palermo costs around €30 each way.

By car Parking is restricted in Monreale's old town and visitors

are advised to use one of the signposted car parks – there's one on Via Cappuccini, below the Duomo and belvedere (from where a pedestrian way leads up past souvenir stalls into the town) and another (Parcheggio Duomo) down Via D'Acquisto to the side of the Palazzo Communale. Parking costs €1 an hour, and it's free overnight after 8pm.

ACCOMMODATION, EATING AND DRINKING

There's only a limited number of **hotels** actually in town, but there are charming **B&Bs** and "rooms" places much nearer the Duomo, especially in the tangle of alleys by the Duomo's apse. There are plenty of **restaurants**, though prices are generally on the high side.

Bricco & Bacco Via B. D'Acquisto 13 ☎ 091 641 7773. A definite cut above the family tourist restaurants in town, this brasserie is serious about its meat. Steaks, chops and

lamb grills are €10–15, and the Angus beef is also available with a classy balsamic vinegar and honey salsa. Lunch & dinner: summer Mon–Sat; winter Tues–Sun.

1

La Ciambra Via Sanchez 23 ☎ 091 640 9565 or ☎ 335 842 5865, ⓦ laciambra.com. A quaint, family-run place wedged into a plant-filled alley, with a great view of the apse. The two rooms here sleep up to four people. No credit cards. **€70**

Peppino Via B. Civiletti 12 ☎ 091 640 7770. Popular local pizzeria tucked away down on a side street off Via Roma, past San Giuseppe church. It has a shady summer terrace, some *antipasti* to start and crisp pizzas (€5–12). Try one of the versions with *mozzarella di bufala*. Mon & Wed–Sun lunch & dinner.

Bagheria and around

The Palermitan nobility of the seventeenth and eighteenth centuries chose to sit out the enervating summer heat in their Baroque country villas scattered around the small town of **BAGHERIA**, 14km east of the city. Here – as described by Dacia Maraini in her memoir *Bagheria* – they enjoyed "the atmosphere of a summer garden enriched by lemon groves and olive trees, poised between the hills, cooled by the salt winds". Some of the villas are open for visits, and Bagheria still has the air of a summer retreat. Give yourself a full day and you can also see the ancient ruins of **Solus** at Solunto and the working fishing port of **Porticello**, the latter boasting a boutique hotel and a ring of harbourside fish restaurants that might just persuade you to make a night of it.

A town map outside the gates of Villa Palagonia shows you the local layout, but basically anything else you need – like drinks and ice cream – is easily found down the pleasant, long, traffic-free Corso Umberto I that runs from the villa.

Villa Palagonia

Via Palagonia • Daily: April–Oct 9am–1pm & 4–7pm; Nov–March 9am–1pm & 3.30–5.30pm • €5 • ☎ 091 932 088, ⓦ villapalagonia.it

Best known – or perhaps that should be most notorious – of Bagheria's Baroque villas is the **Villa Palagonia**, whose grounds boast an eccentric menagerie of grotesque gnomes, giants, gargoyles and assorted mutants. The villa was the work of Ferdinand, Prince of Palagonia, a hunchback who – in league with the architect Tommaso Napoli – took revenge on his wife's lovers by cruelly caricaturing them. Although only 64 of the original 200 statues remain, they certainly add entertainment to a wander around the garden, before you climb the stairs into the crumbling sandstone villa to view a selection of frescoed halls and the dramatic Salone degli Specchi, covered in mirrors and marbling.

Museo Guttuso

Via Rammacca 9 • April–Oct Tues–Sun 9.30am–2pm & 3–7.30pm • €5 • ☎ 091 943 902, ⓦ museoguttuso.it

Some 500m from the train station along the main SS113, **Villa Cattolica** has been restored to hold the **Museo Guttuso**, dedicated to Bagheria's most famous son, Renato Guttuso (1912–87), whose brilliant use of colour and striking imagery made him one of Italy's most important modern artists; his tomb, designed by his friend, the sculptor Giacomo Manzù, is in the garden.

ARRIVAL AND DEPARTURE   BAGHERIA

By bus From Palermo, buses run every half hour to Bagheria, dropping you on Corso Umberto I, from where it's a short, straight walk to the villa.

By train There are frequent trains from Palermo to Bagheria's train station, from where it's a 10min walk to Villa Palagonia

(turn left onto Corso Butera, then left onto Via Palagonia).

By car There's free parking near the villa, though you might find yourself sucked into the narrow streets of the old town trying to find it. Eventually you should be directed into a space by a parking guy (tip a euro).

EATING

Antica Osteria Zza Maria Via Paternò 11 ☎ 091 931 388. All wine barrels and old photos, this atmospheric place is the best option in town for a meal. There's no actual menu (and you might have to hammer at the door for

1

entrance), but you'll get a good plate of home-made *pasta con le sarde* or similar for around €10. Find it by walking down Corso Umberto I to the free-standing columns at Piazza IV Novembre and you'll see the restaurant sign on your right, down Via Pasquale. Mon dinner, Tues–Sun lunch & dinner.

Solus

Mon–Sat 9am–7pm, Sun 9am–2pm, last entry 1hr before closing • €2 • By train from Palermo, get off one stop beyond Bagheria (at Santa Flavia-Solunto-Porticello station), crossing over the tracks and walking down the main road towards the sea; after 300m there's a signposted left turn up the hillside

Beautifully sited on the slopes of Monte Catalfano, ancient **Solus**, a Phoenician settlement, was originally founded in the eighth century BC, resettled in the fourth century BC, and later Hellenized, finally surrendering to Rome after the First Punic War, when its name was changed to Solentum. Ruins at the **site** date mostly from the Roman period, notably the impressive remains of wealthy houses – one, with a standing column, was built on two floors, the stairs still visible, and retains a complete geometric mosaic floor. The main street leads past houses and shops to the agora itself, a piazza with nine clay-red-coloured recessed rooms at the back. Above it sit the fragmentary ruins of a theatre and a smaller odeon, deliberately sited so as to give marvellous views away to the coast. Beyond the agora are the remains of a water cistern and storage tanks – necessary, as Solentum had no natural springs. Two "pavilions" interpret the site and display many of the finds, one at the entrance (before you see the ruins) and one at the exit, though there's nothing in English.

Porticello

With views across the bay towards Cefalù and up to the line of rounded peaks on the horizon, **PORTICELLO**, 6km east of Bagheria, makes a great bolt hole from the city – Palermitani come here at weekends and in summer to eat fish and seafood at the harbourside trattorias, but the place is definitely nice enough to warrant a stay. Fishermen have been working out of the port for centuries, and an old *tonnara* (tuna fishery) is still preserved near the medieval Castello di Solanto, which guards one side of the bay. It's a real, working harbour, and Porticello's fish market is one of the most important in Sicily, with boats unloading here in the early hours before the catch is shipped across Italy and beyond. Ice-house chutes channel ice into containers for the fish, and boats and nets are still hauled under great stone arches back from the harbour to be repaired.

ARRIVAL AND DEPARTURE | PORTICELLO

By bus There is only one direct AST bus daily from Palermo to Porticello, so it's easier to take a bus to Bagheria (see p.78) and another to Porticello. The most convenient services for a day-trip leave Palermo Piazza Lennon at 7am, 8am, 11am and noon, with stops at Piazza Politeama, Via E Amari and Via Balsamo. Return buses from Porticello to Palermo depart at 2.55pm and 7.55pm.

ACCOMMODATION AND EATING

★ **Stenopus Greco** ☎ 091 958 851 or ☎ 320 799 2011, ⓦ stenopusgreco.com. Imbued with real artistic flair by the charming owner Stéfano, this boutique dockside hotel is a surprising find in such a working town,

---

BAGHERIA'S OTHER VILLAS

Several of Bagheria's villas are privately owned, and only open to the public on occasion; check ⓦ bagherianews.com for details. Of these, **Villa Valguarnera** on Piazza Sturzo, another Tommaso Napoli design, displays Bagheria's most sumptuous facade, pink and festooned with a royal coat of arms and Attic statues. **Villa Butera**, on Corso Butera, just off the SS113, has a collection of wax figures in Carthusian apparel within its grounds. Legend has it that their creator, Ercole Branciforti, had promised the erection of a Carthusian abbey in return for the granting of a prayer, and took the crafty way out when the prayer was answered.

SICILY'S BANDIT KING: SALVATORE GIULIANO

Salvatore Giuliano (1922–50) was Sicily's most dashing anti-establishment hero – and villain. Known to his comrades as **Turiddu**, he embodied the hopes and frustrations of the Sicilian people more than any other individual in recent history. Part of his charm lay in his long defiance of the government. Starting out as a petty criminal and black-marketeer, he was a hunted man after his murder of a Carabiniere who had challenged him as he transported stolen grain in 1943. Gathering a band of followers in the mountains around his home in Montelepre, he was pursued by platoons of hand-picked soldiers who combed the maquis for him. As his legend grew, so did his charisma, enhanced by such madcap gestures as writing to President Truman and offering the annexation of Sicily to the United States, in a last-ditch attempt to sever the island from the Italian State.

Giuliano's separatist ambitions led him into some disreputable alliances, and his fall from grace occurred when he was shown to be behind the **massacre** of villagers at Portella della Ginestra in 1947 (see p.82). Just three years later, he was betrayed and killed, his body found in a courtyard in Castelvetrano, in the south. No one knows exactly what happened or who was responsible for his death, though his deputy, Gaspare Pisciotta, chose to confess to the crime. Many doubt that he was the one who pulled the trigger, and Pisciotta himself was on the verge of making revelations at his trial that would have implicated high-ranking Italian politicians, when he too was assassinated in his cell at Ucciardone prison.

Whatever the truth, there's a pungently Sicilian flavour to the affair, full of corruption, betrayal and counter-betrayal, and Giuliano's legend has since grown to Robin Hood dimensions, nowhere more so than in his home territory around the small town of **Montelepre**, where he was born. As his biographer Gavin Maxwell was told: "They should change the name of that village, really – anything else but Montelepre would do. No one can look at it straight or think straight about it now – it just means Giuliano." Giuliano hid out in the hills and caves around the village, slipping into town at night to see family and friends; if you're genuinely interested, you may be able to persuade his nephew to show you around the house in which he lived, to see various personal effects. His nephew also runs the *Castello di Giuliano*, Via Pietro Merra 1, at the top of Montelepere on the road in from Carini (☎ 091 894 1006, ⓦcastellodigiuliano.it; €70), an eccentric hotel and restaurant built to look like a castle, with more Giuliano memorabilia on display and faux-rustic rooms; the baronial restaurant serves pasta, meat and fish grills and pizzas in the evening (full meal €20).

but is perhaps a sign of things to come if plans for a new harbour and marina development for Porticello come to fruition. There are eight lovely rooms in bold colours with terracotta floors and beamed ceilings, original art above the handmade beds, painted ceramics and carved Indonesian chests. Three have harbour-view balconies, others either partial harbour or town views. **€70**

Piana degli Albanesi

Less than an hour's bus ride south of the capital, **PIANA DEGLI ALBANESI** sits placidly in an upland plain above a pleasant lake. The town was founded by fifteenth-century Albanians uprooted from their homes in flight from the Turkish invasions, and the six thousand inhabitants here still follow the Orthodox rite and proudly retain many of their old traditions – signs are in Albanian as well as Italian, and on Sunday mornings there are traditional Orthodox services in the three churches lining the steeply sloping main street, Via Giorgio Kastriota. At Easter, out come the handsome traditional costumes – black with gold brocade on Good Friday, brightly coloured on Easter Sunday.

Museo Civico

Via Giorgio Kastriota • Tues, Thurs & Sat 9.30am–1pm & 4–7pm, Wed & Fri 9.30am–1pm, Sun 10am–1pm • Free

Rural life and local history, as well as Albanian traditions and costumes, are well covered in the fascinating little **Museo Civico**, just off Piazza Vittorio Emanuele, the

1

THE MASSACRE AT PORTELLA DELLA GINESTRA

The mountain pass 4km southwest of Piana degli Albanesi, **Portella della Ginestra**, was the scene of one of the most shocking episodes in recent Sicilian history. On May 1, 1947, when the Albanians and villagers from neighbouring San Giuseppe Jato had assembled for their customary May Day celebrations, gunfire erupted from the crags and boulders surrounding the plain, killing eleven and wounding 55, many of them children. This massacre was the work of the bandit **Salvatore Giuliano**, whose virulent anti-Communist feelings were exploited by more sinister figures high up in the political and criminal hierarchy: only two weeks previously, the people of the town, together with most other Sicilians, had voted for a Popular Front (left-wing) majority in the regional parliament. The cold-blooded killings erased at one stroke the bandit's carefully nurtured reputation as defender of the poor and friend to the oppressed. There's a car park at the pass and the site is marked by a memorial of sculpted rocks inscribed in blood-red lettering – slightly unkempt, and a haunting place still.

---

small square at the top of the main street. There are reconstructions of room interiors containing anything from dental tools to cheese-making equipment as well as grainy photographs and other memorials to the infamous **massacre** at Portella della Ginestra.

ARRIVAL AND DEPARTURE   PIANA DEGLI ALBANESI

By bus Prestia & Commandé buses (direction Santa Cristina) run to Piana from Palermo's Stazione Centrale; the last one back leaves at around 4pm. Buses stop at the top of town, 500m from Piazza Vittorio Emanuele, at the Villa Comunale gardens (there's free parking here too). Cross the road viaduct to reach Via Kastriota and the centre of town.

Ficuzza

South of Piana degli Albanesi, a highly scenic driving route skirts the lake and then winds through rolling hills to reach the junction for the dead-end hamlet of **FICUZZA** after 20km. An information board in the piazza shows the local waymarked **walks** (between 45min and 3hr) on mountain paths that crisscross the wooded heights of Rocca Busambra (1613m), or you can simply grab a drink or a simple meal in one of the two or three bars and trattorias in the piazza.

Palazzo Reale di Ficuzza

Currently closed for restoration · ☎ 091 846 062

Ficuzza is completely dominated by the honey-coloured stone **Palazzo Reale di Ficuzza**, set against a dramatic mountain backdrop. This stately royal palace, fronted by a grassy piazza, was once the hunting lodge of Ferdinand III. Several sections of the building, notably the hunting scenes in the Sala da Pranzo, survived destruction and burning by Mussolini's troops, but at the time of writing the guided group visits of the interior had been suspended and there was no sense of when the *palazzo* might reopen; call for an update.

Corleone

From Ficuzza, another 20km on a quick country highway sees you in **CORLEONE**, a fairly large inland town squeezed between a couple of fortified rocks and girded by crags. It attracts a trickle of tourists, mostly on the scent of the Mafia since the town lent Mario Puzo's fictional Godfather, Don Corleone, his adopted family name. However, it is also the real-life name of Sicily's most notorious Mafia clan, and post-war Corleone was certainly a desperate place of murder and inter-family blood-letting. You wouldn't, of course, know it from the quiet streets today, and if it wasn't for the notoriety there would be no compelling reason to stop in Corleone, pleasant though the town centre is. A flurry of signs do their best to interest you in the various churches and small local museums.

CIDMA

CIDMA Via Orfanotrofio 7 • Open daily, guided tours available, though best to email or call first • ☏ 091 8452 4295, ✉ info@cidma.it • **Corleone, Come and See** ☏ 340 402.5601, ✉ cidmacorleone@gmail.com

Off the central Piazza Garibaldi, close to the *Comune*, **CIDMA** (International Centre for the Documentation of the Mafia and the Anti-Mafia Movement) is an anti-Mafia museum where you can trace the violent history of both Corleone and the Mafia, not only through brutal photographs (taken and donated by photographer Letizia Battaglia) of the so-called "Mafia Wars", but also by examining displays of original documents used in the maxi-trials of the 1980s. It's a sobering experience, though current street names in town at least demonstrate a contemporary *corleonese* desire to make amends (Piazza Víttime della Mafia, Piazza Falcone e Borsellino, etc). And at dusk in the town gardens, when couples, teenagers and families stroll under the soaring palms and flowering oleanders, the dark dealings of earlier times seem an age away. This more enlightened view of town is the one promoted by two local women under the name "**Corleone, Come and See**" who, with a couple of days' notice, can arrange a tailor-made tour with an English-speaking guide and including a typically rustic *corleonese* lunch.

CORLEONE AND THE MAFIA

Whether by luck or with foresight, when Mario Puzo chose the name **Corleone** for his central character in *The Godfather* (published 1969), he picked a little-known place that later came to have a huge significance in Mafia circles, as the native town of many of the so-called *capo di tutti capi* (literally "boss of all the bosses"). Even before Puzo's novel, the name Corleone had a certain resonance, due to the activities of **Luciano Leggio** (also known as Liggio), who had a reputation as a dashing figure and was hailed for his long-running evasion of the forces ranged against him. He was, however, responsible for one of the most notorious political killings of the twentieth century, that of the trade union leader **Placido Rizzoto**, who had been trying to organize peasants into staging occupations of uncultivated Mafia-owned lands. Two years after Rizzoto's disappearance in 1948, the fire brigade hauled out his dismembered corpse from a 30m crevice near Corleone (along with sackfuls of other bodies of Mafia victims). His killers were eventually acquitted for lack of evidence, the most common end to murder charges brought against *mafiosi*. Leggio was finally imprisoned in 1974 and died in jail in 1993.

At the time of his arrest in 1993, Leggio's trusted deputy from Corleone, **Salvatore Riina**, was the most wanted man in Italy, allegedly responsible for ordering at least 150 murders, 40 of which he's said to have committed himself. His capture came as a complete surprise and triggered a wave of accusations, since it became clear that for over twenty years Riina had been living in Palermo while making clandestine visits to his family in Corleone. This, it's said with some justification, could only have been the case if he had enjoyed a degree of high-level protection.

The most notable among several further members of the Corleone clan who have been put away since Riina's arrest is **Bernardo Provenzano**, known as "the Tractor" on account of his brutal methods and also as "the Accountant" for the way in which he increasingly blurred Mafia operations with legitimate business interests. He was finally captured in 2006, having been convicted in absentia of a string of murders, including the 1992 killings of the two anti-Mafia investigators Giovanni Falcone and Paolo Borsellino.

1

THE MAFIA TRAIL

Corleone might only be 60km from Palermo, and still in the same province, but the dry hills, rolling farmland and isolated rural outposts are far removed from the bustling capital. If you're in no hurry, there's a circular driving route back to Palermo that shows you a wilder side of the island, with a few Mafia connections to boot to add a certain *frisson*. It's a quick 25km southeast over the hills on the SS118 to **Prizzi** – the name borrowed for that of a New York mob family in John Huston's 1985 black comedy *Prizzi's Honor*. On Easter Sunday here, giant statues of Christ and the Virgin Mary are taunted by masked figures representing Death and the Devil, to whom onlookers are forced to give money. Another 20km east along the SS189, the main claim of **Lercara Friddi** is as the birthplace in 1897 of the Sicilian-American gangster Lucky Luciano, whose family emigrated in 1907. While in prison in the US, Luciano was enlisted by the Americans to aid their Sicilian campaign (which was fully backed by the Mafia in its desire to end the Fascist rule) and his reward when the war was over was to be freed, on the condition that he returned to Sicily. The town's main piazza was packed to welcome him home in 1946, and he repaid the adulation by opening Lercara Friddi's first cinema – apparently with a screening of the gangster movie, *Little Caesar*. A few kilometres north of Lercara, you pick up the SS121, which winds across the entire length of Sicily from Catania to finish its run in Palermo. One final (signposted) stop is at **Bagni di Cefalà**, eleventh-century Arab baths, still flowing with thermal waters which the locals use for washing clothes, though you can swim here too. Few other examples of Arab architecture in Sicily are in such good condition.

ARRIVAL AND DEPARTURE
CORLEONE

By bus Corleone is 60km from Palermo and there are seven buses daily (AST), taking 1hr 30min. The main bus stop is on the central Piazza Falcone e Borsellino.

EATING AND DRINKING

★ **Azienda Agricola Ridocco del Conte Lo Bue di Lemos** Contrada Ridocco, Campofiorito ☎091 846 1575, �ʷridocco.com. An outstanding *agriturismo* set in the gentle rolling hills above Corleone with rooms in the main house and converted outbuildings of a typical *masseria*, belonging to (and run with grace and enthusiasm by) a local aristocratic family. There are three double rooms with private bathrooms, and an independent apartment with kitchen comprising a double, a twin and a single. There is also a small swimming pool, horseriding and pony-trekking on site, and an excellent restaurant (open to residents only) where the food is simple, genuine and very delicious. Rooms €90; apartments from €90

Leon d'Oro Via Umbertino da Corelone 1 ☎091 846 4287, ⁿleondorocorleone.it. Just off the roundabout on the northern (Palermo) approach road, this three-star, villa-style hotel with swimming pool has spacious and smart rooms, and you can enjoy excellent crisp pizzas (€4–6), pasta and regional cuisine (dishes €6–13.50) in the shady garden courtyard. Restaurant Mon & Wed–Sun lunch & dinner. €70

Ustica

A turtle-shaped volcanic island, 60km northwest of Palermo, **USTICA** is ideal for a few days' rest and recreation. The island's fertile nine square kilometres are just right for a ramble, and what it lacks in sandy beaches it more than makes up for in the limpid waters of a **marine reserve** that many consider to provide the best snorkelling and dive-sites in the Mediterranean. If tourism has rescued isolated Ustica, it has also been at the risk of spoiling its charms – the population of 1300 quadruples in the summer months, and you'll see the island at its best if you can avoid coming in August.

Brief history

Colonized originally by the Phoenicians, the island was known to the Greeks as **Osteodes**, or "ossuary", a reference to the remains of six thousand Carthaginians they found here, abandoned to die on the island after a rebellion. Its present name is derived from the Latin *ustum* – "burnt" – on account of its blackened, lava-like appearance. Ustica had a rough time throughout the Middle Ages, its sparse population constantly harried by **pirates** who used the island as a base. In the Bourbon period the island was commandeered as a **prison** for political enemies, a role it continued to play until well into the twentieth century – Antonio Gramsci, the great theorist of the Italian Communist Party, was interned here in 1926, while Mussolini similarly exiled many other political prisoners. Only in recent decades has Ustica shaken off its chains and become a holiday destination.

Ustica town

USTICA TOWN is built on a steep slope, many of its low buildings covered in fading murals. Despite the veneer of tourism – a handful of hotels, restaurants, diving outfits and souvenir shops – it's not hard to see that life here has always been pretty tough. Most of what passes for entertainment – chatting in the open air, having a coffee in the couple of bars, impromptu games of soccer – takes place in and around the three central squares, piazzas Umberto I, della Vittoria and Vito Longo, which merge into each other, tumbling down the hill from the church.

Museo Archeologico
Largo Granguardia Tanino Russo • ☎ 333 357 4242 • Free

Ustica's museum, the **Museo Archeologico**, is a low-key affair, its collection a motley assortment of crusty anchors, shipwreck oddments and excavated Bronze Age objects. It has recently moved to a new site on Largo Granguardia, near the hospital. To visit, it is necessary to phone the museum guide, Tanino Russo, in advance.

1

Castello Saraceno

To get a sense of Ustica as an island, climb up to the remains of the **Castello Saraceno**, which gives you a good initial view of the island's layout: from the top of the square to the right of the church, the path runs left of the fancy cross at the end of Via Calvario, an easy twenty-minute walk to an old fort pitted with numerous cisterns to catch the precious water.

Guardia dei Turchi

From the Castello Saraceno you can see Ustica's highest point, the **Guardia dei Turchi** (244m), at the summit of a ridge that cuts the island in two, and topped by what looks like a giant golf ball – in fact a meteorological radar system. You can also climb up to the summit from the town, in about an hour or so: take Via B. Randaccio to the right of the church, turn left at the top and then right, and you'll come to the Municipio, where you turn left along Via Tre Mulini for the summit – keep straight ahead on the cobbled path, cutting off to the left when you reach the stepped path.

ARRIVAL AND GETTING AROUND | USTICA TOWN

By boat Siremar (⑩ siremar.it) ferries (€18; 2hr 30min) and hydrofoils (€23.50; 1hr 15min) run to Ustica daily from Palermo (from the Stazione Maríttima); summer departure times from Palermo are 7am, 8.15am, 1pm and 5.15pm, though are liable to change. Note that there's also a summer Ustica Lines (⑩ usticalines.it) hydrofoil service connecting Ustica with the Égadi Islands, Trapani and Naples. The R&S Militello ticket agency, just off the piazza at Via Cap. di Bartolo 15 (☎ 091 844 9002), dispenses all tickets; there's also a ticket kiosk at the harbour, open just before sailings. The island's only port is at Ustica Town, with the town centre up the flight of steps leading from the harbour.

Getting around From Piazza della Vittoria, an efficient minibus service (pay on board) plies the island's one circular road every hour or so until around 7pm.

INFORMATION AND TOURS

Online information There's no tourist office on Ustica, but you can glean some information from ⑩ ustica.net and ⑩ ustica.org.

Bikes, boats and tours Usticamare Noleggio (☎ 339 218 5630) has bikes at €10 per day, boats from €50–180 per day excluding fuel, depending on size, and cars to rent, while the restaurant *Da Umberto* (⑩ usticatour.it) rents out scooters and boats and arranges tours. Boat excursions from the quay cost around €20 per person for three hours – it's best to agree a price beforehand.

ACCOMMODATION

In summer hotels fill up quickly, and in winter only a few remain open. However, there are plenty of opportunities to rent rooms (*camere*) – ask around in the shops or at the *Bar Centrale*, in Piazza Umberto I.

Ariston Via della Vittoria 5 ☎ 091 844 9042, ⑩ usticahotels.it. A smart, central hotel with eleven rooms and impressive sea views. Diving trips and scooter rental can be arranged. Sizeable reductions in winter. No credit cards. **€78**

★ **Caminita Vittorio** Via Tufo 1 ☎ 091 844 9212. Two attractive, self-contained mini-apartments, each with kitchenette, bathroom, terrace and separate entrance, run by friendly, helpful owners. One has a sweeping view down over the town to the sea. It's just a few minutes from the main square – at the church, turn right along Via Calvario, and Via Tufo is the sixth on the left. No credit cards. **€60**

Giulia Via San Francesco 16 ☎ 091 844 9007, ⑩ giuliahotel.com. Open year-round, with ten perfectly acceptable two-star rooms above a lovely restaurant right off the main piazza (single rooms also available). See the website for weekend packages including certain meals and excursions. No credit cards. **€90**

Stella Marina Residence Via Cristoforo Colombo 35 ☎ 091 844 8121, ⑩ stellamarinaustica.it. Seventeen smart, self-catering mini-apartments in a small complex right above the port. There's also a nice big terrace for sun-soaking, and a small spa. Rentals range from €490–990 per week for a two-person apartment, including breakfast, but they're available on a two-nightly basis May–July & Sept–Oct. Nightly rate **€95**

Da Umberto Piazza della Vittoria ☎ 091 844 9542, ⑩ usticatour.it. As well as running the *Da Umberto* restaurant, Gigi Tranchina rents out rooms in over twenty apartments and houses around Ustica, some with great sea views, others more rustic in the middle of the island. Prices depend on size and quality of the accommodation. From **€60**

DIVING ON USTICA

Ustica is well set up for **divers**, and facilities include a decompression chamber, though medical facilities are limited to the pharmacy and the *guardia médica*. The waters are protected by a natural marine reserve, divided into several zones with restrictions on where you can swim, dive and fish. ★ **Profondo Blu** (☎091 844 9609 or ☎349 672.6529, ⓦustica-diving.it), run by an Italo-Belgian couple, is the island's most organized and experienced dive-operator, arranging diving courses, holidays and accommodation in their own self-contained resort with apartments outside town. It is open from May till the end of October, with prices at €470–720 per week for an apartment sleeping two, depending on the season. Meals are available (breakfast €5; dinner €35). There are various diving packages – a single dive costs €43; a ten-dive package €350 and a six-day open water diver PADI course €460.

EATING AND DRINKING

As well as a couple of harbourside bars, there are several places to eat on and around Ustica Town's central squares, and most of the hotels have **restaurants**, often with roof terraces and sea views. Most restaurants not attached to hotels close during the winter. Don't neglect to visit Maria Cristina, just above the piazzas at Via Petriera 5, who sells Ustica lentils, home-made preserves, pestos and sauces, and other island treats to savour, from a tiny room in her home.

★ **Giulia** Via San Francesco 13 ☎091 844 9007. The simple trattoria attached to this hotel is the best bet on the island for genuine home-cooking. Try *pennette al usticese* (with herbs, chilli, garlic, pine-nuts, raisins, anchovies, capers and olives), fish-balls (*polpettine*) with local capers and olives, or *totano* (a big squid) stuffed with shrimp, tomatoes, cheese and breadcrumbs. Fish couscous is available for a minimum of two people, but book a day in advance. Expect to spend around €30–40 per person. No credit cards. Daily dinner only.

Da Umberto Piazza della Vittoria ☎091 844 9542. Tables on the terrace and a menu chiefly consisting of pasta dishes (from €8) and seafood main courses that depend on the day's catch (€12–16). Try the *polpette* of fish spiked with wild fennel, the spaghetti with seafood or a soup of tiny locally grown lentils; or splash out on lobster with spaghetti or a whole fish (such as scorpion fish) cooked with capers and tomatoes (prices depend on weight). Daily lunch & dinner.

DIRECTORY

Bank Monte dei Paschi di Siena, Via Cap. V. di Bartolo, on the left-hand side of the church, has an ATM.
Pharmacy Piazza Umberto I 30 ☎091 844 9382 (Mon–Sat 8.30am–1pm & 5–8.30pm). Closed Wed afternoon

Nov–April.
Post office Largo Ameria off the main piazza (Mon–Fri 8am–1pm, Sat 8am–12.30pm).

Around the island

To explore the rest of Ustica you could use the minibus service that departs from Ustica Town, rent a scooter or bike, or even walk – it doesn't take much more than two or three hours to walk round the entire island. There's a path running right round the rocky coastline, with just a brief stretch where you have to follow the road, and there are ample opportunities to stop for a swim or sunbathe along the northern coast. Keep straight on past the Municipio and then bear off the road to the right, down past the cemetery. The path starts at the remains of a **Bronze Age settlement** – the foundations of the closely packed huts are still clearly visible. From here the path hugs the cliffs along the island's north side as far as the **Punta di Megna** (where path and road converge). There's excellent snorkelling at Punta di Megna and at the offshore rock of **Scoglio del Médico**, where the clear water is bursting with fish, sponges, weed and coral. The road then keeps to the west coast as far as the old *torre* (tower) at **Punta Spalmatore**, where you'll find some of the island's best bathing spots; try below the tower, or – below the nearby lighthouse – at **Punta Cavazzi**, where there's a *piscina naturale*, a perfect, sheltered pool of seawater that can get uncomfortably crowded in high season. Above here, the *Rosa d'Eventi* restaurant-bar offers the only refreshments and shade along the route.

Cefalù and the Monti Madonie

CEFALÙ

Cefalù and the Monti Madonie

Despite being one of Sicily's busiest international beach resorts, Cefalù, just an hour east of Palermo, has a parallel life as a small-scale fishing port. Not only does it have a superb beach, an appealing historic centre, and a stupendous medieval cathedral with some of the best mosaic-work on the whole island, but on its doorstep are the Monti Madonie, a high mountain range and regional park. It's easy to explore the mountains by car – even in just a day-trip from the coast you'll be able to circle the high passes between Castelbuono and the twin towns of Petralia Soprana and Petralia Sottana.

There are plenty of other good day-trips from Cefalù. West, en route to Palermo, lies the archeological site of Greek **Himera**, the old spa town of **Termini Imerese** and the blustery hill-top stronghold of **Caccamo**, which features the best-preserved of Sicily's Norman castles. To the east (towards Messina), it's the Tyrrhenian coast that holds sway, hugged by road, rail and motorway, at its best an eye-catching succession of cliff and cove, sandy strips and citrus groves, though all too often eclipsed by monotonous tourist developments. The ceramics town of **Santo Stefano di Camastra** is a nice little resort, while from **Castel di Tusa** you can trace the mammoth sculptures of the **Fiumara d'Arte** trail. Another appealing base, the town of **Patti** has an untouched historic centre, a lively shingle beachfront, abundant good cheer and a convent serving some of the best – and cheapest – feasts in the region. The most beautiful sands along this stretch of the Tyrrhenian, however, lie below the clifftop sanctuary of **Tindari** at **Marinello** – a coastal nature reserve, with natural (and shifting) salt lakes. **Milazzo**, treated by most as a departure point for the Aeolian Islands, also has hidden charms – among them its recently restored Norman castle, and the coves and beaches of the **Capo di Milazzo**.

GETTING AROUND	CEFALÙ AND THE MONTI MADONIE
By bus and train A good train service makes it easy to see any of the coastal destinations from Cefalù, and buses link to some inland destinations. **By car** A car is definitely required if you're intent on seeing much of the mountains. Driving can be slow on the SS113	coastal road, along which traffic sometimes files at a snail's pace – it's much faster on the A20 autostrada (a toll-road), which features some outstanding feats of road engineering in the form of long tunnels and soaring viaducts.

Cefalù

The finest resort on the long Tyrrhenian coast between Palermo and Messina is CEFALÙ, 70km from the capital, with a long sandy beach and a dramatic setting under the fearsome crag known as La Rocca. Roger II founded a mighty cathedral here in 1131 and his mosaic-filled **church** still dominates the skyline: the great twin towers rear up above the flat roofs of the medieval quarter, with the whole structure framed by the looming cliff behind. The shady tangle of old streets and gift shops, and nearby beach and promenade, are certainly touristy but also retain a real charm. Cefalù, in fact, is nowhere near as developed as Sicily's other main package resort, Taormina. It's busy in

BYZANTINE MOSAIC, CEFALÙ CATHEDRAL

Highlights

❶ Cefalù The Byzantine mosaics in Cefalù's cathedral are one of the glories of Sicily, and the town's long sandy beach is among the island's finest. **See p.93**

❷ Castelbuono The charming old town is the northern gateway to the Monti Madonie – and the food is amazing, too. **See p.100**

❸ Petralia Sottana Pretty mountain town at the heart of the Parco Regionale delle Madonie. **See p.102**

❹ Parco Avventura Madonie Zip-wire through the trees at this climbing park in the Madonie mountains. **See p.104**

❺ Patti Discover the unsung charms of a friendly coastal hill-town with an unrestored historic centre, long shingle beaches, fabulous views of the Aeolians, and one of the best-value restaurants in the region. **See p.108**

❻ Tyndaris and Marinello Explore the Roman remains of Tyndaris, then head down to the enchanting sands of the Marinello coastal nature reserve. **See p.108 & p.110**

❼ Milazzo Before you depart for the Aeolian Islands, take time to explore Milazzo's rambling citadel and the fishermen's stalls along the seafront, then head out to the Piscine di Venere. **See p.110**

HIGHLIGHTS ARE MARKED ON THE MAP ON P.92

CEFALÙ AND THE MONTI MADONIE

HIGHLIGHTS

1. Cefalù
2. Castelbuono
3. Petralia Sottana
4. Parco Avventura Madonie
5. Patti
6. Tyndaris and Marinello
7. Milazzo

July and August, but never overwhelmingly so, and there's a lot to be said for making the town your base. Palermo is less than an hour away by train, and there are smaller beaches and resorts on the rail line to the east, while it's an easy drive into the Monti Madonie to the south. The sandy **beach** is one of Sicily's best, jam-packed in summer, with sheltered swimming in clear waters and marvellous views from the *lungomare* (promenade) over the red roofs of the town.

The old-town streets themselves are the best thing about Cefalù – a cobbled, tangibly Arabic jumble of alleys with rows of washing stretched between houses, hidden arches and flower-filled courtyards. The main Corso Ruggero is lined with attractive buildings in various stages of well-tended decay. The **Osterio Magno**, on the corner of Via Amendola and the Corso, is the surviving part of a medieval palace, now regularly used for art exhibitions, while the **lavatoio** is a relic of the Saracen occupation – a wash-house at the bottom of a curving staircase, with cold water pouring forth into the basins. At the head of the Corso, a **belvedere** gives onto the old Greek walls of Cefalù, largely incorporated into the later sixteenth-century defensive bastion. A modern path has been cut into the rocks below, running in the direction of the hydrofoil port, and you can clamber down here to explore the rock pools and sunbathe on the slabs. Further around the headland, at the **port**, is a bay full of fishing and leisure boats, and more strange rock stacks to investigate.

The Duomo

Piazza Duomo • Daily: summer 8am–7pm; winter 8am–5.30pm

Central to Cefalù's historic existence is its majestic **Duomo**, set back in a pretty square under the cliffs. Apocryphally, it was built in gratitude by Roger II, who found refuge at the town's safe beach in a violent storm, though it's more likely that the cathedral owed its foundation to his power struggle with Pope Innocent II. Shortly after his coronation in 1130, Roger had allied instead with Anacletus, the anti-pope, whose support enhanced the new king's prestige. Roger's cathedral benefited from Anacletus's readily granted exemptions and privileges, and it is at once rich and showy, from the massive, fortress-like exterior to the earliest and best preserved of all Sicilian church **mosaics**. With all the former Baroque decoration finally stripped away after years of "restoration", the impact of the mosaics is profound. Dating from 1148 (forty years older than those at Monreale), they are thoroughly Byzantine in concept and follow a familiar pattern: Christ Pantocrator, right hand outstretched in benediction, open Bible in the left, dominates the central apse; underneath is the Madonna flanked by archangels; then the twelve Apostles, in two rows of six.

Museo Mandralisca

Via Mandralisca 13 • Daily: Jan–July & Sept–Dec 9am–7pm; Aug 9am–11pm • €5 • ☎ 0921 421 547, ⓦ fondazionemandralisca.it

The cathedral is very much the cultural highlight in Cefalù, though just down the road, the **Museo Mandralisca** houses a small collection of quality objects. On the first floor you'll find the star exhibit, a wry and inscrutable *Portrait of an Unknown Man* by the fifteenth-century Sicilian master **Antonello da Messina**. Look out, too, for the quirky Greek *krater* (fourth century BC) showing a robed tuna-fish salesman, knife in hand, disputing the price of his fish.

La Rocca and the Tempio di Diana

Tempio di Diana • Daily: summer 9am–6.45pm; winter closes at least an hour before sunset • Free

Towering above cathedral and town, and accessible by a stepped footpath at the side of the Banco di Sicilia in Piazza Garibaldi, is the mountain of **La Rocca**. A steep twenty-minute climb takes you to the so-called **Tempio di Diana**, a megalithic structure

2

CEFALÙ

■ ACCOMMODATION
B&B Delle Rose	11
Le Calette	3
Camping San Filippo	8
Costa Ponente	9
Dolce Vita	1
La Giara	2
Locanda Cangelosi	7
Palazzo Villelmi	5
Al Pescatore	4
Riva del Sole	6
Villa Cerniglia	10

● CAFÉS AND RESTAURANTS
La Brace	5
Caffè di Noto	2
Le Chat Noir	6
Al Gabbiano	7
La Galleria	4
Lo Scoglio Ubriaco	1
Vecchia Marina	3

● SHOPS
Cantina di Cicerone	4
Farmacia Cirincione	2
A Lumera	1
Robinson	3
Vinum et Ambrosia	5

N

Belvedere

PIAZZA CRISPI

VIA PORPORA

VIA CANDELORO

PIAZZA MESSINA

VIA C.O. DI BORDONARO

VIA VETERANI

PIAZZA MARINA

EMANUELE

VIA PORTO SALVO

Laundry

VIA MANDRALISCA

Museo Mandralisca

VIA XXV NOVEMBRE

Lavatoio

VIA GIOENI

VIA VITTORIO

VIA NICOLA BOTTA

VIA VANNI

VIA AMENDOLA

PIAZZA DUOMO

Duomo

CORSO RUGGERO

VIA DEGLI ANGELI

Ente Parco delle Madonie

VIA COSTA

VIA FRANCAVILLA

Tempio di Diana

ℹ

Osterio Magno

VIA CARBONARI

VIA SPINUZZA

PIAZZA COLOMBO

DISCESA PARAMURO

Police (Carabinieri)

VICOLO SARACENI

VIA CAVOUR

PIAZZA GARIBALDI

VIA DELLA PALESTRA

VIA UMBERTO I

VIA ARCHIMEDE

VIA MATTEOTTI

VIA PINTORNO

VIA S. PASQUALE

VIA MAZZINI

PIAZZA SAN FRANCESCO

VIA FERMI

VIA ROMA

VIA GIGLIO

VIA NOVELLI

VIA MORO

VIA PIETRAGROSSA

VIA GIBILMANNA

PIAZZA STAZIONE

Bus Stop ★

VIA GRAMSCI

Hydrofoil Port, 3 & 4

La Rocca

Post Office (100m)

8, 9 & 10

P

6

7

11

Gibilmanna

0		100

metres

adapted in the fifth century BC by the addition of classical doorways, their lintels still in place. A path continues upwards, right around the crag, through pinewoods and wild fennel, dipping in and out of a surviving stretch of medieval wall to the sketchy fortifications at the very top. You can then cut down to the temple and rejoin the path back into town, the whole walk taking a little over an hour – take water with you, as it's a strenuous climb.

ARRIVAL AND DEPARTURE — CEFALÙ

By train The train station is south of the centre, ten minutes' walk from the main old-town street, Corso Ruggero.
Destinations Messina (12 daily; 2hr 15min–3hr); Milazzo (12 daily; 1hr 40min–2hr); Palermo (1–2 hourly; 1hr); Sant'Agata di Militello (hourly; 1hr); Santo Stefano di Camastra (hourly; 30min); Termini Imerese (1–2 hourly; 25min).
By bus Buses pull into Piazza Stazione outside the train station.
Destinations Caccamo (2 daily; 45min); Castelbuono (7 daily Mon–Sat, 2 daily Sun; 40min); Gangi (1 daily; 1hr 45min–2hr); Geraci (2 daily Mon–Sat, 1 daily Sun; 1hr 25min); Gibilmanna (3 daily; 30min); Palermo (3 daily Mon–Sat, 1 daily Sun; 1hr); Petralia (1 daily Mon–Sat; 2hr).
By car There is residents-only parking throughout the old town, so the best advice is to park on the seafront, either in the metered places along the promenade (€1 per hour, free midnight–8am) or in the patrolled car park (€6/12hr), just after the *Riva del Sole* hotel beyond Via Archimede.

GETTING AROUND

Bike and scooter rental Scooter for Rent, Via Vittorio Emanuele 57 (☎338 230 9008, ⓦscooterforrent.it), has mountain bikes (from €15/day) and scooters (€25–35/half-day, €35–50 /day).

Car rental Siciltravel, Piazza Garibaldi 9 (☎0921 420 090).
Taxis There's a taxi rank outside the train station at Piazza Stazione (☎0921 422 554).

INFORMATION

Tourist information There's a tourist office at Corso Ruggero 77 (Mon–Sat 9am–1pm & 3–7.30pm; ☎0921 421 050), where you can pick up a free town map and an accommodation list, as well as information about boat trips, summer concerts, theatre performances and other events.

Online information The websites ⓦcefaluonline.com and ⓦcefalu.it are also useful for accommodation, restaurants and local services. For information (in Italian) on the Madonie mountains, try ⓦparcodellemadonie.it, which also has details of walks, flora, fauna, events and places to eat and drink.

ACCOMMODATION

HOTELS AND B&BS

B&B Delle Rose Via Gibilmanna ☎0921 421 885, ⓦdellerosebb.it. Charming B&B that has its own parking – the rooms with views and spacious terraces are worth the supplement. The main drawback is its distance from the centre, a 15–20min walk along the continuation of Via Umberto I (up the Gibilmanna road, heading out of town). **€100**
Le Calette Via Vincenzo Cavallaro 12, Contrada Caldura ☎0921 424 144, ⓦlecalette.it. On the eastern side of the headland, overlooking the hydrofoil port, this four-star villa-style hotel is beautifully sited above a little cove, and has its own pool, restaurant and gardens. All rooms face the sea and those on the second floor have large balconies. Good deals online outside the main season. **€230**
⭐ **Dolce Vita** Via C.O. Bordonaro 8 ☎0921 923 151, ⓦdolcevitabb.it. The top choice for B&B – right in the heart of the old town but with the sea on one side, so rooms with a view are nice and peaceful. Two face the street, three the sea, and all are en suite and spacious

(sleeping up to four), with high ceilings and restored tile floors. Best of all is the glorious terrace, a perfect haven with uninterrupted sea views, while the cheery owner can arrange boat trips, airport transfers, etc. Breakfast is taken in a bar in the cathedral piazza. Usually closed two months between Nov and Feb. **€100**
La Giara Via Veterani 40 ☎0921 421 562, ⓦhotel-lagiara.it. The three-star *La Giara* is very central, on an old-town street close to the Duomo, and has decent rooms and a top-floor terrace with town and ocean views. Expect some noise from street-facing rooms. **€144**
Locanda Cangelosi Via Umberto I 26 ☎0921 421 591, ⓦlocandacangelosi.it. The cheapest place in town, this pension has pretty basic facilities. There are four rooms – two with balconies overlooking the busy street – with a shared bathroom, but the better option is one of the four small self-catering apartments in a quieter position. No credit cards. Rooms **€80**; apartments **€100**
⭐ **Palazzo Villelmi** Corso Ruggero 149 ☎0921 923 057 or ☎339 852 0161, ⓦwww.palazzovillelmi.com.

2

2

Stylish, elegant B&B in a beautifully restored old *palazzo* on the main street, very near the Duomo. High painted ceilings give a hint of its former grandeur, and a rooftop breakfast terrace looks right on to the cathedral. €100

Al Pescatore Località Caldura ☎0921 421 572. Around the headland, near the port, this family-run hotel is pretty good value for most of the year, with simply furnished rooms with tile floors offering sea or mountain views. There's no restaurant, though, and it's a fair walk into town. €80

Riva del Sole Lungomare G. Giardina ☎0921 421 230, ⓦrivadelsole.com. The most central seaside hotel has rooms overlooking the promenade and beach, and it's very close to the parking area. As long as you don't mind the summer noise from the bars and restaurants, it's a great location – just steps from the sand and with its own chic terrace café. Half-board only in Aug, at around €100 per person. €160

Villa Cerniglia Lungomare G. Giardina ☎320 306 4275, ⓦvillacerniglia.com. A selection of one-bedroom apartments in a complex right on the seafront. Facilities include access to a lido for those seeking the full Sicilian beach experience. €140

CAMPSITES

Camping San Filippo Contrada Ogliastrillo ☎0921 420 184, ⓦcampingsanfilippo.com. Lovely campsite, a short walk from the beach with tent and caravan pitches under pine trees. Tent pitches €8, plus €8.50 per person and €6 per car

Costa Ponente Contrada Ogliastrillo ☎0921 420 085, ⓦcampeggio-sicilia.it. Big, resort-style campsite with a 33m swimming pool, a variety of sports and activities on offer, and mobile homes for rent as well as tent and caravan pitches. Closed Nov–March. Tents €8, plus €8.50 per person and €5 per car; mobile homes €60

EATING AND DRINKING

There are dozens of **restaurants** in Cefalù, though many trade on their sea view and are overpriced. Menus are broadly similar – fish and seafood, of course, is the local highlight – and the best deals are often in the form of set menus for €20–30 a head. The **cafés** in Piazza del Duomo are a nice place to start the day, with breakfast in front of the cathedral. For sunset drinks and views, there's a line of restaurants, **bars** and *gelaterie* along the prom by the beach, while the local *passeggiata* runs all the way up the main Corso to Piazza Garibaldi and its streetside bars and ice-cream shops.

CAFÉS AND RESTAURANTS

La Brace Via XXV Novembre 10 ☎0921 423 570. A tiny place run by a Dutch mother and son, where you dine to classical music in a room formed by three stone arches. The cuisine is more varied than in many Cefalù restaurants, with beautifully cooked versions of European dishes such as steak tournedos or chicken liver pâté with Madeira joining Sicilian dishes like swordfish *involtini*. Lots of vegetarian options as well. Booking ahead is essential. Mon & Wed–Sun lunch & dinner, Tues dinner only; closed mid-Dec to mid-Jan.

Caffè di Noto Via Bagno Cicerone 3 ☎0921 422 654. This *gelateria* is right at the edge of the *centro storico* and the beginning of the Lungomare, and has fabulous ice creams in flavours including mango, raspberry, prickly pear, and chocolate with chilli. April–Oct daily 10am–late.

Le Chat Noir Via XXV Novembre 17 ☎0921 420 697. An atmospheric setting in the whitewashed, plant-filled courtyard of a sixteenth century building a short walk from the Duomo, and memorable executions of typical Sicilian dishes such as the sweet, unctuous aubergine *parmigiana* with salty ricotta, swordfish *involtini*, and an orange salad spiked with chilli. Count on spending €35 for a full meal including wine if you eat fish, €25 if you opt for meat. Mon–Tues & Thurs–Sun lunch & dinner.

Al Gabbiano Lungomare G. Giardina ☎0921 421 495. Best of the seafront promenade restaurants, this place has a good *antipasto al buffet*, spicy *zuppa di cozze* and pizzas (pizzas €6–10), and fish or seafood mains (mostly €10–12). Daily lunch & dinner; closed Wed Nov–April.

★ **La Galleria** Via Mandralisca 23 ☎0921 420 211, ⓦlagalleriacefalu.it. Billed as a "literary café", and incorporating courtyard bar, exhibition space and cultural centre, *La Galleria* is also a great place for classy, contemporary Sicilian cooking – think chic, white dining room and a menu featuring pasta with swordfish, lemon zest and wild fennel, and tuna sashimi on *caponata* (dishes €8–22). There's a second entrance on Via XXV Novembre. Mon–Wed & Fri–Sun lunch & dinner.

Lo Scoglio Ubriaco Via C.O. Bordonaro 2–4 ☎0921 423 370. The "Drunken Rock" is a slick restaurant with a sea-facing terrace. It's good for fish (with plenty of mains between €8.50 and €13.50), and also serves pizzas (€6–10.50) in the evening. July & Aug daily lunch & dinner; Sept–June closed Tues.

Vecchia Marina Via Vittorio Emanuele 73 ☎0921 420 388. A locals' favourite for a seafood blowout. It's not cheap (pasta and starters €10–15, fish dishes €15–25, catch of the day by weight, generally €50–60 per kilo), though the €29 set menu (including an *antipasto* or pasta, *secondo*, *contorno* and dessert but no drinks) isn't a bad deal. Mon & Wed–Sun lunch & dinner; closed Jan.

SHOPPING

If you're looking for more than *Godfather* T-shirts, Sicilian puppets or mass-produced cookbooks in Japanese and German, you need to dig a bit deeper in Cefalù's old town. It's worth buying sun cream or aspirin just to have a look at the beautifully carved cabinets inside the traditional Farmacia Cirincione, at Corso Ruggero 144.

Cantina di Cicerone Via Vittorio Emanuele 13 ☎ 0921 422 497. A fantastic range of Sicilian wines is on offer at this enoteca. Daily 10am–midnight; closed Dec–Feb.

A Lumera Corso Ruggero 176 ☎ 0921 921 801, ⓦ alumeracefalu.it. A great place to buy traditional Sicilian ceramics, made in nearby Santo Stefano di Camastra (see p.106). Daily, usually 9.30am–10pm.

Robinson Via Madonna degli Angeli 3 ☎ 0921 422 245. A treasure-trove of bric-a-brac, antiques and junk. Mon–Sat 10am–1pm & 5–8pm.

Vinum et Ambrosia Corso Ruggero 15 ☎ 0921 423 156. Artisan pestos, jams, conserves, olive oils and huge chunks of Madonie mountain cheese. Daily 9am–1pm & 3.30–8pm; closed Wed in winter.

DIRECTORY

Hospital Contrada Pietrapollastra ☎ 0921 920 111.
Pharmacies Battaglia, Via Roma 13 (Mon–Fri 9am–1pm & 4.30–8.30pm; ☎ 0921 421 789); Cirincione, Corso Ruggero 144 (Mon–Fri 9am–1pm & 4.30–8.30pm; ☎ 0921 421 209). There's a rota system for evening and late-opening pharmacies posted in their windows.

Police Carabinieri, Discesa Paramuro (☎ 0921 421 412).
Post office Via Vazzana 2, between Via Roma and the seafront (Mon–Fri 8am–6.30pm, Sat 8am–12.30pm).

Himera

Mon–Sat 9am–6.30pm, Sun 9am–1pm • €2 • There's no public transport to Himera. It's around halfway between Cefalù and Termini Imerese – take the Buonfornello exit from the autostrada and keep a keen eye out for signs once you're on the SS113 coastal road.

On the coast around 20km west of Cefalù stands the site of the ancient Greek city of **Himera**, though the visible remains are few and it's probably one for dedicated stone-hunters only. Himera was the first Greek settlement on Sicily's northern coast, founded in 648 BC as an advance post against the Carthaginians, who controlled the west of the island. The town inevitably became a flashpoint, and in 480 BC the Carthaginian leader **Hamilcar** landed a huge force nearby. Pitted against the combined armies of Akragas (Agrigento), Gela and Syracuse, the invading force was demolished and Hamilcar himself perished – either assassinated by Greek spies before the battle, or killed when he threw himself onto the pyre afterwards, depending on whose version you read. The outcome of the battle marked a significant upheaval of the classical world – and, in the case of Sicily, a new balance of power, with the Greeks in the ascendant. But their glory was short-lived: in 409 BC Hamilcar's nephew, **Hannibal**, wreaked his revenge and razed the city to the ground, forcing the surviving citizens west to what is now Termini Imerese.

The site

All that's left of the important Chalcidinian settlement that once stood here is the massive **Tempio della Vittoria**, erected to commemorate the defeat of the Carthaginians – indeed, the labour was carried out by the captured Carthaginians themselves. It's a conventional Doric construction, with six columns at the front and back, and fourteen at the sides. Despite the paucity of the remains, and the proximity of the road and rail line, the solitary ruin does have a powerful appeal. It's said to stand on the very site of the 480 BC battle, and after the victory some of the rich Carthaginian spoils were pinned up inside. The acropolis lay just inland, and, though excavations have uncovered a necropolis and some smaller temples, much work remains to be done at the site. There is a good **museum** (same hours and ticket), housing some of the items dug up at the site (others are in museums in Termini and Palermo), including a few of the striking lion's-head waterspouts that drained the temple's roof. One strangely moving display is of the grave of a married couple, the wife curled up next to her husband, her leg resting on his.

2

Termini Imerese

Around 35km west of Cefalù, **TERMINI IMERESE** is the last major town before the capital, Palermo. The coast on either side is dishearteningly industrial, but Termini has the magnificent backdrop of Monte Calogero (1326m) as some compensation and – once you've negotiated the congested streets – an airy upper town with a stunning belvedere that's worth the trip. Termini was originally settled by Greeks from Zancle (Messina) in the seventh century BC, and grew in importance as it absorbed the influx of survivors from the destroyed city of Himera, 13km to the east. Later, as Therma Himeraia, it flourished under the spa-loving Romans, and today the town is still famous in Italy for its waters, reputed to be good for arthritis and pasta-making.

At the centre of the upper town is a spacious piazza dominated by the monumental, pink-fronted, seventeenth-century **Duomo**. Inside are renowned sculptures by Marabitti, notably his *Madonna del Ponte* in the fourth chapel on the right. Really, though, the views are the thing in Termini, so stroll beyond the Duomo along the palm-fringed **belvedere**, which offers an extensive panorama over town, mountain, port and sea. The promenade continues around the headland to the shady **Villa Palmieri** gardens, which shelter the remnants of a public building from the Roman era as well as the remains of an **Anfiteatro Romano** – this lies just up from the Porta Palermo, the former entrance to the city. Outdoor cafés and kiosks between cathedral, belvedere and gardens offer drinks, ice creams and a shady place to sit.

Museo Civico

Via Marco Tullio Cicerone • Tues–Sat 9am–1pm & 4–6.30pm, Sun 9am–1pm • Free

Opposite the Duomo, down a lane to the side of the Palazzo Margherita, the excellent **Museo Civico** has more art treasures, including work by Antonello Gagini, a fine sixteenth-century Flemish *Annunciation* and some grisly scenes of martyrdom. There are also coins, ceramics and other finds from Greek Himera, as well as the marble bust of an elegant second-century Roman matron.

ARRIVAL AND DEPARTURE   TERMINI IMERESE

By train Termini Imerese is a frequent stop on the line between Palermo, Cefalù and Messina. There are trains approximately every half hour (sometimes more) and journey time is 30–45min. To get to the centre from the station, turn right, walk past Piazza Crispi and down Corso Umberto e Margherita to Via Roma, the stepped street that climbs to the upper town (a good 15min walk).

By bus Buses arrive at and depart from immediately outside the train station, though some also make a stop in the upper town. There is a reasonable service to Caccamo (7–8 daily Mon–Sat; 15min, ⓦ autobusrandazzo.altervista.org) and Castelbuono (Mon–Sat 2 daily; 1hr 30min).

By car Drivers would do best to follow signs for "Museo" and "punto panoramico", as there's plenty of parking up by the belvedere.

Caccamo

Ten kilometres to the south of Termini Imerese, the small town of **CACCAMO**, set amid green hills, is worth visiting chiefly for its remarkable **castello.**

Caccamo itself is not much more than an overgrown village, disturbed only by the weight of traffic along the one main street, Corso Umberto I.

Castello

Via Castello • Mon 9am–1pm & 3–7pm, Tues–Fri 8.30am–1pm & 3–8pm, Sat & Sun 9am–1pm & 3–7pm • €2 • ☎ 091 814 9252

Caccamo's **castello** is a many-splendoured thing, a chalk-white array of towers and battlements dominating the town and commanding the heights above the deep San

Leonardo river valley. Built originally in the twelfth century, the castle has over 130 rooms, though only a fraction are open to the public – there's usually a multilingual guide on hand, able to churn out colourful background stories for a few euros. The highlight is the grand **Sala della Congiura**, where the barons' plot against William I ("the Bad") was hatched in 1160; it has a fine painted wooden ceiling and walls festooned with arms. Other rooms hold more weapons, costumes, coats of arms and reproductions of period furniture, and a **terrace** allows you to savour the glorious views.

Chiesa Madre
Piazza del Duomo • Daily 7am–noon and 3.30–6pm

Behind the castle crag sits the **Chiesa Madre**, with reliefs around the sacristy door attributed to Francesco Laurana, the Renaissance sculptor who left his mark all over the region, particularly in Palermo. Look out, too, for the seventeenth-century **tablet** depicting St George and the Dragon over the main portal.

Chiesa dell'Anime del Purgatorio
Piazza del Duomo • Erratic hours

To the right of the Chiesa Madre as you enter the piazza, the **Chiesa dell'Anime del Purgatorio** is more compelling, specifically for its **catacombs**, reached down crumbling steps. Fully clothed and collapsing bodies lie in niches in the walls, topped by a row of white skulls, the remains of the town's nobility and clergy who made their last journey here between the seventeenth and mid-nineteenth centuries. If the church is closed, ask around for the custodian, who expects a tip for letting you in (though you can get a glimpse of the niches and skulls by peering through the grate beneath the front entrance).

ARRIVAL AND DEPARTURE
CACCAMO

By bus Caccamo is connected by bus with Cefalù (2 daily; 45min); Palermo (4 daily Mon–Sat; 1hr 15min); Termini Imerese (8 daily Mon–Sat; 15min). Buses arrive and depart from Via Porta Euracea on the western edge of the historic centre.

EATING

A Castellana Piazza di Caduti ☎ 091 814 8667. Right by the castle, this medieval granary now houses a popular pizzeria-*ristorante*, with a long list of very reasonably priced grilled meats and pizzas. Tues–Sun lunch & dinner.

Parco Regionale delle Madonie

The Madonie mountain range and valleys south of Cefalù fall within the limits of one of Sicily's most accessible regional parks, the **Parco Regionale delle Madonie**. It's an area of beech and pinewoods, flower-filled upland plains, craggy rocks, high passes and soaring peaks (including the highest mountains in Sicily after Etna). Villages and towns are few and far between, but a couple of places in particular make good bases for tours and walks, while several remote resort hotels and *rifugi* offer a real mountain escape. There's a minor ski scene in winter, though not one for which you'd travel to Sicily.

Northern gateway to the Madonie park (pronounced Mad-on-*ee*-eh) is the attractive town of **Castelbuono**, 20km southeast of Cefalù, while right across the mountains on the south side is the smaller settlement of **Petralia Soprana**.

GETTING AROUND
PARCO REGIONALE DELLE MADONIE

By car You'll need a car to get around the Madonie mountains, particularly as accommodation outside the towns is extremely limited and fairly remote. A good driving route runs from Castelbuono to Geraci Siculo and on

2

> ### EXPLORING THE PARCO REGIONALE DELLE MADONIE
>
> Though largely in Italian, there's useful information on the official **park website**, ⓦparcodellemadonie.it, and at ⓦmadonie.it. There is also a **park information office** in Cefalù at Corso Ruggero 116 (daily: June–Sept 8am–8pm; Oct–May 8am–6pm; ☏0921 923 327). However, it's not as straightforward as it might be to go **walking** in the mountains – you'll be lucky to get any first-hand advice (or English-speaking assistance) in the information offices, while the only available walking **map** (*Carta dei Sentieri e del paesaggio*; 1:50,000), although almost insanely informative, is not of a good enough scale to route-find. There are also some other "geological pathway" route guides, translated loosely into English, for out-of-the-way places like Caltavuturo and Sclafani Bagni – however, they aren't as useful as they seem and require a high degree of tolerance for getting lost. Some local **tour operators** organize hikes, pony treks and other mountain activities, which might be your best bet for getting to grips with the Madonie – check posters and brochures in local information offices.

to Petralia Soprana, before twisting back across the mountains to the ski and hiking area of Piano Battàglia and round again to Castelbuono. You could do this in a day (about a 90km, 3hr, drive), but spending at least one night in the mountains would give you time for a walk, a country picnic or two and endless stunning views.

By bus Buses run between Cefalù and Castelbuono (7 daily Mon–Sat, 2 daily Sun).

Castelbuono

CASTELBUONO – self-styled "capital" of the Monti Madonie – doesn't actually feel much like a mountain town at all, but it is a pretty place that makes a good day-trip from Cefalù, even if you plan to go no further and higher into the Madonie park. It owes its origins to the Ventimiglia family, who made the town something of a thriving cultural centre in the fifteenth century, and their seat was the squat **Castello Ventimiglia** that's visible from many kilometres around.

Castelbuono's main street, **Via Umberto I**, is closed to traffic for much of the day. Like the rest of town, it makes for an enjoyable stroll, with a maze of cobbled streets on either side opening on to occasional churches and shady piazzas. For three days every June, the streets are laid with amazing floral designs and pictures during the **Infiorata Castelbuonese**. The lovely freestanding "Venus and Cupid" **fountain** on Via Umberto I is a good thirst-quencher on a hot day, while if you stroll around for any length of time you'll also probably come across Castelbuono's **eco-donkeys** – the town has replaced its garbage trucks with a unique door-to-door donkey collection service for household waste and recycling.

Matrice Vecchia

Piazza Margherita • Daily 11am–1pm & 5–7pm • Crypt €0.50

From the restored gateway and enclosed castle piazza, a charming tree-lined street runs down to central Piazza Margherita, where terrace cafés overlook the fourteenth-century **Matrice Vecchia**, fronted by a pretty loggia. If it's open, you can pay to descend well-worn steps into the **crypt** to view a series of remarkably well-preserved sixteenth-century frescoes of the *Passion of Christ*.

ARRIVAL AND DEPARTURE

CASTELBUONO

By bus There are regular buses to Castelbuono from outside Cefalù's train station, a 40min ride.

Destinations Cefalù (7 daily Mon–Sat, 1–2 daily Sun; 40min); Collesano (6 daily Mon–Sat; 45min); Gangi (1 daily; 1hr–1hr 20min); Geraci (2 daily Mon–Sat, 1 daily

Sun; 45min); Isnello (1 daily Mon–Sat; 25min); Palermo (3 daily Mon–Sat; 1hr 45min); Termini Imerese (2 daily Mon–Sat; 1hr 30min).

By car If you're staying in Cefalù, you might as well leave the car and take the bus; otherwise, park where you can and walk into the old town area (*"centro storico"*). Traffic loops through town on a convoluted one-way system, and it has to be said that initial impressions of Castelbuono by car are not good; it's much nicer once you're on foot.

ACCOMMODATION

4 Cannola Via Dafni 7 ☎ 0921 671 490 or ☎ 333 242 1018, ⊛ bb-4cannola.it. The town's most central B&B has clean, plain rooms in a restored house just behind the Venus fountain (aka Quattro Cannola or Four Spouts) on the main street. **€60**

★ **Azienda Agrituristica Bergi** Contrada Bergi ☎ 0921 672 045, ⊛ agriturismobergi.com. A laidback organic estate in a gorgeous valley, 3km southeast of town on the SS286 Geraci Siculo road, with spacious, country-style one- and two-room units set around landscaped gardens and a pool. It's a working farm of orchards and olives – home-made preserves and fruit from the trees are served at breakfast, while a good four-course dinner (€25, or included in the €75 half-board per person rate) uses more of their produce. **€110**

Relais Santa Anastasia Contrada Santa Anastasia ☎ 0921 672 233, ⊛ santa-anastasia-relais.it. For a sumptuous stay, try this rather grand restored twelfth-century abbey 8km outside town, with honeyed stone walls, elegant rooms in deep colours, and a glorious outdoor pool. Rates can be high, but contact them for special deals, especially out of season. Dinner in the lovely restaurant is €40 per person. **€360**

Rifugio Francesco Crispi Piano Semprià ☎ 0921 672 279. The nearest mountain refuge to Castelbuono is at 1300m above sea level, and a good two hours' strenuous walk away in the Milocca forest. It's open all year, providing basic accommodation in double rooms. Breakfast is included, and dinner is available. **€60**

EATING AND DRINKING

A line of appealing **cafés** and **restaurants** with outdoor terraces lies between the castle and Piazza Margherita, while yet more places are hidden away in the surrounding alleys. Pork, beef and especially wild mushrooms are typical menu items in this mountain region.

Antico Baglio Piazza Ten. Schicchi 3 ☎ 0921 679 512. It's a couple of hundred metres off the beaten track, but this restored old *baglio* (warehouse) has both a cool interior and shady outdoor deck, where you can sample things like home-made pasta with a sausage-meat and mushroom *ragù* (pasta dishes from €7–9, main dishes from €8–15). At night there are pizzas too. Follow the signs from Piazza Matteotti at the end of Via Umberto I. Tues–Sun lunch & dinner.

Fiasconaro Piazza Margherita 10 ☎ 0921 671 231.

Known throughout Italy for its gourmet panettone and other goodies made with locally grown *pistachio ad manna* (the latter unique to the area), this is a must for foodies. A seat here in the charming old-town square and a home-made ice cream or a dish of strawberry *granita* takes some beating on a hot day. Daily 9am–1pm & 3.15–8pm.

★ **Nangalarruni** Via delle Confraternite 5 ☎ 0921 671 428. The best place in town for serious mountain cuisine, this upmarket rustic tavern does amazing things with wild

A TASTE OF HEAVEN

"And when the dew that lay was gone up, behold, upon the face of the wilderness there lay a small round thing, as small as the hoar frost on the ground. And when the children of Israel saw it, they said one to another, It is manna: for they wist not what it was. And Moses said unto them, This is the bread which the Lord hath given you to eat. This is the thing which the Lord hath commanded, Gather of it every man according to his eating."

Exodus 16:14–16

Famous for the sustenance it gave Moses and the Israelites, **manna** is the sap of the south European flowering ash (*Fraxinus ornus*), cultivated uniquely in several plantations around Castelbuono. The sap is obtained by making incisions with a knife in the trunks of the trees, between July and September. The liquid sap is at first bitter, but it sweetens as it solidifies on the trunk. As well as being a mild laxative and purgative, it is also a cough sedative, an expectorant, a sweetener, and can be used as an eyewash and for softening boils – and according to locals in Castelbuono, it can even bring the dead back to life.

Chewy and tasting like a mixture of honey and maple syrup, manna is put to rather more pleasant use by the *pasticcerie* of Castelbuono, most notably *Fiasconaro* (see above), who use it in their unforgettably delicious panettone, nougat and ice cream.

mushrooms. They appear in soups, sauces and pasta dishes and with pork and beef to follow; finishing with a shot of the sweet local *digestivo*, Elisir di Fontana, is always a good idea. Dishes start at €8, or there are three tasting menus at €23, €25 and (if you are seriously hungry) €30. It's just down Via Umberto I from Piazza Margherita, second alley on the right. Daily lunch & dinner; Jan & Feb closed Wed.

Geraci Siculo

For an initial taste of the mountains, make the half-hour drive from Castelbuono up the winding SS286 to **GERACI SICULO**, 20km away. If ever a town was buttoned up tight against the threat of winter, it's this one, with its packed houses lining streets so narrow that laundry is strung across from balcony to balcony. At the highest point, up back-breaking cobbled alleys, the scant, restored ruins of a castle and an ancient chapel stand amid wild flowers and scented pines. Amazing 360-degree panoramas unfold, while back down the valley Castelbuono and its own mighty castle are easily seen. The road south of town climbs even higher before dropping down to the SS120 Gangi–Petralia road, where you can pick up the route into the central park region.

ARRIVAL AND DEPARTURE   GERACI SICULO

By bus There is a bus to Geraci a couple of times a day from Cefalù via Castelbuono, which then runs on to Gangi, but it really isn't worth the hours of time between one bus and the next. Realistically Geraci is only a coffee stop for drivers.

Piano Zucchi and Piano Battaglia

The heart of the Madonie lies southwest of Castelbuono, in the upland slopes and valleys below the two peaks of Pizzo Antenna Grande (or Pizzo della Principessa, 1977m) and Pizzo Carbonara (1979m). These are the highest of Sicily's mountains after Etna, with a winter ski business based at the two resort areas of Piano Zucchi and Piano Battaglia – though "resort" is pushing it, since there are no villages here and only very limited facilities. Outside winter time, it's an enjoyable drive up into the high mountains, with plenty of places to park up, take a walk through the alpine meadows and have a picnic.

There's nothing much at all at **Piano Zucchi** (1100m), save a little mountain chapel, a children's playground and views of peaks to all sides. **Piano Battaglia**, sited at 1600m (ⓦpianobattaglia.it), is a rather nicer area for walks in the high plains and picnics under the beech trees.

ARRIVAL AND DEPARTURE   PIANO ZUCCHI AND PIANO BATTAGLIA

By car From Castelbuono, drive 9km west to Munciarrati (also known as Mongerati), between Collesano and Isnello, where there's a turn-off up into the mountains. Piano Zucchi is 17km from the junction, with Piano Battaglia 7km further on again. From Piano Battaglia, it's another 20km, or half-hour drive, over the tops and down to the Petralia towns.

Petralia Soprana and Petralia Sottana

The southern edge of the Madonie range is marked by the twin towns of Petralia, which lie on opposite sides of a hill. There are some wonderful views, as you might imagine, from the upper town of **PETRALIA SOPRANA**, which sits at an altitude of nearly 1150m. This was the birthplace of the craftsman Fra Ùmile da Petralia (1580–1639), whose wooden crosses are found in churches all over southern Italy. From the edge of the village you get a long view over the Madonie and Nébrodi mountains, as well as an occasional sight of Etna.

However, it's the lower town, 3km away, **PETRALIA SOTTANA**, that acts as the mountain base for the region. Clinging to the hillside, it's an evocative place with one long main street, Corso Paolo Agliata, lined with weathered medieval churches, small piazzas and shuttered houses, culminating in the usual castle ruins.

OPPOSITE PARCO REGIONALE DELLE MADONIE (P.99) >

Parco Avventura

April–June, Sept & Oct Sat & Sun 10am–6pm; July & Aug daily 10am–8pm • Picnic area €2, adventure course €17 adults, €8 children • ☎ 091 748 7186, ⓦ parcoavventuramadonie.it

For a fabulous day out in the trees above town you can drive to the **Parco Avventura**, 3km beyond Petralia Sottana on the Piano Battaglia road, where as well as picnic areas and marked trails there's a thrilling **high-rope adventure course** through the pines – booking is a good idea in summer and at weekends (especially Sundays).

INFORMATION   PETRALIA SOPRANA AND PETRALIA SOTTANA

Tourist information The tourist office is at Corso Paolo Agliata 100 (daily 8.30am–2pm & 3–8pm; ☎ 0921 641 811, ⓦ petraliasottana.net). The Ente Parco delle Madonie office, at Corso Paolo Agliata 16 (daily 8am–2pm; ☎ 0921 684 011, ⓦ parcodellemadonie.it), should be able to tell you something about hiking, skiing and escorted excursions.

ACCOMMODATION AND EATING

★ **La Locanda di Cadì** A Fuoco Lento Borgo Cipampini, Petralia Soprana ☎ 338 289 0100, ⓦ lalocandadicadi.it. Run with passion and incredible attention to detail, this authentic country inn is really quite a special place, located in a minuscule medieval *borgo* outside Petralia Soprana. It's best known as a place to eat, with mains based on whatever is in season at the time – every ingredient is meticulously sourced or picked from the garden. The quality free-range chickens and Madonie lamb are fragrantly stuffed and oven roasted, and a full meal will be €25–30. There are rooms as well, and staying here is an unforgettable experience. **€80**

Polizzi Generosa

A twenty-minute drive west of the Petralias, the small town of **POLIZZI GENEROSA** is another possible Madonie base. Mountain views aside, the grand old **Chiesa Matrice** contains the area's greatest work of art, a triptych of the *Madonna and Child* flanked by saints. Attributed to a mysterious fifteenth-century Fleming known only as the "Maître au Feuillage brodé", it's reckoned to be his finest achievement.

ARRIVAL AND DEPARTURE   POLIZZI GENEROSA

By bus Polizzi Generosa is connected to Palermo by very infrequent buses (2 daily; 1hr 20min; ⓦ saistrasporti.it).

ACCOMMODATION AND EATING

U Bagghiu Via Gagliardo 3 ☎ 0921 551 111. Serves a great pasta speciality, *penne al Bagghiu* (cheesy penne with tomato and garlic), and pizzas in the evening. Dishes from €6. Mon & Wed–Sun lunch & dinner.

Giardino Donna Lavia Contrada Donna Lavia ☎ 0921 551 104, ⓦ giardinodonnalavia.com. Set within a former Jesuit monastery and the perfect location for a country holiday, with five rooms and a suite with its own terrace in a tower. The restaurant (dinner daily; €23) is exceptional, with locally sourced meats, home-grown veg and pulses, and freshly picked wild greens and herbs. Try the home-made taglietelle with a tasty puree of *fagioli badda* (a dramatic-looking violet and white bean unique to Polizzi), wild borage and wild fennel. Lots of wild mushrooms in season, and a fabulous roast suckling pig. Rooms **€70**, suite **€100**

★ **Santa Venera** Contrada Santa Venera ☎ 0921 649 421, ⓦ santavenera.com. It's worth making the trip to hole up in this place, run by the same family behind *U Bagghiu* and located 7km north of Polizzi Generosa, towards the Scillato autostrada junction. A comfortable farmhouse *agriturismo*, it's surrounded by vineyards and orchards, with seven en-suite rooms, a swimming pool and good views in all directions. You can eat in the restaurant here (daily, dinner only) for €15–25, or there's a half-board deal for €50 per person. **€70**

East of Cefalù

To the east of Cefalù, the rugged Tyrrhenian coast is hugged by rail, road and motorway, and is pretty built up for the most part. There are several resorts tucked along the narrow strip of land between the Nébrodi mountains and the sea, and though most of them are not worth going out of your way for – or indeed getting off your bus or train – there are several spots – ranging from an unusual **art hotel** to the bustling ceramics town of **Santo Stefano di Camastra** – where those travelling by car might want to take a break for a stroll around.

Castel di Tusa

Some 25km east of Cefalù, the coastal village of **CASTEL DI TUSA** features the remnants of a defensive castle and some good rocky beaches. In recent years, however, the place has become rather better known for its modern art, thanks to the efforts of **Antonio Presti** (born in Messina in 1957), who in the late 1980s and early 1990s invited artists from around the world to create a group of large-scale sculptures along the river bed (*fiumara*) and valley of the Tusa River, which flows down from the Nébrodi mountains just east of the village. After a protracted legal battle with the authorities, the sculptures were formally inaugurated as the **Fiumara d'Arte** sculpture park in 2006. You can pick up a brochure and map from Presti's other venture, the equally arresting *L'Atelier Sul Mare* "**art hotel**" (see below), at Via Cesare Battisti 4, which itself has become something of a tourist attraction: non-guests can be shown around the rooms and grounds on guided tours (daily at noon; €5).

Halaesa

Daily 9am–1hr before sunset • €2

Just 3km up the road from Castel di Tusa, on the way to the village of Tusa, are the sparse ruins of **Halaesa**, a fifth-century BC Sikel settlement that enjoyed some success under Rome. The name derives from the Greek *alaomal*, meaning to wander aimlessly, and refers to the original settlers here, the peripatetic Alesini, who had tried settling just about everywhere else. You can make out the chequered layout of the streets, remains of the agora, and – at the highest point – foundations of two third-century BC temples, with lofty views down over the Tusa valley.

ACCOMMODATION

CASTEL DI TUSA

★ **L'Atelier Sul Mare** Via Cesare Battisti 4 ☎ 0921 334 295, ⓦ ateliersulmare.com. Just metres from the sea, many of the rooms here have been given the designer-art treatment by individual artists: one is adorned with Arabic and Italian poetry and sports a mammoth window looking onto the sea, with a shower that works like a car wash, while another is bathed in red glow at night. Other rooms are more conventionally styled, though still with original artworks and furnishings. €140

A TOUR OF THE FIUMARA D'ARTE

All the structures and sculptures along the **Fiumara d'Arte** lie south of Castel di Tusa, and seeing the lot entails a 50km round trip by car through some magnificent countryside. Follow the signposts and you can't go far wrong, starting at the turn off the SS113 for Pettineo, a couple of kilometres east of Castel di Tusa (Santo Stefano/Messina direction). One of the earliest commissions – *La Materia Poteva Non Esserci*, resembling two giant hands joined in prayer – comes almost immediately into view, standing right under the motorway viaduct. It's 6km further up the valley to **Pettineo** itself, a gorgeous little village with the shards of a ruined castle at its highest point and a couple of bars in the old centre for drinks. More signs then direct you another 6km up the nearby mountain to the precariously located village of **Motta d'Affermo** for *Energia Mediterranea* – a graceful concrete curving wave in mottled blue astride a dusty hilltop. Beyond lies the dramatic cliff-top pyramid that is *38° Parallelo* (also known as *La Piramide*), after which you backtrack to Pettineo. There's a further cluster of works a twisting 10km south of Pettineo, in the environs of the striking hilltop hamlet of **Castel di Lucio**, from where you can either return the way you came, back to the coast, or continue on to Mistretta, which offers an alternative way back down to Santo Stefano di Camastra (or on over the mountains to Nicosia).

2

Santo Stefano di Camastra

Cefalù aside, quite the nicest stop along the Tyrrhenian coast is **SANTO STEFANO DI CAMASTRA**, reached by train or via a quick drive along the SS113. It's actually much the better for being split in two – beach and harbour below (where the train station is) and town high above, the latter forming a handsome old grid on a panoramic shelf of land. A steep cobbled path connects the two. Santo Stefano is renowned for its colourful **ceramic work** and the road through town is lined with shops selling platters, plates, cups, jugs, statues, household goods and decorative pottery. Off the main road, the old town is kept largely free of traffic and there's a small public garden, a belvedere with sea views and a pedestrianized main street, **Via Vittorio Emanuele**, of shops, cafés, boutiques and grocery stores. It's touristy certainly, but all very charming, while in the signposted **Museo della Ceramica** (Tues–Sun 9am–1pm & 4–8pm; free), in the handsome Palazzo Trabia, you can admire the best historic examples of the local pottery.

ARRIVAL AND DEPARTURE
SANTO STEFANO DI CAMASTRA

By bus Santo Stefano di Camastra is connected by bus with Mistretta (6 daily Mon–Sat, 3 daily Sun; 35min); and Nicosia (1 daily Mon–Sat; 1hr 30min).

By train Santo Stefano is on the train line between Palermo and Messina, but only a few of the slower regional trains stop here.

Mistretta

Six buses daily ply between Santo Stefano and Mistretta

From Santo Stefano, a high viaduct flies off 16km inland to one of the biggest of the nearby hill villages, **MISTRETTA**. The handsome old centre of eighteenth- and nineteenth-century buildings and cobbled alleys is largely unspoiled by modern construction: wrought-iron balconies and flower boxes overlook the long main street, the seventeenth-century cathedral has the hoary look of a medieval monument, while the population is largely composed of brown-suited pensioners milling around their veterans' associations. There's not much else to it, save some old-fashioned barbers' shops, the public gardens, and castle ruins atop a small hill, but it makes a nice quiet place to stay away from the coast.

Sant'Agata di Militello

SANT'AGATA DI MILITELLO, 28km east of Santo Stefano, is a small Tyrrhenian resort that's moribund for most of the year. In truth, it can hardly be called attractive, though its very long pebbled **beach** and calm sea are popular with holidaying Italian families, who pack the town's apartments for a few weeks each summer. There's a **fishing harbour** at one end, a palm-studded **promenade**, and a gridded town centre set back up the hillside, while a restored **castle** (daily 8.30am–12.30pm & 4–8pm; €2) speaks of more important times.

ARRIVAL AND DEPARTURE
SANT'AGATA DI MILITELLO

By bus There are hourly buses along the coast from Santo Stefano to Sant'Agata.
Destinations Cesarò (1 daily Mon–Sat; 1hr 30min); San Fratello (6 daily; 20min); San Marco d'Alunzio (4 daily; 20min).

By train Sant'Agata is a frequent stop on the coast train line between Palermo and Messina. The station is a 10min walk east of the town centre.
By car Follow the "porto" signs and drive in along the seafront, where there's plenty of free parking.

San Fratello

Fifteen kilometres up in the hills from Sant'Agata, the large village of **San Fratello** was once populated by a Lombard colony, introduced to Sicily by Roger II's queen, Adelaide di Monferrato. On the Thursday and Friday of Holy Week, before Easter, the town puts on the **Festa dei Giudei** (Feast of the Jews) – a unique carnival-type celebration when locals dress up in red devils' costumes, complete with black tongues and horses' tails (a reminder of their traditional trade of horse-raising), to the cacophonic accompaniment of trumpets, bells and drums. Needless to say, the ecclesiastical authorities take a dim view of these proceedings, but have to make do with having the Easter Sunday church congregations in suitably contrite and sober mood. For a panoramic picnic spot, head for the Norman church of **Santi Alfio, Filadelfio e Cirino**, isolated on top of a hill outside the village (follow the rough track from the cemetery). The church is dedicated to three brothers horribly martyred by the Romans: the first had his tongue torn out, the second was burnt alive, and the third was hurled into a pot of boiling tar.

Capo d'Orlando

Some 17km northeast of Sant'Agata, occupying a headland where Aragonese king Frederick II suffered a historic defeat at the hands of a group of rebellious barons in 1299, **CAPO D'ORLANDO** is a slick holiday town surrounded by good rocky and sandy beaches. If you're sufficiently charmed by the **swimming**, which is best on its eastern side (around the San Gregorio area), you might well want to stay. The town has plenty of restaurants, bars and *birrerias*, and a choice of discos in summer.

ARRIVAL AND INFORMATION   CAPO D'ORLANDO

By train Capo d'Orlando is a frequent stop for trains running between Palermo and Messina; the station is a 10min walk from the town centre and beach.

Tourist office For general tourist information, ask at the kiosk on the seafront (summer Mon–Sat 9am–1pm & 3–7pm, extended hours in summer; ☎0941 918 134).

Tours From Capo d'Orlando there are daily excursions to the Aeolian Islands between June and September, with departures around 10am, returning at 9pm: for further information and bookings, contact one of the town's travel agents, such as Agatirso Viaggi, Via Consolare Antica 332 (☎0941 912 756, ⓦagatirso.com).

ACCOMMODATION

Hotel Faro Via Libertà 7 ☎0941 902 466, ⓦnuovohotelfaro.com. 1960s-style hotel with spacious rooms and balconies fronting the beach. Turn right out of the station and walk along Via Crispi, head for the sea at Piazza Matteotti, and it's a few blocks to the right. €115

THE MONTI NÉBRODI

The **Monti Nébrodi** – a sparsely populated expanse of high forest and rocky peaks – covers a huge wedge of land between Santo Stefano di Camastra and Mistretta in the west and Randazzo and the Etna foothills in the east. Much of the mountain range is protected as the **Parco Naturale dei Nébrodi** (the largest such area in Sicily), though it's difficult to get a good impression of the whole by car since few roads connect the scattered villages within the park and even the towns on the periphery are minor attractions for the most part. However, adventurous hikers can follow any number of trails through the hills and valleys – there are some detailed on the useful **park website**, ⓦparcodeinebrodi.it – while there is a road up to the highest peak, **Monte Soro** (1847m), between San Fratello and Cesarò (SS289), from which extensive views reach to the Aeolian Islands to the north and Etna to the southeast. There's plenty more park information on the website, and there are also **visitor centres** in Sant'Agata di Militello (☎0941 702 524), Santo Stefano di Camastra (☎0921 331 199), Cesarò (☎095 773 2061), Randazzo (☎095 799 1611) and several of the mountain villages. Most visitor centres are open weekday mornings only (usually 9am–1pm), and are only intermittently useful – you should be able to pick up maps, accommodation details and walking itineraries, but English-speaking assistance is rare and there's not much more help for hikers than can be gleaned from the printed information. The best single visit is probably to the **Palazzo Zito**, the official headquarters in Sant'Agata di Militello (Mon–Fri 7.30am–2pm, plus Wed 2.30–6pm), which contains a museum covering the park's social and natural history and heritage.

Patti

With its views out to the Aeolian Islands, a crumbling hilltop historic centre, and a general – and infectious – sense of well-being, **PATTI** is an engaging little place, with more charm than many of the centres on this coast. At the top of the semi-restored upper town, the **Cattedrale** has a powerful *Madonna* by Antonello de Saliba and, in the right transept, the tomb of **Adelasia**, much-loved first wife of Roger I, with the date of her death inscribed at the bottom, 1118. Afterwards, you could take one of the frequent buses that depart from outside the hospital just below the old centre to **Patti Marina**, where there's a long, fine pebble beach.

ARRIVAL AND DEPARTURE   PATTI

By train Patti's station (known as Patti–San Piero Patti) is located in the lower town, but connected by regular buses to the upper town; for the *centro storico* get off at Piazza Marconi (the stop after the hospital).

By bus There's one daily bus here from Messina and one from Milazzo (both Mon–Sat). Buses arrive and depart from Piazza Marconi at the foot of the *centro storico*.

ACCOMMODATION AND EATING

BB Casa Rubes Via Magretti 127 ☎ 0941 21 64, ☎ 347 527 5001, ⓦ casarubes.it. An oasis. A lovely, relaxed B&B in a beautifully converted town house in the heart of the old town. Highlights include the flower-filled terrace where breakfast is served at a long table. Gracious, welcoming owners. **€65**

Sacra Famiglia Via Dante Alighieri 1 ☎ 0941 241 622, ⓦ sacrafamiglia.it. A spruce, modern convent perched

atop the old town, with functional rooms and a fabulous, unpretentious restaurant (daily lunch & dinner), where the crowds flock in for the antipasto feast (€15), a seemingly endless series of tasty morsels – hot and cold, and meat-, fish- and vegetable-based – eaten on a terrace looking out to the Aeolian Islands. There are other great fixed-menu deals as well, but make sure you arrive hungry. Closed Easter to late Aug. **€90**

Tindari

Now famous throughout Sicily as the home of a much-revered black Madonna, **Tindari** began life in 396 BC as **Tyndaris**, an outpost of Siracusa. Built and fortified as a defence against Carthaginian attacks along this coast, it was one of the last Greek settlements in Sicily. Almost impregnable thanks to its commanding height, the town continued to prosper under Rome, when it was given special privileges in return for its loyalty.

Santuario di Tindari

Mon–Sat 6.45am–12.30pm & 2.30–7pm, Sun 6.45am–12.45pm & 2.30–8pm; closes 1hr earlier in winter • Free • ⓦ santuariotindari.it

Climbing the hill to the site, the first thing you see, glistening from its cliff-top position, is the **Santuario di Tindari**, a lavishly kitsch temple erected in the 1960s to house the much-revered *Madonna Nera*, or Black Madonna. A plaque underneath this Byzantine icon proclaims *Nigra sum, sed hermosa* ("I am black, but beautiful"), a reference to the esteem in which she has been held for a thousand years since the icon appeared from the east to perform a series of miracles. Pilgrims throng to the sanctuary to pay their respects, especially around the Black Madonna's feast day on September 8. There's a great view from the top, overlooking a long tongue of white sand and the Marinello lagoons below (see p.110).

Tyndaris archeological site

Daily 9am–2hr before sunset • €4

The archeological site of **Tyndaris** lies at the end of a path that starts in front of the sanctuary. Most of the visible remains are Roman, including some houses and shops along the main street, the decumanus – one of them (probably a caldarium, or bathhouse) with traces of plumbing still surviving – and an impressive **basilica** at the eastern end. The basilica would have been the entrance to the agora lying beyond (now covered by tourist shops). It was restored in the 1950s, using modern materials, though it still retains a certain grandeur. You can just about make out the manner of its construction, bridging Greek and Roman building techniques, and designed in such a way that the central gallery could be shut off at either end and used for public meetings, with the market traffic diverted along the side passages.

The decumanus has streets running off it, and at the bottom of one is the **Casa Romana**, a Roman house in good condition, with mosaic floors. At the other end of the main street, the **teatro**, cut into the hill, boasts a superb view over the sea, as far as the distant Milazzo promontory. A part of the stage remains from the original third-century BC Greek edifice, but most of the rest is Roman, dating from the Imperial Age when the theatre was converted for use as a gladiatorial arena. Later, it was partly dismantled to furnish stone for the **city walls** that once surrounded the settlement, of which a good portion remains. You'll have seen some of them on the road up, including the ancient city's **main gate**, built to the same "pincer" design as the one at the Euryalus castle outside Siracusa.

The site's **museum** contains some of the best finds from the excavations, including a massive stone head of Augustus. There's also a reconstruction of the theatre's scene-building, and some eighteenth-century watercolours showing how the basilica looked before its overhaul.

TINDARI (TYNDARIS)

Teatro
DECUMANUS
Museum
Casa Romana
Entrance to Site
Basilica
Agora
Greek Walls
Santuario
Main City Gate ★ Bus Stop
N
0   100
metres
Riserva Naturale Laghetti di Marinello & Patti

2

> **ANCIENT THEATRE AT TINDARI**
>
> Each year from late May until mid-June, **classical dramas** are staged in the ancient theatre at Tyndaris on alternate evenings, and between late July and late August, there is also a season of theatre and **concerts** here. Performances normally start at 9pm, and **tickets** cost around €20. Ask at the ticket office by the entrance to the archeological site or contact the **box office** directly (☎0941 240 912 or ☎800 031 922, ⓦteatrodeiduemari.net) for details. You can also pick up a programme from the Tindari tourist office (see below).

Riserva Naturale Laghetti di Marinello

Directly below Tindari and west of Oliveri lies one of Sicily's most entrancing **beaches**, forming part of the **Riserva Naturale Laghetti di Marinello**, where saltwater lagoons, sand dunes and dramatic rocky cliffs provide a sanctuary for migratory birds. The lagoons, fine sand and clean water are irresistible, and there are bars and a campsite (see below), but precious little shade on the beach.

ARRIVAL AND INFORMATION   TINDARI

By bus Frequent buses from Patti stop in the car park over 1km from the sanctuary, from where minibuses shuttle every 10min or so up to the foot of the church (return tickets €0.60). The car park charges €1/hr.
By train The closest train station to Tindari is Oliveri-

Tindari, a good 3km (uphill) walk.
Tourist information Tindari has a tourist office right next to the site on Via Teatro Greco (Mon–Fri 9am–1pm; ☎0941 369 184, ⓦpattietindari.com).

ACCOMMODATION

Marinello Località Marinello ☎0941 313 000, ⓦwww.villaggiomarinello.it. Perfectly located for the Laghetti di Marinello, this well-equipped campsite is at the bottom of the cliffs holding the Tindari sanctuary, within

steps of the lovely sandy beach and with bungalows and mini-apartments rentable by the week. Tent pitch €13, plus €5–10 per person; bungalows €50

Novara di Sicilia

Branching inland into the mountains at the nondescript village of San Biaggio, the SS185 to Giardini-Naxos (see p.177) is the only road connecting the Tyrrhenian and Ionian coasts. One of the most dramatic routes on the island, the road climbs gently into the hills through some handsome countryside to **NOVARA DI SICILIA**, whose main street is dotted with bars and shops that sell the strong local sheep's cheese, *maiorchina*.

The dense woods above the village, with expansive views over the sea, are a favourite spot for the locals, who come out here on a Sunday armed with picnic hampers and portable stoves, though there are enough shady nooks and glades to find your own space. Soon after Novara, the road climbs to 1270m before descending, in sight of Etna's dramatic slopes, to Francavilla and Castiglione (see p.178).

EATING   NOVARA DI SICILIA

La Pineta Via Nazionale ☎0941 650 522. A traditional trattoria, where you can sample the local ricotta, deep-fried

crespelle (little pancakes) stuffed with fresh vegetables, and home-made pasta. Tues–Sun lunch & dinner.

Milazzo

If it weren't for the industry besieging **MILAZZO**, it wouldn't be a bad-looking place. A long plane- and palm-tree-lined promenade looks across the sparkling sea, while behind the town a rambling old castle caps Milazzo's ancient acropolis. Most people, though, are put off by the unsightly oil refinery that occasionally produces a yellow smog overhead, and only stop long enough to get out again, taking the first ferry or hydrofoil to the Aeolian Islands (see p.116), for which Milazzo is the major embarkation point.

Historically, the site's strategic importance made it one of the most fought-over towns in Sicily. The Greeks arrived in 716 BC, after which the town was contested by successive armies, from the Carthaginians to the Aragonese. It even became a base for the British during the Napoleonic Wars, while fifty years later Garibaldi won a victory here that set the seal on his conquest of Sicily. If you get stuck here, there's a fair bit to see and do, ranging from a great **castle**, to the surprisingly gorgeous **Capo di Milazzo**, with a beguiling cove and lovely beaches.

If you're in a hurry, Milazzo is easy enough to handle. You could be on an outward-bound ferry or hydrofoil within an hour of arriving. But there's enough in and around town to make it an enjoyable overnight stop, before or after your Aeolian trip.

The lower town

Milazzo's **lower town** has a nice, brisk feel. It is not really a place to sightsee, more a place to go for a stroll, coffee or aperitivo while you wait for your ferry or hydrofoil. Given the inflated prices on the islands, anyone self-catering is well advised to do a little food shopping. There is a daily morning **market** behind the post office on Via G. Medici. If you have time to kill, the best thing to do on a sunny day is to walk along the shore, passing little booths and tables where fishermen sell their daily catch. Carry on long enough (around 20min), and you'll reach a small sandy beach with refreshments.

Duomo Nuovo

If you fancy a touch of sightseeing, the silver-domed **Duomo Nuovo** has some Renaissance paintings in the apse: four panels of Sts Peter, Paul, Rocco and Thomas Aquinas; between the last of these, an *Adoration of the Child* by Antonello de Saliba, and an *Annunciation* by Andrea Giuffrè above that.

The citadel

The **Borgo**, Milazzo's old hilltop **citadel**, dominates the town. Here, the views open out over bay and plain, while the higher you climb, the older and more decrepit the buildings become – some churches and *palazzi* on the approach to the castle are little more than precariously balanced shells. To appreciate the citadel's size, walk round to the north side, where the formidable defences erected by the Spanish still stand almost in their entirety. The massive walls are magnificent, pierced by a suitably imposing tunnelled gateway.

Also within the citadel's walls are the **Duomo Antico**, with Byzantine fragments, a central Norman keep, the old Sala del Parlamento and the remains of the Palazzo dei Giurati, later used as a prison. Outside the

CAFÉS AND BARS
Albatros	3
Bar Dama	1
Il Spizzico	2

RESTAURANTS
Bagatto	4
La Casalinga	3
Il Covo del Pirata	2
Giardino di Sicilia	1

ACCOMMODATION
Cassisi	3
Giardino di Sicilia	1
Orchidea	6
Petit	4
Solaris	5
Il Vicolo	2

MILAZZO

walls, opposite the castle's entrance, the Dominican **Chiesa del Rosario** was formerly a seat of the Inquisition.

The castello

Via del Castello • Guided tours: July Tues–Sun 9.30am–1.30pm & 4.30–10pm; Aug Tues–Sun 9.30am–1.30pm & 4.30pm–midnight; rest of the year check times at the tourist office, as they vary according to staffing levels • Free • ☎ 090 922 1291

The **castello** itself is steeped in military history: built by Frederick II in the thirteenth century on the site of the Greek acropolis and on top of Arab foundations, it was enlarged by Charles V, and restored by the Spanish in the seventeenth century. Recently restored, excellent information boards in English and Italian recount the history of the site, which retains the pile holes made by Bronze Age huts, and a recently excavated medieval quarter with a complex system of cisterns.

Capo Milazzo

Bus #6 runs to the cape, departing from the stop to the left as you leave the hydrofoil station

Some 6km north of Milazzo, the thin **Capo Milazzo** promontory is the focus of most of the summertime activity. There are plenty of good little **beaches** here, but the loveliest spot to swim and snorkel is right at the tip of the cape, where the road ends and a path leads down to a natural sea-pool known as the **Piscina di Venere**, or pool of Venus. From here, a path runs along the west coast to a longer, sand and shingle beach, which is rarely busy, even in the summer.

ARRIVAL AND DEPARTURE

MILAZZO

By train Trains running on the main Palermo–Messina line stop at Milazzo. The train station is a good 3km south of the centre. Local buses are scheduled to run into town via the port every 30min or so during the day, but the service is not entirely reliable. Buy tickets (€0.85) aboard, or take a taxi (☎ 340 628 7546) for around €10. There are usually a few enterprising locals offering an unofficial taxi service in dodgy-looking cars. If you want to risk it, establish a price first.

By bus Buses (including the Giuntabus service from Messina, whose timings are pretty much organized to tie in with hydrofoil arrivals and departures) stop on the port-side car park – turn right as you disembark from the hydrofoil.

Destinations Messina (approx hourly; 50min).

By ferry and hydrofoil Milazzo is the main departure point for ferries and hydrofoils to the Aeolian Islands. Via dei Mille runs along the port, with pedestrian and car access to the queues for the ferries. All hydrofoils now depart from the new departure terminal at the north end of Via dei Mille, right by the Giuntabus stop. Details of ferry and hydrofoil services are given in Chapter 3 (see p.120).

INFORMATION AND TOURS

Tourist information Milazzo's tourist office is just back from the harbour at Piazza Duilio 20 (Mon–Fri 8.30am–1.30pm & 3.30–6pm, Sat 8.30am–1.30pm; ☎ 090 922 2865).

Boat tours During the summer there are daily cruise excursions to the Aeolians from Milazzo, usually sailing from Milazzo at 8.15am or 9am, stopping at two or three of the islands, and returning at around 6pm. Tickets are €40–60, and the trips are run by Navisal, Via dei Mille 27 (☎ 090 922 4926, ⓦ navisal.com), and Tar.Nav, Via dei Mille 17 and 43 (☎ 090 922 3617 or ☎ 340 070 7285).

ACCOMMODATION

★ **Cassisi** Via Cassisi 5 ☎ 090 922 9099, ⓦ cassisihotel .com. Elegant, minimalist, family-run hotel, with a deft touch of contemporary oriental style. The buffet breakfast is abundant, with local cheese and salamis, typical pastries and biscuits, and lots of fresh fruit. A 5min walk from the port, and close to the main shopping area. **€130**

Giardino di Sicilia Via Santa Maria Maggiore 29 ☎ 090 922 2191. Five rooms with en-suite facilities belonging to one of Milazzo's most appealing restaurants. The location is perfect for those who want to discover the hidden delights of Milazzo, right at the foot of the Borgo, a few steps from the seafront, and a short walk to the first beach of Capo Milazzo. **€80**

Orchidea Via Nino Bixio ☎ 090 928 8004, ⓦ beborchidea.it. Clean, functional B&B in a modern *palazzo*, overlooking the port and sandwiched between Via XX Luglio and Via Nino Bixio. The rooms won't win any design awards, but they are clean, serviceable and four have sea views, and there's a kitchen for guests' use. There are also two family suites with a twin room, double room and bathroom. Signposted from the port. Rooms €45; suites from €50

★ **Petit** Via dei Mille 37 ☎ 090 928 6784, ⊛ petithotel .it. Eco-archictectural hotel in a nineteenth-century building on the seafront. Staff go out of their way to be helpful, and breakfasts include local salamis and cheeses, organic yogurt, eggs and jams, and home-made cakes. €110

Solaris Via Colonello Berte 70 ☎ 333 605 0091, ⊜ bedandbreakfast.milazzo.info. Bright and welcoming

B&B a block from the port, with five cheerfully decorated rooms with a/c and fridges. All the rooms have balconies and one has a small covered terrace. €90

Il Vicolo Via Salemi 14 ☎ 349 504 6851, ⊛ ilvicolobeb .it. Located in a quiet side street on the Ponente (eastern) side of town, 30m from the beach and just a 5min walk from the port, this B&B has three spick-and-span rooms with en-suite bathrooms, and a fourth with a bathroom outside. All have use of a fully equipped kitchen, and there's a courtyard for outside dining. Facilities include a washing machine, and the use of bikes. €80

EATING AND DRINKING

There's a small but worthy range of **restaurants and trattorias** in Milazzo's centre; those furthest from the port tend to do the best food. The town's *passeggiata* is one of the liveliest in Sicily, with baby buggies, scooters and cars clogging up Lungomare Garibaldi, and a swarm of couples and families dropping in for ice cream at the **bars** along the way, most of which stay open late in summer. There are plenty of pubs dotted around the Borgo, too, open every evening in summer, at weekends in winter.

RESTAURANTS

★ **Bagatto** Via M. Regis 11 ☎ 090 922 4212. You can sample local salami and cheeses as well as more substantial dishes (€10–16) at this chic wine bar and restaurant. Try the tagliata of seared, thinly sliced rare beef (€16). There's a great selection of wines and a cool, laidback ambience, with some tables outside. Mon–Tues & Thurs–Sun aperitivo & dinner.

La Casalinga Via R. D'Amico 13 ☎ 090 922 2697. Local favourite for fish, where the speciality is spaghetti *polpa di granchi* (with crab sauce). First courses are €8 or €9, mains €7–16. Worth booking. Daily lunch & dinner; closed Sun Oct–April.

Il Covo del Pirata Lungomare Garibaldi 47–48 ☎ 090 928 4437. With wooden ceilings, stone walls and piratical decor, this has more atmosphere than most local eateries, and the food is occasionally superb. Downstairs is a pizzeria, but you should go upstairs for the sea view. First courses include *linguine tuttomare*, a seafood extravaganza (€14) – other pasta dishes are around €10. Closed Wed. Mon–Tues & Thurs–Sun lunch & dinner.

★ **Giardino di Sicilia** Via Santa Maria Maggiore 29 ☎ 090 922 2191, ⊛ giardinidisicilia.net. Amiable family-run restaurant and pizzeria, where you eat in a garden courtyard in summer, serving what may be one of the best

pizzas (from €4) you ever eat, their crisp, tasty feather-light bases the result of a dough fermented for 48 hours and a man who knows how to get the best out of a *forno a legna*. The emphasis on quality ingredients is evident right across the menu, making even a simple *pepata di cozze* (peppered mussels; €9) an unforgettable experience. Daily lunch & dinner.

CAFÉS

Albatros Via dei Mille 38 ☎ 090 928 3666. Once the classic café in which to hang out while waiting for your ferry or hydrofoil, and though the dock has moved 100m up the street, Aeolians and old-timers still flock here for nostalgia's sake and for the great barman. Yummy pastries (try the *nastrino*, a raisin twist, or the *cornetti* with apple and crema), plus good savouries and ice cream. Or make the waiting easier with a deftly mixed martini. Daily 10am–8pm; Nov–May closed Tues.

Bar Dama Piazza Battisti (no phone). Excellent little café for a daytime snack, with a few outdoor tables. The fruit *granite* are terrific. Closed Mon Oct–June.

Il Spizzico Via dei Mille s/n (no phone). Right next to the Ustica Lines office, this takeaway does the best *arancini* hereabouts, including versions filled with aubergine or spinach and mozzarella. Open daily.

The Aeolian Islands

LIPARI

The Aeolian Islands

The Aeolian Islands, or Isole Eolie, are a mysterious apparition when glimpsed from Sicily's northern coast. Sometimes it's clear enough to pick out the individual white houses on their rocky shores; at other times they're murky, misty and only half-visible. D.H. Lawrence, on his way to Palermo by train in bad weather, was clearly not in the best of moods when he wrote that they resembled "… heaps of shadow deposited like rubbish heaps in the universal greyness". The sleepy calm that seems to envelop this archipelago masks a more dramatic existence: two of the islands are still volcanically active, and all are buffeted alternately by ferocious storms in winter and a deluge of tourists in summer. But their unique charm has survived more or less intact, fuelled by the myths associated with their elemental and unpredictable power.

Closest island to the mainland is the day-tripper magnet of **Vulcano**, with its mud baths, hot springs, black-sand beaches and smoking main crater. Across the channel lies the main island, **Lipari**, which is the hub of the ferry and hydrofoil system. It also has the widest choice of accommodation and restaurants, and is the only island with any kind of life outside the main summer season. Of the central group of islands, **Panarea** is the smallest and most elite, and in August the conspicuously rich float in to commune with nature from their multi-million-euro yachts and villas and €500-a-night hotel rooms, overlaying the gentle lapping of the waves with a cacophony of extremely loud music. Though the regular fireworks of its volcano bring droves of trekkers to **Stromboli**, this island too attracts its share of fashionistas – Dolce and Gabbana have a house here – while the chic whitewashed Piscità quarter is full of stylish villas. Twin-peaked **Salina** springs perhaps the best surprise – second in size only to Lipari, it attracts a less flamboyant crowd, and being unusually fertile, remains green year-round, making walking in its mountains pleasant at all times. **Filicudi**, long favoured by the trendy left, has something of a radical-chic feel, though it is all very understated and relaxed; wandering its mule tracks, it's not hard to get a taste of what life in the archipelago was like twenty – or a hundred – years ago. If this is what you are looking for, make the effort to get out to distant **Alicudi**, an uncompromising kind of place and, some would say, the hardest to like. Individual identity aside, each Aeolian island is embraced by water of a limpid quality rarely found along the coast of Sicily. Most of the beaches are pebble – sandy stretches are sparse, and tend to be ash-black – but **boat tours** (available at every Aeolian harbour) provide access to any number of secluded coves, hidden caves and quiet snorkelling and scuba-diving waters.

Brief history

The first historic settlers exploited the volcanic resources, above all the abundance of **obsidian**, a hard glass-like rock that can be worked to produce a fine cutting edge, and

ALICUDI

Highlights

❶ Upper town, Lipari The ancient citadel, high above two harbours, shelters the island's magnificent archeological museum. **See p.123**

❷ Lingua, Salina With its traffic-free piazza and promenade overlooking protected pebble beaches, this relaxed little village is the perfect destination for families with children. **See p.135**

❸ Panarea diving Snorkel or dive in sparkling waters above bubbling fumaroles and Roman remains, and explore the craggy uninhabited offshore islets. **See p.140**

❹ The ascent of Stromboli Don't miss the guided climb up one of the world's most active volcanoes. **See p.146**

❺ Lidalina, Filicudi It's not quite the lido at the end of the world, but this disarming, eco-friendly oasis is hard to beat. **See p.149**

❻ Zucco Grande, Filicudi This remote village, abandoned to emigration, makes a great target for a hike along the mule tracks of Filicudi. **See p.150**

❼ A sojourn in Alicudi Few places in Europe are more remote than Alicudi. Join its population of eighty in low season for a true isolation experience. **See p.150**

HIGHLIGHTS ARE MARKED ON THE MAP ON P.118

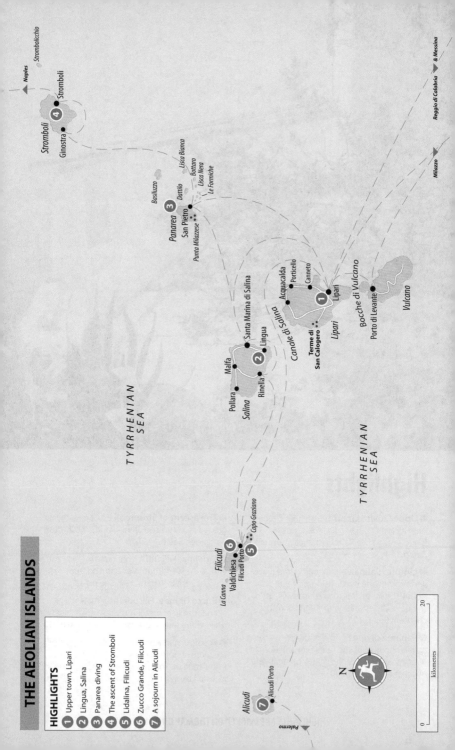

THE AEOLIAN ISLANDS

HIGHLIGHTS

1. Upper town, Lipari
2. Lingua, Salina
3. Panarea diving
4. The ascent of Stromboli
5. Lidalina, Filicudi
6. Zucco Grande, Filicudi
7. A sojourn in Alicudi

was traded far and wide, accruing enormous wealth to the archipelago. The islands were drawn more closely into the Greek ambit by the arrival, around 580 BC, of **refugees** from the wars between Segesta and Selinus (Selinunte). Those Greeks based at the fortified citadel of Lipari later allied themselves with Carthage, which made Lipari its base during the First Punic War. For its pains, Greek Lipari was destroyed by the Romans in 251 BC and the islands became part of the Roman province of Sicily, paying hefty taxes on exports of obsidian. The islands subsequently changed hands several times before being abandoned to the frequent attacks of wide-ranging North African **pirates**, culminating in a terrible slaughter that took place in 1544 at the hands of Khair ed-Din, or Barbarossa, who consigned all the survivors of the massacre to slavery – a figure estimated to have been as high as 10,000.

Political prisoners, emigration and Il Postino

Italian unification saw the islands used as a **prison** for political exiles, a role that continued right up to World War II, with the Fascists exiling their political opponents to Lipari. The last political detainee to be held here was, ironically, Mussolini's own daughter, Edda Ciano, in 1946. By the 1950s **emigration**, especially to Australia, had reduced the Aeolian population to a mere handful of families, when the release of **Rossellini**'s *Stromboli: Terra di Dio* (1949) and the story of his affair on the island with star Ingrid Bergman put the archipelago under the spotlight. The curious began to visit the islands, many of them buying properties for a song, while other film-makers followed, many of them pioneers in underwater photography. Today's economy is based on **tourism**, with hotels sprouting on previously barren ground, and running water and electricity installed (almost) everywhere. Nonetheless, enough primitive splendour has remained for the islands to continue to attract film crews, and Michael Radford's *Il Postino* (1994), filmed on Salina, and Nanni Moretti's *Caro Diario* (1994) still draw tourists in their droves. Since 2000, the Aeolians have been listed as a UNESCO World Heritage Site.

3

VISITING THE AEOLIANS

Aeolian food is among the most distinctive in Italy, fish of course providing the mainstay but with the traditional crops of capers, olives and mountain herbs flavouring most dishes, while the malvasia grapes provide one of Sicily's more ancient wines. Other foods (as well as much of the water on some islands) have to be imported, so restaurants tend towards the expensive, as do hotels and B&Bs. **Accommodation rates** in the Aeolians fluctuate a lot more than in other parts of Sicily. Prices for August are at least double those charged in low season, and often rates can as much as triple. For example, a hotel charging €200 for a double room with breakfast in August would probably cost €60 in early spring and late autumn, €80 in May or October, €100 in June or September, €120 in July. Many places also insist on half board (*mezza pensione*, ie dinner, bed and breakfast) and multi-night stays in high season. It's wise to book ahead if you plan on visiting at this time – but thankfully August is arguably the least appealing month for non-Italians to visit, with the heat and crowds making it hard to get a sense of the true identities of the islands.

  Ferries and **hydrofoils** ply between the islands year-round – their arrival is often the high point of the day in a place like Alicudi, with a permanent population of around a hundred. Services are reduced out of season (basically Oct–May), but you should still be able to reach most islands daily. Indeed, visiting outside **peak season** is highly recommended, since there's a refreshing absence of other tourists, and accommodation rates plummet accordingly. However, be warned that many hotels and restaurants close their doors for the entire **winter**, while if the weather turns, you're in danger of being stuck for days – the archipelago is frequently lashed by **storms** between October and March. Even in summer high winds and storms can strike, and heavy seas can mean the cancellation of ferry and hydrofoil services to both the mainland and the other islands. If this happens, there's no alternative to sitting and waiting the storm out.

  There are **ATM**s on all the islands except Alicudi. **Power cuts** are commonplace, caused by storms in winter, and in August by over-demand, so a torch is a good idea, especially in winter. Don't be surprised if hotels ask you to be sparing with the water, as it's imported by tanker.

3

AEOLIAN LEGENDS

Volcanoes have always been identified with the mouths of hell, and legend has it that Jupiter's son, **Vulcan**, had his workshop in the Aeolians. Vulcano is named after this god of fire and metalworking, while another island takes its name from Liparus, whose daughter Ciane married **Aeolus**, ruler of the winds and master of navigation; Aeolus, in turn, lent his name to the whole archipelago. These winds were kept in one of the Aeolians' many caves, and were presented to Odysseus in a bag to take on his travels. His curious crew opened the bag and, as a result, blew his ship straight back to port.

GETTING TO THE AEOLIAN ISLANDS

BY FERRY AND HYDROFOIL

Essentials The main embarkation point is Milazzo, from where ferries (*navi* or *traghetti*) and hydrofoils (*aliscafi*) depart year-round (weather permitting), with more frequent departures during the high season (June–Sept). There is also a twice-weekly year-round ferry service from Naples, and a daily year-round service from Messina. In summer there is also one daily hydrofoil connection with Palermo and Naples. The car-carrying ferries take roughly twice as long to most destinations as the hydrofoils, but are around sixty percent cheaper. Hydrofoils are also more prone to cancellation in bad weather, particularly out to the more distant islands, and the low-season ferry to Naples is subject to frequent cancellations.

Ferry and hydrofoil operators Services from Milazzo are with three main companies, all of which have offices at the port: Siremar (ferries and hydrofoils; ⓦsiremar.it), Ustica Lines (hydrofoils only; ⓦusticalines.it), and NGI (ferries only; ⓦngi-spa.it). Hydrofoil services to Naples are run by SNAV (ⓦSNAV.it).

Tickets Tickets are sold at the companies' harbourside offices before departure, and timetables are posted at every office; up-to-date schedules are also available online on the company websites. In July and August, and at the beginning and end of public holidays you might need to buy tickets in advance (for which there is a surcharge); otherwise, services are rarely full.

Fares Sample one-way high-season fares from Milazzo are around €16 by hydrofoil or €10 by ferry to Lipari; €21/14 to Stromboli; and €28/16 to Alicudi. Hydrofoils from Messina to Lipari cost around €23, while from Palermo you'll pay around €26 to Alicudi, €38 to Lipari and €54 to Stromboli. Transporting a car on the car-ferry starts at around €30 one-way (Milazzo to Lipari), while on all services children under 4 go free and under-12s go half-price.

DEPARTURES FROM MILAZZO

Getting to Milazzo Milazzo (see p.112) is 50min from Messina by bus (ⓦgiuntabustrasporti.com); arrivals are timed to coordinate with hydrofoils, and drop you right by the hydrofoil dock. Be sure to take a bus that goes via the autostrada; if not, journey time is 90min. Several companies run minibus shuttle services between the port and Catania airport, costing €25 per head. There is also a direct bus to

and from Catania airport at least twice daily from April to October (ⓦgiuntabus.com). Trains are not as convenient, as Milazzo station is on the edge of town and the buses to the port infrequent. There are rarely taxis outside the main summer season, though plenty of dodgy guys in beat-up cars offer an unofficial taxi service. If you need to book an official taxi call Francesco (☎347 189 3440).

Ferry destinations (June–Sept) Alicudi (7 weekly; 6hr); Filicudi (7 weekly; 5hr); Ginostra (4 weekly; 5hr 20min); Lipari (5–8 daily; 2hr–2hr 30min); Naples (2 weekly; 17hr); Panarea (4 weekly; 4hr 20min); Rinella (8 weekly; 3hr 30min); Santa Marina (4–5 daily; 3hr–3hr 30min); Stromboli (6 weekly; 5hr 50min–6hr 40min); Vulcano (5–8 daily; 1hr 30min–2hr).

Ferry destinations (Oct–May) Alicudi (6 weekly; 6hr–6hr 30min); Filicudi (6 weekly; 5hr 10min); Ginostra (3 weekly; 5hr 45min); Lipari (3–5 daily; 2hr–2hr 30min); Naples (2 weekly; 17hr 30min); Panarea (4 weekly; 4hr 10min–5hr); Rinella (6 weekly; 3hr 45min); Santa Marina (2–4 daily; 3hr–3hr 30min); Stromboli (5 weekly; 5hr 45min–7hr); Vulcano (3–5 daily; 1hr 30min–2hr).

Hydrofoil destinations (June to mid-Sept) Alicudi (2 daily; 2hr 35min–3hr 15min); Filicudi (2 daily; 2hr 20min–2hr 35min); Ginostra (4 daily; 1hr 20min–2hr 30min); Lipari (16 daily; 1hr); Palermo (1 daily; 5hr 15min–6hr); Panarea (8 daily; 1hr 15min–2hr); Rinella (7 daily; 1hr 35min–1hr 40min); Santa Marina (13 daily; 1hr 25min); Stromboli (8 daily; 1hr 5min–2hr 50min); Vulcano (15 daily; 40min).

Hydrofoil destinations (mid-Sept to May) Alicudi (1 daily; 2hr 35min); Filicudi (1 daily; 2hr); Ginostra (2 daily; 1hr 20min–2hr 30min); Lipari (12 daily; 1hr); Panarea (4 daily; 1hr 40min–2hr 5min); Rinella (8 daily; 1hr 40min–2hr 20min); Santa Marina (12 daily; 1hr 20min–2hr); Stromboli (4 daily; 1hr 5min–2hr 45min); Vulcano (12 daily; 45min).

DEPARTURES FROM MESSINA

Getting to Messina Departures from Messina (see p.160) are more convenient if you're coming directly from Catania airport out of season. The port is a 7min walk from the train station, where buses also stop. Ferry departures are frequent, and Ustica Lines runs hydrofoils out to the islands all year (at least once daily even in winter), and also operates summer connections from Reggio di Calabria on the other side of the straits of Messina. Some hydrofoils call at Stromboli and Panarea before heading on to Santa Marina Salina, Lipari and Vulcano – excellent if you are heading to Stromboli or Panarea, but less fun if you are going elsewhere. Other routes call first at either Lipari or Santa Marina Salina.

Ferry destinations (Oct–May) Lipari (5 daily 2hr 35min); Panarea (3 daily; 2hr–2hr 50min); Rinella, Salina (2 daily 2hr 20min–3hr); Santa Maria Salina (4 daily 2hr 10in–2hr 45min); Stromboli (3 daily 1hr 25min–3hr 30min); Vulcano (5 daily 2hr 30min–3hr 20min).

Ferry destinations (June to mid-Sept) Vulcano (1 daily; 1hr 30min); Lipari (1 daily; 1hr 50min), Santa Marina Salina (1 daily; 1hr 25min); Rinella (1 daily; 1hr 45min).

DEPARTURES FROM PALERMO

Getting to Palermo Coming from the west of Sicily (or arriving at Palermo airport), it makes far more sense to use the Ustica Lines hydrofoil services from Palermo (see p.68), which run daily in summer. However, note that these services are routed first via Alicudi and Filicudi, which makes for a long and expensive trip (with a change at Lipari) if you're heading directly for Panarea or Stromboli, for example. Note also that this route – much of it out in the unprotected open sea – is particularly subject to delays, so don't cut things too close if returning from the Aeolians to take a flight from Palermo.

Hydrofoil destinations Alicudi (1 daily; 2hr); Filicudi (1 daily; 2hr 30min); Lipari (1 daily; 4hr); Milazzo (1 daily; 5hr 30min); Panarea (1 daily; 4hr 40min); Rinella (1 daily; 3hr 15min); Santa Marina Salina (1 daily; 3hr 30min), Stromboli (1 Daily; 5hr 20min).

DEPARTURES FROM NAPLES

By ferry The most direct way to get to the islands from central Italy is by ferry from Naples, with departures twice weekly (Tues & Fri) throughout the year at 8pm (weather permitting); ferries return to Naples on Mon and Thurs. If you're heading to or departing from Salina, note that ferries alternate between using the ports of Rinella and Santa Marina, though in winter the choice of port will depend on weather conditions. The Friday service from Naples is the only one that calls at Filicudi – on all other services you will need to change at Rinella or Santa Marina Salina. Note that delays of a couple of hours or so are not unusual.

Ferry destinations Filicudi (1 weekly; 13hr, 15min); Ginostra (2 weekly; 10hr 20min); Lipari (2 weekly; 13hr 30min–15hr 30min); Milazzo (2 weekly; 16hr–18hr); Panarea (2 weekly; 11hr 15min); Rinella (1 weekly; 14hr 20min); Santa Marina Salina (1 weekly; 12hr 30min); Stromboli (2 weekly; 9hr 40min); Vulcano (2 weekly; 14hr 15min–16hr 10min).

GETTING AROUND

Inter-island ferries and hydrofoils Travelling between the Aeolians is easy, as ferries and hydrofoils link all the islands. The schedules detailed in this chapter are for year-round services; visit the company websites to get details of the increased summer sailings, which vary from year to year. In winter, services are reduced, and in rough weather may be cancelled altogether, particularly on the routes out to Stromboli, Alicudi and Filicudi.

Ferries can sail in stormier conditions than hydrofoils, but even these are cancelled on occasion. However, as long as your schedule is not too tight, travelling around the islands out of season is perfectly feasible – especially if you base yourself on Vulcano, Lipari and Salina, taking side trips to remoter islands when conditions permit. Reliable sources for weather forecasts include Ⓦ windfinder.com.

DRIVING IN THE AEOLIANS

In a measure designed to cut down on the density of tourist traffic on the islands, **cars** are banned from Stromboli, Panarea and Alicudi. In July and August, cars belonging to non-residents can disembark from ferries to Lipari, Vulcano and Filicudi only if drivers can prove they are staying on the island for at least a week, whether in a hotel or in private accommodation. Ferry companies will ask for proof of a hotel booking before issuing tickets to those wanting to take their own car.

However, it's easy enough to manage without your own transport. Lipari and Salina have a good **bus** network, while you can **rent bicycles**, **mopeds** and **scooters** on all the main islands, or simply walk around the smaller ones.

If you need to leave a car in Milazzo, you can do so at one of several **garages**, the most convenient of which are also listed below; expect to pay around €15 per day (worth negotiating for longer periods). Some offer a shuttle service to the port.

GARAGES

Central Garage Via Cumbo Borgia 60 ☎ 090 928 2472. By the Duomo Nuovo, 5min from the port.
Mil Nautica Via Acquaviole 49 ☎ 090 928 1912.

South of the port, on the road to the train station.
Ullo Via Nino 40 ☎ 090 928 3309. Signposted up Via Minniti from the port.

Lipari

LIPARI is the busiest, biggest and most diverse island in the Aeolian archipelago, with a long history of settlement and trade. The main town – also called Lipari – is a thriving little port, dominated by impressive castle walls that surround an upper citadel housing the bulk of the archeological remains and a terrific museum. The road that circles the island from town takes in several much smaller villages, some good beaches and excellent views out to the neighbouring islands, though development has not been carefully controlled. While parts of the island are beautiful and unspoilt, getting there inevitably means passing through villages cluttered with brassy holiday houses, or with rusting machinery and ghostly abandoned factories – relics of the island's now defunct pumice mining industry.

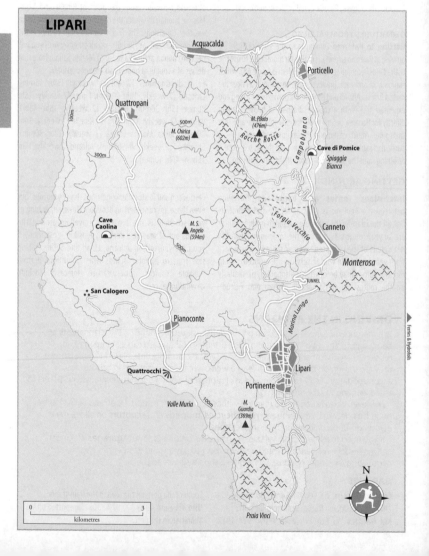

LIPARI

Acquacalda

Porticello

Quattropani

M. Pilato
(476m)

500m
M. Chirica
(602m)

Rocche Rosse

Campobianco

Cave di Pomice

Spiaggia
Bianca

100m

300m

Cave
Caolina

M. S.
Angelo
(594m)

Forgia Vecchia

Canneto

500m

Monterosa

San Calogero

TUNNEL

Marina Lunga

Ferries & Hydrofoils

Pianoconte

Lipari

Quattrocchi

Portinente

Valle Muria

100m

M.
Guardia
(369m)

N

0   3
kilometres

Praia Vinci

Historically, it has always been Lipari that has guided the development of the Aeolians. In classical times, after obsidian had been superseded by metals, the island's prosperity was based on its sulphur baths and thermal waters, while its alum, too, was much prized, and was found more abundantly here than anywhere else in Italy. More recently, its main industry was mining pumice – the reason why huge chunks of the mountains on the east coast are missing – but under the auspices of UNESCO this has now been banned, and today the economy is firmly based on tourism.

Lipari Town

LIPARI TOWN is split into upper and lower sections. Virtually everything of historic interest lies in the upper town, or **citadel**, protected by the sturdy walls of the castle, while all the shops and services are in the lower town, mostly along and off the attractive, colourful main **Corso Vittorio Emanuele**, with the town's two **harbours** at either end. The most impressive approach from lower to upper town is from Via Garibaldi, from which long steps cut straight up through the thick defensive walls, emerging right outside the Duomo.

Most of what remains of Lipari's formidable **citadel** is sixteenth-century Spanish in style, though it incorporates fragments of earlier medieval and even Greek buildings. Until the eighteenth century, this upper zone was the site of Lipari town itself, which explains the presence of the island's most important church, the **Duomo**, along with the dilapidated ruins of several other Baroque churches. Scattered in between are the excavations of superimposed layers of occupation, from the Neolithic to the Roman age, a continuous record covering almost two thousand years and a unique sequence that has allowed archeologists to date other Mediterranean cultures.

Parco Archeologico
Via Castello • Mon–Sat 9am–dusk • Free

At the southern end of the citadel walls, the **Parco Archeologico** has some Greek and Roman tombs on display, as well as a modern amphitheatre. It also makes a good place to lay out a picnic and enjoy the views over the rooftops and Marina Corta.

Museo Eoliano
Via Castello 2 • Daily 9am–1.30pm & 3–7pm • €6 • ☎ 090 988 0174, ⓦ www.regione.sicilia.it/beniculturali/museoeolipari/pagina.asp

All the finds from the Parco Archeologico are displayed in Lipari's superb **Museo Eoliano**, which is housed in various buildings on either side of the Duomo. Despite the official opening hours, most of the sections are usually only accessible in the mornings – only the **Sezione Classica** tends to keep the full opening times.

BOAT EXCURSIONS FROM LIPARI

Tour operators all over town offer year-round **boat excursions**, both around Lipari and to all the other islands, which offer an easy way to do some sightseeing without bothering about bus timetables and hydrofoil schedules. The boats mostly run from Marina Corta, but agencies are prominent at the main port too. Universally recommended is Da Massimo, Via Maurolico 2 (☎ 090 981 3086, ⓦ damassimo.it), where there will be someone who can speak English, and where boats are clean, well maintained, and have freshwater showers and canopies. Prices are pitched roughly the same everywhere, from €15 for a Lipari and Vulcano tour, €25 for Lipari and Salina, and from €30 from Lipari to Panarea and Stromboli. Da Massimo also work with the excellent Magmatrek (see p.146) for boat trips to Stromboli, including a night ascent of the volcano (from €70). If you want to rent a **gommone** (rubber boat) and putter around yourself, expect to pay around €100 per day for a 5m-long boat with shower and canopy and space for six people. Most operators also run **beach shuttles** in summer to good beaches on Lipari that are otherwise tricky to reach, like Praia Vinci.

Sezione Classica

The **Sezione Classica** holds classical and Hellenic material retrieved from various necropoli, and includes re-creations of both a **Bronze Age burial ground** and of the **Lipari necropolis** (eleventh century BC), where bodies were either buried in a crouching position in large, plump jars or cremated and placed in bucket-shaped jars (situlae). Most eye-catching of all are the towering banks of **amphorae**, each 1m or so high, dredged from shipwrecks under Capo Graziano (Filicudi), many still encrusted with

3

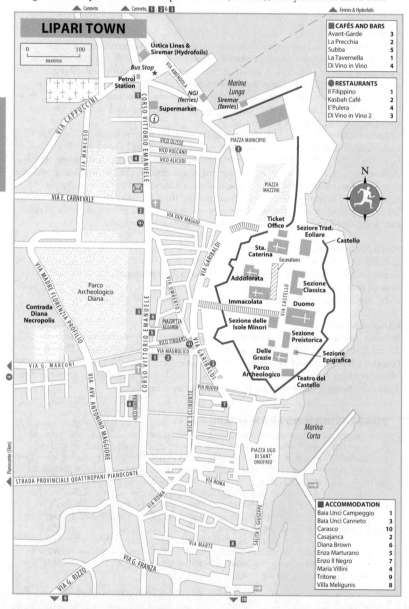

LIPARI TOWN

Canneto ▲   Canneto, **1**, **2** & **3** ▲   Ferries & Hydrofoils ▲

0 ──── 100
metres

Petrol Station

Bus Stop

Ústica Lines & Siremar (Hydrofoils)

VIA AMENDOLA

VIA CAPPUCCINI

CORSO VITTORIO EMANUELE

NGI *(ferries)*
Siremar *(ferries)*

Supermarket

Marina Lunga
Siremar *(ferries)*

VIA MANCUSO

VICO ULISSE
VICO VULCANO
VICO ALICUDI

PIAZZA MUNICIPIO

PIAZZA MAZZINI

VIA E. CARNEVALE

VIA XXIV MAGGIO

N

Ticket Office

Seziore Trad. Eoliare
Castello

Sta. Caterina
Excavations

VIA MADRE FLORENZIA PROFILO

Parco Archeologico Diana

Contrada Diana Necropolis

CORSO VITTORIO EMANUELE

VIA UMBERTO

VIA GARIBALDI

Addolorata

Immacolata

Sezione delle Isole Minori

VIA CASTELLO

Sezione Classica

Duomo

Sezione Preistorica

Sezione Epigrafica

PIAZZETTA AUSTRIA

VICO TINDARIS

VIA MAUROLICO

VIA G. MARCONI

VIA GARIBALDI

Delle Grazie

Parco Archeologico

Teatro del Castello

VIA NUOVA

VICO HIMERA

VIA TITO OTTO

VIA AVV. ANTONINO MAGGIORE

Marina Corta

STRADA PROVINCIALE QUATTROPANI PIANOCONTE

Pianoconte (5km)

PIAZZA UGO DI SANT' ONOFRIO

VIA ROMA

VIA ROMA

SALITA S. GIUSEPPE

VIA MARTE

VIA G. FRANZA

VIA G. RIZZO

┃ **CAFÉS AND BARS**

Avant-Garde	3
La Precchia	2
Subba	5
La Tavernella	1
Di Vino in Vino	4

● **RESTAURANTS**

Il Filippino	1
Kasbah Café	2
E'Pulera	4
Di Vino in Vino 2	3

┃ **ACCOMMODATION**

Baia Unci Campeggio	1
Baia Unci Canneto	3
Carasco	10
Casajanca	2
Diana Brown	6
Enza Marturano	5
Enzo Il Negro	7
Maria Villini	4
Tritone	9
Villa Meligunis	8

barnacles. There are also shelves of **vases** decorated in polychrome pastel hues – showing sacrifices, bathing scenes, mythical encounters and ceremonies – with many identified as those of an individual known as the Lipari Painter (300–270 BC) and his pupils and rough contemporaries. Other poignant **funerary goods** include toy vases and statuettes from the grave of a young girl, and delicate clay figurines of working women using mortar and pestle or washing children in a little bath.

The Sezione Classica, however, is best known for the oldest and most complete range of Greek **theatrical masks** in existence. Many are models, found in fourth-century BC graves, and covering the gamut of Greek theatrical life from the tragedies of Sophocles and Euripides to satyr plays and comedies. One room has a collection of small terracottas grouped in theatrical scenes, while there are also statuettes representing actual dancers and actors – nothing less than early Greek pin-ups of the period's top stars.

Sezione Preistorica

Set in the seventeenth-century bishop's palace, the **Sezione Preistorica** traces the early exploitation of **obsidian**, made into blades and exported all over the western Mediterranean – glass cases contain mounds of shards, worked flints, adzes and knives. Meanwhile, the **pottery** finds from ancient burial sites allowed archeologists to follow the development of the various Aeolian cultures, as burial techniques became gradually more sophisticated and grave goods more elaborate – as in the lid of a mid-sixth-century BC bothros, or sacred repository of votive articles, embellished with a reclining lion.

The rest of the museum

Other museum sections cover subjects as diverse as vulcanology and Aeolian traditions and customs, while the **Sezione Epigrafica** contains a little garden of tombs and engraved stones, and a room packed with more inscribed Greek and Roman tombstones and stelae. Unless you're really keen, though, there are diminishing returns to be had from soldiering on to the bitter end.

Corso Vittorio Emanuele

The **Corso Vittorio Emanuele** runs the length of the lower town – it is closed to traffic in summer during the evening passeggiata, when its cafés come into their own. Most of the gift shops are found along here, but tourism has never completely dominated life in Lipari, so among the carved obsidian trinkets, coral jewellery and Etna postcards there are still shops selling screwdrivers, fishing tackle and goldfish, along with a very useful supermarket and some great bakeries.

Marina Corta

Overlooked by parasol-shaded cafés and pastel-facaded *palazzi*, the little harbour of **Marina Corta** is the departure point for most boat excursions. There's a beguiling and very photogenic little **chapel** right on the water (which is sometimes open for art exhibitions), while beyond the pavement cafés, steps climb up from the south side of the port into the narrow alleys and courtyards of the old **fishing quarter**.

ARRIVAL AND DEPARTURE	LIPARI TOWN

By ferry and hydrofoil Hydrofoils and ferries dock to either side of Marina Lunga (sometimes called Porto Sottomonastero), at the north end of town. The services detailed below are year-round; schedules increase during the summer months.

Ferry and hydrofoil companies Dockside offices sell tickets and post timetables; for hydrofoils, Siremar (☎090 981 2200) and Ustica Lines (☎090 981 2448) have ticket offices in the same building, just up from the gangways leading from the hydrofoils. For ferry tickets, Siremar (☎090 981 1312) have an office on the other side of the port, while NGI (☎090 981 1955) sell tickets from a kiosk in the port car park.

Ferry destinations Alicudi (2–3 weekly; 4hr); Filicudi (2–3 weekly; 3hr); Ginostra (2–3 weekly; 3hr); Milazzo (5 daily; 2hr); Naples (2 weekly; 15hr); Panarea (2–3 weekly; 2hr); Santa Marina Salina (5 daily; 1hr); Stromboli (2–3 weekly; 3hr 40min); Vulcano (5 daily; 30min).

3

3

Hydrofoil destinations Alicudi (1 daily; 1hr 45min); Filicudi (2 daily; 1hr); Ginostra (1 daily; 1hr 30min); Messina (1 daily; 1hr 25min); Milazzo (14 daily; 1hr); Panarea (2 daily; 1hr); Rinella (9 daily; 30min–1hr); Santa Marina Salina (13 daily; 20–40min); Stromboli (2 daily; 1hr 45min); Vulcano (15 daily; 10min).

INFORMATION

Tourist information The tourist office, Corso Vittorio Emanuele 202 (Mon–Fri 8.30am–1.30pm, plus Mon, Wed & Fri 4–7.30pm; ☎090 988 0095), is the most reliable place for information on all the islands, and can advise on accommodation, boat excursions and current events; there's also lots of material in English on the website.

GETTING AROUND

By bus From Lipari Town, buses operated by Urso Guglielmo (☎090 981 1262) run in two directions around the island: clockwise to Quattropani, and anticlockwise to Canneto, Porticello and Acquacalda. Services depart approximately every hour (every 15–30min in summer for Canneto, less often on all routes on Sun and outside July and Aug); nowhere is more than a 30min ride away. The bus stop is at Marina Lunga, opposite the petrol station and close to the quayside ticket agency. Current timetables are posted at the kiosk window; you can buy tickets on board, and tickets and information are also available from a booth at the port, directly across from the hydrofoil ticket office.

By bike, scooter and car Rental agencies line the dockside at Marina Lunga (the ferry and hydrofoil port); you'll have to leave your passport, credit card or a hefty deposit as security. Bikes cost from €10/day, scooters €15–20, and small cars from €40 for most of the year, with prices skyrocketing in August.

ACCOMMODATION

HOTELS AND B&BS

Carasco Porto delle Genti ☎090 981 1605, ⓦcarasco .org. Superbly located three-star hotel, with its own terraces, rocky cove, good pool and sparkling views. There's a wide range of rooms, though not all standard rooms have sea views. It's out of the centre, but not too far from Portinente beach and the Marina Corta. Closed Nov–March. €220

Casajanca Marina Garibaldi 109, Canneto ☎090 988 0222, ⓦcasajanca.it. If you don't mind being out at Canneto, you might prefer this boutique-style place to the resort hotels in town. It's a charming townhouse hotel, three-star standard, 20m back from the beachfront promenade, with ten stylish rooms and personal service. You can also ask about their simpler B&B in Canneto. €200

★ **Diana Brown** Vico Himera 3 ☎090 981 2584 or ☎338 640 7572, ⓦdianabrown.it. Run by a jovial South African and her Sicilian husband, this is a really friendly and well-organized B&B, located in a tiny lane parallel to Corso Vittorio Emanuele. Seven smart rooms have a/c, heating, fridges and kettles, while another five also have small kitchenettes, and there's a great roof terrace where you eat breakfast. There's wi-fi, a book exchange and laundry service available, while Diana and her family know lots about the island, and can advise about walks and boat tours. Breakfast is €5, though is not available in Aug. €100

Enza Marturano Via Maurolico 35 ☎368 322 4997, ⓦenzamarturano.it. Four bright, modern rooms with a/c, cooking facilities and views, ranged around a communal lounge, with a terrace overlooking the Corso. No credit cards. €120

Enzo Il Negro Via Garibaldi 29 ☎090 981 3163, ⓦenzoilnegro.com. "Enzo the black" takes its name from the bronzed owner's local nickname. Just up from Marina Corta, its eight rooms, all with a/c and fridge, share one of the best private roof terraces in town. €100

Maria Villini Via Salina 27 ☎090 981 2784. Nice little B&B with a shady roof terrace on a plant-filled, pedestrian-only alleyway off the main Corso Vittorio Emanuele. There are five rooms, two of which have cooking facilities, one with a private terrace. All guests have the use of a fridge, either in their room or in the corridor outside. €80

Tritone Via Mendolita ☎090 981 1595, ⓦeolie experience.it. This superior five-star on the southern edge of the town centre is the best of the resort-style hotels, set away from the town bustle amid quiet gardens, and extremely competitively priced. There's a good pool, a

---

DIVING OFF LIPARI

The most spectacular dives in the Aeolians are off Panarea, Stromboli and Filicudi, all accessible on day-trips from Lipari. Closer at hand, there's always plenty to see in the straits between Lipari and Vulcano. Many of the larger hotels can put you in touch with a **diving school**, or contact Diving Centre La Gorgonia, Salita S. Giuseppe, Marina Corta ☎090 981 2616 or ☎335 571 7567, ⓦlagorgoniadiving.it). Single dives start at €30 (€50 including equipment); three dives from €85 (€125 including equipment), PADI courses from €350.

lovely spa, a superb restaurant, and rooms all have a balcony or terrace. **€280**

★ **Villa Meligunis** Via Marte 7 ☏090 981 2426, �ⓦvillameligunis.it. A converted *palazzo*, this elegant central four-star has excellent views of the citadel and sea from its rooftop restaurant, which sports a pool alongside. Rooms are tastefully turned out, many with sea views and balconies; there is also a beautifully restored eighteenth-century annexe with apartments. Apartments **€130**; rooms **€168**

HOSTEL AND CAMPSITE
Baia Unci Campeggio Via Marina Garibaldi s/n, Località Canneto ☏090 981 1909, ⓦcampingbaiaunci

.it. The island's only campsites is across from the long beach at Canneto, and has one-bedroom bungalows available, as well as tent pitches and its own bar and restaurant. Camping prices include water and parking space. No credit cards. Closed Oct–March. Camping **€15** per person; bungalows **€90**

Baia Unci Canneto Via Marina Garibaldi s/n, Località Canneto ☏090 981 1540, ⓦliparicasevacanze.it. A hostel next door to the island's campsite, occupying a townhouse above the beach at the southern end of the seafront, with two five-bed dorm rooms sharing a kitchen and terrace area. Advance reservations are essential; their bus picks up guests from Lipari harbour. Closed Nov–March. Dorm beds **€20**

EATING AND DRINKING

There's a fair choice of **restaurants** in Lipari town, though many close between October and March. Prices are on the high side, but a couple of the restaurants rank among the best in the archipelago. **Bars** along the Corso fill up from early evening onwards, as the *passeggiata* swings into action. Alternatively, for a drink with a sea view, head down to the Marina Corta where a line of tables belonging to late-opening bars spills out across the harbourfront.

RESTAURANTS
★ **Il Filippino** Piazza Municipio ☏090 981 1002, ⓦeolieexperience.it. This stupendous fish restaurant – Lipari's best, in business since 1910 – really knows its stuff. It's in the upper town and has a shaded outdoor terrace where you can eat classy Aeolian specialities like borlotti bean, sardine and fennel soup, *risotto nero* (coloured with squid ink), grouper-stuffed *ravioloni* and local fish in a *ghiotta* sauce (tomatoes, onions, celery, capers and olives). Choose carefully and you might get away with €40 a head, though you could easily spend €70 – and more if you give any serious thought to the massive wine list. Daily lunch & dinner; closed mid-Nov to Dec, and Mon Oct–Nov & Jan–March.

★ **Kasbah Café** Vico Selinunte 45 ☏090 981 1075, ⓦkasbahcafe.it. Chic but unpretentious restaurant with a beautiful garden; the Anglo-Aeolian owner will advise on the best ways to sample the fresh fish. *Antipasti* (€8–9) and *primi* (€10–12) make creative use of local ingredients – try *treccine* with local shrimps, aubergine and cherry tomatoes, or *tagliolini* with clams, zucchini flowers, basil and black pepper. They also make their own bread and the island's best pizza (€6–8.50), using stone-ground flour. Daily dinner only; Oct–March closed Wed.

E'Pulera Via Diana ☏ 090 981 1158, ⓦeolieexperience.it. A romantic courtyard-garden restaurant specializing in classic Aeolian food: swordfish *involtini*, caper salads, home-made pasta with wild fennel and prawns, almond biscuits and malvasia wine. The super cuisine is well worth the highish prices, and it stays open till late (kitchen closes at midnight). Expect to pay €40 plus per head excluding wine. Daily dinner only; closed Oct–March.

Di Vino in Vino 2 Via Garibaldi 34 ☏090 988 0554. This

enoteca serves full meals as well as snacks – ingredients are rigorously sourced and cooked by the owner's wife. There's pizza *bianca*, a wide range of inventive sandwiches and bruschetta, plates of salami, hams and cheeses served with home-made bread, figs, nuts, honey and jams (€14), and dishes such as *paccheri* with swordfish, mint and pistachio (€15), pasta with fresh Vulcano ricotta (€8), and spaghetti with mussels and prawns (€12). Fish of the day is €18, and desserts include a delectable strawberry or banana and rum tiramisu (€5). Conclude in style with cigars, fine rums and grappas. Daily 8am–3am; closed Dec–Feb.

CAFÉS AND BARS
Avant-Garde Corso Vittorio Emanuele 135 ☏090 988 0505. You get a huge plate of nibbles here at evening aperitivo time, where there are tables outside (along with a rowdy TV), plus DJs and live jazz on most summer evenings. Daily 7am–late; closed mid-Jan to mid-Feb.

La Precchia Corso Vittorio Emanuele 191 ☏090 981 1303. A cosy spot in winter for a glass of wine or any of a vast range of hot chocolates, from white chocolate to dark chocolate with chilli, chocolate and hazelnut or chocolate and orange – a treat if you've done the night trip to Stromboli. Not a bad place for breakfast, too. Daily 7am–late.

★ **Subba** Corso Vittorio Emanuele 92 ☏090 981 1352. Open since 1930, this is the island's best and most traditional café, with a nice shaded terrace at the rear in the square. Try *Lulus*, clouds of *crema*-filled choux pastry, or the pistachio- and almond-studded *eoliana* ice cream. Mon & Wed–Sun 7.30am–8.30pm, closes later in summer.

La Tavernella Corso Vittorio Emanuele 271 ☏360 268 512. On the main Corso just round the corner from the port,

3

this little *tavola calda* is perfectly located for a snack while you wait for a ferry or hydrofoil. Great spinach frittata, and a daily choice of *pasta al forno* and other hot dishes. Daily 8am–10pm.

Di Vino in Vino Corso Vittorio Emanuele 102 ☎ 334 110 8455. This classy enoteca has a well-researched range of wines, along with hams and cheeses from the Nébrodi mountains (tasters of which appear with your glass of wine at aperitivo time). They also serve a choice of salads, bruschetta and toasted sandwiches. Daily 9am–late; closes early in winter, and for most of Feb.

ENTERTAINMENT

Theatre and live music Every summer (June–Sept), Lipari's council sponsors several theatre performances and concerts, including some spectacularly sited events at the Teatro del Castello, the modern Greek-style theatre up at the citadel's Parco Archeologico. Ask at the tourist office for details.

Festivals There are annual processions in town at Carnevale (Feb/March) and at Easter, but Lipari's main festival, dedicated to the island's patron, St Bartholomew, takes place over three days around August 24.

DIRECTORY

Banks and exchange There are plenty of ATMs down the main Corso, and you can exchange cash at the post office and some travel agencies. It's best to make sure you have enough cash before you set off island-hopping, as other island ATMs do occasionally run out of money.

Hospital Ospedale Civile, Via Sant'Anna ☎ 090 98 851. The hospital also has a walk-in 24hr first aid service on ☎ 090 988 5267. Or for emergencies or an ambulance, call ☎ 118.

Left luggage The Siremar/Ustica Lines office at Marina Lunga has a small left-luggage facility (daily from 8.30am until the last hydrofoil departs; €4 for 12hr).

Pharmacies Cincotta, Via Garibaldi 60 (☎ 090 981 1472); Internazionale, Corso Vittorio Emanuele 28 (☎ 090 981 1583); Sparacino, Corso Vittorio Emanuele 95 (☎ 090 981 1392). Pharmacies open late according to a rota system, detailed on the doors of the shops.

Police Carabinieri, Via Madre Florenzia Profilio, near Via G. Marconi ☎ 090 981 1333.

Post office Corso Vittorio Emanuele 207 (Mon–Fri 8.30am–6.30pm, Sat 8.30am–1pm).

Around the island

It's well worth taking time to explore the rest of Lipari. Buses (see p.126) from town are frequent enough to enable getting around the whole island in a single day; and it's also possible to scoot or drive around Lipari's winding roads in a couple of hours flat, stopping at places like Monte Guardia, Quattrocchi, Quattropani and Monterosa for some amazing views out across the archipelago. With its mountains tumbling straight into the sea, the island's **west coast** is perhaps the more alluring, largely undeveloped and with some lovely **walks**, especially between the **Terme di San Calogero** and the **Caolina quarries**. Exploring the **east coast** offers a chance to see the relics of Lipari's pumice and obsidian mining industries. It may not be the idyllic Aeolian island scenery of your dreams, but if industrial archeology holds any appeal, a few hours here – with a camera at the ready – is a must. Bring mask and snorkel to explore the extraordinary deep blue waters of **Porticello**, with their bed of white-pumice sand.

Canneto

It's around 3km north from Lipari town to the nearest village, **Canneto**, a shabby resort set on a wide bay on the other side of the headland. A long stony beach fronts the village, which has a rather abandoned feel outside summer when most businesses are closed, which may however be preferable to the gaudiness and noise when they are open. For more secluded swimming, head to the Spiaggia Bianca, signposted from the northern end of town, along a stepped path that runs up, around and down to the **Spiaggia Bianca**, an expansive sand-and-pebble beach that is worth the effort to reach. Refreshments and parasols are available here in summer.

Campobianco and Monte Pilato

North of Canneto at **Campobianco**, pumice workings have left huge white scars on the hillside. For 2–3km all around, the ground looks as if it's had a dusting of talcum powder, while years of accumulation of pumice sediment on the sea bed have turned the water a piercing aquamarine colour. Above Campobianco, a path leads up the slopes of **Monte Pilato** (476m), thrown up in the eruption from which all the pumice originally came. The last explosion occurred in around 700 AD, leading to the virtual abandonment of Lipari town and creating the obsidian flows of Rocche Rosse and Forgia Vecchia, both of which can be climbed. Although it's overgrown with vegetation, you can still make out the outline of the crater at the top, and you may come across the blue-black veins of obsidian.

Porticello

From the bus stop above the stony beach at **Porticello**, a road (and a quicker, more direct path) winds down to a small bay, which sunbathers share with the forlorn Heath Robinson-style pumice-work machinery that connects the white hillside with the pier. After storms, this is ripe hunting ground for hunks of obsidian, washed up on the strand. There's no shade here, and the pebble beach soon reaches scalding temperatures. A couple of vans sell cool drinks and snacks in the summer.

Quattrocchi

Three kilometres west of Lipari town is **Quattrocchi**, a noted viewpoint over Vulcano and the spiky faraglioni rocks, which puncture the sea between the two islands. The curious name (meaning "Four Eyes") is said to derive from the fact that newly wedded couples traditionally come here to be photographed, so gracing every shot with two pairs of eyes.

San Calogero

Just before the fragmented village of Pianoconte, a side road slinks off down to the old Roman thermal baths at **San Calogero**. It's a particularly pleasant route to follow on foot, across a valley and skirting some impressive cliffs, with the baths hidden behind a long-disused spa hotel: there's usually an unofficial guide to show you around and allow you a dip, if you dare, in the scummy 57°C Roman pool.

Cave Caolina

For a really great coastal hike, head to the **Cave Caolina**, a quarry of multicoloured clays used as pigments by the ancient Greek artist responsible for the polychrome painted vases in Lipari's museum, known simply as "the Lipari painter". From here an easy-to-follow path leads down through the quarry, and back to San Calogero, passing sulphurous fumaroles, a hot spring, and a couple of places where you can scramble down the cliffs for a swim.

Vulcano

Closest of the Aeolians to the Sicilian mainland, and just across the narrow channel from Lipari, **VULCANO** is the usual first port of call for ferry and hydrofoil services from Milazzo, and as such suffers the bulk of the archipelago's day-trippers. As on more distant Stromboli, volcanic action defines the island, with the main crater hanging menacingly over its northern tip and constant vapour trails issuing from its flanks. It's a very old volcano, in the last, smoking, phase of its life, and you often don't even have to disembark to experience its other apparent trait – the disconcerting sulphurous, rotten-egg smell that pervades the island's entire inhabited area when the wind is in the right direction.

The **volcano** was threatening enough to dissuade anyone from living here before the eighteenth century, since when there have been some hasty evacuations – subterranean activity is still monitored round the clock, as Vulcano is felt to be more potentially dangerous than the constantly active Stromboli. In the nineteenth century a Scot called Stevenson bought the island to exploit the sulphur and alum reserves, but all his work was engulfed by the next major **eruption**. Although the volcano's last gasp of activity occurred between 1886 and 1890, its presence gives Vulcano an almost primeval essence. Everything here is an assault on the senses, the outlandish saffron of the earth searing the eyes, as violent as the intense red and orange of the iron and aluminium sulphates that leak out of the ground in the summer, to be washed away with the first autumn rains.

However, none of the summer trippers and B-list celebs bronzing themselves on Vulcano's **black-sand beaches** are discouraged, while many others come to dip themselves in the sulphurous **mud baths**. That said, it's difficult to recommend a night's stay, even if the lingering smell doesn't put you off. Accommodation is overpriced, while restaurants tend to command exorbitant prices for barely edible food. In fact, you can climb the crater, and cycle or bus across the island and back, all on a day-trip from the far pleasanter Lipari, just a ten-minute hydrofoil ride away.

3

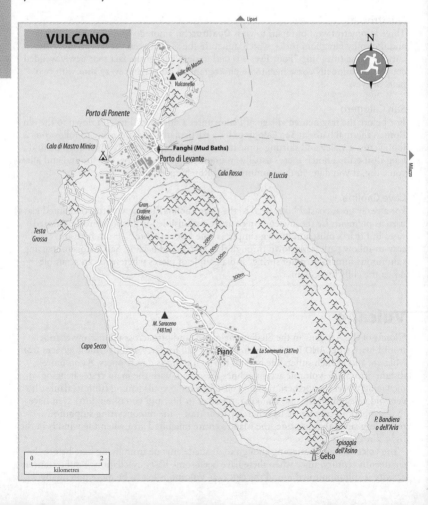

Porto di Levante

Porto di Levante has the flimsy feel of a hastily erected film set, consisting of a couple of ramshackle streets lined with whitewashed cubes that house restaurants, bars and lots of tacky souvenir shops. If you need provisions, there's a small supermarket tucked into an alley at the end of the main street.

ARRIVAL AND DEPARTURE PORTO DI LEVANTE

By ferry and hydrofoil Ferries and hydrofoils dock at Porto di Levante, the main harbour; ticket offices are located near the dock. All ferries, and virtually all hydrofoils, stopping at Lipari also call at Vulcano. The services detailed below are year-round; schedules increase during the summer months.
Ferry departures Alicudi (2–3 weekly; 3hr 30min); Filicudi (2–3 weekly; 2hr 30min); Ginostra (2–3 weekly; 2hr 30min); Lipari (5 daily; 35min); Milazzo (5 daily; 1hr 30min); Naples 2 weekly (15hr 30min); Panarea (2–3 weekly; 1hr 30min); Santa Marina Salina (5 daily; 1hr 30min); Stromboli (2–3 weekly; 3hr).
Hydrofoil departures Alicudi (1 daily; 1hr 45min); Filicudi (1 daily; 1hr 15min); Ginostra (1 daily; 1hr 15min); Lipari (15 daily; 10min); Messina (1 daily; 1hr 45min); Milazzo (14 daily; 40min); Panarea (2 daily; 50min); Rinella (9 daily; 1hr); Santa Marina Salina (13 daily; 40min); Stromboli (2 daily; 1hr 30min).

GETTING AROUND

By bus From the Porto di Levante dockside, buses run year-round to Piano (Mon–Sat 7–8 daily; 10min), and in summer to Gelso (mid-June to mid-Sept Mon–Sat 3 daily; 20min).
Bike and scooter hire Da Paolo (☎090 985 2112) and Sprint (☎090 985 2208), in the centre of the village on the main Strada Comunale Porto Levante, rent out mountain bikes and scooters (€5/15 per day).
Boat tours The boat trips (around €15 per person) offered at the Porto di Levante in summer visit the caves and bays on the island's west side.

The fanghi

Via Porto Levante snc • Easter–Oct daily 7am–9pm • €3

Located directly to the north of Porto di Levante, a brief walk between the multicoloured rock pinnacles, are the famed **fanghi** or **mud baths**, more exactly one pool containing a thick yellow soup of foul-smelling sulphurous mud, in which people flop belly-up, caking every centimetre of their bodies with the stuff. The smell is indescribable, and the degree of radioactivity makes it inadvisable to immerse yourself for any length of time, and unsuitable for young children or pregnant women. Avoid contact with the eyes (it stings mightily) and remove contact lenses as well as any silver or leather jewellery, which will be ruined just by coming into contact with the sand hereabouts. When you've had enough, hobble over to rinse yourself off in the nearby sea, where natural hot water springs bubble up. Note that outside of the summer season, you can just walk in and wallow for free.

The Gran Cratere

Daily daylight hours • €3 in summer • Follow the road immediately to the left of Porto di Levante dock for 500m or so until you're directed off the road to the left and up the slope to the crater

Vulcano's main crater, the **Gran Cratere**, is just to the south of Porto di Levante. It takes an hour to walk up to the crater, and it's a toughish climb, on a slithery path that's totally exposed to the sun – do it early or late in the day in the summer months, and wear strong shoes. The only vegetation consists of a few hardy gorse bushes on the lower slopes, nibbled at by goats whose bells echo across the scree. The first part of the path ascends a virtually black-sand dune before reaching the harder volcanic crust, where it runs above the rivulets caused by previous eruptions. Reaching a ledge with views over all the other Aeolian islands, you look down into the vast **crater** itself, where vapour emissions – acrid and yellow – billow from the surrounding surfaces. Follow the crater in an anticlockwise direction, so you are going downhill rather than up through the clouds of sulphurous emissions on the northern rim, where nerves are not exactly steadied by the admonitory notices at the start of the climb reading "Do not sit down, do not lie down".

3

Porto di Ponente

A narrow neck of land separates Porto di Levante from **Porto di Ponente**, a fifteen-minute walk past the fanghi. Here, a perfect arc of fine black sand lines a bay looking onto the towering pillars of rock that rise out of the channel between Vulcano and Lipari. There are a couple of seafront cafés here, and some large hotels set back from the sands. From the beach, the only road heads north through the trees to **Vulcanello**, thrown up out of the sea in a famous eruption in 183 BC, and joined to the main island by another flurry of activity a few centuries later. The walk takes less than an hour.

ACCOMMODATION   **PORTO DI PONENTE**

★ **Eden Park** Via Porto Ponente 10 ☎ 090 985 2120, ⓦ isolavulcano.it. This agreeable holiday site, set in its own peaceful grounds on the south side of the bay and slightly inland, is by far the island's best budget option. Campers can pitch tents on real grass, or even bivouac on the lawn, while there are also single-room apartments with terrace, shower and kitchen; and "economic" double rooms with two bunk beds and a shared bathroom. Note that prices double for ten days on either side of the *ferragosto* (Aug 10–20). Breakfast is available, and campers

pay extra for showers. No credit cards. Closed Dec–Feb. Camping per person **€16**; double rooms **€40**; apartments **€120**

Orsa Maggiore Via Porto Ponente 4 ☎ 090 985 2018, ⓦ orsamaggiorehotel.com. It's a few hundred metres from the black-sand beach, but this small hotel does have a very nice pool, surrounded with chic decking, terrace and gardens. Prices are raised by €40 overnight for ten days on either side of the *ferragosto* (Aug 10–20). Closed Nov–March. **€140**

Gelso

At the far south of Vulcano, 15km from Porto di Levante, the coastal hamlet of **Gelso** is named for the mulberries that grow here, along with capers. There's a tiny patch of black sand (with a seasonal trattoria, *Da Pina*), and a better beach at **Spiaggia dell'Asino**, a larger cove accessible from a steep path which you'll have passed on your way into Gelso. This is a great spot for a swim, with a summer café, and umbrellas and deckchairs available.

Salina

The ancient name of **SALINA** was Didyme, or "twin", referring to the two volcanic cones that give the island its distinctive shape. Both volcanoes are long extinct, but their past eruptions, combined with plenty of ground water – unique in the Aeolians – have endowed Salina with the most **fertile** soil of all the islands. The slopes are verdant, the island's tree cover contrasts strongly with the denuded crags of its neighbours, and both capers and malvasia grapevines – classic Aeolian staples – are vigorously cultivated. The island's central position in the archipelago makes it a good alternative base to Lipari for exploring the others, while Salina itself holds a network of **hiking trails**, some good **beaches** and several distinct **villages**. Tourism here is fairly sophisticated, with some charming boutique-style accommodation and excellent restaurants, especially in the main port, **Santa Marina Salina**, and in the town of **Malfa**, but the island certainly isn't a summer fleshpot like Vulcano or Panarea. It's quieter, more relaxed and still very much part of the ebb and flow of traditional Aeolian life, which makes it many people's favourite island.

There are two **ports** on Salina: Santa Marina Salina in the east and smaller **Rinella** on the south coast. Not all ferry and hydrofoil services call at both ports, so it's essential to check timetables carefully if time is tight and connections crucial. There is, however, a regular bus service between both ports, vaguely timed to connect with arrivals, though if your boat is late, don't expect the bus to have waited.

Santa Marina Salina

On the east coast, **Santa Marina Salina** is Salina's main port and the location of most of the island's services. A village of whitewashed Aeolian houses and elegant townhouses built in the nineteenth century by those who made their fortunes with Malvasia wine, it's a relaxed place, with a couple of pebble beaches. A long lungomare reaches north from the harbour, running from the town **beach** to the more secluded **Punta Barone**, backed by the relics of an ancient Roman fish farm. Running parallel to the water but one block back, the narrow pedestrianized main street, **Via Risorgimento**, holds chic boutiques that mingle with grocery shops, fruit shops and butcher and baker. A couple of the gift shops sell a decent map of the islands.

ARRIVAL AND INFORMATION · SANTA MARINA SALINA

By ferry and hydrofoil The Siremar (☎090 984 3004) and Ustica Lines/NGI (☎090 984 3003) ticket offices stand close to the dock on the waterfront piazza, on either side of the church, and usually open 30min before sailings. The services detailed below are year-round; schedules increase during the summer months.

Hydrofoil destinations Alicudi (1 daily; 1hr 15min); Filicudi (1 daily; 40min); Ginostra (1 daily; 45min); Lipari (14 daily; 20min); Messina (1 daily; 2hr 35min); Milazzo (10 daily; 1hr 20min); Panarea (1 daily; 20min); Rinella (9 daily; 10min); Stromboli (1 daily; 1 hr); Vulcano (10 daily; 40min).

Ferry destinations Alicudi (2–3 weekly; 3hr 30min); Filicudi (2–3 weekly; 2hr 30min); Ginostra (2–3 weekly; 2hr 30min); Lipari (5 daily; 1hr); Milazzo (5 daily; 3–4hr); Naples (1 weekly; 13hr 30min); Panarea (2–3 weekly; 1hr 30min); Stromboli (2–3 weekly; 3hr); Vulcano (5 daily; 1 hr 30min).

Tourist information There is a seasonal tourist information point in Santa Marina (usually July & Aug daily 9am–1pm & 4–8pm), just up the hill from the piazza, on Via Cristofero Colombo, below *Bar La Vela*.

Services Santa Maria has a clinic with emergency doctors and ambulance, a pharmacy, the post office, an internet point and a bank with ATM (with another ATM on the seafront just beyond the Ustica Lines office).

GETTING AROUND

By bus The bus stop for Lingua is by the Siremar office; buses to Malfa, Rinella and Pollara stop on the other side of the piazza, right by the port, opposite the *La Cambusa* bar. Buses cover all points on the island; departures to all

3

destinations are roughly every 90min, hourly in summer, and you pay on board. In winter you may have a lengthy wait in Malfa, the island hub, for an onward connection to Pollara or to Leni and Rinella.

By bike, moped and car Nino Bongiorno, Via Risorgimento 222 (☎ 090 9843 409, ⓦ rentbongiorno.it), at the beginning

of the road to Lingua, rents bikes, mopeds and cars.

Boat tours Booths in the piazza by the port sell tickets for half-day cruises around the island (€25 per person), as well as day-trips further afield to Panarea and Stromboli, Filicudi and Alicudi, and Lipari and Vulcano (from €45 per person), all with plenty of chances for swimming and sightseeing stops.

ACCOMMODATION

I Cinque Balconi Via Risorgimento 38 ☎ 090 094 3508, ⓦ icinquebalconi.it. Simple rooms in a nineteenth-century townhouse on Santa Marina's pedestrianized shopping street, whose most striking feature is the subtle, carefully preserved original floor tiles. Behind the hotel, you can while away afternoons in an enchanting secluded garden, shaded by citrus and fig trees. There are eight rooms, several with sea views, and in the evenings aperitivo is served at tables on the street outside. **€150**

★ **Mamma Santina** Via Sanità ☎ 090 984 3054, ⓦ mammasantina.it. The affable Mario presides over a highly personal, boutique-style restaurant-with-rooms, set on wide terraces above the town. The sixteen rooms are in bright seaside colours, with gorgeous Mediterranean tile

floors and big bathrooms with walk-in showers, while guests can lounge in hammocks or around the pool. Call to be picked up from the port, or follow the signposts off Via Risorgimento (after no. 66). Closed mid-Dec to mid-March. **€250**

Mercanti di Mare Piazza Santa Marina 7 ☎ 090 984 3536, ⓦ hotelmercantidimare.it. Harbourfront three-star hotel with nine white, airy rooms and an attractive terrace overlooking the water. **€200**

Da Sabina Via Risorgimento 5c ☎ 090 984 3134 or ☎ 333 272 6025, ⓦ bbsalina.it. Classy B&B at the far end of the village from the port, a 10min walk from the centre. Three smart en-suite rooms open onto a big sea-view terrace, where breakfast is served. No credit cards. **€140**

EATING AND DRINKING

RESTAURANTS

Batana Via Rinascente 17 ☎ 090 984 3311. A peaceful location above the port, sweeping views from an airy roofed terrace and engaging owners make this Santa Marina's top choice for a relaxing meal or extended aperitivo. The food is excellent: the *fritto misto* (€10) of calamari, tiny *ciciarelli* and locally netted prawns is faultless, and the gently spiced and succulent swordfish kebab (€16) literally melts in the mouth. Desserts are all home-made, and include an apple crumble which may challenge your mum's. Pizza too, from €4.50. Daily dinner only.

★ **Mamma Santina** Via Sanità ☎ 090 984 3054. The restaurant at the lovely *Mamma Santina* hotel is a marvellous spot, with outdoor service for most of the year. The emphasis is on island specialities, like a grilled *antipasto* platter of vegetables and seafood, spaghetti with a pesto of fourteen herbs, or grilled sea bass (pasta from €10, fish from €14). Daily lunch & dinner; closed mid-Dec to mid-March.

Nni Lausta Via Risorgimento 188 ☎ 090 984 3486. Cool bar-restaurant whose New York-trained owner-chef gives an adventurous twist to local dishes – try raw tuna dressed

---

WALKING ON SALINA

There are well-maintained, waymarked **hiking trails** right across Salina, in particular to the heights of Monte Fossa delle Felci and the sanctuary of Madonna del Terzito. It's great walking country, since most of the island has been zealously protected: wild flowers are much in evidence, and hunting and shooting are banned, which helps keep the bird numbers high.

For a good day out on the tops, first take the bus to the sanctuary – all buses except those between Malfa and Pollara pass right by. **Madonna del Terzito** is set in the saddle between the two peaks of Salina, with fine views over the sea. A signposted track leads up to the summit of **Monte Fossa delle Felci** (962m), the archipelago's highest peak. It's a steady climb through forest and mountain parkland, which takes the best part of two hours – only in the latter stages does it become tougher, with a final 100m clamber over rocks to reach the stone cairn and simple wooden cross at the top, from where the views are magnificent.

You can come back the same way to the sanctuary and catch the return bus, but signposts point out alternative approaches and **descents** to Malfa, Lingua or Santa Marina. However, not all the tracks are clear, they can be very steep, and soil erosion and the crumbling volcanic underlay can make getting a grip a tricky business, so if you are not an experienced walker, it's best to stick to the main track. Count on another two hours back down, whichever descent you follow.

with wild fennel and capers, or crispy fish cakes made from the day's catch. A full meal will cost at least €45 without wine, though you can just have a drink at the bar (until 2am) – €5 will buy you a glass of decent Salina wine, with crostini and home-made dips, pestos and salsas. Daily lunch & dinner; closed Nov–March.

Porto Bello Via Lungomare 2 ☎ 090 984 3125. Set right above the harbour, and with a terrace looking out to the lights of Lipari, this reliable and longstanding restaurant serves excellent local *antipasti* and is a good choice if you want to splash out. It's worth trying the *pasta al fuoco*, with cherry tomatoes, chilli and grated oven-baked ricotta, or the raw prawns with a yogurt salsa (€16). Main courses include standards such as deep-fried squid (€16), but this is a place to go for the catch of the day (priced by weight at €75 per kilo). If they have *scorfano* (scorpion fish), ask to have it hard-fried, otherwise owner Teodoro or his son Dario will recommend a fish and cooking method that suits. A four-course meal will cost at least €50 without wine. Daily lunch & dinner; closed winter.

CAFÉS AND BARS

Papagayo Piazza Santa Marina ☎ 333 141 0974.

Minuscule bar owned by a local sculptor, with a terrace that spills out onto Santa Marina's seafront piazza. Good music, generous cocktails and a laidback vibe – this is the kind of place where spontaneous parties develop. Olives, crostini and local cheeses to accompany drinks at aperitivo time. Daily usually 6pm–late.

Portobello Sea Lounge Via Lungomare 2 ☎ 090 984 3125. With its whitewashed walls and white-resin floors, sea terrace, chilled soundtrack and driftwood decor, this is Santa Marina's most chic hangout, though service can be lackadaisical at times. Cocktails are served with an array of snacks of a quality you'd expect of one of the island's best restaurants. For once, they are served at your table, instead of the usual buffet. If you're lucky there will be tuna carpaccio, a delectable aubergine parmigiana, crostini with *caponata*, and courgette-flower fritters. Daily 6.30pm–late.

La Vela Via Risorgimento 135 ☎ 090 984 3541. Great hazelnut pastries, along with traditional biscuits featuring lots of almonds, pistachios and a sticky *cedro* (citrus) jam; *cannoli* are filled to order. There's also a decent range of savoury snacks such as *arancini* and pizza, all best enjoyed on the terrace overlooking the sea. Daily: summer 7.30am–late; winter 7.30am–1pm & 4–8pm.

Lingua

Three kilometres to the south of Santa Marina, **Lingua** is a prettier base, and its traffic-free waterfront makes it ideal if travelling with young children. It's connected to Santa Marina by bus, though the undulating road makes a fine forty-minute stroll, weaving around the coves in between the two settlements. Lingua itself is not much more than a seafront promenade and a narrow beach, backed by a tiny cluster of hotels and trattorias facing the shore of Lipari. At the end of the road is the **salt lagoon** from which Salina takes its name, and a car park where locals used to gather after bumper anchovy catches to salt fish en masse. Overlooking the lake, two typical Aeolian houses have been converted into museums: a small **ethnographic museum** (May–Oct Tues–Sun 9am–1pm & 3–6pm; free) holds examples of rustic art and island culture – mainly kitchen utensils and mill equipment, much of it fashioned from lava rock, while the **archeological museum** (May–Oct Tues–Sun 9am–6pm; free) has finds from Bronze Age and Roman Salina.

ACCOMMODATION   LINGUA

A Cannata Via Umberto I ☎ 090 984 3161 or ☎ 339 575 4240, ⓦ acannata.it. Set a few metres back from the sea near the church, there are simple rooms above a decent restaurant, and several apartments of various sizes and styles to rent around the village, starting from around €500 a week in mid-season (€350 in low). Rooms €120

Il Delfino Via Marina Garibaldi 5 ☎ 090 984 3024, ⓦ ildelfinosalina.it. Smart new rooms with marvellous terraces and views, set back from Lingua's lungomare; and older rooms opening directly onto it, which are a good bet if you have children. €160

Il Gambero Piazza Marina Garibaldi ☎ 090 984 3049, ⓦ gamberosalina.it. Above *Il Gambero* restaurant (see p.136), the three simple, sparkling rooms with bathrooms

here share a fabulous terrace with 360-degree views of Lipari, Panarea, Stromboli and Monte Fossa. The family live half the year in Australia, so speak perfect English. €100

La Salina Borgo di Mare Via Manzoni ☎ 090 984 3441, ⓦ lasalinahotel.com. This impressive four-star hotel is set in the restored buildings of the old salt-works, by Lingua's lagoon. The lovely rooms are individually furnished, and most have sea views and private terraces, while public areas are enhanced by traditional tiles and stonework. There's good swimming from below the hotel, with sunbeds set out on the rocks. No restaurant, but you can eat at nearby *Il Gambero* on a half-board basis (an extra €30 per person). €220

Villaggio Eoliano Via Umberto I 52 ☎ 335 666 0777 or

☎ 329 796 6120. A tiny complex of funky apartments on the main road through the village, overlooking the lagoon,

which offers some of the best-value accommodation on the island. Lovely owners, and lots of cats. Closed Oct–April. **€80**

EATING AND DRINKING

★ **Da Alfredo** Piazza Marina Garibaldi ☎ 090 984 3075. Right on the seafront piazza, this little café is famous throughout Italy for its fresh fruit *granitas* – the summer yachties and boat-trippers queue up for a taste. The other speciality is *pane cunzato*, a huge round of grilled bread piled with various combinations of home-cured tuna, capers, tomatoes, baked ricotta and olives (€8–11). Daily 8am till last customer leaves; closed Dec–Easter.

Il Delfino Via Marina Garibaldi 5 ☎ 090 9843 024, ⊛ ildelfinosalina.it. Lovely restaurant, with tables on the Lungomare, well known for its antipasto buffet (arrive

around 8pm to make the most of it). The signature dish is the stuffed calamari braised with onions and malvasia wine (€15), but check out daily specials as well. Daily lunch & dinner; closed Dec–Easter.

Il Gambero Piazza Marina Garibaldi ☎ 090 984 3049. This restaurant serves excellent fish – try the mixed fish *antipasto* (€15) and *involtini di pesce spada* (€15) – as well as pizza and *pane cunzato*, and all-day snacks and aperitivo in summer. There's also a fixed-price menu at €15 (€20 in Aug). Daily lunch & dinner; closed Dec–Easter.

Malfa

Six kilometres from Santa Marina, reached along Salina's sole, tortuous coast road, **Malfa** is the island's biggest village, spilling down from the gentle, neatly cultivated vineyards on the lower slopes of Monte Fossa. At the centre of the village is the main church and a large **piazza** with views out to sea, inlaid with a *rosa dei venti* or compass rose, which names the eight prevailing Mediterranean winds.

A devilishly twisting road runs down from here to the **port**, across which cuts a more direct series of paths and steps. A little further along, by the *Punta Scario* hotel, steps lead down to Malfa's boulder **beach**, Punta Scario, picturesquely backed by vertiginous cliffs. In summer there is an appealing little beach bar here selling cold drinks, sandwiches and *pane cunzato*, as well as renting out mattresses, lilos and umbrellas.

ARRIVAL AND INFORMATION

By bus The bus stops on the main road by the bank, then down in the village by the main piazza, and again a few hundred metres below, directly above the path that leads down to Punta Scario beach.

Tourist information In summer an enterprising somebody usually opens a little information office

somewhere along Malfa's main street.

Boat tours There are booths in the main piazza with information on boat tours around the island and to other islands. If you're confident enough to putter about yourself, you can rent a small *gommone* (rubber dinghy) in the port for a day or half-day (from €40 per half-day, excluding petrol).

ACCOMMODATION

Capo Faro ☎ 090 984 4330, ⊛ capofaro.it. Some 3km east of Malfa at the Tasca d'Almerita malvasia wine estate, the stunning, contemporary rooms here occupy seven Aeolian-style houses that look down across the vineyards. Facilities are top-notch, from magnificent pool to classy bar and restaurant, and you can tour the vineyards on request. No children under 12. **€370**

★ **Signum** Via Scalo 15 ☎ 090 984 4222, ⊛ hotel signum.it. Style and luxury deftly balanced with friendly

and relaxed service – island hotels don't come much better than this. Thirty comfortable rooms (some classed as superior and deluxe) display a seamless blend of antique furniture and contemporary style and have either terraces or balconies, sea or garden views. Night swimming in the splendid infinity pool and catching sight of Stromboli's eruptions across the water takes some beating, and the exquisite spa, tapping into a hot volcanic spring, is also not to be missed. **€300**

EATING AND DRINKING

A Lumeredda Via San Lorenzo ☎ 090 984 4130. Hidden down one of Malfa's myriad flower-lined alleyways, this is exactly what an island restaurant should be – relaxed and unpretentious with wooden tables on a simple, shady terrace. Come for a deftly cooked crispy-edged pizza (from

€4.50), and a carafe of house wine or a beer, and for once you won't break the bank. Daily lunch & dinner; closed Dec–Easter.

Maracaibo Punta Scario beach (no phone). Beach hut with a shady, flower-filled covered terrace serving a couple of kinds of fresh fruit *granitas* (usually lemon and watermelon), plus salads (€4–6) and sandwiches (€3.50–4) that make copious use of local ingredients such as capers, sun-dried tomatoes and tuna. Daily mid-morning till sunset; closed winter.

Ravesi Via Roma 6 ☎ 090 984 4385, ⓦ hotelravesi.it. Good drinks and a help-yourself buffet of nibbles served in the candlelit garden of this elegant hotel – a must for aperitivo junkies. In mid-Aug there's a programme of aperitivo-hour concerts. Daily 7–9pm; closed winter.

★ **Signum** Via Scalo 15 ☎ 090 984 4222, ⓦ hotel signum.it. Enthusiastic, attentive staff and great cooking ensure dinner at *Signum* is always special: candlelit and subdued, but refreshingly relaxed. Let sommelier Vincenzo guide your choice of wine – he'll listen to exactly what you like, and come up with one of the cellar's real treasures. Signature dishes include an unguent sformata of raw prawns with pistachios; the crispest, lightest and most succulent fish polpette imaginable; and home-made ravioli stuffed with ricotta, orange and lemon zest, sprinkled with finely chopped lemon leaves. Fish of the day will depend on what's in season. Hotel guests have priority, but it is worth phoning early to get on the waiting list. Expect to pay at least €50 per head. Easter–Oct daily lunch & dinner.

Pollara

Just above Malfa, a minor road (served by several buses a day) snakes off west to secluded **POLLARA**, raised on a cliff above the sea and occupying a crescent-shaped crater from which Salina's last eruption took place some 13,000 years ago. Scenes from Michael Radford's 1994 film *Il Postino* were shot in a house here and down on the narrow beach at the base of cliffs below the village, but film pilgrims and the many boat tours that pitch up here have caused severe erosion over the years, and the beach has recently been closed. You can swim instead from ramps in front of the so-called *balate*, caves in which fishermen traditionally kept their boats and equipment; or clamber and splash along the rocky coast to more private swimming spots. In summer two enterprising locals rent kayaks, lilos, mattresses and sun umbrellas at the ramps.

ACCOMMODATION AND EATING   **POLLARA**

Al Cappero Pollara Via Chiesa 38 ☎ 090 984 3968. Simple, family-run place, with something of a Greek taverna feel, where you should be sure to arrive in time to watch the sun sink over the isles of Filicudi and Alicudi. *Frittelle di zucchine* (deep-fried courgette fritters) come free, after which there will be two or three pasta dishes of the day (€7–10), inevitably including one dressed with a pesto of their own capers. Fish (€8–12) comes grilled or fried, but the signature dish is a tasty *coniglio in agrodolce* (€12), rabbit stewed in a typical Sicilian sweet-sour sauce. Wines from €12. Daily lunch & dinner.

La Locanda del Postino Via Picone 10 Pollara ☎ 090 984 3958, ⓦ lalocandadelpostino.it. A great choice if you want to turn your back on the world and collect sunsets. The best rooms are no. 7 and no. 10, with large, private terraces (terraces of other rooms are divided by potted planes and are pleasant but lack privacy). Discounts for longer stays. Dinner is €35 per person à la carte with water and house wine included. Specialities include linguine with local wild fennel, anchovies, pine nuts, raisins and toasted breadcrumbs; and fresh fish, with set dishes costing around €14 and whole fish priced at €40 per kilo. You could also come for an aperitivo with snacks – timed to coincide with sunset. Restaurant daily lunch & dinner; closed Nov–Easter. **€200**

L'Oasi Piazza Sant'Onofrio (no phone). Set in an immobile caravan, Pollara's only bar offers home-made lemon and watermelon *granitas*, along with wine, beer, soft drinks, ice cream and sandwiches (€3–4.50), plus salads making good use of local capers and tomatoes. It is also a nice place to come and watch the sunset over an aperitivo (€5 for a drink and finger food). There is a shady terrace – position yourself at the back, and you can keep an eye on the hairpin road for the arrival of the bus – it takes at least 5min for the bus to make its way down to the village: plenty of time to finish your drink. Daily 9.30am–9.30pm; closed winter.

Valdichiesa and Leni

In the saddle between Salina's two mountains, sprinkled between malvasia vineyards and smallholdings of fruit trees and vegetables, **Valdichiesa** is lush, cool and green all year. Dominated by the twin-towered church of Santa Maria del Terzito, this sparse scattering of whitewashed houses is also the starting point for the easiest ascent of Monte Fossa, the trailhead kicking off from directly behind the church. There is also a paved track below the church running down to the port and beach of Rinella, via the village of Leni. There are

3

no shops or bars, making it the most peaceful place to stay on the island – even in high summer. The silence is shattered just once a year, on July 21–22, when the festival of **Madonna del Terzito** is celebrated with the usual music, market, fireworks and dancing.

The village of **Leni**, a couple of kilometres beyond, spills along a ridge above Rinella. Though not quite as away-from-it-all as Valdichiesa, it has an appealingly sleepy feel, and fantastic views over to Lipari and Vulcano.

ACCOMMODATION AND EATING

VALDICHIESA

Vacanza a Salina Via Piano Croce ☎331 575 2677, ⓦvacanzeasalina.it. Simple, tasteful studios and one- and two-bedroom apartments with kitchens in a traditional winemaker's house, set in a garden with lovely views of the valley and the distant sea. Utterly peaceful, and owners who respect guests' privacy. Studios and one-bed apartments €50

Agriturismo Galletta Via Ruvoli 7 ☎333 367 1706. The restaurant of this simple *agriturismo* gives a gutsy taste of traditional Aeolian life, surrounded by vineyards, vegetable gardens and fruit trees. There are six simple rooms with en-suite bathrooms, and a kids' playground, but it's best as a place to eat (daily lunch & dinner). The

owners keep island traditions alive, preserving fruit and veg, making wine and, in summer, cooking up tomato sauce on their terrace in huge cauldrons. Pasta dishes kick off at €6 for a simple spaghetti with cherry tomatoes, and you'll pay €8–10 for pasta with home-made caper pesto, or with swordfish, capers, tomatoes, olives, aubergine, pine nuts and wild mint. The outstanding choice is the grilled lamb seasoned with local herbs (€12), though there are fish dishes as well, including stuffed calamaretti (€12). Follow it with a salad, and wind up with a home-made liqueur of wild fennel, wild mint or apple and rose petal (€3). Book in advance in low season. Rooms €80

Rinella

On the island's south coast, 15km from Santa Marina, the tiny port of **RINELLA** consists of a cluster of houses, a sandy **beach** and a quay at the very bottom of a steep and winding road. It has clear water, and the beach is popular, so it gets a fair number of visitors in summer, though it's otherwise rather remote in feel. To escape the crowds, take the path from behind the former campsite (recognisable by several half-constructed concrete structures) to the stone boulder beach of **Praia Venezia**. The walk takes about twenty minutes, and there is a bar en route in the summer.

ARRIVAL AND DEPARTURE

RINELLA

By ferry and hydrofoil Rinella is Salina's second port, and first port of call if you are arriving from Palermo, Filicudi or Alicudi. The ticket office is on the dock, right by the bus stop. Buses call here several times a day, but don't always coincide with ferries and hydrofoils, so unless you have accommodation in Rinella, it's far better to disembark at Santa Marina. Note that the services detailed below are year-round; schedules increase during the summer months. Ferry destinations Alicudi (1 daily; 2hr 20min); Filicudi (1–2 daily; 1hr 10min); Ginostra (1 daily; 2hr); Lipari (1–2

daily; 1hr 40min); Milazzo (1–2 daily; 1hr 35min–2hr); Santa Maria Salina (6 daily; 10min); Naples (1 weekly; 13hr 30min); Panarea (1 daily; 1hr 15min); Stromboli (1 daily; 4hr); Vulcano (1–2 daily; 2hr 20min).

Hydrofoil destinations Alicudi (2 daily; 1hr); Filicudi (2 daily; 25min); Ginostra (1 daily; 2hr 45min); Lipari (10 daily; 25min); Messina (1 daily; 2hr 20min); Milazzo (7 daily; 1hr 40min); Panarea (1 daily; 2hr 20min); Santa Marina Salina (6 daily; 10min); Stromboli (1 daily; 3hr); Vulcano (8 daily; 25min–1hr).

ACCOMMODATION

L'Ariana Via Rotabile ☎090 980 9075, ⓦhotelariana .it. A hotel and restaurant above the port to the left, occupying an old villa with a frill of terracotta busts around its roof. The interior doesn't quite live up to expectations

– and high-season rates are not worth paying – but the location is unbeatable, and it's just a couple of minutes' walk from the sandy beach. €168

EATING AND DRINKING

L'Ariana Via Rotabile ☎090 980 9075, ⓦhotelariana .it. *Bar Papero* run a laidback aperitivo bar on the terrace

below the hotel in the evenings, with occasional live jazz and DJ sets. It's an excellent place for sunset watching, and those

3

who can't be bothered to change out of their beach clothes won't feel out of place. Daily 11am–late; closed winter.

★ **Bar Papero** Piazzetta Anna Magnani (no phone). Run with verve and passion by three siblings, this friendly bar does a great *tavola calda* of home-cooked food (and yummy cakes for afterwards), ideal for lunch or an after-beach aperitivo. Opening hours are flexible and closing times depend on clients. Daily from early morning till evening.

Chiosco Punta Megna Via Pra Venezia snc ☎ 339 612 4585. With a shady terrace and sea views, this wooden kiosk above Praia Venezia serves reasonably priced chilled soft drinks and beer, along with sandwiches and salads. Book ahead, and they will stay open to barbecue you a simple dinner of grilled fish, salad, wine and seasonal fruit (€20 per head, or €25 with a pasta course). Daily mid-morning until sunset.

Da Marco Via Rotabile ☎ 090 980 9120. Just up the road from *L'Ariana*, this excellent pizzeria offers some inspired inventions involving wild fennel fronds from about €5. Easter–Nov daily lunch & dinner; limited opening in winter.

Seaside Via Rotabile ☎ 090 980 9206. Highly recommended *granitas*, especially fig (€2.50) or malvasia (€3), along with mega salads (€7–13) and an excellent *tavola calda* – try the stuffed escarole (€6) if they have it. Opening hours revolve around the arrival and departure of hydrofoils. Daily early morning till late.

Le Tre Pietre Via Rotabile 72 ☎ 090 980 9081. Amiable restaurant and pizzeria; the TV is always on, and it serves up a nice line in fresh fish. *Antipasti* include simple island staples such as anchovies with capers (€5), while among the spaghetti dishes (€6–10), there are several with an authentic Aeolian feel – try the *finochietto*, dressed with a pesto of wild fennel. The fish menu depends on the day's catch, but the island speciality of *polpette di totano* (deep-fried patties of flying squid) is a regular feature. March–Nov daily lunch & dinner.

Panarea

Only 3km by 1.5km, **PANAREA** is the smallest, loveliest and, sadly, the most painfully stylish and ridiculously expensive of the Aeolians: in summer, its harbours, hotels and villas overflow with an international crowd of designers, models, pop stars, actors, royalty and their lackeys. In low season, however, the island is an utter delight. Come in spring or autumn and you'll find accommodation prices relatively sane and beaches and bays uncrowded, while the weather should be cool enough to follow the path that hugs the entire length of Panarea's fractured **coastline**, one of the most stunning anywhere in Italy.

BOAT TOURS AND DIVES AROUND PANAREA

The islets and rocks off Panarea make for a great day out. You can either go on a **tour** (from around €15 per person) – there'll be plenty of time for swimming – or **rent your own boat** (from around €100 for a half-day excluding fuel). Check out the seafront kiosks at San Pietro or look for the signs advertising "*Noleggio barche*" (boat rental) in nearly every bar, shop and restaurant.

The nearest of the islets to Panarea, **Dattilo**, points a jagged, pyramidal finger skyward and has a minuscule beach. There's better swimming at **Lisca Bianca**, the stark setting of Antonioni's 1960 film *L'Avventura*, where the tranquil water is sheltered by **Bottaro** opposite. Just offshore, submarine fumaroles, created during the last major eruption of Stromboli in 2002, send columns of bubbles rising to the surface – a great snorkelling experience – though check before leaving if access is permitted, as gas emissions can occasionally be dangerous. Nearby Lisca Nera and Le Formiche (The Ants) are mere wrinkles on the sea surface, albeit a constant hazard to shipping. The largest islet is **Basiluzzo**, which retains the remains of a Roman fort and port (the latter now submerged) but is currently only used for caper cultivation.

There are some great **dives** too: take a day out with Amphibia (☎ 335 613 8529, ⓦ amphibia.it) to see what appears to be a submarine snowstorm – the water is full of blobs of a weird white bacteria that grows on sulphur and has the consistency of eggwhite – and to dive the remains of a British cargo ship deliberately sunk during the Depression as an insurance scam – for the past fifteen years it has been inhabited by a giant fish (about 80kg). Amphibia also offers introductory and PADI diving courses, plus **snorkelling** and **children's activities**.

Cars are banned, and the only transport is by Vespa or electric golf car. Panarea's couple of hundred year-round inhabitants live in three linked hamlets on the eastern side of the island, **Iditella**, **San Pietro** and **Drauto**, with the boats docking at San Pietro.

San Pietro and Iditella

The core of Panarea's settlement is **San Pietro**, tucked onto gentle terraces and backed by gnarled outcrops of rock. It's here that you'll find most of the accommodation, restaurants and facilities, while just to the north, passing through **Iditella**, you'll see evidence of volcanic activity in the steaming gas emissions (*fumarole*) on the sand-and-pebble beach below here, the **Spiaggia Fumarole**, or Calcara.

3

ARRIVAL AND DEPARTURE
SAN PIETRO AND IDITELLA

By ferry and hydrofoil All boats dock at San Pietro harbour, where the Siremar (☎090 983 007) and Ustica Lines (☎090 983 344) ticket offices are almost next door to each other. The services detailed below are year-round; schedules increase during the summer months.
Ferry destinations Ginostra (2 weekly; 1hr 40min); Lipari (2 weekly; 1hr); Milazzo (2 weekly; 3hr 40min); Naples (12hr 15min); Stromboli (2 weekly; 1hr); Vulcano (2 weekly; 1hr 40min).

Hydrofoil destinations Ginostra (2 daily; 25min); Lipari (4 daily; 50min); Milazzo (4 daily; 1hr 40min); Rinella (1 daily; 35min); Santa Marina Salina (2 daily; 25min); Stromboli (2 daily; 35min); Vulcano (4 daily; 1hr 20min).
By helicopter If they don't have their own yacht, celebs use Air Panarea's helicopter service (☎090 983 4428 or ☎340 366 7214, ⓦairpanarea.com), which runs a summer scheduled service from Reggio di Calabria airport (from €200 one-way), plus panoramic fly-overs of Stromboli and the other islands.

INFORMATION

Tourist information Although there's no tourist office, you can get information at ⓦpanarea.com (in Italian), which has links to a few hotels and rooms places.
Services San Pietro has a pharmacy, an ATM and a summer-only police post and *guardia medica*, while in the

warren of alleys behind the harbour is a little supermarket, two or three *alimentari* and a bakery. The little electric buggies down at the harbour act as taxis. However, all the hotels provide a free pick-up service.

ACCOMMODATION

Lisca Bianca Via Lani, San Pietro ☎090 983 004, ⓦliscabianca.it. This typical Aeolian building – covered wide terraces, blue shutters, white walls – has some gorgeous views, with stylish rooms overlooking either the sea or the bougainvillea-clad gardens and port. You can see Stromboli from the breakfast terrace, and the bar is one of the best on the island. If you can avoid August, prices aren't too bad at all; check the website for deals. Closed Nov–March. **€210**
Pippo and Maria Soldini Via Iditella, Iditella ☎090 983 061 or ☎334 703 5010. Up the hill behind the port in Iditella, beyond the Carabinieri barracks, the rooms here

are one of the least expensive places to stay on Panarea. They are spotlessly clean, have their own terraces, are set in a garden, and out of season owners Pippo and Maria will cook for you. **€90**
Quartara Via San Pietro, San Pietro ☎090 983 027, ⓦquartarahotel.com. Very classy four-star boutique hotel run by a cheerful family, whose thirteen fashionable rooms have elegant wood furniture and stone floors. A terrace jacuzzi out the back overlooks the port and there's a well-regarded restaurant. Closed Nov to March. **€360**
Raya Via San Pietro, San Pietro ☎090 983 013, ⓦhotelraya.it. Opened in the 1960s, this is the hotel that

put Panarea on the party map, and it remains the hippest, sexiest and most expensive hotel in Sicily – even though the owner's refusal to install TVs and telephones means that it has only two stars. It's built entirely of natural materials, and the food is organic, though its claim to be a simple retreat for nature lovers seems a little disingenuous when the place is crawling with party animals. Rooms (whitewashed walls, teak furniture, hand-batiked textiles, citronella candles) are built into the hillside above the village, with great views to the sea over groves of olives, hibiscus and bougainvillea; there are also some cheaper rooms in town above the *Raya*'s boutique. **€540**

EATING AND DRINKING

Da Adelina Via Comunale Mare, San Pietro 28 ☎ 090 983246. Intimate candlelit restaurant with a romantic roof terrace overlooking Panarea's port. Relaxing and unpretentious, with a simple menu of seasonal dishes such as *moscardini* (tiny octopus cooked with tomato, capers, wild fennel and chilli; €14) appearing alongside year-round dishes like *pennette adelina*, dressed with anchovies, aubergine, capers, olives, mint and basil (€10). For the main course opt for the mixed fish of the day, either fried or grilled (€18). Daily lunch & dinner; closed Nov–Feb.

Da Francesco Via San Pietro, San Pietro ☎ 090 983 023, ⊛ dafrancescopanarea.com. Overlooking the harbour, and pretty good value for meals of pasta (around

€12), including the signature dish "*disgraziata*", with peppers, chilli, capers, olives, aubergine, tomatoes and baked ricotta, plus fish from €15. Daily lunch & dinner; closed Dec–Feb.

Da Paolino Via Iditella 75, Iditella ☎ 090 983 008. A 10min walk north of the port towards Iditella, this family-run restaurant has a terrace with fine views of Stromboli. You'll spend quite a bit if you eat a whole meal, but you can have a very unpretentious meal of pasta and salad and a glass of wine here for around €25 – try the rich *mille baci* pasta with greens (€10); and the fish is whatever the family has caught that day. Daily lunch & dinner; closed Nov–March.

Drauto and Zimmari beach

South of San Pietro through the tangle of lanes, a gentle thirty-minute stroll above the coast leads to the mainly stone beach below **Drauto**. Just beyond here, the path descends to **Zimmari**, a popular, dark-gold sandy beach – the only one on the island – overlooked by a seasonal (and expensive) bar-trattoria. Steps at the far end of the beach climb up and across to the headland of **Punta Milazzese**, passing the trailhead of a waymarked path (look for the signposts) that wends into Panarea's interior, passing below the island's highest peak, the craggy **Punta del Corvo** (421m), before descending back to San Pietro – a hike of two to three hours on a path that is easy to follow.

ACCOMMODATION   DRAUTO

Albergo Girasole Via Drauto ☎ 090 983 018 or ☎ 328 861 8595, ⊛ hotelgirasole-panarea.it. Family-run hotel out on the way to the sandy beach at Zimmari. Great place to stay in low season, but even this part of the island is chocca in August, the skinny road buzzing with electric cars and *motorini*. **€220**

Villaggio Preistorico

Beautifully situated on a craggy headland above Zimmari, atop Punta Milazzese and overlooking two rocky inlets, the **Villaggio Preistorico** is the archipelago's best-preserved Bronze Age village. The 23 huts here were discovered in 1948, and the oval outlines of their foundation walls are easily visible. The site is thought to have been inhabited since the fourteenth century BC, and pottery found here (displayed in Lipari's museum) shows a distinct Minoan influence – fascinating evidence of a historical link between the Aeolians and Crete that goes some way towards corroborating the legends of contact between the two in ancient times.

Cala Junco

Steps descend from Punta Milazzese to **Cala Junco**, a spectacular stony cove whose aquamarine water, scattered stone outcrops and surrounding coves and caves make it a popular spot for snorkelling.

Stromboli

The most spectacular of all the Aeolian Islands, **STROMBOLI** is little more than a volcanic cone thrust out of the sea. It's very much alive and kicking, throwing up showers of sparks and flaring rock from the craters every twenty minutes or so, while a handful of more serious **eruptions** over the last century have caused major lava flows. That of 1930 led to serious damage to many homes and sparked a spate of emigration from the island, while threatening eruptions in 2002 and 2003 spewed volcanic rock into the sea, spawning tsunami and ejecting rocks onto rooftops. In 2007, two new craters opened on the summit, creating new lava streams into the sea, and in July 2010 fiery boulders set the mountain alight, though the fire was swiftly extinguished. A flow of lava is often visible from afar, slowly sliding down the northwest side of the volcano into the sea.

Amazingly, perhaps, people have chosen to live here for centuries, reassured that, historically, the main lava flows have been confined to the channel of the Sciara del Fuoco, down the western side of the island. This leaves the eastern parishes of San Vincenzo, San Bartolo and Piscità (often grouped together simply as **Stromboli village**), and the solitary southern community of **Ginostra**, to lead something of a charmed life, their white terraced houses adorned with bougainvillea, plumbago and wisteria, remote from the fury of the craters above. The island's permanent population numbers perhaps five hundred, plumbing is often rudimentary, and access sometimes restricted because of winter storms, but despite this, Stromboli has become a chic resort, attracting an eclectic moneyed crowd that ranges from gay fashionistas to hip intellectuals, a mix leavened with a generous dose of holidaying families and hardy mountain types. Its black-sand **beaches** are overlooked by attractive terraced hotels, while thrill-seekers come from all over the world to climb one of the planet's most accessible volcanoes.

GETTING AROUND   **STROMBOLI**

By taxi Stromboli has no public transport – indeed the only transport on the island is by three-wheeler pick-up (the Ape, or bee, known as a *lapa* hereabouts), motorbike or electric car – so if your hotel is any distance from the port you may need a taxi. Though unofficial *lapas* may offer their services, the only official taxis are the electric golf carts; however, as these take ten hours to charge for every two hours' driving, demand quite often simply outstrips supply. As a precaution, ask your hotel at the time of booking if they have, or can organize, transport for you. Of the official taxis, Sabbia Nera (☎ 090 986 399), based near the port, are reliable and friendly. In high season, consider booking one in advance to meet you on arrival.

Stromboli village

The main settlement of **Stromboli** spreads for a distance of around 2km between the lower slopes of the volcano and the island's beaches. It's an utterly straightforward layout of two largely parallel roads and steep, interconnecting alleys, though the profusion of local place-names keeps visitors on their toes. From the scruffy quayside area known as **Scari**, the lower coastal road (Via Marina and Via Regina Elena) runs around to the main beach of **Ficogrande**, a long black stretch overlooked by several hotels. Further on is **Piscità**, around 25 minutes' walk from the port, with the island's most beautiful and secluded ashy beach at its far end. There's also a sand-and-stone stretch south of Scari, past the fishing boats, and if you clamber over the rocks at the end of this beach, there's a further sweep of lava-stone beach that attracts a fair bit of nude sunbathing.

Pottering around Stromboli village as you go about your daily business is one of the great pleasures of being on the island. The other road from the quayside cuts up into what could loosely be described as "the village", where, as Via Roma, it runs as far as the church of **San Vincenzo**, whose square offers glorious views of the Strombolicchio basalt stack. Beyond the square, it's another fifteen minutes' or so walk to the second church of **San Bartolo**, above Piscità, just beyond which starts the path to the crater. Once you've got this far, you've seen all that Stromboli village has to offer. The only "sight", apart from the

3

STROMBOLI VILLAGE

ACCOMMODATION
Casa del Sole	2
Locanda del Barbablù	4
La Sirenetta Park	3
Villaggio Stromboli	1

CAFÉS AND RESTAURANTS
La Lampara	1
Lapillagelato	3
Locanda del Barbablù	2
Zurro	4

churches, is the house in which **Ingrid Bergman** lived with Roberto Rossellini in the spring of 1949, while making the film *Stromboli: Terra di Dio*. A plaque records these bare facts on the pink building, just after San Vincenzo church, on the right.

ARRIVAL AND INFORMATION

STROMBOLI VILLAGE

By ferry and hydrofoil Several ferry and hydrofoil services from Lipari call first at Ginostra (see opposite), though the main port is Stromboli village. Siremar (☎090 986 016) and Ustica Lines (☎090 986 003) both have ticket offices by Stromboli harbour. The services detailed below are year-round; schedules increase during the summer months.
Ferry destinations Lipari (2 weekly; 1hr 45min); Milazzo (2 weekly; 3hr); Naples (2 weekly; 11hr); Panarea (2 weekly; 25min); Vulcano (2 weekly; 2hr).

Hydrofoil destinations Ginostra (1 daily; 10min); Lipari (4 daily; 1hr 20min); Panarea (4 daily; 25min); Vulcano (4 daily; 1hr 30min); Milazzo (4 daily; 2hr 30min).
Information Libreria sull'Isola bookshop on Via Vittorio Emanuele (June–Sept daily 10am–1pm & 5–8pm, sometimes opens much later; ☎090 986 5755), and several other shops in town, sell a good map of Stromboli showing local hiking trails.
Services There's internet access at the Libreria dell'Isola bookshop.

ACCOMMODATION

Casa del Sole Via Soldato Cincotta, Piscità ☎090 986 300. A cheapie in an old building within metres of the sea. Simple four- to six-bed apartments are available all year, and accommodation is pretty flexible, whether you want an off-season single or multi-bedded room in summer. Kitchen facilities are available, and there's a sun terrace. No credit cards. Doubles **€60**
Locanda del Barbablù Via Vittorio Emanuele 17 ☎090 986 118, ⬤barbablu.it. This old Aeolian house provides the most relaxed accommodation on Stromboli, with antique rooms, four-poster beds and original tile floors. It's combined with a restaurant where you can dine under the stars (see opposite). Closed Nov–Feb. **€290**

La Sirenetta Park Via Marina 33, Ficogrande ☎090 986 025, ⬤lasirenettahotel.it. Four-star hotel set opposite the black sands of Ficogrande, with a decent-sized outdoor pool, a summer nightclub and access to watersports facilities. The room rates drop considerably outside summer and at the beginning or end of the season you can stay for around €120. Closed Nov–March. **€240**
Villaggio Stromboli Via Regina Elena ☎090 986 018, ⬤villaggiostromboli.it. With simple rooms jutting up against the breaking waves, this pleasant, quiet place offers one of the island's nicest seaside stays; it also has a good terrace restaurant where you can gaze out over the water. **€190**

EATING, DRINKING AND ENTERTAINMENT

CAFÉS AND RESTAURANTS
La Lampara Via Vittorio Emanuele ☎090 986 009. Dine on pizza, pasta and grilled meat and fish on the large

raised terrace under a pergola of climbing vines among huge pots of basil and rosemary. Pizza from €6. Daily lunch & dinner; closed Nov–March.

STROMBOLI BOAT TOURS

The main daytime boat tour from Stromboli is the **round-island excursion** (2hr 30min; around €30 per person), calling at Ginostra and Stromboli's extraordinary basalt offspring, Strombolicchio. You usually get half an hour to scramble around Ginostra, which is plenty of time to see it, while at Strombolicchio there's swimming and a 200-step climb up the battlemented rock to the lighthouse on its top.

At night, the stock-in-trade is the cruise to see the **Sciara del Fuoco** (1hr 30min; around €25 per person), the lava channel rising sheer out of incredible deep-blue sea water. Boats aren't allowed to dock on the shoreline, since it's too unpredictably dangerous, but through the gloom you'll see orange and red flashes from the crater above.

You can book tours at any of the stands by Stromboli Town harbour (prices are broadly similar on all the boats), where you can also charter a boat for longer tours or rent your own, or from Paola and Giovanni (☎338 431 2803) who work from opposite the *Sirenetta* hotel in Ficogrande.

Lapillagelato Via Roma snc ☎333 320 8966. Artisan ice cream made with natural ingredients and no hydrogenated fats, added colours or preservatives. Try the fig, the vanilla with caramel or the dark chocolate with cinnamon. Daily 3.30–11pm; closed winter.

Locanda del Barbablù Via Vittorio Emanuele 17 ☎090 986 118, ⊛barbablu.it. Stylish restaurant specializing in fresh fish and vegetables, which keeps things simple by offering just three choices that change every day. Choose between a selection of four *antipasti* created from the fish of the day; a pasta dish with fresh fish; or two fish dishes (no pasta) with vegetables. Each "choice" costs €25, wine and dessert are extra. Mid-June to mid-Sept daily dinner only; rest of the year open on request.

Zurro Via Marina s/n ☎090 986 283. Not exactly romantic, with its startlingly bright lights and sliding aluminium framed windows, but you eat well at *Zurro*. It's named for its bearded, piratical-looking chef, a one-time fisherman who shocked his mates by tampering with traditional recipes, but opened a restaurant nevertheless. Try razor-thin slices of raw aubergine, flecked with chilli flakes and served with balsamic-dressed rocket and parmesan; *spaghetti alla strombolana*, with cherry tomatoes, anchovies, mint, chilli and garlic (€14), or *pietre di mare*: black ravioli stuffed with *ricciola* (amberjack) and dressed with capers, cherry tomatoes and basil (€14). The chocolate cake is a must. Daily lunch & dinner; closed Nov–Feb.

Ginostra

Without seeing its name on boat timetables, you might not even be aware of the existence of **Ginostra**, the hamlet on the southwest side of Stromboli. From the minuscule harbour, zigzag steps climb into a cluster of typical white Aeolian houses on terraces. It's a refreshingly simple place: donkeys are tethered to posts outside homes; ancient exterior stone ovens lie idle; and cultivated hedges and volcanic stone walls snake up the hillside. Hydrofoils run to and from Stromboli town in summer, though a boat tour is a more realistic way to see Ginostra (unless you fancy actually staying here at the one small hotel). A century ago, there was also a maintained path that skirted the shore back to Stromboli, but assault by the elements has done for most of it. However, following the coast anticlockwise, you don't need to go very far to find spots where you can swim off the rocks.

ARRIVAL AND DEPARTURE   GINOSTRA

By ferry and hydrofoil Weather permitting, a couple of hydrofoils run to and from Stromboli town per day in summer (once daily in winter), weather permitting of course, continuing to Panarea, Santa Marina, Lipari, Vulcano and Milazzo. There is also a ferry to the same places daily except Saturday. The twice weekly ferry to Naples stops at Ginostra.

Ferry destinations Lipari (3 weekly; 3hr); Milazzo (3 weekly; 5hr 25min); Naples (2 weekly; 12hr); Panarea (3 weekly; 45min); Santa Marina Salina (1 weekly; 2hr); Stromboli (1 weekly; 30min); Vuicano (3 weekly; 3hr 45min).

Hydrofoil destinations Lipari (2 daily; 1hr 15min–3hr 15min); Milazzo (3 daily; 2hr 15min–4hr 25min); Panarea (30min–2hr 20min); Santa Marina Salina (1 daily; 3hr 35min); Stromboli (2 daily; 10min); Vulcano (3 daily; 1hr 15min–3hr 35min).

3

CLIMBING STROMBOLI'S VOLCANO

Climbing Stromboli's **volcano** is big business. Public access was only reopened in 2005 (after the eruptions of preceding years), and while you can freely walk along the trails below 400m, you have to be accompanied by a licensed guide to go any higher. Numbers at the crater are also limited, so it's essential to reserve a place on an **organized excursion** (around €30; see below) as soon as you can – calling on the day is usually fine for most of the year, but advanced booking is advised in high summer – and be prepared for the trip to be postponed because of poor weather or other climatic or geological reasons. You need to be in decent health, have proper hiking boots and clothes (you can rent these in the village), and carry plenty of water and sun protection. Guides usually supply helmets.

If you want to see eruptions without the effort or expense of climbing to the summit, follow the track a few minutes' walk beyond San Bartolo church at the far end of Piscità, climbing to the first orientation point, L'Osservatorio, a bar-pizzeria (closed in winter) which has a wide terrace and a view of the volcano. Beyond, you'll see the frighteningly sheer **Sciara del Fuoco** lava outflow plunging directly into the sea. This is a huge blistered sheet down which thousands of years' worth of volcanic detritus has poured, scarring and pock-marking the hillside. Menacing little puffs of steam dance up from folds in the bare slope, where absolutely nothing grows.

THE CLIMB

Most excursions leave in the late afternoon, taking around five or six hours – this lets you catch the amazing sunsets and gives you around an hour or so at the top, watching the fireworks. The **ascent** takes three hours, and you are expected to go at a fair whack; at first, it's no different from walking up any mountain, then suddenly all vegetation stops, giving way to black ash strewn with small jagged boulders spewed out by the volcano. Once at the top, all you see at first are clouds of white steam – then suddenly there will be a resounding clash, the clouds glow red, and spouts of fire shoot up into the air, the glowing boulders drawing tracks of red light across the night sky. The **descent** takes around two hours – for the most part trudging down a steep slope of lava-sand.

GUIDES, EQUIPMENT AND INFORMATION

Gruppo Nazionale Vulcanologia ☎090 986 708, ⓦgnv.ingv.it. Near the harbour, the national vulcanology organization has an office with useful background information on the volcano. It's open most days and shows a video about Stromboli, while the national website has photos, technical information and some scary seismograph readings from previous eruptions.

★ **Magmatrek** Via Vittorio Emanuele, just off the piazza ☎090 986 5768, ⓦmagmatrek.it. Local climbing guru, Zazà, and his colleagues have daily volcano treks throughout the year. Guides are knowledgeable and experienced and in constant contact with the vulcanological centre.

Totem Trekking Piazza San Vincenzo 4 ☎090 986 5752. Useful little shop that sells and rents out hiking equipment and accessories.

ACCOMMODATION AND EATING

Petrusa ☎090 981 2305. Ginostra's only official accommodation has three large rooms with their own terraces, sharing a bathroom. Half-board is obligatory in July and Aug; you can eat at their bar-restaurant, L'Incontro (July & Aug daily lunch & dinner), which has fairly high prices (everything has to be shipped in) but is pretty good. No credit cards. Closed Oct to April. **€110**

Filicudi

The larger of the Aeolians' two most westerly islands, **FILICUDI** is a fascinating place, the contours of its sheer slopes traced with steep stone terraces and crisscrossed by stone mule tracks. It's an island best explored on foot – which is just as well, as there's no public transport. The tarmac road that connects Filicudi's small settlements gives a false impression of the island, making villages seem far apart even if they're just a few minutes' walk from each other – at least if you're fit. Most of the tracks are pretty steep, following and cutting up and down between the ancient terraces carved into slopes of maquis and prickly pear.

Climb away from the port, up the flight of steps opposite the jetty, and you're in another world. The well-kept **paths** are lined with volcanic boulders interspersed with great flowering cacti, whose pustular blooms erupt upon elephant-ear leaves. You can clamber down to pebble **beaches** and swim in deserted coves and at the archipelago's loveliest **lido**; make your way around the terraced headlands to phenomenal **viewpoints**, or hire a little wooden boat (a *gozzetto*) for the day and snorkel around splintered offshore rocks and hidden sea caves.

Filicudi's sheer slopes are all painstakingly lined with stone **terracing**, a reminder that before mass emigration in the 1950s and 1960s there was a great deal of agricultural activity here. Many terraces were subsequently abandoned, and cultivation is now down to a few vines and olives, but they do serve to reduce soil erosion. Today, there are only 250 or so permanent island residents, and while this number swells perhaps tenfold in August with visitors, a coterie of left-wing villa owners (including former Rome mayor Francesco Rutelli), and returned *emigranti*, Filicudi is still a long way from being overdeveloped.

GETTING AROUND

FILICUDI

By taxi There is no public transport on Filicudi. There's usually a minibus taxi (*bus navetta*) waiting at the harbour, which will take you where you want to go on the island. It costs €12 to Pecorini Mare, less per head if there's a group of you. If it's not there, call D&G Servizio Navetta (☏ 347 757 5916 or ☏ 347 517 1825).

By car and scooter There's scooter rental (€25/day) at the port and from I Delfini at Pecorini Mare (☏ 090 988 9077or ☏ 340 148 4645), who also rent cars (€40/day).

Filicudi Porto

Filicudi's main settlement is **Filicudi Porto**, a functional place with a few colour-trimmed whitewashed cubes containing a couple of shops, hotels, basic services and two or three bar-restaurants, with terraces overlooking the water and Salina in the distance. Staying here won't really allow you to key into the magic of the island, however, so unless you have an early morning ferry or hydrofoil, it's far better to base yourself elsewhere.

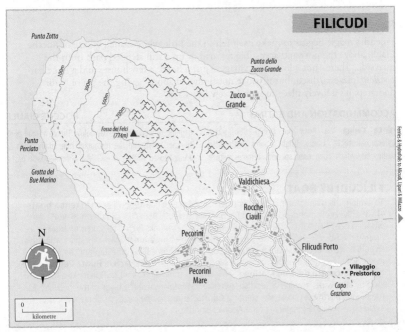

ARRIVAL AND INFORMATION

FILICUDI PORTO

By ferry and hydrofoil Filicudi Porto is an hour by hydrofoil from Lipari, and three hours from Palermo. The Siremar (☏ 090 988 9960) and Ustica Lines (☏ 090 988 9949) ticket offices are on the dockside, both open before departures. Although there is one weekly ferry from Naples to Filicudi, there are no direct services back to Naples from here – you'll need to connect to another ferry at Rinella or Santa Marina Salina. The services detailed below are year-round; schedules increase during the summer months.

Ferry destinations Alicudi (1 daily; 1hr 10min); Lipari (1 daily; 2hr 50min); Milazzo (1 daily; 5hr); Rinella (1 daily; 1hr); Santa Marina (1 daily; 1hr 50min); Vulcano (1 daily; 3hr 20min).

Hydrofoil destinations Lipari (2 daily; 1hr); Rinella (2 daily; 30min); Santa Marina Salina (2 daily; 45min).

Services The one-street port has a pharmacy (limited opening), general store and ATM. One of the bar-restaurants here, *Da Nino sul Mare* (☏ 090 988 9984), also sells ice cream, postcards and island maps (€5) showing Filicudi's footpaths.

ACCOMMODATION AND EATING

Da Nino sul Mare ☏ 090 988 9984. The seafront terrace of this bar and *pasticceria* is the focal point of life in the port. Come for breakfast, a lunchtime snack or aperitivo at sunset. April–Oct daily 7.30am–midnight.

Phenicusa ☏ 090 988 9946, ⊛ hotelphenicusa.com. The only hotel right by the village harbour opens for just four months a year – it's a traditional three-star, with reasonable rooms, though not all have sea views (and you pay a supplement for those that do). Breakfast is served on the sun-soaked terrace, and the decent restaurant has the same sea and harbour views. Half board is required in Aug. Closed Oct–May. Per-person half board €110

Capo Graziano

Signposted off the main road from Filicudi Porto, it's a pleasant twenty-minute walk along a steep stone path to **Capo Graziano**. Here, on a grassy plateau, high above the harbour, are the remains of a dozen or so oval **prehistoric huts**, dating from the eighteenth to the thirteenth century BC. The site is always open, and though there's not much to see, it's a fine place from which to watch the comings and goings at the harbour below, and there are several rocky places to swim from on the south side of the cape.

Rocche Ciauli

Filicudi's magic begins to make itself felt in the little whitewashed village of **Rocche Ciauli**, above the port and accessible by road or up a stiff stepped path from the quayside. There's not a lot to the village – just a hotel, a few houses and a huge bar/ *pensione*/pizzeria/disco, but if you're not bothered about having the sea on your doorstep, it's a lovely place to spend a few lazy days.

ACCOMMODATION AND EATING

ROCCHE CIAULI

★ **La Canna** Via Rosa 43 ☏ 090 988 9956, ⊛ lacannahotel.it. Lovely bright rooms with tiled bathrooms, which open onto spacious terraces with a magnificent view over the bay below. There's a small pool (summer only), and the restaurant here (daily lunch & dinner, closed winter) is excellent – home-made pasta

---

FILICUDI BY BOAT

To explore the island's uninhabited northern and western coasts you'll need to **rent a boat**. The highly recommended I Delfini at Pecorini Mare (☏ 090 988 9077 or ☏ 340 148 4645) rent wooden boats (€100/day), rubber dinghies (€120/day), kayaks (€15/day), and offer boat tours around the island (€15 per person; minimum 4 people). In summer, there's usually someone at Filicudi Porto or Pecorini Mare touting for custom; any hotel, shop or restaurant can point you in the right direction too. The main sights include the fine natural arch of **Punta Perciato** and the nearby **Grotta del Bue Marino** ("Seal Grotto" – there aren't any), a wide rocky cavity 37m long by 30m wide, its walls of reddish lava barely visible in the pitch black of the interior. Near the island's northwest coast, the startling **Canna**, a rugged obelisk 85m tall, is the most impressive of all the *faraglioni* of the Aeolian Islands.

TO PECORINI MARE BY MULE TRACK

It is an 18km drive by road from Filicudi Porto to Pecorini Mare, but by **mule track** it's a mere 3km. From the port, go up the steps by the Postamat bank machine, and follow the cobbled track until you come to a fork. The right fork leads to *Villa La Rosa* (see below), but for Pecorini Mare bear left until you hit the tarmacked road. Head right along the road; at the first bend there is an electricity cabin – a little dirt path from here leads down to a good swimming track, while the main, cobbled mule track heads right towards Pecorini, following a terrace. Keep on along this track until you come to a white house, from where a track heads uphill to Valdichiesa; the path to Pecorini Mare squeezes past the wall of the white house, before descending to the village.

(€9), fresh fish (€13), local caper salads (€4) and plenty of home-produced wine and fruit. In Aug, half board is obligatory in rooms with a sea view. It's a stiff climb up the steps from the port; call ahead and they'll pick you up from the dock. €150

Villa La Rosa Via Rosa 24 ☎090 988 9965, ⓦvillalarosa.it. Open all year, *Villa La Rosa* is, inevitably, the social hub of Filicudi, where locals gather to watch sports matches, play pool or ping pong, eat a pizza, buy a loaf of bread (they make their own) or boogie the night away. There is even a rudimentary selection of groceries (pasta, tinned tomatoes, eggs, oil and the like). Cook Adelaide Rando produces some great dishes (and has written a book on Filicudari cuisine). Try the lasagne with fresh tuna and wild fennel; the herbed rabbit; *involtini*; swordfish wrapped in lemon leaves; or the prickly pear pudding. Expect to pay €25–30 a head for a full meal. Baked in a wood oven, pizzas kick off at €6. Restaurant opens daily for lunch & dinner; call ahead out of season. There are also rooms in a couple of houses nearby. €130

Pecorini Mare

Eighteen kilometres from Filicudi Porto, at the foot of a narrow switchback road below the hamlet of **Pecorini** (no more than a few houses grouped around a church), is the little harbour of **Pecorini Mare**, a mere scrap of a fishing hamlet with a small dockside, a Carabinieri post, a "saloon" selling drinks and *gelati*, a fine trattoria (see below), a marvellous grocery shop with fresh fruit and veg and genuine local produce (bottled tuna, anchovies, honey, capers, almonds and various conserves) and a lovely desert-island-feel **lido** (€10 per person per day). It's a gorgeous, end-of-the-line place, with a long pebble beach backed by fishermen's houses and holiday homes, and perfectly clear water. In the evenings take a slow stroll up the hill (preferably with a bottle of wine) and out to the clifftop belvedere above to watch the sun set over the offshore rock known as La Canna, the Italian slang for joint (which may clue you in to the mindset of Filicudi's first wave of tourists back in the 1970s).

ACCOMMODATION AND EATING   PECORINI MARE

★ **Lidalina** ☎349 361 7577, ⊜info@filicudicase vacanze.it. A desert-island lido at the far end of the Pecorini Mare beach, with straw parasols and a little bar selling snacks, salads and artisan *granitas*. There's no music and a single electric cable serving the fridge, so at night tables are lit with oil lamps. Daytime, food is self-service and includes *arancini* of rice-flower *spaghettini* with squid ink (€3), *polpette* of vegetables (€2 each), tuna or prawns (€2.50 each), octopus salad (€8) and a fine *caponata* (€6). In the evenings it becomes a restaurant, with a simple menu of fish carpaccio (around €10) and grilled or roast fish (€12–15). There are books and magazines in a variety of languages for the use of clients. Anglo-Polish owner Alina also has several houses and studio apartments in the village (all with kitchens or cooking facilities, sleeping from 2–8 people). Closed Oct–May. Houses from €60

Saloon ☎347 047 4914. The quayside below the *Saloon* is the social hub of Pecorini Mare, and on a summer evening folk gather outside in their hundreds for a sundowner. It has been going since the 1950s, and little has changed: inside there's a fridge, a kitchen and a table where you pay your bill. Early June to mid-Sept daily 10.30am–2pm & 5–11pm.

★ **La Sirena** ☎090 988 9997, ⓦpensionelasirena.it. An oasis you won't want to leave, this cosy inn is run with relaxed flair and sits right on the Pecorini Mare seafront, with the fishing boats drawn up alongside. Rooms above the restaurant have little waterfront balconies, and there's a couple right on the beach itself. Out on the shaded terrace is the island's most relaxed restaurant (daily lunch &

FILICUDI'S ABANDONED VILLAGE

There are plenty of good **walks** along the ancient mule tracks of Filicudi: one of the nicest is out to the abandoned village of **Zucco Grande**. From the port, walk up to *La Canna* hotel (see below), following the well-kept stone mule track that begins from a point almost opposite the hydrofoil and ferry dock, then continue until you meet the tarmacked road. The path continues on the other side of the road, heading towards the settlement of Valdichiesa. After about 20min, the path forks, and you'll see the first of several signs to Zucco Grande. The path is well marked, following the contours through a prickly terrain of gorse, lentisk, prickly pear and euphorbia. Another 20min brings you to the village, abandoned forty years ago when its last inhabitants left for Australia. A couple of pioneering souls have bought ruins here, which are being renovated, but at the moment there is just one inhabitant, Giovanni (☎ 347 813 2579 or ☎ 368 407 544), who has a couple of **rooms** (haggle hard over the price as he pitches high) and can provide a basic dinner.

---

dinner). It gets very busy in Aug, but at most times of the year all you can hear is the sound of lapping water as you tuck into things like spaghetti with almond sauce (€15), orange-scented *involtini* of swordfish (€15) and an unforgettable Sicilian-style tuna hamburger spiked with fennel seeds, raisins and almonds (€15). In high season there are two dinner sittings, at 8pm and 10pm. There's wi-fi and a fine Mac for the use of clients. Closed Oct–Easter. Half board obligatory in July and Aug. Per person half board €130

Alicudi

Ends-of-the-line in Europe don't come much more remote than **ALICUDI**. Two and a half hours from Milazzo by hydrofoil, or five by ferry, the island forms a perfect cone, a mere Mediterranean pimple, and its precipitous shores are pierced by numerous caves. Up the sheer slope behind the only settlement, terraced smallholdings and white houses cling on for dear life, decorated with tumbling banks of flowers. Indeed, Alicudi's ancient name of Ericusa was the word for the heather that still stains its slopes purple in spring. Its rocky isolation was formerly exploited by the Italian government, who used the island as a prison for convicted Mafiosi, but now it's virtually abandoned by all but a few farmers and fishermen. It's this solitude, of course, that attracts tourists; not many, it's true, but enough for there to be some semblance of facilities in the village to cater for visitors. Electricity arrived at the start of the 1990s, so now there's TV, too. There are two general stores, plenty of fancy boat hardware, even a car or two parked at the dock (though, since there are no navigable roads, it's not clear whether this is bravado or forward planning on behalf of the owners). You have to walk to reach anywhere and the network of volcanic stone-built paths behind the village is extremely steep and tough – all the heavy fetching and carrying is still done by donkey or mule, whose indignant brays echo across the port all day.

Once you disembark at **Alicudi Porto**, things to do are simply enumerated. The most exhausting option is the hike up past the castle ruins to the island peak of **Filo dell'Arpa** (675m). The path runs up through the village houses from the port and there's a proper stone-built track most of the way. Unfortunately, the track looks as though it was created by a malevolent giant emptying a bag of boulders from the top and letting them fall where they will.

There's absolutely no shade, and it will take at least two hours to get up, though the magnificent views make it worthwhile.

Otherwise, you'll probably get all the exercise you need clambering over the rocky **shore** to the south of the port. The path soon peters out beyond the island's only hotel and the power station, but the rocks offer a sure foothold as they get larger the further you venture. The water is crystal clear and, once you've found a flat rock big enough to lie on, you're set for more peace and quiet than you'd bargained for. The only sounds are the echoed mutter of offshore fishermen, the scrabbling of little black crabs in the rock pools and the lap of the waves.

ARRIVAL AND INFORMATION

By ferry and hydrofoil Ferries and hydrofoils arrive at the only port, Alicudi Porto. Set in the cave-like dwellings to the left of the dock are the ticket offices (open just before departures) for Siremar (☎ 090 988 9795) and Ustica Lines (☎ 340 301 5047). Even in summer, when hydrofoil services increase to a maximum of four daily, it's usually necessary to change at Lipari if you're travelling onto Vulcano, Milazzo, Panarea or Stromboli. The only direct service to Milazzo is the daily summer Ustica Lines service from Palermo; in summer there's also one hydrofoil daily to Palermo. The services detailed below are year-round; schedules increase during the summer months.

ALICUDI

Ferry destinations Filicudi (4–5 weekly; 1hr); Lipari (4–5 weekly; 4hr); Milazzo (4–5 weekly; 6hr 15min); Rinella (4–5 weekly; 2hr 10min); Santa Marina Salina (4–5 weekly; 2hr 50min); Vulcano (4–5 weekly; 4hr 40min).
Hydrofoil destinations Filicudi (2 daily; 25min); Lipari (2 daily; 1hr 35min); Rinella (2 daily; 55 min); Santa Marina Salina (2 daily; 1hr 10min).
Services Alicudi has just two little grocery stores, both near the port. Supplies of fresh fruit and vegetables are limited at the best of times, so you'd do well to bring what you need with you. Self-catering carnivores should also bring a coolbox of fresh meat, as there is no butcher.

ACCOMMODATION AND EATING

Ericusa Hotel ☎ 090 988 9902, ⊛ alicudihotel.it. A modern twelve-room hotel of little architectural charm, a 5min walk south of the port along the shore. Compensating are sea views, spacious terraces and a restaurant. Closed Oct–May. Offers half board only; rates are per person. From €75
Casa Mulino ☎ 090 988 9681, ⊛ alicudicasamulino.it. Small apartments with cooking facilities and rooms with terraces sleeping two, four or six people. Rooms €80; apartments €100
Da Rosina Alla Mimosa Via Vallone 3 ☎ 090 988 9937 or ☎ 368 361 6511, ⊛ rosina-barbuto.it. Named after a huge mimosa tree that was uprooted by a recent tornado, the glassed-in terrace of this *agriturismo* (decorated with abundant artificial flowers) is the best place to eat in Alicudi. Virtually everything is produced or – in the case of rabbit and fish – caught by the family: a raisiny rough red wine, good olive oil, fruit, vegetables and meat (cows and sheep are grazed way up the mountain, goats and rabbits run wild,

chickens are free-range). In autumn there are wild mushrooms, and from autumn to spring wild pickings such as fennel and borage. Menus are set (€25 per head); a typical dinner would include an *antipasto* of grilled vegetables or frittata (with ricotta and borage if you're lucky), pasta, grilled meat or fish, salad and fruit. There are also a handful of simple rooms to rent. No credit cards. Closed Oct–March, though open on request at other times. €60
Signore Silvio Taranto Via Regina Elena snc ☎ 090 988 9922. It's well worth calling in on Signore Taranto, who lives up the hill behind the Siremar office (anyone can point you in the right direction). He cooks dinner on request – spaghetti, fresh fish, salad, fruit and wine – for around €25 a head, served on his bougainvillea-covered terrace in the company of whoever else happens to turn up, which in summer will include other tourists, in winter a motley array of builders, technicians, doctors and others who come to the island to work. Daily dinner only.

HIKING ON ALICUDI

Most of Alicudi's **hiking** is up stepped tracks that seem to have been designed with giants in mind, so be prepared for a good deal of calf-work. If you don't fancy hauling yourself to the top of the island (675m; 2hr), you'll still get plenty of exercise climbing up to the church of **San Bartolomeo**, where controversy rages over the removal of a statue of the saint to a more easily accessible church lower down the hill (it is said that since the statue was moved, the island has had bad luck). Otherwise, follow the path north out of the port behind the church of the Carmine from where it's an easy walk to the narrow stony beach of **Bazzina**, with a couple of smallholdings behind it.

Messina, Taormina and the northeast

TEATRO GRECO, TAORMINA

Messina, Taormina and the northeast

With its dramatic backdrop of mountains, Sicily's northeastern corner includes the island's most visually exotic coastline, crammed with brilliant displays of vegetation. With beaches of fine quartz shingle, the coast is also dominated by an almost unbroken ribbon of development, for this is one of Sicily's most popular resort areas, with both Italian and foreign tourists lured by the stunning views down to a cobalt sea. Once the decadent retreat of D.H. Lawrence and Oscar Wilde, Taormina is now the most illustrious resort on the entire island, and its famous ancient theatre, grand hotels and engaging small-town charm captivate most visitors. The local beaches are all a short ride below town, including the extensive sands that line the curving bay at Giardini-Naxos.

It's **Messina**, just across the busy Straits from mainland Italy, that's the major city in this region, though an unfortunate history has left only scant attractions. Inland, you can leave the crowds behind in the venerable old hill-villages of **Savoca** and **Forza d'Agrò**, where many scenes from the *Godfather* films were shot, as well as taking in the area's most gruesome attraction – the mummified bodies on display in Savoca's Cappuccini monastery. Further south, beyond Taormina, the **Alcantara valley** with its spectacular gorge is the best target hereabouts for those seeking outdoor adventure – while beguiling, unspoilt **Castiglione di Sicilia** is the hill-town most likely to pull at the heartstrings of those yearning to begin a new life in rural Sicily.

GETTING AROUND   MESSINA, TAORMINA AND THE NORTHEAST

By bus Fast buses are the most convenient link between Messina and Milazzo. Travelling south down the coast, local buses get snarled up in the succession of towns and villages along the coast – an excruciatingly slow ride passing pretty much nowhere you would want to stop (or even see). Far better to take one of the fast buses via the autostrada whenever you can.

By train Palermo-bound trains running west from Messina stop at Milazzo and Capo d'Orlando. The line traces the shoreline pretty much all the way, allowing sparkling views across to Calabria on a clear day.
By road The toll autostradas (the A18 south and A20 west) are the fastest way to get around the northeast, plunging through some fairly dramatic scenery as they cruise above the sea.

Messina

MESSINA may well be your first sight of Sicily, and from the ferry it's a fine one, stretching out along the seaboard, north of the distinctive hooked harbour from which the city took its Greek name – Zancle (Sickle). The natural beauty of its location, looking out over the Straits to the forested hills of Calabria, is Messina's

VARA AT MESSINA FERRAGOSTO

Highlights

❶ Messina by night Climb the Via Panoramica to the floodlit sanctuary of Cristo Re for magical views over the lights of the city and the Straits to mainland Italy. **See p.159**

❷ Ferragosto The Vara, an opulent silver scaffolding mounted on iron skis showing the Madonna ascending to Heaven, is hauled through the streets of Messina's historic centre. **See p.164**

❸ Savoca This hill-village offers a gruesome set of mummified bodies and the chance to scope out locations from *The Godfather* movies. **See p.165**

❹ Teatro Greco, Taormina The island's most dramatically sited classical theatre makes a superb summer venue for concerts, films, opera and classical Greek dramas. **See p.170**

❺ The Gole dell'Alcantara Wade through the water in the deep gorge of the Alcantara River. **See p.178**

❻ Castiglione di Sicilia Clustered below a castle, this mellow medieval village has a gentle pace of life and great views of Etna. **See p.179**

HIGHLIGHTS ARE MARKED ON THE MAP ON P.156

THE TRIALS AND TRIBULATIONS OF MESSINA

Messina straddles a fault-line which has been responsible for several centuries of catastrophic **earthquakes**. The most devastating occurred in 1783 and 1908; on the latter occasion the shore sank by half a metre overnight and around 80,000 Sicilians lost their lives (plus around 15,000 across the Straits in Calabria). Few Messinese families were untouched by the quake, and almost everyone you meet will have some earthquake story – of miraculous escapes, or of people driven insane by the loss of loved ones and their city – passed down from grand- or great-grandparents.

As if that wasn't enough, the few surviving buildings, along with everything that had been painstakingly reconstructed in the wake of the earthquake, were subsequently the target of **Allied bombardments**, when Messina achieved the dubious distinction of being the most intensely bombed Italian city during World War II.

best point; Shakespeare (who almost certainly never laid eyes on the city) used it as the setting for his *Much Ado About Nothing*. Yet the city itself holds only a few buildings of any historical or architectural interest, dotted along streets that are either traffic-choked or used as racetracks by drivers who rank among the most reckless in Sicily. The unedifying appearance is not entirely Messina's own fault: the congestion is largely the result of the surrounding mountains, which squeeze the traffic along the one or two roads that link the elongated centre with the northern suburbs. Messina's modern aspect is more a tribute to its powers of survival in the face of a record of devastation that's high even by Sicily's disaster-prone standards (see box above). Consequently, the attractions of Messina itself are limited, and can be seen quickly.

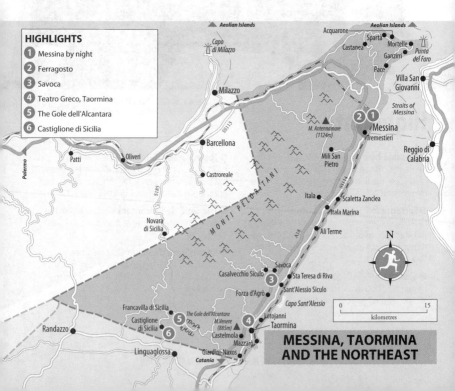

HIGHLIGHTS

1. Messina by night
2. Ferragosto
3. Savoca
4. Teatro Greco, Taormina
5. The Gole dell'Alcantara
6. Castiglione di Sicilia

MESSINA, TAORMINA AND THE NORTHEAST

If you're here in summer, you'll notice the passage of the tall-masted *felucche*, or **swordfish boats**, patrolling the narrow channel, attracted to these rich waters from many kilometres up and down the Italian coast. You can enjoy their catch the same day in the city or a little way north at **Ganzirri**, where gaudy lakeside fish restaurants provide some relief from the city. Beyond, and around the corner of **Punta del Faro**, lidos line the coast at **Mortelle**, whose beaches, bars and pizzerias are where the city comes to relax. Messina's wide remodelled boulevards, the best of them lined with trees and Liberty-style *palazzi*, have a certain bourgeois charm, but much of the city centre is given over to charmless buildings, more or less anti-seismic, depending on the honesty of whoever was responsible for their construction. The treasure-trove of art contained in the **Museo Regionale** makes up for what the rest of the city lacks.

The Duomo

Piazza del Duomo • Mon–Fri 9am–7pm, Sat & Sun 9am–noon & 3.30–7.30pm

Messina's most important monument, the **Duomo**, epitomizes the city's phoenix-like ability to re-create itself from the ashes of its last disaster. It's the reconstruction of a twelfth-century cathedral erected by Roger II, one of a series of great Norman churches that included the sumptuous cathedrals of Palermo and Cefalù. Formerly, the building dominated medieval Messina, and was the venue for Archbishop Palmer's marriage of Richard the Lionheart's sister Joan to the Norman-Sicilian king, William II. Devastated by the earthquake in 1908, it was rebuilt in the years following World War I, only to fall victim to a firebomb in 1943 that reduced it once more to rubble. What you see today is mostly a faithful copy, which took years to complete, with few elements remaining of the original fabric.

The Romanesque facade is its best aspect, the lower part mostly authentic and dominated by a richly decorated, late Gothic **central portal**, extravagantly pointed and flanked by two smaller contemporary doors. Almost everything in the undeniably grand **interior** is a reproduction, from the marble floor to the elaborately painted wooden ceiling. Two rows of sturdy columns line the nave, topped by cement capitals faithfully copied from originals, some of which survive in the Museo Regionale. The **mosaic work** in the three grand apses holds most interest, though it pales into insignificance beside the island's other examples of the genre, and only the mosaic on the left – of the Virgin Mary with St Lucy – is original. All the same, try to find someone to switch on the lights, as the mosaics then take on a majesty that's entirely lost in the gloom that normally shrouds the cathedral's interior. Little else here predates the twentieth century, apart from some salvaged tombs, most handsome of which is that of Archbishop de Tabiatis from 1333, on the right of the altar and heavily graffitied.

4

MESSINA'S ROARING CLOCKTOWER

The Duomo's detached **campanile**, or belltower, claims to be the largest astronomical clock in the world, and puts on its best show at noon every day, when a bronze lion (Messina's ancient emblem) unleashes a mighty roar over the city – quite alarming if you're not expecting it. On the side facing the cathedral two dials show the phases of the planets and the seasons, while above them a globe shows the phases of the moon. The elaborate panoply of moving gilt figures facing the piazza, activated on the hour, half-hour and quarter-hour, ranges from representations of the days of the week and the four Ages of Man to Dina and Clarenza, two semi-legendary women who saved the city from a night attack by the Angevins during the Wars of the Vespers.

You can climb to the top of the tower to enjoy a great **view** of the piazza and city (mid-April to mid-Sept Mon–Sat 9am–1pm & 4.30–6.30pm, Sun 10am–1pm & 4.30–6.30pm; mid-Sept to Oct Mon–Sat 9am–1pm, Sun 10am–1pm; Nov to mid-April Sun 10am–1pm; €3.50, or €5 including the tesoro).

The tesoro

Aug daily 9.30am–1pm & 4–7.30pm, other times usually Mon–Sat 9.30am–1pm • €3.50, or €5 including campanile

The Duomo's **tesoro** holds precious reliquaries, highlight of which is the *Manta d'Oro* – a holy adornment designed to "dress" an icon of the Madonna and Child on special occasions, festooned with jewellery donated by aristocrats and royalty. In a similar decorative vein is the Stendardo banner, designed to be carried in sacred processions and encrusted with brooches, rings, chains, necklaces and even watches.

MESSINA

SHOPS
| Oviesse | 2 |
| Salumeria Nucita | 1 |

CAFÉS
| Billé | 6 |
| Irrera | 7 |

RESTAURANTS
Le Due Sorelle	1
Fratelli La Bufala	4
Al Gattopardo	8
Osteria Etnea	2
Al Padrino	9
Shawarma	3
Trattoria del Popolo	5

ACCOMMODATION
Blu Mediterranea	1
Lepanto	2
Messina Guest House	5
Sole Luna	3
Town House Messina	4

MESSINA BY NIGHT

Messina can be particularly beautiful by **night**, especially from the high **Via Panoramica** – from here, with the city at your feet, there's a long, sparkling view across to mainland Italy. Via Panoramica changes its name along its route west of the centre from Viale Gaetano Martino to Viale Principe Umberto and Viale Regina Margherita. From the centre, the closest sections of this route are the Viale Principe Umberto and Viale Regina Margherita stretch, where there are bars and pizzerias around two floodlit sanctuaries (Cristo Re and Montalto) and plenty of scope for pleasant evening strolling.

Fontana di Orione

Piazza del Duomo

In front of the cathedral, the graceful **Fontana di Orione** was daintily carved in the mid-sixteenth century by Montorsoli, a Florentine pupil of Michelangelo. The fountain depicts Orion, the city's mythical founder, surmounting a collection of cherubs, nymphs and giants, and surrounded by four figures (representing the rivers Nile, Ebro, Camaro and Tiber) reclining along the balustrade. The upper part was carefully restored after earthquake damage in 1908.

Chiesa Annunziata dei Catalani

Via Garibaldi 111 • Usually Mon–Sat 9.30–11.30am, but often closed; call to check • ☎ 090 675 175

Just back from the Duomo, the truncated section of the twelfth-century **Chiesa Annunziata dei Catalani** squats below pavement level, and is Messina's only surviving example of Arab/Norman church-building. The blind arcading around the apses and the Byzantine-style cupola are the perfect antidote to the ugly cement **facade** surrounding its three portals, and the **interior** is suitably simple, with the transept and apse true to their original construction. In front, a martial statue by the sculptor Andrea Calamecca (Calamech) stands half-hidden under the trees, depicting a proud Don Giovanni of Austria, victor of the Battle of Lepanto (the victorious Christian fleet sailed from Messina in 1535).

4

The harbour

Messina is one of Sicily's major ports, and the city is at its most atmospheric down by the **harbour**, with its combination of constant activity and compelling vistas over the Straits. Sicily's deepest natural harbour is a port of call for freighters and cruisers of all descriptions, as well as for frequent NATO warships. But the greatest traffic consists of ferries, endlessly plying back and forth, which are Sicily's chief link with the mainland.

Museo Regionale

Via della Libertà 465 • Tues–Sat 9am–7pm (last entry 6.30pm), Sun 9am–1pm (last entry 12.30pm) • €3 • ☎ 090 361 292, ⓦ www.regione.sicilia.it • Tram #28 to the terminus, Annunziata, or a 45min walk along Via della Libertà; the museum lies on the left, immediately after the Regina Margherita hospital

Messina's **Museo Regionale** is a repository for some of the city's greatest works of art, many of them carefully rescued from earthquake rubble, and includes what is perhaps Sicily's finest collection of fifteenth- to seventeenth-century art. A much larger museum building is being built next door, where the collection is due to be transferred (ring for an update): until then, the layout of the museum is as described below. In addition, many more items will be displayed in the new building, including an ethereal statue of the *Madonna and Child*, attributed to Francesco Laurana, and a collection of mainly ecclesiastical silverware, an art at which Messina once excelled.

The displays

The collection starts with some lovely Byzantine work, larded with a good helping of Gothic, well evident in a fourteenth-century triptych of the *Madonna with Child between Saints Agatha and Bartholomew*, and a remarkably modern-looking wooden crucifix from the fifteenth century, with a sinuous, tragic Christ. The highlight is **room 4**, which holds marvellous examples of fifteenth-century art, notably the museum's most famous exhibit, the *St Gregory* polyptych, by Sicily's greatest native artist, **Antonello da Messina** – a masterful synthesis of Flemish and Italian Renaissance styles that's a good example of the various influences that reached the port of Messina in the fifteenth century. The statue of *Scilla*, the classical Scylla who terrorized sailors from the Calabrian coast (as described in Homer's *Odyssey*), is on display in **room 6** – an alarming spectacle, with contorted face and eyes awash with expression. Sculpted by Montorsoli in 1557, it was once adjoined to an imperious figure of Neptune in the act of calming the seas, a copy of which stands on the seafront just up from the hydrofoil terminal. Also here are a couple of large shadowy canvases by **Caravaggio**, commissioned by the city in 1609, the better of which is the atmospheric *Raising of Lazarus*. The last room on the ground floor has a monstrous ceremonial carriage from 1742, hauled out for viceregal and other high-ranking visits. Though faded and tarnished, its gilt bodywork is still awesomely grandiose, showing an impressive array of detail.

ARRIVAL AND DEPARTURE
MESSINA

BY TRAIN

Train stations Arriving by train, disembark at Stazione Centrale, Piazza della Repubblica, unless you're coming on the train ferry from the mainland, in which case you might as well get off at the Stazione Marittima – even if you're changing trains, as it takes a good hour to reassemble trains from the ferry – and walk 100m on to the Stazione Centrale. If arriving from elsewhere in Sicily, with a hydrofoil or ferry to catch, get off at Stazione Centrale and walk along the platform to the Stazione Marittima. The hydrofoil dock is straight across the road from the station entrance. Allow 10min on foot if you have luggage. On no account take a taxi from outside the station – drivers will attempt to charge €15.

Destinations Catania (1–2 hourly; 1hr 30min–2hr); Cefalù (12 daily; 2–3hr); Milan (8–10 daily, most with change at Villa S. Giovanni and Rome; 11hr–17hr 45min); Milazzo (10–14 daily; 20–35min); Naples (7–10 daily, most with change at Villa S. Giovanni; 5–7hr); Rome (10 daily, most

with change at Villa S. Giovanni; 7–10hr); Palermo (8–11 daily; 2hr 30min–4hr); Taormina (1–2 hourly; 40min–1hr 10min).

BY BUS

Bus terminus Piazza della Repubblica is where most of the local and long-distance buses arrive and depart, including buses to Milazzo for the Aeolian Islands.

Destinations Barcellona (1–2 hourly Mon–Sat; 1hr–1hr 30min); Capo d'Orlando (12 daily Mon–Sat; 1hr 15min–1hr 45min); Catania (11–19 daily Mon–Sat, 8 daily Sun; 1hr 35min); Catania airport (9–15 daily Mon–Sat, 8 daily Sun; 1hr 50min); Forza d'Agrò (1 daily Mon–Sat; 1hr 35min); Giardini-Naxos (8–9 daily Mon–Sat; 45min–2hr); Milazzo (fast service hourly Mon–Sat, 3 daily Sun; 50min); Naples (2 daily; 6hr 30min–7hr); Palermo (4–8 daily Mon–Sat, 4 daily Sun; 2hr 40min); Patti (1–2 hourly Mon–Sat; 1hr–1hr 20min); Rome (3 daily; 9hr–9hr 20min); Santa

---

MESSINA BUS COMPANIES

AST ☎090 662 244 or ☎840 000 23, ⊛azienda sicilianatrasporti.it. Departing from Piazza della Repubblica for Barcellona and Patti.

Giuntabus ☎090 675 749, ⊛giuntabustrasporti .com. Departing from Piazza della Repubblica 52 for Milazzo.

Interbus ☎090 661 754, ⊛interbus.it. Departing from Piazza della Repubblica 6 for the coast south to Letojanni and Taormina.

Jonica ☎090 771 400, ⊛insicilia.com. Departing Autosilo Cavallotti (for Forza d'Agrò, Itala, Santa Teresa

di Riva and Savoca.

SAIS Autolinee ☎090 771 914, ⊛saisautolinee.lt. Departing from Piazza della Repubblica 6 for Palermo, Catania and Catania airport, also regular connections to Umbria, Tuscany, Bologna and Milan.

SAIS Trasporti ☎091 617 1141, ⊛saistrasporti.it. Departing from Piazza della Repubblica for Catania, Naples and Rome.

TAI/Magistro ☎090 675 184, ⊛autolineetai.it. Departing from Via Santa Maria Alemanna, near the train station for Capo d'Orlando, Patti and Tindari.

Teresa di Riva (13 daily Mon–Sat; 1hr); Taormina (5–8 daily Mon–Sat, 2 daily Sun; 1hr 45min).

BY FERRY

Arrivals and tickets Ferries from Villa San Giovanni dock at the Stazione Marittima, apart from Caronte ferries which pull in further up, adjacent to Via della Libertà (10min walk north along the harbour). All tickets across the Straits are on sale at the respective terminals; for Villa San Giovanni, contact Caronte (☎ 800 627 414, ⓦ carontetourist.it) or the train ferry Bluvia, which also takes foot passengers (☎ 090 678 6478, ⓦ rfi.it).

Destinations Salerno (1–2 daily; 8hr); Villa San Giovanni (Bluvia 1–2 hourly, Caronte every 20min or every 40–60min at night; 20–30min).

BY HYDROFOIL

Arrivals and tickets Hydrofoils (from the Aeolian Islands, Villa San Giovanni and Reggio di Calabria) dock at the terminal in the port area signposted "aliscafi". If you're driving, follow the signposts from the autostrada. There is one hydrofoil daily to Reggio di Calabria and the Aeolian Islands throughout the year, and several daily in summer (mid-June to mid-Sept). Tickets to Reggio di Calabria, Villa San Giovanni and the Aeolians are on sale at the hydrofoil terminal (☎ 0923 873 813). Timetables and online booking are available at ⓦ metromaredellostretto.it or ⓦ usticalines.it.

Destinations Lipari (5 daily June to mid-Sept, 1 daily mid-Sept to May; 1hr 20min–3hr 25min); Panarea (3 daily June to mid-Sept; 2hr 5min); Reggio di Calabria (15 daily; 15–25min); Santa Marina Salina (4 daily June to mid-Sept, 1 daily mid-Sept to May; 2hr–2hr 45min); Stromboli (3 daily June to mid-Sept; 1hr 25min); Villa San Giovanni (14 daily; 20min); Vulcano (3 daily June to mid-Sept, 1 daily mid-Sept to May; 1hr 20min–2hr 50min).

BY CAR

Getting to the centre Driving into Messina, leave the autostrada at the Boccetta exit for the centre and ferries (which are fairly well signposted).

Car rental Avis, Via Garibaldi 109 (☎ 090 679 150); Maggiore, Via Vittorio Emanuele II 75 (☎ 090 675 476); Sicilcar, Via Garibaldi 187 (☎ 090 46 942).

BY PLANE

Aeroporto dello Stretto The nearest airport is on the mainland outside Reggio di Calabria, on the other side of the Straits (☎ 0965 640 517, ⓦ sogas.it). There's a year-round bus service linking the airport with Reggio's port.

GETTING AROUND

By tram You can walk easily from the station or harbour to the centre of town, but to venture anywhere further, take the city's single tram line (#28), running between Annunziata in the north (for the Museo Regionale) to Gazzi in the south, with departures from Piazza della Repubblica, Piazza Cairoli and Piazza Municipio every 10min (30min on Sun).

By bus Useful routes include the #79 to Ganzirri, and the #81 (*barrato*) to Ganzirri and Mortelle, which you can pick up on Via 1 Settembre.

Bus and tram tickets All city buses and trams are run by ATM (☎ 090 228 5263, ⓦ www.atmmessina.it), with tickets (€1.25 valid 90min; €1.70 valid 2 journeys per day, or €2.60 all day) available at *tabacchi* and from Autosilo Cavallotti, the terminal for most services.

Taxis Ranks at Piazza Cairoli (☎ 090 293 4880), Piazza della Repubblica, outside Stazione Centrale (☎ 090 673 703), and at the Caronte terminal; there's also a 24hr radio taxi (☎ 090 6505).

INFORMATION

Tourist information The main tourist office is just outside Stazione Centrale on Piazza della Repubblica (Mon & Wed 9am–1.30pm & 3.30–6.30pm, Tues & Thurs 9am–1.30pm & 3–5pm, Fri 9am–1.30pm; ☎ 090 672 944), where good English is spoken.

Travel agents Albertours, right opposite the train station at Piazza della Repubblica 25 (☎ 090 712 035), sells all air, rail and sea tickets.

ACCOMMODATION

Blu Mediterranea Viale Libertà 341 ☎ 090 914 8777, ⓦ blumediterraneobb.com. Three vibrant, pristine rooms in an apartment a little out of town, overlooking the Straits. Though there are no views from the rooms, there is a pleasant inner courtyard (with shower) and Messina's nearest lido is a 10min walk away. There is a tram stop right outside, so whizzing in and out of the centre is easy. **€65**

Lepanto Via Lepanto 7 ☎ 090 669 528, ⓦ bedandbreakfastmessina.com. Five rooms in a Liberty *palazzo* overlooking the Catalana church, close to the Duomo, so an excellent location for anyone coming to Messina for a touch of sightseeing. Rooms are comfortable and traditionally furnished, and breakfast is served on site. **€75**

Messina Guest House Via Reitano Spadafora 1 ☎ 090 958 6266, ⓦ guesthousemessina.it. Smart, stylish B&B occupying the first floor of an apartment on the

4

CROSSING THE STRAITS FROM THE MAINLAND

Crossing the **Straits of Messina** is arguably the most evocative entry into Sicily. The main embarkation point is **Villa San Giovanni**, but you can also travel by hydrofoil from **Reggio di Calabria**, 12km further south towards the tip of Italy's boot.

Caronte also operates a ferry service direct to Messina **from Salerno**, 77km south of Naples, leaving once or twice daily all year and taking eight hours; fares are €20 for foot passengers, more for an armchair or berth, and €43 for a car.

TRAVELLING FROM VILLA SAN GIOVANNI

From **Villa San Giovanni** there are two **ferry** services, the state-railway-run Bluvia (☎090 678 6478, ⓦrfi.it) and the private firm Caronte (☎800 627 414, ⓦcarontetourist.it), and one hydrofoil (*aliscafo*) service, Metromare (☎0923 873 813, ⓦmetromaredellostretto.it).

Drivers should follow signs from the Villa San Giovanni autostrada exit, a straightforward run with ferry ticket offices clearly marked. The most frequent service is operated by Caronte, which has two ticket kiosks en route to the port; the second one, past the railway, can be a bit of a scramble, with nowhere to park. The FS/Bluvia ticket office lies across the square from here, with plenty of parking space. **Tickets** are €37 for a car one-way, or a day-return including three passengers; returns valid for 90 days cost €73 (including three passengers), three-day returns €42 (including three passengers). The queue for boarding involves an average wait of around 15min – even in the peak times of August and rush hour, it's rarely more than 25min.

Travelling **by train**, you might want to stay on it if you're crossing at night (though you'll probably be woken by the clanking din as the train is loaded onto the Bluvia ferry), but by day it's quicker to leave the train at Villa San Giovanni station and skip the shuttling operation, boarding an earlier ferry by foot. In this case, follow the signs from the platform and descend to sea level, where there are ticket offices for Bluvia ferries (one-way tickets €1.50) and Metromare hydrofoils (€2.50). Overhead signs tell you which bay leads to the first departure, or follow everyone else. There are enough Bluvia ferries (1–2 an hour) to make it unnecessary to walk the 500m to the Caronte ferries; hydrofoil departures are roughly hourly (Sat & Sun 4–5 daily).

Journey time for crossings is 20–40min on Bluvia and Caronte ferries; hydrofoils take 20min. On ferries, a bar on board serves snacks (including some good *arancini*), coffee and refreshments. Drivers might as well leave their vehicles, though look sharp as the ferry approaches Messina, as disembarkation is a rushed affair (and a suitable introduction to driving in Messina).

TRAVELLING FROM REGGIO DI CALABRIA

From Reggio di Calabria to Messina, there are **hydrofoil** services from the port, a couple of hundred metres back from Reggio Lido station, operated two or three times daily by Ustica Lines (☎346 011 6552, ⓦusticalines.it) and roughly hourly (Sat & Sun 5 daily) by Metromare, taking about 15min and 30min respectively. Tickets cost €3.50. Meridiano Lines (☎0965 810 414, ⓦmeridianolines.it) runs a **car ferry service** from Reggio di Calabria to Messina, departing on Saturday only. The crossing takes 40min and tickets, costing just €15 per car including passengers, can be bought before departure from the kiosk at the port.

---

boulevard-like Corso Europa. Rooms are soundproofed, with custom-made contemporary dark-wood fittings and furniture, contrasting with creamy upholstery and soft furnishings, and there are prints on the walls by local artist Felice Canonico, a pupil of Guttuso. Bathrooms are spacious with fabulous showers. **€80**

Sole Luna Via Solferino 9 ☎328 678 7901, ⓦbbsoleluna.info. In a perfect location, on a little street between Viale San Martino and Via Garibaldi, just a hop and a skip from both the hydrofoil port and Piazza Cairoli, this cheerfully decorated little B&B has three rooms, one of

them with a spacious, sheltered balcony. It is cosy, and spotlessly clean, with nice bathrooms, and free wi-fi. Breakfast is in a nearby bar. **€65**

Town House Messina Via Giordano Bruno 66 ☎090 293 6097, ⓦtownhousemessina.it. Bijou B&B just off Piazza Cairoli, with gently minimalist rooms decorated in shades of white, grey and mink, fabulous bathrooms (including one with a sexily exposed glass shower) and a changing selection of contemporary art on the walls. Breakfast is at *Billé* (see opposite). The word is out, so it can be difficult to get a room. All rooms have free wi-fi. **€90**

EATING AND DRINKING

Messina has a good range of inexpensive **restaurants**, though you should head away from the port and Piazza Cairoli for a more relaxed atmosphere. If you're here in early summer, make a point of sampling the local **swordfish**; May and June are the height of the swordfish season. The streets around Piazza Lo Sardo (also known as Piazza del Popolo) hold a good mix of rough-and-ready trattorias and more serious eating places, while the area around Piazza Cairoli is best for **bar life**, though some of the bars close in August when everyone's at the beach.

CAFÉS

Billé Piazza Cairoli 7 ☎ 090 240 3059. One of Piazza Cairoli's two long-established cafés – both of them Messina institutions. Good range of *cornetti* and other pastries for breakfast, savouries for lunch and cakes for tempting afternoon teas. There are seats outside across the road in the piazza – though service is not always up to scratch. Mon & Wed–Sun 7.30am–11pm, later on Fri and Sat.

Irrera Piazza Cairoli 12 ☎ 090 673 823, ☺ irrera.it. Founded in 1910, this historic *pasticceria* makes typical Sicilian biscuits, cakes, pastries, *cornetti* and *cannoli* that are, if anything, even better than at *Billé*, while slick service during lunch (good sandwiches) and the aperitivo hour make this a popular spot throughout the day. Daily 8am–8.30pm.

RESTAURANTS

Le Due Sorelle Piazza Unione Europea 4 ☎ 090 44 720. With only nine tables, this is a small and select trattoria. Specialities such as *padella* – a local version of paella – and *couscous con pesce* cost about €16, with main courses up to €20. Booking advised. Mon–Fri lunch & dinner, Sat & Sun dinner only; closed Aug.

Fratelli La Bufala Corso Vittorio Emanuele 1 ☎ 090 662 513, ☺ fratellilabufala.eu. A branch of the superior Neapolitan pizza chain committed to using no hydrogenated fats, glutamates or GM ingredients. Handy for the hydrofoil dock, it serves up great pizza (with buffalo mozzarella, of course) along with buffalo-meat *secondi* and Campanian wines. Two could eat a pizza and have a glass of wine for less than €20. Daily lunch & dinner.

Al Gattopardo Via Santa Cecilia 184 ☎ 090 673 076. With tables outside on a lovely tree-lined avenue, *Al Gattopardo* is a Messinese institution. The pizzas are some of the best in town (try the Messinese with escarole, mozzarella, anchovies and black pepper; €7), but there are other tempting choices such as raw prawns (€12), *zuppa di cozze* (mussel soup; €9), and a delicious lemon risotto with prawns and *cernia* (grouper; €12). Meat is carefully sourced too, and even includes steaks of Irish Angus (€14). Daily lunch & dinner.

Osteria Etnea Via A Martino 38 ☎ 393 898 7144. Abundant portions and low prices (all dishes €6–12) make this tidy little place near Piazza Lo Sardo popular with locals. The menu is long (specializing in fish) and the service brisk. Mon–Sat lunch & dinner.

★ **Al Padrino** Via S. Cecilia 54–6 ☎ 090 292 1000. This bare, frill-free neighbourhood trattoria specializes in traditional Sicilian fare, such as *maccu* (mashed fava or broad beans), *melanzane al Padrino* (aubergines stuffed with fresh pasta and ricotta) and *pasta con legumi riposata* (pasta with beans, left to rest a while after cooking so that broth thickens and flavour develops), both €6–8. A three-course meal will cost under €20. Mon–Fri lunch & dinner, Sat dinner only.

★ **Shawarma** Via M. Giurba 8 ☎ 090 712 213. Tagines, couscous and a range of potato dishes share menu space with (less recommendable) pizzas at this popular trattoria off Piazza Lo Sardo, with some outdoor seating. Hubble-bubbles and occasional belly-dancing (usually Fri & Sun) add to the atmosphere. You can eat well for under €20. Tues–Sat dinner only.

Trattoria del Popolo Piazza Lo Sardo ☎ 090 671 148. You can eat outside at this friendly trattoria, making the most of the rare calm of this corner of the city. Dishes include *sarde allinguate* (fried sardines dressed with vinegar) and *franceschini* (baby squid fried in breadcrumbs); pasta dishes cost €5–7, mains €6–10. Mon–Sat lunch & dinner; closed late Aug.

4

FOOD SHOPPING IN MESSINA

Messina is renowned for its pastries and biscuits. There's a cluster of classy **pasticcerie**, most notably *Billé* and *Irrera* (see above) on Piazza Cairoli. If you want to try something really local, look out for the *pignolata*, a sugary confection covered with brown or white icing. It is not as delicious as it looks. Oviesse is a convenient **supermarket** for food, clothes and other items on Piazza Cairoli (daily 9am–1pm & 4–8pm), while the lanes running off the square hold smart boutiques and leather shops. For a picnic lunch, tasty panini and other cold snacks are on offer at Salumeria Nucita, an *alimentari* at Via Garibaldi 125 (Mon–Wed & Sat 9am–1pm & 4–8pm, Thurs 9am–1pm).

FERRAGOSTO

If you're in Messina in midsummer, you might catch the festivals around the Feast of the Assumption, or **ferragosto**. Although all the villages on both sides of the Straits hold festivals around this time, with some pretty spectacular fireworks lighting up the sky on any one night, Messina's festivities are grander, beginning around August 12, when two plaster giants (**giganti**) are wheeled around town, and finally stationed near the port opposite the Municipio. These are said to be Messina's two founders, Mata and Grifone, one a white female, the other a burly Moor, and both mounted on huge steeds. On *ferragosto* itself, August 15, another towering carriage, the **Vara**, is hauled through the city centre. It's an elaborate column supporting dozens of papier-mâché cherubs and angels, culminating in the figure of Christ stretching out his right arm to launch Mary on her way to Heaven. This unwieldy construction is towed on long ropes, pulled by hundreds of penitents – semi-naked if they're men, all in white if they're women – and cheered on by thousands of people along the way. The whole thing is a sweaty and frenetic performance, finishing up at Piazza del Duomo, where flowers are thrown out to the crowds, many of whom risk being crushed in the mad scramble to gather these luck-bearing charms. Late at night, one of Sicily's best **firework displays** is held on the seafront near Via della Libertà.

NIGHTLIFE AND ENTERTAINMENT

Exhibitions and classical concerts take place near the port at the church of Santa Maria Alemanna (Via I Settembre), while free **concerts** of light music are staged in Piazza del Duomo in July and August. Though they're not put on every year, July and Aug also see free **film screenings** (usually at 8.30pm), generally in the Villa Mazzini public gardens near the hydrofoil dock, or nearby next to the church of San Giuliano off Via della Libertà, around the Fiera di Messina – though venues may change. If films are showing, arrive early, as these events tend to get crowded. Ask at the tourist office for details of all of the above events.

DIRECTORY

Hospital Ospedale Policlinico, Via Consolare Valeria 1 (☎090 2211); take the tram to the Bonino terminus. For emergencies call ☎113.
Left luggage The office on Platform 1 at the train station (Mon–Fri 6am–4pm, Sat & Sun 6am–2pm) charges €3 per bag for 12hr, then €2 for every subsequent 12hr.
Pharmacy There's an all-night service on a rotating basis: consult any pharmacy window to find out current

farmacie notturne.
Police Carabinieri, Via Nino Bixio (☎112 or 090 771 330); Questura, for the police, Via Placida 2, near Villa Mazzini (☎113 or 090 3661).
Post office Main office at Corso Cavour 138, behind Piazza Duomo (Jan–July & Sept–Dec Mon–Fri 8am–6.30pm, Sat 8am–12.30pm; Aug Mon–Fri 8am–1.30pm, Sat 8am–12.30pm).

North of Messina

Several mountain or coastal destinations, all well worth a visit, are less than thirty minutes from the centre of Messina by bus or car. **Mortelle** is the focus for Messina's bronzed youth in summer, who throng the orderly lidos and sleek bars and pizzerias, filling the air with the screech of motorbikes. Fine sandy **beaches** extend west from here, most easily accessed from such villages as **Acquarone** (also called Acqualadrone). If you're driving, you might wish to follow the high-level **Via Panoramica** north rather than the congested coastal road, which is the route the bus takes; but make a point of taking this lower road – an extension of Via della Libertà – at least once, passing fishermen's houses that back onto short sandy strips in areas that must once have justified their idyllic names of Paradiso, Contemplazione and Pace. In Pace, look out for the British cannons lining the esplanade, pulled out of the Straits where they were sunk during the Napoleonic Wars.

Ganzirri

Buses #79, #80 and #81 run to Ganzirri from Messina

Wedged between a salt lake (where mussels are farmed) and the sea, 10km north of central Messina, is the ramshackle fishing village of **GANZIRRI**. Messinese flock here in summer to eat fresh shellfish, swordfish or whatever else has been hauled in that day by the many boats operating on the lake and in the Straits. It's a pleasant spot for a meal, though prices can be high and quality variable. Bear in mind too that traffic can be hell in the summer – whether you get here by bus or car, expect to spend quite some time in jams. Most of the **trattorias** are squeezed in between the lake and sea, and you can eat outside at nearly all of them.

EATING GANZIRRI

★ **Lilla Currò** Via Lido di Ganzirri 10 ☎ 090 395 064. Signposted on the right side of the lake, it's well worth seeking out *Lilla Currò* for its very reasonably priced, exquisitely cooked seafood dishes – you can enjoy a feast for €25. Booking is essential for evening meals, and service can be slow. No credit cards. Tues–Sun lunch & dinner.

La Sirena di Mancuso At Via Lago Grande 96 ☎ 090 391 268. Fifty metres further up from *Lilla Currò*, *La Sirena di Mancuso* also puts on a very good spread, again at low prices, with lake views from its covered veranda. Lunch & dinner Mon, Tues & Thurs–Sun.

Punta del Faro

Punta del Faro (also called Capo Peloro) is the very tip of Sicily, the nearest point to mainland Italy, and on summer evenings it's the venue for open-air **free films**. The lighthouse here (the *faro*) is dwarfed by one of the two towering electric pylons that flank either side of the Straits. No longer in use (Sicily is now tethered to the mainland electricity grid by underwater cables), the pylons remains a much-loved landmark, decked out with multicoloured lights each Christmas. Here, too, was the whirlpool where the legendary **Charybdis** once posed a threat to sailors – along with the rock of Scylla on the opposite shore – still remembered in the locality's name of Cariddi.

Savoca

Around 30km south of Messina, the small resort of Santa Teresa di Riva is the jumping-off point for the evocatively situated **SAVOCA**. The village sits at the end of a winding 4km run up from the coast, its houses and three churches perched on the cliffsides in clumps, and with a tattered castle (originally Saracen) topping the pile. Two pincer-like streets, Via San Michele and Via Chiesa Madre, reach around to their respective churches, the grandest being the square-towered thirteenth-century **Chiesa**

ON THE GODFATHER TRAIL

Many scenes from Francis Ford Coppola's **Godfather** movies were filmed in Savoca and Forza d'Agrò, both deemed rather more picturesque than Corleone, the actual setting of Mario Puzo's novel. Fans of the film are spoilt for choice when it comes to **guided tours** of locations: key stopoffs are *Bar Vitelli*, which displays a collection of photographs taken during the filming of *Godfather II* – the table where Micheal Corleone sat to ask the *padrone* for the hand of his delightful daughter Apollonia is still in situ. You can also see the Chiesa Madre in the piazza, where they married on screen. The best tours continue to the crows'nest village of **Forza d'Agrò**, perched on a spur of the Peloritani Mountains high above the sea, which featured in the third Godfather movie.

For a tour run by enthusiastic, well-informed English-speaking guides contact Sicily Travel (☎ 360 397 930, ⓦ sicilytourguides.net/Godfather_tour.htm).

Madre. Seated on a tiny ridge between two opposing hills, it's a fine vantage point from which to look down the valley to the sea and across the surrounding hills. Spare a glance, too, at the house next door, lovingly restored and displaying a fifteenth-century stone-arched double window; the house is one of many in the village that have had a facelift as outsiders move in to snap up run-down cottages as second homes. These days, Savoca lies within the Taormina commuter belt and most of the people who live here work elsewhere. That's to its advantage: during the day the streets and hillside alleys are refreshingly empty, and the medieval atmosphere still intact.

Cappuccini monastery

April–Sept Tues–Sat 9am–1pm & 4–7pm, Sun 4–7pm; Oct–March Tues–Sat 9am–1pm & 3–6pm, Sun 3–6pm • Donations requested

Signs in Savoca point you to the **Cappuccini monastery**, whose **catacombs** contain a selection of gruesome mummified bodies. These are the remains of local lawyers, doctors and the clergy: two hundred to three hundred years old, they stand in niches dressed in their eighteenth-century finery, the skulls of less complete colleagues lining the walls above. An added grotesque touch is the green paint with which the bodies have been daubed, the work of vandals and hard to remove without damaging the cadavers. Ask the custodian and you'll probably be shown the church **treasury** as well, which holds a small collection of liturgical books and seventeenth- and eighteenth-century Bibles.

ARRIVAL AND DEPARTURE

SAVOCA

By bus Frequent Jonica buses (Mon–Sat only) connect Messina with Santa Teresa di Riva, from where there are six connections daily to Savoca. From Taormina, take an Interbus service to Santa Teresa and change there for Savoca and Casalvecchio.

EATING AND DRINKING

★ **Bar Vitelli** Piazza Fossia 7 ☎ 334 922 7227. Set in an appealing wood-panelled, stone-flagged eighteenth-century building, this offbeat delight was used as the setting for Michael Corleone's betrothal to Apollonia in *The Godfather*. A few words of Italian might nudge the woman behind the bar into recounting her memories of the shoot – she's something of an expert on all the *Godfather* films. There are numerous mementoes of other episodes in the bar's past inside, and tables under the pergola outside. In summer, the signora will probably persuade you to sample her delicious lemon *granita*, which she makes daily, along with a range of snacks. Daily, usually 8am–8.30pm.

Casalvecchio Siculo

2km from Savoca • Served by bus from Santa Teresa Riva via Savoca

The only road beyond Savoca along the ridge runs the 2km to **CASALVECCHIO SICULO**, which has even better views of the valley from its terraces. There's not much to detain you here, except the quiet village atmosphere, but walk through Casalvecchio and, after about 500m, a rough (signposted) road drops away to the left, snaking down into a lush, citrus-planted valley. It's about a twenty-minute hike to the Norman monastery of **Santi Pietro e Paolo**, gloriously situated on a high bank above the river. Built in the twelfth century, its battlemented facade and double domes are visible from a distance through the lemon groves. Though considered Sicily's best example of Basilian architecture, the church betrays a strong Arabic influence, particularly in the polychromatic patterns of the exterior. If it's locked, there should be someone around in one of the adjacent buildings with a key.

From the church, either head back up to the main road and wait for the return bus to pass, or continue downhill for a longer **walk**, beyond the monastery to the River Agrò. It's about another hour's tramp, alongside the wide (and mostly dry) river bed to Rina, back towards the sea. The main (SS114) coastal road is signposted from Rina, and in another twenty minutes, through a small tunnel, you're back in Santa Teresa di Riva, on the Messina–Catania bus route.

Forza d'Agrò

The nicest spot on the coast south of Messina is the **Capo Sant'Alessio**, where a pinnacle cliff supports a sturdy castle; you can climb up to it, but you can't get in. Four kilometres inland of here, atop a corkscrew road, is **FORZA D'AGRÒ**. Like so many Sicilian villages, it's a breezy place defiantly crumbling all around its mostly elderly inhabitants, and with little left of the Norman **castello** that crowns it. A memorable clamber will take you up to the top: the streets become ever more perilous, and the stone cottages increasingly neglected and held together by rotting spars of wood. The lower parts of the village are better maintained, but not much – shops are tucked into tiny cottage interiors, and a couple of churches are locked and decrepit.

Still, this is close enough to Taormina to attract the tour buses, which deposit their passengers in the village square, where there are a couple of bars to help idle the time away.

ARRIVAL AND DEPARTURE   FORZA D'AGRÒ

By bus Four daily Interbus buses run to Forza d'Agrò from Taormina and Letojanni.

ACCOMMODATION AND EATING

O Dammuseddu Via Heros Cuzari 2 ☎ 0942 98 030. The perfect hill-town restaurant. Go for the abundant house *antipasto*, then follow with a wild mushroom dish, or some herby grilled meat. Expect to spend around €20 for a meal without wine. Tues–Sun lunch & dinner.

Villa Souvenir Viale delle Rimembranze ☎ 0942 721 078. If you're tempted to overnight in Forza d'Agrò, the small and simple *Villa Souvenir* hotel is a reasonable option. It also has a decent restaurant, with half-board deals available on request. **€70**

Taormina

TAORMINA, dominating two grand, sweeping bays from high on Monte Tauro, is Sicily's best-known and classiest resort. Although it has no beach of its own – they are all sited quite a way below town – the outstanding remains of the classical theatre and the sheer beauty of the town's site, framed by a distant Etna, amply compensate. Beloved of writers, artists and celebrities across the decades, it's an expensive place, but the air of exclusivity at least is only skin-deep – at heart, what was once a small hill-village still can't seem to believe its good luck. Much of its late medieval character remains intact, with the one main traffic-free street presenting an unbroken line of aged *palazzi*, flower-decked alleys and intimate piazzas. The downside is that most of the time, and particularly between June and September and at New Year and Easter, Taormina simply seethes as the narrow alleys are filled shoulder-to-shoulder with tourists. Things get a little quieter in winter, and this is also the time when the views of Etna – snowcapped to boot – are incomparably clearer, while the spring brings flamboyant hillside displays of flowering plants and shrubs. Entering Taormina's old centre from Porta Messina, you'll find yourself immediately on the town's axis, Corso Umberto I, magnificently heralded by the turreted **Palazzo Corvaja**.

Palazzo Corvaja

Corso Umberto I • Museo Siciliano di Arti e Tradizioni Popolari Tues–Sun 10am–1pm • €2.60 • ☎ 0942 6101

Palazzo Corvaja began life back in the tenth century as a defensive tower built by the Arabs. The tower still forms the body of the *palazzo*, while in the courtyard, Arab-style ogival windows harmonize perfectly with Gothic elements such as a staircase crowned by a Romeo-and-Juliet-style balcony.

Within Palazzo Corvaja is the chamber where the so-called Sicilian "parliament"– actually a group of Aragonese nobles – met in 1410 to choose the next king. It now houses the tourist office (see p.171) and the engaging **Museo Siciliano di Arti e Tradizioni Popolari**, a collection of quirky folklore items ranging from painted Sicilian carts to cork-and-wax Nativity scenes. One of the highlights is the 25 panel paintings of the 1860s showing people being saved by miraculous intervention from such terrible fates as falling onto a stove or being attacked by cats.

TAORMINA

Monte Tauro

Castello Saraceno

Madonna della Rocca

Lumbi

San Pancrazio

Market

Porta Messina

Bus stop

Teatro Romano

Santa Caterina

Palazzo Corjava & Museo Siciliano de Arte

Palazzo dei Congressi

La Naumachia

San Giuseppe

Torre dell'Orologio

Sant' Agostino

Porta Catania

Duomo

Porta Catania

San Domenico

Giardino Pubblico

SS 114

Stazione Taormina-Giardini

■ **CAFÉS & BARS**

Arco Rosso	2
Bam Bar	1
Daiquiri Lounge	7
Al Grappola d'Uva	3
Morgana Bar	4
Re di Bastoni	5
Wunderbar Café	6

● **RESTAURANTS**

Casa Grugno	9
La Cisterna del Moro	5
Al Duomo	7
Al Giardino	4
Maffei's	8
Mamma Rosa	1
Vecchia Taormina	6
Vicolo Stretto	2
A'Zammara	3

Castelmola (3km)

D.H. Lawrence's Villa

Autostrada

Messina, Catania & Motorway

Giardini-Naxos (2km)

Santa Caterina

Corso Umberto 1 • Daily 9am–8pm

Opposite Palazzo Corvaja, the church of **Santa Caterina** was built almost on top of a small, brick-built odeon, known as the **Teatro Romano** (originally used for musical recitations): peer down at it through the railings around the back, and then enter the church to take a closer look at bits of the theatre exposed in the floor of the nave.

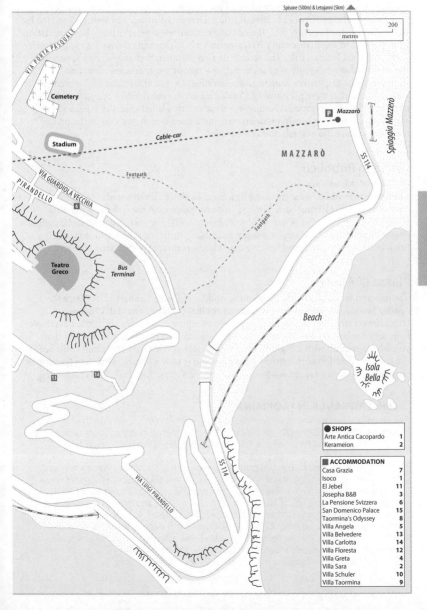

Teatro Greco

Via del Teatro Greco • Daily 9am–1hr before sunset • €8

The crowds flowing from Piazza Vittorio Emanuele past an unbroken parade of tourist shops will point you towards Taormina's **Teatro Greco**, one of Sicily's unmissable sights – and best visited in the early morning or near closing time to avoid the throngs. Nothing, however, can detract from the site's natural beauty. Carved out of the hillside, the theatre gives a complete panorama of the Sicilian coastline, the mountains of southern Calabria across the water and of snowcapped Etna – a glorious natural backdrop for the audiences of classical times. Despite its name, and though founded by Greeks in the third century BC, the existing remains are almost entirely Roman, dating from the end of the first century AD, a period when Taormina enjoyed great prosperity under Imperial Roman rule. The reconstruction completely changed the character of the theatre, though not always for the better – the arched apertures, niches and columns of the impressive Roman scene-building, for example, must have obscured the views of Etna that were presumably a major reason for the theatre's original siting. As the spectacles of the Imperial Roman era were strictly gladiatorial, the stage and lower seats were cut back to provide more room, and a deep trench was dug in the orchestra to accommodate the animals and combatants.

Giardino Pubblico

Via Bagnoli Croce • Daily dawn–dusk • Free

The **Giardino Pubblico** were endowed by a Scot, Florence Trevelyan, who settled in Taormina in 1899 having been "invited" to leave England in the wake of a romantic liaison with the Prince of Wales, the future Edward VII. She also contributed the curious *apiari* ("beehives") – pavilions, variously resembling rustic log cabins and stone- or brick-built pagodas, and now holding caged birds, plants and a children's play area.

Piazza IX Aprile

Tourists and locals all collide bang in the middle of Corso Umberto I at **Piazza IX Aprile**, Taormina's "balcony". The restored twelfth-century Torre dell'Orologio (clocktower) straddles the Corso here, while sweeping views from the terrace overlook Etna and the bay. It's hard to resist the lure of a café seat here – just be warned that you'll be presented with a big bill, even for an *espresso*. There are two small churches in the square: squat fifteenth-century **Sant'Agostino** is now a library, while **San Giuseppe**'s seventeenth-century facade is adorned with plaques depicting skulls and crossbones.

> ### D.H. LAWRENCE IN TAORMINA
>
> If you've got twenty minutes to spare you could turn literary sleuth to see the villa in which **D.H. Lawrence** lived for three years in the 1920s – though there's nothing to see except the back of a house. From Porta Messina, follow Via Cappuccini and then Via Fontana Vecchia, before dropping down to Piazza Franz Pagano. Following the road around a steep left fork – Via David Herbert Lawrence – puts you on the right track for the villa, up the hill and just around the corner. On the right-hand side of the road, the pink- and cream-coloured building, now a private house, is marked by a simple plaque reading: "D.H. Lawrence, English author, lived here 1920–1923". He wrote many of his short stories and essays here, and much of *Lady Chatterley's Lover*, which was supposed to have been inspired by the exploits of an Englishwoman living in Taormina who had fallen for a local farmer. Lawrence wasn't always enamoured of the town; in a letter of December 1921 he described Corso Umberto as "one long parade of junk shops … things dearer than ever, more faked, food tiresome as it always was. If only Etna would send down 60,000,000 tons of boiling lava over the place and cauterise it away."

A WALK TO THE CASTELLO SARACENO

It's well worth taking a walk up above Taormina to the the cliff-top chapel of **Madonna della Rocca** and the remains of the town's tumbledown medieval **Castello Saraceno**. There are glorious views over the theatre and town to the coast, and a couple of restaurants and cafés here that are perfect for a sundowner. Buses taking just a few minutes run up the winding road once or twice hourly from town, but it's more evocative to walk up – there's a steep processional path to the chapel (signposted "Castel Taormina/Via Crucis") from Via Circonvallazione, starting just past the Q8 petrol station, and taking around twenty minutes.

Piazza Duomo

Duomo daily 8.30am–8pm

Taormina's intimate **Piazza Duomo**, set on a quirky slant, makes it very clear just how small-scale Taormina was until fairly recently. Entered via an arch in the clocktower, and with a pretty seventeenth-century fountain in its centre, the square contains the battlemented **Duomo**, originally built in the thirteenth century, though much restored since. The interior is simple – the pink marble columns along the nave are thought to have come from the Greek theatre, while the beamed wooden ceiling is decorated with Arab-Gothic motifs.

ARRIVAL AND DEPARTURE   TAORMINA

By train One of Italy's most attractive stations, in Sicilian-Gothic style with Art Nouveau decoration, Taormina-Giardini train station is way below town, on the water's edge. To get up to town, you either need to take a taxi (around €15) or catch one of the Interbus buses leaving once or twice hourly (fewer on Sun) from outside the station; buy your ticket from the driver.

Destinations Castiglione di Sicilia (6 daily Mon–Sat; 45min–1hr 10min); Catania (1–2 hourly; 45min–1hr); Francavilla di Sicilia (8 daily Mon–Sat, 1 daily Sun; 30–55min); Gole dell'Alcantara (9 daily Mon–Sat, 1 daily Sun; 35–50min); Messina (1–2 hourly; 40min–1hr); Randazzo (4–5 daily Mon–Sat, 1 daily Sun; 55min–1hr 40min); Siracusa (4–7 daily; 2hr–2hr 30min).

By bus Most buses stop in Taormina's bus station on Via

Luigi Pirandello. Buses to the Alcantara and Randazzo leave from outside the train station, while local bus services depart hourly from Piazza San Pancrazio up to Madonna della Rocca (for the castle) and Castelmola, and down to the beach at Spisone/Letojanni.

Destinations Castelmola (hourly Mon–Sat, 9 daily Sun; 15min); Castiglione di Sicilia (2 daily Mon–Sat; 1hr 20min); Catania (1–2 hourly Mon–Sat, 12 daily Sun; 1hr 10min–1hr 50min); Catania airport (15 daily Mon–Sat, 11 daily Sun; 1hr 25min); Forza d'Agrò (2 daily; 40min); Francavilla di Sicilia (3 daily Mon–Sat, 1 daily Sun; 1hr); Giardini-Naxos (1–2 hourly Mon–Sat, every 1–2hr Sun; 15min); Gole dell'Alcantara (4 daily Mon–Sat, 1 daily Sun; 1hr); Messina (6–7 daily Mon–Sat, 2 daily Sun; 55min–1hr 45min); Santa Teresa di Riva (8–9 daily Mon–Sat, 3 daily Sun; 35min).

GETTING AROUND

Taxis There are ranks at the train station (☏ 0942 51 150), at Porta Catania (☏ 0942 628 090), in Piazza San Pancrazio and in Piazza Vittorio Emanuele (☏ 0942 23 000).

Car and scooter rental Avis, Via S. Pancrazio 7

(☏ 0942 23 041); California, Via Bagnoli Croce 86 (☏ 0942 896 203); City, Piazza Sant'Antonio 5 (☏ 0942 23 161); Italia, Via Luigi Pirandello 29 (☏ 0942 23 973); Sicily By Car, Via Apollo Arcageta 4 (☏ 0942 21 252).

INFORMATION AND TOURS

Tourist information There's a small tourist office (Mon–Fri 9am–2pm; ☏ 0942 52 189) in the train station, and another inside Palazzo Corvaja, off Piazza Vittorio Emanuele (Mon–Fri 8.30am–2.15pm & 3.30–7pm; ☏ 0942 23 243, ⊛ gate2taormina.ns0.it). Staff are extremely well informed.

Tours From Taormina, there are lots of tours are offered to Etna, the Alcantara gorge and Siracusa, or further afield to places like the Valley of the Temples and Piazza Armerina, from around €35 for a day for the Alcantara gorge and the Etna foothills to €75 for an Etna summit jeep tour. The tourist office has flyers and brochures.

4

PARKING IN TAORMINA

Unless there's parking at your hotel, drivers will have to use one of the long-stay **car parks** signposted on the approaches to Taormina, notably outside Porta Catania at the southwestern end of town or at the Lumbi car park northeast of the centre; Lumbi car park is further from the centre, and is a lengthy walk up steps to Via Cappuccini, though a free **minibus service** (*bus navetta*) shuttles from Piazza San Pancrazio (just below Porta Messina) to and from the Lumbi car park and saves you the 10min climb. Alternatively, park near the coast at Mazzarò, and take the cable car up to town. **Tariffs** (€5–7 for 2hr 30min, €12.50–16 for 24hr, €20.50–28 for 48hr) are slightly higher at Porta Catania, and higher at all car parks in August.

ACCOMMODATION

Nowhere else in Sicily can match Taormina for its range of gorgeously sited places to stay (many of them elegant old villas) with sweeping views of sea and mountain. Although there are excellent deals to be had online if you book in advance, prices can be steep if you arrive on spec. Drivers should enquire whether their hotel has parking facilities, as otherwise cars have to be left in one of the car parks (see box above). Note that a city tourist tax ranging from €1 to €2.50 per person per night (depending on the category of hotel) will be added to the room rate.

HOTELS

★ **Isoco** Via Salita Branco 2 ☎ 0942 23 679, ⓦ isoco.it. The five rooms in this small boutique hotel are quirkily themed on such artists as Botticelli and Keith Haring, and each has its own entrance, a/c, safe and minibar, with a private bathroom across the corridor. Amazing breakfasts are served round a large table in the shady garden, where there's also a hot tub, while the roof terrace has sunbeds and views extending north up the coast as far as Calabria. Free wi-fi. No credit cards. Closed Dec–Feb. €98

El Jebel Salita Palazzo Ciampoli ☎ 0942 625 494, ⓦ hoteleljebel.com. Taormina's brand-new shrine to conspicuous consumption, its nine suites occupying three floors of a dandified fifteenth-century *palazzo* up from the main corso. Inside it's all very Hollywood-Dubai: lavish bathrooms caked in treacly, liquorice-veined marble, gold taps, claw-foot baths and enough mirrors to make narcissists feel they've died and gone to heaven. The rooms themselves are more subdued, spacious and very comfortable. Service is excellent, and waiter-served breakfasts exceptional. Expect to feel exceedingly (but discreetly) pampered, especially at the spa. Excellent deals via the website. €300

La Pensione Svizzera Via Pirandello 26 ☎ 0942 23 790, ⓦ pensionesvizzera.com. Just up from the bus terminal and cable-car station, this comfortable hotel has lovely views from its spacious rooms (with prices increasing by €5–10 for a sea view), 24hr bar service, free wi-fi throughout and a shuttle to a private beach. Excellent value for money. €115

San Domenico Palace Piazza San Domenico 5 ☎ 0942 613 111, ⓦ thi.it. The last word in luxury, and one of the most celebrated hotels in Italy, housed in a fifteenth-century convent with gorgeous formal gardens, unsurpassable views, a Michelin-starred restaurant and stratospheric prices. Refreshingly, staff are both relaxed

and gracious. Luxuriate in one of the €3000-per-night suites, and you feel you've died and gone to heaven, but do check the website as there are deals on rooms for a fraction of that. Rooms €316

★ **Villa Angela** Via Leonardo da Vinci ☎ 0942 27 038, ⓦ hotelvillaangela.com. Ever wondered what rock stars do in their spare time? Jim Kerr of Simple Minds, a devotee of Taormina, plumped for opening a four-star boutique hotel, high on the Castelmola road above town. It's a swish, contemporary take on a traditional villa, with terrific views from soaring picture windows, a pool and a terrace restaurant. The staff are especially friendly. It's a steep walk from Taormina itself, but there's an efficient shuttle to town and beach, and a bus stop directly outside. €220

Villa Belvedere Via Bagnoli Croce 79 ☎ 0942 23 791, ⓦ villabelvedere.it. Comfortable rooms in soothing pastels, most of them with balconies with fantastic views over the marvellous pool and lavish gardens to Etna and the sea. There are also several garden suites as well as mini-apartments with cooking facilities. Look out for good deals online. Rooms €195; apartments and suites €300

Villa Carlotta Via Pirandello 81 ☎ 0942 626 058, ⓦ hotelvillacarlottataormina.com. Splendidly sited above the sea among abundant subtropical vegetation – the roof garden has spectacular views of Mount Etna and the sea (very romantic and candlelit at night), and a terraced garden with a small pool is set among citrus and olive trees, bougainvillea and mint, lying between the walls of an old chapel and remains of a Romano-Byzantine cemetery. There's a comfortable, homey sitting room with books, games and snooze-inducing sofas, and all the stylish rooms but one have bathtubs. Good deals on the website. €220

Villa Schuler Piazzetta Bastione ☎ 0942 23 481, ⓦ villaschuler.com. This lovely old hotel has been in the same family of German émigrés for a century, and retains

FROM TOP TAORMINA (P.167); ISOLA BELLA (P.177) >

the feel of an elegant family-run *pensione* (they take no tour groups). Decor retains a quiet vintage feel, without being overstated, there are great views from its rooms and terrace, and a beautiful garden behind. Worth checking the website for special offers. **€150**

Villa Taormina Via T. Fazzello 39 ☎ 0942 620 072, ⓦ hotelvillataormina.com. A superior four-star that oozes old-fashioned charm – and with only eight antique-filled rooms, the feel is more private house party than hotel. It's also blessedly quiet, off the main drag, and with a terrace that has a hot tub and excellent views. Check online for the best last-minute deals. Parking and beach shuttle available. Closed Nov–Feb. **€220**

HOSTELS AND B&BS

Casa Grazia Via Iallia Bassia 20 ☎ 0942 24 776, ⓦ casagrazia.com. You won't find accommodation much cheaper than this in the centre, nor with such positively mothering management. Most of the basic but clean rooms have fridges, private bathrooms and balconies – the best ones are at the top, with use of a panoramic terrace. Free wi-fi. No credit cards. **€70**

Josepha B&B Vico Zecca 31 ☎ 0942 628 871 or ☎ 348 844 2971, ⓦ bbtaormina.com. In a little courtyard, through a hacked-out archway immediately inside the Porta Messina, this has two doubles and two singles, sharing two bathrooms. There's also a kitchen, a terrace and laundry facilities for guests. It's pretty flexible, since families or groups can rent all or part of the building.

Breakfast is taken at a nearby bar. No credit cards. **€70**

Taormina's Odyssey Via Paternò di Biscari 13 ☎ 0942 24 533 or ☎ 349 810 7733, ⓦ taorminaodyssey.com. Near Porta Catania, this homely and comfortable place is more of a B&B than a hostel, with four double rooms (some with bunk-beds) and two dorms. All rooms have a/c and TV, and there's a kitchen and even a terrace. It is understandably popular, so book well ahead. Dorms **€20**; bunk-bed doubles **€48**; doubles **€60**

Villa Floresta Via Damiano Rosso 1 ☎ 0942 620 184 or ☎ 331 708 0115, ⓦ villafloresta.it. Pleasant, family-run B&B in a nineteenth-century *palazzo*, tucked into a courtyard with a crumbling fifteenth-century staircase behind Piazza del Duomo. Most rooms have balconies, with a choice between a view of the sea or the Duomo. **€90**

Villa Greta Via Leonardo da Vinci 41 ☎ 0942 28 286, ⓦ villagreta.it. A 15min walk out of town on the road up to Castelmola, this family-run place has superb balcony views, as well as a dining room with good home cooking. In winter, there's tea with complimentary home-made cakes and biscuits. **€108**

★ **Villa Sara** Via Leonardo da Vinci 55 ☎ 0942 28 138, ⓦ villasara.net. This exceptional B&B is a 15min walk (or a brief bus ride) up the road to Castelmola. It doesn't look much from the outside, but behind the bare walls is a gracious two-storey apartment where a friendly family rent out three spacious rooms, each with its own bathroom and large terrace commanding great views over Taormina, Etna and the sea. **€90**

EATING AND DRINKING

Eating out in Taormina can be very expensive, though there are plenty of places offering competitively priced set menus. While there are lots of **restaurants**, menus are pretty standard across the board, although a few at the top end stand out as pretty special. Because of the demand, **pizzas** are widely available here at lunchtime too (unlike most other places in Sicily), usually costing €8–10. Taormina's **cafés** and **bars** are particularly pricey, though. Barring a few chic retreats, Taormina's drinking scene isn't especially exclusive, with people milling around the streets all night in summer, hopping from bar to bar until the small hours. There's also a fairly discreet gay scene, mostly centred on the style bars around Piazza Paladini. At least the buzzing evening *passeggiata* along the Corso is free.

RESTAURANTS

Casa Grugno Via Santa Maria dei Greci ☎ 0942 21 208, ⓦ casagrugno.it. Still finding its feet after the departure

of Michelin-starred chef Andreas Zangerl, but the courtyard remains a lovely romantic place for fine dining. There are three fixed-price menus, at €40, €50 and €60, excluding

---

TAORMINA'S FESTIVALS

Taormina stages **festivals** and parades at Christmas and Carnevale, but summer is the best time for cultural events. Between June and September, **Taormina Arte** (ⓦ gotaormina.com) features a varied theatre, music and dance programme, from rock bands and symphony orchestras to classical dramas, held either at the spectacular Teatro Greco or the Palazzo dei Congressi in Piazza Vittorio Emanuele. Tickets cost from around €15. The events kick off with the **Taormina FilmFest** (ⓦ taorminafilmfest.it), which runs for a week every June, previewing new movies from around the world in their original versions on a big screen at the Teatro Greco (tickets €8–12).

Tickets for all events are available online or at the Palazzo dei Congressi, Piazza Vittorio Emanuele.

SHOPPING IN TAORMINA

Corso Umberto I can lay fair claim to be the flashiest shopping street in southern Italy, and here you'll have no trouble tracking down a Gucci bag, a €10,000 necklace or a genuine Baroque candelabra. Of course, you can also pick up mass-produced ceramic dishes, Sicilian puppets, model Etnas and AC Milan football shirts. The bulk of the out-and-out tourist gift shops are up Via Teatro Greco on the way to the theatre, but for quirkier boutiques and souvenirs, delve into the side alleys and stepped streets off the Corso.

A few outlets are especially worth seeking out. The **ceramic workshop** at Kerameion, Corso Umberto I 198 (daily 9am–8.30pm; closed Sun Nov–March; ☎ 339 207 9032, 🅦 kerameion.com), turns out tiles, plates, vases and espresso cups, among other items. At Corso Umberto I 27, corner Via F. Ingegnere (daily 9am–9.30pm; ☎ 0942 23 544, 🅦 cacopardoarteantica.com), Signor Pancrazio's grandmother first opened the Arte Antica Cacopardo **antiques** store in 1902 (he's got postcards showing her sitting outside it), and he continues to set out the furniture, porcelain and *objets* on the pavement every day, rain or shine.

There's also a daily indoor **market** (Mon–Sat) for fruit and veg off Via Cappuccini, and a weekly **Wednesday market** for household items, above town at Parcheggio von Gloeden, off Via Leonardo da Vinci; both are morning affairs, open till around 1.30pm. The Upim/Punto SMA supermarket (Mon–Sat 9am–1pm & 4–8pm) is outside Porta Catania (and to the right) on Via Apollo Arcageta.

wine. Closed lunchtime; Nov–April closed Sun, also closed Jan & Feb.

La Cisterna del Moro Via Bonifacio 1 ☎ 0942 23 001. This is basically an all-day pizza joint – they are good and crisp – though with the low lights and a bougainvillea-draped terrace it's also a romantic spot for local couples on a night out. Pizzas €6.50–10. Daily noon–midnight; closed Nov.

Al Duomo Vico Ebrei 11 ☎ 0942 625 656, 🅦 ristorantealduomo.it. Pleasant restaurant with a commitment to local ingredients and local dishes such as *maccu* (broad bean soup), lamb stew and pasta with sardines and wild fennel. Mains cost €20–23, and the tasting menu rings in at €60. There's a lovely terrace above the Duomo square and a simple, pretty interior. Daily lunch & dinner; closed Mon Nov–March.

Al Giardino Via Bagnoli Croce 84 ☎ 0942 23 453, 🅦 algiardino.net. With pasta at €8–10 and standard meat and fish dishes from €10, this is what passes for inexpensive in Taormina. It's in an out-of-the-way spot opposite the public gardens, and is usually busy, with amiable and enthusiastic service. Daily lunch & dinner.

★ **Maffei's** Via San Domenico de Guzman 1 ☎ 0942 24 055, 🅦 ristorantemaffeis.com. If you want one really good fish meal, this formal but not overpowering restaurant is the place. From sea bass to lobster, the day's specials (from €18, whole fish €6 per 100g) are written on the board, while oysters, sea urchins, pastas and *carpaccios* are offered as appetizers. English-speaking staff guide you through the menu, and all you can hear on the bougainvillea-covered terrace is the gentle clatter of cutlery and contented murmurs. It's small, so book ahead in the evening. Daily lunch & dinner.

Mamma Rosa Via Naumachia 10 ☎ 0942 24 361. This does a roaring trade in *forno a legna* pizzas (€6.50–10), served at tables spilling down the stepped alley. There's also a full menu, though you'll easily pay €30 a head for a couple of courses and wine. Daily lunch & dinner; closed Tues Nov–Feb.

★ **Vecchia Taormina** Vico Ebrei 3 ☎ 0942 625 589. This bustling pizzeria has a stack of olive wood outside the door for the fire, and tables outside in a sheltered courtyard. Pizzas (from €6.90) are light, crispy, blisteringly hot and also available at lunchtime. Daily lunch & dinner.

Vicolo Stretto Vicolo Stretto 6 ☎ 0942 625 554. Reached up the slimmest of alleys off the Corso, by Piazza IX Aprile, this is a chic place to try "real Sicilian cuisine", from pasta with swordfish and mint to beef in a Nero d'Avola wine sauce; mains range €16–22, though fresh fish is sold by weight (around €6 per 100g). There's a small terrace for eating *al fresco*. Daily lunch & dinner.

★ **A'Zammara** Via Fratelli Bandiera 15 ☎ 0942 24 408, 🅦 azammara.it. Romantic place where you sit in a garden of orange trees eating the likes of home-made *tagliolini* with prawns and pistachios, the latter grown in nearby Bronte (€12.50); or *involtini di pesce spada*, swordfish wrapped around cheese and breadcrumbs (€16). Expect to pay around €40 for a full meal including wine. Daily lunch & dinner; closed Wed Oct–July.

CAFÉS AND BARS

Arco Rosso Via Naumachia 7 (no phone). This proper little old-fashioned bar is quite a rarity. Tucked down steps just off the Corso, it sells wine by the glass or bottle and doesn't charge the earth for it. Scrummy bruschetta and

4

sandwiches too. Mon–Tues & Thurs–Sun 8am–8pm.

Bam Bar Via Di Giovanni 45 ☎0942 24 355. Taormina's no. 1 spot for ice cream and *granitas*, coming in a lip-smacking range of flavours – recommended choices include watermelon, coffee with almond and nutella. The owner will show you photos of all the celebs who have dropped by. Daily 9am–late.

Daiquiri Lounge Piazza Duomo ☎0942 625 703. Specializing (as you might guess) in daiquiris, this pleasant, perfectly located bar makes a nice place for an aperitivo (served with a generous selection of nibbles) or an after-dinner drink. Daily 7pm–late.

Al Grappola d'Uva Via Bagnoli Croce 6–8 ☎0942 625 874. Friendly, unpretentious wine bar – a good place to sample Etna wines with olives and local cheeses as you sip a good glass of wine (€4 including nibbles). They can also organize tours of Etna's vineyards. Daily 11am–late.

Morgana Bar Scesa Morgana 4 ☎0942 620 056. International party place off Corso Umberto I, for serious cocktail consumption. Sexy violet velvet inside, a cool outdoor space, and nightly DJ sets. Daily 7pm–late.

Re di Bastoni Corso Umberto I ☎0942 23 037. Funky, Bohemian pub that is quite alternative for Taormina, and attracts a lively crowd. Daily, usually 6pm–late; closed Mon in winter.

Wunderbar Café Piazza IX Aprile ☎0942 625 302. Once the haunt of Garbo and Fassbinder, this remains Taormina's favoured spot for the see-and-be-seen brigade, with outdoor seats beneath the clocktower and a determinedly elitist pricing policy. The piano is wheeled out every night for ivory-tinkling beneath the stars. Go for an Aperol spritz, and sip it slowly as you people-watch. Daily 9am–late.

DIRECTORY

Hospital Ospedale San Vincenzo, in Via Crocefisso, Contrada Sirina, south of Porta Catania (☎0942 5791; for emergencies ☎0942 579 297).

Pharmacy British Pharmacy, Corso Umberto I 152, corner of Piazza IX Aprile (June–Sept daily 8.30am–9.30pm, Oct–May Mon–Fri 8.30am–1pm & 3.30–8pm; ☎0942 625

735); outside these hours pharmacies operate according to a rota system, indicated on pharmacy doors.

Police Carabinieri, Piazza Vittorio Emanuele 4 (☎0942 23 232 or ☎112).

Post office Piazza Sant'Antonio, outside Porta Catania (Mon–Fri 8am–6.30pm, Sat 8.30am–1pm).

Around Taormina

Taormina is overlooked by the lofty mountain village of **Castelmola**, visited for the superb views in all directions, and an easy trip from town. The **coastline** below Taormina, north and south, is immensely appealing – a mixture of grottoes, rocky coves and good sand beaches – although much of it is either sectioned off as private lidos (which you have to pay to use; prices vary from around €5 to €15 a day) or simply gets very packed in summer. Easiest to reach, by bus or cable car, are the small, stony stretches around **Mazzarò**. For decent expanses of sand you'll have to travel to **Giardini-Naxos**, a 5km, fifteen-minute bus ride south of Taormina. Cheaper and less pretentious than Taormina, it's very much a separate town, with its own holiday trade and nightlife.

Castelmola

Drivers should park in the car park before entering the village; hourly buses from Taormina (15min) stop 200m below the main square. To walk up from the Castello Saraceno (around 1hr), take the signposted concrete path

Some 5km above Taormina, the tiny hill-village of **Castelmola** seems to sprout out of the severe crag beneath it, with just a jumble of precipitous alleys to explore and the remnants of a long-demolished castle. Hardly surprisingly, it is entirely given over to tourism, with souvenir shops and up to a dozen bars and restaurants flanking the cobbles.

Above Castelmola, intrepid hikers can embark on the roughly two-hour climb to the top of **Monte Vénere** (885m), the highest peak hereabouts. The **walk down** from Castelmola is *much* easier than the ascent, and the views are better, too; it's an easy fifteen minutes to Madonna della Rocca, thirty minutes to town.

EATING AND DRINKING **CASTELMOLA**

Bar San Giorgio Piazza Sant'Antonio ☎0942 28 228. This bar in the main square is the doyen of Castelmola, purveying drinks and views for decades, as the old newspaper cuttings in the corner attest. Try a glass of *vino alla mandorla* (almond wine) here, the sweet local brew. Daily, usually 8am–10pm.

Bar Turrisi Piazza Duomo ☎0942 28 181. The decor here is dedicated to the phallus in all its manifestations, and without the slightest hint of irony. The views from the terrace are good too – but probably best not to take the kids. Daily, usually 10am–1am.

Mazzarò

There's a cable-car (*funivia*) service from Taormina to Mazzarò (Mon 8.45am–8pm, Tues–Sun 8am–8pm, until 1am daily in summer; €3, weekly pass €30); the station is on Via Luigi Pirandello, between Porta Messina and the bus terminal

The closest beaches to Taormina are the scintillating pebbled coves at **MAZZARÒ**, which you can reach by cable car (*funivia*) from Via Luigi Pirandello in Taormina. There's also a steep path, which starts just below the cable-car station. Of the two beaches, the southernmost is usually the most packed, fronting its much-photographed islet, the **Isola Bella**, protected as a marine-life sanctuary. The waters are remarkably clear, and you can rent boats, snorkelling and scuba gear down here.

Spisone

Hourly buses from Taormina's Piazza San Pancrazio run to Spisone, passing Isola Bella and Mazzarò on the way; there's also the Linea beach bus, departing from Piazza San Pancrazio (7daily; €1).

A little further north from Mazzarò are the beach bars and restaurants at **SPISONE**, which you can either walk to from Mazzarò (10min) or directly down from Taormina (around 30min); take the path from below the cemetery, off Via Guardiola Vecchia.

Giardini-Naxos

The best sand beaches close to Taormina are those at **GIARDINI-NAXOS**, south of town, where a long strip of sand curves around the wide bay, backed by a busy promenade of bars, cafés, restaurants and hotels. It's much more of a resort in the Italian style than Taormina – packed and noisy until late September each year, and then largely drawing up the shutters until the following spring. Half of the beach is free ("*spiaggia libera*"), although the better sands further around the bay towards the cape are partitioned off as private lidos, complete with sun-loungers, shades, watersports gear, bars and restaurants.

Greek colony excavations

Daily 9am until 1hr before sunset • €3

Significantly, Giardini-Naxos bay was the site of the first **Greek colony** in Sicily. As an obvious stop for ships sailing between Greece and southern Italy, there was a settlement here by 734 BC, named **Naxos** after the Greek island from which the colonists came, though it was never very important. The **excavations** on the site of the ancient settlement lie right on the cape, Capo Schisò, with the entrance right by *La Sirena* restaurant, overlooking the harbour. The remains are disappointingly sketchy, though they stretch across a large area of the cape and it's pleasant to stroll through the olive and lemon groves around the site. There's scarcely any interpretation of what you're seeing – scant foundations of a large, gridded town and a long stretch of ancient, lava-built city wall – and the small museum on site that houses some of the finds doesn't really help either.

4

VISITING THE ALCANTARA GORGE

There are numerous tours to the **Alcantara gorge** on offer in Taormina, but you can do the trip yourself easily enough, as four buses a day (1 on Sun) run out this way from Taormina's bus terminal. It's an hour's ride to the main entrance to the **Gole dell'Alcantara**, where there's a car park, bar and restaurant. The gorge is protected as the Parco Fluviale dell'Alcantara (W parco alcantara.it), but access (daily 9am–sunset) is controlled by the Terralcantara office at the main entrance, where you pay €8 to descend in a lift to the bottom and to follow a geological and botanical itinerary extending for 1.5km above the river. There's also a free public entrance, 200m beyond the main entrance (Francavilla direction), though it's 200 steps down and back. Within the gorge, you can rent waders and wetsuits in summer in order to slosh along the river (it's always icy) through pools and into the main gorge. Terralcantara (T 0942 985 010, W terralcantara .it) organizes **river-trekking and canyoning expeditions** (€18 and €40 respectively) which you can book at the ticket office. Note that the last bus back to Taormina leaves at 6.15pm.

The Alcantara valley

Around 2400 BC, an eruption of the Monte Moia volcano, at the head of the **Alcantara valley**, smothered the river and filled the valley with lava. Over four millennia, the Alcantara river has carved its way through the deposits of slick grey basalt, forming the magnificent gorge, the **Gola di Alcantara**, and scooping the rock into all manner of strange, sculptural formations. It is a lovely drive from Taormina, some 20km to the east, through gentle hills covered with citrus groves, olive trees and wild flowers, and there are a couple of beguiling towns to visit, namely **Francavilla** and, more notably, **Castiglione di Sicilia**. The road through the valley runs over and alongside the river, and the various bridges are a reminder that the name, Alcantara, is a corruption of the Arabic word for bridge.

Francavilla di Sicilia

If you want to escape the crowds at the Alcantara gorge, continue another 4km to the largely modern town of **Francavilla di Sicilia**. Set alongside the river and overlooked by the few surviving walls of its toothy old hillside **castle**, this was the site of one of the bloodiest battles fought in Sicily, when the Austrian army (given logistical support by the British) engaged with the Spanish in 1719, with obvious result apart from the loss of some 8000 lives. There's a path up to the ruins, and although much of the town is newly built there's a fair amount of interest in the couple of old central streets. From below the castle a well-marked path winds down to the river at **La Gurne**, through groves of citrus and nut trees. Here you'll find a series of waterfalls and natural round ponds where you can swim without the crowds.

Convento dei Cappuccini

Easter–Oct daily 11am–1pm & 3.30pm–sunset; in winter call ahead as hours vary • €2.50 • T 0942 981 017 or T 338 941 8324

Taking the signposted right turn as you approach Francavilla di Sicilia, you might drop in to the **Convento dei Cappuccini** that peers over town and river, where a modest little **museum** shows how the monks – now reduced to two – passed their time in baking, brewing and crafting. You can also inspect the herbarium and buy some of their honey, perfumes or almond- or lemon-flavoured liqueurs.

ACCOMMODATION   **FRANCAVILLA DI SICILIA**

Hotel d'Orange d'Alcantara Via dei Mulini T 0942 981 374, W hoteldorange.it. On the way into Francavilla from the Alcantara gorge, this friendly, family-run three-star has a small pool and a restaurant-pizzeria; the hotel can rent you a car, book you onto local tours and dispense advice about hikes in the area. Excellent deals via the website. €55

Castiglione di Sicilia

The nicest place to stay (and eat) in the Alcantara valley is **Castiglione di Sicilia**. Fused to a hilltop high above the valley, the town's lovely weather-eroded houses with pantiled roofs cluster below the remains of its castle. The numerous church spires and the lofty, ruined rock-built castle make an inviting target as you approach up the switchback road, and it's easy to spend a couple of hours just wandering the quiet streets of this old mountain settlement. You can meander up as far as a small piazza at the top of town – with fabulous views of Etna – where there's a flight of steps leading up to the shattered castle, or **Fortezza Greca** (always open), supposedly founded in the fifth century BC by Greek exiles from nearby Naxos and offering grand panoramic views.

Just outside Castiglione in the valley below (and signposted from town) is a perfectly restored Byzantine chapel known as **La Cuba** for its perfect symmetry. Behind La Cuba, a path leads to the river where there are little waterfalls and pools.

ACCOMMODATION AND EATING CASTIGLIONE DI SICILIA

Alcantara Formaggi Via Federico II ☎0942 984 268. A small artisan cheese factory where the Camiglia family produce and sell a range of traditional and inventive cheeses, mostly made of local sheep's milk. Mon–Sat 8am–1pm & 4.30–6pm.

Belvedere d'Alcantara ☎0942 984 037. A short walk beyond the piazza, and well signposted all over town, this excellent restaurant has a rooftop terrace that takes full advantage of the soaring views, as well as a €20 tourist menu and pizzas in the evening. Tues–Sun, lunch & dinner.

Hotel Federico II Via Maggiore Baracca 2 ☎0942 980 368, ⓦhotelfedericosecondo.com. A chic, smart and reasonably priced little hotel with an excellent restaurant just off the main piazza. The restaurant, *Sine Tempore (*daily lunch & dinner; closed Wed if there are no hotel guests), serves local produce to great effect in simple, tasty dishes. The mixed *antipasto* (€10) is a great way of trying lots of local goodies, while to follow there is *tagliatelle Federico Secondo* (with porcini mushrooms, courgettes and pancetta; €9) or hand-made ravioli dressed with pistachios from Bronte (€10). If you're lucky there will be fresh ricotta warm from the factory at lunchtime and breakfast. **€100**

Catania, Etna and around

5

Catania, Etna and around

Bang in the middle of the Ionian coast, with Mount Etna looming high above it, Catania is Sicily's second-largest city, a major port and transport hub and a thriving commercial centre. Its airport is the point of arrival for many of the island's foreign visitors, though few stay long. Those who do are usually pleasantly surprised, however. An intensely vibrant city, Catania has a uniformly grand appearance, its historic centre full of jaunty Baroque buildings of black lava and creamy white limestone built in the wake of the 1693 earthquake that wrecked the whole region. There's an iconic fish market, plenty of good restaurants, an easy-going drinking and nightlife scene and just enough historical sights to pique your interest without being overwhelming.

The jagged volcanic coast to the north sustains a series of small resort-villages around the Baroque town of **Acireale**, while to the south the main driving routes to Siracusa, Ragusa and Enna cross the fertile plain of the **Piana di Catania**. This rich agricultural region was known to the Greeks as the Laestrygonian Fields after the Laestrygonians, a race of cannibals who devoured several of Odysseus's crew. It's a pretty enough ride through the flat, windmill-dotted fields, but the only detour of interest is to the archeological museum at **Lentini**, one of the earliest Greek colonies to be founded in Sicily.

There's absolutely no mistaking the single biggest draw in the province, namely **Mount Etna**, Europe's highest volcano, whose foothills start a few kilometres north of Catania. It's still highly active and its massive presence dominates the whole of this part of the coast, with every town and village in the neighbourhood built at least partly from the lava that it periodically ejects. A road and a small single-track railway, the **Ferrovia Circumetnea**, circumnavigate the lower slopes, passing through a series of hardy towns, such as **Randazzo**, almost foolishly situated in the shadow of the volcano and surrounded by swirls of black volcanic rock. Meanwhile, higher villages and ski stations like **Nicolosi** and the **Rifugio Sapienza** are the base for escorted tours and ascents to the **summit craters**. Depending on the weather and volcanic conditions, you should be able to experience the heights of Etna at first-hand between April and May and September to October.

Catania

First impressions don't say much at all for **CATANIA** – there's heavy industry here, a large port and some depressing suburbs, while the traffic-choked city centre is largely constructed from suffocating, black-grey volcanic stone. Indeed, the influence of

PESCHERIA, CATANIA

Highlights

❶ Pescheria, Catania Eat a sea urchin, buy some swordfish, have spaghetti and clams for lunch – Catania's raucous fish market is Sicily's best. **See p.187**

❷ Teatro Massimo Bellini, Catania Enjoy a night at the opera with the music of Catania's most famous native son. **See p.196**

❸ The ascent of Etna The smoking cone of Etna dominates much of eastern Sicily, and invites an ascent of its blackened upper slopes, not least for the awesome views. **See p.199**

❹ Ferrovia Circumetnea A day-trip by public transport that takes some beating – riding the volcano-train for over 100km around the base of Mount Etna. **See p.200**

❺ Nicolosi The best base on Etna's south side, ideal for winter skiing or summer walking. **See p.203**

❻ Castello Nelson, Bronte An English country house with a fascinating history, deep in the Sicilian countryside. **See p.207**

HIGHLIGHTS ARE MARKED ON THE MAP ON P.184

5

Etna is pervasive, with the main thoroughfare named after the volcano, which looms threateningly just to the north. Yet Catania is well worth a day or two's visit. It is first and foremost a commercial place, boasting arguably the island's best two **markets**, while if you look beyond the darkened shadows of the buildings you'll detect some of the finest Baroque architecture in Sicily. A large student population enlivens the centre, and the thronged piazzas and bars make for one of the island's most exuberant evening promenades. In early February Catania devotes itself to

CATANIA, ETNA AND AROUND

HIGHLIGHTS

1 Pescheria, Catania
2 Teatro Massimo Bellini, Catania
3 The ascent of Etna
4 Ferrovia Circumetnea
5 Nicolosi
6 Castello Nelson, Bronte

celebrating the festival of its patron, **Saint Agatha**, with a passion and intensity diminished not a jot by the fact that this is Sicily's most outward-looking, contemporary and international city.

Catania is a major **transport terminus**, with buses (from the central bus station and the airport) to just about every major destination on the island. The train service is less comprehensive, though the lines south to Siracusa and north to Taormina and Messina are useful. If you're Etna-bound by public transport you'll have to leave from Catania itself – drivers usually choose to see the volcano from the prettier towns and villages to the north. You could see the whole of central Catania in a busy day's strolling, but the city really deserves more time if you can spare it. Most of the sights are confined within a small area, centred on **Piazza del Duomo** and the cathedral, from where the wide main avenue, **Via Etnea**, steams off to the north up to the city's **Bellini gardens**. **Fish market** and **castle** lie to the south, and the landmark **Teatro Bellini** to the east. Much of this entire area, sections of Via Etnea included, is closed to traffic, so walking around is quite enjoyable, especially at night when certain areas become bar and café zones.

Brief history

Some of the island's first **Greek colonists**, probably Chalcidinians from Naxos, settled the site as early as 729 BC, becoming so influential that their laws were eventually adopted by all the Ionian colonies of Magna Graecia. Later, the city was among the first to fall to the **Romans**, under whom it prospered greatly. Unusually for Sicily, Catania's surviving ancient relics are all Roman (albeit lava-encrusted, after successive historic eruptions). In the early Christian period Catania witnessed the martyrdom of **Agatha**, who, having rejected the improper advances of the praetor, Quintianus, was put to death in 252. She was later canonized (becoming the patron saint of Catania), and it was her miraculous intervention that reputedly saved the city from complete volcanic destruction in the seventeenth century. Even with the saint's protection, Catania has had its fair share of disasters: Etna erupted in 1669, engulfing the city in lava, while the **great earthquake** of 1693 devastated the whole of southeastern Sicily. But making full use of the lava as building material, the eighteenth-century architect **Giovanni Battista Vaccarini** gave central Catania a lofty, noble air that endures today.

Piazza del Duomo

Piazza del Duomo is one of Sicily's most elegant Baroque piazzas, rebuilt completely in the first half of the eighteenth century by the Palermitan Giovanni Battista Vaccarini, who was made Catania's municipal architect in 1730. With the majestic cathedral as his starting point, he produced a dramatic open space – kept traffic-free today – softened by the addition of a central fountain, no less than a **lava elephant** supporting an Egyptian obelisk on its back. The elephant has been the city's symbol since at least the thirteenth century, a talismanic protection against Etna eruptions, and this one also features an inscription, *Agatina MSSHDEPL* – an acronym for "The mind of St Agatha is sane and spontaneous, honouring God and liberating the city".

The Duomo

Piazza Duomo • Daily 9am–noon & 4–6pm

Agatha herself is both Catania's patron saint and the dedicatee of Vaccarini's grandest project, the **Duomo**, which flanks the eastern side of the piazza. The original cathedral here was founded in the eleventh century, and built on the site of earlier Roman baths, but of this medieval church only the beautifully crafted apses survived the 1693 earthquake; you can see them through the gate at Via Vittorio Emanuele II 159.

5

Vaccarini added an imposing Baroque facade, on which he tagged granite columns filched from Catania's Roman amphitheatre, while the interior is adorned with a rich series of chapels. The **Cappella di Sant'Agata** is to the right of the choir, and houses the relics that are paraded through the city on the saint's festival days. Next to it, entered through a fine sixteenth-century doorway, the **Cappella della Madonna** holds a Roman sarcophagus that contains the ashes of the Aragonese kings – Frederick II, Louis and Frederick III. The tomb of the composer **Bellini**, a native of the city, is set in the floor before the second column on the right as you enter, inscribed with a phrase from his opera, *La Sonnambula* (The Sleepwalker).

Museo Diocesano and the Terme Achilliane

Piazza Duomo • Mon–Fri 9am–2pm, Sat 9am–1pm • Museum €7, Terme Achilliane €5 • ☎ 095 281 636, Ⓦ museodiocensanocatania.com

To the right of the Duomo, the **Museo Diocesano** houses the cathedral's collection of religious art and silverware, with items dating back to the fourteenth century, including pieces recovered from the pre-1693 cathedral. Beautifully presented as the museum is, most people will find more appeal in the remains of the **Terme Achilliane**, Catania's Imperial Roman baths, which form part of the museum. They're perhaps not quite as alluring as they were in the days of eighteenth century French traveller Jean Houel, who, discovering a hall covered with stuccoes of Cupids, vines, grapes and animals, concluded that it must have been a Temple to Bacchus. Delightful as the idea of a temple devoted to the most decadent of Greek gods might be, it's pretty obvious that the building was a baths complex, as testified by a huge marble pool in what is thought to have been the Frigidarium. Originally stretching right across the piazza as far as the Pescheria (where remains of the Caldarium were discovered), water was provided by the River Amenano, which still flows below the city.

The Pescheria

Piazza Pardo and Piazza Alonzo de Benedetto • Mon–Sat, usually 7am–2pm

Catania's best-known food and fish market, the **Pescheria**, is reached from the back of Piazza del Duomo by nipping down the steps behind a gushing marble fountain. This takes you right into the main part of the fish market, where vendors shout across slabs and buckets full of twitching fish, eels, crabs and shellfish. Brandishing wicked-looking knives, they slice off swordfish steaks to order, while others shuck oysters, mussels and sea urchins for browsing customers. The side alleys off the fish market are dense with fruit, vegetable and dried goods and herb stalls, as well as cheese counters and bloody butchers' tables.

Via Vittorio Emanuele II

On the other side of the Duomo, across busy Via Vittorio Emanuele II, the church of **Sant'Agata** is another of Vaccarini's works, though the lighter, pale grey Rococo interior post-dates his death. A little further up the street, at no. 140, there's the minor curiosity that was the home of Catanese erotic poet and philosopher **Domenico Tempio** (1750–1821). It's now desperately neglected, though you can still make out the raunchy figures of men and women playing with themselves, which support the balcony above the blackened doorway.

THE FESTA DI SANT'AGATA

Catania's biggest annual festival, the **Festa di Sant'Agata**, takes place each year between February 3 and 5. It's a 500-year-old celebration of the life and death of the virtuous Agatha, born in the city around 230 AD and destined for dreadful tortures once she had spurned the unwelcome advances of the Roman praetor, Quintianus, in 252 AD: prison, whipping, mutilation and burning followed. The three days of the festival see hundreds of thousands processing through the streets following a silver, bejewelled reliquary that holds the relics of the saint. There's also a procession of decorated candlesticks, up to 6m high, carried for hours at a time by groups representing different trades. On the morning of February 5, the saint's relics are carried back into the Duomo, where they remain until the following year. Meanwhile, there are fireworks, food stalls, special services and concerts throughout the *festa*.

5

Teatro Romano
Via Vittorio Emanuele II 260 • Daily 9am–6.30pm • Free

The **Teatro Romano**, built in the second century AD, is an intimate little theatre, which preserves much of the Roman seating and underground passageway. A small antiquarium here displays finds from the site. The smaller **Odeon**, adjacent, was used for music and recitations.

Castello Ursino and the Museo Civico
Museo Civico Mon–Fri 9am–1pm & 2.30–7pm, Sat 9am–8pm • €6 • ☎ 095 345 830

Beyond the Pescheria, Via Plebiscito winds through a dilapidated though appealingly neighbourly quarter to Piazza Federico di Svevia, dominated by the **Castello Ursino**, once the proud fortress of Frederick II. Originally the castle stood on a rocky cliff above the sea, but a 1669 eruption of Etna resulted in this entire area becoming landlocked, and left just the keep standing. The castle still presents a formidable appearance, and now houses the **Museo Civico**, part of whose ground floor is taken up with temporary exhibitions, while permanent exhibits include retrieved mosaic fragments, stone inscriptions, elegant painted Greek amphorae and terracotta statuettes. Upstairs the **Pinacoteca** (art gallery) holds mainly religious art from the seventeenth century.

Via Crociferi

The best place to appreciate the eighteenth-century rebuilding of Catania is along its most handsome street, **Via Crociferi**, where the wealthy religious authorities and private citizens competed with each other to construct dazzling houses, palaces and churches. They were building using the very bones of the Roman and medieval city: the arcaded **Piazza Mazzini** (straddling Via Garibaldi) was constructed from 32 columns that originally formed part of a Roman basilica.

Via Crociferi begins to the north of Piazza San Francesco, running under an imposing Baroque arch that announces the start of a series of arresting religious and secular buildings, little-changed since the eighteenth century. Amble up the narrow street and you can peer into the courtyards of the *palazzi* (one holds a plantation of banana trees) and poke around the churches. About halfway up on the right, the finest of these, **San Giuliano** (usually only open for services), has a facade by Vaccarini and an echoing elliptical interior.

Museo Belliniano
Piazza San Francesco d'Assisi 3 • Mon–Sat 9am–1pm • Free • ☎ 095 715 0535

At the bottom of Via Crociferi, opposite San Francesco church, the house where the composer Vincenzo Bellini was born in 1801 is now open as the **Museo Belliniano**, displaying photographs, original scores, his death mask and other memorabilia. Born into a musical family, Bellini supposedly composed his first work at the age of 6, and later studied in Naples, where he produced his first opera in 1825. Ten more operas followed during the next decade – his first big success was *Il Pirata* (1827) – with

---

STAYING SAFE IN CATANIA

Of all Sicilian cities, Catania has the worst reputation for **petty crime**. Hoteliers and locals often warn tourists to be on their guard against pickpockets and, without being too alarmist, it doesn't do any harm to follow their advice. If you're happy with security at your hotel, leave your passport and valuables there before going out. Be careful on your own at night, and don't flash your cash, phones or cameras in run-down areas or in the middle of the teeming markets.

Bellini living largely in Milan until his early death in Paris, aged only 33. His body was transported back to his native Sicily to be buried, and Catania subsequently did her favourite son proud, with the airport, a piazza, the city's main theatre and a park all named after him, as well as the ultimate accolade – a pasta dish, *spaghetti alla Norma*, cooked with tomato and aubergine and named after Bellini's famous 1831 opera.

San Nicolò

Piazza Dante • Mon–Sat 9am–1pm

Opposite the peculiar crescent-shaped Piazza Dante looms the unfinished facade of **San Nicolò**, studded by six enormous, lopped columns. It was conceived on a ridiculously grand scale, and the work was ultimately curtailed by earthquake damage and soaring costs. What's left is a stark 105m-long **interior**, virtually undecorated save for the sculpted choir stalls and a meridian line etched in marble across the floor of the transept, embellished with zodiacal signs. The famous organ, admired by earlier visitors, was destroyed in the nineteenth century.

The church is part of an adjoining **Benedictine convent**, with equally impressive dimensions – it's the second-largest convent in Europe after Mafra in Portugal. Through a gate to the left of the church lie the remains of some **Roman walls**, and, behind, the massive conventual buildings. These are now used by the university's language and literature faculties, but you should be able to stroll in for a look around the once grand cloistered courtyards.

Via Etnea and around

The main city thoroughfare, **Via Etnea**, runs north from Piazza del Duomo and out of the city. Following its full length would eventually lead you right to the foothills of Mount Etna – and from the street's northern end there are photogenic views of the peak in the distance.

The first square off the street, Piazza dell'Università, holds some outdoor cafés and the main building of the **University**, founded by the Aragonese kings in the fifteenth century. The earthquake postponed its completion until the 1750s. The tangled streets off to the east form the heart of the student nightlife zone, converging eventually on the restored Piazza Bellini, overlooked by the flagship **Teatro Massimo Bellini** (see p.196), built in 1890.

Anfiteatro Romano

Piazza Stesicoro • Tues–Sun 9am–1pm & 3–7pm • Free

Halfway up Via Etnea, **Piazza Stesicoro** marks the modern centre of Catania, with its western side almost entirely occupied by the sunken black remains of the **Anfiteatro Romano**, built from lava blocks in the second or third century AD. Much is still concealed under the surrounding buildings, but a diagram shows the original dimensions of the theatre, which could hold sixteen thousand spectators – it's quite evident that the section you can walk through represents only one tiny excavated corner.

Sant'Agata al Carcere

Piazza Santo Carcere • No set hours

Behind the Anfiteatro Romano is the twelfth-century church of **Sant'Agata al Carcere**, built on the site of the prison where St Agatha was confined before her martyrdom at the hands of the Romans. When it's open (hours are sporadic), a custodian will let you into the third-century **crypt** and show you the chapel's medieval stone doorway, topped by evil, grinning, sculpted heads and ape-like creatures.

5

Fera o Luni market

Piazza Carlo Alberto • Mon–Sat usually 7am–2pm

Off the east side of Via Etnea, at Piazza Stesicoro, the stalls are out from early in the morning ranged up Via San Gaetano alla Grotta, heralding the city's rambunctious **Fera o Luni market**, which is centred on the broad Piazza Carlo Alberto. As well as fruit, veg and fish, all kinds of clothes (new and secondhand), shoes, accessories and household goods are sold here, from tat piled high on a wooden cart to cut-price designer labels (or copies thereof), all accompanied by the constant patter and haggling of cheery traders. The market is a great spot for souvenir-hunting, even more so on Sundays when an **antiques fair** takes over the space.

Villa Bellini

For tourists Via Etnea finishes at the **Villa Bellini**, just beyond the post office, a large, ornamental public garden that provides a welcome touch of greenery. The stand-up drinks bar here is where the local police hang out, whiling away time between meal breaks; rather touching photos of the regulars are pinned up, posing stiffly in uniform on horseback or motorbikes.

Zo: the centre for contemporary culture

Piazzale Asia 6 • **Museo del Cinema** Tues–Sun 9am–12.30pm, plus Tues & Thurs 3–4.30pm • €4 • **Museo Storico dello Sbarco in Sicilia 1943** Tues–Sat 9am–12.30pm, plus Tues & Thurs 3–5pm • €4 • ☎ 095 816 8912, ⓦ zoculture.it

In the east of the city, up Viale Africa near Stazione Centrale, Catania's former sulphur works, Le Ciminiere, has been transformed into a cultural centre known as **Zo**. The original red-brick chimneys and lava-block walls have been wrapped in a contemporary glass-and-steel frame, while inside are theatre and performance spaces and a café-restaurant. It's an interesting place to visit even if you don't come for an exhibition or event, and it holds two museums as well, both self-explanatory: the **Museo del Cinema**, and the **Museo Storico dello Sbarco in Sicilia 1943**, or the Museum of the Allied Invasion of Sicily. The latter is a winner with kids, who get to walk through a replica of a typical Sicilian village piazza, take cover in an air-raid shelter as the siren sounds, and emerge at all-clear into a bombed version of the same piazza.

ARRIVAL AND DEPARTURE   CATANIA

BY PLANE

From Fontanarossa airport, 5km south of the city, the cheapest way into the centre is the Alibus #457 (every 20min, daily 5.30am–midnight) from right outside, which runs to the central Piazza Stesicoro (on Via Etnea) and to Stazione Centrale in around 20min (longer in heavy traffic); buy tickets (€1) from the machine or the bookshop, both in the Arrivals hall. Most regional express buses (to Siracusa, Taormina, Ragusa, Agrigento, Enna, Messina and Palermo) also stop at the airport, and from April to October you can get a direct bus from the airport to Milazzo (for the Aeolian Islands). A taxi ride to the centre costs around €20.

BY TRAIN

Stazione Centrale Trains pull in at Stazione Centrale in Piazza Giovanni XXIII, just east of the centre. It's easy to jump on a city bus outside to reach Piazza del Duomo or Via

Etnea (see p.189), or to take a taxi (around €10). Otherwise, it's a 20min walk to the Duomo. For information and timetables call ☎ 892 021, or visit ⓦ ferroviedellostato.it. For Circumetnea services, note that there is a reduced service in July and Aug, and no trains on Sundays and holidays in winter.

Mainline destinations Acireale (1–2 hourly; 10min); Caltagirone (6 daily Mon–Sat; 1hr 45min); Caltanissetta (3–4 daily; 2hr); Enna (4 daily Mon–Sat, 3 daily Sun; 1hr 20min); Gela (5 daily Mon–Sat; 2hr 10min–2hr 45min); Giarre-Riposto (1–2 hourly; 30min); Lentini (11 daily Mon–Sat, 5 daily Sun; 30min); Messina (1–2 hourly; 1hr 30min); Palermo via Caltanissetta or Messina (4 daily; 3hr–6hr 40min); Siracusa (11 daily Mon–Sat, 5 daily Sun; 1hr 30min); Taormina (1–2 hourly; 45min).

Stazione Catania Borgo The other city station, the Stazione Catania Borgo on Via Caronda, off the northern end of Via Etnea, is for trains on the Ferrovia Circumetnea,

5

CATANIA CITY TOURS AND ETNA EXCURSIONS

To see a lot of Catania in a short time and without too much walking, join one of the **bus tours** operated by Katane Live (☎095 354 704, ⓦkatanelive.it), which offers a hop-on hop-off service (daily 9am–7pm; €5, plus €2 for audioguide; tickets sold on board) around the centre, taking in Via Etnea, Piazza del Duomo and Villa Bellini, with additional stops at the train station, Piazza Stesicoro and Piazza Verga, among other places. Alternatively, there's the **Trenino Turistico** (☎095 820 4281), a mini-train on wheels, of special appeal to children, which leaves from Piazza Duomo and performs a wide 35min circuit of the centre including Via Vittorio Emanuele II, Via Etnea and Via Crociferi (€5, €3.50 for children over 7).

Of the numerous **tours to Etna**, Geo Etna Explorer (☎349 610 9957, ⓦgeoetnaexplorer.it) and Etna Experience (☎349 305 3021, ⓦetnaexperience.com) offer a range of half- and full-day tours from around €55, with pick-up points in the city centre (some operators will pick you up from your hotel). Ask the tourist office for the full list of Etna excursions.

the round-Etna line (☎095 541 250, ⓦcircumetnea.it; see p.200); it's connected by metro (see below) with Stazione Centrale. A taxi to the centre is around €12.

Circumetnea destinations Adrano (14 daily; 1hr); Bronte (11 daily; 1hr 30min); Maletto (11 daily; 1hr 45min); Paternò (16 daily; 30min); Randazzo (11 daily; 2hr); Riposto (4 daily; 3hr 10min).

BY BUS

Essentials Virtually all long-distance buses stop at the airport as well as at the bus station – a far easier place to change buses if you are not intending to spend time in the city. The bus station is a grotty 5min walk from the train station, up Viale della Liberta, on Via Archimede, and the ticket offices are currently inconveniently located on the other side of Viale della Liberta, so buy them before going in to the station.

Bus companies The major companies have terminals around Stazione Centrale, including: AST, Via L. Sturzo 230 (☎840 000 323 or ☎095 723 0535, ⓦaziendasiciliana trasporti.it), for services within Catania province, including Etna; Interbus/Etna, Via d'Amico 187 (☎095 530 396, ⓦinterbus.it), for Acireale, Caltagirone, Enna, Giardini-Naxos, Messina, Nicosia, Noto, Piazza Armerina, Ragusa, Siracusa and Taormina; SAIS Autolinee, Via d'Amico 181 (☎095 536 168, ⓦsaisautolinee.it), to Palermo, Messina, Enna and Caltanissetta; SAIS Trasporti, Via d'Amico 213 (☎095 536 201, ⓦsaistrasporti.it), to Messina, Agrigento, Caltanissetta and mainland destinations.

Destinations from Catania Acireale (1–3 hourly; 35min–1hr 15min); Agrigento (approx hourly; 2hr 50min); Caltagirone (1–2 hourly Mon–Sat, 4 daily Sun; 1hr 30min);

Enna (12 daily; 1hr 30min–2hr 25min); Gela (8–10 daily Mon–Sat, 6 daily Sun; 1hr 45min); Giardini-Naxos (5 daily Mon–Sat, 2 daily Sun; 1hr 30min); Lentini (1–2 hourly Mon–Sat; 1hr–1hr 15min); Messina (1–2 hourly; 1hr 35min); Nicolosi (hourly; 40min); Nicosia (4–5 daily Mon–Sat, 2 daily Sun; 2hr–2hr 45min); Noto (7 daily; 2hr 25min–2hr 15min); Palermo (hourly; 2hr 40min); Piazza Armerina (3–6 daily; 1hr 50min); Ragusa (12 daily; 2hr); Randazzo (1–2 hourly Mon–Sat; 1hr 45min); Rifugio Sapienza (1 daily; 2hr); Rome (2–3 daily; 11hr); Siracusa (approx hourly; 1hr 20min); Taormina (16 daily; 1hr 40min).

Destinations from Catania airport Agrigento (hourly Mon–Sat, 10 daily Sun; 2hr 40min); Enna (9 daily Mon–Fri, 6 daily Sat, 3 daily Sun; 1hr 15min); Messina (13 daily Mon–Fri, 8 daily Sat & Sun; 1hr 50min); Milazzo (1–2 daily April–June & Oct; 4 daily July–Sept; 1hr 50min); Palermo (hourly Mon–Sat, 9 daily Sun; 2hr 30min); Siracusa (8 daily Mon–Fri, 6 daily Sat & Sun; 1hr 15min); Taormina (hourly Mon–Sat, 11 daily Sun; 1hr 25min).

BY FAST FERRY AND HYDROFOIL

Essentials There is a hydrofoil and fast-ferry service at least four times a week between Catania and Malta in summer (☎095 703 1211, ⓦvirtuferries.com). TTT Lines (☎800 915 365 or ☎081 580 2744, ⓦtttlines.it) run a daily ferry to Naples, taking 12 hours; most travel agents have timetables and can sell tickets. The port is a 5min walk along Via VI Aprile, southwest of the train station, and is also served by a stop on the Metropolitana (Stazione Porto).

Destinations Naples (1 daily; 12hr); Valletta, Malta (1–5 weekly; 3hr).

GETTING AROUND

By bus AMT city buses (☎800 018 696 or ☎095 751 9111, ⓦamt.ct.it) have terminals at Stazione Centrale and Piazza Borsellino, where there's a stop for the airport. Central pick-up points are Piazza del Duomo and Piazza Stesicorot. Tickets (€1) are valid for any number of journeys within

90min and are available from *tabacchi*, the newsagents inside Stazione Centrale or the booth outside the station. The same outlets also sell a *biglietto giornaliero* (€2.50), valid for one day's unlimited travel on all local AMT bus routes.

By metro The city has a metro system, operated by the

same folk who run the Circumetnea line, which operates every 15min (7am–8.30pm) on a limited route running from the main Stazione Centrale (beyond Platform 11) south to Catania Porto and north and northwest to Catania Borgo, the terminal for the Stazione Circumetnea on Via Caronda. Bus tickets are valid on metros and must be punched at machines before boarding the train.

By car Driving into Catania isn't too difficult (just follow signs for "centro" for Via Etnea), but driving around the city is a different matter thanks to chaotic traffic, the fiendish one-way system and the utter impossibility of parking. Some hotels have their own parking or arrangements with nearby garages, but as you really don't need a car in Catania, the best advice if you're renting a car is to do so on the day you leave the city, and to consider picking it up from the airport, connected by frequent local buses with the centre.

Car rental All the big-name agencies – Avis (☎095 340 500, ⓦavis.com); Europcar (☎095 348 125, ⓦeuropcar.it); Hertz (☎095 341 595, ⓦhertz.it); Maggiore (☎095 340 594, ⓦmaggiore.it); Sixt (☎095 340 389, ⓦsixt.it) – have outlets at the airport (opposite the bus stops outside arrivals) and in the city. However, you may find prices from local operator Hollywood (☎095 281 161) beat even the car rental broker websites.

By taxi There are taxi ranks at Stazione Centrale, Piazza del Duomo and Via Etnea (Piazza Stesicoro); call ☎095 330 966 or ☎095 338 282 for 24-hour service.

INFORMATION

Tourist office The most convenient tourist offices are located up by the side of the Villa Bellini gardens at Via Beato Bernardo 5 (Mon–Fri 9am–1pm, plus Wed 3–7pm; ☎095 747 7415), and close to the Duomo at Via Vittorio Emanuele II 172 (Mon–Sat 8.15am–1.15pm; ☎800 841 042 or ☎095 742 5573, ⓦwww.comune.catania.it/turismo).

Listings information For what's on check out the Catania editions of daily newspapers *Giornale di Sicilia*, *La Sicilia* and the *Gazzetta del Sud*, and the comprehensive, free fortnightly arts and entertainment leaflet, *Lapis* (ⓦlapisnet.it), available at the tourist offices and elsewhere.

ACCOMMODATION

Catania's **hotels** have raised their game in recent years, with grubby old pensioni replaced by renovated three- and four-star hotels and a few stylish boutique places. It's always wise to reserve in advance, especially in July and August and during the Sant'Agata celebrations, with prices usually determined by availability. There's also a burgeoning number of city-centre **B&Bs** – you'll see several signposted just by walking up Via Etnea – and a couple of excellent central **youth hostels**. Catania is the first city in Sicily to introduce a **tourist tax** of €1–1.50 per day (for the first three days), depending on the kind of hotel or B&B you stay in.

HOTELS AND B&BS

B&B 5 Balconi Via del Plebiscito 133 ☎338 727 2701, ⓦ5balconi.it. This clean, relaxed B&B has artistically decorated rooms with vintage furnishings and plenty of personality; and as the name implies, it has five balconies. The young Anglo-Sicilian couple who run it are full of local tips. Bathrooms are shared, and there's a/c and free wi-fi. It's on a busy road, but noise intrusion is minimal. Breakfast includes traditional Catanese pastries. No credit cards. **€55**

B&B BaD Via C. Colombo 24 ☎095 346 903, ⓦbadcatania.com. Four vibrant rooms and an apartment with cooking facilities and a terrace with a view of Etna, all set in a funky, self-styled B&B with 1960s and 1970s furniture and walls covered with psychedelic geometries and optical illusions. It's conveniently located behind the Pescheria and Piazza del Duomo. Rooms **€80**; apartment **€100**

B&B Bianca Via S. Tomaselli 43 ☎095 989 0989, ⓦbiancabb.com. B&B behind the Giardino Bellini, where the young, friendly owners make sure guests are well informed about what's going on in Catania. There are two rooms, at present with shared bathroom. The communal area is a cheerful place to hang out and chat, with white walls and fittings, scarlet chairs, and a tangerine sofa where you can flop and watch a DVD. **€70**

★ **B&B Casa Barbero** Via Caronda 209 ☎095 820 6301, ⓦcasabarbero.it. Contemporary colours and design in a beautifully restored Liberty-era *palazzo* with six quiet rooms set around a courtyard. Breakfast is served either in the courtyard, or in the elaborately stuccoed and frescoed dining room, at tables elegantly laid with Japanese-style ceramics and modern pewter. Bikes for guests' use (free but €100 deposit). **€90**

Etnea 316 Via Etnea 316 ☎095 250 3076, ⓦhoteletnea316.it. Real care has gone into the maintenance of this charming old B&B, where ten spruced-up rooms retain their original tile floors and lofty proportions. There's a pretty lounge and breakfast room, and a calm air envelops all. **€65**

Holland International Via Vittorio Emanuele 8 ☎095 533 605, ⓦhollandintrooms.it. Old-fashioned *pensione*, convenient for the station and charging competitive prices for rooms on the first floor of an old *palazzo* with vaulted frescoed ceilings. Rooms come with and without bathroom and all have a/c, satellite TV and tea- and coffee-making facilities. There is free wi-fi, and the friendly Dutch owner speaks good English. **€60**

5

Hotel Gresi Via Pacini 28 ☎ 095 322 709, ⓦ gresihotel .com. Newly refurbished traditional hotel, with a pleasantly old-fashioned atmosphere, where the spacious rooms with frescoed ceilings offer exactly what you'd expect of a three-star hotel – charmless veneer furniture, plain furnishings, phones, fridges and a/c. Good location between Via Etnea and the bustling Piazza Carlo Alberto market. **€70**

Liberty Hotel Via San Vito 40 ☎ 095 311 651, ⓦ libertyhotel.it. Intimate and romantic hotel in an early twentieth-century *palazzo*, a 10min walk from Via Etnea. Wonderfully refurbished in carefully researched Liberty style, the hotel has a calm atmosphere and a trellis-shaded courtyard, and is an ideal place to recuperate after a long journey. There are good-value discounts and packages including trips to Etna via the website. There's no restaurant, but a local pizzeria will deliver to the hotel. **€180**

Una Hotel Via Etnea 218 ☎ 095 250 5111, ⓦ unahotels .it. Chic designer hotel belonging to a national chain, whose decor reflects the dominant black-and-white of the city's Baroque (and of snowcapped Etna): floors of Etna lava and Comiso limestone; beds laid with cream cotton and black velvet; and Baroque-style chairs sprayed gold and upholstered in black velvet. Facilities include roof terrace and restaurant-bar with spectacular views of Etna, and a gym with steam bath. Check the website for offers, especially weekend packages. **€160**

La Vetreria Via Grimaldi 8 ☎ 095 281 537, ⓦ residencelavetreria.com. Occupying a 1920s mirror factory, this popular complex of serviced rooms and apartments (sleeping 1–5 people) has tasteful furniture, spacious rooms, and cooking facilities. The breakfast room with toy cupboard and little table and chairs signals straight away that this is a place where kids are genuinely welcomed. There's an official minimum stay of two weeks, but this is flexible. From **€300** per week

HOSTELS

★ **Agorà** Piazza Currò 6 ☎ 095 723 3010, ⓦ agorahostel.com. Fantastic but nonetheless secluded location near the Pescheria fish market (follow the signs), though its restaurant, bar and night-time events (see opposite) mean that it can get noisy. The basic dorms (six to ten beds) have bunks and lockers, with separate bathrooms for men and women, and there are some small private double rooms. Free internet access, use of kitchen, washing facilities and bike rental are also offered, and there's 24hr access. Dorms from **€16**; rooms **€55**

C.C.Ly Piazza Falcone ☎ 095 746 2399, ⓦ ccly-hostel .com. On the top floor of a nineteenth-century *palazzo*, this hostel – pronounced "Sicily" – created by two couchsurfing veterans, is fantastically kitsch, the swirling decor harking back to the 1960s – but it's very friendly and has low prices and a central location close to the bus station. The eight beds in each single-sex dorm share a bathroom, and there are also en-suite doubles. Guests have lockers, internet access, use of a kitchen, laundry facilities and parking. Dorms from **€15**; doubles **€40**

EATING, DRINKING AND NIGHTLIFE

Catania's streets teem until late, especially in summer. **Restaurants** are pretty good value, thanks to the presence of so many students, who also go a long way to ensuring the island's best **nightlife**. The whole ambience is helped by the fact that the *Comune* closes old-town streets and squares to traffic (the so-called *café concerto*) and bars spill tables outside until the small hours. Of the outdoor **cafés**, those in Piazza del Duomo and Piazza dell'Università have the best views in the most touristy locale, while the cooler **bars** are found around Piazza Bellini (particularly down Via Teatro Massimo, in Via Rapisardi and in adjacent piazzas Ogninella and Scammacca). The sole exception is the funky, most un-Sicilian café, bar and restaurant at the *Agorà* youth hostel, near the Pescheria market (see opposite). In summer, there are open-air venues for **dancing** until the early hours along the coast on the outskirts of town – ask around and look for posters and flyers for the latest spots.

CATANIA'S STREET FOOD

The Catanese do a lot of eating on the hoof, from grazing on raw mussels and sea urchins in the Pescheria to eating ice cream as they parade up Via Etnea in the evening. February's Festa di Sant'Agata sees food stalls selling traditional **nougat** (*torrone*) and confections of **marzipan and sweet ricotta** (including little cakes with a cherry on top, known as *Minne di Sant'Agata*, or Saint Agatha's boobs), while during summer kiosks offer that thirst-quenching Catania speciality, soda water and crushed lemon, served with or without salt (*seltz e limone con/senza sale*). In autumn the **roast-chestnut** vendors are out in force, and around San Martino's Day (November 11) it's the time for **crispelle** – fritters of flour, water, yeast and ricotta or anchovies. A great place to try these and other traditional fried snacks is *Friggitoria Stella*, Via Monsignor Ventimiglia 66 (Mon–Sat 7pm–late; closed in summer; ☎ 095 535 002), a backstreet establishment off Via Giovanni di Prima that's been going for years.

5

SHOPPING IN CATANIA

Via Etnea is the central spine of the city and its major shopping street, with department and chain stores, designer labels, boutiques and brands. Off here, just before the Villa Bellini, **Via Pacini** is devoted to cheap clothes, shoes, underwear and accessories, along with purveyors of spices and other exotic goodies (ranging from Heinz baked beans and Marmite to fresh lemongrass and *kecap manis* sauce).

At the far end it melds into the unmissable **Fera o Luni market** (Piazza Carlo Alberto; see p.190). The nearest daily **supermarket** is Punto SMA, Corso Sicilia 50 (Mon–Sat 8.30am–8.30pm, Sun 8.30am–1.30pm; ☏ 095 326 099). The other daily market, the **Pescheria** (see p.187), mainly trades in food (not just fish; it's also great for buying things like salted capers, sun-dried tomatoes, hunks of pecorino cheese or bags of wild oregano), though on the fringes you'll find clothes and jewellery too – **Via Vittorio Emanuele II** has a few "ethnic" shops with carvings, beads and fabrics. Across Piazza del Duomo, in the arches under the Porta Uzeda gateway, there are two or three well-stocked Sicilian souvenir stores, for puppets, postcards, ceramics, painted carts and almond wine. And around the back of the Duomo, in the old Palazzo Biscari at Piazza San Placido 7, look for the historic main branch of the now-ubiquitous **Nonna Vincenza** (Mon–Sat 8am–9pm, Sun 8am–2pm; ☏ 095 715 1844), the most traditional place in the city to buy artisan sweets in gorgeous packaging.

As for **books**, Feltrinelli, Via Etnea 285 (Mon–Sat 10.30am–1.30pm & 4.30–8.30pm; ☏ 095 352 9001), has a good range of English books; there's also a branch of Mondadori at Piazza Roma 18 (Mon–Sat 9am–8pm; ☏ 095 716 9610).

RESTAURANTS

★ Da Aldo Piazza G. Sciuti 2 ☏ 095 311 158. The best choice near the Fera o Luni market, this is an amiable first-floor lunchtime grill-house where bustling waiters reel off the daily specials (*pasta alla Norma*, stuffed squid or a simple grilled sea bass or steak). It's great value, less than €20 for a full meal. From Piazza Carlo Alberto, take the first left off Via Pacini, down Via al Carmine. No credit cards. Mon–Sat lunch only.

Antica Marina Via Pardo 29 ☏ 095 348 197. Trattoria bang in the heart of the fish market where you can eat reasonably priced fresh fish on tables laid with paper cloths. Go for one of the set menus – a mixed *antipasto* plus two kinds of pasta, or *antipasto* plus mixed fried fish – at €25 including a lemon sorbet and coffee. Mon–Sat lunch & dinner.

Camelot Piazza Federico di Svevia 75 ☏ 095 723 2103. Lively place where you can feast for a song on Sicilian *antipasti* (€5) or barbecued sausages and meat (from €3 per sausage), and drink local wine from plastic cups. Dinner only Tues–Sun.

De Fiore Via Coppola 24 ☏ 095 316 283. Cosy, family-run trattoria, serving good, traditional Sicilian food at moderate prices. The *spaghetti alla Norma* with hand-made pasta (€6) is wonderful. Daily lunch & dinner; closed Mon in winter.

Oxidiana Via Conte Ruggero 4a ☏ 095 532 585, ⓦ oxidiana.it. Scores of different sushi and California rolls, along with *tataki*, tempuras, stir-fries and a marvellous sesame-crusted tuna (best in May and June, the height of the tuna season). There are vegetarian options and lots of gluten-free dishes, plus fab cocktails and over sixty different rums for the trying. A great place, and they deliver too (daily 6.30–8.30pm only). Daily, dinner only.

★ La Paglia Via Pardo 23 ☏ 095 346 838. Simple trattoria (wipe-clean tablecloths, panel-board walls) that's the best place in town for a reasonably priced fish-market lunch – when the *signora* runs out of something at lunchtime she just bellows through the kitchen window at the stallholders for more. *Antipasti* cost €5–10, pasta dishes such as spaghetti and clams are €7–10, and mains – grilled tuna, perhaps – €10–15. The house wine is the kind that you can run your car on. Mon–Sat lunch & dinner.

Sicilia in Bocca Via Dusmet 35 ☏ 095 250 0208. One of the nicest places in town to sit outside, this is pizzeria one side, restaurant the other (though in practice you can mix and match menus), sharing a shaded terrace. It's set in the old arched sea wall (through Porta Uzeda from Piazza del Duomo and turn left), and service is friendly and English-speaking. Pizzas are €6–10, pasta dishes €8–12, mains €12–20. Mon dinner, Tues–Sun lunch & dinner.

★ La Siciliana Viale Marco Polo 52a ☏ 095 376 400. Renowned as one of eastern Sicily's best restaurants, with a thoroughly traditional menu, strong on fish and local specialities like rice with squid ink and fresh ricotta; they also make their own sensational pastries and desserts. In summer there's outdoor garden-terrace seating. It's expensive, however: count on spending €45 for a full meal without wine. You'll need to take bus #628 *rosso* from the station or a taxi as it's way up in the north of the city. Tues–Sat lunch & dinner, Sun lunch only.

CAFÉS AND BARS

Agora Piazza Currò 6 ☏ 095 723 3010, ⓦ agorahostel .com. Lively pub that attracts a mix of locals and travellers from the youth hostel (see opposite). Non-guests come

5

here for the restaurant, to catch a DJ or gig (check the website for upcoming events), sit out at the laidback outdoor terrace or drink in the unique cellar wine bar (housed in a natural lava-cave with one of Catania's underground streams running through it). They make nice bruschetta too to soak up the booze. Daily noon–late.

La Cartiera Via Casa del Mutilato 8 ☎ 347 637 2592, ⊛ brassjazzclub.it. Long-established jazz club just off Piazza Bellini, with good food (pasta for around €9) as well as live music. Check out the website for concerts. Mon & Wed–Sun 8.30pm–late.

La Collegiata Via Collegiata 3 ☎ 095 321 230. A laidback, studenty place with a pleasant terrace for an evening drink or daytime snack. Daily 11.30am–4.30pm & 5.30/6pm–late.

★ **Nievski** Via Alessi 15–17 ☎ 095 313792. They love Che in this "*pub-trattoria alternativo*", where you can come for a plate of organic food, a Fair Trade coffee or a beer. There's internet access, all kinds of concerts and events, and more goatees than you can shake a stick at. It's on the Alessi steps up to Via Crociferi. Tues–Sat noon–late, and Sun eve.

Savia Via Etnea 302 ☎ 095 322 335. Opposite the main entrance to the Villa Bellini, this is the city's most notable *pasticceria*, open since 1897 and always busy with folk digging into savoury *arancini*, ricotta-stuffed *cannoli*, real *cassata* and the like. Tues–Sun 7am–8pm.

ENTERTAINMENT

While the Bellini theatre is the traditional centre of opera, music and ballet, Catania's new focus for **culture and the arts** is the Zo centre (see p.190). Summer is the best time for **concerts and events**, from open-air jazz in the Villa Bellini gardens to classical concerts in churches and theatres across the city. To find out what's on, check the listings information in several local publications (see p.193).

CULTURE AND THE ARTS

Teatro Massimo Bellini Via Perrotta 12 ☎ 095 730 6111 or ☎ 095 715 0921, ⊛ teatromassimobellini.it. Facing Piazza Bellini, Catania's impressive opera house has a concert season that runs from Oct until May, which includes classical music and ballet as well as opera.

Zo Viale Africa ☎ 095 533 871, ⊛ zoculture.it. Catania's centre for contemporary arts is the place for cutting-edge theatre, electronic and world music, experimental art shows, off-the-wall installations and offbeat festivals. It's a 2min walk from Stazione Centrale.

DIRECTORY

Hospital Ospedale Garibaldi, Piazza S. Maria di Gesù 7 ☎ 095 759.1111, emergencies ☎ 095 759.4368.

Internet Internetteria, Via Penninello 44 (Mon–Fri 9am–1am, Sat & Sun 5pm–1am; may close earlier in winter). There's a cluster of other points on Via Vittorio Emanuele II and Via Garibaldi.

Left luggage At Stazione Centrale, Piazza Giovanni XXIII (daily 7.30am–1.30pm & 2.30–8.30pm; €3 per bag for 12hr).

Pharmacies Caltabiano, Piazza Stesicoro 36 (☎ 095 327 647); Croce Rossa, Via Etnea 274 (☎ 095 327 232); Europa,

Corso Italia 111 (☎ 095 383 536); Cutelli, Via Vittorio Emanuele II 54 (☎ 095 531 400). All open daily 8.30am–1pm & 5–8pm; late openings are indicated by a rota posted in the shop windows.

Police In emergencies call ☎ 112. Otherwise, the Carabinieri are at Via Teatro Greco 111 (☎ 095 326 666); Questura (for police) is at Via Manzoni 8, Piazza S. Nicolella (☎ 095 736 7111).

Post office Main post office is close to the Villa Bellini at Via Etnea 215 (Mon–Fri 8am–6.30pm, Sat 8am–12.30pm).

Catania's beach resorts

The main sandy beaches lie south of Catania, on the wide **Golfo di Catania** (Viale Kennedy), but it's actually the coast north of the city that's the most popular **resort area**. The lava streams from Etna have reached the sea many times over the centuries,

THE SCOGLI DEI CICLOPI

Aci Castello marks the beginning of the so-called Riviera dei Ciclopi, named after the jagged points of the **Scogli dei Ciclopi** that rise from the sea just beyond town. Homer wrote that the blinded Polyphemus slung these rocks (broken from Etna) at Ulysses as he and his men escaped from the Cyclops in their ships. The largest of the three main sharp-edged islets – also known as *faraglioni* – sticks some 60m into the sky.

5

ACIREALE DRESSES UP

Acireale is known throughout Italy for its celebrations during **Carnevale** (Feb/March), when it hosts one of Sicily's best festivals, with extraordinarily elaborate flower-decked floats and fancy-dress parades clogging the streets for five noisy days. The town also has a long tradition of Sicilian **puppet theatre**, with regular shows performed in summer by its surviving theatre companies, like that of Turi Grasso at Via Nazionale 195 (☎ 095 764 8035, ⓦ operadeipupi.com), which also has a small **museum** at the theatre (Wed, Sat & Sun 9am–noon & 6–9pm in summer or 3–6pm in winter; free).

turning the coastline into an attractive mix of contorted black rocks and sheer coves, excellent for swimming. Consequently, what was once a series of small fishing villages is now a fair-sized strip of hotels, lidos and restaurants, idle in the winter but swarming in summer with day-trippers. Incidentally, the prefix "Aci", given to a number of settlements here, derives from the local River Aci, said to have appeared following the death of the herdsman Acis at the hands of the giant, one-eyed Polyphemus, for having the temerity to fall in love with Galatea, with whom the giant was also in love. The river is no longer identifiable.

The resorts

The first stop on trains heading north along the coast, **OGNINA** is a small suburb on the northern outskirts of Catania, built on lava cliffs formed in the fifteenth century. It holds a few restaurants, overlooking the little harbour, as well as a campsite.

Continuing up the coast, **ACI CASTELLO**, 9km from Catania, is a striking place, its castle rising high above the sea in splinters from a volcanic rock crag. The base of the rebel Roger di Lauria in 1297, it's remarkably well preserved, despite many threatening eruptions and the destruction wrought by Frederick II of Aragon, who took the castle from Roger by erecting a wooden siege-engine adjacent. The ragged coastline to the north is popular for sunbathing and swimming and, in summer, a wooden boardwalk is built over the lava rocks (you pay a small fee to use the changing rooms and showers).

You could always walk the couple of kilometres north along the rough coast from Aci Castello to **ACI TREZZA**, the fishing village at the heart of nineteenth-century Sicilian novelist Giovanni Verga's masterpiece *I Malavoglia*. It is a pleasant resort, with bars, *gelaterie* and seafood restaurants ranged along the lungomare.

ARRIVAL AND DEPARTURE

CATANIA'S BEACH RESORTS

By bus AMT bus #534 runs from Catania's Piazza Borsellino to Aci Castello and Aci Trezza. The beaches of the Golfo di Catania are reached by taking bus #427 from Stazione Centrale or summer bus #D from Piazza Borsellino.

By train Regular trains (approximately hourly) from Catania's Stazione Centrale make the 5min journey to Ognina.

Acireale

ACIREALE, 16km north of Catania, has a marvellous site, high above the rocky shore and the surrounding lemon groves. It's a location best appreciated from the public gardens at the northern end of town, from where you can look right back along the Riviera dei Ciclopi. Known since Roman times as a spa centre (the thermal baths are still heavily used), Acireale is also another striking example of Sicilian Baroque town planning. This is the fourth successive town on the site, rebuilt directly over the old lava streams after the 1693 earthquake, and, as in Catania, it relies on grand buildings, a handsome central square and Duomo and some long thoroughfares for its effect.

5

Santa Maria la Scala

The nicest place to while away a few hours in Acireale – especially over lunch – is the tiny hamlet of **Santa Maria la Scala**, 2km below town, huddled around a minuscule harbour full of painted fishing-boats, where three or four trattorias overlook the bay. To get here on foot, go down Via Romeo (to the side of the Municipio), across the busy main road and then down the steep rural path to the water.

ARRIVAL AND DEPARTURE   ACIREALE

By bus Buses to Acireale from Catania (1–3 hourly) stop outside the public gardens or near the Duomo.

By train Trains run regularly (1–2 hourly) between Acireale and Catania. The train station is well to the south of town, near the thermal baths, and a long walk into the centre along Via Vittorio Emanuele II.

Lentini

Half an hour or so south of Catania by road, **LENTINI** has a long pedigree that puts it among the earliest of the Greek settlements in Sicily, and the first of all the inland colonies. Established in 729 BC as a daughter city of Naxos, Lentini (Leontinoi) flourished as a commercial centre for two hundred years, before falling foul of Hippocrates of Gela. Later, the city was absorbed by Syracuse, sharing its disasters but never its prosperity. It was Leontinoi's struggle to assert its independence, by allying itself with Athens, that provided the pretext for the great Athenian expedition against Syracuse in 415 BC. Another attempt – this time an alliance with the Carthaginians during the Second Punic War – resulted in the Romans beheading two thousand of its citizens, a measure that horrified the whole island, as no doubt it was intended to do. By the time Cicero got round to describing the city, Lentini was "wretched and empty", though it continued as a small-scale agricultural centre for some time, until the great earthquake of 1693 completely demolished it.

Carlentini

Noisy, sprawling, modern Lentini has little to recommend it, and the extensive remains of the ancient city are a few kilometres out of town and easier to reach from the upper town of **Carlentini**, which itself has a fairly pleasant central square with a few bars. Some of the finds from ancient Lentini are on display in the **Museo Archeologico** (Tues–Sun 9am–6pm; €4), at Piazza Studi, east of central Carlentini off Via Piave. However, the best artefacts have been appropriated by the museums at Catania and Siracusa.

Zona Archeologica

Daily 9am–1pm • Free • The site is a 20min walk south of Carlentini; most Lentini buses also stop in Piazza San Francesco on the outskirts of Carlentini, closer to the Zona Archeologica, as do local buses from Lentini's train station, from where the site is a 5min walk

The **Zona Archeologica** is spread over the two hills of San Mauro and Metapiccola. The first of these is the more interesting, holding the ancient town's **acropolis** and the substantial remains of a vast **necropolis** nearby. You'll see the pincer-style south gate immediately, part of a well-conserved system of fortifications that surrounded the town. Together, the hills make a good couple of hours' rambling, while a dirt road to the side of the main entrance climbs around the perimeter fence to allow views over the whole site and down to Lentini in the valley below.

ARRIVAL AND DEPARTURE   LENTINI

By train Most trains between Catania and Siracusa stop at Lentini.

By bus Buses from Catania run to Lentini approximately half-hourly.

EATING

Navarria Via Conte Alaimo 8 ☏ 095 941 045. For a snack in Lentini, seek out this fabulous *pasticceria* (anyone can point the way), where pastries and *granitas* are to die for. Tues–Sun 7am–9.30pm.

Mount Etna

One of the world's largest volcanoes, **Mount Etna** (3323m) dominates much of Sicily's eastern landscape, its smoking summit an omnipresent feature for travellers in the area. The main crater is gradually becoming more explosive and more dangerous, with spectacular eruptions (see box, p.205) in 2001 and 2002 far eclipsing those of the preceding decade. Despite the risk, the volcano remains a remarkable draw, though the unpredictability of eruptions – they may be expected, but cannot be pinpointed to a precise time – means that it's often impossible to get close to the main crater.

Etna was just one of the places that the Greeks thought to be the forge of Vulcan, a fitting description of the blustering and sparking from the main crater. The philosopher Empedocles studied the volcano closely, living in an observatory near the summit. This terrifying existence was dramatized by Matthew Arnold in his *Empedocles on Etna*:

> *Alone! –*
> *On this charr'd, blacken'd melancholy waste,*
> *Crown'd by the awful peak, Etna's great mouth.*

Certainly, it all proved too much for Empedocles, who in 433 BC jumped into the main crater in an attempt to prove that the gases emitted would support his body weight. They didn't.

The higher reaches of Etna resemble a lunar landscape, the ground underfoot alternately black, grey or red depending on the age of the lava. The most recent stuff lies in great folds; below, the red roofs and green fields of the lower hills stretch away to the sea. You'll not be in any danger, provided you stay within the limit that is currently deemed safe to reach. Note that **ascending the volcano** is only possible between about May and October; the rest of the time, it's swathed in snow. For obvious reasons, access to the upper reaches of Etna, around the craters, is strictly controlled – current volcanic activity and weather conditions will dictate how far up you'll be able to go.

However you go, at whatever time of year, take warm clothes, good shoes or boots and glasses to keep the flying grit out of your eyes. You can **rent boots and jackets** cheaply from the Etna Sud cable-car station. Food up the mountain is poor and overpriced, so you might want to bring a picnic.

Approaches to Etna

A ring of villages circles the lower slopes of Etna, including the ski-centres of **Linguaglossa** (on the Circumetnea rail route) and **Nicolosi**, which hold the bulk of the

---

SNOW, ICE AND THE BISHOP

Even in winter, the **snow** on Etna's southern side tends to lie only in patches, partly melted by the heat of the rocks. On the northern side, however, hollows in the ground are filled year-round with snow. From here, the **ice** used to be cut, covered with ash and then transported to the rest of the island, the mainland and even Malta, for refrigeration purposes – a peculiar export that constituted the main source of revenue for the Bishop of Catania, who owned the land until comparatively recently.

5

THE FERROVIA CIRCUMETNEA

Although there's nothing to beat an ascent of Etna, you can experience something of the majesty of the volcano along the route of the **Ferrovia Circumetnea** (☎095 541 250, ⓦcircumetnea.it), or Circumetnea railway. This is a private line, 110km long, starting in Catania and circling the base of Etna as far as Riposto on the Ionian coast, 30km north of Catania. It's a marvellous ride, running through fertile vegetation – citrus plantations, vines and nut trees – and past the strewn lava of recent eruptions, with endless views of the summit en route. If you don't have time to do the whole circuit, some of the best views of Etna are between Adrano and Bronte, as the railway line climbs ever closer to the lava flows.

You can easily do the whole round-trip in a day from Catania, although the medieval town of Randazzo also makes an interesting overnight stop. The Circumetnea ends its run 20km southeast of Linguaglossa at Riposto, where you switch to the mainline station Giarre-Riposto for frequent trains south to Catania (or north to Giardini-Naxos).

Circumetnea trains depart from Stazione Catania Borgo, on Via Caronda in Catania. They take two hours to Randazzo, three to Linguaglossa and three and a half to Riposto (no Sunday service; timetables available on the website), and **tickets** cost €6.85 one-way, €11 return. Occasionally, sections of the line are under repair, in which case a replacement bus service operates.

accommodation, restaurants and tour facilities. The two main approaches to the summit are from north and south. Some of the best scenery is on the north side (signposted "**Etna Nord**"), and if you have your own transport, the circular road that leads up from Linguaglossa to Piano Provenzano, and then to the Rifugio Cutelli, is highly recommended – though the road beyond **Piano Provenzana** is strictly controlled in snowy weather, and even with a 4WD you may be strongly encouraged to leave your vehicle and take an organized jeep trip. From the south side ("**Etna Sud**"), beyond Nicolosi, the chief departure point is the mountain refuge-hotel of **Rifugio Sapienza**, connected by daily bus from Catania.

If you're short on time, the easiest way to see the volcano and climb its slopes is by **organized tour**. 4WD minibuses and guided hikes operate out of Piano Provenzana and Rifugio Sapienza, though many tourists simply book an all-day tour via their hotel or B&B in places like Taormina, Giardini-Naxos, Catania and Siracusa. If you're pushed for time or unable to ascend higher due to adverse conditions, you'll have to make do with the glimpses of Etna's peak and hinterland from the **Circumetnea railway** (see above).

Etna Nord

If you have a car, head to the town of **LINGUAGLOSSA** and drive through the town following the brown signs to **Etna Nord**. There are several picnic places with barbecues along the road, and buying some good local meat before you leave Linguaglossa is probably the only reason to stop in town.

The road up the mountain is at its most spectacular in winter, when the peak of Etna is covered in snow. As you drive along, look out for ungainly lumps of solidified lava colonized with lichen, protruding through the undergrowth. Beyond **Rifugio Ragabo** (1425m), follow the sign for **Piano Provenzana**, whose hotels and ski-lifts were devastated by the most recent major eruption of 2002. Today the scorched skeletons of trees still protrude from a vast river of solidified lava. Going back to the main road, continue until you come to a side road marked **Rifugio Citelli** (1750m). On a clear day the views stretch across the Nébrodi mountains, to Taormina, and across the Ionian Sea, to the Aspromonte mountains in Calabria. The Refugio isn't always staffed, but when it is, basic food is available, as are treks up the volcano (snow shoes are provided

5

THE ASCENT OF ETNA FROM RIFUGIO SAPIENZA

From *Rifugio Sapienza*, there are two ways **up the volcano**. The **Funivia dell'Etna cable car** (daily: summer 9am–5.30pm, winter 9am–3.30pm; €17.00 one-way, €29.50 return; Ⓦfuniviaetna.com) reaches an altitude of 2500m at Monte Montagnola, from where SITAS **minibuses** leave for the crater (April–Oct daily 9am–5pm, weather permitting; ☏095 914 141). The total journey (cable car plus minibus) takes around 2.5hr and costs €57.50. When the wind is up, or conditions are otherwise difficult, the entire journey is undertaken from *Rifugio Sapienza* by minibus.

Conditions permitting, it's also possible to **walk to Etna's summit** from *Rifugio Sapienza*, for which you need to contact Etna Touring (☏095 791 8000 or ☏347 783 8799, Ⓦetnatouring .com). Expeditions without an authorized guide are extremely unwise.

---

during winter). The descent takes you through a black moonscape of lava and back along the foothills of Etna to Linguaglossa.

ACCOMMODATION AND EATING   ETNA NORD

Rifugio Ragabo Pineta Bosco Ragabo ☏095 647 841, Ⓦragabo.it. Simple, cosy pine-wood *rifugio*-hotel, high up on Etna near Linguaglossa, which makes a perfect base for an active mountain holiday – winter or summer – with cosy doubles and family rooms and a pleasant restaurant serving hearty mountain fare that is open to all. Half board is available (€50 per person); otherwise rates include breakfast. Closed Nov. <u>€70</u>

Etna Sud

More built-up and touristy than the north slope, **Etna Sud** offers the easiest approach to the volcano via public transport, with buses connecting Catania with the *Rifugio Sapienza*, at the foot of the cable car to the summit and at the end of the negotiable road up the south side of Etna. The ride up Etna to the *rifugio* throws up some truly bizarre scenery: the green foothills give way to wooded slopes, then to bare, black-and-grey seas of volcanic debris, spotted with the hardy endemic plants – yellow-green *spino santo* and Etna violets – that are the only things to grow on the heights of the volcano. The most recent lava streams lie to the right of the road, where you'll also see earlier spent craters, grass-covered on the lower reaches and no more than black pimples further up.

Torre del Filosofo

In the autumn of 2013, as this book went to press, eruptions from a crater in the southeast destroyed the so-called **Torre del Filosofo**, a tower that was said to have been the observatory of Empedocles (see p.199), though more likely to have been a memorial built by the Romans to celebrate the emperor Hadrian's climb to the summit. At the time of writing, excursions to this area were suspended.

ARRIVAL AND DEPARTURE   ETNA SUD

By bus One or two buses a day from Catania go to *Rifugio Sapienza*, the mountain refuge/hotel that marks the end of the negotiable road up the south side of Etna. The year-round service leaves from Piazza Giovanni XXIII, outside Catania's Stazione Centrale, daily at 8.15am, with a stop at Nicolosi; an additional summer service (mid-June to mid-Sept) leaves daily at 11.20am, and necessitates a change at Nicolosi. Altogether, it's a two-hour journey; tickets cost around €5. (You can, of course, catch the bus at Nicolosi, from where departures to the refuge are at 9.15am and – in summer – 12.30pm, an hour-long trip.) The return bus from *Rifugio Sapienza* leaves for Catania at 4.30pm.

ACCOMMODATION

Hotel Corsaro ☏095 914 122, Ⓦhotelcorsaro.it. Ski-lodge-type place popular with tour groups, advertising itself as Etna's highest lodging. It has a restaurant and offers half-board deals (€70 per person). <u>€120</u>

★ **Rifugio Sapienza** ☏095 915 321, Ⓦrifugio sapienza.com. At 1400m below the summit, this is the cheapest place on this side of Etna to spend the night, so it's always wise to ring ahead and book. Its modern rooms have

clean lines and en-suite bathrooms, and there's a restaurant (excursions can also be arranged from here). **€110**

Nicolosi

The tidy little resort of **NICOLOSI** (698m), which had a narrow escape in the 2002 eruption, is a popular winter ski-centre and the most useful base in the foothills on the south side of the volcano. With several hotels and some good places to eat, it also has good bus connections from Catania. It gets pretty busy around here, even in summer, with some good walking possibilities in the area. Best of these, certainly if you're going no further, is the hike up to the **Monti Rossi** craters, around an hour each way. Formed in the eruption of 1669, they're the most important of the secondary craters that litter the slopes of the volcano.

Five kilometres or so east of Nicolosi, **Trecastagni** is worth a look for its main church, the Chiesa Madre, a fine Renaissance building probably designed by Antonello Gagini, and the marvellous views over the coast from its elevated position. Frankly, though, you're hardly likely to come here for just these; better, if you're driving, to look upon Trecastagni as a coffee-stop.

ARRIVAL AND INFORMATION NICOLOSI

By bus Nicolosi is the last main bus stop before the steeper slopes begin; AST buses run hourly from Catania, taking 40min.
Tourist office There's a helpful tourist office on Piazza

Vittorio Emanuele (Mon–Fri 9am–1pm, plus Mon, Wed & Thurs 4–6pm; ☎ 095 914 488), just off the main road that runs through town.

ACCOMMODATION AND EATING

Camping Etna Via Goethe ☎ 095 914 309. Nice campsite in a shady pinewood with a pool (summer only), is on Via Goethe, signposted from town just past the hotels. Open all year. Tent pitch plus two people **€22**
Al Centro Storico Via Garibaldi 26 ☎ 095 910 735 or ☎ 348 266 4310, ⓦ alcentrostorico.it. A good, central B&B with antique-style touches, along with fridges, TV and wi-fi, just off Piazza Vittorio Emanuele. **€60**
Etna Garden Park Hotel Via della Quercia 7 ☎ 095 791 4686 or ☎ 347 877 9969, ⓦ etnagardenpark.com.

Subdued rooms in a capacious chalet-type building with a garden full of colonnades and statues. The friendly owners will help you organize the whole gamut of Etna-based activities, from mountain-biking and horseriding to tours based around food or wine. **€85**
★ **Nero di Cenere** Via Garibaldi 64 ☎ 095 791 8513. Wine bar and restaurant serving taster-plates of local cheeses and salami, along with pastas and various vegetarian dishes, which you can enjoy *al fresco* on the terrace. Closes late if custom demands. Mon & Wed–Sun 7–9pm.

ETNA NORD BY ORGANIZED TOUR

If you don't have your own vehicle, you'll need to take a taxi from Linguaglossa to Piano, from where **tours** aboard 4WD minibuses operated by STAR (daily May–Oct, weather permitting; ☎ 095 371 333 or ☎ 347 495 7091) shuttle up and down the upper slopes. At present there is just one option, costing €48.50: a two-hour excursion that brings you to Pizzi Deneri (at a height of 2800m), where there is a 10min pause; you then descend to 2400m for another stop, then down again to 2100m for a 30min walk to a minor crater. If the current regulations change (the situation on the slopes is constantly monitored), there may be other options that bring you closer to the main crater (3200m). The early morning and early evening tours are the best – Etna at dawn or sunset is a spectacular sight – but need booking. The minibuses don't run to a fixed timetable; they simply take off when full, and the operation is a lower-key affair than on the southern side.

You can also join an **organized hike** to the summit from Linguaglossa or Piano Provenzana – contact Guide Etna Nord for details: Via Roma 93, Linguaglossa (☎ 095 777 4502 or ☎ 348 012 5167, ⓦ guidetnanord.com). Solo expeditions are not encouraged.

5

Zafferana Etnea

The most appealing of the villages on Etna's southeastern side, **ZAFFERANA ETNEA** is surrounded by vineyards and citrus groves, and is renowned for its honey, the smell of which lingers in the air. Parts of the outskirts were damaged by lava in 1992, when the village became the operational hub of the effort to halt the flow from the volcano. The centre, however, was untouched, and it retains an eighteenth-century air in its buildings and churches, making it a pleasant stop, perhaps for a coffee in the bar on the corner of the elegant central piazza. The previous eruption to threaten Zafferana occurred in 1792, halted on that occasion – according to local tradition – by the intervention of Our Lady of Divine Providence, whose name was again invoked by God-fearing locals during the last volcanic ructions.

Zafferana has acquired a reputation as a low-key hill-resort, and the population of around seven thousand practically doubles at weekends and holidays as the trippers arrive. Certainly, there's some good walking to be done in the green hills behind the village, and if you fancy a longer stay there's a choice of **hotels**, all north of the centre. A road from Zafferana Etnea winds directly up the mountain to *Rifugio Sapienza* (see p.202), a drive of around 45 minutes, while a lower road leads 15km north past various old lava flows – of 1852, 1950 and, near Fornazzo, of 1979 – to Linguaglossa.

ARRIVAL AND INFORMATION   ZAFFERANA ETNEA

By bus Buses run hourly Mon–Sat (4 daily Sun) from Catania to Zafferana Etnea, taking 1hr 15min.
Tourist information There's a tourist office at Piazza Luigi Sturzo 3 (summer Mon–Sat 9am–1pm & 4–8pm; winter Mon–Sat 9am–1pm & 3–7pm; ☎ 095 708 2825, ⓦ zafferana-etnea.it).

ACCOMMODATION

Primavera dell'Etna Via Cassone 86 ☎ 095 708 2348, ⓦ hotel-primavera.it. Large, well-equipped hotel, a bit shabby at the seams. It's more popular with Italians than foreigners, with fabulous views of Etna and the sea from its terraces, and lovely grounds with a tennis court and solarium. Rooms can be a bit old-fashioned, but the location is great, staff friendly and there is a restaurant too serving local fare, with half-board, deals should you so wish. **€100**

THE WINES OF ETNA

Thanks to mineral-rich volcanic soil, an extremely low yield and a varied climate (temperatures can range from 30°C to 0°C in a single day), the **vineyards** on Etna's foothills have the potential to produce some of Italy's most interesting **wines**. They were also some of the only vineyards in Europe to survive the phylloxera epidemic of the late nineteenth century – the virus couldn't pass through volcanic powder, sand or snow. The richness and complexity of the grapes grown here has led several producers to rebel against the trend of ageing wines in small wood *barriques*, preferring instead to use stainless-steel vats or even ceramic amphorae, so that there is nothing to interfere with the natural taste of the grape. At the vanguard of this movement are the highly talented Tuscan wine-producer **Andrea Franchetti**, whose Etna vineyards produce the international award-winning Passopisciaro (☎ 366 358 9926, ⓦ passopisciaro.com); and eccentric Belgian **Frank Cornelissen** (no phone; ⓦ frankcornelissen.it), who spurns the use of sulphates in wines such as Magma and Munjibello, which now enjoy a cult following (especially in Japan) for their extreme unpredictability. These days Etna even has a celebrity winemaker in **Mick Hucknall** of Simply Red, who owns the Il Cantante vineyard (☎ 095 716 9255, ⓦ ilcantante .com and ☎ 393 189 8430, ⓦ quincunx.it) on the eastern slope of Etna, near Sant'Alfio, and who is working with one of the volcano's most highly regarded winemakers, the pioneer, environmentalist and visionary Salvo Foti, who has an almost mystical approach to winemaking. You can get a (free) tour of all the above vineyards by appointment.

5

MOUNT ETNA'S ERUPTIONS

Of the scores of recorded **eruptions** of Etna since the 475 BC one described by Pindar, some have been disastrously spectacular: in 1169, 1329 and 1381 the lava reached the sea, while in **1669**, the worst year, parts of Catania were wrecked and its castle was surrounded by molten rock.

During the twentieth century, the Circumetnea railway line was repeatedly ruptured by lava flows, the towns of the foothills were threatened, and roads and farms destroyed. The **1971** eruption destroyed the observatory supposed to give warning of such an event, while in **1979** nine tourists were killed by an explosion on the edge of the main crater. During the **1992** eruption, which engulfed the outskirts of Zafferana Etnea, the American navy joined Italian forces in an attempt to stem the lava flow by dropping reinforced concrete blocks (so-called "Beirut-busters", used to defend military camps) from helicopters into the fissures.

In **2001**, the military helicopters were out again in force, this time water-bombing the forest fires and blazing orchards. Regarded as the most complex in the last three hundred years, the 2001 eruption spewed forth from six vents on Etna's northern and southeastern sides and sent vast, fiery fountains of lava to the skies. Drivers found the roads blocked and air passengers were forced to divert to other island airports, while Catania suffered a rain of black ash day and night. Luckily there were no fatalities; the cluster of buildings around *Rifugio Sapienza* narrowly escaped and the lava flow petered out 4km short of Nicolosi, though the upper cable-car station was destroyed and the hut that held the monitoring live-cam was incinerated (somehow the equipment was saved).

Triggered by an earthquake, the eruption of **2002** saw lava streams pouring down both north and south flanks, destroying restaurants, hotels and a cable car in the ski resort of Piano Provenzana, and threatening the villages of Nicolosi and Linguaglossa below. Emergency teams, however, succeeded in diverting the flow, and a major catastrophe was averted. Some local villagers, on the other hand, preferred to place their faith in parading statues of the Virgin Mary before the volcano, although the devout were far outnumbered by the flocks of sightseers who made excursions as close as they dared, until curtailed by the authorities.

More eruptions followed in **2006**, **2007** and **2008**, the latter accompanied by minor local earthquakes and continuing at a low intensity for some six months, making it the longest of the eruptions since 2000. A significant eruption of ash also occurred in **2010**, producing an ash plume that rose to a height of 800m above the crater.

In late **2013**, Etna began erupting again, with most of the activity centred around the southeast crater. Pulsating lava fountains reached 600m height, and explosions of giant magma bubbles ejected liquid lava for hundreds of meters, destroying the Torre del Filosofo and entering the Valle del Bove. As the volcano was still in activity when this book went to press, we recommend that anyone intending to visit Etna first consults the regularly updated English-language **website**, ⓦ volcanodiscovery.com for an update on current conditions.

Milo

Five kilometres or so north of Zafferana, **Milo** offers impressive views of the Valle del Bove above. Maps show a road from Milo that climbs northwest, up the volcano to the *Rifugio Citelli* (see p.200) and back towards Linguaglossa, but frequent landslides often make this route impossible. You should be able to get some of the way up though, for more striking views of the summit and the coastline below.

Etna Adventure

Parco Sbargaglio, Via Acque del Vescovo • Daily 10am–sunset; sometimes closed weekends mid-Sept to mid-June, call ahead to check • Courses start at €15 • ☎ 329 918 8187, ⓦ etnaadventure.it

If you've kids in tow, you may get no further than **Etna Adventure**, just outside Milo on the road to Linguaglossa. An excellent adventure park, it has challenging Tarzan-like obstacle courses for adults and children (from age 2 and up) slung among the trees. They also organize all manner of activities on and around Etna, including snow-shoe trekking, whitewater rafting, potholing and jeep tours.

5

Randazzo

Great rivers of volcanic rubble clutter the slopes on all sides of **RANDAZZO**, the closest town to the summit of Etna, just 15km away as the crow flies. Walls belonging to former orchards or vineyards are occasionally visible through the black debris. Despite its dangerous proximity, the town has never been engulfed, though an eruption in 1981 came perilously close. Randazzo has not escaped entirely unscathed, however: as one of the main forward positions of the German forces during their defence of Sicily in 1943, the town was heavily bombed, and most of the lava-built churches and palaces you'll see here, originally dating from the wealthy thirteenth- to sixteenth-century era, are the result of meticulous restoration. The result is a handsome old centre, with enough to occupy a half-day's exploration – and Randazzo is easily the best place to break your Circumetnea trip if you fancy a night in the sticks.

In medieval times, three churches took turns to act as Randazzo's cathedral, a sop to the three parishes in town whose inhabitants were of Greek, Latin and Lombard origin. The largest, **Santa Maria**, on the main Via Umberto I, is the modern-day holder of the title, a severe Catalan-Gothic structure with a fine carved portal with vine decoration. Further up the road, facing a small square, the blackened tower that forms part of the old city walls is all that survives of Randazzo's Castello Svevo, which did duty as a prison from around 1500 until 1973.

Museo Vagliasindi

Via Castello 1 • Tues–Sun 9am–6pm • €2.60

Museo Vagliasindi holds a good collection of objects from a nearby Greek necropolis, including wine jugs in the form of women's heads, and a vessel in the shape of a spunky little rat. Downstairs you'll find ranks of dangling Sicilian puppets, variously sporting armour, a velvet cloak or a deer-stalker cap – typically for eastern Sicily, they are taller than the puppets you may have seen in Palermo. The museum's other rooms, including the bare, minuscule cells where inmates once rotted, display agricultural tools and other rustic items.

ARRIVAL AND INFORMATION

RANDAZZO

By Circumetnea train Arriving on the Circumetnea, walk straight up Via Vittorio Véneto to reach the central Piazza Loreto, with the medieval town further on, down Via Umberto I.

Destinations Catania (up to 7 daily Mon–Sat; 2hr 20min); Linguaglossa (4 daily Mon–Sat; 35min); Riposto (4 daily Mon–Sat; 1hr 10min).

By bus The bus station is a couple of blocks back from Piazza Loreto off Via Vittorio Véneto. There are frequent connections with Catania (1–2 hourly Mon–Sat; 1hr

45min), and limited services (early morning and lunchtime) to several other places you might want to visit, such as Bronte, Castiglione di Sicilia and Gole Alcantara. There's also a morning bus (leaving at 8am) to Taormina.

Tourist information You'll find a limited amount of information on Etna and the surrounding area at the Parco dei Nébrodi tourist office, on the way to the museum at Via Umberto I 197 (daily 9am–1pm & 3–7.30pm; ☎ 095 799 1611, ⓦ parcodeinebrodi.it).

ACCOMMODATION, EATING AND DRINKING

Ai Tre Parchi Bed and Bike Via Tagliamento 49 ☎ 095 799 1631 or ☎ 329 897 0901, ⓦ aitreparchibb.it. Excellent place offering B&B rooms and self-catering apartments, plus bike rental and local bike tours. To reach Via Tagliamento, turn left off Via Vittorio Véneto from the station. Doubles **€80**

Da Antonio Via Pietro Nenni 8 ☎ 095 799 2534. Best place in town for typical local dishes and pizzas (€6–10); the house *antipasto* is really good, too. The restaurant is a few hundred metres from Piazza Loreto – walk down the Linguaglossa road, past the petrol

stations, and it's up a side road on the right. Tues–Sun lunch & dinner.

San Giorgio e Il Drago Piazza San Giorgio 28 ☎ 095 923 972. Cosy trattoria housed in a nineteenth-century wine cellar, run by Samantha and Daniele Anzalone with food cooked by their two mothers. In spring, there's the chance to eat home-made pasta with wild asparagus; in autumn, look out for dishes using porcini mushrooms collected from the woods of Etna; and in winter sausage fried with wild greens. Expect to pay around €30 per head for a full meal. Mon & Wed–Sun dinner only.

BRONTE'S PISTACHIOS

The mineral-rich volcanic soil of Bronte produces what are considered to be the best **pistachios** in Italy, grown in the exquisitely tended orchards that stretch around the town. In fact, Sicily is the only place in Italy where the pistachio tree grows, and Bronte itself is responsible for eighty percent of the production. There is no shortage of places to sample the striking violet-and-green nut in town – and indeed throughout Sicily; take home a jar of pistachio pesto, or a box of pistachio biscuits, or taste either *in situ* at one of the cafés lining Bronte's main corso, such as *Conti Gallenti*, Corso Umberto 1 (Mon & Wed–Sun 6am–10pm; ☎ 095 691 165), an unassuming little place that has changed little since the 1970s, famous for its pistachio *arancini* and ice cream.

Castello Nelson

Daily 9am–1pm & 2.30–5pm, summer until 7pm • €3, gardens only €1.50

About 12km west of Randazzo, just off the SS120, lies the estate given to Lord Nelson as part of his dukedom, granted by King Ferdinand in gratitude for British help in repressing the Neapolitan revolution of 1799, which had forced the Bourbon court to flee to Palermo. Although Nelson never got round to visiting his Sicilian property, his family, the Bridports, only relinquished control in 1978. Surrounded by a wooded estate, it's now owned by the *Comune*, but is still known (and signposted) as the **Castello Nelson**. Its original name was Maniace, after the convent founded here in 1174 on the site of a victory over the Arabs by George Maniakes. The 1693 earthquake destroyed much of this building, but as you pass through the walls you'll see the restored thirteenth-century chapel with its chunky lava columns and Byzantinesque icon, the so-called *Madonna di Maniace*. As for the **house** itself, were it not for the beautiful tiled floors, restored to match the original pattern in yellow, rose and blue, it could easily be mistaken for an English country residence. Its style and furnishings – wallpaper, maritime paintings – were defined by Alexander Hood, one of the Bridports, who lived here for sixty years until the 1930s. The same Englishness is evident in the well-tended **garden**, planted with box hedges, magnolias and palm trees.

On the other side of the river lies the only part of the estate still owned by Nelson's descendants, the English cemetery. Its most celebrated occupant is the Scottish author William Sharp (1855–1905), who wrote under the name of Fiona Macleod and was a regular visitor here.

Bronte

A small, unassuming town with a noble past, **BRONTE** lies half an hour's drive southwest of Randazzo along the SS284. It was founded by Charles V in 1535, and many echoes of its original layout survive, particularly in the numerous battlemented *campanili* that top its ageing churches. The town gave its name both to the dukedom bestowed upon Nelson (see above) and to Yorkshire's trio of novelists, the Brontë sisters, whose father, the Rev Patrick Prunty, harboured such an obsession for Nelson that he changed his name to Brontë (and added an umlaut). Otherwise, Bronte's sole claim to fame these days is as the centre of Italy's **pistachio** production: the plantations around town account for 85 percent of the country's output, but are only harvested in the early autumn of odd-numbered years. The nuts are widely used in Sicilian pasta dishes (including a famously tasty shrimp and nut concoction), while not surprisingly the town's cafés do a great line in pistachio *granitas*, ice cream and other goodies.

Siracusa and the southeast

NOTO

Siracusa and the southeast

Sicily's southeast has always ranked among the island's most alluring regions, and in Siracusa it boasts a city whose long and glorious history outshines all others on the island. Indeed, Siracusa was once the most important city in the Western world, though with most business activity located elsewhere and all political power centred on Palermo, its status today is as a provincial capital. Yet it remains the most interesting destination in this part of the island, charged with historical resonance, and a useful base for visiting many other regional highlights, few more than 45 minutes' drive from the city.

6

Inland, the southeast is characterized by the rough and wild **Monti Iblei**, riven by spectacular ravines, or *cave*, which are riddled with rock-cut tombs that prove occupation of the area as far back as the thirteenth century BC. The most famous is **Pantalica**, northwest of Siracusa, Sicily's greatest necropolis, while at the **Cava Grande del Fiume Cassibile**, near Avola, you can peer into the distant depths of Sicily's own "Grand Canyon". Greek colonists later appropriated many early Neolithic sites, founding towns at **Megara Hyblaea**, on the coast north of Siracusa near **Augusta**, and inland at **Akrai**, just outside the attractive small town of **Palazzolo Acreide**. Several other much smaller archeological sites lie strung along the coast, often set beside otherwise unsung sandy beaches.

However dramatic the natural scenery, it's the built environment that most defines the southeast. **Earthquakes** have repeatedly afflicted the area, none so destructive as that of January 11, 1693, which devastated the entire region. This catastrophe did, however, have one lasting effect: where there were ruins, a confident new generation of architects raised planned towns, displaying a noble but vivacious Baroque style that endures today. **Noto** and **Ragusa Ibla** have some of the most spectacular Baroque cityscapes, though nearby **Modica** and **Scicli** hold Baroque centres of varying refinement. Local authorities have slowly awoken to the tourist potential hereabouts: the southeast holds more B&Bs than any other region of Sicily, many housed in restored Baroque mansions, while tours and activities are increasingly available, from mountain-biking to gorge-walking.

The **coast** is a mixed bag, virtually off-limits north of Siracusa thanks to the petrochemical industry that disfigures the **Golfo di Augusta**. To the south, sandy beaches have spawned small-scale dormitory towns aimed squarely at a local clientele – none has much architectural charm, but the beaches are good. The only real exception is the coastline south of Noto, from **Avola** to Sicily's southern cape, **Capo delle Correnti**, in between which lie assorted pristine beaches, old tuna-fishing villages and market-garden towns, with the undisputed highlight being the lagoons, paths and bird hides of the **Riserva Naturale di Vendicari**. West of the Capo, there is no shortage of

Highlights

① Piazza del Duomo, Siracusa Sicily's most graceful piazza is surrounded by Baroque palaces and has an Ancient Greek temple embedded in its Duomo. **See p.217**

② Siracusa's Teatro Greco Classical dramas are still staged in the theatre where Aeschylus attended performances of his own plays. See p.231

③ Noto The apotheosis of Baroque town planning, Noto offers glorious vistas at every turn, from extravagantly balconied palazzi to soaring church facades. **See p.235**

④ Cava Grande del Fiume Cassibile Eagles soar high above the Cassibile River canyon, while a track leads down to secluded swimming spots. **See p.239**

⑤ Riserva Vendicari Have a swim and see the pink flamingos fly at this idyllic coastal nature reserve. **See p.240**

⑥ Chocolate-tasting, Modica Sample the goods at Sicily's oldest chocolate manufacturer. **See p.244**

⑦ Ragusa Ibla Spend the night in a classy B&B in Ragusa's chic Baroque old town. **See p.249**

⑧ Sampieri beach Follow in the footsteps of Inspector Montalbano and the artists of the Gruppo di Scicli with a walk on the southeast's most beautiful beach. **See p.251**

HIGHLIGHTS ARE MARKED ON THE MAP ON P.212

long sandy beaches, such as Marina di Modica and Marina di Ragusa, but the finest is at **Sampieri**, a modest little resort which still retains a core of cobbled streets lined with cubic fishermen's houses.

Siracusa

6

More than any other Sicilian city, **SIRACUSA** (ancient Syracuse) has a past that is central not just to the island's history, but to that of the entire Mediterranean. Its greatest splendour belongs to antiquity. Syracuse established its ascendancy over other Sicilian cities for more than five hundred years, and at its height was the supreme power in Europe, home to at least three times its present population. Its central position on the major trade routes ensured that even after its heyday the port continued to wield influence and preserve its prestige. All this is reflected in a staggering diversity of monuments, spanning the Hellenic, early Christian, medieval, Renaissance and Baroque eras – the styles are often shoulder-to-shoulder, sometimes in the same building. It's one of the most enjoyable cities in Sicily, with a fascinating old town and outlying archeological and leisure areas that can easily occupy three or four days, if not a week, of your time.

As for two and a half thousand years, the city is still divided between its ancient hub, the island of Ortigia, and the four mainland quarters of Achradina, Tyche, Neapolis and Epipolae. **Ortigia** is the heart and soul of Siracusa, a predominantly medieval and Baroque ensemble of mansions and palaces, and home to most of the city's best B&Bs, hotels, cafés and restaurants. Across the bridge on the mainland, the modern city is centred on **Achradina**, now, as in Greek times, the busy commercial centre, traversed by the main street of Corso Gelone. North of Achradina, the old residential quarter of **Tyche** holds Siracusa's celebrated **Museo Archeologico** and the extraordinary Santa

HIGHLIGHTS

1. Piazza del Duomo, Siracusa
2. Siracusa's Teatro Greco
3. Noto
4. Cava Grande del Fiume Cassibile
5. Riserva Vendicari
6. Chocolate-tasting, Modica
7. Ragusa Ibla
8. Sampieri beach

SIRACUSA & THE SOUTHEAST

Lucia and San Giovanni **catacombs** – after those in Rome, Siracusa's catacombs constitute the largest system of subterranean tombs in Italy, and are the oldest in Sicily. **Neapolis** is the site of the **Parco Archeologico**, containing remains of the Greek city's theatres and some extensive quarries, while spread over the ridge to the west of town, **Epipolae** holds the old defensive walls and the remnants of the **Euryalus fort**. Other obvious trips out of the city are to the local beaches, particularly that at **Fontane Bianche**, or a cruise along the **Fiume Ciane** (Ciane River).

Brief history

6

The **ancient city** grew around Ortigia, an easily defensible offshore island with fresh springs, natural harbours on either side and access to extensive trade routes. Though Corinthian colonists arrived here in 733 BC, apparently at the behest of the Delphic oracle, it wasn't until the start of the fifth century BC that the city's political position was boosted by an alliance with Greeks at Akragas (Agrigento) and Gela. With the transfer of Gela's tyrant, **Gelon**, to Syracuse and the crushing victory of their combined forces over the Carthaginians at Himera in 480 BC, the stage was set for the beginning of the city's long supremacy. The grandest extant monuments are from this period, and more often than not were built by slaves provided from the many battles won by Syracuse's bellicose dictators.

The colony rebels

Inevitably, the city's ambitions provoked the intervention of Athens, which dispatched one of the greatest fleets ever seen in the ancient world. This **Great Expedition** was scuppered in 413 BC by a mixture of poor leadership and astute defence: "to the victors the most brilliant of successes, to the vanquished the most calamitous of defeats", commented the historian Thucydides. But Syracuse earned the condemnation of the Hellenic world for its seven-year incarceration of the vanquished Athenians – in appalling conditions – in the city's notorious quarries.

Tyrants, dramatists and philosophers

Throughout this period Syracuse was in a state of constant tension between a few overweening but extremely capable rulers, and sporadic convulsions of democracy. Occasionally the tyrants displayed a yearning for cultural respectability that sat uncomfortably beside their vaulting ambition. **Hieron I** (478–466 BC), for instance, described by the historian Diodorus as "an utter stranger to sincerity and nobility of character", invited many of the luminaries of the age to his court, including **Pindar**, and **Aeschylus** – who possibly witnessed the production of his last plays, *Prometheus Bound* and *Prometheus Released*, in the city's theatre. **Dionysius the Elder** (405–367 BC) – "cruel, vindictive and a profane plunderer of temples" and responsible for the first of the **Euryalus** forts – comically harboured literary ambitions to the extent of regularly entering his poems in the annual Olympic Games. His works were consistently rejected, until the Athenians judged it politic to give him the prize, whereupon his delirious celebrations were enough to provoke the seizure that killed him. His son **Dionysius II** (367–343 BC) dallied with the "philosopher-king" theories of his tutor **Plato** until megalomania turned his head and Plato fled in dismay. Dionysius himself, recorded Plutarch, spent the end of his life in exile "loitering about the fish market, or sitting in a perfumer's shop drinking the diluted wine of the taverns, or squabbling in the streets with common women".

Rarely, the rulers themselves initiated democratic reforms – men such as **Timoleon** (343–337 BC), who arrived from Corinth to inject new life into all the Sicilian cities, and **Hieron II**, who preserved Syracuse's independence from the assertions of Rome by a novel policy of conciliation, abandoning expansion in favour of preserving the status quo. His long reign (265–215 BC) saw the construction of such monuments as the **Ara di Ierone II**, and the enlargement of the **Teatro Greco** to more or less its existing proportions.

6

Neapolis & Parco Archeologico

Catania & Epipolae

VIALE TERACATI

VIALE AUGUSTO

VIALE PAOLO ORSI

SIRACUSA

N

Fontane Bianche & Noto

VIA SAN SEBASTIANO

VIA AUGUSTO VON PLATEN

VIA POLITI LAUDIEN

Latomia dei Cappuccini

PIAZZA CAPPUCCINI

Catacombs

TYCHE

Basilica di San Giovanni

Museo Archeologico

VIALE TEOCRITO

VIA DEL SANTUARIO

VIA LATINA

Stadio Comunale

RIVIERA DIONISIO IL GRANDE

Hospital

Santuario della Madonna delle Lacrime

VIA BIGNAMI

PIAZZA DELLA VITTORIA (excavations)

VIA GORIZIA

Basilica di Santa Lucia

VIA TESTAFERRATA

VIA ALGERIA

VIA DI NATALE

VIA M. CARABELLI

CORSO TIMOLEONTE

VIALE LUIGI CADORNA

VIA ENNA

VIA RAGUSA

VIA AGRIGENTO

VIA CALTANISETTA

PIAZZA S. LUCIA

VIA MONTE GRAPPA

VIA EURGETTA

VIA ADIGE

CORSO GELONE

VIA TRAPANI

VIA STATELLO

PIAZZA REPUBBLICA

VIA MOSCO

ACHRADINA

Edificio Termale

Arsenale

VIA BRENTA

V. EPICARMO

VIA F. CRISPI

Stazione Centrale

VIA ARSENALE

Bus Station

CORSO UMBERTO I

PIAZZA MARCONI

VIA CATANIA

VIALE A. DIAZ

VIA DANTE

VIA R. MARGHERITA

Porto Píccolo

VIA ELORINA

Foro Siracusano

CORSO UMBERTO I

VIA MALTA

VIA PALERMO

VIA BENGASI

VIA RODI

PIAZZA DELLA POSTA

VIA TRIESTE

VIA TRENTO

PIAZZA PANCALI

LARGO XXV LUGLIO

Porto Grande

RIVA GARIBALDI

RIVA NAZARIO SAURO

VIA BELVALLE

VIALE SETTEMBRE

VIA SAVOIA

VIA MAZZINI

VIA RESALIBERA

ORTIGIA

VIA MIRABELLA

LUNGOMARE VITTORINI

VIA DIONE

CORSO MATTEOTTI

VIA VITTORIO VENETO

VIA G. CARCALLO

VIA CAVOUR

PIAZZA ARCHIMEDE

VIA LANDOLINA

VIA MAESTRANZA

FORO ITALICO

VIA ROMA

VIA GIUDECCA

PIAZZA DEL DUOMO

VIA LARGA

VIA NIZZA

VIA PICHERALI

VIA CAPODIECI

VIA CASTELLO MANIACE

Castello Maniace

SEE "ORTIGIA" MAP FOR DETAILS

■ **ACCOMMODATION**

Caol Ishka	3
Giuggiulena	1
Lol Hostel	2
Paradiso del Mare	4
Rinaura	5

0   200
metres

The end of the glory days

Following the death of Hieron II, Syracuse, along with practically every other Sicilian city, sided with Carthage against Rome in the Second Punic War. For two years the city was besieged by the Romans, who had to contend with all the ingenious contrivances devised for its defence by **Archimedes**, though Syracuse eventually fell in 211 BC, an event that sent shockwaves rippling around the classical world. The city was ransacked, and Archimedes himself – the last of the great Hellenic thinkers – was hacked to death, despite the injunctions of the Roman general Marcellus.

Syracuse languished under Roman rule, though its trading role still made it the most prominent Sicilian city, and it became a notable centre of early Christianity, as attested by its extensive **catacombs**. The city briefly became the capital of the Byzantine empire when Constans moved his court here in 663 AD, but otherwise Syracuse was eclipsed by events outside its control and played no active part against all the successive waves of Arab, Norman and other medieval conquerors. The 1693 **earthquake** laid low much of the city, but provided the impetus for some of its Baroque masterpieces, notably the creations of the great Siculo-Spanish architect **Giovanni Vermexio**, who contributed an imposing facade to the Duomo, itself adapted from the bones of an early Greek temple and later Norman cathedral – and thus a building that encapsulates perfectly the polyglot character of modern Siracusa.

Ortigia

The ancient nucleus of Siracusa, **Ortigia** best conserves the city's essential spirit, with the artistic vestiges of over 2500 years of history concentrated in a space barely 500m across and 1km in length – and all within an easy stroll through quiet streets and alleys. Although parts of Ortigia were badly neglected in the past, there's been a lot of sensitive restoration and development in recent years, which has helped to restore the old town's lustre.

You can **swim and sunbathe** from Ortigia off Largo della Gancia, where there are rocks, wooden decks and handy nearby bars, or from a paying beach below the Talete car park, where sunloungers and parasols are available.

Tempio di Apollo
Largo XXV Luglio

Siracusa announces its long history immediately across the narrow ribbon of water that severs the island from the mainland. The **Tempio di Apollo** is thought to have been the first of the great Doric temples built in Sicily (seventh-century or early sixth-century BC) and, though not much survives apart from a couple of columns and part of the south wall of its cella, it's a dignified old ruin. A **scale model** in Siracusa's archeological museum (see p.222) shows you what it looked like in its heyday – the arched window in the wall dates from a Norman church that incorporated part of the temple into its structure. To help you make sense of what remains here, imagine the entrance with a double row of six columns, topped by a pediment at the eastern (far) end, and seventeen columns along each side. Visiting in the eighteenth century, the French writer Vivant Denon reported finding one of the columns embedded in the wall of a bedroom in a house on the adjacent Via Resalibera, part of it hacked away by the owner to make more room.

Ortigia market
Via de Benedictis · **Ortigia market** Mon–Sat from 7am until around 2pm · **Farmers' market** Sun 8am–1pm

Ortigia's weekday **market** spreads along Via de Benedictis, running north of the temple of Apollo toward the sea. One of the best stalls is run by Claudio Romano, who sells the wild herbs he collects near Pantalica, and fresh ricotta. At the far end is a cluster of unofficial stalls where locals sell fish, sea urchins and whatever wild vegetables are in

6

ORTIGIA

season. On Sunday's there is a **farmers' market** in the Renaissance-style courtyard of the nineteenth-century Antico Mercato, which backs onto Via de Benedictis, but has its entrance on parallel Via Trento.

Piazza Archimede

Lined with Fascist-era *palazzi* housing clothes and shoe shops, Corso Matteotti leads uphill from Largo XXV Luglio to **Piazza Archimede**, its centrepiece a twentieth-century **fountain** depicting the nymph Arethusa (the symbol of Ortigia) at the moment of her transformation into a spring. The square is surrounded by restored medieval *palazzi*, while down the skinny Via Montalto you can admire the facade of the **Palazzo Montalto**, graced by immaculate double- and triple-arched windows, and a star of David cut into the stonework. This is one of the few buildings in this style to have survived the 1693 earthquake– an inscription dates its construction to 1397.

6

Arkimedeion

Piazza Archimede 10 · Daily 10.30am–7pm · €6 · ☎ 0931 61 121, ⊛ arkimedeion.it

Occupying two floors of the recently restored Palazzo Pupillo, the high-tech **Arkimedeion** museum is devoted to Siracusa's most famous son, Archimedes. There are replicas – many of them interactive – of his inventions, including a **parabola microphone** in the courtyard, or you can try your hand at the Tangram-like **Stomachion puzzle**, with 536 solutions. Replicas of his most famous inventions – including a catapult, a human lever and the hydraulic screw – are due to arrive in 2014.

Piazza del Duomo

Ortigia's most impressive architecture belongs to its Baroque period, and nowhere does this reach such heights as in the city's (some would say Sicily's) loveliest square, the **Piazza del Duomo**. It's been gloriously restored, and the traffic kept out, so that the encircling seventeenth- and eighteenth-century buildings are now seen at their best from the pavement cafés, notably the **Municipio** (corner of Via Minerva) and the **Palazzo Beneventano** opposite.

The Duomo

Piazza Duomo · Usually daily 8am–7pm; may close earlier, and at lunchtime in winter · €2

The great age of Siracusa's **Duomo** is first glimpsed from around the side in Via Minerva, where stout Doric columns (part of an earlier Greek temple) form the very skeleton of the structure. The site was already sacred when the Greeks started work on an Ionic temple to Athena here in about 530 BC, though this was abandoned when a new temple was begun in thanksgiving for the victory over the Carthaginians at Himera. The extravagant decoration that adorned this building spread its fame throughout the ancient world, and tantalizing details of it have come down to us through **Cicero**, who visited Syracuse in the first century BC and listed the temple's former contents as part of his prosecution of the Roman praetor and villain Verres, who appeared to have walked off with a good proportion of them – part of the booty he plundered from many Sicilian temples. The doors were of ivory and gold, and its walls

---

GOING UNDERGROUND

An entrance on the Piazza Duomo in the Palazzo Arcivescovile, next to the cathedral, leads down into the **Ipogeo di Piazza Duomo** (Tues–Sat 10am–1pm; €4). This series of underground tunnels and water cisterns, dating back centuries, was used by the *siracusani* as an air-raid shelter during the heavy Allied bombing of 1943, and a small exhibition tells you something of the inhabitants' day-to-day experience. You can follow one of the tunnels right the way under the piazza, to emerge by the harbour on the Foro Italico, close to the Fonte Aretusa.

painted with military scenes and portraits of various of Syracuse's tyrants – claimed to be the earliest examples of portraiture in European art. On the temple's roof stood a tall statue of the warrior-goddess Athena carrying a golden shield which, catching the sun's rays, served as a beacon for sailors out at sea.

Although all this rich decoration has vanished, the main body of the temple was saved further despoliation thanks to its conversion into a Christian church, which was elevated to cathedral status in 640 AD. A more drastic overhaul was carried out after the 1693 earthquake, when the Norman facade collapsed and was replaced by the present formidable Baroque front, with statues by Marabitti. This is in sharp contrast to the more muted **interior**, in which it's the frame of the ancient temple that is still prevalent. The aisles are formed by the massive Doric columns, while the cella walls were hacked through to make the present arched nave. Along the **north aisle**, the distorted pillars give some inkling of how close the entire structure came to toppling when the seventeenth-century earthquake hit Siracusa. The Duomo's **south aisle** shows more characteristic Baroque effusion in the series of richly ornate chapels, though the first one (nearest the main door, on the right) – actually the baptistery – is from an earlier age. Enlivened by some twelfth-century arabesque mosaics, it contains a Norman font that was cut from a block still marked with a Greek inscription, and is supported by seven bronze lions.

Santa Lucia alla Badia

Piazza Duomo • Tues–Sun 11am–2pm

With its twisted barley-sugar columns, intricate wrought-iron balcony, and stone as delicately worked as silver, the facade of **Santa Lucia alla Badia** is one of Ortigia's prettiest. The original church, built by Queen Isabella of Castille on the site where it was thought Santa Lucia had been raped, was completely destroyed in the 1693 earthquake. Dedicated to Siracusa's much-loved patron saint, it was the focus of celebrations for the **miracle of Santa Lucia** in May. The mother superior clearly understood the resonance of this site for the people of Siracusa, and immediately after the earthquake requested that a shack was erected among the rubble, as a temporary church.

Her request was denied, so that work could start on the new church straight away. The building was supposed to be completed within two years – another sign of how important this church was felt to be for Siracusa – although in the end, it wasn't completed until 1703. The nuns – belonging to a closed Cistercian Order – returned, and there are still poignant indications of what life was like for them here, notably the oval *parlatorio* (to the left as you enter) with grills set in the wall so that nuns could talk to their families without being seen.

THE MIRACLE OF SANTA LUCIA

In the mid-seventeenth century, Sicily was suffering from **famine**. Under Spanish rule, the island was in a parlous state: rural areas were neglected by the aristocracy and fleeced by farm managers known as *gabelloti*, and urban centres riven with poverty. In Palermo these conditions gave rise to a riot; in Siracusa, in May 1646, people gathered instead in the cathedral to pray to **Santa Lucia**. As they were praying, a dove flew into the Duomo, shortly followed by the news that a ship laden with grain had arrived in the harbour. According to tradition, people were so hungry that there was no time to grind the wheat into flour, so they ate the grains boiled in a kind of porridge, known as **cuccia**. These days *cuccia* has been vastly improved – the wheat berries are served mixed with sweetened ricotta, candied fruit and chocolate; while Santa Lucia is still celebrated with processions and fireworks on her feast day, December 13, and in May, when quails are released in Piazza Duomo to record the miraculous news-bearing dove.

DUOMO, SIRACUSA >

The Burial of Santa Lucia

For the past few years Santa Lucia alla Badia has been the temporary home of one of Siracusa's most prized works of art, *The Burial of Santa Lucia* by **Caravaggio**. Having escaped from prison in Malta, Caravaggio arrived in the city in October 1608 and received an immediate commission to have a painting of Santa Lucia ready for her festival on December 13. Some scholars think the fact that the upper two-thirds of the canvas are taken up by a bare wall may have more to do with lack of time than aesthetics, for as Caravaggio was painting it, he was in fear of his life, pursued, it's thought, by the Knights of Malta.

The canvas was designed not for this church, but for the church of Santa Lucia across in the Borgata, scene of the saint's martyrdom, and home of her tomb (if not her body, which has been in Venice since the time of the Crusades). Bathed in shafts of sunlight, dwarfed by stark, scorched bare plaster walls, two mighty gravediggers brace themselves to lower the corpse of the saint into her tomb, watched by a bishop and mourners. One tradition is that the bearded gravedigger to the left is a portrait of Alof de Wignacourt, Grand Master of the Knights of Malta – and that painting him in this role was Caravaggio's way of taking revenge on the man who had had him imprisoned. Paranoid and persecuted, Caravaggio slept fully dressed and fully armed whilst painting the work, and fled from Siracusa as soon as it was finished, not even waiting for the painting to be unveiled at the feast of Santa Lucia.

Fonte Aretusa
Largo Aretusa

Down from the Duomo toward the seafront, the freshwater spring known as the **Fonte Aretusa** is probably the next most photographed part of the island. Planted with papyrus, and filled with bream below the water and ducks above, it's a compulsory stop on the evening *passeggiata*. It's ringed by cafés, while the terrace above offers sweeping views across the bay. The **spring** was mentioned in the original Delphic directions that brought the first Greek settlers here, and the number of myths with which it's associated underlines the strong sentimental links that continued to bind the colonists to their motherland. This was where the nymph Arethusa rose after swimming across from the Peloponnese, having been metamorphosed into a spring by the goddess Artemis to escape the attentions of the predatory river-god Alpheus; all in vain, though, for the determined Alpheus pursued her here to mingle with her in a watery form. Other legends declared that the spring's water would stain red at the time of the annual sacrifices at the sanctuary of Olympia, and that a cup thrown into the river there would rise here in Ortigia.

Porto Marina

The promenade runs both ways from the Fonte Aretusa, south towards the castle and north along the tree-lined Foro Italico (also known as Foro Vittorio Emanuele II) to **Porta Marina**, a fifteenth-century gateway surmounted by a curlicued Spanish heraldic device. The vast, still pool of the **Porto Grande** spreads out beyond, dotted with fishing-boats, liners and tankers, and the odd millionaire's yacht.

Galleria Regionale di Palazzo Bellomo
Via Capodieci 14–16 • Tues–Sat 9am–7pm, Sun 9am–1pm • €8 • ☎ 0931 69 511

Siracusa's tradition of architectural hybridism is again apparent in the **Palazzo Bellomo**, with a courtyard that features thirteenth-century arcading and a Spanish-style stairway leading up to the loggia. The palace is the home of the city's **Galleria Regionale di Palazzo Bellomo**, whose most treasured exhibit is an Annunciazione by Antonello da Messina, painted for a church in Palazzolo Acreide, with the Hyblaean mountains visible through the windows behind the angel and the Madonna. Early Christian **sculpture** and a fine collection of **altarpieces** and **icons** are also fascinating evidence of the enduring Byzantine and Gothic influence in Sicily. As late as the sixteenth century, while the rest of Italy was swept by the Renaissance, Siracusa's artists were still painting heavily stylized Byzantine or Gothic works.

San Martino

Via San Martino • Usually open Sunday mornings as the local Scout group meets here

The church of **San Martino** is among Siracusa's oldest. Originally a sixth-century basilica, it was rebuilt in the fourteenth century and smartened up with a good-looking rose window and Gothic doorway. It's not often open, but the dusky **interior** is a treat – plain stone columns leading to a tiny mosaic half-apse with a fifteenth-century triptych to the right of the choir.

6

Castello Maniace

Via del Castello Maniace • Tues–Sat 9am–1pm • €4 • ☎ 0931 464 420

The dangling southern limb of Ortigia is entirely taken up by the parade grounds and buildings of the stout **Castello Maniace**, a defensive bulwark erected around 1239 by Frederick II, but named after George Maniakes, the Byzantine admiral who briefly reconquered Syracuse from the Arabs in 1038. Now that the military has moved out, the barracks buildings are used by the university's archeological department, while visitors are allowed to enter through the imposing main gate and wander the echoing halls, chambers and defensive ramparts. Restoration work continues to shore up the neglected castle interior – one of the rooms displays a copy of the famous bronze ram statue, known as *L'Ariete*, a pair of which once guarded the castle gates. The original is now in Palermo's archeological museum.

Mainland Siracusa

Modern development in the mainland quarters of Siracusa makes it difficult to picture the ancient city that Plutarch wept over when he heard of its fall to the Romans. Much of the new building dates from after World War II, when Siracusa was bombed twice over – once by the Allies, then, after its capture, by the Luftwaffe in 1943. But even so, some extraordinary relics survive, both in **Achradina**, the nearest mainland quarter to Ortigia, but far more impressively in the northern district of **Neapolis**, where the main archeological park is sited. There's plenty more to see too in **Tyche**, the location of the city's unsurpassed **archeological museum**, while that district in particular is riddled with underground **catacombs**. Regular city buses run to all these places, departing from Riva della Posta on Ortigia or Via Rubino off Corso Umberto I, or you can walk to the museum, catacombs or archeological park in under half an hour from Ortigia.

On the mainland, you'll find congenial spots for **swimming and sunbathing** if you head north along Riviera Dionisio il Grande, or south at **Isola**, on the far side of Porto Grande, reachable by bus #23 from Piazza Pancali.

Foro Siracusano

Corso Umberto I • No set hours • Free

Over the bridges from Ortigia, the main drag of Corso Umberto I runs up to the small urban park known as the **Foro Siracusano**, once site of the old town's agora. There's not much to see today, though the gardens (and playground) are not a bad place for a shady picnic.

Ginnasio Romano

Via Elorina • Not usually open to the public, though sometimes open without notice

Set in an unprepossessing position on busy Via Elorina, the main road out to the beaches, the diminutive **Ginnasio Romano** was never actually a gymnasium at all but a small Roman theatre, probably built in the first century AD when the ancient city's much grander Greek theatre was requisitioned for blood sports. All you can see from the road is the shape of the semicircular *cava*; if you do happen to find the building open, it's worth slipping inside for a closer look.

Arsenale and Edificio Termale

Via Arsenale • Closed to the public

Over on the eastern edge of Achradina, close by the crowded huddle of boats in the Porto Piccolo, you'll find a much less recognizable ruin, the **Arsenale** provisions centre, where ships were refurbished, hoisted up from the port by devices that clamped into the ground – the slots that engaged them are about the only thing to look at here. Adjacent, visible below the apartment block built above it, is the **Edificio Termale**, a Byzantine bathhouse claimed to be the very same one in which, in 668 AD, the Emperor Constans was assassinated, knocked on the head by a servant wielding a soap dish. It lies under a modern block of flats, and only a few piles of stones are visible.

Basilica di Santa Lucia

Piazza Santa Lucia • **Basilica** Mass daily 5pm, and Sun morning • Free • **Catacombs** English and Italian guided tours every 30min Mon–Sat 11am–1pm & 2.30–5.30pm • €8 • ☎ 0931 64 694, ⓦ kairos-web.com

At the northern end of the huge Piazza Santa Lucia, the church of **Santa Lucia**, built in 1629, supposedly marks the spot where St Lucy, Siracusa's patron saint, was martyred in 304 AD. Within is a fine wooden ceiling, but you don't need to enter to admire its Norman tower or, from the piazza outside, Giovanni Vermexio's octagonal chapel of **San Sepolcro**, where the mortal remains of St Lucy were originally preserved before being carried off to Constantinople by the Byzantine admiral Maniakes in 1038, and later shipped to Venice as part of the spoils plundered by the Venetian "crusaders" in 1204.

If you like **catacombs**, be sure to take one of the guided tours of the labyrinthine complex below the church, full of the tombs of those who wanted to be buried close to the sight rendered holy by Santa Lucia's death.

Santuario della Madonna delle Lacrime

Viale Teocrito and Via del Santuario • Daily 7am–1pm & 3–8pm

The gargantuan **Santuario della Madonna delle Lacrime**, fronting Viale Teocrito, dominates the skyline on most approaches to Siracusa. It was completed in 1994 to house a statue of the Madonna that allegedly wept for five days in 1953 (*delle Lacrime* means "of the tears"), and the church was apparently designed to resemble a giant teardrop (it actually resembles one of Tracy Island's missing Thunderbirds). As you can't sink a spade into the ground in Siracusa without turning up a relic or two, it came as no surprise during the building work to discover the extensive remains of **Greek and Roman houses** and streets, which are fenced off but visible just to the south in Piazza della Vittoria.

Museo del Papiro

Viale Teocrito 66 • Tues–Sun 9am–2pm • €2 • ☎ 0931 22 100, ⓦ museodelpapiro.it

Across the main Viale Teocrito from the Madonna delle Lacrime, next to the archeological museum grounds, the small **Museo del Papiro** is worth a visit to see papyrus art, ancient and modern, including models of boats and even sandals made of the stuff. Ever since papyrus was introduced to Siracusa in the reign of Hieron II, there's been a thriving papyrus industry here, and gift shops on Ortigia are awash with it.

Museo Archeologico

Via Teocrito 66 • Tues–Sat 9am–6pm, Sun 9am–1pm; last entry 1hr before closing • €8, combined ticket with Parco Archeologico €13 • ☎ 0931 489 511

If you have any interest at all in the archeological finds made in this extraordinary city, then all roads lead to Siracusa's **Museo Archeologico**. It was purpose-built for Sicily's most wide-ranging collection of antiquities, and it's certainly worth seeing, though there are caveats. It's often extremely confusing to find your way around, with notes in English either nonexistent or mind-numbingly detailed and academic, and to cap it all sections are sometimes closed as continuing renovations attempt to address its organizational shortcomings. The museum is basically split into four sections: prehistoric (section A); items from Syracuse, Megara Hyblaea and the Chalcidinian colonies (B); finds from Gela, Agrigento, Syracuse's subcolonies and the indigenous Sikel centres (C); and Greek and Roman Siracusa (D).

6

Section D

It's **section D** that's the easiest to understand, where Siracusa in the **Greek and Roman age** is laid bare in an extraordinary series of tomb finds and public statues, none more celebrated than the statue of **Venus Anadiomene**, also known as *Landolina* after the archeologist who discovered her in 1804. *Anadiomene* means "rising from the sea", which describes her coy pose: with her left hand she holds a robe, while studs show where her broken-off right arm came across to hide her breasts. Probably Roman-made in the first century AD, from a Greek model, the headless statue has always evoked extreme responses, alternately exalting the delicacy and naturalism of the carving, and condemning her knowing sensual attitude that symbolized the decline of the vigorous classical age and the birth of a new decadence. By the statue's feet, the dolphin, Aphrodite's emblem, is the only sign that this was a goddess. Of the tomb finds, pride of place is given to the superb **Sarcofago di Adelfia**, a finely worked fourth-century marble tomb found in the catacombs below San Giovanni. It held the wife of a Roman official, the couple prominently depicted and surrounded by reliefs of scenes from the Old and New Testaments.

Section B

Elsewhere, eyes will possibly glaze over at the thousands of pottery shards, burial urns, amphorae, statues, figures and temple fragments. However, **section B** does at least put many of the finds into context, showing where excavations occurred in the city, and even reconstructing useful models of the fallen temples. Among the earlier Hellenic pieces, the museum has some excellent **kouroi** – toned, muscular youths, one of which (from Lentini) is one of the most outstanding fragments still extant from the Archaic age of Greek art – around 500 BC. A striking image from the colony of Megara Hyblaea dates from the same period: a **mother/goddess suckling twins**, its absorbed roundness expressing a tender harmony as close to earth and fertility rites as the *Venus Landolina* is to the cult of sensuality.

Basilica di San Giovanni catacombs

Piazza San Giovanni • Daily 9.30am–12.30pm & 2.30–5.30pm • Tours depart every 30min • €8 • ☎ 0931 64 694, ⓦ kairos-web.com

Close to the Museo Archeologico, below the ruined **Basilica di San Giovanni** off Via San Sebastiano, lies the most extensive series of catacombs in the city, their presence explained by the Roman prohibition on Christian burial within the city limits (Siracusa having by then shrunk back to its original core of Ortigia). Fronted by a triple arch, most of the church was toppled in the 1693 earthquake and the nave is now open to the sky, but you can still admire the seventh-century apse and a medieval rose window. San Giovanni was once the city's cathedral, built over the crypt of St Marcian, first bishop of Siracusa, who was flogged to death in 254.

The tours take you down into the **crypt** to see Marcian's tomb, the remnants of some Byzantine frescoes and an altar that marks the spot where St Paul is supposed to have preached, when he stopped in the city as a prisoner on his way to Rome. Then you're led into the **catacombs** themselves, labyrinthine warrens hewn out of the rock, though often following the course of underground aqueducts, disused since Greek times. Numerous side-passages lead off from the main gallery (decumanus maximus), often culminating in *rotonde*, round caverns used for prayer;

other passages are forbiddingly dark and closed off to the public. Entire families were interred in the thousands of niches hollowed out of these walls and floors, anxious for burial close to the tomb of St Marcian. Most of the treasures buried with the bodies have been pillaged, though the robbers overlooked one – an ornate Roman-era sarcophagus unearthed from just below the floor in 1872 and now on show in the archeological museum.

Parco Archeologico della Neapolis

Viale Paradiso • Daily 9am–2hr before sunset • €10 • ☎ 0931 66 206 • Take any bus that goes up Corso Gelone, and get off at the hospital at the top of Corso Gelone, from where it's a 10min walk along Viale Augusto and Viale Paradiso to the site entrance

Siracusa's **Parco Archeologico** encompasses the classical city district that was Neapolis. This contained most of the ancient city's social and religious amenities – theatres, altars and sanctuaries – and was thus never inhabited, though these days it's in danger of disappearing under the sheer weight of visitors. The **ticket office** is hidden beyond a street market of souvenir stalls and ice cream stands, catering to the busloads of tourists that arrive every few minutes in the summer.

Anfiteatro Romano

As you enter the Parco Archeologico, a path to the left leads down to the **Anfiteatro Romano**, a large elliptical arena built in the third century AD to satisfy the growing lust for circus games. The rectangular **tank** in the centre of the arena is too small to have been used for aquatic displays, and is more likely to have been for draining the blood and gore spilled in the course of the combats. But not before the spectators had had their fill: at the end of the contests the infirm, ill and disabled would attempt to suck warm blood from the bodies and take the livers from the animals, in the belief that this would speed their recovery.

HEAR HEAR

The **Orecchio di Dionisio** owes its name to the painter **Caravaggio**, who was taken to visit the cave during a visit to Siracusa in October 1608. Said to have been used as a prison by the ancient Greek tyrant, Dionysus, the cave's natural acoustics amplified every sound, and from their base above a crack at the apex, sentries could eavesdrop on the prisoners hundreds of metres below. Having just escaped from prison and fled to Siracusa, Caravaggio was deeply disturbed by this ingenious quirk. He noted that the cave amplified sound in the same way as the human ear – which led recent biographer Andrew Graham Dixon to speculate that Caravaggio saw the "speaking cave" as an image of his own contracting world, where every movement was monitored by spies, every remark overheard by eavesdroppers.

6

Ara di Ierone II

No public access

On the main path into the Parco Archeologico, past the turnoff to the Anfiteatro Romano, the ruined base of the **Ara di Ierone II** is a 200m-long altar erected by Hieron II in the second half of the third century BC. It commemorated the achievements of Timoleon, who liberated the city from tyranny and decline, and was the biggest construction of its kind in all Magna Graecia. It was also the venue for some serious sacrificing: Diodorus records that 450 bulls were led up the ramps at either end of the altar to be slaughtered in the annual feast.

Teatro Greco

You may be asked to show your ticket again at the office at the foot of the steps leading up to the **Teatro Greco**, Siracusa's most spectacular monument. One of the largest and best-preserved Greek auditoriums anywhere, its site has been home to a theatre since at least the fifth century BC, though it was frequently added to at different periods. Hieron II expanded it to accommodate 15,000 people, in nine sections of 59 rows (of which 42 remain). The **inscriptions** around the top of the middle gangway on the west side of the theatre – faint but still visible – date from the third century BC, giving the names of the ruler and his family, with Zeus Olympios in the middle. Most of the alterations carried out by the Romans were made to adapt the arena for gladiatorial combat, and they also installed some marble-faced seats for privileged spectators, while the seventeenth row was removed, possibly to segregate the classes. The high terrace above the theatre contains the **Nymphaeum**, a large artificial grotto (fed by water from an ancient aqueduct) where a number of statues were found. To the left of here, the overgrown **Via dei Sepolcri** (Street of the Tombs) is deeply rutted by the carts that plied to and fro, and is flanked by more votive niches.

Latomia del Paradiso

From the ticket office at the foot of the steps to the Teatro Greco, a path descends to the largest of Siracusa's huge *latomie* (pits or quarries), from which the rock for the city's multifarious monuments was excavated. Now planted with citrus, oleander and bay trees, the so-called **Latomia del Paradiso** is more garden than quarry, and a steady stream of tour parties troops down mainly to see the remarkable ear-shaped cavern known as the **Orecchio di Dionisio** (Ear of Dionysius), which is over 60m long and 20m high. A second cave, the **Grotta dei Cordari**, was used by the ancient city's ropemakers, who found that its damp air prevented rope strands from breaking under stress.

Latomie dei Cappuccini

Largo Latomie 3 • Mon–Fri 9.30am–1.30pm, Sat & Sun 10am–1pm & 4.30–7.30pm • €3 • ☎ 0931 411 394

Gouged out of the hillside below the Cappuccini monastery and *Grand Hotel Villa Politi*, the wide, vertically walled quarries of the **Latomie dei Cappuccini** provided a harsh but effective prison for the 7000 Athenian prisoners of war following the fiasco of the Great

Expedition. The quarries were acquired by Capuchin monks in the sixteenth century, who turned them into both market garden and contemplative retreat, which is why the cavern floors are so lush. Sinuous paths wind through the overgrown quarries, past natural rock pillars, huge caverns and early Christian tombs – there's even a cavern-theatre down here, sometimes used for performances, usually advertised by posters around town.

Epipolae and the Castello Eurialo

Castello Eurialo Daily: April–Oct 9am–7pm; Nov–March 9am–5pm • €4 • A 20min ride on bus #11 or #25 to the village of Belvedere, from Corso Gelone and outside the Parco Archeologico

The outlying area of **Epipolae**, 7km west of the city, was the site of ancient Siracusa's military and defensive works. These heights were first fortified by Dionysius the Elder in about 400 BC, and subsequently modified and extended over a couple of centuries. What remains today consists of a great wall, which marked the city's western limit, and the **Castello Eurialo**, just before the village on the right. This is the major extant Greek fortification in the Mediterranean, most of it dating from Hieron II's time, when Archimedes, as his General of Ordnance, must have been actively involved in its renovation. Despite the effort and ingenuity that went into making this site impregnable, the castle has no very glorious history: ignored altogether by the attacking Carthaginians, it surrendered without a fight to the Roman forces of Marcellus in 212 BC.

Assailants had to cope with three defensive **trenches**, designed to keep the new artillery of the time at bay, as well as siege-engines and battering rams. The first of the trenches (approached from the west, where you come in) lay just within range of catapults mounted on the five towers of the castle's keep, while in the trench below the keep you can see the high piers supporting the drawbridge that once crossed it. Long galleries burrow beneath the walls into the keep, serving as supply and escape routes, and also enabling the defenders to clear out by night the material thrown in by attackers during the day.

Epipolae gate

Behind the keep is a long, wedge-shaped fortification, to the north of which is the main gateway to the western quarter of the city. This, the **Epipolae gate**, was built indented from the walls, allowing the defenders to shower attackers with missiles, and is reminiscent of the main gate at Tyndaris, a city that shared the same architects. The longest of the underground passages surfaces here stretches 180m from the defensive trenches. From the gate, you can stroll along Dionysius' extensive walls, looking down over the oil refineries and tankers off the coast north of the city, and back over Siracusa itself, with Ortigia clearly visible pointing out into the sea.

THE FIUME CIANE

Just southwest of Siracusa, the source of the **Fiume Ciane** (Ciane River) forms a pool said to have been created by the tears of the nymph Cyane when her mistress Persephone was abducted into the underworld by Hades. The pool and the river banks are overgrown by thickets of papyrus, apparently the gift of Ptolemy Philadelphus of Egypt to Hieron II, making this the only place outside North Africa where the plant grows wild. **Boat cruises** operate between early March and November from the bridge over the Ciane, a 5km signposted drive from Siracusa on the SS115; you can also take bus #21, #22 or #23 from Piazza Pancali. There are daily departures between 10am and 6pm, with tickets costing around €10 per person (minimum three people); call ☎ 346 159 9635 or ☎ 368 729 6040 for information. As well as the river, you'll also see the scant but evocative remains of the **Olympieion**, or Tempio di Giove Olimpico, a Doric temple built in the first half of the sixth century BC. The hillock the ruin stands on, a vital strategic point in classical times, was often occupied by Siracusa's enemies when the city was under attack. The pestilential air of the Lysimelia marshes below saved the day on more than one occasion, infecting the hostile armies with malaria.

PARKING IN SIRACUSA

As in the rest of Italy, **parking** in Siracusa is free for everyone on the **white lines** along the Lungomare Levante between the junction with Via Maestranza, though you'll be lucky to find a place. For streets with **blue lines**, payment (€0.60/hr) is often required; on Riva Nazario Sauro, fees are charged all day, every day, but everywhere else in the city, you pay only Mon–Fri between 9am–1pm & 4–8pm. There are no parking meters and no ticket machines in Ortigia; instead, parking tickets are sold at tobacconists and newsagents, and cost €0.60 per hour.

The **Talete car park** is at the end of Via Trieste (look for the sign) on the lungomare (Mon–Sat: 7.30am–2.29pm & 10pm–7.29am fixed charge of €1; 2.30–9.59pm €0.60 per hour; Sun and hols 7.30am–9.59pm €0.60 per hour; 10pm–7.29am fixed charge of €1. Talete is an easy walk from the centre of Ortigia, though look out for the free shuttle-bus (*navetta*) which in theory leaves from outside every fifteen minutes, dropping passengers in Piazza Pancali and Piazza Archimede.

The other car park is at the Molo San Antonio, on the mainland across the bridge from Ortigia, daily 8am–9.59pm, €0.60 per hour; 10pm–7.59am, fixed rate of €1.

6

ARRIVAL AND DEPARTURE

By train Siracusa is at the beginning of two train lines: the main line running up to Catania, Taormina and Messina, and a little branch line to Gela via Noto, Sampieri, Scicli, Modica, Ragusa and several other small Baroque towns. The city's train station is on the mainland at the end of Via Francesco Crispi. You can walk from here to Ortigia in around 20min, and there's a taxi rank outside the station. Depending on the financial circumstances of local bus company AST (see below), there may or may not be free shuttle minibuses to Ortigia, leaving every 15min or so from a bus stop, a couple of minutes' walk away on (the second parallel street) Via Rubino.

Destinations Catania (7–11 daily; 1hr 15min); Lentini (7–11 daily; 45min); Messina (7–9 daily; 3hr); Modica (4 daily Mon–Sat; 1hr 45min); Noto (7 daily Mon–Sat; 1 daily Sun; 30min); Ragusa (2 daily Mon–Sat; 2hr); Sampieri (4 daily Mon–Sat; 1hr 20min); Scicli (4 daily Mon–Sat; 1hr 25min).

By bus All regional buses stop across the road from the train station, on the parallel streets Corso Umberto I and Via Rubino. AST (📞 0931 462 711, 🌐 aziendasicilianatrasporti .it) has services to and from Lentini, Catania, Comiso, Ispica, Modica, Noto, Palazzolo Acreide, Ragusa, Sortino and Vittoria; while Interbus (📞 0931 66 710, 🌐 interbus.it) runs to Avola, Catania, Noto, Pachino and Palermo.

Destinations Avola (7 daily Mon–Sat, 1 daily Sun; 40min); Catania (1–2 hourly; 1hr 25min); Catania airport (6–7 daily; 1hr 15min); Ferla (1 daily Mon–Sat; 1hr 35min); Lentini (11 daily Mon–Sat; 1hr–1hr 30min); Modica (8 daily Mon–Sat, 3 daily Sun; 1hr 45min–3hr); Noto (12 daily Mon–Sat, 4 daily Sun; 55min); Pachino (6 daily Mon–Sat, 2 daily Sun; 1hr 20min); Palazzolo Acreide (1–2 hourly Mon–Sat, 2 daily Sun; 1hr 10min–2hr 15min); Palermo (3 daily; 3hr 20min); Piazza Armerina (1 daily Mon–Sat; 4hr); Ragusa (4 daily Mon–Sat, 2 daily Sun; 2hr 15min–3hr); Sortino (Mon–Sat 10 daily; 1hr 15min).

GETTING AROUND

By bus City buses are run by AST (📞 0931 462 711, 🌐 aziendasicilianatrasporti.it) and depart from Piazza Pancali in Ortigia. All services run on circular routes. Tickets cost €1.20 for 120min, and €1.80 for two days, and should in theory be available at *tabacchi* and newsstands displaying an AST sticker. However, thanks to internal problems within AST, the availability of both tickets and buses may be erratic. At the time of writing, only the buses out to the beaches are reliable. If they do start running again, the most useful buses for getting to the Archeological Zone are #1, #3, #12; plus #4 for the Museo Archeologico and #25 and #26 for Castello Eurialo.

By car Siracusa's drivers are as undisciplined as any in

Sicily, but nevertheless drivers will find the city a breeze after Palermo and Catania. Parking on the street in Ortigia is almost impossible, so leave your car at the covered Talete car park to the east of the island (see box above). Ortigia is completely closed to traffic (except for residents) on Sundays and on certain other occasions – a traffic signal at the foot of Corso Matteotti indicates whether access is permitted or not. When access is not permitted, you can either turn left and drive around the coast road to Talete (for a scenic route, and the rare chance of picking up a free parking place), or turn right and go directly to Talete.

By taxi There are ranks in Piazza Pancali (📞 0931 60 980) and at the train station (📞 0931 69 722).

INFORMATION AND TOURS

Tourist information For maps, accommodation, details of performances in the Greek theatre, and other information, head for the extremely helpful and well-informed InfoPoint, inside the provincial offices at Via Roma 31 on Ortigia (Mon–Sat 8am–8pm, Sun 9.15am–6.45pm; 📞 0931 462 946 or 📞 800 055 500, 🌐 provsr.it).

Boat trips Ortigia Tours (☎ 368 317 0711, ⓦ ortigiatour .com) offers daily cruises around the city's harbours and nearby coastline. Boats leave from near the bridge on Ortigia (from 9am in summer, 10am in winter, weather permitting), and trips last an hour or so; tickets are €10 per person (minimum 4 people). In summer, a kiosk on the quayside provides tickets and information. For a more exclusive experience, book a day or evening cruise with lunch or dinner on Fiesta (☎ 333 329 3732; from €90 per person), a classic wooden 30ft sailing ketch.

ACCOMMODATION

Siracusa holds a lot of **accommodation**, much of it in the old town on Ortigia, which is by far the best place to stay, with scores of **B&Bs** in the backstreets and a cluster of four-star **hotels** on the waterfront. Note that in high summer and during the theatre season (May–June), it's wise to book in advance. Unless your chosen establishment has private parking, it's best to leave the car overnight in the Talete garage (see p.227). The cheapest beds are at the **hostel** by the train station; **camping** is available at a very basic site outside the city or at a much better-equipped site down the coast towards Avola. For **apartment rentals** contact ⓦ lacasadellefate.it.

HOTELS AND B&BS

Algilà Via Vittorio Veneto 93 ☎ 0931 465 186, ⓦ algila .it; map p.216. Recently opened hotel on the eastern seafront of Ortigia, with all the comforts of a four-star plus friendly, helpful staff. Styled by Siracusa-born theatre director, Manuel Giliberti, the design has a Maghreb feel, with Tunisian tiles in the bathrooms, *kilims* on the floors, watercolours of sun-scorched palms and North African piazzas, and a tiny decorative courtyard with fountain. **€300**

★ **Alla Giudecca** Via Alagona 52 ☎ 0931 22 255, ⓦ allagiudecca.it; map p.216. A stunning renovation in the old Jewish quarter has brought an interconnected series of medieval houses back to life as an exquisite little boutique hotel. There's exposed stone, soaring arches, colourful tapestries and dried flowers everywhere, while the 23 rooms feature eye-catching wrought-iron beds, stone-flagged floors and antique furniture. **€120**

★ **L'Approdo delle Sirene** Riva Garibaldi 15 ☎ 0931 24 857, ⓦ apprododellesirene.com; map p.216. Smart B&B in a tastefully renovated waterfront *palazzo* overlooking the channel between Ortigia and the mainland. Owned and run by a charming mother-and-son team: Fiora runs cooking courses in her apartment next door and Friedrich, who has trained as a pizza chef, is opening a pizzeria. Great home-made breakfasts with abundant fresh fruit are served on a terrace overlooking the sea. Facilities include mini-laptops in rooms, free wi-fi and bikes for guests' use. **€125**

Ares Via Mirabella 49 ☎ 0931 461 145, ⓦ ares bedandbreakfast.it; map p.216. Comfortable B&B on a quiet street, a skip and a jump from the sea and in the less touristy east side of Ortigia. Rooms are smart and spotless, there's a lovely roof terrace, and owner Enzo will go out of his way to make sure guests have all the information they need on Ortigia. Breakfast is by voucher at the fabulous *Bar del Duomo* opposite the cathedral, just a few minutes' walk away. **€80**

★ **Caol Ishka** Via Elorina, Contrada Pantanelli ☎ 0931 69 057, ⓦ caolishka.it; map p.214. Minimalist chic in a cluster of traditional stone farm buildings, all painted the same lavender-mink grey as the sky at dusk. The rooms have resinated cement floors, and spacious bathrooms with showerheads the size of soup plates. The grounds are ample, with a good-sized pool, and there is a superb restaurant. It's about 2km west of Siracusa; the little beaches at nearby Isola and boat excursions along the River Ciane make it an ideal choice for anyone who wants to alternate sightseeing with lazy days by the beach or pool. **€230**

Domus Mariae Via Vittorio Veneto 76 ☎ 0931 24 858, ⓦ www.sistemia.it/domusmariae; map p.216. Occupying a former religious school, this three-star hotel is still owned and run by an order of nuns. Half of the rooms have views to the sea and all are efficiently maintained, if a little plain. There's a fitness centre, a roof terrace, parking and, of course, a chapel. They have expanded across the road, transforming another convent into a hotel and spa. **€160**

★ **Giuggiulena** Via Pitagora da Reggio 35 ☎ 0931 468 142, ⓦ giuggiulena.it; map p.214. Chic but friendly and relaxed B&B in a clifftop villa, along the eastern seafront of Siracusa and ideal for families. Flooded with light from floor-to-ceiling windows, the main living/eating area has a glass cube suspended above the ocean and a bookcase stuffed with English paperbacks. All six rooms have balconies overlooking the sea, and you can swim off rocks or forage in rock pools (the hotel has a supply of chairs, mats and beach shoes), yet Ortigia is just a 15min walk away. Breakfasts are abundant and delicious, and eaten on a balcony overhanging the sea. **€80**

★ **Gutowski** Lungomare Vittorini 26 ☎ 0931 465 861, ⓦ guthotel.it; map p.216. Chic simplicity and intelligent design make this hotel overlooking the sea on the eastern edge of Ortigia a good restful choice. It's worth booking in advance to secure one of the rooms with private terrace. Great breakfasts, with freshly squeezed orange juice and, in summer, home-made almond *granita*. There is also a little wine bar, and private dinners can be arranged for four or more guests. **€110**

★ **Palazzo del Sale** Via S. Teresa 25 ☎ 0931 69 558, ⓦ palazzodelsale.it; map p.216. Stylish, relaxed B&B in a nineteenth-century salt-merchant's home and warehouse on a quiet street behind Piazza del Duomo. Six spacious rooms with wooden floors, architect-designed beds, and intriguing touches such as mirrors framed with driftwood and lamps with palm-bark shades. Breakfasts are superb, and service is unfussy and friendly. Free wi-fi – though the hefty stone walls mean that the signal can be weak – and a PC for guests' use. **€110**

Roma Via Roma 66 ☎0931 465 626, ⓦhotel romasiracusa.it; map p.216. A serene four-star oasis in the old centre, the chic *Roma* presents spacious, contemporary rooms with wood-block floors and excellent bathrooms. Staff are charming, breakfast is an extensive buffet spread, and there's also a fine-dining restaurant, fitness area and sauna. Excellent deals online, even in high season. **€125**

HOSTELS AND CAMPSITES

Lol Hostel Via Francesco Crispi 92 ☎0931 465 088, ⓦlolhostel.com; map p.214. This smart, modern youth hostel in a converted old *palazzo* is just a few steps down from the train station, with dorms holding up to ten beds as well as private singles and doubles, all air-conditioned and with en-suite bathrooms. Reception is 24hr, no membership is required, and there's internet access and the cheapest bike rental in town, plus use of a kitchen. Dorms **€22**; doubles **€50**

Paradiso del Mare Contrada Gallina Fondolupo, Avola ☎0931 561 147, ⓦparadisodelmare.it; map p.214. The best-equipped local campsite lies 22km south of Siracusa off the SS115, in a small secluded spot under trees and close to a great beach. To get here by public transport, take any bus for Avola, get off at Ospedale di Maria and walk a couple of kilometres back up the road – or call for a pick-up. Closed Nov–March. Camping **€6.50** per person, plus **€6.50** per pitch

Rinaura Località Rinaura ☎0931 721 224, ⓦcampingrinaura.it; map p.214. Some 4km south of Siracusa, this is a very basic campsite – more a couple of fields, really, with little shade. The washing facilities are fine, though, and there are electric hook-ups as well as self-catering bungalows. Take bus #21, #22 or #23 (also #24 or #25 in summer) from Corso Umberto I; it's less than a 10min walk from the stop on the SS115 (signposted to the right after the *Albatros* hotel). Camping **€5** per person, plus **€4** per pitch; bungalows **€50**

EATING AND DRINKING

Ortigia holds the city's best array of **cafés** and **restaurants**, most within a short walk of each other. Prices are on the high side for Sicily, though there are few nicer places in Sicily to sit outside in a medieval street or courtyard and while the evening away. Ortigia also has excellent **bars** – from Italian-style pubs to cocktail joints – and most of the late-night action is concentrated on the streets and alleys near the Fonte Aretusa, particularly around Piazzetta San Rocco and along Lungomare Alfeo.

CAFÉS

Caffè d'Ortigia Largo XXV Luglio ☎349 628 9674 ; map p.216. Opposite the Temple of Apollo, on bustling Largo XXV Luglio, this is not only a great spot for people-watching, but has friendly staff and great *cornetti* filled with fresh ricotta. Daily 6am–9pm.

Gran Caffè del Duomo Piazza del Duomo 18 ☎0931 21584; map p.216. Bang in front of the cathedral, this is the place to sit and watch life pass by over a lazy breakfast or aperitif – staff are friendly and attentive and its prices are so reasonable that even street-sweepers and dustmen stop by for a coffee on their morning rounds. *Cornetti* here are more like brioche than croissants – try them filled to order with fresh ricotta. Tues–Sun 8am–late.

Viola Via Roma 43 ☎331 861 8415; map p.216. Light and buttery, the best *cornetti* in town are made by *Viola*, though if you hang out here for any length of time, you will realize that constant repetition of their sole Norah Jones CD is a torture to rank alongside anything dreamed up by Japanese game-show directors. Daily 7.30am–9pm.

RESTAURANTS

Apollonion Via Campisi 18 ☎0931 483 362 or ☎349 535 4189; map p.216. You'll feast on some of the best seafood in town at this quietly elegant family-run eatery, though there's no menu. Instead, you'll be pampered with a succession of superbly prepared dishes – from such starters as a mix of sardines, swordfish and shrimps in olive oil to mussels in a garlicky broth, baked langoustines and *fritto misto*, served with delicious rustic bread – all for €35. There's a small lunchtime à la carte menu as well. Booking recommended. Mon–Tues & Thurs–Sun lunch & dinner.

Arrusti e Mangia Ronco Cristina 3 ☎333 644 0847; map p.216. Hidden in a dead-end Ronco behind Corso Umberto, just across the bridge from Ortigia, this is a very simple place, run and owned by butcher Ciccio and his childhood friend Mauro. It offers a fixed-price set menu (€18) of *antipasti*, charcoal-grilled meats and wine. It is always full. At present only the interior is open, but they have applied for permission to put tables outside in the Ronco. Thurs–Sat 8pm–midnight, Sun 1–3pm.

Castello Fiorentino Via del Crocifisso 6 ☎0931 21 097; map p.216. The finest pizzas in the city centre – people queue out of the door waiting for tables. It's really good value, and the in-your-face waiters, blasting TV and general mayhem at peak times are all part of the charm. Pizzas are €3–10, other dishes – pastas, seafood and meat – €7–10. There's a takeaway service too. Tues–Sun lunch & dinner.

6

SHOPPING IN SIRACUSA

At Fonte Aretusa, shining like a pearl among the tourist tat, is **Circo Fortuna**, Via Capodieci 10 (Mon–Sat 10am–1pm & 5–7pm; ☎ 347 216 3374, ⓦ circofortuna.it; map p.216), where Caroline Van Riet creates quirky and original ceramics that will make you think of Ortigia and smile, when you get back home. Alessia Genovese's workshop-store, **Artesania**, behind the temple of Apollo at Via dell'Apollonion 5 (Mon–Sat 10am–1pm & 5–8pm; ☎ 0931 21 778; map p.216), is the source of the inspired furniture and smaller objects made from driftwood and reclaimed window frames, beams, doors, planks – that you will find in Ortigia's boutique hotels and bars. She and her collaborators also create gorgeous textiles and knits – dyeing the yarns themselves from esoteric potions of Mediterranean plants. At **Sete d'Incanto**, Via Roma 27 (Mon–Sat 11am–2pm & 6–8.30pm; ☎ 333 594 4518, ⓦ silkinortigia.wordpress.com; map p.216), owner-artist Elene Moreau is inspired by Ortigia's architectural forms and natural elements to produce her hand-painted silk scarves and wall-hangings. For carefully sourced clothes and shoes from niche designers, head to **Via Cavour 38** (Mon–Wed & Fri–Sun 11.30am–8pm; no phone; map p.216); for designer and high-street clothes, try the shops along Corso Matteotti.

Don Camillo Via della Maestranza 96 ☎ 0931 67 133, ⓦ ristorantedoncamillosiracusa.it; map p.216. If locals want to impress visitors, they bring them to this refined restaurant in the fifteenth-century vaults of a former convent. The fish is fantastically fresh, and the menu emphasizes unusual Sicilian specialities, like pasta with tuna, mint and tomatoes; or a whole fish baked inside a crust of golden bread. It also has Siracusa's finest wine cellar. Prices are high at around €16 for pastas and from €20 for mains, and there's a tasting menu for €55. Mon–Sat lunch & dinner; closed part of Feb, July & Aug.

★ **La Foglia** Via Capodieci 21 ☎ 0931 66 233, ⓦ lafoglia.it; map p.216. The city's most idiosyncratic eatery, from the antique shop/art gallery furnishings to the hippy-chic tableware and place settings. It's actually quite romantic, and a very laidback place to sample Mediterranean and vegetarian cooking, from rustic soups and home-made ravioli to veggie platters or fish *matalotta* (with tomatoes, onions, capers and olives). You'll pay €12–15 for most dishes, up to around €22 for seafood. Daily lunch & dinner.

★ **La Gazza Ladra** Via Cavour 8 ☎ 340 060 2428; map p.216. Most restaurants around Via Cavour are very similar, but the "thieving magpie" tries to do things a little differently. A friendly family-run *osteria*, it has just eight tables and concentrates on authentic Sicilian cuisine with a homestyle touch, using staple ingredients like courgettes, aubergines, tuna, capers, olives, mint and oregano to great effect in *antipasto* platters and pasta dishes. Mains of the day (mostly fish) are chalked on the board. A meal will cost around €25, or you can just drop in for a salad, panino and a drink. Tues–Sat dinner only; closed July & Aug.

Al Mazari Via G. Torres 7 ☎ 0931 483 690; map p.216. Run by a family from Mazara del Vallo, this sophisticated yet cosy restaurant is the place to come for a romantic meal for two, or if you just need a treat. Carefully sourced ingredients are used to prepare dishes such as an excellent fish couscous (€20), handmade pasta with prawns and cherry tomatoes (€12), or *casarecce* pasta with swordfish, aubergine, wild mint and breadcrumbs (€12) that are typical of western Sicily. Daily lunch & dinner; sometimes closed Sun in winter.

★ **Zsa** Via Roma 73 ☎ 0931 22 204; map p.216. Good pizza – the dough is made with a light touch, and comes blistered from the wood oven, and the quality ingredients on top are abundant. They kick off at €4, but for a bit more you can feast on a *vegetariana*, laden with succulent grilled vegetables laced with radicchio, or a *stufata*, scattered with chilli and fennel-seed scented sausages and potatoes. In summer try the range of Philadelphia pizzas (made with cream cheese). In summer there is pizza at lunchtime too, though the choice of seafood pasta might divert you. Take-away available too. Tues–Sat lunch & dinner.

BARS

Bar Collo Via Pompeo Picherali 10 ☎ 0931 24 580; map p.216. Set in the courtyard of a *palazzo*, with wrought-iron filigree furniture on a candle-lit terrace below a bougainvillea-covered wall, *Bar Collo* is probably the most romantic place on the island for an early evening aperitivo. Later things hot up and the party crowd arrives. Outdoor heaters in winter. Daily 6.30pm–late.

Blu Via Nizza 50 ☎ 0931 445 052; map p.216. Don't leave Ortigia without tasting a seasonal fresh-fruit prosecco or daiquiri at *Blu*. It's also one of the few places where you can sit outside and watch the open sea. Owner Seby plays a laidback and eclectic range of music, and provides delicious home-made nibbles, as well as full meals featuring fresh fish. During the day there are fresh fruit *gremolatas* and *pane cunzato* to eat on the terrace or on the swimming rocks across the road. April–Oct daily 11am–late; Nov–March Mon–Sat 6.30pm–late.

Tinkite Via della Giudecca 61–63 ☎348 597 5369; map p.216. In the heart of the Giudecca, *Tinkite* attracts a rather hip crowd, and with gas-heaters and blankets, it's one of the few places in Ortigia where you can sit outside comfortably in cold weather. Help yourself from the buffet of snacks to accompany your drink. If you're not in the mood for alcohol, there's a huge choice of speciality teas (served with little biscuits) along with hot chocolate, and, of course, coffee. Daily:

April–Oct 9.30am–1.30pm & 7–11pm; Nov–March 8.30am–1pm & 5–10pm; closed Wed morning year-round.

Il Sale Via Amalfitania 56 ☎0931 483 666; map p.216. Atmospheric place for an aperitivo or for partying till late, this is one of three bars on a hidden courtyard off Via Amalfitania. Whitewashed stone vaults, candles and semi-outdoor seating. There are often live bands on Thursdays. Daily 7pm–late.

ENTERTAINMENT

Siracusa is one of the easiest places to catch a traditional Sicilian **puppet theatre** performance, though the best-known cultural entertainments on offer are the open-air classical **Greek dramas** performed in the Teatro Greco. Focusing on contemporary music and performance art, the **Ortigia Festival** in September has lapsed, though may be revived.

Istituto Nazionale del Dramma Antico (INDA) Palazzo Greco, Corso Matteotti 29 ☎800 542 644 or ☎0931 487 200, ⊚indafondazione.org. Classical Greek drama is performed each year (May and June, usually Tues–Sun from around 6.45pm) at the Teatro Greco in the Parco Archeologico. It's a real spectacle, though performances are in Italian only. Tickets range from €32 to €64, but vary from performance to performance according to availability, with cheaper last-minute tickets available for some performances. Get details on the INDA website or

from Siracusa's tourist offices; tickets are available at the INDA box office or online.

Piccolo Teatro dei Pupi Via della Giudecca 17 ☎0931 465 540 or ☎328 532 6600, ⊚pupari.com. Traditional puppet shows by the Vaccaro-Mauceri family, Siracusa's pre-eminent puppeteers, are held at least twice weekly between March and Oct (twice daily in Aug, and daily late Dec to early Jan) in their thriving theatre. You can check up-to-date schedules on the website; behind-the-scenes tours and special shows take place throughout the year. Tickets €7.50.

DIRECTORY

Hospital Ospedale Umberto I, Via Testaferrata, near Madonna delle Lacrime church (☎0931 724 111); for the 24hr accident and emergency service call ☎0931 724 285.
Internet There's free wi-fi in many central bars, and (provided by the council) on Piazza del Duomo: apply with a passport at the Municipio (9am–2pm).
Pharmacies Farmacia Centrale, Via Maestranza 42 (☎0931 65 320); and Gibiino, Via Roma 81 (☎0931 65

760). Outside normal working hours, pharmacies open on a rota system that's posted outside, and is also available at ⊚www.comune.siracusa.it.
Police For police, call ☎0931 495 111; call ☎112 in an emergency. There's a Carabinieri post in Piazza San Giuseppe, Ortigia (☎0931 441 344).
Post office The main post office is at Piazza delle Poste 15, Ortigia (Mon–Fri 8am–6.30pm, Sat 8am–12.30pm).

BEACHES NORTH OF SIRACUSA

North of Siracusa, much of the coast has been contaminated by noxious chemicals, but there are popular swimming spots south at **Arenella** (bus #23 from Piazza Pancali), mostly consisting of private lidos, but with a free, sandy beach a 5min walk along a cliff path heading back in the direction of Siracusa, and a rocky cape to the south where the inlets create clear pools that are good for snorkelling.

On the other side of the cape – a 30min walk away – is **Ognina**, a small fishing port and marina, also accessible by bus. It has no beach, but lots of appealing little coves.

Fontane Bianche, 20km south of Siracusa (buses #21 or #22 from Piazza Pancali), is another very popular spot with the locals, with a wide arc of sand ringed by hotels, bars and restaurants, though there is a stretch of free public beach as well. An unofficial coastal path heads off south along the cliffs, taking you to a handful of swimming spots, but no beach. If you get off the bus at the junction between the road to Fontane Bianche and the main SS113 (whether you arrive here before or after arriving in Fontane Bianche depends on the route), a 10–15min walk along the main road brings you to the utterly lovely **La Marchesa** beach, backed by orange groves. There is a charge for access during the summer, but if you speak nicely to the custodian in low season he will usually let you in.

North of Siracusa

The coast north of Siracusa, the **Golfo di Augusta**, sports one of the largest concentrations of chemical plants in Europe. This mammoth industrial zone employs one-tenth of the local population, and fills the air with acrid fumes and the sea with chemicals. Hardly surprisingly, it figures on no holiday itineraries, though the industrial port of **AUGUSTA** – half an hour by train or bus from Siracusa – does at least offer the compensation of a handsome, if crumbling, Baroque centre. Despite the town's superficial resemblance to Siracusa – its old centre detached from the mainland on its own islet, surrounded by two harbours – the port has never attained the same importance and didn't even exist until 1232. Frederick II, who founded Augusta, characteristically stamped his own personality on it in the form of a castle (no public access), though everything else of the medieval town was destroyed by the 1693 earthquake. The **Villa Comunale** below the castle is a shady public garden, on both sides of which are views out to sea, on one side over the port and tankers, on the other to the headland. A few blocks down the main Via Principe Umberto, a piazza holds the eighteenth-century **Duomo** and a solemn **Palazzo Comunale**, its facade crowned by Frederick II's imperial eagle.

Megara Hyblaea

Daily: June–Sept 9am–7pm; Oct–May 9am–1hr before sunset; last entry 1hr before closing · €4

The extensive (and well-signposted) remains of **MEGARA HYBLAEA** are considered to be the most complete model of an Archaic city still surviving. The settlement prospered as a Greek colony after the Sikel king of Hybla had granted land alongside his own to Greeks from Megara (near Athens). By the middle of the seventh century BC, the population had done so well out of trade and their high-quality pottery that they were able to found some minor colonies of their own, including Selinus in the west, though their city was eventually submerged by Syracusan ambitions and destroyed by Gelon in 482 BC. The town flourished again later in the fourth century BC, but was finally levelled by the Romans in the same avenging campaign that ended Syracuse's independence in 214 BC. Most of the **ruins** belong to the fourth-century revival, but the fortifications were erected a century later, interrupted by the Romans' arrival. Various buildings lie confusingly scattered over a wide area, though all the finds are in Siracusa's Museo Archeologico.

Pantalica

Always open · Free

PANTALICA, Sicily's greatest **necropolis**, lies in the folds of the Monti Iblei, around 40km northwest of Siracusa. Here, in the deep gorge of the River Anapo, you can follow tracks past several thousand tombs hollowed out of the valley sides at five separate locations. Several skeletons were found in each tomb, suggesting that a few thousand people once lived in what is now largely a craggy wilderness. It's an extraordinary location, designated a UNESCO World Heritage Site, but it's virtually impossible to get to Pantalica by public transport; by car, the approaches are from the small towns of **Sortino** or **Ferla**, at either end of the gorge, with parking at various points near both places; the northern necropolis, approached via Sortino, makes the most dramatic introduction to the area.

The site was first used between the thirteenth and the tenth centuries BC by Sikel refugees from the coast. After the eighth century BC, it is thought to have been the location of the city of **Hybla**, whose king invited Megarian Greeks to colonize Megara Hyblaea; remains from this era are visible, but all pale into insignificance in contrast with the five thousand or so tombs hewn out of the gorge below. In some were found the traces of several separate skeletons, probably of the same family, while others show evidence of habitation – though much later, when the Syracusans themselves were forced to flee inland from barbarian incursions. The atmosphere is primeval and almost sinister – for Vincent Cronin, even something terrifying: "Here is Sicily of the stone age, intent on nothing higher than the taking of food and the burial of its dead." For Cronin, the free play of nature in this ravine embodied Sicily's own particular contribution to the man-made wonders bestowed later by the island's conquerors, and as such – symbolized by a honeycomb he came across in one of the caves – the object of the quest described in his book, *The Golden Honeycomb* (1954).

6

The site

The road ends at a parking area at the entrance to the **northern necropolis**, 6km from Sortino (follow the signs). An obvious but rocky path leads around a plateau, then down to the river and up the other side (where there's another parking area, but this time accessed from Ferla – the road was originally planned to span the gorge, but never completed). You'll soon see the **tombs**, first just dotting the walls of the valley in clusters and finally puncturing the whole vertical cliff face – this last view is about 1km, or a thirty-minute walk, from the parking area. There are superb views from the higher reaches, and the path and rock-cut steps remain good all the way.

You can continue down across the river and up the other side of the gorge, where the road begins again and runs west to Ferla, another 9km beyond. This is the upper road to Ferla, with a parking area allowing access to the foundations of the **Anaktoron**, or prince's palace, a building from ancient Hybla, and to the **southern necropolis**, where more rock tombs are visible. A lower road from Ferla has another parking area, from where you can stroll easily along the bottom of the gorge for a while.

ACCOMMODATION AND EATING   **PANTALICA**

Il Giardino di Pantalica Via Orazio Motta Tornabene 3 ☎ 095 712 2680, ⓦ pantalica.it. An *agriturismo* on an estate within the Pantalica natural reserve; to get there take the Siracusa road from Ferla, and enter (after 3km) via the park entrance. There are one- and two-bedroom apartments and a summer swimming pool, and as for food, there are barbecue facilities and a restaurant (open daily if there are guests) specializing in local meat, where you can eat for €20–25 per head. No credit cards. **€70**

Palazzolo Acreide

Set on a hill some 40km west of Siracusa, **PALAZZOLO ACREIDE** is a mainly Baroque town with the remains of the ancient city of **Akrei**, one of the province's classical sites, lying just outside the modern settlement. Palazzolo makes a good excursion from Siracusa, or a rather quiet overnight stop if you have your own transport (the nicest places to stay are in the surrounding countryside).

Palazzolo's main square, **Piazza del Popolo**, is the heart of the Baroque town, with two sides dominated by the handsome church of San Sebastiano and the gleaming town hall. From here lanes radiate down past opulent facades, hidden courtyards and gargoyled balconies, eventually leading to a trio of fine Baroque **churches**, the Chiesa Madre, San Paolo and the Annunziata. Everything you will want to see is within walking distance of the centre, though it is quite a slog up the hill to Akrei, especially in the height of summer.

Casa-Museo di Antonino Uccello

Via Machiavelli 19 • Mon–Sat 9am–6.30pm, Sun 9am–12.30pm • €2 • ☎ 0931 881 499, ⓦ casamuseo.it

Palazzolo's main focus of interest – at least for anyone curious about the roots of Sicilian culture – is the **Casa-Museo di Antonino Uccello**, tucked away in a house in the old centre. The fruit of one man's thirty-year obsession to preserve the traditions of rural Sicily, it constitutes an important documentation of folk art, showing trousseaux, ceramics, olive presses, puppets, reconstructions of houses and stables, and anything else judged by Uccello to be in danger of extinction.

Akrai

Daily 9am–5pm • €4 • A 20min walk up from Palazzolo Acreide town centre, or you can park close to the entrance

The first inland colony of Siracusa, ancient **Akrai** thrived during the peace and security that characterized Hieron II's reign during the third century BC. It declined under the Romans, but later re-emerged as an important early Christian centre (as shown by the number of rock-cut tombs in the area), only to be eventually destroyed by the Arabs.

Many remains give little impression of their former grandeur. You'll have a job identifying the excavated Roman **Tempio di Persefone**, above the Greek theatre, an unusually round chamber that was formerly covered by a cupola. Equally fragmentary is the much older **Tempio di Afrodite**, sixth or fifth century BC, lying at the head of what was the agora. From here you can look straight down into one of the two quarries from which the stone to build the city was taken. Later they were converted into Christian burial chambers, and in the first of them, the **Intagliata**, you can plainly see the recesses in the walls: some of them catacombs, others areas of worship, the rest simply rude dwellings cut in the Byzantine era. The narrower, deeper quarry below it, the **Intagliatella**, holds more votive niches and a relief cut from the rock-face, over 2m long, that combines a typically Greek scene – heroes banqueting – with a Roman one of heroes offering sacrifice. It's thought to date from the first century BC.

There are more niches and chambers in a lower quarry, the **Templi Ferali**, though you'll have to ask the custodian to let you see this.

Teatro Greco

Of the visible remains, the most complete is the small **Teatro Greco**, built towards the end of Hieron's reign. A perfect semicircle, the theatre held six hundred people and retains traces of its scene-building. Behind the theatre to the right is a small **senate house**, or bouleuterion, a rectangular construction that was originally covered. Beyond lies a 200m stretch of decumanus that once connected the two gates of the city. Crossed at regular intervals by junctions and paved in lava rock, it's in better condition than many of the more recent roads in the area.

Santoni

Currently closed for refurbishment; call for an update • ☎ 0931 876 602 • The sculptures are a 15min walk from the main Akrai site

Comprising twelve rock-cut sculptures (carved no later than the third century BC), the **Santoni** represent the fertility goddess Cybele, a predominantly eastern deity whose origins are steeped in mystery. There's no other example of so rich a complex relating to her worship, and the local name tagged to these sculptures – *santoni*, or "great saints" – suggests that the awe attached to them survived until relatively recently.

Parcallario

June–Sept daily 10am–sunset; Oct–March weekends or by appointment 10am–sunset, but always call first • €9 • ☎ 333 921 8145, ⓦ parcallario.it • There are no buses to the park, so you'll need your own transport

Half an hour's drive northwest of Palazzolo on the Vizzini–Caltagirone road (the SS124), set in cool, shady woods outside the little village of Buccheri, the well-run **Parcallario** offers the opportunity to head up into the tree canopies. There are currently four routes of varying difficulty (and more in the pipeline), with rope-walks, zip wires and swinging wooden bridges, as well as a fun course for young children. There are also barbecues (Buccheri and Palazzolo are famous for their butchers), picnic tables and a small bar selling freshly grilled sausage sandwiches and powerful local red wine.

ARRIVAL AND INFORMATION
PALAZZOLO ACREIDE

By bus AST buses from Siracusa pull up in the central Piazza del Popolo in the heart of the historic centre.
Tourist information There's a tourist office on Piazza del

Popolo (daily 9am–1pm & 3–7pm, 4–8pm in summer; ☎ 0931 472 181).

ACCOMMODATION AND EATING

Anapama Contrada Fiumara ☎ 0931 24 011, ⓦ anapama.it. Three apartments on a rambling country estate with lush gardens and masses of space for children to play. There's a swimming pool fed by a freshwater spring, bikes for guest use and three horses which guests can ride. If you don't like dogs, give it a miss, however. **€70**
Fattoria Giannavi Contrada Giannavi ☎ 0931 881 776, ⓦ fattoriagiannavi.it. A farm with rooms, pool and a restaurant serving home-grown, home-cooked food, with good deals if you stay on a full- or half-board basis. It's set high on a bluff with extensive views, 8km from Palazzolo on the Giarratana/Ragusa road (10min drive). Camping also available here. Camping **€10** per person; rooms **€60**

Il Portico Via Orologio 6 ☎ 0931 881 532. Grandly renovated old *palazzo*, with painted ceilings and period furnishings – dining here is something of an occasion. The menu includes such dishes as fresh pasta and grilled meats, and prices are excellent: pizzas are €4–10, all other dishes are €7–15, and tasting menus are €35 and €40. Mon & Wed–Sun dinner only.
Lo Scrigno dei Sapori Via Maddalena 50 ☎ 0931 882 941. A great spot for a lunch or more substantial dinner, where the inventive menu is strong on meats, for example ravioli with a hare and nut sauce, pork with a pistachio crust, stuffed rabbit, and lamb's ribs, all at reasonable prices. There are pizzas in the evening too. Tues–Sun lunch & dinner.

Noto

Some 32km southwest of Siracusa, the exquisite town of **NOTO** represents the apogee of the wholesale renovation that took place following the cataclysm of 1693, a monument to the achievement of a few architects and planners whose vision coincided with the golden age of Baroque architecture. Although a town called Noto, or Netum, has existed in this area for centuries, what you see today is in effect a "New Town", conceived as a triumphant symbol of renewal. The fragile Iblean limestone used in its construction was grievously damaged by modern pollution, but years of restoration work have gradually shaken off the grime and most of the harmonious buildings have regained their original honey-hued facades. Some characterful B&B accommodation, and traffic-free old-town streets that are at their most charming as the lights come on at dusk make this one of the island's essential stopovers.

Brief history

Noto was flattened by the earthquake on January 11, 1693, and a week later its rebuilding was entrusted to a Sicilian-Spanish aristocrat, **Giuseppe Lanza, Duke of Camastra**, on the strength of his work at the town of Santo Stefano di Camastra, on the Tyrrhenian coast. Lanza visited the ruins, saw nothing but "*un monton de piedras abandonadas*" (a mountain of forsaken rocks), and quickly decided to start afresh, on a new site 16km to the south. In fact, the ruins weren't abandoned; the city's battered population was already improvising a shantytown, and even held a referendum when Lanza's intentions became known, rejecting the call to relocate their city. But partly motivated by the prestige of the undertaking, partly by the need to refurbish the area's defences, Lanza ignored the local feeling, even pulling down their new constructions and the old town's remaining church.

With the help of the Flemish military engineer Carlos de Grunemburg, Lanza devised a revolutionary new **plan**, based on two gridded sections that were to be almost completely separated from each other – a lower area for the political and religious establishment, the upper town for the people. The best **architects** were to be used: Vincenzo Sinatra, Paolo Labisi and the master craftsman Rosario Gagliardi – not innovators, but men whose enthusiasm and experience enabled them to concoct a graceful synthesis of the latest architectural skills and forms. Their collaboration was so complete that it's still difficult to ascribe some buildings to any one person. Within an astonishingly short time the work was completed: a new city, planned with the accent on symmetry and visual harmony, from its simple street plan to the lissom figures adorning its buildings. It's easily the most successful post-earthquake creation, and, for a time, in the mid-nineteenth century, the new Noto replaced Siracusa as the region's provincial capital.

AMONG THE RUINS OF NOTO ANTICA

Until finally abandoned in 1693, the original town of Noto had several times been a significant historical stronghold: one of the few Sicilian towns to resist the looting of the Roman praetor Verres, it was also the last bastion of Arab Sicily before the Norman conquest of the island. Only sparse remnants of the old town survive, but **Noto Antica** makes a fascinating side-trip nonetheless. It's 16km northwest of Noto, signposted from the western end of the Corso in town (there's no bus) – the turn-off to the site is also that for the convent of Santa Maria delle Scale, with Noto Antica another 5km past the convent. You park outside the surviving gate of the **castle** (occupied from the eleventh to the seventeenth century), where renovation work has rebuilt some of the circular tower. Early Christian **catacombs** honeycomb the rock beneath the tumbled walls that line the valley cliff. An unsurfaced country lane pushes on through the castle gate past the now-puzzling, completely overgrown remains of an **abandoned city** – square-cut stone blocks, shattered arches, bramble-covered courtyards and crumbling walls. If you come out here, you might as well plan the day to take in the Cava Grande canyon, too (see p.239), which is only another twenty minutes' drive away – back past the convent to the main road, turn left and look for the signposted right turn.

6

Porta Reale

From the public gardens on the eastern side of town, the centre of Noto is approached through the monumental **Porta Reale**, built in 1838 and topped by the three symbols of the town's allegiance to the Bourbon monarchy: a dog, a tower and a pelican (respectively, loyalty, strength and sacrifice). The main **Corso Vittorio Emanuele**, running from here through the heart of the lower, patricians' quarter, is lined with some of Sicily's most captivating buildings. Now the traffic's kept out you can stand back and admire them at will, while floodlights, many set into the pavement, show them off to glorious effect at night.

The Duomo

Piazza del Municipio • Usually daily 10am–1pm & 5–7pm

Mid-way along Corso Vittorio Emanuele, **Piazza del Municipio** forms the dramatic centrepiece of the town's design, with the imposing twin-towered **Duomo** magnificently restored following the dramatic collapse of its dome in 1996. First completed in 1776, it's said to have been inspired by models of Borromini's churches in Rome – the story of its reconstruction, and some of the Duomo's treasures, are on display around the back of the cathedral.

Palazzo Ducezio

Piazza del Municipio • Opening hours vary, and the Hall of the Mirrors is sometimes closed for civic events; check with the tourist office • €4

Piazza del Municipio is bordered by gleaming buildings restored to look as they must have done when first built. Opposite the Duomo and currently serving as the Municipio (town hall), the **Palazzo Ducezio** presents a lovely, convex front of columns and long stone balconies. The **interior** is well worth a visit to see the so-called Hall of Mirrors, with its splendid trompe l'oeil ceiling.

Via C. Nicolaci

West of the Duomo, the steep **Via C. Nicolaci** culminates in the elliptical **Monte Vergine** church. It's a perfectly framed view that's enhanced during the annual **Infiorata** flower festival (third weekend of May), when flower petals are laid up the entire street in a swirl of intricate designs. **Palazzo Villadorata**, the palace that flanks the west side of the street, also makes rather an unusual, not to say eccentric, sight. Onto a strictly classical front six extravagant balconies were grafted, supported by the last word in sculpted buttresses – griffins, galloping horses and bald and bearded figures with fat-cheeked cherubs at their bellies. The *palazzo* is sometimes open for guided visits – ask at the tourist office.

ARRIVAL AND INFORMATION

By bus All buses stop at the Giardino Pubblico at the eastern end of town, close to the Porta Reale.
Destinations Avola (1–2 hourly; 15min); Eloro (2–4 daily Mon–Sat; 20min); Ispica (9 daily Mon–Sat, 6 daily Sun; 45min); Siracusa (11 daily Mon–Sat, 4 daily Sun; 55min).
By train The train station is a good 10–15min walk away down Via Principe di Piemonte, has no facilities – not even a bench – and is often unstaffed. If you have luggage, you may need a taxi (☎0931 838 713 or ☎338 945 8206).
Destinations Ragusa (1 daily Mon–Sat; 1hr 40min); Siracusa (8 daily Mon–Sat, 1 daily Sun; 35min).
By car Traffic through town is all one-way and while it's

easy enough to drive in (follow "centro" signs) or out (destinations are all well signposted), finding a particular spot while driving can be difficult. The best advice is to park first (there's a free waste-ground car park behind the stadium, among others) and get your bearings. Many hotels and B&Bs are signposted through town as well.
Tourist information There's a well-informed tourist office in Piazza XVI Maggio, set back from the Corso behind the Hercules fountain (April–Oct Mon–Sat and most Sundays 9am–1pm & 2.30–7.30pm; Nov–March daily 8.30am–1pm & 2.30–7pm; ☎0931 573 779, ⓦcomune .noto.sr.it), which has a full list of accommodation.

ACCOMMODATION

★ **Il Castello** Via Fratelli Bandiera 2 ☎320 838 8869, ⓦostellodinoto.it. Youth hostel housed in a converted *palazzo* in the upper part of town with wonderful views, large dormitories, excellent showers and laundry service; there are some family rooms too, sleeping four. It's accessible from the centre in a few minutes up signposted steps from Via Cavour, behind the Duomo. Dorms €16; beds in family rooms €19.50
La Fontanella Via Rosolino Pilo 3 ☎0931 894 735, ⓦalbergolafontanella.it. Thirteen rooms in a sympathetically restored nineteenth-century *palazzo* on a busy road on the northern edge of Noto Alta. It's a three-star place, and the only hotel (rather than B&B) within walking distance of the centre (10min), but there's no restaurant. Often cheaper than the B&Bs, though lacking some of their charm. Parking is for once easy around here. €60
Liberty Rooms Via Francesco Ferruccio, corner Corso Vittorio Emanuele ☎338 230 4042. This beautiful Art Nouveau "palazzetto" on Noto's central Corso has gracious rooms furnished with antiques. A kitchen for guests' use and a huge roof terrace on which to eat mean there's no need to dine out. €100

Macrina Vico Grillo, corner Via Fabrizi ☎0931 837 202, ⓦb-bmacrina.com. Family-run B&B in a neighbourly street, with three spacious and airy rooms, each with its own terrace. There's also a huge walled garden with a couple of swings plus use of a barbecue, making this a good choice if you have kids. The small breakfast terrace is useful if you want to rustle up a snack or aperitivo. €75
★ **Montandon** Via A. Sofia 50 ☎0931 836 389 or ☎339 524 4607, ⓦb-bmontandon.com. A real gem, this B&B in a grand *palazzo* in the upper town has three huge rooms, each with its own terrace. Guests have access to an enchanting garden (with swings), which makes a welcome summer retreat from heat and crowds. The owner is a marvellous host, and serves outstanding breakfasts, including eggs, local ricotta, salami, ham, pastries, fruit and home-made jams. €80
Villa Canisello Via Cesare Pavese 1 ☎0931 835 793, ⓦvillacanisello.it. An old farmhouse on the western outskirts of town in a quiet residential suburb; rooms open to a patio or terrace, and there's parking. Signs lead you right there from the western end of the Corso – it seems like a bit of a slog, but it's actually only a 10min walk to the centre. Closed Nov–Easter. €80

EATING, DRINKING AND ENTERTAINMENT

Although there are surprisingly few **restaurants** in the centre of Noto, you'll be able to ring the changes over a couple of days, and prices are pretty reasonable. The cafés along the Corso come into their own during the evening *passeggiata*, while the local authorities put on a full range of **concerts** and **events** throughout the year, from religious processions at Easter to summer music festivals – get details from the tourist office (see above).

CAFÉS AND RESTAURANTS
Caffè Sicilia Corso Vittorio Emanuele 125. You really shouldn't leave Noto without sampling the ice creams at its rival prize-winning *gelaterie*, *Costanzo* (see opposite) and

Sicilia. This is the more radical of the two, with flavours such as lemon and saffron, and even basil. Daily 8am–8pm, closes later in summer.
★ **Carmine** Via Ducezio 1 ☎0931 838 705. Locals flock

6

CAVA GRANDE DEL FIUME CASSIBILE

A spectacular winding route northwest of the ramshackle agricultural town of Avola climbs past the Convento di Avola Vecchia to the magnificent gorge and nature reserve of the **Cava Grande del Fiume Cassibile**. There's parking by a sensational viewpoint over the Cassibile River gorge, which really is quite Grand Canyon-esque, with sheer rock walls visible across the divide, birds of prey circling, and the river glistening far below. The very steep path that leads down to the bottom of the valley is closed at times of high fire risk, and you need to be properly shod, fit enough to climb back out, and to carry plenty of water. The round-trip requires a good three hours, plus any time you spend splashing in the natural swimming pools or following the footpath alongside the river, which runs for most of the gorge's 11km length. If you don't fancy going right down to the bottom, follow the gentler path that hugs the canyon walls, branching off to the left about halfway down the steps. At the top, at the parking area, you can get a drink or a meal from a rustic tavern, the *Trattoria Cava Grande* (no phone; June–Sept Tues–Sun lunch & dinner; Oct–May Sat & Sun lunch only).

Cava Grande is not accessible on public transport. It's a 15km drive from Avola, or you can also approach from Noto up the SS287, past the turn-off for Noto Antica. For **walking tours** with an English-speaking guide, including transport, call ☎333 329 3732.

to this trattoria for a good meal at low cost and it's certainly pretty remarkable value, with rustic *antipasto* and pasta dishes running at €6–7, grilled fish from around €11, and a mixed grill at €13. It perfectly defines the phrase "cheap and cheerful", though the downsides are that it's too brightly lit, the house wine is challenging to say the least and the interconnected rooms get very busy. Daily lunch & dinner; closed Mon Sept–June.

Costanzo Via Silvio Spaventa 7–11. A well-known *pasticceria* and *gelateria*, known for producing what may be the best ice cream in Italy (the other contender is *Sicilia*) in flavours such as mandarin, ricotta, jasmine and rose (depending on the season), as well as sweets and pastries, including dreamy *cassata*. The almond milk is joyous. Mon–Tues & Thurs–Sun lunch & dinner.

Emily's Wine Via Cavour 34 ☎0931 838 028,

⊛enotecanoto.com. A nice place for a glass of good wine (€6) and tasty snacks such as *crostini* with ricotta and honey, an unctuous *caponata* (€9), *foccace* (€2–3), and local cheeses and hams (€3 per portion). They also have several pasta dishes daily (€5.50–6.50) and a range of lentil and pulse soups to eat in or take away and heat up at home – useful if you have an apartment. Daily 11am–3pm & 4pm–late; winter closed Wed.

Trattoria Baglieri Il Crocifisso Via Principe Umberto 46 ☎0931 571 151. Fine trattoria using seasonal local ingredients in ways that make the taste-buds zing: spaghetti with prawns and wild asparagus (€12), rabbit in *agrodolce* with orange-blossom honey, wild greens, celery, carrot and peppers (€12), or tuna in a pistachio and sesame crust (€14). Mon–Tues & Thurs–Sun lunch & dinner.

South of Noto

South of Noto lies the most undeveloped stretch of coast on the east side of the island, sheltering excellent sand beaches – like **Noto Marina** and **Eloro** – and the extensive **Vendicari** nature reserve. Minor roads run all the way south to the Capo delle Correnti, the southernmost point of Sicily, while in between the old restored fishing villages of **Marzamemi** and **Portopalo di Capo Passero** serve as small-scale summer resorts. There are several good rural **accommodation** options in the area, though with a car, you could see the whole of the coast – as far as the cape and back – from Noto in a day, but public transport is practically nonexistent.

Noto Marina and Eloro

Eloro Mon–Sat 9am–1.30pm • Free • Buses operated by Caruso (☎0931 836 23) run from Noto to Noto Marina

Noto's local beach, 5km southeast at **NOTO MARINA** (also called Lido di Noto), is fine for a swim and a bite to eat (in summer at least). You can walk from here (though it's easier to drive) just south to the seaside ruins of Helorus, or **Eloro**, a Syracusan colony founded in the seventh century BC at the mouth of the Tellaro River. It's all a bit ramshackle, and the few remains are quite difficult to make head or tail of, but its position right above the shore is very attractive. The broad expanse of sand below offers good swimming, but direct access is tricky from the site: a road to the south, across the river, leads directly to the **beach**.

The Riserva Naturale di Vendicari

Daily: April–Oct 7am–8pm; Nov–March 7am–6.30pm • Free, parking €2.50 • ☏ 0931 67 450, ⓦ oasivendicari.net

Some 10km south of Noto is the magical **Riserva Naturale di Vendicari**, an enchanting landscape of marshes, lagoons, dunes and saltpans. There's parking at the entrance, but no other facilities. Loads of waterbirds can be seen from the hides, including herons, cranes, black storks and even pelicans, though the more than three hundred flamingos can be elusive at times, while sandy tracks and boardwalks fan out north and south through the marshland, leading to some splendid sand crescents. The reserve takes its name from the brick tower, the Torre Vendicari, which looms over a part-restored *tonnara* (tuna-fishing village) by one of the beaches. Its internal courtyards and sandstone pillars gleam brightly against a turquoise sea. Another good beach, signposted **San Lorenzo**, lies just a short drive further south of the reserve, down the main Pachino road, and has very clear water and a small summer lido.

ACCOMMODATION
RISERVA NATURALE DI VENDICARI

Agriturismo Cala Mosche Riserva Naturale l'Oasi di Vendicari ☏ 347 858 7319. This agriturismo with six rooms and a restaurant is set right inside the reserve (take the Cala Mosche entrance), in walking distance of the beaches. Ideal for families. €50

Il Roveto Contrada Roveto-Vendicari ☏ 338 742 6343, ⓦ roveto.it. This beautifully restored old farmhouse is signposted at the Riserva Naturale turn-off on the SP19 Pachino road. The five self-contained apartments with kitchen sleep either two, four or six people, and you're only 800m from the pristine Torre Vendicari beach. Three-night minimum stay. From €90

Terre di Vendicari Contrada Vaddeddi ☏ 346 359 3845, ⓦ terredivendicari.it. Minimalist chic in a country hotel at the heart of the Vendicari nature reserve, with views out to sea over its olive and lemon groves. Rooms are cool and stylish, with freestanding Philippe Starck baths and abundant bathtime products. Fabulous swimming pool, too. €230

Villa Romana del Tellaro

Contrada Vaddeddi • Daily 9am–7pm • €6 • ☏ 0931 573 883, ⓦ villaromanadeltellaro.com

In 1971 the remains of the **Villa Romana del Tellaro**, an Imperial-era Roman country villa dating back to the fourth century AD, were discovered on land above the River Tellaroo, about 2km inland from Vendicari. Though on a smaller scale than the Villa Romana del Casale (see p.270), Tellaro too has some fantastic **mosaics**, including scenes from the Odyssey, and a wonderfully realized wild-animal hunting scene in which people and animals are shown wading through water. There is a magnificent tiger too – suggesting that these mosaics, like those at Casale, were the work of North African craftsmen.

Marzamemi

MARZAMEMI, prettily set around a crescent harbour backed by the port's old *tonnara*, is still renowned for its tuna dishes, and is home to a **film festival** in late July (ⓦ cinemadifrontiera.it), showing international contemporary and vintage films in open-air venues. Behind the shell of a church and *palazzo*, the restored *tonnara* square shelters bars and restaurants that come into their own in high summer, when tourists descend on the village in droves.

CLOCKWISE FROM TOP LEFT RAGUSA IBLA (P.247); ORECCHIO DI DIONISIO, NEAPOLIS (P.225); RISERVA VENDICARI (P.240) >

La Cialoma Piazza Regina Margherita 23 ☎ 0931 841 772. Immediately appealing, cosy little restaurant run by a family of women, occupying one of the diminutive buildings of the *tonnara* complex and specializing not just in tuna, but in several local varieties of blue fish, served in hearty and tasty traditional dishes with a light creative touch. Daily lunch & dinner; closed Nov, and Tues Dec–Feb.

Portopalo di Capo Passero

Eight kilometres south of Marzamemi down the rugged coastal road, **PORTOPALO DI CAPO PASSERO** is another low-key summer resort. You might be able to persuade someone to row you over to the little islet that lies just offshore, complete with a seventeenth-century castle. Otherwise, follow the minor cape road out to the southeastern point of **Isola delle Correnti** (the tiny islet just off the cape, linked to it at low tide). You're on the southernmost tip of Sicily here, with nothing between you and Africa.

Ispica and the Cava d'Ispica

Inland from the cape at **ISPICA**, 18km southeast of Modica, human settlement can be traced back 4000 years, to the cave dwellings and tombs carved out of the wide gorge of the **Cava d'Ispica**. These were later used by generations of Sikels, Greeks and early Christians to bury their dead, while during medieval times a strong fortified castle, town and churches were built on the rocky bluff above the southern section of the gorge. Then, in 1693, disaster struck, as the great quake levelled thousands of years of habitation in one swift blow. A new town was rebuilt on the neighbouring hill, which is where modern Ispica thrives today, a rather sprawling place set around a central kernel of restored squares and Baroque churches, including the rather special elliptical **Piazza Santa Maria Maggiore**.

Parco Archeologico della Forza

Daily 9am–1 hour before sunset • Free • ☎ 0932 951 133 • You can walk here from the centre of Ispica: follow signs to Rosolini, and at the foot of the town the road forks – the left fork is marked Parco Archeologico della Forza, where there's a car park

Ispica lies at the head of a dramatic limestone **gorge**, some 12km long and honeycombed with rock-cut tombs and dwellings. The area nearest to Ispica, designated as the **Parco Archeologico della Forza**, has a well-marked path taking you past the broken remains of palaces and churches and into the southern section of the gorge itself, where caves were used as houses, storerooms, stables, workshops and cemeteries, right up until 1693. The nearest water supply was the river at the bottom of the gorge, reached by 3300 steps, no less. A separate path from the parking area leads to the church of **Santa Maria La Cava**, cut into the rock and dating back to the very earliest days of Christianity in Sicily – some medieval frescoes can be seen inside.

In the week before Christmas, **tableaux vivants** are staged in the caves of the Parco della Forza, with locals dressed up as peasants, reviving old traditions such as making ricotta and shoeing horses.

Cava d'Ispica Nord

April–Oct daily 9am–1hr before sunset; Nov–March Mon–Sat 9am–1.30pm • €4

The Ispica gorge actually runs for 13km northwest towards Modica, with rock-cut dwellings and tombs lining the entire route. It's possible to walk through the gorge, starting either at Ispica or at the northern section, the **Cava d'Ispica Nord**, which is around 7km east of Modica (and very clearly, indeed almost obsessively, signposted).

From the entrance (where there's a café), a landscaped **path** descends into the gorge, where towering fronds of bamboo and wild fennel grow amid the fig, pomegranate and walnut trees. There are **catacombs** immediately below the site entrance, while the path meanders back through the site past tombs and dwellings cut into the cliff face. The route through the gorge starts on the other side of the road from the entrance, running under the road bridge.

Molino ad Acqua

6

Via Cava d'Ispica 89, Modica • Daily 9am–7pm • €3 • ☏ 0932 771048, ⊛ cavallodispica.it

Heading to Cava d'Ispica Nord from either Modica or Ispica, you may like to make a stop at the fascinating working watermill of **Molino ad Acqua** – just follow the many signs. Here you can watch the mill – set on the horizontal, rather than the vertical, so that it could still work when water levels were low – grinding wheat into flour, and visit the cave-house (with bed, laundry and kitchen) where members of the family who ran it lived until the 1950s.

Modica

The small but busy town of **MODICA**, 17km northwest of Ispica and 18km south of Ragusa, is enjoying a new lease of life as a select tourist destination, based again on its remarkable late Baroque heritage. A powerful medieval base of the Chiaramonte family, and later the Cabreras, it was once far more important than Ragusa itself, though ironically, following the reconstruction after 1693 (which has earned it UNESCO World Heritage status) it never regained its erstwhile prestige. There's really not much to see to Modica – a night would do it full justice – but it is an enjoyable place to visit. There's interest enough in simply strolling the Corso and window-shopping in the boutiques, fancy shoe shops, *enotecas* and gourmet delis.

Corso Umberto I

Modica's upper and lower towns are divided by the long main drag of **Corso Umberto I** – which originally was a river until a flood of 1902 prompted the authorities to cover it over. The Corso is flanked by a run of handsome *palazzi*, whose balconies are buttressed by gargoyles, twisted heads and beasts, while its churches make grandiose Baroque statements of intent. That of **San Pietro**, for example, has a wide flight of steps framing the life-sized statues of the Twelve Apostles.

Modica Alta

The warren-like upper town of **Modica Alta** holds some genius in the shape of the magnificent eighteenth-century facade of **San Giorgio**, a worthy rival to the church of the same name in Ragusa Ibla. It's thought that architect Rosario Gagliardi was responsible for this, too: the elliptical facade is topped by his trademark, a belfry, while the approach is characteristically daring – twin flights of stairs zigzag up across the upper town's hairpins, ending in a terrace before the church. From here, and from the tight streets above San Giorgio, you can look back over the grey-tiled roofs and balconies of the town, built up two sides of a narrow valley. There are more views from the remains of the **castle** and its clocktower, which perches on a rocky spur above the main part of town.

ARRIVAL AND INFORMATION   **MODICA**

By bus Regional buses drop you right in Modica's centre on Corso Umberto I.

Destinations Catania (9 daily Mon–Sat, 4 daily Sun; 2hr 10min); Catania airport (9 daily Mon–Sat, 4 daily Sun; 1hr

6

SICILY'S CHOCOLATE CITY

Mention Modica to most Italians and they'll think **chocolate**. The great Sicilian writer Leonardo Sciascia declared that "Modican chocolate is unparalleled … tasting it is like reaching the archetype, the absolute … chocolate produced elsewhere, even the most celebrated, is an adulteration, a corruption of the original." In fact, the chocolate sold here is unlike most other chocolate you'll have encountered, from its grainy, crunchy texture to the undertones of cinnamon, orange, vanilla, honey, almonds and even salt and pepper. You can sample it in a myriad of ways, from ice cream to Modica's famous **hot chocolate**, but it's most readily available in the traditional **chocolate bar** format available from numerous shops in the town. Above all, seek out Sicily's oldest chocolate manufacturer, the **Antica Dolceria Bonajuto**, up an alley at Corso Umberto I 159 (daily 9am–8pm; ☎0932 941 225, ⊕bonajuto.it), which has been making the stuff since 1880. The shop's a beauty, filled with old display cabinets, and you can sample from dainty little tasting dishes on the counter before you buy.

55min); Ispica (9 daily Mon–Sat, 1 daily Sun; 30min–1hr 10min); Noto (hourly Mon–Sat, 6 daily Sun; 1hr 25min); Ragusa (1–2 hourly Mon–Sat, 4 daily Sun; 25min–1hr); Scicli (1–2 hourly Mon–Sat, 4 daily Sun; 30–40min); Siracusa (10 daily Mon–Sat, 4 daily Sun; 2hr–2hr 40min).

By train The train station is a good 10min walk away from the town centre.

Destinations Noto (4 Mon–Sat only; 1hr 15min); Ragusa (4 Mon–Sat only; 15min); Scicli (4 Mon–Sat; 20min); Siracusa (4 Mon–Sat; 1hr 45min).

By car Drivers can park on the street, but in most central areas you need to buy a parking voucher (from *tabacchi*) to put in your window (€0.75/hr, half day €2.50; charges apply Mon–Sat 9am–1pm & 4–8pm). Note also that if you're going to the Cava d'Ispica, you can drive directly to the northern section closest to Modica (there's a brown sign at the ornamental fountain) – you don't need to take the main road to Ispica itself.

Tourist information The tourist office is at Corso Umberto I 141 (Mon–Sat 8am–1.30pm & 3–7pm; ☎346 655 8227).

ACCOMMODATION

Casa Talia Via Exaudinos 1 ☎0932 752 075, ⊕casatalia.it. Occupying a cluster of restored houses in what was once Modica's Jewish ghetto, *Casa Talia* is far removed from the city-centre bustle, yet just a 5min walk down a series of steps and alleyways from the main Corso. A garden planted with fruit trees adds to the feeling of seclusion. Rooms, designed by the architect owners who live on-site, are stylish and practical, and breakfasts are excellent (freshly squeezed juices, home-made cakes, jams and breads), served in a nook-and-crannied whitewashed room occupying what were once caves used as a cistern and stables. **€130**

L'Orangerie Vico de Naro 5 ☎0932 754 703 or ☎347 067 4698, ⊕lorangerie.it. Tranquil, refined B&B with three huge suites (with kitchens) and four spacious rooms, in a *palazzo* with frescoed ceilings and private flower-filled terraces. Doubles **€96**; suites **€126**

Palazzo Il Cavaliere Corso Umberto I 259 ☎0932 947 219, ⊕palazzoilcavaliere.it. A down-to-earth aristocratic family run their eighteenth-century palace as a B&B. The setting is splendid and authentic – original Caltagirone tiled floors, frescoed ceilings and antique furniture, and

three of the eight rooms open on to a courtyard. **€88**

Palazzo Failla Via Blandini 5 ☎0932 941 059, ⊕palazzofailla.it. Reborn as a comfortable four-star hotel, this handsome upper-town palace by the Santa Teresa church retains its intimate, aristocratic feel. The seven rooms are elegant and traditional, with tiled floors, high frescoed ceilings and antique beds. There are also three contemporary minimalist rooms in an annexe across the road by the trattoria *La Locanda del Colonnello* (see opposite). Check the website for good last-minute deals. **€109**

I Tetti di Sicliando Via Cannata 24 ☎0932 942 843, ⊕sicliando.it. Simple, friendly and unpretentious budget hotel, popular with backpackers and set in the tangle of historic streets above Corso Umberto I. Rooms are pretty basic, but it's very reasonably priced and sociable. The owners are very helpful, and have rental bikes (€15/day) and can help organize bike tours of the surrounding area. Look for the sign opposite the Agip petrol station towards the top of the Corso (where you'll have to park), and follow the steps up around the passageway for the signposted "bed, bike and breakfast". **€35**

EATING AND DRINKING

La Gazza Ladra Via Blandini 5 ☎0932 755 655, ⊕ristorantelagazzaladra.it. Top-class restaurant that's part of the *Palazzo Failla* hotel, offering creative and

exquisitely presented Sicilian cuisine (spaghetti with anchovies, candied orange, wild fennel flowers, chilli and wild-onion greens; a fillet of Nébrodi mountain pork, with a cream of pine nuts and asparagus). *Degustazione* menus at €65 and €80 a head plus drinks. Daily lunch & dinner.

La Locanda del Colonnello Vico Biscari 6 ☎0932 752 423. Done up like a traditional *locanda*, with chequered tiled walls, a *pietra pece* (local limestone, naturally impregnated with petroleum) floor below cantilevered white vaults, and evocative photos of old Modica on its walls. Heavy napery and good service, however, remind you that this is a *Palazzo Failla* enterprise. The mixed *antipasto* (€9) is highly recommended: sardine *polpettine* with wild fennel, a crisp *scacce* (savoury pastry) with a reduced tomato filling, pepper- and fennel-seed studded salami, a *sformatino* of asparagus, and a miniature *arancino*. *Primi* are all €9, and make great use of legumes in dishes such as *maccu*, a traditional fava bean puree/soup, or pasta with chickpeas. *Secondi* (€10) include sausages and pancetta in a stickily reduced tomato sauce. Mon– Tues & Thurs–Sun lunch & dinner.

Osteria dei Sapori Perduti Corso Umberto 1 228–30 ☎0932 944 247. Right on the Corso, offering reasonably priced rustic dishes with a strong emphasis on beans and pulses. The abundant mixed *antipasto* (€7.50) is a good way to start, and enough for two people, followed by *lolli con le fave* (handmade pasta with fava bean puree) or pasta with broth and meatballs. *Primi* are around €6. The menu is in Sicilian, but translations are available, and it's marvellous value – you can walk away with a full stomach for €10–15. Mon & Wed–Sun lunch & dinner.

Taverna Nicastro Via S. Antonino 30 ☎0932 945 884. For traditional meat (and especially pork) dishes, try this delightfully old-fashioned and very reasonably priced trattoria with tables outside on a flight of steps in Modica Alta. Specialities include sausages and salamis made on the premises, good hearty legume dishes, and classic Modican fare such as ricotta ravioli with a sauce of tomato, pancetta, sausage and pork. *Secondi* highlights include rabbit with potato, olives, tomato and pork, and lamb stewed with tomato, capers, cherry tomatoes and onion. You could eat a four-course meal (including a *cannolo* or a lemon, cinnamon or almond jelly) for under €20, while house wine is €4 per litre. *Nicastro* is signposted from outside San Giorgio, but it's quite a walk, and you will probably still have to stop several people to ask the way before you find it. Tues–Sat dinner only.

Scicli

Ten kilometres south of Modica, **SCICLI** is dramatically pitched against the bottom of a knobbly limestone bluff. Like southeast Sicily's other Baroque towns, it has seen quite a restoration in recent years, most strikingly on the main **Piazza Italia** and the pedestrianized **Via Mormina Penna** – a scenographer's dream of a street, lined with exuberant and painstakingly restored Baroque churches and *palazzi*, including the Municipio fronted by a marvellous sculptural staircase and a small bandstand.

If it is open, be sure to step inside the church of **San Giovanni Battista**, which holds one of the strangest images of Christ you are likely ever to see, standing before a crucifix dressed in what appears to be a long white skirt. Dating back to the seventeenth century, it originated in the Spanish city of Burgos, where representing Christ in a skirt (actually his death shroud) was normal, and was given to the city by a Spanish nobleman. Gender norms are challenged once again in the town's main church, Sant'Ignazio or the Chiesa Madre, which holds Italy's only representation of the Madonna as a belligerent horseriding warrior.

PUZZLING PLAQUES

Intrigued by the **plaques** that appear in various spots throughout the Siracusa and Ragusa area, featuring a portrait of a bald man, architectural notes, strange quotations and photographs of crime scenes? The explanation is that Italy's most popular TV crime series **Montalbano**, based on books penned by Antonio Camilleri (see box, p.292), is filmed in the area, especially Scicli itself, which serves as the town of Vigata in the books and TV series. The building used as Montalbano's house is on the beach at the nearby resort of Punta Secca, while Scicli's Municipio plays the part of the police HQ.

Numerous Scicli-based **Montalbano tours** such as the summer-only Il Treno di Montalbano (€45 per person; ⓦgogreensicily.blogspot.it), which departs Siracusa by train, and includes a walking tour of Scicli, a Montalbano lunch, and a bus to various nearby locations including Punta Secca.

Around Piazza Italia

Just off Piazza Italia is one of Scicli's Baroque showpieces, the **Palazzo Beneventano**, complete with spectacularly grotesque grinning faces with lolling tongues and bald heads tucked under the balconies and clinging to the walls. Beyond the *palazzo*, the voluptuously curvy Baroque church of **San Bartolomeo** stands embraced by the towering limestone gorge. Walking on, you'll find yourself in the honeycomb of the old town, clamped to the sides of the gorge, with dwellings at times almost indistinguishable from the natural caves. Although it has a fair number of abandoned houses, the area is by no means deserted, and several of the buildings are now undergoing restoration.

San Matteo and around

Continuing up the stepped path above Palazzo Beneventano, you can enjoy grand views over Scicli from the terrace of the abandoned church of **San Matteo**. Just below the church, a further stepped path (signposted "Chiesa S. Lucia") leads to the remains of another church; at the top of the ridge here, you're standing right above a series of abandoned **cave-dwellings** that litter the hills around, used from Neolithic times until fairly recently. From the vantage point you can make out bricked-up entrances, caves and doorways in the tree-dotted cliffs below.

ARRIVAL AND INFORMATION   SCICLI

By car Scicli is an easy stop by car en route to or from Modica or Ragusa. There is a tricky one-way route through town, so you may prefer to park at the train station.
By bus Regional buses from Modica and Ragusa drop you in the centre on Piazza Italia.
By train Scicli is a stop on the Siracusa–Gela train line. The train station is a 15min walk from the centre, along Corso Mazzini.
Tourist information The tourist office is in the Municipio, Via Mormino Penna (Mon–Fri 8am–1pm, plus Tues & Thurs 3–6pm; ☎ 0932 839 608, ⓦ comune.scicli.rg.it).

ACCOMMODATION, EATING AND DRINKING

Baqqala Piazzetta Ficili ☎ 0932 931 028. On the steps above Palazzo Beneventano, this shabby-chic *osteria* has lunchtime snacks and fuller meals in the evening (most dishes €8–10). But it's most fun for a drink at night, when you can lounge on the divans outside, soaking up the mellow soundtrack. Tues–Sun lunch & dinner.
Conte Ruggero Piazza Italia 24 ☎ 0932 931 840, ⓦ conteruggero.it. Smart old B&B in a restored palace on the main square, fine for a night or two. The spacious rooms have a/c, and some have minibars and balconies. **€90**

IL GRUPPO DI SCICLI

Sampieri beach, down the road from Scicli, is the spiritual home of a group of artists known as the **Gruppo di Scicli**. For over thirty years they met here every morning, to walk together on the strand before starting work. They walk less often now – the oldest members of the Gruppo are over eighty and the younger ones live away in Modica or Catania – but they still come down for a stroll occasionally.

Since its beginnings in the 1980s, the Gruppo di Scicli has shrunk and grown and shrunk again, accommodating and adapting, like an extended family. At present it has nine members. Operating outside the mainstream of contemporary art, the Gruppo has no manifesto or ideology. The artists were brought together by their shared approaches to painting, sculpture, light and landscape and, not least, in how they wanted to live.

Having exhibited widely – in group and solo shows – all over Italy, October 2012 saw the first Gruppo di Scicli exhibition abroad, at the Bernaducci Meisel Gallery in New York. In Scicli, their works can be seen on the walls of the *Hotel Novecento* (see opposite), and often at the **QUAM art gallery**, Via Mormino Penna 79 (Tues–Sat 10am–1pm & 4.30–8pm, Sun and hols 5.30–8.30pm; ☎ 0932 931 154, ⓦ tecnicamista.it), recently opened within the vaults of a restored monastery refectory. If it's open (hours vary), poke your head in too at the cosy Brancati Associazione Cuturale, also on Via Mormino Penna, founded by members of the group back in the 1980s.

★ **Novecento** Via Duprè 11 ☎0932 843 817, ⓦhotel900.it. Occupying a Baroque *palazzo* in the heart of town, this stylish hotel has fully equipped rooms with architect-designed beds and arty but sumptuous bathrooms with Bisazza mosaic tiles. The tone is contemporary and cultured, and staff are friendly and helpful. **€90**

Satra Via Duca degli Abruzzi 1 ☎0932 842 148. This recently opened place in the vaulted cellars of a former convent has a seasonally changing menu featuring innovative versions of traditional dishes. There is a tasting menu priced at €75, but choosing à la carte you can eat for considerably less. Try handmade spaghetti flavoured with chilli, saffron and wild fennel, served with sardines, pine nuts and toasted breadcrumbs. Mon & Wed–Sun lunch & dinner.

Scidi Albergo Diffuso Reception at Via Mormino Penna 15 ☎0932 185 555, ⓦscidialbergodiffuso.it. A great idea this – accommodation on a B&B or self-catering basis in one of eleven restored houses scattered around the historic town centre. Two-person apartments **€75**

6

Ragusa

A Baroque town laid out on a grid system over a mountain plateau, **RAGUSA** has two very distinct identities. The 1693 earthquake destroyed many towns and cities that were then rebuilt in a different form, but the unique effect on Ragusa was to split the city in two. The old town of **Ragusa Ibla**, on a jut of land above its valley, was comprehensively flattened, and within a few years a new town on a grid plan emerged on the higher ridge to the west, known simply as Ragusa (or **Ragusa Superiore**). However, Ibla was stubbornly rebuilt by its inhabitants, following the old medieval street layout. Rivalry between the two was commonplace until 1926, when both towns were nominally reunited.

Ragusa Ibla

The original lower town of **Ragusa Ibla** is totally charming, its appealing, stepped alleys and dead-end courtyards a delight to wander around. Over the past decade or so, Ibla (spurred on by European funding) has undergone a renaissance, with the renovation of historic buildings and the opening of some stylish hotels and restaurants. Something of a magnet for Americans and northern Europeans tired of the charms of Tuscany and Pugli, Ibla is, however, something of a charmed and slightly unreal museum town, with just 2000 inhabitants (out of a total of around 72,000) and little in the way of everyday Sicilian life. It is, however, undeniably gorgeous, and wandering along its limestone pavements, past the grand facades of golden palaces and town houses, is like walking onto a film set. What's more, Ibla is virtually traffic free, and certainly makes for a very agreeable night or two's stay.

San Giorgio

Piazza del Duomo • Mon & Wed–Sun 10am–12.30pm & 4–6.30pm, Tues 4–6.30pm • Enter up the steps to the left-hand side

The central focus of Ragusa Ibla is the sloping **Piazza del Duomo**, split by six palms, which ends in impressive wrought-iron fencing, beyond which broad steps lead to the church of **San Giorgio**. A masterpiece of Sicilian Baroque, it's the work of Rosario Gagliardi – one of Noto's chief architects – and took nearly forty years to complete. Its three-tiered facade, with sets of triple columns climbing up the wedding-cake exterior to a balconied belfry, is an imaginative work, though typically not matched inside. As with Gagliardi's other projects, all the beauty is in the immediacy of the powerful exterior. The architect gets another credit for the elegant rounded facade and bulging balconies of **San Giuseppe** in Piazza Pola, 200m below San Giorgio.

The Giardini Ibleo and around

The main **Corso XXV Aprile** runs down the hill through the restored heart of town, past stores selling designer sunglasses, "slow food" gourmet delis, galleries and wine bars. At the foot of town, the **Giardino Ibleo** public garden is a favourite spot for an evening stroll and a drink in the nearby cafés. You can enjoy dramatic views from the very edge of the spur on which the town is built, while the violet-strewn flowerbeds set off the remains of three small churches, abandoned in the grounds. To the right of the garden's entrance stands the **Portale San Giorgio**, a surviving Gothic church portal whose badly worn stone centrepiece depicts a skeletal St George killing the dragon.

Ragusa Superiore

If you're driving – in which case you can head straight to Ibla – you might not visit the upper town of **Ragusa Superiore** at all, though that's where most of the city's shops and services are located. It's built on a grid plan, slipping off to right and left on either side of the sloping Corso Italia, just off which stands the sombre Duomo, completed in 1774. Although Baroque Ragusa received its share of good-looking buildings (like the few grand *palazzi* down Corso Italia), most of the architects' efforts seem to have been devoted to keeping the streets as straight as possible, and the town's most striking vistas are where this right-angled order is interrupted by a deep gorge, exposing the bare rock on which the city was built.

If you're walking back down to Ibla, you could make a stop on the terrace by the restored fifteenth-century church of **Santa Maria della Scala** (which features the remains of an unusual exterior pulpit). A mighty view lies beyond, of the weatherbeaten roofs of Ragusa Ibla straddling the outcrop of rock, rising to the prominent dome of San Giorgio. From the church terrace, steps descend beneath the winding road to another church, the **Chiesa del Purgatorio**, from where winding alleys climb back into the heart of Ragusa Ibla.

ARRIVAL AND INFORMATION   **RAGUSA**

By train The station is just off Piazza del Popolo in Ragusa Superiore, a short walk from Ponte Nuovo and Via Roma.
Destinations Comiso (5 daily Mon–Sat; 30min); Gela (5 daily Mon–Sat; 1hr 20min); Ispica (4 daily Mon–Sat; 1hr); Modica (4 daily Mon–Sat; 20min); Noto (4 daily Mon–Sat; 1hr 30min); Scicli (4 daily; 35min); Siracusa (2 daily Mon–Sat; 2hr); Vittoria (5 daily Mon–Sat; 45min).

By bus Buses stop next the the train station.
Destinations Catania airport/Catania (10 daily Mon–Fri, 6–7 daily Sat & Sun; 1hr 45min–2hr); Chiaramonte Gulfi (Mon–Sat 7 daily; 50min); Gela (3 daily Mon–Sat, 1 daily Sun; 1hr 30min); Ispica (6 daily Mon–Sat, 1 daily Sun; 55min–1hr 40min); Kamarina (6 daily; 1hr); Marina di Ragusa (hourly; 1hr); Modica (Mon–Sat 1–2 hourly, Sun 3 daily; 30min–1hr 10min); Noto (6 daily Mon–Sat, 4 daily Sun; 1hr 45min–2hr 15min); Palermo (Mon–Sat 4–5 daily,

Sun 2 daily; 4hr); Scicli (9 daily Mon–Sat; 1hr–1hr 50min); Siracusa (6 daily Mon–Sat, 2 daily Sun; 2hr 45min).
By car Drivers can follow the signs to Ragusa Ibla, where there's a capacious car park below Piazza della Repubblica.
Tourist information Ragusa Superiore has a small tourist office in front of the Duomo on Piazza San Giovanni (Mon–Fri 9am–7pm, Sat 8.30am–2pm; ☎ 0932 684 780, ⓦ comune.ragusa.gov.it), where you can pick up a map and an accommodation booklet.

6

GETTING AROUND

By bus The most useful city buses are #11 and #33 (both every 30–60min; buy tickets in advance from any *tabacchi*), which ply between the upper and lower towns along Via Roma and Corso Italia, stopping outside both Santa Maria and Purgatorio churches, and ending their run in Ibla outside the Giardino Ibleo.

On foot If you're based in the upper town, the best advice is to walk down to the lower town – less fatiguing and you can enjoy the magnificent view – and catch the bus back. The walk down to Ibla takes about half an hour, heading down Corso Italia and the narrow Via XXIV Maggio.

ACCOMMODATION

It's infinitely preferable to stay the night in Ibla than in Superiore, where you can stroll the traffic-free streets in the evening and hop from bar to trattoria. Ibla holds more than two dozen **B&Bs** alone, as well as a handful of small, stylish **hotels** – all signposted – and most can find you a parking space outside or nearby. There's a similar number of B&Bs in the upper town, as well as a few largely colourless business-type hotels.

Il Barocco Via Santa Maria la Nuova 1, Ragusa Ibla ☎ 0932 663 105, ⓦ ilbarocco.it. A very charming old-town hotel set around a bright courtyard – the rooms are in traditional style, with tile floors and oak furniture,

but it's a modern place, all very tasteful and understated. **€125**
Eremo della Giubiliana Contrada Giubiliana ☎ 0932 669 119, ⓦ eremodellagiubiliana.it. Some 7.5km south

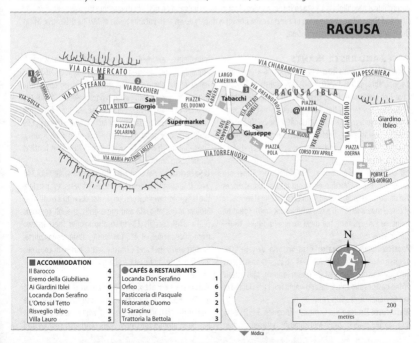

RAGUSA

N

0 ⸻ 200
metres

▼ Módica

6

of Ragusa on the Marina di Ragusa road, this five-star country property is housed in the restored buildings of a feudal estate and hermitage dating back to the twelfth century. Rooms (converted from monks' cells), suites and self-contained estate cottages all feature traditional Sicilian furnishings, the grounds are ravishing, and you can dine on their own organically grown food. It's no surprise to find it also has its own airstrip and private beach, plus pool, nature trails and all sorts of tours and activities available. Rooms €211

Ai Giardini Iblei Via Normanni 4, Ragusa Ibla ☎0932 246 844 or ☎338 640 1238, ⊚aigiardini.it. Right next to the town gardens, the three sunny rooms here have private bathrooms and are simply but tastefully furnished. Free internet. €70

★ **Locanda Don Serafino** Via XI Febbraio 15, Ragusa Ibla ☎0932 220 065, ⊚locandadonserafino.it. Beautifully set within the hefty stone walls of a row of carefully restored Baroque cottages, the reception area here is tucked under exposed limestone vaults and paved with chocolate-brown *pietra pece* (a kind of limestone suffused with petroleum). Rooms combine rustic stone vaults (and in one case a Gothic arch that survived the earthquake) with boxy cream leather furniture. Best of all

is the room in what was once the stables, with its shower inside a cave. €148

L'Orto sul Tetto Via Tenente Distefano 56, Ragusa Ibla ☎0932 247 785 or ☎338 478 0484, ⊚lortosultetto.it. A short walk from the Duomo, this warm, friendly place, run by a mother and son, has three serene bedrooms. Breakfasts are served on a roof terrace full of plants and include pastries fresh from the bakery. €110

★ **Risveglio Ibleo** Largo Camerina 3, Ragusa Ibla ☎0932 247 811 or ☎335 804 6494, ⊚www .risveglioibleo.com. A very friendly welcome awaits at this elegant townhouse with four studio apartments (for couples or families), either in the main house (for more character) or just around the back. The rooms are stylishly decorated, with small kitchenettes, and you come up to the owners' second-floor rooms for a breakfast of fresh bread, home-made preserves and honey, served on the terrace in summer. No credit cards. €85

Villa Lauro Via Ecce Homo, Ragusa Superiore ☎0932 655 177, ⊚villadellauro.it. Minimalist style within the exposed limestone walls of an eighteenth-century *palazzo* in the historic part of Ragusa Superiore. Excellent choice in summer, when you can while away afternoons in the serene, stylish garden with swimming pool. €170

EATING, DRINKING AND ENTERTAINMENT

Good **restaurants** are easy to find in Ibla, while a few cafés put out tables in Superiore's Piazza del Duomo – as night falls, and the lights come on, it's not too much of an exaggeration to suggest that this is the prettiest square in Sicily. The annual entertainment highlight is **L'Estate Iblea**, a series of concerts, recitals and events held throughout the town between late June and September, culminating in a spectacular fireworks display down at the nearby resort of Marina di Ragusa; ask at the tourist office for more information.

CAFÉS AND RESTAURANTS

Locanda Don Serafino Via Avvocato G Ottaviano, Ragusa Ibla ☎0932 248 778. This stylish and costly cave-like restaurant, lit as deftly as an exclusive fashion boutique, is among the best places to eat in town, offering a modern take on traditional dishes – things like grilled vegetable pie, beef fillet flavoured with tobacco, or rabbit with bacon and pistachios. Mon & Wed–Sun lunch & dinner.

★ **Orfeo** Via Sant'Anna 117, Ragusa Superiore ☎0932 621 035. Worth seeking out for traditional dishes like broad bean soup, stuffed sardines or the local speciality of *cavati ragusana* (fresh pasta with a pork *ragù*). Count on spending €20–25 for a full meal excluding drinks. Mon–Sat lunch & dinner.

Pasticceria di Pasquale Corso Vittorio Veneto 104, Ragusa Superiore ☎0932 624 635, ⊚pasticceria dipasquale.com. The best ice cream in town, plus utterly divine pastries and cakes. Just downhill from the Duomo of San Giovanni. Tues–Sun 7am–9pm.

Ristorante Duomo Via Capitano Bocchieri 31, Ragusa Ibla ☎0932 651 265. Meticulously sourced Sicilian

ingredients reworked to stunning effect, in what is arguably Sicily's greatest restaurant. Put yourself in the hands of the chef Ciccio Sultano, and opt for one of the tasting menus (€160), with wines selected from the copious cellar to match each course. At lunchtime, the simpler three-course tasting menu (€45 without wine, €59 with) is a very good deal. April–Oct Mon dinner only, Tues–Sat lunch & dinner; Nov–March Tues–Sat lunch & dinner, Sun lunch only.

U Saracinu Via del Convento 9, Ragusa Ibla ☎0932 246 976. *U Saracinu* has been here donkey's years, even before the fancy old-town restoration, and sticks with a traditional Sicilian menu of pasta and meat grills, though couscous (€8) and fish specials (€8–9) are also on offer. There are two fixed-price menus, at €15 (*antipasto*, pasta, main course, dessert and wine) and €18 (the same, but with couscous and fish instead of pasta and a main). Mon–Sat lunch & dinner.

Trattoria la Bettola Largo Kamarina, Ragusa Ibla ☎0932 653 377. A rarity in Ibla: a simple, inexpensive family-run trattoria with red-and-white tablecloths that has been around for thirty years. *Antipasti* cost €4 and include deep-fried and breadcrumbed morsels of local cheeses, aubergine *polpette* and a lemon-scented *tortino* of courgettes. *Primi* (all €7) include tagliatelle with cream and saffron, *secondi* (€7–9) feature *maiale* *ubriaco*, pork braised in wine and wild herbs, in winter, and pork chops with citrus in summer. There is horsemeat as well, if you feel like going totally local. Tues–Sun lunch & dinner.

Around Ragusa

6

To the south and west of Ragusa, the largely unsung Baroque towns of **Comiso** and **Vittoria**, the views from **Chiaramonte Gulfi** or the low-key resorts and beaches along the local **coast** can fill another day's touring, but these are all mere sideshows compared with Ragusa itself. By public transport, to be frank, it's barely worth the trouble to visit any of the places covered below.

Chiaramonte Gulfi

Twenty kilometres north of Ragusa, **CHIARAMONTE GULFI** merits a visit largely for its far-reaching **views**. This is one of several places dubbed the "balcony of Sicily" and, though hazy in summer, the panorama (west towards Gela and north to Etna) embraces dun-coloured farmland interspersed with solitary villages – a still, silent scene, but for the occasional dog's bark or the whine of a Vespa.

Sampieri

There's more to the province of Ragusa than its feted Baroque towns. Head down to the coast from Modica or Scicli and you'll strike the magnificent beach of **Sampieri**, a stunning 2km sweep of sand running between the dramatic Gothic ruins of an abandoned brick factory (which fans of Montalbano will recognize). Sampieri **village**, a small and pleasantly low-key local resort, retains a core of traditional cubic fishermen's houses, built of the same gleaming limestone as the cobbles on the streets. In summer a couple of small lidos open on the beach, but for the rest of the year it's a marvellous place to spend a few days if you want to do nothing but swim and take long beach walks.

ACCOMMODATION   SAMPIERI

If you want to rent a **house** or **apartment** in Sampieri, the Abitare Solemare agency (📞334 633 4423, 🌐abitaresolemare.it) has the widest choice, with high-season prices starting at €500 per week for two people – and low season prices around half that.

Poggio Bellavista 📞0932 939 068, 🌐poggio-bellavista.com. If you want to stay in Sampieri you couldn't do better than this welcoming and comfortable B&B, with five pretty rooms, perched on the hillside 1km outside town. The English-speaking owners go out of their way to make guests feel at home. **€80**

Marina di Ragusa

Southwest of Ragusa, it's a straight 24km run down to the coast, and the start of the so-called "riviera", which extends as far as Gela. the small resort of **MARINA DI RAGUSA** is a typical Sicilian mix of private lidos and apartments, and bars and restaurants that really only do business for four or five months of the year. A coastal road westwards (served by Tumino buses) offers access to more beaches near Punta Secca (not to be confused with the Punta Secca of Montalbano fame, which is just beyond Sampieri) and Punta Braccetto, almost as far as the desolate remains of ancient **Kamarina** (also spelt Camerina), a Syracusan colony founded in 599 BC. It lies on a headland overlooking beaches on either side, and has a small **Museo Archeologico** (daily

9am–1pm & 3–5.30pm; €4). Behind the antiquarium is all that's left of a fifth-century BC Tempio di Atena, surrounded by the rubble of city walls and the various ruins of the Hellenistic-Roman city.

ARRIVAL AND DEPARTURE   **MARINA DI RAGUSA**

By bus Marina di Ragusa is served by Tumino buses from Ragusa (☎ 0932 623 184, ⓦ tuminobus.it),

Gela

GELA couldn't present a worse aspect: drivers have to negotiate a tangle of untidy backstreets, while the train line weaves through a mess of futuristic steel bubbles and pipes. Despite a few fine dune-backed beaches in the vicinity, it's no place to bathe; this is one of the most polluted places in Sicily, with a worryingly high rate of certain cancers, and a chemical tang to the air. But it was not always so. Gela was one of the most important of Sicily's Greek cities, founded in 688 BC, and under Hippocrates in the fifth century BC it rivalled even ancient Syracuse as the island's political hub. Its artistic eminence attracted literary stars, including the world's first cookery-book writer, Archestratus, and the dramatist Aeschylus, who, according to legend, met his end here when an eagle dropped a tortoise on him, apparently mistaking his bald head for a stone on which to dash its prey. However, Gela's heyday was short-lived. Hippocrates' successor, Gelon, transferred his power and half the city's population east to Syracuse in 485 BC, the deep-water harbour there being more to the tyrant's liking. Gela was later smashed by the Carthaginians and the Mamertines, its walls razed in the third century BC and abandoned to the encroaching sands. Modern Gela was the first Sicilian town to be liberated by the Allies in 1943, but otherwise – beyond an excellent **archeological museum** and a fine set of Greek defensive walls at the **Capo Soprano** archeological zone – is almost entirely without interest.

Museo Archeologico

Corso Vittorio Emanuele • Daily 9am–6.30pm • €4, includes entry to Capo Soprano archeological zone • ☎ 0933 912 626 • The museum is a 20min walk from the centre along the Corso

At the eastern end of the Corso, the **Museo Archeologico** is notable largely for its important collection of **painted vases**, on the upstairs floor. Mainly seventh to fifth century BC, the black- and red-figure jugs and beakers were Greek Gela's speciality: most major world museums tend to feature one or two, but the bulk are here. Other impressive finds include an animated sculpture of a horse's head (sixth century BC),

---

COMISO CONNECTS

In September 2013, the little town of **Comiso** was given what could turn out to be a new lease of life, when its previous military **airport** (ⓦ aeroportodicomiso.it) opened to civil flights, kicking off with Ryanair routes to London Stansted, Brussels Charleroi and Rome Ciampino. What the effect this will have on sleepy Comiso, with its dusty Baroque core, remains to be seen, but there's likely to be a rash of new B&Bs (details will be posted on the airport website). However, most folk are so far using the airport to get to the area's more established tourist attractions, most notably Ragusa.

At the time of writing **transport links from the airport** were still in the developmental stage, with the website publishing new services as (or if) they are added, and the only bus routes from the airport ran to Catania Airport and Catania (1 daily Mon–Wed, Fri & Sun) and Ragusa (1 daily except Thurs), but note that departures don't tie in with flight timings. A **taxi** to Ragusa from the airport should cost around €40, while there are also two local car-rental outfits: Morgan Service (☎ 393 426 6443, ⓦ morganservice.it) and Gianni Motors (☎ 0932 721 851, ⓦ giannimotors.it).

> **THE GELA PAINTER**
>
> Many major museums throughout the world have black-figure ware by the so-called **Gela Painter**, a prodigiously prolific potter and painter of jars who was working from around 510–480 BC. This anonymous Gelan has been criticized by academics for being more interested in composition and symmetry than in the narrative content of his paintings – it has even been suggested that, being a Sicilian, his knowledge of Greek myths left much to be desired. In recent years, however, the aesthetic merit of his compositions has come to be more and more appreciated.

6

and Corinthian and Athenian ceramics unearthed from various necropolises belonging to Geloan dependencies, illegally excavated in the late nineteenth century. Outside the museum, a small **acropolis** has been uncovered, consisting of a few walls and a single temple column from the fifth century BC, though the small site is drained of all romance by the brooding, dirty industrial plant that dominates the beach below.

Capo Soprano and the archeological zone

Viale Indipendenza, Contrada Scavone • Mon–Sat 9am–1hr before sunset • €4, includes entry to Museo Archeologico • ☎ 0933 930 975 • Head along the Corso and take a left fork (Via Manzoni), which runs parallel to the sea as far as the red gates of the site, a distance of almost 4km

Gela's main archeological site occupies the unexpectedly lovely **Capo Soprano**, at the western end of town. The **Greek fortifications** here date from the fourth century BC. Preserved by the sand dunes under which they were discovered, the **walls**, built under the tyrant Timoleon, stand nearly 8m high in parts, made up of perfectly fitted stone blocks topped by a layer of brick and now covered in protective glass panels. It's a beautiful site, and you're free to wander around the line of the walls: in some places you can make out the remains of **watchtowers** and **gateways**, while waves crash onto a duned stretch of **beach** below. If you've come this far out of town, you may as well nip around the corner (back towards the centre and left, by the hospital), to Via Europa, to see the remains of Gela's fourth-century BC **public baths**, the only ones from Greek times discovered in Sicily and still equipped with their original seats.

ARRIVAL AND INFORMATION   GELA

By bus Buses stop directly outside the train station (tickets and information from the bar across the square); regular departures serve Licata and Agrigento, Vittoria, Caltanissetta and Siracusa. From the station, turn right down the main road and, at the junction, bear right for the town centre and Corso Vittorio Emanuele.

By train Gela is at the far end of the train line that runs from Siracusa via the Baroque towns of Noto (4 daily; 3hr), Ispica (4 daily; 2hr 50min), Scicli (2 daily; 2hr 15min), Modica (4 daily; 1hr 40min) and Ragusa (5 daily; 1hr), and consequently

is a feasible day-trip from any of these places, especially if you bring a bike to get to Capo Soprano. There are no trains on Sundays, and journeys may involve a change.

By car Driving into town, simply follow the signs for museum and fortifications – it's slow going on the SS115, which cuts right through the centre.

Tourist information The tourist office is at Via Pisa 65, off Via Bresmes, which cuts across Corso Vittorio Emanuele (Mon–Fri 8am–2.15pm, plus Wed 2.45–6.15pm; ☎ 0933 913 788, ⓦ comune.gela.cl.it).

Enna and the interior

PERGUSA COUNTRYSIDE

Enna and the interior

… for the last five hours all they had set eyes on were bare hillsides flaming yellow under the sun … They had passed through crazed-looking villages washed in palest blue; crossed dry beds of torrents over fantastic bridges; skirted sheer precipices which no sage and broom could temper. Never a tree, never a drop of water; just sun and dust.

Giuseppe Tomasi di Lampedusa, The Leopard

7

It is in Sicily's vast and mountainous interior – thoroughly depleted by mass emigration – that you can truly begin to get off the tourist trail. Outside just three or four decent-sized towns, bunched together almost in the centre of the island, much of the land is burnt dry during the long summer months. The extensive cornfields have been a feature of the Sicilian landscape since Greek times, but the rolling hills are mostly silent and empty, punctuated only by occasional moribund towns and villages wrapped around easily defensible heights. Even crossing through the centre via the Catania–Palermo motorway gives a powerful flavour of the rural Sicily in Lampedusa's books. However, travelling slowly through this land has its rewards, not least the fascinating glimpses of a way of life that has all but disappeared in the rest of the island. This is true not just of the countryside, but of the cities too – perhaps manifested most intensely during religious festivals, such as Easter. Indeed, one of the most evocative times to visit the area is Holy Week, which sees costumed processions in Caltagirone, Troina, Caltanissetta and, most striking of all, Enna.

Symbol of the entire interior is the blustery mountain settlement of **Enna**, easy to reach from both Catania and Palermo. It's a historic place, with a mighty castle and some even mightier views, and deserves a night's stay. Routes north (towards the Tyrrhenian coast and Palermo) or east (Etna and Catania) head through minor mountain towns and villages on the fringes of the Nébrodi and Madonie mountains, and make good driving circuits provided you don't mind potholed roads and a middle-of-nowhere feel. The largest town in the region is actually **Caltanissetta**, gateway to the south coast and the deep west, though it's also the most disappointing and devoid of much charm. The treasures of the interior are all in the southeast, especially the single biggest draw: the lavish Roman mosaics at the **Villa Romana del Casale**. This lies just outside the enjoyable Baroque town of **Piazza Armerina**, which could also be your base for seeing the extensive and unsung Greek ruins of **Morgantina** and the fabulous collection of the Archeological Museum in **Aidone**. Further south, ceramic-studded **Caltagirone** makes a handy departure point for the Baroque towns of the southeast.

MOSAIC DETAIL, VILLA ROMANA DEL CASALE

Highlights

❶ Enna Spend the night high up in the hill-town of Enna and watch the sun set from its spectacular terraces or visit on Good Friday to see thousands take part in traditional processions. **See p.258**

❷ Piazza Armerina The old Baroque town of Piazza Armerina is an undiscovered gem. **See p.266**

❸ Villa Romana del Casale The extraordinary mosaics in this ancient Roman villa, created by artists from North Africa, are unmatched anywhere in Italy. **See p.270**

❹ Museo Archeologico, Aidone See the incredible ancient Greek sculptures and silverware recently returned to Sicily after a protracted legal battle. **See p.272**

❺ Morgantina A little-known Greek archeological site in gorgeous rural surroundings. **See p.274**

❻ La Scala, Caltagirone In a town famed for its ceramics, these 142 steps are adorned with beautiful patterned tiles. **See p.275**

HIGHLIGHTS ARE MARKED ON THE MAP ON P.258

GETTING AROUND

By car The interior's main roads at least are pretty good and distances not too large, and with a car you could pick any of the towns and use it as a base for seeing the rest of the region.
By bus Enna, Caltanissetta and Piazza Armerina are the only towns with frequent bus connections to the rest of Sicily, so if you're relying on public transport, you're pretty much limited to these places plus a side-trip from Piazza Armerina to Aidone and Morgantina. It's more difficult to travel north and west into the mountains by bus, though there are services out of Enna along the two major routes, the SS120 and SS121.

Enna

From a bulging V-shaped ridge almost 1000m up, **ENNA** lords it over the surrounding hills of central Sicily. One of the most ancient towns on the island, Enna has only ever had one function: Livy described it as "inexpugnabilis", and, for obvious strategic reasons, the town was a magnet for successive hostile armies, who in turn besieged and fortified it. The Arabs, for example, spent twenty years trying to gain entrance to Enna before eventually, in 859, resorting to crawling in through the sewers. The approach to this doughty mountain stronghold is still formidable, the road climbing slowly out of the valley and looping across the solid crag to the summit and the town.

Enna remains a medieval hill-town at heart, with a tightly packed centre of narrow streets, small squares and hemmed-in churches, where occasional gaps through the

HIGHLIGHTS

1. Enna
2. Piazza Armerina
3. Villa Romana del Casale
4. Museo Archeologico, Aidone
5. Morgantina
6. La Scala, Caltagirone

ENNA AND THE INTERIOR

LAGO DI PERGUSA

The **Lago di Pergusa** was the site of Hades' abduction of Persephone to the underworld. The story has it that Persephone, surrounded by nymphs, was gathering flowers on the lush banks of the lake when Hades emerged from a chasm beneath the water and spirited her away. Demeter searched in vain for her daughter, and her grief at the loss of Persephone prevented the corn from growing. To settle the matter, Zeus ruled that Persephone should spend half the year as queen of the underworld, and live for the other six months in Sicily with her mother as one of the island's goddesses. In her gratitude, Demeter, as goddess of grain and agriculture, made the corn grow again – a powerful symbol in a traditionally fertile land. These days, sadly, the Pergusa road is choc-a-bloc with apartments, hotels and holiday developments, while the lake is encircled by a motor-racing track. It's hard now, despite the pleasant wooded banks beyond the water, to imagine a less romantic spot. Mary Taylor Simeti's journal, *On Persephone's Island*, labels the Lago di Pergusa "a brilliant example of the Sicilians' best efforts to ruin their landscape".

There's really no point coming to the lake for any glimpse of the truth behind the legend, though it does make a possible base near Enna, especially if you fancy a retreat with Moleskine and pencil to ★ *La Casa del Poeta* at Contrada da Parasporino, 1km from Lago di Pergusa (329 627 4918 or 328 657 2731, lacasadelpoeta.it; €100), a nineteenth-century villa, where you're invited to immerse yourself in literature from their library or write in their "writing room". Those suffering from writer's block can seek inspiration as they lounge by the pool.

7

buildings reveal swirling drops down into the valleys below. Most of Enna's churches – even the ones in use – have cracked facades and weeds growing out of improbable places, but there are some that catch the eye, like fourteenth-century **San Giovanni** (behind the much larger San Giuseppe, on Piazza Coppola) which has a Catalan-Gothic facade and a tower crowned by a little cupola. When all is said and done, apart from the **castle**, the all-encompassing **views**, and the usual desultory pleasures of provincial town life (like the little street market on Piazza Coppola), there's little to keep you here more than a night. However, that night is very definitely worth it – with some stupendous vantage points from which to watch the sun set, summer evenings here must count among the most enjoyable in Sicily. Come in winter and you should expect snow, the wind blowing hard through the streets, and the white slopes beyond blending with the anaemic stone buildings.

Castello di Lombardia

Via Nino Savarese • Daily: April–Oct 8am–8pm; Nov–March 9am–5pm • Free

Despite numerous wars and attacks over the years, most of Enna's medieval remains are in good condition. Dominating the easternmost spur of town is the thirteenth-century **Castello di Lombardia**, built by Frederick II who, according to some sources, spent his summers here. There's a huge area inside enclosed by the walls, split into various courtyards, while six surviving towers (out of an original twenty) provide lookouts. Climb the tallest, **Torre Pisana**, for some great views of Enna, the rugged countryside in all directions, and across to Mount Etna.

Rocca di Cerere

Via Nino Savarese • Daily: April–Oct 8am–8pm; Nov–March 9am–5pm • Free

Up above Enna's castle is the **Rocca di Cerere**, an exposed outcrop where some scattered foundations are presumed to be the remnants of a temple erected by Gelon in 480 BC. Enna was the centre of the Greek cult of **Demeter**, the fertility goddess (her Roman counterpart was Ceres, hence the rock's name), and the most famous of the myths associated with the goddess – the carrying off of her daughter, Persephone, to the underworld – is supposed to have taken place just a few kilometres away, at Lago di Pergusa.

ENNA

ACCOMMODATION	
Bianko & Bianko	2
Da Pietro	1
Grande Albergo Sicilia	4
Prosperina	3

CAFÉS & RESTAURANTS	
Ariston	3
Al Kenisa	5
Centrale	4
Grotta Azzurra	1
Marro Caffè	2

The Duomo

Piazza Duomo • Daily 9.30am–1pm & 3.30–8pm

Enna's **Duomo** fronts a shady little square, which has been rebuilt several times since its foundation in 1307. It's not much to look at from the outside, but the sixteenth-century interior is a different story, with every surface covered in ornamentation. Look closely at the bottom of the huge supporting dark-grey columns, the bases of which are carved with snarling heads with human hands and snake bodies. Treasures from the cathedral are kept in the adjacent Museo Alessi, which was closed for "works" at the time of writing.

Piazza Vittorio Emanuele

The western extremity of Via Roma is marked by the sloping, rectangular **Piazza Vittorio Emanuele**, focal point of the evening *passeggiata*. Off here, a long cliff-edge promenade looks out to the little rust-coloured town of Calascibetta over the valley. The plain, high wall of the church of **San Francesco**, which flanks the piazza, has a massive sixteenth-century tower, previously part of the old town's system of watchtowers that linked the castle with all Enna's churches.

Torre di Federico II

Via Torre di Federico • Mon–Sat 8am–6pm, Sun 9am–1pm • Free

An octagonal watchtower, 24m high, the **Torre di Federico II** is linked by a (now hidden) underground passage to the castle. Built in the thirteenth century by Frederick II, it now stands in isolation amid the **Giardino Pubblico** in the largely modern south of the town. You can climb to the top of the tower for more great views.

Calascibetta

6km from Enna • Buses every two hours from the terminal but only two on Sunday

The small town you can see from Enna's terraces, hugging a lower hill to the north across the valley, is **Calascibetta**, and it hints at what Enna would be like without the tower blocks. Once a Saracen town, it was fortified by Count Roger in his successful attempt to take Enna in 1087, and the tangled streets seem straight from that age. The tightly packed red-stone buildings perch above a sheer drop on the eastern side, rising to the restored Chiesa Madre at the very top.

ARRIVAL AND DEPARTURE   ENNA

By bus The terminal is on Viale Diaz, just out of the old centre and a 10min walk from the Piazza Vittorio Emanuele. All bus companies are at the bus terminal: SAIS (☎0935 500 902, ⓦsaisautolinee.it) covers Calascibetta, Caltanissetta, Catania, Catania airport, Messina, Palermo and Piazza Armerina; Interbus (☎0935 22 460, ⓦinterbus.it) covers Agira, Catania, Leonforte and Nicosia; and ISEA (☎095 464 101, ⓦiseaviaggi.it) Cesarò, Nicosia and Troina.

Destinations Calascibetta (8–12 daily Mon–Sat, 2 daily Sun; 30min); Caltagirone (2 daily Mon–Fri, 1 daily Sun; 1hr 25min); Caltanissetta (4–5 daily Mon–Sat; 55min); Catania (8–10 daily Mon–Sat, 5 daily Sun; 1hr 15min); Gela (3–4 daily; 1hr 15min); Leonforte (8 daily Mon–Sat, 2 daily Sun; 35–45min); Nicosia (3 daily Mon–Sat; 1hr 30min); Palermo (3–5 daily; 1hr 35min); Pergusa (4–9

daily Mon–Sat, 4 daily Sun; 20min); Piazza Armerina (4–6 daily; 30min).

By train The train station is 5km north of town: a local bus runs roughly hourly to the town centre and back (less frequently on Sun), or a taxi costs around €15.

Destinations Caltanissetta (7 daily Mon–Sat, 5 daily Sun; 35min); Catania (6 daily; 1hr 20min); Palermo (2 daily Mon–Sat, 1 daily Sun; 2hr 20min).

By car Having whizzed up the road from below town with comparative ease, the traffic in Enna is among the most congested in all Sicily, and you really don't want to drive around more than you have to. There's a car park just off Viale Diaz, by the Cappuccini cemetery and near the bus terminal (look for the blue "P" sign), and plenty of free parking up by the castle (follow "castello" signs); from either place it's a 10min walk to the old town.

GETTING AROUND

By bus Everywhere in Enna itself can be reached very easily on foot, though local buses run out to places like Pergusa, Calascibetta and the train station – you'll need to buy a ticket (valid for 1hr) in advance from *tabacchi*.

By taxi Ranks can be found along Viale Diaz, near the bus terminal, and at Piazza Vittorio Emanuele; alternatively, call ☎0935 500 905.

INFORMATION

Tourist information You can pick up a good town map and accommodation details at the Info Point at Via Roma 413 (Mon, Tues & Thurs–Sat 8.30am–1.30pm, Wed 8.30am–7pm; ☎0935 528 288), or at the larger office on Piazza Colaianni (Mon–Fri 8am–2pm, plus Wed

2.45–6.15pm; ☎0935 500 875), off Via Roma next to the *Grande Albergo Sicilia*.

Online information There's information on Enna at ⓦennaturismo.info and ⓦturismoenna.it, but only in Italian.

ACCOMMODATION

★ **Bianko & Bianko** Via Longo 15 ☎331 329 4288 or ☎327 159 8426, ⓦbiankoebianko.it. An effortlessly cool and uncluttered B&B in a nineteenth-century townhouse, with three spacious, light-filled rooms in stylish white. It's handy for the old town, just to the right of the steps of San Cataldo church at the bottom of Via Vittorio Emanuele. There's no one on the premises (you have to call first), and breakfast is taken at the bar around the corner. **€55**

Grande Albergo Sicilia Piazza Colaianni ☎0935 500 850, ⓦhotelsiciliaenna.it. This easy-to-find pile in the centre, close to the Duomo, is the best of Enna's two central hotels. It's a traditional place, with an Art Deco lobby and nicely refurbished rooms, some with hand-painted Sicilian country furniture and others with rooftop views. You can also park right outside, which is a definite bonus. Online

bookings and last-minute deals can bring the price down. **€120**

Da Pietro Contrada Longobardi, Calascibetta ☎0935 33 647 or ☎340 276 5763, ⓦbbcalascibetta.it. Surrounded by a garden, this pleasant B&B has a wide terrace with great views where breakfast is served. It's 6km north of Enna and well signposted on the approach to the village of Calascibetta. No credit cards. **€50**

Prosperina Piazza Scelfo 108, corner Via Sant'Agata ☎333 299 1957, ⓦbbenna.it. A tall townhouse B&B right in the historic centre, with seven polished rooms perched on top of one another and reached by lift. They sleep from one to four (including a good family room, with separate bunk beds), and there's a dining room and little covered terrace area for breakfast. Among services on offer are tours of the city centre by vintage Ape. Doubles **€55**

7

EATING AND DRINKING

There's only a limited choice of restaurants in the old part of Enna, but enough for a night or two. The cafés and bars around Piazza Vittorio Emanuele fill up during the evening, while during the *passeggiata* dawdling locals hold up the traffic all along Via Roma.

RESTAURANTS

Ariston Via Roma 353 ☎ 0935 26 038. Longstanding, reliable place for fresh pasta and good, authentic Sicilian fish dishes, this is a typically formal provincial place; it's set inside an old-fashioned shopping arcade, which does its gloomy terrace tables no favours. Expect to pay €30 a head for a meal, though there are pizzas at night, too. Mon–Sat lunch & dinner.

Centrale Piazza VI Dicembre 9 ☎ 0935 500 963. Attracts a largely local crowd, and has a shady terrace off the main street. The *antipasti* table is impressive, and dishes on a wide-ranging menu cost €6–18 for meat and €25 for fish, or there are four fixed-price menus (priced €15–€23). Daily lunch & dinner; closed Sat in winter.

★ **Grotta Azzurra** Via Colaianni 1 ☎ 0935 24 328. Run for over fifty years by the charming Giuseppe and Maria, this tiny, no-frills basement trattoria serves the cheapest meals in town: from €3.50 for *primi* and €5.50 or €6 for *secondi*. It's nothing fancy (baked pasta, simple grills and roasts,

omelettes, and fruit for dessert), and the house wine could fuel a mission to Mars, but it's a real taste of the past. It's at the very bottom of Via Roma, past Piazza Vittorio Emanuele and down an alley on the left (there's a sign). No credit cards. Daily lunch & dinner; closed Sat in winter.

CAFÉS

Al Kenisa Via Roma 481 ☎ 0935 500 972, ⓦ alkenisa .blogspot.it. This old church has been stripped bare and revamped as a cultural centre and café. There are warm stone walls, art exhibitions and books inside, and Arab-style lounging outside on the cobbles at low tables and cushions. Tues–Sat 3pm–1am.

Marro Caffè Piazza Vittorio Emanuele 22 ☎ 0935 502 836. *Marro Caffè's* outdoor deck is the best perch on the main square. When you get tired of people-watching, someone has thoughtfully Googled song lyrics for you to read on the back of every chair. Tues–Sun usually 8am–8pm.

DIRECTORY

Emergencies Ambulance ☎ 118; police ☎ 113.
Hospital Ospedale Umberto I, Contrada Ferrante in Enna Bassa, on the road to Pergusa (☎ 0935 45 111).
Pharmacies Librizzi, Piazza Vittorio Emanuele 20 (☎ 0935 500 908); Farmacia del Centro, Via Roma 315 (☎ 0935 500

650). Both open Mon–Sat 8.30am–1pm & 4.30–8pm, and a late-opening rota is posted in all pharmacy windows.
Police Questura at Via San Giuseppe 4 (☎ 0935 522 111).
Post office Via A. Volta, off Piazza Garibaldi (Mon–Fri 8am–6.30pm, Sat 8am–12.30pm).

Northeast of Enna

There's a great driving route northeast of Enna, along the minor **SS121** which runs all the way to Adrano and the Etna foothills. It's rolling countryside for the most part, punctuated by a succession of viewpoints and sleepy little towns and villages such as **Leonforte** and **Cesarò**, and with an occasional coffee and a stretch of the legs the route can occupy half a day. The road is in a bit of a state, with the surface breaking up here and there, though it's perfectly drivable with care. Buses come this way too, though with services timetabled to take local kids to school in Enna, you might find yourself spending longer than you'd want in many of the towns – generally you can expect to have to leave Enna after school finishes for the day around 2pm, and then to return the next day at the crack of dawn.

Forty kilometres north of Enna, the small hill-town of **Nicosia** is the main stop on the trans-mountain **SS120**, which cuts across some of the remoter stretches of the Sicilian interior. It's hardly a major destination its own right, though onward routes from Nicosia are all dramatic, especially north over the Madonie mountains to Gangi, Mistretta and the Tyrrhenian coast (see Chapter 2) and east along the SS120 through a bare landscape dominated ever more dramatically by the giant silhouette of Etna. Again, the road isn't in great condition, with slips and wash-outs common, but it's no problem if you heed the signs and drive carefully.

Leonforte

Some 20km from Enna along the SS121, **LEONFORTE** is typical of the small towns hereabouts, with its roots firmly in the seventeenth century and an attractive central square that sprouts bars in profusion. Other than the impressive Duomo and the domineering Palazzo Baronale, Leonforte's most noteworthy sight is **La Granfonte**, overlooking the hills on the edge of town. Built in 1651, it's not so much a fountain as a row of 24 waterspouts set in a sculpted facade of carvings and inscriptions. Once you've filled your water bottle, it's time to move on, unless you fancy stocking up on the lentils for which the town is famous.

Nicosia

Sitting under looming crags, **NICOSIA** is a medieval mass of cracked *palazzi* topped by the remains of a Norman castle. Traffic all funnels up to the chatter-filled Piazza Garibaldi, the site of Nicosia's lovely old cathedral, **San Nicola**, a stately construction with a fourteenth-century facade and belltower, and a handsome sculpted Gothic portal. To the side of the cathedral (left side, as you face the church), Via Francesco Salamone rises steeply to the former Saracen district of the town, a jumble of streets occupying one of the four hills on which Nicosia is built.

Santa Maria Maggiore

Via Francesco Salamone

Founded in 1267 but rebuilt after an eighteenth-century landslide, **Santa Maria Maggiore** has the bells from its campanile piled up outside – they fell down after another earthquake and the sound of them is now electrically reproduced. Inside, amid "No Spitting" notices, you'll find an impressive marble polyptych by Antonello Gagini and a throne used by Charles V when he passed through here in 1535, on the way back from his Tunisian crusade. The views from outside encompass the town's other three promontories, on the highest of which sits the ruined castle.

ARRIVAL AND DEPARTURE   NICOSIA

By bus Buses drop you a few minutes' walk below Piazza Garibaldi.

Destinations Catania (5 daily Mon–Sat, 1 daily Sun; 2hr); Enna (3 daily Mon–Sat; 1hr 30min); Gangi (4–7 daily Mon–Sat, 2 daily Sun; 40min); Leonforte (4–5 daily Mon–Sat, 1 daily Sun; 40min); Palermo (4 daily Mon–Sat, 2 daily Sun; 3hr 10min); Petralia Soprana (4–5 daily Mon–Sat, 2 daily Sun; 1hr 10min); Petralia Sottana (4–5 daily Mon–Sat, 2 daily Sun; 1hr 20min); Polizzi Generosa (2 daily; 2hr); Sperlinga (4–7 daily Mon–Sat, 2 daily Sun; 15min).

By car You might be able to park near the square for a short while, but it's better to use one of the signposted parking areas as you drive into the centre.

ACCOMMODATION

Baglio San Pietro Contrada San Pietro ☎ 0935 640 529 or ☎ 335 876 7396, ⊛ bagliosanpietro.com. Some 1km west of Nicosia and signposted off the Sperlinga road, this is a restored farm estate originally dating from the seventeenth century. The comfortable rooms here make a good base for the surroundings, as the farm has its own restaurant, pool and gardens. **€90**

Sperlinga

Some 10km west of Nicosia, **SPERLINGA** owes its name to the numerous cave-dwellings (from the Latin *spelunca*, cave), some hundreds of years old, that pit the sandstone slopes below the town. Several were inhabited until recently, furnished with mod cons such as microwaves and fridges.

THE SIEGE OF TROINA

In the summer of 1061, **Count Roger** marched his troops across the mountains from Messina, holing up in Troina, the highest place around. There he posted soldiers, and left his wife, **Judith**, while he went on to try and seize Nicosia from the Arabs. Unfortunately, Troina had a large population of Byzantine Greeks, who hated the Normans even more than they hated the Arabs, and one night they attempted to kidnap Judith, which resulted in rioting on the streets. Roger rushed back and, in the face of a united Arab and Byzantine attack, took refuge in Troina's **fortress**. Roger and Judith spent four months of a freezing winter in the castle, with no fuel, and just one cloak between them, which they used as a blanket at night. One particularly freezing evening, Roger and Judith's troops, starving and frozen, hearing the Arabs and Byzantines partying on wine in the town below, could stand no more, crept out over the snow and slaughtered them, finally bringing the siege to an end.

The castello

Daily 9.30am–1.30pm & 4–6.30pm • €2

With its storerooms, cellars, stables and steps hewn out of the rock, Sperlinga is dominated by a formidable battlemented **castello**. Sperlinga was the only town in Sicily to open its doors to the Angevins, bloodily expelled from other Sicilian towns during the thirteenth-century Wars of the Vespers: barricading themselves inside the castle, the French held out for a year before surrendering. Just below the castle, a small archeological and ethnographical **museum** (same ticket and times as castle) contains the usual motley collection of historical items and old agricultural and domestic artefacts.

ARRIVAL AND DEPARTURE   SPERLINGA

By bus There is one daily bus to Sperlinga from Enna, run by SAIS (⚑ saisautolinee) and departing Mon–Sat during school term-time only from Enna's bus terminal, via Calascibetta, leaving at 2.10pm. The return is the following day at 6.20am.

Troina

From a distance, **TROINA** appears like a thimble perched on a hill, 1120m high. A twisting 30km ride from Nicosia, the town has long played a strategic role in the various wars and power struggles that have racked Sicily, initially coming to prominence during the reconquest of Sicily from the Arabs, when it became one of the first cities to be taken by the Normans. Count Roger withstood a siege here (see box above) in 1061 that nearly put paid to his Sicilian adventures, a victory commemorated by founding the monastery of **San Basilio**, now in ruins. The top of town features an eleventh-century **cathedral** with an adjacent fifteenth-century **church** dedicated to San Giorgio (notice the relief of George and the Dragon above the door under the cupola). The wide piazza-terrace in front has a simply magnificent Etna view, while beyond stretches the main street. It's laid out along a high ridge, and it makes for an atmospheric stroll down a narrow thoroughfare between noble mansions with a steep drop to either side.

Cesarò

CESARÒ stands under fearsome crags at the crossroads of the SS120 and the SS289, the road that runs north across the Nébrodi mountains to the coast at Sant'Agata di Militello (see Chapter 2). On a clear day there are remarkable views over to Etna as you approach town, though the hemmed-in streets of Cesarò itself give no hint of the grandeur of its setting – for a panorama, you must climb or drive up to the mammoth bronze statue of Jesus, the **Cristo Signore della Montagna**, in the cemetery above town.

ARRIVAL AND DEPARTURE

CESARÒ

By bus Isea Viaggi buses (◍ iseaviaggi.it) run once daily to Cesarò from Enna via Leonforte, Nicosia and Troina, leaving Enna at 2pm, with return buses departing from Cesarò at 5.20am the following day.

ACCOMMODATION AND EATING

Hotel Fratelli Mazzurco S.S. 120 Via Conceria ☎ 095 773 2100, ◍ hotelmazzurco.it. The *Mazzurco* not only has decent rooms but also the town's finest restaurant (Aug daily lunch and dinner; rest of the year closed Thurs), specializing in local produce (namely mushrooms, pork and pistachios). Portions are huge, so make sure you are very hungry before ordering the fixed-price menu at €30. There's a garden-courtyard for *al fresco* meals and some scintillating views from the front of the hotel. **€70**

Caltanissetta

With twice as many inhabitants as Enna, the provincial capital of **CALTANISSETTA** (35km to the southwest) is easily the largest town in the interior, though little else about it is remarkable. Moreover, its sprawling modern suburbs give way suddenly to rolling empty fields beyond – the town is very much the last gasp before the almost ghostly rural expanses of Sicily's western interior.

The largely traffic-choked centre breathes a sigh of relief around the prettily restored **Piazza Garibaldi**, with its splashing fountain, handsome Duomo and the wedding-cake confection that is the church of San Sebastiano. The churches may well be locked but they form a pleasing ensemble, while the nearby sandstone and salmon-pink **Sant'Agata**, at the other end of Corso Umberto I, is equally easy on the eye. You can also take a spin around the imposing walls of the seventeenth-century **Palazzo Moncada** two blocks to the north of Piazza Garibaldi, an aristocratic mansion belonging to one of Sicily's great feudal dynasties. Down behind the Duomo (follow Via Pugliese Giannone and Via San Domenico) it's less than ten minutes' walk to one of the island's stranger castle ruins, the **Castello di Pietrarossa**, improbably balanced on an outcrop of rock. It's off-limits and looks like it should have fallen down years ago, though it's finally getting some belated attention as restoration work continues on the adjacent church and monastery.

Museo Archeologico

Via di Santo Spirito • Tues–Sun 9am–1pm & 3.30–7pm; closed last Sun of month • €4 • ☎ 0934 567 062 • Take a bus from the train station (direction Villaggio Santa Barbara), and ask to get off near the museum; the stop is about 300m from the museum; if driving, follow the brown "Museo Archeologico" signs from town, though it's easy to get lost

Located 3km north of the centre, the **Museo Archeologico** is a vast circular bunker straight out of the Thunderbirds school of architecture, and contains some of Sicily's earliest finds (from the Bronze Age to the fourth century BC), including treasures like an unusual votive clay model of a temple. It's all beautifully presented, with clear English notes throughout, and there's unlikely to be another soul around save the slumbering attendants.

Santo Spirito

Alongside the Museo Archeologico, the restored twelfth-century abbey church of **Santo Spirito** was founded by Count Roger and – a rare thing in Sicily – is purely Norman in form. The plain structure is only enlivened by three tiny apses at the back, though the interior has a fifteenth-century fresco over the central apse and a twelfth-century font. If the church is locked, you can try ringing at the door on the right (home of the parish priest).

ARRIVAL AND DEPARTURE CALTANISSETTA

By bus Caltanissetta's bus station is at Piazza Roma, outside the train station, about a 10min walk from Piazza Garibaldi.

Destinations Agrigento (3–4 daily Mon–Sat, 1 daily Sun; 1hr 35min); Catania (13 daily Mon–Sat, 8 daily Sun; 1hr 35min); Enna (4–5 daily Mon–Sat; 50min); Palermo (7–10 daily Mon–Sat, 4 daily Sun; 1hr 40min); Piazza Armerina (5–8 daily; 30min).

By train Although buses are usually faster and more frequent, Caltanissetta has reasonable train connections with Enna, Palermo, Catania and Agrigento, but if you're heading to Enna it's easier to take the bus, as the town's train station is a long way out from the centre. Going the

other way, the railway line meanders northwest, ultimately to Palermo, through empty upland plains, one of the most desert-like of Sicilian journeys.

Destinations Agrigento (5–6 daily Mon–Sat, 2 daily Sun; 1hr 25min); Catania (7–8 daily Mon–Sat; 1hr 40min); Enna (7 daily Mon–Sat, 5 daily Sun; 35min); Gela (3–4 daily; 2hr); Grammichele (7–9 daily Mon–Sat; 15min); Licata (3–4 daily; 1hr 20min); Palermo (4 daily; 2hr).

By car There's currently cheap on-street parking all over town. Note that there is no entry to the Piazza Garibaldi or surrounding streets between 5pm and 8.30pm, while the evening *passeggiata* is in progress.

ACCOMMODATION AND EATING

★ **Azienda Agricola Silvia Sillitti** ☎ 0934 930 733 or ☎ 338 763 4601, ⓦ sillitti.it. Some 12km out of town off the SS640 Agrigento road, this wonderful *agriturismo* is set on a working organic farm of olive and almond groves, wheat fields and vegetable plots. There are rustic rooms in three apartments, expansive terraces with views on all sides, hammocks in the shade and a sparkling swimming pool. Silvia is a charming host who prepares excellent Sicilian dinners on request (€25), using produce from her estate. Two-person apartment €90

Gran Caffè Romano Corso Umberto I 147 ☎ 0934 21 402. Best café in town, with an 8m-long counter full of almond *mandorle* biscuits (the local speciality), *cannoli* and other treats, and chunky leather sofas outside on the pavement. Daily 8am–8pm.

Piazza Garibaldi Piazza Garibaldi 11 ☎ 0934 680 510 or ☎ 340 379 5803, ⓦ piazzagaribaldi11.it. A first-class B&B in a restored palace opposite the Duomo, with colourful bedrooms sporting idiosyncratic murals. €60

Piazza Armerina

The small town of **PIAZZA ARMERINA** lies amid thickly forested hills. A quiet, unassuming place, it is mainly seventeenth- and eighteenth-century in appearance, with a skyline pierced by towers and houses that huddle together under the joint protection of decrepit castle and pristine cathedral. Despite the dense traffic that fills its lanes and thoroughfares, it's a charming place that deserves a detour and even an overnight stop, though many visitors bypass it altogether, given the enticement of the mosaics at the nearby Villa Romana del Casale (see p.270).

The town's central core is small enough to cover in a morning's stroll. Restoration has pretty much started and stopped in **Piazza del Duomo**, but the rest of Piazza Armerina is an endearing jumble of cobbled steps and faded grandeur, dilapidated yet graceful churches and *palazzi*, narrow streets and skinny alleys. There are noble mansions in varying stages of decay along **Via Monte**, formerly the medieval town's main street, while down Via Floresta (to the side of Palazzo Trigona) you soon reach the closed and tumbledown **castello**, built at the end of the fourteenth century and surrounded by once-rich *palazzi* with broken windows and tattered wooden shutters.

Piazza Duomo

Duomo Daily 8am–noon & 4–7pm

Piazza Armerina's best views are from the terrace of **Piazza Duomo**, at the very top of town. The town's elegant seventeenth-century **Duomo** has a marvellously cool, blue-and-white stuccoed interior accessible through the small green door on the Via Cavour side of the building. Across from the cathedral campanile, and its blind Catalan-Gothic windows, stands the spruce facade of the eighteenth-century **Palazzo Trigona**, its simple brick exterior crowned by a spread-eagle plaque.

Castellina

The **Castellina** quarter, off Via Mazzini, is a fascinating area to explore, with steep residential alleys dropping down to the **Porta Castellina**, a surviving part of the medieval town wall – with a rough arch hacked through it for traffic access. From pretty **Piazza Garibaldi**, Via Mazzini, Via Garibaldi and Via Umberto I are the main old-town shopping streets, all leading eventually to the large twin squares that separate old town from new, with the **Giardino Garibaldi** gardens beyond.

ARRIVAL AND INFORMATION

PIAZZA ARMERINA

By bus Buses drop you off at Piazza Senatore Marescalchi, a large square on the main road in the lower, modern town, a 15min walk from the old centre. For bus information and tickets to Aidone, Caltagirone, Catania and elsewhere, ask in the *Bar della Stazione* in Piazza Senatore Marescalchi, or the AST office next door.

Destinations Aidone (6–13 daily Mon–Sat, 2 daily Sun; 15min); Caltagirone (5 daily Mon–Sat; 1hr–1hr 30min); Catania (3–6 daily Mon–Sat, 2 daily Sun; 1hr 40min); Enna (3–6 daily; 30min); Gela (3–4 daily; 40min); Palermo (3–5 daily; 2hr 15min).

By car There's metered on-street parking in the lower town, but you can get closer to the sights by following the signs for "centro" and then "Duomo". The narrow streets may seem challenging, but a fairly sensible one-way system runs along Via Mazzini to Piazza Garibaldi and then dog-legs up Via Cavour to the Duomo – there's a fair amount of metered parking on the way, and free parking in Piazza Duomo itself.

Tourist information There's a tourist office at Viale Generale Muscarà 47 (Mon–Fri 8am–2pm; ☎0935 680 201).

ACCOMMODATION

B&B Umberto 33 Via Umberto 33 ☎0935 683 344 or ☎340 558 6002, ⊛umberto33.com. A centrally located B&B on one of the old town's main shopping and strolling streets, with three handsome en-suite rooms. **€60**

Gangi Via Generale Ciancio 68–70 ☎0935 682 737, ⊛hotelgangi.it. A three-star hotel housed in a sympathetically restored old *palazzo* in the lower town, featuring exposed stone walls, a cobbled courtyard and straightforward rooms. You can park nearby as well. **€70**

Ostello del Borgo Largo San Giovanni 6 ☎0935 687 019, ⊛ostellodelborgo.it. This refurbished fourteenth-century Benedictine convent has both hostel beds (Hostelling International card required) and sixteen other private rooms (singles, doubles and family rooms, with en-suite bathrooms), all converted from former nuns' cells and thus fairly spartan but quiet and clean. Dorm beds **€17**; doubles **€60**

Park Hotel Paradiso Contrada Ramaldo ☎0935 680 841, ⊛parkhotelparadiso.it. It's out of the historic centre, 1km beyond the church of Sant'Andrea (signposted from town), but if you want a resort-style stay this is the place. It's a modern four-star with echoing public spaces aimed at the convention-and-wedding market, but the rooms are pretty spacious and well equipped, and there's a pool, sauna, gym and formal restaurant. **€80**

★ **Suite d'Autore** Via Monte 1 ☎0935 688 553, ⊛suitedautore.it. Offbeat is hardly the word: fabulously quirky accommodation in a redesigned old *palazzo* across from the Duomo (rooms with views cost extra), where the themes come thick and fast ("Strangeness", "Magic and Irony", "Fluidity", etc) in fun-filled rooms that mix contemporary design, stylish artefacts, retro objects, original art and photography. If you're especially taken by your Star Wars bedside table or Philippe Starck chair, everything is also for sale. The top-floor bar, for breakfast and evening drinks, has fabulous town and country views, and there's free parking right outside in the square. **€100**

EATING AND DRINKING

The old-town **restaurants** have the most atmosphere and are handy for the B&Bs. The liveliest cafés and bars though are those around **Piazza Generale Cascino**, in front of the Garibaldi gardens. This is where to come at *passeggiata* time for a stroll, an ice cream or a beer.

CLOCKWISE FROM TOP PIAZZA ARMERINA (P.266); SPERLINGA (P.263); CALTAGIRONE (P.274) >

★ **Amici Miei** Largo Capodarso 5 ☎ 0935 683 541. "My friends" has charming terrace seating outside and a rustic brick-walled dining room, plus a menu that's especially good for seafood, from baked bream to sauteéd clams and mussels. Pastas and mains are €7–12, or there are also really good pizzas (€2.50–8) at night. Daily lunch & dinner; closed Thurs in winter.

Al Teatro Via del Teatro 6 ☎ 0935 85 662. It takes a bit of finding (easiest from the end of Via Garibaldi), but it's worth it for the terrace tables with nice views over the old theatre and town rooftops. Try the home-made *pappardelle*, or one of the thirty-odd different types of pizza (most dishes €6–10). Daily lunch & dinner; closed Wed in winter.

Da Totò Via Mazzini 29 ☎ 0935 680 153. House speciality in this local institution is the *bocca di lupo*, a steak with prosciutto, aubergine and mozzarella (€12). Otherwise, pastas and main dishes cost between €8 and €15, or go for pizza at night. Daily lunch only; closed Mon in winter.

Trattoria del Goloso Via Garao 4 ☎ 0935 685 693. Good-value trattoria (most dishes €6–10) just off Piazza Garibaldi, with a little outdoor terrace. Try the home-made pasta (for a treat look out for pasta dishes featuring pistachios) and follow up with deftly herbed grilled local lamb. Daily lunch & dinner; closed Wed evening in winter.

Villa Romana del Casale

Daily: April–Oct 9am–7pm; Nov–March 9am–5pm; last entry 1hr before closing • €10 • ⓦ villaromanadelcasale.it

Built on terraces in a sparsely inhabited neighbourhood 5km southwest of Piazza Armerina, the **Villa Romana del Casale** dates from the early fourth century AD and remained in use right up until it was covered by a mudslide in the twelfth century. It was then hidden from view for seven hundred years until excavations began in 1950, revealing multicoloured mosaic floors that are unique in the entire Roman world for their quality and extent. A roof and walls were added to indicate the original size and shape of the villa, and the mosaics are now protected from the elements, with walkways leading through the various rooms and chambers. It's an essential visit on any trip to Sicily, but the continuous stream of coach parties and tour groups hardly makes for a relaxing trip. If you can, it's best to come early or late in the day in order to avoid the heat and the crowds – the whole visit takes around an hour. In addition, there are ongoing restoration works and it pays to check the website, or ask at Piazza Armerina tourist office, before setting out to see the mosaics.

The site

Conflicting theories surround the function of the **villa**, but the most convincing explanation of its deeply rural location is that it was an occasional retreat and hunting lodge. That theory is supported by the many mosaics of animals and birds, including two specific hunting scenes. It's also immediately clear from the extent of the remains that the villa complex belonged to an important owner, possibly **Maximianus Herculeus**, co-emperor with Diocletian between 286 and 305 AD. There are four separate groups of buildings, built on different levels of the hillside and connected by passageways, doors and courtyards. Nearly all of what you see would have been occupied by the family for which it was built – slaves' housing and other outbuildings are still to be excavated properly.

While there are other splendid Roman villas in Italy, none has anything like the extraordinary interior decoration of the Villa Casale. The floors of almost the entire building are covered with bright **mosaics** of excellent quality, stylistically belonging to an early fourth-century Roman-African school, which explains many of the more exotic scenes and animals portrayed. Their design also contains several hints as to their period and patron, though given their extent they're likely to have taken fifty or sixty years to complete.

The main building

The villa's **main entrance** gives one of the best impressions of its former grandeur, with the approach leading through the remains of a columned arch into a wide courtyard. Today's site entrance, though, is through the adjacent **thermae** (or baths): a typical

VILLA ROMANA DEL CASALE

N

Ticket Office

Site Entrance

Circus Scene

Great
Hunting Scene

Small
Hunting Scene

Private
Apartments

Tepidarium

Calidariaa

Thermae

Basilica

Children's
Hunting Scene

Frigidarium

Peristyle

Atrium

Mosaic of
Ten Girls

Latrine

Main
Entrance

Triclinium

Xystus

0   25
metres

7

arrangement of dressing/massage rooms and plunge-baths around an octagonal **frigidarium**, its central mosaic a marine scene of sea nymphs, tritons, and little cherubs rowing boats and spearing fish. A walkway leads out of the baths and into the villa proper, to the massive central courtyard or **peristyle**. This is where guests would have been received, and the vestibule displays a fragmented mosaic depicting a formal welcome by an attendant holding an olive branch. The corridor around the four sides of the courtyard is covered with a series of animal-head medallions: snarling tigers, yapping dogs and unicorns. Just off here, a balcony looks down upon one of the most vivid pictures, a boisterous circus scene showing a chariot race. Starting in the top right-hand corner, the variously coloured chariots rush off, overtaking and crashing at the turns, until finally there's victory for the green faction. The next room's mosaic shows a family attended by slaves on their way to the baths. Period detail – footwear, hairstyles and clothes – helped archeologists to date the rest of the mosaics.

Small rooms beyond, on either side of the peristyle, reveal only fragmentary geometric patterns, although one displays a **small hunting scene**, an episodic adventure that ends with a peaceful picnic in the centre. Another room contains what is the villa's most famous image, a two-tiered scene of **ten girls**, realistically muscular figures in Roman "bikinis", taking part in various gymnastic and athletic activities. One of the girls, sporting a laurel wreath and a palm frond, is clearly the winner of the competition.

The great hunting scene

The peristyle is separated from the private apartments and public halls beyond by a long, covered corridor, which contains the best of the villa's mosaic works. The **great hunting scene** sets armed and shield-bearing hunters against a panoply of wild animals, on sea and land. Along the entire 60m length of the mosaic, tigers, ostriches, elephants and even a rhino, destined for the games back in Rome, are pictured being trapped, bundled up and down gangplanks and into cages. The caped figure overseeing the operation is probably Maximianus himself. Much of the scene is set in Africa, Maximianus's main responsibility in the Imperial Tetrarchy, while an ivy-leaf symbol on the costume of the attendant to his right is that of his personal legion, the Herculiani.

The rest of the site

Family apartments and public halls beyond the great hunting scene are nearly all on a grand scale. A large courtyard, the **xystus**, gives onto the **triclinium**, a dining room with three apses, whose mosaics feature the labours of Hercules. One bloody scene portrays his fight against the giants, all struck by arrows, who writhe and wail with contorted faces. A path leads around the back to the **private apartments**, based around a large basilica, with mosaics echoing the spectacular scenes of the main building: a **children's circus**, where the small chariots are drawn by colourful birds, and a **children's hunt**, the tiny tots being chased and pecked by the hares and peacocks they're supposed to snare.

ARRIVAL AND DEPARTURE   VILLA ROMANA DEL CASALE

By bus From Piazza Armerina, a bus (May–Sept) leaves Piazza Senatore Marescalchi for the Villa Romana on the hour between 9am and noon, and between 3pm and 6pm, with a stop at Piazza Generale Cascino; it's a half-hour ride, and the return service is on the half-hour, starting at 9.30am.

By taxi A taxi from Piazza Generale Cascino in Piazza Armerina costs around €10 each way.

ACCOMMODATION AND EATING

Mosaici da Battiato Contrada Paratore ☏ 0935 685 453, ✉ hotelmosaici.com. Located at the turn-off to the Villa Romana, this country inn has reasonable rooms at low prices, and a terrace-restaurant that's subject to an influx of tour groups at lunch. Closed Nov & Dec. **€50**

Trattoria La Ruota Contrada Paratore ☏ 0935 680 542. In an attractive rustic setting a little way up the road from the Villa Romana, this handsome former watermill offers shaded outdoor seating and excellent regional food, from home-made pasta to local sausage, lamb and rabbit (mains €98). The best place to eat near the mosaics. Daily lunch only.

Around Piazza Armerina

The extraordinary remains of the Greek city of **Morgantina**, which was at its height in the fourth century BC, lie 15km northeast of Piazza Armerina. That it's not better known is a shame, but also a boon as your visit will be mercifully free of the tourist shenanigans associated with the famous Casale mosaics. Unfortunately, buses from Piazza Armerina only run as far as the pretty village of **Aidone** (site of Morgantina's museum), with the archeological site itself another 5km beyond.

Aidone

Museo Archeologico Daily 9am–7pm • €6, or €10 with Morgantina • ☏ 0935 87 307 • Buses for Aidone leave from Piazza Senatore Marescalchi in Piazza Armerina at least six times daily

With its quiet central square and thoroughly laidback air, **AIDONE** is a charming little spot. There are a couple of agreeable bars on the square and a crumbling church, but the true reason for a visit is the **Museo Archeologico**, impressively housed in a former Capuchin monastery on Largo Torres Trupia – it's signposted, right at the top of the village. It makes an indispensable adjunct to seeing the Morgantina archeological site, since it's here that you'll find everything that was removed from the ancient city – from ceramics, statuettes and busts to coins, candle-holders and domestic artefacts. Aerial photos and plans also provide a useful idea of the layout of the site. The highlights, however, are the objects recently returned to Sicily from America, after years of legal battles: the exquisite **Morgantina Venus** (now known as the Dea di Morgantina, as it's thought she is, in fact, Demeter); the so-called **Eupolemo Silver**, fifteen pieces of tableware dating from the third century BC; and the acroliths of Demeter and Persephone, the heads, hands and feet of sixth-century BC **statues** of the Goddess Demeter, and her daughter Persephone, or Kore (see box below).

THE RETURN OF THE GODDESSES

When Greeks began to arrive in Sicily during the eighth century BC, attracted by the island's legendary fertility, their cults of **gods and goddesses** found fecund ground among the local inhabitants, who lived side by side with the Greeks in provincial towns such as Morgantina. Over time, indigenous fertility cults of death and rebirth centred on the annual cycle of harvests became intertwined with the Greek fertility cult focusing on the goddess **Demeter** and her daughter, **Persephone**, abducted by Hades and taken to the underworld. According to the myth, the summer months (when nothing grows in Sicily) occur when Persephone is in the underworld; then, at the beginning of autumn, when the seeds of the old crop are scattered, she returns to earth to be reunited with Demeter. (Interestingly, when the myth is retold in English, Persephone is absent from the earth in winter, and returns in spring, the myth having to be adapted to the exigencies of climate.) That Morgantina, in the agricultural interior of Sicily, where survival depended on the vagaries of the weather, should have been home to an immense temple to Demeter and Persephone, is thus no surprise.

In the summer of 1979, rumours began to circulate in Aidone about the secret discovery of several **marble sculptures**. They had been found, the story went, by illegal excavators, sponsored by the Mafia and working close to the site of Morgantina, a few kilometres away. A short while later, legal excavations revealed the foundations of a vast sanctuary at Morgantina dedicated to fertility goddess, Demeter. But there was no sign of any statues. A few years later, word spread among the New York art world of the acquisition, by an anonymous collector, of several elements of ancient Greek statuary. Then in 1986, hitherto unknown fragments of ancient Greek statues were exhibited at the **Paul Getty Museum** in Malibu, on loan from a private and still anonymous collector; American archeologist Malcolm Bell, director of the legal excavations at Morgantina, was able to establish that the pieces had been **stolen** from Morgantina.

In 1988 Enna's Public Prosecutor, Silvio Raffiotta, established that the pieces had been sold to multimillionaire **Maurice Tempelsman**, last husband of Jackie Onassis, via London art dealer Robin Symes. The Italian Ministry of Culture attempted to negotiate for the statues' return to Sicily, but with no result. In 2002, however, Tempelsman donated the sculptures to the Bayly Art Museum of the University of Virginia, on three conditions: the donation had to receive no publicity, the donor had to remain anonymous, and the sculptures could not be returned to Italy for five years.

In early 2008, the university finally succumbed to pressure and agreed to return the statues to their rightful home, and in late 2009 the **acroliths of Demeter and Persephone** were put on public display in Aidone's museum for the first time, "dressed" by innovative fashion designer Marella Ferrara. The exhibition marked the beginning of a series of **restitutions** to Sicily of antique objects scavenged from the site of Morgantina and sold to the Metropolitan Museum New York and Paul Getty. **Euploemo silverware** arrived in January 2010, followed in 2011 by the most important of all Morgantina antiquities: the so-called **Morgantina Venus**, a superb example of late fifth-century BC sculpture, showing a mighty goddess, with her drapery blown against her muscular, almost masculine, body.

Morgantina

Daily 9am–1hr before sunset • €6, or €10 including Museo Archeologico at Aidone

Five kilometres northeast of Aidone, at the end of a long cobbled lane, the **site of Morgantina** occupies two quiet hillsides with gorgeous views of the valley below. The car park is just under the east hill, and it's around a 500m walk down to the main entrance and ticket office, where you're given a brochure and map: all the signs on the site are in Italian and English.

After its demise in around 211 BC, the city became buried and forgotten for almost two thousand years, and even after the site's discovery it wasn't identified as Morgantina until 1957. To date, only a fraction of the city has been excavated, but the finds have shed much light on the island's pre-Hellenic Sikel population, who inhabited central Sicily from the ninth century BC. In the sixth century BC, Chalcidian Greeks settled here and lived in harmony alongside the Sikels until the city became the centre of a revolt led by the Sikel leader Ducetius, who destroyed it in the mid-fifth century BC. Swiftly rebuilt on a grid plan with walled and towered defences, Morgantina reached its apogee in the fourth and third centuries BC under the protection of Syracuse, and many of the surviving buildings date from this period. A couple of hundred years later the city was in decline, and was soon abandoned altogether.

The agora and the teatro

Heading left into the site from the main entrance leads directly to Morgantina's most distinctive ruin, the **agora**, bounded by three stepped sides that served as seats for public meetings. The small **teatro** to its right was built in the third century BC, but reconstructed in Roman times. Concerts, Greek plays and modern drama are sometimes held here in the summer – you can get more information from the tourist offices in Enna (see p.261) or Piazza Armerina (see p.268).

The santuario and Fornace Grande

Other buildings here include a fourth-century BC **santuario** of Demeter and Kore, while on the level ground behind the agora is a granary and square slaughterhouse, beyond which stretches the 100m-long **east stoa**. A great kiln, the **Fornace Grande**, is one of the biggest ancient kilns ever excavated, and probably produced heavy-duty roof tiles, massive storage jars and the like. Further up the hillside in the residential quarter stand the ruins of some Hellenic **houses**, with two mosaic floors. One, the "House of Ganymede", has an illustration of the youth Ganymede being carried away to Olympus by Zeus's eagle to become the cupbearer of the gods.

The west hill

There's an awful lot more of the site to explore, though in summer the heat might dissuade you. A path leads up to excavations on the **west hill**, which, though less revealing, include the fairly substantial remains of houses, roads and walls in what was another large residential area. In recent years, the remains of a second temple and a spring and aqueduct have also been unearthed.

Caltagirone

Around 35km southeast of Piazza Armerina, **CALTAGIRONE** is a curious place. One of the most ancient of Sicilian towns, it was settled well before the arrival of the Greeks, and has an Arabic name (from *kalat*, "castle" and *gerun*, "caves"), yet an overwhelmingly Baroque aspect, dating from the dramatic rebuilding after the 1693 earthquake that flattened the area. The Arabs, though, had one extraordinary and lasting influence on the town, introducing local **ceramic craftsmen** to the glazed polychromatic colours – in particular, blues and yellows – that subsequently became typically Sicilian in execution. Until the great earthquake, the town supported a population of around 20,000, of whom perhaps five percent were actively engaged in the tiled decoration of churches and public buildings. The Baroque rebuilding saw a further burst of creative construction, while later, during the nineteenth century, came the principal period of ceramic figurative work. Caltagirone's traditional industry is still flourishing, with scores of ceramicists displaying work at galleries across the town, while public buildings, churches, house balconies and gardens all feature ceramics in every nook and cranny – not to mention the famous tiled steps of **La Scala**, Caltagirone's pride and joy. The old centre is small and easy to see in half a day, but there's an upbeat air here (and plenty of shopping opportunities) that makes a night an enjoyable prospect.

La Scala

Emblem of Caltagirone is undoubtedly the 142 steps of **La Scala**, which cuts right up one of the town's three hills to the sorely neglected church of Santa Maria del Monte at the top. The staircase was originally conceived at the turn of the seventeenth century as a road between the church (then the cathedral) and the town centre below; the steps were added once it was clear that the incline was too steep. The risers in between each

7

▲ Piazza Armerina, Palermo, Catania & Gela

CALTAGIRONE

VIALE REGINA ELENA
San Giorgio
P
VIA S. SALVATORE
VIA S. SOTIA
Santa Maria del Monte
VIA CAPPUCCINI
LA SCALA
VIA CIRCONVALLAZIONE DI LEVANTE
Municipio
Gesù   PIAZZA MARCINNO
San Giacomo
VIA VITTORIO EMANUELE
PIAZZA MUNICIPIO
Galleria Luigi Sturzo
Duomo   PIAZZA UMBERTO
Corte Capitaniale   Museo Civico
PONTE SAN FRANCESCO
VIA ACQUANUOVA SECONDA
San Francesco all'Immacolata
PIAZZA SAN FRANCESCO
N
VIA ROMA

BAR	
Giardino Spadaro	1

ACCOMMODATION	
Il Piccolo Attico	3
La Pilozza Infiorata	1
Tre Metri Sopra il Cielo	2

RESTAURANTS	
Il Locandiere	1
I Marchesi di Santa Barbara	2

0 ——— 200
metres

Giardino Pubblico   **Museo della Ceramica**

Train Station & Bus Station

step are covered with hand-painted ceramic patterns, added in the 1950s, no two the same. Having puffed your way up, your reward is the magnificent **view** down across town to the distinctive spire of the Sicilian Baroque church of San Francesco all'Immacolata, with the plain stretching away into the distance beyond. At night the steps are lit, and couples and families spread out on them, chatting away. In May, there are floral decorations laid up the entire length, while on July 24 and 25 every year La Scala is lit by thousands of coloured paper lamps as part of the celebrations for the feast of St James (San Giacomo).

Piazza Municipio

The main square of the old town is **Piazza Municipio**, where the sturdy seventeenth-century **Corte Capitaniale**, decorated by the Gagini family, is used for temporary art exhibitions. Named after the locally born mayor, reformer and anti-Fascist Luigi Sturzo (1871–1959), modern **Galleria Luigi Sturzo** is another exhibition venue.

Museo Civico

Carcere Borbonico, Via Roma 10 • Tues–Sun 9.30am–1pm, plus Tues & Fri–Sun also 4–7pm • €4 • ☎ 0933 41 812

Off Piazza Umberto, the square building with grilled windows and spike-studded metal doors was a Bourbon prison in the eighteenth century, but now houses the **Museo Civico**. There's nothing essential to see inside, just the usual intriguing collection of local curios, folklore items and architectural fragments, plus paintings by the Vaccaro family who renovated the cathedral in the nineteenth century.

Museo della Ceramica and the Giardino Pubblico

Via Roma • Daily 9am–6.30pm • €4 • ☎ 0933 58 418

The road to the newer town crosses the **Ponte San Francesco** – studded with ceramic flowers and emblems – and then runs down towards the large **Giardino Pubblico** (a 10min walk), where you'll find the last word on the 5000-year-old tradition of local ceramics in the **Museo della Ceramica**. The gardens themselves are worth a whirl in any case, the centrepiece being a wonderful Art Nouveau bandstand, overlooked by a couple of kiosk cafés. This is one of several elegant examples in Caltagirone of the "Liberty" style – you'll also pass the Art Nouveau theatre outside the main entrance to the gardens.

ARRIVAL AND INFORMATION   CALTAGIRONE

By bus The bus station is in the lower town, 2km below the old centre and connected to it by half-hourly local bus. Destinations Catania (1–2 hourly Mon–Sat, 4 daily Sun; 1hr 30min); Enna (2 daily Mon–Fri, 1 daily Sun; 1hr 25min); Gela (2 daily Mon–Sat; 1hr–1hr 10min); Grammichele (2 daily Mon–Sat; 30–40min); Piazza Armerina (5 daily Mon–Sat; 1hr–1hr 20min); Ragusa (2

daily Mon–Sat; 2hr).
By train The train station is adjacent to the bus station. Destinations Catania (7–8 daily Mon–Sat; 1hr 40min); Gela (5 daily; 1hr); Grammichele (5 daily; 15min).
By car Driving right into the upper town is best avoided, and parking is easiest at the large free space off Viale Regina Elena, near San Giorgio church, from where it's a

THE CITY OF CERAMICS

All the way up La Scala staircase, and in the alleys on either side, are ceramicists' **workshops and galleries**, though you'll also find shops and showrooms all over town. Some are huge warehouses, others just a room in an old house, selling copies of traditional designs or original work – plates, vases, jars, figurines – from just a few euros to a few thousand. The other Caltagirone specialities are sculpted terracotta **whistles** and **presepi**, or Nativity crib scenes; again, you can find examples in shops and galleries all across town.

A GEOMETRIC DIVERSION

Just fifteen minutes east of Caltagirone by train, twenty by car (via the Ragusa road), **Grammichele** ranks among the strangest and most ambitious of the new towns built after the 1693 earthquake that flattened much of this land. At its heart is a hexagonal design centred on an imposing central piazza with six radial streets, each bisected by secondary piazzas. The shape is no longer entirely perfect, due to a surfeit of new building around the edges of town, but it makes for an intriguing couple of hours' stroll, with all the streets in each segment corresponding exactly to their neighbours in dimension and appearance. It's disconcertingly easy to lose your bearings and, despite the grand design, Grammichele remains a predominantly rural-looking, old-fashioned town. Piazza Carafa, the main square, has a handful of *circoli*, or clubs, where most of the town's over-60s gather, while a café has ringside seats for all the comings and goings.

5min walk down Via Luigi Sturzo into the centre.
Information The main tourist office, Via Volta Libertini 4 (Mon–Fri 8am–2.30pm & Wed 3–6.30pm; ☏ 0933 53 09), is down an alley just off Piazza Umberto, and there's a useful information desk inside Galleria Luigi Sturzo, Piazza Municipio (Mon–Sat 9am–7pm, Wed 8am–2.30pm & 3–6.30pm, Sun 9am–1pm & 3–7pm; ☏ 0933 41 365, ⓦ comune.caltagirone.ct.it).

ACCOMMODATION

Il Piccolo Attico Via Infermeria 82 ☏ 0933 21 588 or ☏ 320 077 3315, ⓦ ilpiccoloattico.it. One large double room with a bathroom, and one attic apartment composed of two double rooms, with great views on all sides, taking in Etna. Generous breakfasts. **€60**
La Pilozza Infiorata Via San Salvatore 97 ☏ 0933 22 162 or ☏ 339 735 2861, ⓦ lapilozzainfiorata.com. Rather fancy B&B in a restored "Liberty"-style *palazzo* with six individually styled en-suite rooms, three with cooking facilities. There's no view to speak of – the house is tucked into an old-town street – but the rooms are spacious and comfortable, and there's a small terrace. **€75**

★ **Tre Metri Sopra il Cielo** Via Bongiovanni 72 ☏ 0933 193 5106 or ☏ 392 213 3228, ⓦ bbtre metrisoprailcielo.it. Caltagirone's best B&B is this perfectly situated place right on La Scala steps, near the top. Helpful owner Gaetano has three simple rooms in his charming house (you may have to share a bathroom, depending on numbers), but he can also find space in up to half a dozen other rooms in adjacent buildings. Everyone gets to take breakfast on the top-floor terrace, which has a stupendous view over the town and surrounding hills. **€80**

EATING AND DRINKING

Giardino Spadaro Via San Giuseppe 5 ☏ 0933 21 331. Lamp-lit garden bar just up an alley off the bottom of La Scala, which is cool and shady by day, often thronged in the evening when the music is turned up. Mon & Wed–Sun usually 8am–8pm.
Il Locandiere Via Luigi Sturzo 55 ☏ 0933 58 292. A tastefully restored old restaurant that's primarily a fish place, though there are good vegetarian *antipasti* and pastas. The menu depends on what's off the boat, though fish couscous is usually available. Mains are €9–16. May be closed Sun if they run out of fish. Daily lunch & dinner.
I Marchesi di Santa Barbara Via San Bonaventura 22 ☏ 0933 22 406. Located within a cavernous aristocratic mansion, with meals served in the echoing dining room or out in the internal courtyard. There's an upmarket regional menu with reasonable prices (first courses €6–8, mains €10–16, and pizzas in the evening), offering things like pasta with pistachios and almonds, or pasta *Marchese*, with tomatoes, wild fennel and breadcrumbs. Tues–Sun lunch & dinner.

Agrigento and the southwest

TEMPIO DI GIUNONE, VALLE DEI TEMPLI

Agrigento and the southwest

Set on a ridge below the town of Agrigento, the golden Doric temples of the Valle dei Templi are Sicily's prime tourist destination. Throughout the year, charabancs disgorge their hoards here, but only a fraction of visitors see anything else of this area. This is a shame, as this part of Sicily has its own fascination, especially for fans of Inspector Montalbano. The fictional detective's creator, Andrea Camilleri, was born in Porto Empedocle, and wove instantly recognizable elements of both his home town and Agrigento into his detective novels and other writings. You could spend a happy day or so in the southwest just searching out the authentic Montalbano locations – which are very different from the romanticized locations of the TV series.

This is a part of Sicily that will appeal to realists, not romantics, a land where decaying 1970s apartment buildings encircle crumbling historic centres; of dusty roads running through sleepy, shabby villages; and of abandoned settlements at the top of parched hills. The long south coast, from **Licata** to **Sciacca**, is sparsely developed, its marvellous sandy beaches and low-key Mediterranean ports and resorts barely known to Italians, let alone tourists. Sporadic concentrations of spectacularly ugly industrial development along the coast put off many people, while the sea is heavily polluted in some areas. But there's good swimming to be had here nonetheless, and on the coast to either side of Agrigento, isolated sandy **beaches** – packed with locals on summer weekends – warrant the occasional trip off the busy SS115 main road. One of the best beaches lies just below the Hellenic site of **Eraclea Minoa**, to the north of Agrigento, while the port of **Licata**, to the south, offers a few old-town diversions to go with its sand and sea. Of the other coastal towns, **Sciacca** is perhaps the most enjoyable, a fishing port and summer resort with amazing cliff-top views, and a good base for detours into the tall and craggy mountains that back this part of the coast. Those seeking Sicily's romantic side could take the midnight ferry from **Porto Empedocle** to the remote island of **Linosa**, closer to Africa than Europe, while if solitude is not your style, the larger island of **Lampedusa** (with its own airport, no less) has fantastic beaches and a lively summer season.

GETTING AROUND

By public transport Agrigento is connected by bus with most major Sicilian cities, and as ever, buses are usually far quicker than trains. However, as many buses are timed to bring kids to school in the towns in the early mornings, and return them at 2pm, you may end up spending nights in one-horse villages if you rely on them. The nearest airport to Agrigento is Catania, a 3hr journey by bus, around 2hr if you're driving. Regular trains and buses link the coastal towns and villages, though services to the inland towns are less frequent.

ERACLEA MINOA

Highlights

❶ Valle dei Templi, Agrigento Take a walk through ancient Akragas, with its sandstone Greek temples dramatically sited between town and sea. **See p.285**

❷ Montalbano tour, Porto Empedocle Take a tour of the places that inspired Andrea Camilleri, creator of Inspector Montalbano, and discover aspects of Sicily few tourists ever see. **See p.292**

❸ Torre Salsa Several kilometres of unspoilt sands, backed by cliffs of crystalline selenite and a nature reserve – sheer bliss. **See p.293**

❹ Eraclea Minoa A superb sandy beach overlooked by the impressive remains of a Greek city. **See p.296**

❺ Sciacca With a labyrinthine Arabic upper town and spas that have been offering cures since antiquity, this vital, salty Mediterranean port town is a fascinating place to visit. **See p.297**

❻ Isola dei Conigli, Lampedusa Paddle or swim across to this idyllic desert-island nature reserve, with its pristine white sands and crystal-clear blue waters. **See p.304**

❼ Linosa Six hours by ferry from Porto Empedocle, Sicily's most remote island is completely unspoilt, with only the briefest of tourist seasons. **See p.306**

HIGHLIGHTS ARE MARKED ON THE MAP ON P.282

AGRIGENTO AND THE SOUTHEAST

0 — 20 kilometres

HIGHLIGHTS

1. Valle dei Templi, Agrigento
2. Montalbano tour, Porto Empedocle
3. Torre Salsa
4. Eraclea Minoa
5. Sciacca
6. Isola dei Conigli, Lampedusa
7. Linosa

N

PELAGIE ISLANDS

0 — 20 kilometres

Pelagie Islands

Linosa

To Porto Empedocle

Lampedusa

Lampione

Lampedusa

Agrigento and the Valle dei Templi

No one comes to **AGRIGENTO** for the town, though its worn medieval streets and buildings soak up the thousands of tourists who come every year to marvel at the **Valle dei Templi**. The substantial remains of **Akragas**, Pindar's "most beautiful city of mortals", these Doric temples strung along a ridge facing the sea, a couple of kilometres below town, are the most captivating of Sicilian Greek remains, unique outside Greece. This is a big and very beautiful site, and it is a shame to see it (as most tourists do) in a single day. Take it easy, with time to sit around and relax among the ruins or in the shade of a tree, and you'll enjoy it all the more. And if your visit coincides with the summer night-time opening of the three main temples, you're in for a truly magical experience.

Agrigento

Despite (or perhaps because of) the undoubted pulling power of the temples which fills the town with tourists for much of the year, **AGRIGENTO** has little sense of identity. Although it retains a historical core of a certain charm, ugly modern suburbs and road viaducts on the coast below lack all sense of proportion and are creeping ever closer to the temples themselves. Meanwhile, government statistics show Agrigento to be one of Italy's poorest towns. Consequently it comes as no surprise to learn that the Mafia has an undue local influence.

Via Atenea and Rabato

Agrigento's main shopping street, the semi-pedestrianized **Via Atenea** is pleasant enough, with a tangle of steep, narrow side streets harbouring ramshackle *palazzi* and minuscule *cortili* (courtyards). At the far end of Via Atenea is Piazza Sinatra, beyond which is the **Rabato** district, the old (and now very dilapidated) Arab quarter, still showing signs of a landslide in 1966 that destroyed much of the historic centre and left 7500 homeless. Although there are a handful of B&Bs in Rabato, full-blown gentrification is dragging its heels.

Santo Spirito

Piazza Santo Spirito • If closed, ring the bell at Piazza Santo Spirito 8

The **Santo Spirito** church and its adjoining convent began life as part of a grand Norman palace belonging to the Chiaramonte family, and were bequeathed to the Cistercian order in the thirteenth century by a widowed baron mourning the death of his young wife. There is usually a young nun about to show you around the **interior**, where florid early eighteenth-century monochrome stuccoes by Serpotta sprawl across the walls and domed trompe l'oeil ceiling.

Back on Piazza Santo Spirito, if you ring the bell at no. 8 and ask for "*dolci di mandorla*", a nun will bring you a tray of almond cakes, which are expensive, chewy, and worth the experience. If you are lucky there will also be sweet couscous (*cuscus dolce*), made to a recipe the nuns inherited – along with seven Tunisian servants – back in the thirteenth century.

SAN PIETRO AND THE BELLS

Pirandello (see p.291) spent much of his boyhood in a house overlooking Piazza Jose Maria Escriva and the church of **San Pietro**. The story goes that Pirandello's father, a supporter of Garibaldi and committed anti-clericist, was so incensed by the racket of the **bells** chiming, that he took a rifle and shot at them. These days, the church is usually closed, but the piazza is a nice place to sit, with views down to the sea.

Museo Civico

Piazza Santo Spirito • Mon–Sat 9am–1pm & 3.30–7.30pm • €2.50 including guided tour

An enticing muddle of Romanesque, Byzantine, Norman, Gothic and Spanish building styles and motifs, with a cloister sliced in half to give the nuns (who live in a modern convent overlooking it) a private garden, the restored remains of the Chiaramonte family's Norman palace now house the **Museo Civico**. The friendly, well-informed custodian will take you to see a chapterhouse with a zigzag Gothic arch, and the tower, with beautiful faded Byzantine frescoes – the holes in the painted saints were created when American soldiers, billeted here during World War II, drilled holes to hang up their kit. The most enticing part of the museum, however, is the **Ethno-anthropological section**, crammed onto the top floor. Created in the 1990s with everyday objects donated by ordinary Agrigentini, it's a fascinating collection, with items ranging from an exam-busting ammunition belt (with cheat-notes instead of ammo), recipe notes, an old-fashioned ice-cream maker and a clothes drier fuelled by almond shells. Don't miss the marvellous **views** of the temples across the fields from the museum windows.

ACCOMMODATION

Arco Ubriaco	3
Atenea 191	5
Camere a Sud	6
Fattoria Mosè	9
Mille e Una Notte	4
Peppe e Romina Melisenda Giambertoni	8
Le Scalette	2
Terrazze di Montelusa	1
Villa Pirandello	7

CAFÉS & RESTAURANTS

L'Ambasciate di Sicilia.	3
Antica Panelleria Musicò	4
Caffeteria Nobel	5
Capotavola	6
La Corte degli Sfizi.	1
Le Cuspidi	7
Per Bacco	2
Posata di Federico Secondo	8
Terra	9
Trattoria dei Templi	10

Santa Maria dei Greci
Via Santa Maria dei Greci • Key from the guardian at Via Santa Maria dei Greci 15

The narrowest and steepest of Agrigento's streets spread up the hill from Piazza Duomo, passing the church of **Santa Maria dei Greci**, built over a Greek temple of the fifth century BC. The flattened columns can be seen in the nave, and through glass panels set into the floor, while outside, visible from an underground tunnel in the flower-filled courtyard, the stylobate and column stumps are incorporated into the church's foundations. Inside are the remains of Byzantine frescoes. Just up from here, Via Duomo leads past a line of decrepit *palazzi* to the massive **Duomo**, set on a terrace at the top of the hill and fronting a spacious, if slightly forlorn, piazza. It has been closed for years.

The Valle dei Templi

The astonishingly well-preserved temples of the **Valle dei Templi** are the most captivating of Sicily's Greek remains. Magnificently strung along a fertile ridge high above the coast, **Akragas** was one of Sicily's richest and most powerful Greek cities – visitors reported that people had ivory furniture, abundant silver and gold, and even made elaborate tombs for their pets. Silver, gold and ivory may have gone, but the sandstone temples are stunning, and the site itself is beautiful too – especially when the almond trees blossom in January and February, and when it's carpeted with wild flowers in the spring.

A road winds down to the Valle dei Templi from Agrigento, passing the **Museo Regionale Archeologico**, a treasure-trove of magnificent artefacts recovered from the site. If you're intent upon doing the temples and museum in one go, you'll need to allow a full day, and arrive as the site opens. It makes sense to start with the **eastern zone**, home to the three major temples, then see the museum, and wind up in the **western zone**, with a restorative wander through the **Giardini di Kolymbetra**.

There are several basic places offering refreshments at the site entrances, and a few nearby restaurants mostly aimed at coach parties, but it's far more pleasant to buy a picnic in Agrigento before coming down to the site.

Brief history
In 581 BC, colonists from nearby Gela and Rhodes founded the city of **Akragas** between the rivers of Hypsas and Akragas. This was the concluding act of expansion that had seen Geloans spread west along the high points of their trade routes, subduing and Hellenizing the indigenous populations as they went. They surrounded the new city with a mighty wall, formed in part by a higher ridge where they placed the acropolis (and where, today, the modern town stands). The southern limit of the ancient city was a second, lower ridge, and it was here, in the so-called **Valle dei Templi** (Valley of the Temples), that the city architects erected their sacred buildings during the fifth century BC. They were – and are – stunning in their effect, reflecting the wealth and luxury of ancient Agrigento: "Athens with improvements", as Henry Adams had it in 1899.

The eastern zone
The **eastern zone** is the more popular, and is at its least crowded in the early morning, or when it's floodlit in striking amber light at night. From the eastern entrance, a path climbs up to the **Tempio di Giunone** (Juno, or Hera), an engaging structure, half in ruins, standing at the very edge of the spur on which the temples were built. A long altar has been reconstructed at the far end of the temple; the patches of red visible here and there on the masonry denote fire damage, probably from the sack of Akragas by the Carthaginians in 406 BC.

VISITING THE VALLE DEI TEMPLI

The Valle dei Templi and the Museo Regionale Archeologico are open daily 8.30am–7pm. An €10 **entry fee** covers both the eastern and western sites, though not the Giardino della Kolymbetra (see opposite); there's also an €13 **combined ticket** covering the temples and the archeological museum.

The easiest way to **get to the temples** is by bus; **buses** #1, #1/, #2, #2/ and #3/ leave every 20min or so from Piazza Rosselli in Agrigento (also stopping outside the train station), and drop off at the museum or at the main car park in between the eastern and western sites. **Taxis** charge about €15 from the city centre to the eastern entrance or museum.

The Giunone, Concordia and Ercole temples are also open for **evening sessions** (July, Aug & Sept Mon–Fri 7.30–10pm, Sat & Sun 7.30pm–midnight; €15). There's a small night-time entrance directly above the Tempio di Giunone, which is best reached from the main site entrance by taxi (€2 per person); there's no public transport to the Giunone entrance, and it's quite a walk. Note that the site is cleared before evening entry is allowed, so you cannot stay inside between 7pm and 7.30pm. Tickets for the evening session go on sale at this ticket office only, from 7.15pm, with a queue forming rapidly.

Hiring a **guide** can bring the history of the site to life and greatly enhance your visit. The talented and informed Michele Gallo (☎380 397 930, ⒲valleyofthetemples.com) is highly recommended. Tours start at €10 per person, plus entry fee.

In August and September, it's also worth looking out for posters advertising open-air **concerts** on the southeastern edge of the archeological zone at Piano San Gregorio, with tickets from €30, though the average price is nearer €50: call ☎0922 20 500 for details of the programme, or ask at the tourist office.

8

Tempio della Concordia

Following the line of the ancient city walls that hug the ridge, Via Sacra leads west to the **Tempio della Concordia** (Concord), dating from around 430 BC. Perfectly preserved and beautifully situated, with fine views to the city and the sea, the tawny stone lends the structure warmth and strength. It's the most complete of the temples, and has required less renovation than the others, mainly thanks to its conversion in the sixth century AD to a Christian church. Restored in the eighteenth century to its (more or less) original layout, the temple has kept its simple lines and slightly tapering columns, although sadly it's fenced off from the public. Circle the temple at least once to get a decent view, and stand well back to admire its elegant proportions.

Tempio di Ercole

From the Tempio della Concordia, Via Sacra continues past the site of the city's ancient necropolis and across what remains of a deep, wheel-rutted Greek street to the oldest of Akragas's temples, the **Tempio di Ercole** (Hercules). Probably begun in the last decades of the sixth century BC, it's a long structure, with nine of the original thirty-eight columns re-erected, and everything else scattered around like a half-finished jigsaw puzzle.

Tempio di Esculapio

No set hours • Free

The quickest way to reach the **Tempio di Esculapio** (Asclepius) is to climb over the wall to the side of the Tempio della Concordia and scramble down to the SS115, from which a dusty track leads down to the undersized temple, which has solid walls instead of a colonnade.

The western zone

The **western zone** is less impressive than the eastern end of the site, though its vast tangle of stone and fallen masonry from an assortment of temples is still engaging.

Most notable is the mammoth pile of rubble that was the **Tempio di Giove** (Jupiter, or Zeus). The largest Doric temple ever known, it was never completed, left in ruins by the Carthaginians and further damaged by earthquakes and the removal of stone to build the port of Porto Empedocle to the south. Still, the stereobate remains, unnaturally huge in scale, while on the ground, face to the sky, lies an 8m-high telamone: a supporting column sculpted as a male figure, arms raised and bent to bear the weight of the temple. As excavations continue, other scattered remains litter the area, not least piles of great column drums marked with a U-shaped groove, which enabled them to be lifted with ropes.

Tempio dei Dioscuri

Beyond the Tempio di Giove, behind the excavated gates and walls of the Greek city, is the earliest sacred site, the **Sanctuary of the Chthonic Deities**, dedicated to the gods of the underworld and marked by two altars (one square and fire-reddened, the other round), dating from the seventh century BC, before the official foundation of the colony. Considerably more romantic-looking are the ruins of the so-called **Tempio dei Dioscuri** (also known as Tempio di Castore e Polluce, or Castor and Pollux), assembled in 1832 from various columns and other random architectonic fragments discovered nearby.

Giardino della Kolymbetra

Daily: April–June 10am–6pm; July–Sept 10am–7pm; Oct to early Jan & Feb–March 10am–5pm • €3

Behind the Temple dei Dioscuri is the entrance to the **Giardino della Kolymbetra**, for which you need a separate ticket. Part of the city's irrigation system in the fifth century BC, it's now an extensive sunken garden, lush and green amid the aridity of the rest of the archeological zone. There is nothing monumental here, but it makes a pleasant relief from temple-touring, the olive, almond and citrus groves overlooked by honey-toned calcareous cliff walls draped with cactus and pitted with caves. It also holds banana, pistachio and pomegranate trees, all meticulously labelled and explained, and a reedy stream.

Museo Regionale Archeologico

Tues–Sat 9am–1pm & 2–7pm, Mon & Sun 9am–1pm • €8, audioguide €5 • ☎ 0922 401 565

The road between town and the temples runs past the excellent **Museo Regionale Archeologico**. It holds an extraordinarily varied collection, devoted to finds from the temples, the ancient city and the surrounding area. There are brief notes in English throughout, and an informative audioguide.

Rooms 1–6

Unusually for an archeological museum, much of what's here holds artistic merit as well as historical interest. You could skip most of the initial local prehistoric and Bronze Age finds, though in **room 1** look out for the gold signet rings, engraved with animals. **Rooms 3 and 4** feature an outstanding vase collection, beguiling sixth- to third-century BC pieces, one of which depicts the burial of a warrior. The highlight is a stunningly detailed white-ground *krater* from 440 BC portraying a valiant Perseus freeing Andromeda. But it's the finds from the temples themselves that make this collection come alive: leaving room 4, you'll pass a series of sculpted lion's-head waterspouts, a common device for draining the water from the roofs of the city's temples, while **room 6** is given over to exhibits relating to the Tempio di Giove, with three enormous stone heads from the temples sitting in the recessed wall. Some useful wooden model reconstructions help to make sense of the disjointed wreckage on the ground, although the prime exhibit is a reassembled telamon stacked against one wall: all the weather damage can't hide the strength implicit in this huge sculpture.

8

Rooms 10–15

The finest statue in the museum is in **room 10**, where the Ephebus, a naked Greek youth, displays a nerveless strength and power that suggests that the model was probably a soldier. Rooms beyond hold coins, inscriptions and finds from local necropolises; typical is an alabaster child's sarcophagus in **room 11** showing poignant scenes from his life, which was cut short by illness. The last couple of rooms contain finds from the rest of the province, one of which, in **room 15**, is the equal of anything that's gone before, amply demonstrating the famed Geloan skill as masters of vase-ware: a fifth-century BC *krater* displays a graphic scene from Homer in which Achilles slays the queen of the Amazons at the moment when he falls in love with her.

San Nicola and the Hellenistic-Roman quarter

In the grounds of the Museo Regionale Archeologico, look out for the Gothic doorway of the adjacent church of **San Nicola**. From the terrace outside, you get an invigorating view over the temple valley, while just beyond is a small odeon (third century BC), used for public meetings, during which the participants stood rather than sat in the narrow rows. Nip over the road on the way out of the museum, too: the **Hellenistic-Roman quarter** opposite (daily 9am–1hr before sunset; free) contains rows of houses, inhabited (on and off) until the fifth century AD, many with mosaic designs still discernible.

San Biagio and the Santuario di Demetra

Via Demetra

Heading back up the road towards town from San Nicola and the Hellenistic-Roman quarter, you'll pass the Norman chapel of **San Biagio**, built over the visible remains of another ancient Greek temple. If you're fortunate, a custodian may appear to lead you down the cliff behind the chapel to the eerie **Santuario di Demetra** (be prepared to tip), where a stone-built chambered shrine hides two dingy caves that stretch 20m into the hillside. The thin corridor between building and caves was a sort of vestibule with niches for water so that worshippers could wash themselves. The most ancient of Agrigento's sacred sites, it was once devoted to the cult of Demeter and Persephone, and in use even before Akragas was founded. A mysterious and evocative place, it's at its best as the sun sets, when shadows flit across the dark and silent caves.

ARRIVAL AND DEPARTURE	AGRIGENTO AND THE VALLE DEI TEMPLI

By bus Services operating from the bus terminal at Agrigento's central Piazza Rosselli include: Camilleri (☎0922 29 136, ⊛camilleriargentoelattuca.it) and Cuffaro (☎091 616 510, ⊛cuffaro.info) to Palermo; Lattuca (☎0922 36 125, ⊛autolineelattuca.it) to Sant'Angelo Muxaro; SAL (☎0922 401 360, ⊛autolineesal.it) to Licata, Gela, Palma di Montechiaro and Porto Empedocle (for the Pelagie Islands); SAIS Trasporti (☎0922 29 324, ⊛saistrasporti.it) to Caltanissetta, Catania and Naro; Salvatore Lumia (☎0922 20 414, ⊛autolineelumia.it) to Castelvetrano, Cattolica Eraclea (for Eraclea Minoa), Marsala, Mazara, Menfi, Sciacca and Trapani. There's a SAIS bus ticket/information office in the corner of the piazza. Otherwise, buy tickets on the bus. Timetables are posted in front of the various companies' stops.

Destinations Caltanissetta (hourly Mon–Sat, 10 daily Sun; 1hr 15min); Catania (hourly Mon–Sat, 10 daily Sun; 2hr 50min); Cattolica Eraclea, for Eraclea Minoa (6 daily Mon–Sat, 1 daily Sun; 1hr–1hr 30min); Licata (14 daily Mon–Sat; 1hr); Palermo (14 daily Mon–Sat, 5 daily Sun; 2hr); Palma di Montechiaro (14 daily Mon–Sat; 35min); Porto Empedocle (1–2 hourly Mon–Sat, 6 daily Sun; 20min); Sant'Angelo Muxaro (3 daily Mon–Sat; 1hr 10min); Sciacca (11 daily Mon–Sat, 2 daily Sun; 1hr–1hr 40min); Trapani (3 daily Mon–Sat, 1 daily Sun; 3hr 20min–4hr).

By train Trains pull in at the edge of the old town at Stazione Centrale, unusually fronted by a garden – don't make the mistake of getting out at Agrigento Bassa, 3km north of town.

Destinations Caltanissetta (5 daily Mon–Sat, 3 daily Sun; 1hr 30min); Enna (3 daily; 1hr 50min–2hr 25min); Palermo (12 daily Mon–Sat, 8 daily Sun; 2hr 15min).

By car The one-way system in Agrigento's old town is a nightmare. Some hotels are signposted, but you may well not be able to park anywhere near where you're staying (ask about *parcheggio* when you book). You can usually bag a space on Viale della Vittoria or Via F. Crispi.

GETTING AROUND

By bus From outside the train station on Piazza Marconi, city buses depart for the temples and the beach at San Leone; buy tickets prior to boarding from kiosks, *tabacchi* or the station bar (€1.10, or €3.30 for ticket valid all day); kiosks stand to either side of Piazza Marconi, though they're not always open on Sundays. You can buy single tickets on board the bus for €1.65.

By taxi There are ranks at Piazzale Aldo Moro (☎0922 21 899) and outside the train station (☎0922 26 670).

Car rental Avis, Piazzetta San Calogero 11, near train station (☎0922 26 353); Hertz, Via Empedocle 35 (☎0922 556 090).

INFORMATION

Tourist information Agrigento holds a couple of tourist offices, with one focusing on the town at Via Atenea 272 (Mon–Fri 9.30am–1.30pm, also Tues & Thurs 3.30–7.30pm; ☎0922 596 168), and one covering the whole province, located inside the Prefettura building at the back of Piazzale Aldo Moro (Mon–Fri 8am–2pm & 3–7pm, Sat 8am–1pm; ☎0922 593 227 or ☎800 236 37); both can supply useful maps and brochures. There's also a desk at Stazione Centrale (Mon–Fri 9am–1pm) and a kiosk at the Valle dei Templi western zone car park (Mon–Sat 9am–1.30pm).

ACCOMMODATION

Finding **accommodation** in Agrigento itself is rarely a problem, although in peak season the nearby coastal resorts fill fast. All the budget choices, primarily small family-run establishments, are in the old town above the temples, and there are several B&Bs signed on the main Via Atenea. Tour groups tend to stay in the grander hotels a few kilometres east of town at **Villaggio Mosè**, an unattractive traffic-choked suburb on the coast road into Agrigento, though the hotels themselves – glossy, three- and four-star holiday palaces – are fine. The nearest **campsites** lie 6km south of town at the unappealing coastal resort of San Leone, also the site of a good B&B.

Arco Ubriaco Via Sferri 12 ☎335 745 6532, ⓦarcoubriaco .com. Three rooms in a warm, welcoming family house on the edge of Rabato, named for the tilting medieval arch leading off the living room. There's wi-fi, and all rooms have bathroom, a/c and a fridge. The motherly owner is adept at making all guests feel part of the family. **€60**

Atenea 191 Via Atenea 191 ☎0922 595 594, ⓦatenea191.com. A real find, this B&B on the main drag has huge, tastefully designed en-suite rooms, with balconies offering distant views of the sea. One room has frescoed walls and ceiling. Breakfast is served on the roof terrace in summer. No a/c but ceiling fans in all the rooms. **€85**

Camere a Sud Via Ficani 6 ☎349 638 4424, ⓦcameresud.it. This bijou B&B in an alley off Via Atenea has charming hosts, three vividly coloured en-suite rooms with a/c, paintings by Catanese artist Antonio Recca and a roof terrace for breakfasts. Internet access available; no credit cards. **€70**

Fattoria Mosè Via M. Pascal 4, Villaggio Mosè ☎0922 606 115, ⓦfattoriamose.com. On an estate run by the same family for 200 years, this *agriturismo* midway between the sea and the temples (signposted from the SS115) offers a simple B&B option as well as self-catering apartments in a converted stable block. Rooms are on the spartan side but there's a huge garden and a small swimming pool. Breakfasts and meals (€10 for lunch, €25 for dinner) are mostly home-produced and organic, and the family also run cookery courses. There's free internet and a laundry service. Closed Nov–Feb. Rooms **€96**

Mille e Una Notte Via Garibaldi 46 ☎320 483 5856, ⓦmilleeunanottebeb.it. Sensitively run B&B on the fringe of the evocative Rabat quarter, with spick-and-span rooms including two sleeping four and five and a small apartment with cooking facilities. Doubles **€88**

★ **Peppe e Romina Melisenda Giambertoni** Via Passeggiata Archeologica 29 ☎348 762 2790, ⓔcasinagiambertoni@gmail.com. There is simply no better place to stay in Agrigento than these three simple apartments on the ground floor of a nineteenth-century country villa set just between an olive grove and the Roman-Hellenistic area of the archeological zone, a short walk from the museum. They may not be luxurious, but you have everything you need, and the opportunity to sit outside your apartment at night, looking at the temples, is without a price. Weekly rates from **€500**

Le Scalette Salita Iacono 3 ☎335 745 6532, ⓦbeblescalette.com. Run by the same people as *Arco Ubriaco*, this house is higher up in town, close to Santo Spirito. There are four small but clean rooms, and a kitchen-dining room for the use of guests. **€60**

Terrazze di Montelusa Piazza Lena 6 ☎0922 28 556, ⓦterrazzedimontelusa.it. Smart, clean and airy second-floor B&B at the far western end of the old town, with large, fully equipped rooms and a charming,

8

knowledgeable host who will offer useful tips for the area and even trot out a few tunes on the piano if you ask nicely. There are great views from the roof terraces, where a garden is being planned. Free internet. No credit cards. **€80**

★ **Villa Pirandello** Via Francesco Crispi 34 **☎** 0922 22 275, **🌐** bbvillapirandello.it. A Sicilian-Yorkshire family run this B&B in a nineteenth-century villa where the dramatist Luigi Pirandello's wife lived (and apparently chucked furniture out of the windows at the barracks next door during one of the spells of madness to which she was prone). With five rooms, a shady garden and a sunny terrace, a more therapeutic post-temples spot is hard to imagine. And you don't even need to leave for dinner, as the *La Terra* restaurant (see below) is in its garden. Breakfasts are superb, featuring fresh fruit and artisan pastries. **€75**

EATING AND DRINKING

Agrigento has a fairly good choice of **restaurants**, many clustered around Via Atenea and offering some kind of *menu turistico*. Unsurprisingly, they tend to be a bit touristy, though prices are usually low. There are two distinct areas for **cafés** and **bars**. The town-centre *passeggiata* focuses on Via Atenea, and once the shops reopen in the late afternoon the whole street is packed. To watch the action, choose a seat at one of the little bars in Piazzale Aldo Moro, at the beginning of Via Atenea, a nice place to sit in the early evening, despite the occasional burst of organ music from a local crooner. For sunsets and views, stroll along the leafy Viale della Vittoria, where four or five cafés cater to a local family crowd.

L'Ambasciate di Sicilia Via Giambertoni 2 **☎** 0922 20 526. Fairly standard food in folksy surroundings, though tables on the outdoor terrace provide one of the few good views in town. The *antipasto rustico*, house pasta and *involtini* are good choices (mains €7–9 for meat, €13–17 for fish dishes). Tues–Sun lunch & dinner, plus Mon dinner Aug.

Antica Panelleria Musicò Viale della Vittoria s/n (no phone). This little van parked at the beginning of Viale della Vittoria is an Agrigento institution, selling *pane e panelle* (chickpea-flour fritters in soft bread rolls) since 1954. Daily 8.30am–1pm & 5–8.30pm.

Caffeteria Nobel Viale della Vittoria 11 **☎** 0922 24 562. A relaxing spot for breakfast (amazing pastries), an ice cream or a beer under the shady trees of the avenue. Daily 8am–late.

Capotavola Viale della Vittoria 15–17 **☎** 0922 21 484. Perfect for families – it even has a designated play area screened from the main restaurant by a glass window, so you can keep an eye on the kids while you eat in peace. There are pizzas (€5–8, with mini-pizzas at a euro less), including the crowd-pleasing *ricottina*, with mozzarella, ricotta, ham and parmesan, plus risotto with shellfish and *cedro* (*citron*), spaghetti with seafood and toasted breadcrumbs, and fish dishes featuring red prawns from Mazara, further up the coast. From Tuesday to Friday there is a *giropasta* – you get as much pasta as you want (though you have to finish one plate before qualifying for another) for €15 per head including a drink. Otherwise a full meal will cost around €35. Daily lunch & dinner.

La Corte degli Sfizi Cortile Contarini 169 **☎** 349 579 2922. Little trattoria opposite Via Atenea with a summer walled courtyard where you can eat tasty pasta (like *cavatelli* with aubergines), or dishes such as grilled sausage or swordfish, and there's pizza in the evening.

Nice staff and very reasonable food for the price. Fixed-price menus including wine cost €20 (meat) and €22 (fish). Mon & Wed–Sun lunch & dinner, plus Tues dinner in summer.

Le Cuspidi Piazza Cavour 19 **☎** 0922 24 562. Come to this *gelateria* for the best ice creams in town – try the fresh ricotta, pistachio or almond. Daily 9am–late.

Per Bacco Vicolo Lo Presti **☎** 0922 553 369. Fish dominates the menu in this small, smart trattoria favoured by locals. There's a good selection of salads (€5–6) and risottos (€7–9). Expect to pay around €30 for a full meal including drinks. Tues–Sun dinner only.

★ **Posata di Federico Secondo** Piazza Cavour 19 **☎** 0922 28 289. Lovely, elegant restaurant, just off tree-lined Viale della Vittoria. The food is superb, strictly seasonal, with the menu divided according to the main ingredient (artichoke, veal etc) rather than the usual *primi* and *secondi*, so you may need a little help deciphering it. There's no pressure to order a four-course meal – try it for dinner, and you may well decide to come back for a light *antipasto* lunch or plate of pasta the next day. The signature dish is beef fillet with gorgonzola and honey – amazing! Expect to pay €35–40 for a full meal, but you could have a nice light lunch for under €15. Mon–Sat lunch & dinner.

La Terra Via Francesco Crispi 34 **☎** 0922 29 742 or **☎** 329 091 4850. Lovely relaxed setting in the garden of playwright Luigi Pirandello's former summer villa, with a well-researched but unpretentious menu and wine list inspired by the Slow Food ethos. Menu is seasonal, making great use of Sicilian produce – a fillet of dentex (similar to sea bass) in a potato crust, or linguine lightly dressed with mussels, cherry tomatoes and *tenerumi* (courgette plant fronds). Desserts include a Modica chocolate mousse. Around €45 a head for a full meal. Tues–Sun: summer lunch & dinner; winter dinner only.

Trattoria dei Templi Via Panoramica dei Templi 15 ☎ 0922 403 110. Fresh seafood in a traditional restaurant halfway between town and the Valle dei Templi. Among their ample pasta dishes, opt for *panzerotti della casa* (ravioli with seafood sauce; €7), or splash out on the *fettuccine all'aragosta*, served with a chunk of lobster (€14). Mon–Sat lunch & dinner; winter closed Fri & Sun.

DIRECTORY

Banks and exchange ATMs at banks along Via Atenea.
Hospital Ospedale Civile San Giovanni di Dio, Contrada Consolida, just outside town (☎ 0922 442 111, or for emergencies ☎ 0922 591 221).
Internet Internet Train, Cortile Contarini, opposite *La Corte degli Sfizi* (Mon–Sat 9.15am–1.15pm & 3.30–9pm); you can also log on at the provincial tourist office in the Prefettura (first 15min free).
Pharmacies Averna, Via Atenea 325 (☎ 0922 26 093); Maria Teresa Indelicato, Piazza Vittorio Emanuele 13 (☎ 0922 23 889); Minacori, Via Atenea 91 (☎ 0922 25 089). All are open Mon–Fri 9am–1pm & 4–8pm, Sat & Sun; the usual late-opening rota system is in operation, with details posted outside all pharmacies.
Police Call ☎ 112 or ☎ 113, or contact the Questura on Piazza Vittorio Emanuele (☎ 0922 483 111), or the Carabinieri at Piazzale Aldo Moro 2 (☎ 0922 499 000).
Post office Piazza Vittorio Emanuele (Mon–Fri 8am–6.30pm, Sat 8am–12.30pm).

Around Agrigento

The area around Agrigento has several places worth visiting that can be easily seen in day-trips from the town, and that are of interest in particular to fans of Sicilian literature – the highlights being **Caos**, birthplace of Luigi Pirandello, **Porto Empedocle**, birthplace of Montalbano creator Andrea Camilleri, and the ancestral seat of **Giuseppe Tomasi di Lampedusa**, author of *The Leopard*.

8

Caos

Southwest of Agrigento, at the end of the flyover leading out towards Porto Empedocle, the suburb of **CAOS** was the birthplace of writer **Luigi Pirandello** and the inspiration for the Taviani Brothers' film, *Kaos*, based on four of Pirandello's short stories. One of the greats of twentieth-century Italian literature, Pirandello is best-known for his dramatic works, such as *Six Characters in Search of an Author* and *Henry IV*, though his 1934 Nobel Prize was awarded as much for his novels and short stories. He had a tragic life: his wife was committed to an asylum, having lapsed into insanity following the ruin of her family and the birth of their third son, and for much of his life Pirandello was forced to write to supplement his frugal living as a teacher. His drama combines elements of tragedy and comedy with keenly observed dialogue, and the nature of identity and personality, reality, illusion and the absurd are all recurring themes. Pirandello's ideas – and innovations – formed the blueprint for much subsequent twentieth-century drama.

Casa Natale di Luigi Pirandello

Contrada Caos, just off the SS115 and past the Valle dei Templi • Daily 9am–1pm & 2–7pm • €4 • ☎ 0922 511 826, ⓦ lavalledeitempli.it • Bus #1/ runs here from Agrigento

Although he left Agrigento while still young, Pirandello spent time here every summer at the **Casa Natale di Luigi Pirandello**, where you can see the study in which he wrote, crammed with foreign editions of his works. As well as a couple of murals he painted, it holds stacks of photos, including one sent by George Bernard Shaw, and a fifth-century vase, depicting a bearded man attacking a young woman, that was formerly used as an urn for Pirandello's ashes. After seeing the house, with its bamboo and daub interior, you can wander down through the **grounds** to where the writer's ashes are interred, though the views he once enjoyed over the sea are now ruined by a patch of industrial horror.

Porto Empedocle

Six kilometres southwest of Agrigento, **PORTO EMPEDOCLE** is mainly of interest as the departure point for ferries to the Pelagie Islands (see p.300) – unless, that is, you happen to be a fan of **Andrea Camilleri**, who was born here. Porto Empedocle is Camilleri's Vigàta, the fictional home to many characters including the beguiling **Inspector Montalbano** (see box below), whom Camilleri based at the police station here, and who lived on the beach at nearby Marinella. Indeed, if you enter town from the south, you will pass a sign recently erected by the local council proclaiming "Vigàta (Porto Empedocle)".

Though it's an unprepossessing, functional port, much of it dominated by an enormous cement works, Porto Empedocle's workaday ambience makes a welcome

---

THE MONTALBANO PHENOMENON

Inspector Salvo Montalbano is the most famous policeman in Italy, and his creator, **Andrea Camilleri**, a chain-smoking octogenarian native of Porto Empedocle, is the country's most successful writer. The Montalbano books – twenty novels and four collections of short stories – have sold well over eleven million copies in Italy, while episodes of the Montalbano TV series regularly attract an astonishing nine million viewers here. Montalbano fever is fast becoming an international phenomenon, too. The TV series has been broadcast in fifty countries, including the UK and Australia; *The Potter's Field*, the latest Montalbano novel to be translated into English, won the UK Crime Writers' Association International Dagger award in 2012; and intriguingly, Police HQ Scotland Yard in London recently requested copies of the entire TV series for use in "professional training courses".

A very human policeman, Montalbano lives on a beach, begins every morning with a swim, savours what he eats in silence with an almost religious passion, and suffers from bad digestion. Although the setting for the novels is contemporary, the core of Montalbano's world remains the provincial Sicily of Camilleri's youth, a fictional place in which elements of modern life, such as the mobile phone and computer, can at times seem anachronistic.

When it came to filming the TV series, however, director Alberto Sironi decided to re-create Camilleri's Sicily not in Agrigento, but in the province of Ragusa, perhaps because Agrigento and Porto Empedocle were deemed a little too real for the tastes of TV viewers. Below are **locations** in Agrigento and Porto Empedocle that you could easily visit yourself, though keen Montalbano fans are unlikely to regret splashing out on a guided tour of the sites with Michele Gallo (☎ 360 397 930, ⊛ sicilytourguides.net); group prices start at €150 for a half-day tour.

MONTALBANO LOCATIONS

Questura The Police Headquarters (and base of the irascible Commissioner Bonetti Algheretti and his odious assistant Lattes) is in fact Agrigento's police station, on Piazza Municipio at the beginning of Via Atenea.

Rabato Semi-destroyed by a landslide, Agrigento's Arab quarter, just to the north of Via Garibaldi, serves as the home of Montelusa lowlifes including the Tunisian prostitute mother of Montalbano's almost-adopted son.

La Mannara The car park and abandoned factory used as a base by Gigi and his prostitutes lie behind the ENI, at the edge of Porto Empedocle on the road to Agrigento.

The "dwarf skyscrapers" A frequently recurring cityscape detail of the TV shows, these occupy the ridge above the port at Porto Empedocle.

Montalbano's flat rock The place the inspector comes to digest both his lunches and the complexities of his current case lies at the end of the dock in Porto Empedocle.

Chiesa Madre This church on Via Roma, the main street of Porto Empedocle, provides the setting for several funerals, some of them Mafia affairs.

Via Granet This little street off Porto Empedocle's Via Roma serves as the site of former restaurant *San Calogero*, and the home of the observant Maestra Clementina and the melancholy violinist.

Bar Kenia, Marinella A favourite meeting place for Montalbano and his Swedish soul mate (and occasional lover) Ingrid, this bar is still functioning at the end of Marinella beach.

Scala dei Turchi Meeting place for Montalbano and his informer and ex-schoolmate, Gigi.

Da Enzo Montalbano's favourite restaurant is open for business in Porto Empedocle (see opposite).

antidote to tourist-ridden Agrigento. If you're waiting for a ferry, you can enjoy a pleasant stroll along the town's spruced-up pedestrian walkway to check out the statue of Detective Montalbano on the main street (inspired by the books, not the TV series, with moustache and cigarette), or dine at good, inexpensive fish **restaurants** including (if you're lucky) the eccentric fish trattoria so beloved of Montalbano (see below).

ARRIVAL AND DEPARTURE

PORTO EMPEDOCLE

By bus SAL buses for Porto Empedocle leave once or twice hourly from Agrigento's bus and train stations, six times on Sunday (a 15–20min journey), dropping you in Piazza Italia, one block from the waterfront; the last bus from Agrigento leaves at 9pm (7pm on Sun).

By ferry and hydrofoil Services to Lampedusa and

Linosa leave from the town's dock.

Ferry destinations Lampedusa (6 weekly; 8hr 15min); Linosa (6 weekly; 5hr 45min).

Hydrofoil destinations Lampedusa (May–Oct 6 weekly; 4hr 15min); Linosa (May–Oct 6 weekly; 3hr).

By taxi A taxi from Agrigento will cost about €25.

EATING AND DRINKING

La Lampara Via F. Crispi 3 ☎ 339 490 6833. Housed in what looks like a long wooden shed, a few minutes' walk from the port along the seafront, offering an abundant three-course meal plus good local wine for around €25. Open erratically for lunch & dinner.

Il Timone da Enzo Via Garibaldi 11 ☎ 334 342 7177. This trattoria is more engagingly idiosyncratic in reality than it is in the pages of Camilleri. Located on a hill above the port, you can't miss it – it's the shack with the battered boat on its roof, several hastily erected

chipboard walls and the broken plastic (once-illuminated) sign on which you may (or may not) be able to make out the word "ENZO". It usually opens in the evenings, doesn't usually open at lunchtime, and often has the kind of dishes that would bring tears of joy and nostalgia to the eyes of Montalbano ... *polpette* made of *neonati* (newborn fish), spaghetti *al nivuru di siccia* (with squid ink) and glistening fresh *triglie* (red mullet). About €25 per head, including carafes of the strong local plonk. No set hours.

8

Scala dei Turchi

About 7km west of Porto Empedocle, following signs for Realmonte, the stunning **Scala dei Turchi** beach lies at the bottom of furrowed and gleaming-white cliffs. Prone to landslides, the road above it collapsed in the winter of 2013, and was barricaded off to traffic at the time of writing (though you can still walk down to the beach). This only adds to the traffic congestion during the summer and on sunny weekends. If you want cliffs and sands without the crowds, continue on to Torre Salsa (see below).

ARRIVAL AND DEPARTURE

SCALA DEI TURCHI

By car As there are no bus connections to Scala dei Turchi from Agrigento, the easiest way to get here is by car.

ACCOMMODATION AND EATING

Lido Scala dei Turchi Scala dei Turchi, Realmonte ☎ 0922 814 563. At the top of the steps leading down to Scala dei Turchi beach, this lido restaurant provides welcome sustenance in the form of delicious seafood meals for less than €25. Daily lunch & dinner; closed Mon Sept–June.

Scala dei Turchi Via Grande 171, Realmonte ☎ 0922 816 238. A little B&B in the village of Realmonte – the main attraction being that it is close to the stunning white cliffs of Scala dei Turchi and the unspoilt beaches at Giallonardo, near Siciliana, and Torre Salsa, between Siciliana Marina and Eraclea Minoa. **€50**

Torre Salsa

Protected by a WWF nature reserve, and stretching for endless kilometres, the long sandy beach of **Torre Salsa**, backed by cliffs of mark and selenite crystal, has none of the crowds of Scala dei Turchi. For most of the year, underground springs make the dirt road to the beach inaccessible by car, though if you don't mind a muddy walk, you could park once the going gets too tough for your car, and continue to the beach on foot; just follow signs for the Ingresso Pantano. If you want to drive all the way to the beach you will need to enter via the *Agriturismo Torre Salsa*, which charges €3 entrance per person. Both are well signposted from the SS115.

ARRIVAL AND DEPARTURE TORRE SALSA

By car Torre Salsa is off the SS115 between Agrigento and Sciacca; turn off at the junction marked Montallegro/Bovo Marina /Torre Salsa.

ACCOMMODATION

Agriturismo Torre Salsa Torre Salsa ☎336 945 967, ⓦtorresalsa.it. German-run *agriturismo* with several rooms and apartments as well as parking places on the beach for campers. The motto is *mente sana in corpo sano* ("a healthy mind in a healthy body"), and there's an emphasis on energetic healthy pursuits such as Nordic walking and mountain biking, with several marked trails. There is a restaurant, and home-cultivated organic vegetables are on sale for self-caterers. Rooms **€116**

Palma di Montechiaro

Shabby **PALMA DI MONTECHIARO**, half an hour's dive southeast of Agrigento, was once the seat of the Lampedusa family, the last of whom – **Giuseppe Tomasi di Lampedusa** – wrote the acclaimed novel, *The Leopard*. He died in 1957 (*The Leopard* was published a year later), but the palace in Palma had lain derelict for a long time before that. Indeed, far more resonant for *Leopard* fans are the ruins in the western Sicilian town of Santa Margherita di Belice (see p.358). Today, the only echoes of the great feudal family recorded in the novel are to be found in Palma's imposing seventeenth-century **Chiesa Matrice**, built by one of Lampedusa's ancestors and approached by a wide flight of crumbling steps, and the ruined site of the **Castello di Palma**, a few kilometres west of town at the end of a small track.

Naro

The medieval hill-town of **NARO** makes a good destination for a scenic drive inland. The finest of the buildings are the Chiaramonte **castello** at Naro's highest point, and the nearby ruins of the old cathedral; other churches in this walled and battlemented town are emphatically Baroque. Architecturally harmonious though Naro is, the real attraction is not so much the end destination as the drive itself from Palma, which is rewarded by extensive sweeping views down to the coast.

Licata

LICATA is a pleasant little port town some 50km down the coast from Agrigento, though there's certainly nothing left of ancient Phintias, the settlement founded here in 280 BC by Greeks from Gela, whose own city had been destroyed in successive attacks. Instead, Licata's historic centre is largely Baroque, with a lower town split into two distinct halves. Pavement cafés line the two wide avenues – Corso Roma and Corso Umberto – that form an L-shape at the heart of town meeting at Piazza Progresso. Behind here, the narrow crisscrossed alleys of the old town reach back to the harbour. There's a lido and **beach** just up from the harbour, though as Licata is still a working port, full of maritime hardware, it's not exactly enticing. For a view over the harbour, climb to the top of the town from the main Corso Roma and then work your way around the hill to reach an imposing sixteenth-century **castello**. Other strolls can take in the lively old-town **market** (Mon–Sat from early morning till around 2pm), held in the cobbled square in front of the church, and some of Licata's good *palazzi*, the most prominent being the gargoyle-studded **Palazzo Canarelli** on Corso Roma. Housed in a sixteenth-century convent on Piazza Sant'Angelo, and reached by walking down Via Dante off Corso Umberto, the **Museo Archeologico** displays a good deal of local prehistoric and Greek material, as well as medieval art, but has been closed for a lengthy renovation for some years now, though there are rumours that it is due to reopen shortly; call for an update (☎0922 77 6263).

ARRIVAL AND DEPARTURE
LICATA

By bus Buses pull up on Corso Roma, right in the centre; the bar at Corso Roma 36 posts timetables and sells tickets for the regular daily departures to Agrigento, Gela, Catania (and Catania Airport) and Palermo. Main bus companies are Etnabus, Interbus, SAIS and SAL.

By train Licata is served by far fewer trains than buses; principal destinations are Caltanissetta and Gela. The train station is a 5min walk from the bus station.

ACCOMMODATION AND EATING

Antica Dimora San Girolamo Piazza San Girolamo ☎0922 875 010, ⌨dimorasangirolamo.it. This is a great little B&B in the heart of the old fishing quarter, La Marina, housed in an old building full of character on an atmospheric square where, in fine weather, guests are served first-class breakfasts *al fresco*. €50

La Madia Corso Re Capriata 22, off Corso Serrovia ☎0922 771 443, ⌨ristorantelamadia.it. A pricey, critically acclaimed restaurant where world-class but distinctly Sicilian dishes can be sampled on a tasting menu for €80. Summer Mon & Wed–Sat lunch & dinner, Sun dinner only; winter Mon & Wed–Sat lunch & dinner, Sun lunch only.

L'Oste e il Sacrestano Via Sant'Andrea 19 ☎0922 774 736. A small, smart but unpretentious *hostaria* and wine bar near the Duomo and Corso Vittorio Emanuele, where the tasting menu of five small courses (€48) is highly recommended. Tues–Sat lunch & dinner, Sun lunch only.

8

North of Agrigento

The lively spa and port town of **Sciacca** and the lovely ancient site of **Eraclea Minoa** are the best-known destinations to the north of Agrigento, but if you have a car, Sciacca makes a good base for a day's circular drive, taking in a few minor inland towns, including the superbly sited village of **Caltabellotta**. Local buses also make certain simple excursions into the hinterland possible.

Sant'Angelo Muxaro

Some 30km north of Agrigento, in the steeply sloping Platani River valley, the small agricultural centre of **SANT'ANGELO MUXARO** boasts a number of local *tholos* (tombs) hollowed out of the rock in dome-shaped caves. The earliest date from the eleventh century BC, but most are from around the eighth to the fifth centuries BC, and recall Minoan and Mycenaean examples in design. You'll spot them as you approach the bare

---

THE *ALBERGO DIFFUSO* EXPERIENCE

Sant'Angelo boasts a great **accommodation** option which transforms the village from a day-trip destination into a place where you might well be tempted to stay a night or two. Run by the Val di Kam agency, who have a "reception" at Piazza Umberto I 31 (☎0922 919 670 or ☎339 530 5989, ⌨valdikam.it), it's known as an **albergo diffuso** – a hotel that is "diffused" throughout the village, with en-suite rooms (€60) in a number of different houses – it's a formula that's becoming increasingly popular in Sicily, and it's proving to be a great way of reviving small rural centres. Breakfast is usually a grand affair with local delicacies, served in your room, and the agency can also arrange local dinners in private houses. Val di Kam also organize **hiking**, **caving** and **archeological trips** around Sant'Angelo (from around €50 per person), can arrange pick-ups from Agrigento and is a mine of useful information on the area.

hillside on which the village stands: the road leads up past a ramshackle brick wall, beyond which a path heads along the sheer rock to the "beehive" caves. At the bottom, the largest is known locally as the **Tomba del Principe**: later converted into a Byzantine chapel, it's half-hidden by overhanging trees and you may have to backtrack to get inside. Like all the others, it's empty now, the finds scattered in various museums around Europe.

ARRIVAL AND DEPARTURE   SANT'ANGELO MUXARO

By bus From Agrigento, buses for Sant'Angelo run by Lattuca (☎ 0922 36 125, ⌨ autolineelattuca.it) leave from Piazza Vittorio Emanuele (Mon–Sat at 10.30am, 2.10pm & 6.30pm; the last bus back leaves at 4pm).

By car Drivers should take the SS189 branching off westward for Aragona and Sant'Angelo, or choose the more wriggly but faster SS118 via Raffadali.

Eraclea Minoa

Thirty-five kilometres along the coast northwest of Agrigento is the ancient Greek site of **ERACLEA MINOA**. According to the historian Diodorus, this was originally named Minoa after the Cretan king Minos, who chased Daedalus from Crete to Sicily and founded a city where he landed. The Greeks settled here in the sixth century BC, later adding the tag Heraklea. A buffer between the two great cities of Akragas, 40km to the east, and Selinus (Selinunte), 60km west, Eraclea was dragged into endless border disputes, but flourished nonetheless. Most of what's left dates from the fourth century BC, the city's most important period, three hundred years or so before it fell into decline.

While you're here, you'll be hard put to resist a trip down to the **beach**, one of the finest on Sicily's southern coast, backed by pine trees, chalky cliffs and a strip of holiday homes. It's hideously busy in July and August; unless you get here early, you'll never find a space to park.

The site

Daily 9am–1hr before sunset; may close Sun in winter, call to check • €4 • ☎ 0922 846 005

The **site** sits on a ridge high above a beautiful arc of sand, with the mouth of the River Platani on the other side. Among the most attractive of all Greek sites in Sicily, it occupies a headland of which only around a third has so far been excavated. What there is to see is the fruit of successive excavations by foreign universities, who, together with the local *Comune*, have landscaped the remains to good effect. Don't stray too far off the paths, though, as snakes lurk in the undergrowth.

Apart from the city **walls**, once 6km long and with a good part still standing, the most impressive remains are of the sandstone **theatre**. Now restored to its former glory after years of deterioration of the seats (which are made of very soft stone), the theatre is protected from the worst of the elements by a plastic roof.

Above the theatre, excavations have also revealed tombs and traces of a Greco-Roman temple, while below stand the ruins of a grand house, with fragments of Roman mosaics, though these are covered and inaccessible. Many of the finds are displayed in a small on-site **museum**.

ARRIVAL AND DEPARTURE   ERACLEA MINOA

By bus You can get here between June and September by bus from Cattolica Eraclea, which has bus connections from Agrigento, but outside the summer months you're going to have to take any bus running between Agrigento and Sciacca and ask the driver to let you off at the turning on the SS115: from here, you'll have to walk the 3.5km to the site. Heading on, walk back to the SS115, where you should be able to flag down any bus bound for Sciacca.

ACCOMMODATION

Eraclea Minoa Village ☎ 0922 846 023 (summer), ☎ 0922 29 101 (winter), ⌨ eracleaminoavillage.it. Pine-shaded campsite a few steps from the sea which also has one- and two-bedroom bungalows and a bar, pizzeria, restaurant and disco. Camping **€7** per person, plus **€10** per pitch; bungalows **€70**

Sciacca

Just over 30km further up the coast from Eraclea Minoa, **SCIACCA** is a working fishing port that conceals a good-looking upper town which is virtually untouched by tourism. A spa town for nearby Selinus in ancient times, it enjoyed great prosperity under the Arabs, from whom its modern name is thought to derive (the Arabic *xacca* meaning "from the water"). The town was at the centre of a feud between Catalan and Norman families that simmered on for a century, resulting in the deaths of a good half of the local population. Several notable buildings are scattered about, which infuse Sciacca's agreeable Mediterranean air with more than a passing historical interest and make for some pleasant strolling through the weaving streets.

The town is the main centre of **ceramic** production on Sicily's south coast, and you'll see colourful plates, vases and ornaments on sale everywhere. Its spa waters are still potent, and Sciacca remains a popular destination for Italians seeking all manner of cures, many of which are available on the state. There's also a decent arc of sandy **beach** 1km west of the centre at the end of Via Gaie di Garaffe.

The upper town

The still-walled upper town can be entered through any of the three grand gates remaining of the original seven. The westernmost, **Porta San Salvatore**, leads onto the **Chiesa del Carmine**, whose facade is lent a skew-whiff air by an off-centre Gothic rose window. Past the church, up Via P. Gerardi, the fifteenth-century **Palazzo Steripinto** is even more ungainly, its embossed exterior only partially offset by some slender arched windows.

From Palazzo Steripinto, the main **Corso Vittorio Emanuele** runs right the way down to the lovely **Piazza A. Scandaliato**, a large terrace with some good cafés, enhanced by wide views over the port and distant bays. The most enduring Arab legacy in town is the street layout and, back from the piazza, above the **Duomo**, a Moorish knot of passages and steep alleys leads up to the rather feeble remains of the fourteenth-century **Castello Conti Luna**, which belonged to one of the feuding families that disrupted medieval Sciacca. A little way down from here, the twelfth-century church of **San Nicolò** is a tiny construction with three apses and some elegant blind arcading.

The port

Steps from Piazza A. Scandaliato lead down the cliffside to the lower town and **port**, whose most distinctive feature is the hexagonally steepled modern church of **San Pietro**. Just north of the church you'll see further steps, each riser decorated with contemporary ceramic **tiles**, some depicting sea life, some just patterned, and each one different. Fishing vessels lie tied up at the quayside, lorries unload salt by the bucketful for anchovy- and sardine-processing, and repairmen, foundry workers and chandlers go about their business, breaking off work for a drink in some scruffy portside bar.

ARRIVAL AND INFORMATION

SCIACCA

By bus Buses pull up by the Villa Comunale (the town gardens) at the eastern end of Sciacca. Bus tickets are sold at the *Bar Giglio* on Viale della Vittoria for Lumia services to Agrigento, Caltabellotta, Castelvetrano and Trapani, and from the *Antico Chiosco* bar in the centre of Piazza Santa Friscia for Gallo services to Palermo.

Destinations Agrigento (9 daily Mon–Sat, 2 daily Sun; 1hr 10min–1hr 40min); Caltabellotta (4 daily Mon–Sat; 45min); Castelvetrano (3 daily Mon–Sat, 1 daily Sun; 40–55min); Palermo (8–10 daily Mon–Sat, 5 daily Sun; 1hr 45min);

Trapani (3 daily Mon–Sat, 1 daily Sun; 2hr–2hr 20min).

By car Parking is problematic in Sciacca – ask locals for advice.

Tourist information Both of the town's tourist offices are on Corso Vittorio Emanuele, at no. 84 (Mon–Fri 9am–1pm, also Wed 3.30–7pm; ☎ 0925 22 744) and no. 94 (Mon–Fri 8am–2pm, extended opening in summer; ☎ 0925 20 478, ⓦ comunedisciacca.it), and can supply maps, public transport timetables, accommodation lists and information in English, though not everything is up to date.

Castello Incantato, Monte San Calógero, Eraclea Minoa, ▲ Agrigento, Campsite & 2

SCIACCA

N

■ ACCOMMODATION	
Allai	4
Casa Jacaranda	2
Conte Luna	3
Grand Hotel delle Terme	5
Locanda al Moro	1

● RESTAURANTS	
La Lampara	2
Porto San Paolo	3
La Vela	1

SS115

VIA G. CUSMANO

VIA E. RAVASIO

VIA DELLE NUOVO TERME

Giardino delle Terme

VIA FIGULI

Stabilimento Termale

VIA DELLA VITTORIA

VIALE DELLA VITTORIA

VIA VALVERDE

VIA AGATOCLE

Porta San Calogero

Castello Conti Luna

Bus Stop ★

Bus Stop ★

Villa Comunale

PIAZZA S. FRISCIA

Rocca Regina

VIA GIGLIO

VIA CIACCIO

VIA AMATO

San Nicolò

PIAZZA S. NICOLÒ

PORT A S. PIETRO

VIA S. PIETRO

VIA MADONNUZZA

VIA S. CATERINA

CORSO SAN PAOLO

VIA SCAGLIONE

PIAZZA G. NOCETO

VIA S. NICOLA

FRISCIA

VIA S. CATERINA

VIA GIUSEPPE LICATA

EMAN. UELE

PIAZZA S. FRISCIA

VIA VETRANO

VIA P. PUCCIO

S. MICHELE

Duomo

CORSO VITTORIO

VIA CALOGERO

VIA QUEVLA

FILIPPO TOMMASO FAZELLO

VIA GIRILO

VIA MASCOLO

VIA MICHELE

PIAZZA PURGATORIO

PIAZZA DUOMO

VIA PORTA DI MARE

Chiesa del Collegio

VIA ROMA

PIAZZA A. SCANDALIATO

VIA PORTA DI MARE

CORSO

CORSO

VIA S. SALVATORE PASSAGGIO

VIA RAMI

VIA GARIBALDI

PIAZZA MATTEOTTI

ⓘ ⓘ

VIA CARICATORE

VIA ALBERO

PIAZZA MURA DI VEGA

VIA GORITA

VIA CITADELLA

VIA CAPPELLINO

PIAZZA M. ROSSI

VIA CALLEORA

LUNGOMARE C. COLOMBO

VIA SCALA S. VENERA

VIA GIUSEPPE LICATA

CORSO VITTORIO EMANUELE

VIA INCISA

VIA AL MORO

San Pietro

VIA CAPPUCCINI

PIAZZA D. L. STURZO

PIAZZA MARCONI

Porta Palermo

VIA P. GERARDI

Palazzo Steripinto

Chiesa del Carmine

PIAZZA CARMINE

VIA MORI

VIA ALLA STAZIONE

VIA MULINI

VIA GAIE DI GARAFFE

Selinunte ▲

Porta San Salvatore

SS115

8

Castelvetrano & Selinunte ▲

Beach ▼

0   200   metres

ACCOMMODATION

Aliai Via Gaie de Garaffe 60 ☎ 0925 905 388, ⒲ aliai .com. First-rate B&B facing the sea in the lower town. The smartly renovated rooms boast antique touches, wood-beamed ceilings and free wi-fi, and one has its own terrace. **€100**

Casa Jacaranda Via delle Sequoie, Contrada Isabella ☎ 392 812 3231, ⒲ casajacaranda.it. This ultramodern B&B lies 2km east of town, but just 30m from the bus stop for the frequent service into the centre. It has designer decor, boldly coloured rooms equipped with LCD TV, a/c, wi-fi and scented towels, and a gazebo in the semi-tropical garden where breakfast is served. Good deals for longer stays. No credit cards. **€100**

★ **Conte Luna** Vicolo Gino 1 ☎ 0925 993 396 or ☎ 348 120 3647, ⒲ contelunasciacca.com. Excellent value for money, this is a welcoming B&B in an old *palazzo* in the heart of the upper town (off Via Licata), where two of the seven en-suite rooms have cooking facilities, and all have fridges and a/c. The top room is best, with a large balcony and panoramic views. There's also a spacious lounge and a terrace, and in summer, a minibus service is available to carry guests to nearby beaches. Breakfast is at a nearby café. No credit cards. **€60**

Grand Hotel delle Terme Via Agatocle ☎ 0925 23 133, ⒲ grandhoteldelleterme.com. This spa hotel offers a wide range of beauty treatments and massages as well as more serious physical therapies and cures in its spa building and in the wonderful steamy caves at San Calogero. There's a garden with an area for kids, too, as well as restaurants and bars where you can hone your Italian medical vocabulary by eavesdropping on fellow residents chatting about their ailments and treatments. All in all, a thoroughly Italian experience. Half board obligatory. Doubles, per person **€85**

★ **Locanda al Moro** Via Liguori 44 ☎ 0925 86 756, ⒲ almoro.com. Set in a thirteenth-century Moorish tower in the heart of town, this is an excellent B&B, modern and clean, and run by a Sicilian-German couple. The only downsides are the difficulty in finding it by car (ask directions and don't attempt to negotiate the surrounding narrow lanes) and the stairs. Rooms – some small – have a/c, and there's free internet. Local wine tours can be organized. **€100**

EATING AND DRINKING

La Lampara Lungomare C. Colombo ☎ 0925 85 085. Slightly pricier than some other places at Sciacca's port, and better quality, with a fancy upstairs dining area where you can enjoy your meal overlooking the boats. First courses such as *pasta con sarde* and *risotto ai frutti di mare* go from €10, as do fish mains (though can naturally rise far higher for prized fish), and there's a good wine list. Daily lunch & dinner; closed Mon in winter.

★ **Porto San Paolo** Largo San Paolo 1 ☎ 0925 27 982. Come here for the fine views over the harbour from the terrace, and delicious dishes such as seafood risotto and lobster fettuccine, as well as pizza in the evening. You'll pay around €40 for a full meal excluding drinks. Arrive early for the best tables, and in any case book ahead in summer. Daily lunch & dinner; closed Wed Sept–July.

La Vela Via Gaie de Garaffe 60 ☎ 0925 23 971. This quayside eatery serves a €25 set menu, which includes two first and two second courses plus dessert, but not drinks – all very abundant and usually exquisite. Booking advisable. Daily lunch & dinner; closed Wed Sept–July.

Caltabellotta

Twenty kilometres northeast of Sciacca, and an impressive ride past sparkling fresh streams and jagged outcrops of rock, the village of **CALTABELLOTTA** perches magnificently on three jutting fangs of rock 950m above sea level. Tremendous **views** stretch out on all sides, apparently taking in 21 villages. On the highest pinnacle, you can pass through the solitary surviving entrance of the Norman **castello** (always open; free) that once stood here, and climb up steep, rock-cut steps to the very top, from which the village below appears as a patchwork of grey roofs. The castle itself, ruined by an earthquake, was where the Angevins and Aragonese signed the peace treaty that ended the Wars of the Vespers in 1302. Immediately below sit the Norman **Chiesa Madre** and the Gothic **Chiesa di San Salvatore**, both wonderfully sited against a rocky backdrop.

ARRIVAL AND DEPARTURE   CALTABELLOTTA

By bus Lumia buses run direct to Caltabellotta from Sciacca four times daily (not Sun), the last one back leaving at 3.40pm.

ACCOMMODATION

Mulè Via Venezia 5 ☎ 0925 951 145 or ☎ 329 377 6740, ⓦ bbmule.it. The perfect B&B for anyone interested in staying right off the beaten track. It's set in a typical village dwelling, close to the entrance to the castle, and the plain rooms share a bathroom. You can also taste and buy local oil and other rural products, and view changing collections of local arts and crafts. No credit cards. **€50**

Sambuca di Sicilia

The Arab past of **SAMBUCA DI SICILIA**, around forty minutes' drive northwest of Sciacca, atop a hill to the west of the Arancio lake, is just about discernible in its convoluted old-town layout. A sixteenth-century church in Piazza della Vittoria, the **Chiesa del Carmine**, is the home of a statue that's reputed to be by Antonello Gagini, and you can **eat** at two or three very cheap trattorias. In addition, a 10km detour north enables you to see the low-key excavations (always open; free) at **Monte Adranone**, a Greek city of the sixth century BC which fell to Carthage in the fourth.

The Pelagie Islands

The remote **Pelagie Islands** (Isole Pelagie) are little more than dry rocks set bang in the middle of the Mediterranean, over 200km from Sicily's south coast and lying even further south than Malta or Tunis. Throughout history they've been neglected, often abandoned or uninhabited, although the largest island, **Lampedusa**, now makes its living as a summer resort for an increasing number of Italians, who are attracted by its wonderfully clear waters and remote, end-of-the-line feel. Tiny, tranquil, volcanic **Linosa** is the perfect place most of the year for anyone wanting a few hours, days or weeks away from it all. B&Bs and restaurants are all seasonal, but there are always houses to rent for a song. The tiniest islet, **Lampione**, is uninhabited and mostly visited on dive and fishing trips.

In 1943 the Allies bombed Lampedusa prior to springing into Sicily, and Colonel Gaddafi of Libya nearly gave a repeat performance in 1987 when he retaliated against the American bombing of Tripoli by targeting missiles at the US base on Lampedusa. Italian troops were mobilized and Sicily was on a virtual war-footing for three days, though in the event the missiles dropped into the sea short of the island. In recent years, the island has been the site of detention centres for enormous numbers of **immigrants** from Africa, either dumped here by unscrupulous people-traffickers, or intercepted at sea by naval vessels. Often they stay for months on end – kept firmly out of sight of tourists – until the legal processes for their inevitable repatriation are completed.

GETTING TO THE PELAGIE ISLANDS

The quickest way to Lampedusa is to **fly from Palermo or Catania** with Darwin Airline (ⓦ darwinairline.it). Tickets cost from €60 one-way, and are cheapest booked online. Otherwise, there are ferries and hydrofoils **from Porto Empedocle** (6km southwest of Agrigento and connected to it by frequent buses). Siremar (ⓦ siremar.it) **ferries** leave Porto Empedocle year-round at midnight daily except Friday, calling at Linosa (5hr 45min) and Lampedusa (8hr 15min). You can buy tickets online or at the port, with one-way tickets starting at around €40 to Linosa, or €50 to Lampedusa, including use of a *poltrona* (reclining chair); shared and exclusive-use cabins are also available. Ustica Lines (ⓦ usticalines.it) operates **hydrofoils** six times a week (not Tues) from May to October, departing Porto Empedocle at 3pm and arriving in Linosa three hours later and Lampedusa about four hours later; one-way tickets are around €40 to Linosa, €60 to Lampedusa.

Lampedusa

LAMPEDUSA is the largest of the Pelagie Islands (23 square kilometres), and is inhabited by around 5000 people, most based in the town of the same name. Many still earn a living from fishing, but most depend on the influx of tourists who swell the population to around 20,000 every August. This is a comparatively recent phenomenon, since Lampedusa has either been largely uninhabited or long-neglected by Sicily's rulers. In 1667 it passed into the hands of the Tomasi family (as in Giuseppe Tomasi di Lampedusa, of *The Leopard* fame), one of whose descendants attempted to sell the island to Queen Victoria in 1839, when it still had only twenty or so inhabitants. The queen lost out on the sale (at a cost of twelve million ducats) to Ferdinand II, the Neapolitan king, who was finally stirred into action at the prospect of losing such a scraggy but strategically important island.

Lampedusa is long, thin, flat and very dry, though the pristine waters offer some of the best **swimming**, **snorkelling** and **diving** in the Mediterranean. There are excellent **beaches**, almost all found on the south coast, and some fantastic swimming coves and grottoes. Dolphins are often seen, there's a sperm whale migration in March, and an offshore nature reserve where turtles come to lay their eggs. Bear in mind that it's a small, exposed island, so summer evenings are cooler than on the mainland. It's also not really somewhere you'd want to holiday in winter, when the wind whips across the barren landscape.

Lampedusa Town

Its location – set back from two curving harbours – is the best thing about **LAMPEDUSA TOWN**, as otherwise it is nothing special to look at. Low concrete buildings hug a dusty grid of streets between airport and harbours, though things improve along the wide, main **Via Roma**, which is largely closed to traffic and lined from top to bottom with gift shops, pavement cafés and restaurants. On summer evenings, as the temperature drops, out come the wicker café chairs, souvenir stalls, jewellery hawkers and fruit-and-veg stands, and a real street-market atmosphere develops. Indeed, there are far more people on the street at 11pm than 11am. You can buy the usual beach gear, postcards and T-shirts, but there's also a thriving trade in souvenirs like turtle carvings, sculpted beach rocks and hand-crocheted Arab caps. Enterprising local kids sell polished shells from

> ### LAMPEDUSA'S FAUNA AND FLORA
>
> When Lampedusa became a Bourbon colony in the 1840s, one of the first actions of the new settlers was to strip the land of its indigenous Mediterranean maquis, in order, it was thought, to render the island cultivable. The result was one of Europe's most extreme examples of **deforestation**, resulting in massive soil erosion that accounts for the arid state of the land today. However, a progamme of conservation and reforestation is gradually having some effect and, while Lampedusa still appears devoid of greenery at first glance, a closer look reveals a wide range of **plant life**. Date palms are dotted along otherwise barren stretches, and, at Cala Galera in particular, look out for the Phoenician juniper, carob and wild olive trees, all survivors of the original maquis. Rare plants include the *Caralluma europaea*, a cactus-like plant with star-shaped flowers, and the *Centaurea acaulis*, from the centaury family, while during spring the flowering squills, irises, crocuses, orchids, echinops and thyme make up a vibrant display. Meanwhile, the nature reserve of Isola dei Conigli is the only habitat in Italy of the *Psammodromus algirus* **lizard** – a common species in North Africa – and Lampedusa and Linosa are among the few surviving nesting places in Italy of the **turtle** *Caretta caretta*. During summer evenings, the turtles deposit between 100 and 150 eggs in deep holes, from which the babies stagger out after sixty days. The nests are individually fenced off, but that doesn't help protect them from peregrine falcons. Injured turtles are cared for at the World Wildlife Fund's **Centro Recupero Tartarughe Marine** on the island's east coast at Cala Creta, before being released back into the sea.

the beach, while **island produce** – sun-dried tomatoes, mountain capers, wild oregano and fennel seeds, hand-made cheese – is widely available from stalls and grocery stores.

A twenty-minute walk around the large **Porto Nuovo** harbour leads to the busy main beach, **Spiaggia della Guitgia**, backed by bars, hotels and restaurants. There's a stretch of fine sand, and good swimming in gently shelving water, though it's always packed here in summer; for a change of view try the next bay west, **Cala La Croce**. The other place you can explore from town is the smaller harbour, **Porto Vecchio**, where the ferries and hydrofoils dock, which also has a few bars and restaurants, and fishing boats coming and going during the day.

Isola dei Conigli and the south coast

Hourly buses for Isola dei Conigli depart from Lampedusa town bus station, off Via Roma

The best single beach destination on the island is at **Isola dei Conigli** (Rabbit Island), 5km to the west of Lampedusa town. From the cliff-top road you clamber down the jagged path to a stretch of fine, white sand and gorgeous aquamarine waters. Just offshore is the little island itself, which you can reach either on foot or by swimming, depending on the tide. Conigli island, and much of the rest of Lampedusa's **southern coast**, is protected as a nature reserve and there are various access places along the cliff-top road to viewpoints and short signposted footpaths. With a bike or scooter you can find more windswept vantage points and hidden bays if you continue along the road past Isola dei Conigli, or you can turn inland opposite the Conigli parking area and loop back towards town high above the **north coast**. However, you can only swim on the north side of the island from a boat – it's mostly sheer cliffs, tiered like a wedding cake, and pierced by deep gorges and grottoes.

Cala Creta

Buses for Cala Creta depart from Lampedusa town bus station, off Via Roma; ask to get off at Cala Creta, and follow the signpost down a dusty track

Some 3km to the east of Lampedusa town, **Cala Creta** is a magnificent swimming cove, where steps lead from a tiny rock apron directly into stunning waters. It gets busy in summer, but it's a pretty spot with a sophisticated beach bar on the rocks – Cala Creta is a cut above the other island beaches, overlooked by pristine *dammusi* houses and a holiday village.

ARRIVAL AND DEPARTURE   LAMPEDUSA

By plane Lampedusa's airport (☎0922 970 006) is on the edge of town, a 10min walk to Via Roma and the centre – most hotels have courtesy buses for guests. Taxis charge €10; Salvatore (☎333 345 6062) is a recommended driver. Destinations Catania (1 daily, 1hr); Palermo (2–4 daily; 1hr).

By ferry and hydrofoil Ferries and hydrofoils dock at Porto Vecchio; a bus meets arrivals in summer, or you can jump in a taxi. The Siremar ferry (Ⓦsiremar.it) to Linosa/ Porto Empedocle departs daily (not Sat) at 10.15am, with one-way tickets from around €50. The Ustica Lines hydrofoil

(Ⓦusticalines.it) departs May–Oct daily except Tues at 7.30am (one-way tickets around €60). There's also an extra morning and afternoon hydrofoil to Linosa (6 weekly between April and Oct, and at least 4 weekly throughout the year; one-way ticket around €20). Full timetables available on the websites.

Ferry destinations Linosa (6 weekly; 1hr 45min); Porto Empedocle (6 weekly; 7hr 45min).

Hydrofoil destinations Linosa (2–3 daily, 4 to 6 days a week; 1hr); Porto Empedocle (May–Oct 6 weekly; 4hr 15min).

GETTING AROUND

By bus The bus station is on Piazza Brignone in the centre of the town, off Via Roma. Timetables are posted, but basically there are buses every hour (roughly 8am–8pm) to Isola dei Conigli and the south coast, and to Cala Creta and the east coast.

By bike, scooter or quad It's much easier to see the whole island by renting some form of transport, either a bike (from €7 a day), scooter or quad (from €25) or a mini-moke (€40), with all prices cheaper by the week or outside July and Aug. There are lots of rental agencies around town and harbour, or ask at your accommodation. Bike rental in particular is a great idea – you can easily do a complete circuit of the island in a day, and even in the hottest months a refreshing breeze blows constantly. You can also rent your own self-drive motorboat from various harbour agencies, for around €80 per day plus fuel.

INFORMATION AND TOURS

Tourist information There's online information (in Italian) at ⓦ lampedusa35.com and ⓦ lampedusa.it, while on the island you can call in at the environmental agency, Legambiente, Via Vittorio Emanuele 25 (highly erratic hours, and usually closed in winter; ☎ 0922 971 611). Some English is spoken here, and you can pick up an island sketch map and information about the nature reserve and hiking trails.

Tours Boat trips and cruises (from €35 per person) mostly depart from the Porto Nuovo, particularly the part of the harbour by the petrol station. Departures are usually around 10.30am, returning at 5.30pm, and options include round-island cruises with swimming stops and lunch included (from €30 per person), or more specialist tours like dive trips to Lampione or night-fishing for squid.

Diving centres The larger hotels can all book you onto dive trips, or contact one of the operators direct; try Blue Dolphins (☎ 338 819 4489, ⓦ bluedolphins.it), Lo Verde Diving (☎ 329 178 6723, ⓦ loverdelampedusa.it), or Moby Diving Center (☎ 335 528 1984, ⓦ mobydiving.it). Single dives are from €35, open-water dive courses from €330, and most places are open April–Nov.

ACCOMMODATION

The season on Lampedusa runs from Easter to the end of October, and you'll generally have no problem finding a room; however in **August**, advance booking is essential and half or full board is often obligatory. There are several **hotels** in the town itself, another half a dozen within a stone's throw of the port and Spiaggia della Guitgia beach, and others just outside town and near Cala Creta. **Self-catering** accommodation (usually by the week) is available either in apartments or in one of Lampedusa's stone-built **dammusi** – updated versions of the traditional dome-roofed, thick-walled shepherd's hut, typical of Sicily and North Africa. *Dammusi* are found all over the island, some in village-style developments, and prices vary wildly (some are very boutiquey in style) – there's more information from agencies like Servizi Mikael (ⓦ servizimikael.com), Licciardi (ⓦ lampedusa-licciardi.it) and Dammusi di Borgo Cala Creta (ⓦ calacreta.com).

Baia Turchese Via Lido Azzurro ☎ 0922 970 455, ⓦ lampedusa.to. This cheery four-star seaside hotel has the best location at Spiaggia della Guitgia beach, a skip across from the sands, which explains the high prices. Rooms are always on a half-board basis, with an extra charge if you want a terrace and sea view. **€205**

★ **Belvedere** Piazza Marconi 4 ☎ 0922 970 188, ⓦ hotelbelvederelampedusa.it. In town, rather than by the beach, this is a friendly, family-run place overlooking the harbour (rooms with a view cost extra), with a good panoramic dining room and terrace restaurant to boot. It's pretty good value for most of the year. Closed Nov–Feb. **€150**

Cupola Bianca Via Madonna ☎ 0922 971 274, ⓦ hotelcupolabianca.it. A luxury outfit 2km out of town, with a North African feel and plush rooms as well as upmarket *dammusi*-style accommodation. There's a fabulous pool and terrace, plus a restaurant and all sorts of boat trips and excursions available. At least half board is required. Closed Nov–April. Half-board doubles **€400**

Nautic Via delle Grotte ☎ 0922 971 531, ⓦ lampedusanautichotel.it. This chic little four-star hotel off Via Roma is the classiest town-centre choice, with only a dozen rooms and a light, stylish touch throughout. There's a decent restaurant too, with a corner terrace. **€200**

Paladini di Francia Via Alessandro Volta ☎ 0922 970 550, ⓦ hotelpaladinidifrancia.com. Contemporary three-star resort hotel and restaurant on the harbour, close to the beach, with rooms set around bright, white courtyards, the four at the front with port-side balconies. There are flight-and-accommodation packages from Milan Linate, Bologna and Bergamo available by the week. Closed Nov–Feb. **€160**

Vega Via Roma 19 ☎ 0922 970 099, ⓦ lampedusa -hotelvega.it. There's nothing wrong with the cheapest hotel in town – in fact, it's quite cheery, with perfectly decent en-suite rooms – but it just doesn't have much of an island or seaside feel. That said, B&B rates are always available, some rooms have distant port views, and it's in the middle of town so ideally located for bars, restaurants and services. **€120**

EATING AND DRINKING

There are lots of **restaurants** in Lampedusa town, and more around the harbours, and while prices are much higher than on most of the Sicilian mainland, the quality is largely excellent. In fact, you're unlikely to have a bad meal, given the abundance of fresh-off-the-boat fish and the exacting standards of Italian holidaymakers. Specialities available everywhere include fish couscous, grilled tuna and swordfish (often simply served with a garlic, olive oil, lemon and parsley *salsa*), and whole sea bream or bass baked with potatoes. At night, the whole of Via Roma is basically one long

8

open-air **café**, with hundreds of chairs and tables spread out down the traffic-free road. Some places are more **bar** than café, with DJs and music, and it's a pretty lively scene until well into the small hours. Most cafés and restaurants close from mid-October to mid-May, but you'll find something open whenever you come.

Il Balenottero Via Sbarcatoio 40 ☎0922 970 830. A family-run place near the old port that's nice and cool inside but also has an outdoor terrace. It's a standard seafood-pasta and grilled fish place, with squid, shrimp, clams, mussels, tuna, swordfish and bream on the menu, and most dishes under €15. Daily lunch & dinner; closed Dec–Feb.

Bar del Amicizia Via Vittorio Emanuele 34 (no phone). Not exactly a secret, but you have to know it's here to come this far down the street. Inside is a huge array of stuffed pastries, simply amazing ice cream and a dozen flavours of *granita* (from strawberry to watermelon), plus a large terrace that overlooks Lampedusa's back gardens to the sea beyond. Daily lunch & dinner; closed Nov–Easter.

★ **U' Calacciuni** Spiaggia della Guitgia ☎339 435 0300. Summer-season beach-shack trattoria that's great for whiling away the hours over typical *lampedusani* dishes. There's no menu but you'll be offered pasta (say with clams and mussels, or *con le sarde*, with sardines and wild fennel), followed by the day's catch, like a slab of grilled tuna with a breadcrumb and pistachio crust. Dishes cost between €10 and €20. Daily lunch & dinner; closed Nov–April.

La Cambusa Piazza Municipio ☎0922 970 826. Down an alley just off Via Vittorio Emanuele, this cavernous underground restaurant serves the best pizzas (€5–8) in town, straight from the wood-fired oven. It's also a great place for fish (dishes €9–16); try the pasta with scampi, tomato, garlic and parsley. Daily dinner only; closed Nov–Easter.

★ **Al Gallo d'Oro** Via Vittorio Emanuele 45 ☎0922 970 249. A cheerful trattoria, with seats inside and out, serving a fish and seafood menu that's a cut above most in town. Typical dishes are pasta tossed with fresh tuna, cherry tomatoes and parsley, followed by oven-roast bass with potatoes. Expect to pay €30 a head for a full meal à la carte, or go for the €25 tourist menu. Daily dinner only; closed Oct–May.

★ **Gemelli** Via Cala Pisana 2 ☎0922 970 699. Near the airport, and worth the short walk for a menu full of Tunisian flavour – from appetizers like *brik* (stuffed savoury pastries) and *merguez* sausage to couscous. It's also excellent for fish, and well worth the higher-than-normal prices (expect to pay around €50 a head for a full meal). Reservations essential in Aug. Daily dinner only.

Trattoria del Porto Via Madonna 20 ☎0922 970 516. Best place on the main harbour, with a breezy upper terrace that affords a bird's-eye view of the port. There's a summer salad menu for lunch, as well as a choice of classic fish and seafood dishes, from spaghetti with clams to marinated tuna with wild fennel (*primi* €7–12, *secondi* €15–20). Daily lunch & dinner; closed mid-Oct to May.

DIRECTORY

Banks There are banks and ATMs along Via Roma.
Hospital Via Grecale, Lampedusa town (☎0922 970 604).
Pharmacy Dottore Inglisa, Via Vittorio Emanuele 35 (Mon–Sat 9am–12.45pm & 5–7.30pm, Sun 10am–noon

& 6–7.30pm; ☎0922 970 195).
Police Carabinieri, Via Roma 37 (☎0922 970 001 or 112).
Post office Piazza Piave, Lampedusa town (Mon–Fri 8am–1.30pm, Sat 8am–12.30pm).

Linosa

Fifty kilometres north of Lampedusa, and easily visitable as a day-trip by hydrofoil, **Linosa** is basically the tip of a submerged **volcano**, with four extinct **craters** and some **lava beaches** to explore, and not much else in the way of actual sights. It's much smaller than Lampedusa (just five square kilometres), and the only **village** has just a few hundred inhabitants, rather fewer cars and a minimal road system. Until the advent of tourism, the only time the tranquillity was disturbed was when the government in Rome sent their latest star Mafia prisoner to be detained on the island's **prison** pending trial, a practice suspended since the holiday trade picked up. Some Italian families come here year after year, revelling in the peace and quiet. If you take the tracks that lead away from the brightly coloured houses on either side of the port, you can clamber around the cliffs and coves, and reach a couple of black-sand beaches with crystal-clear water. **Swimming** and **diving** here are, of course, fantastic, and there are all sorts of dive trips, courses and excursions on offer (see opposite). Don't expect the island to be fully up and running until July, and be prepared for things to be winding down in September – arrive in May and you could easily be the only tourist.

ARRIVAL AND INFORMATION LINOSA

By ferry and hydrofoil Linosa is only an hour from Lampedusa by Ustica Lines hydrofoil. There are two or three departures a day, the first at 7.30am or 8am, leaving six days a week (not Mon or Tues, depending on the service) from April to October and four days a week (not Tues, Thurs or Sun) from November to March; one-way tickets are around €20. The Siremar ferry is cheaper (around €15), leaving Lampedusa daily (not Sat) at 10.15am, arriving at noon. The hydrofoil from Linosa to Porto Empedocle leaves daily except Tues at 8.45am (May–Oct only), and the ferry (not Sat) leaves at 12.15pm.

Ferry destinations Lampedusa (6 weekly; 1hr 45min); Porto Empedocle (6 weekly; 5hr 45min).

Hydrofoil destinations Lampedusa (2–3 daily, 4 to 6 days a week; 1hr); Porto Empedocle (May–Oct 6 weekly; 3hr).

Diving Operators such as Linosa Blu Diving (☎ 333 965 4595, ⓦ linosabludiving.it) and Terra Ferma (☎ 347 343 5027, ⓦ terrafermadiving.it) offer all sorts of dive trips, courses and excursions.

ACCOMMODATION AND EATING

You might find **B&B rooms** offered on arrival in the summer, and restaurants and several locals let out apartments. The local website ⓦ linosa.biz has a few lovely little houses to rent. There are half a dozen **trattorias** and bars all closed except between June and September – only *Bar Dammuso* stays open all year.

Bar Dammuso Via V Alfieri 5 ☎ 0922 97 2195. The heart and soul of Linosa, this friendly bar is where locals gather all year round, happily joined by tourists in the summer. They have *cornetti* in the morning, and snacks such as cheese and ham or bruschetta to accompany drinks. Daily 8am–late.

Residence La Posta Vicolo Pisa 3 ☎ 320 601 0556 or ☎ 339 741 0705, ⓦ linosaresidencelaposta.it. Linosa's only conventional hotel, with smartly furnished, air-conditioned rooms in the heart of the village. Closed Nov–May. **€160**

8

Trapani and the west

ETTORE E INFERSA SALTPANS

9

Trapani and the west

Closer to North Africa than the Italian mainland, Sicily's western reaches are traditionally poor and remote, the economy dependent on fishing and small-scale farming. Since the opening of the A29 autostrada in the 1970s, connecting it with Palermo, the region has become more integrated with the rest of Sicily, but even today, access by public transport is limited. Indeed, much of the appeal of the area lies in the fact that it's still very different from the rest of the island. Historically, the region has always been distinct, influenced by a strong Phoenician and Arab culture rather than the Greek and Norman traditions that prevail elsewhere in Sicily. The Arab influence can still be tasted in its food – couscous is a local favourite – and visually too, the flat land, dotted by white cubic houses, is strongly reminiscent of North Africa.

On the northern coast, the **Golfo di Castellammare** is only an hour by train or road from Palermo. Despite patches of industrial development along the gulf, it still manages to offer some empty beaches and a couple of unspoiled villages at its western end. In particular, the coastline between the old tuna-fishing village of **Scopello** and the resort of **San Vito Lo Capo** encompasses the beautiful **Zingaro** nature reserve. The capital of the province that encompasses this entire area, **Trapani**, is a congenial port town within sight of the flat saltpans on which its wealth was based. It is also a departure point for the **Egadi Islands**, and makes a good base for visiting the mountain town of **Erice** – originally a centre of Punic influence, though diverging from the region's dominant trend in its uniform Norman and medieval character. The pattern re-establishes itself a little way down the coast at **Mozia**, Sicily's best-preserved Phoenician site, while further south the Moorish imprint is discernible in the secretive alleys and courtyards of **Marsala** and **Mazara del Vallo**.

Although the Greeks never wielded much influence in the area, the Hellenic remains at **Segesta** and **Selinunte** (Selinus) count among the island's most stunning. Between the two, the Valle del Belice delineates the region struck by an earthquake in 1968, which left a trail of destruction still visible in many towns and villages. This is most notable at **Gibellina**, abandoned in its ruined state as a powerful reminder, and at the little town of **Santa Margherita di Belice**, whose once-proud palace and church were immortalized in that quintessential Sicilian novel, *The Leopard*. There could be no greater contrast to this disorder than the peaceful island of **Pantelleria**, a distant outpost just a short hop away from the African coast, mountainous and wind-blown, and adopted as a chic resort by a few high-profile glitterati.

SAN VITO LO CAPO

Highlights

❶ Riserva Naturale dello Zingaro Hike the footpaths or swim from isolated pebble coves within Sicily's loveliest nature reserve. **See p.317**

❷ Segesta The most romantic of all Greek sites on the island, the theatre and temple here are beautifully positioned amid rolling hills. **See p.318**

❸ Funierice cable car to Erice This stately ascent from Trapani to the hilltop town of Erice opens up a stunning panorama. **See p.326**

❹ Swimming at San Vito Lo Capo Hidden away on Sicily's northwestern tip, the idyllic beach at this appealing resort boasts a dramatic mountainous backdrop. **See p.331**

❺ Hiking on Marettimo Take some panoramic walks on the most remote of the Egadi Islands, and end the day with a fish supper overlooking the port. **See p.339**

❻ Pantelleria Though there's not a beach in sight, this craggy island en route to Tunisia still makes an enticing place to unwind. **See p.358**

HIGHLIGHTS ARE MARKED ON THE MAP ON P.312

By public transport You'll find getting around the coast a simple matter, as frequent buses cover the short distances between all the towns and villages. Trains are useful for the main towns (Trapani, Marsala, Mazara del Vallo and Castelvetrano) and also for getting to Segesta. Inland, what interior bus services there are depart from Marsala or Castelvetrano.

By car Apart from the two arms of the A29 autostrada there are only two other main roads, the SS115 following the coast between Trapani and Castelvetrano and the inland SS188 between Marsala and Salemi.

The Golfo di Castellammare

Backed by a forbidding wall of jagged mountains, the wide bowl of the **Golfo di Castellammare** is almost entirely made up of small holiday towns. Some are

HIGHLIGHTS

1 Riserva Naturale dello Zingaro

2 Segesta

3 Funierice cable car to Erice

4 Swimming at San Vito Lo Capo

5 Hiking on Marettimo

6 Pantelleria

PANTELLERIA   **TRAPANI AND THE WEST**

uncomfortably close to industrial plants, though these disappear as you progress west. The main train line from Palermo (and the SS187 road) skirts the bay from Trappeto to **Castellammare del Golfo**, but despite the ease of access and the consequent development the resorts have not entirely shrugged off their original role as fishing villages – though they have completely lost the mean look they had when fishing was the only source of income. If you're after a beach, **Trappeto**, **Balestrate** or **Alcamo Marina** make a reasonable place to stop off, with popular summer pizzerias, fish restaurants and hotels, but there's no real reason to stay: in summer it's just too busy and in winter too funereal. In July and August you would be wise to stay on the train, unless playing sardines on the sands is your thing. Otherwise, the train ride is as fair an entertainment, hugging the coast at the base of massive wedges of rock, often of a raw red colour, echoed by smaller, weathered nuggets poking out of the sea.

Alcamo

Just inside the Trapani provincial boundary, **ALCAMO** was founded by Frederick II early in the thirteenth century. Good wine is made from Alcamo grapes, and the town, spread across a low hill with views towards the coast, has also become known thanks to the atmospheric descriptions in **Mary Taylor Simeti**'s classic memoir *On Persephone's Island* (1986), much of which is set hereabouts. Otherwise, Alcamo will mainly be of interest to fans of medieval castles: adjacent to the broad main Piazza della Repubblica, the fourteenth-century **Castello dei Conti di Modica** in Piazza Castello has a small collection of archeological scraps and farming items as well as the headquarters of the regional wine association; however, the building was closed for restoration at the time of writing following the appearance of cracks in its walls. Alcamo also boasts some fine ecclesiastical architecture, its largely Baroque **churches** all found along and around the lengthy main street of the old town, Corso VI Aprile. The Chiesa Madre on the Corso is typical, with its bold frescoes and elaborate sculptures by members of the Gagini family.

If you have your own transport, **Monte Bonifato** (825m), 5km south of Alcamo – a well-signposted climb up a corkscrew road – is worth the drive for the panoramic views from the top.

DANILO DOLCI: THE "SICILIAN GANDHI"

Today, the two villages of Trappeto and Balestrate, down on the coast northeast of Alcamo and just 5km apart (and both on the train line), display a tidy sense of well-being that's in sharp contrast to the poverty found by social reformer **Danilo Dolci** (1924–97) when he came to the region in 1952. Regarded in Sicily as something of secular saint, Dolci was born near Trieste, and having first worked among the poor in Tuscany, he moved to Trappeto in 1952, determined to settle in "the poorest place I had ever known". His *Sicilian Lives* records his first impressions of Trappeto: "Coming from the North, I knew I was totally ignorant. Looking all around me, I saw no streets, just mud and dust. Not a single chemist – or sewer. The dialect didn't have a word for sewer." He **campaigned** tirelessly but nonviolently (including by fasting and "reverse strikes") to draw attention to the local conditions, and to have a dam built outside nearby Partinico – something that was resisted at every turn by the Mafia and their political clients, who controlled the existing water supplies. Inevitably, Dolci stirred up the opposition not just of the Mafia, but of the police, the church, and – eventually – even local people, who accused him of publicity-seeking and ill-conceived campaigns, and though twice nominated for the Nobel Peace Prize, he spent the last twenty years of his life in obscurity. Today, the area presents a far more prosperous face, and the beaches on either side of Trappete and Balestrate, backed by orange groves, are regularly visited by Palermitan holidaymakers. However, this economic reversal is more a reflection of the general improvement in Sicilian standards of living during the late twentieth century than of Dolci's campaigning.

9

ALCAMO'S SPAS

Alcamo's excellent, good-value **spas** may well tempt you to spend a few days here. The **Stabilimento Termale Gorga** (☎0924 23 842, ⊛termegorga.com), is a thermal spa where you can bathe in the exquisitely hot pool (€7) or take other treatments such as a mud bath (€15) or sauna (€12). You can also stay comfortably here (double €60) – guests have free access to the pool – and there's a ristorante-pizzeria. It's just a couple of hundred metres along the right-hand dirt track from the train station (don't go down under the bridge). At a second spa, **Terme Segestane** (☎0924 530 057; no credit cards), five to ten minutes' drive west, mud treatments (June to mid-Nov only) cost €20, and entrance to the pool (closed 2 weeks in Dec) is €8.

ARRIVAL AND INFORMATION   ALCAMO

By bus There are frequent bus connections to Palermo with Segesta (⊛segesta.it), which also operate a Trapani bus, though these are less frequent than you might hope, and they all leave before 9am. Russo Autoservizi buses (⊛russo autoservizi.it) run to and from San Vito del Capo and Valderice.

By train The nearest train station is down on the coast at Castellammare del Golfo, from where a few buses run up to Alcamo daily.

Tourist information Alcamo's tourist office is on Piazza Mercato, near Piazza Ciullo (Mon–Sat 9am–1pm, plus Mon, Wed & Thurs 4–7pm summer, 3.30–6.30pm in winter; ☎0924 22 301).

EATING

Bar 900 Corso VI Aprile 105 (no phone). Founded in 1937, this Alcamo institution has the best pastries in town – including a fabulous choice of miniature morsels – and an excellent *tavola calda* at lunchtime, where a full meal is priced at €12 per head. The ice cream is excellent as well.

Tues–Sun 8am–9pm; opens later in summer.

Salsapariglia Via Libertà 1 ☎0924 508 302. Abundant fish dishes such as pasta with seafood, fish couscous and mussel and clam soup, all of them delicious. In the evenings they have pizza too. Tues–Sun lunch & dinner.

Castellammare del Golfo

CASTELLAMMARE DEL GOLFO, on the coast about twenty minutes' drive northwest of Alcamo, is the biggest of the local fishing ports, entirely surrounded by high hills and built on and around a hefty rocky promontory that's guarded by a squat castle from which the town takes its name. Castellammare's incredible pedigree of bloodshed once gave it one of the worst reputations in Sicily for **Mafia** violence. The writer Gavin Maxwell, who lived locally during the 1950s, claimed that in that period eighty percent of the town's adult males had served prison sentences, and one in three had committed murder; coupled with this are the official statistics for the same period that classify one family in six as destitute. Needless to say, all of this is extremely hard to believe today: strolling down the sloping Corso Garibaldi towards the castle and harbour, past handsome *palazzi* interspersed with bars and shops selling beach gear, it seems a most benign place, ideal for a few days' relaxation. Originally Norman but much remodelled in later centuries, the **castello** (Tues–Sat 9am–1pm & 3.30–7.30pm; free) today contains well-presented collections dedicated to the history, archeology and maritime culture of the area.

Beneath the castle walls, on the harbourside, the row of cafés and restaurants that face the fishing boats is a nice place to kill time and eat lunch. There's a scrappy sand beach at the harbour, though you may prefer the fine sands 2km east of the centre, between the town and train station, while the coastline northwest of Castellammare is perhaps the most beautiful in the whole of Sicily, abounding in unspoiled coves and white pebble beaches, connected by paths to the road above. The road passes **Baia di Guidaloca**, a small bay that some people believe to be the spot where Nausicaä found the naked, shipwrecked Odysseus and finally set him on the last leg of his journey home to Ithaca. Legends apart, it's a pretty beach with a stream running into the water and pleasant swimming. Away from the sea, the pinewood slopes of Monte Inici, accessed from the SS187 2km west of town, are a popular spot for picnics and views. They provide some relief from the summer heat, and there is a restaurant here.

ARRIVAL AND DEPARTURE

CASTELLAMMARE DEL GOLFO

By bus The bus station is in the upper part of the town on Via della Repubblica, which runs off Via Segesta. Regular services operated by Russo (🌐 russoautoservizi.it) run from here to Scopello,; summer services run by Tarantola (🌐 tarantolabus.it) carry on to Lo Zingaro.;

Destinations Alcamo (12 daily Mon–Sat; 25min); Calatafimi (5 daily Mon–Sat; 30min); Palermo (5–9 daily Mon–Sat, 1–3 daily Sun; 1hr 10min–1hr 40min); San Vito

Lo Capo (2–4 daily Mon–Sat, 1–3 daily Sun; 1hr–1hr 30min); Scopello (4–8 daily Mon–Sat, 4 daily Sun in summer only; 30min); Segesta (2 daily; 40min); Trapani (4 daily Mon–Sat; 1hr–1hr 20min).

By train The local train station is 4km east of town; a bus meets arrivals and shuttles you into Castellammare, passing the campsite on the way, and dropping off passengers at the bus station.

INFORMATION AND TOURS

Tourist information The tourist office is inside the castle (Mon–Sat 9am–1pm & 3.30–7.30pm; ☎ 0924 30 217).

Tours Between June and September, there are boat tours

up the coast to Zingaro and San Vito Lo Capo, leaving from Castellammare port every morning, returning in the afternoon (around €35 including lunch; ☎ 331 868 6242).

ACCOMMODATION

Cala Marina Via Don Leonardo Zangara 1 ☎ 0924 531 841, 🌐 hotelcalamarina.it. In a prime position right by the marina and beach, this smart, modern hotel provides a relaxed atmosphere. Ask for one of the three bright rooms with balconies and sea views (costing extra). **€110**

★ **Case d'Anna** Corso Garibaldi 120 ☎ 0924 31 101 or ☎ 339 661 0722, 🌐 casedanna.it. The large, clean rooms in this intimate, centrally located family-run place are beautifully and meticulously decorated with Art Deco or

Victorian furnishings, and come with a/c, minibars and wi-fi. You'll pick up loads of helpful tips from the friendly host family, and breakfast includes home-made pastries. No credit cards. **€90**

Nonna Giò Via A. Mario 28 ☎ 334 594 1224, 🌐 sicilianelgolfo.it. Four good-value, en-suite and air-conditioned rooms are available in this place just up from Piazza Petrolo and the seafront. Breakfast is taken on the roof terrace. No credit cards. **€80**

EATING AND DRINKING

Most of the **restaurants** around the centre of Castellammare or down by the harbour feature *cuscus a pesce* (fish couscous). The harbour is also the place for an evening stroll and **drink**, with a selection of late-opening bars.

La Cambusa Via Don Luigi Zangara 67 ☎ 0924 30 155. Very nice harbourside fish restaurant that does a lovely fish couscous, and makes all its own pasta. You can also choose your own fish (on display) to have cooked *al cartoccio* (dressed with herbs and baked in a parcel). First courses go for €7–12 and second courses €8–17. Arrive early or book for the best tables. Daily lunch & dinner.

★ **A Muciara du Rais** Via Don Sturzo 12 ☎ 0924 30 604. Backstreet trattoria just down the steps from the town gardens, with a vaulted stone interior and a few tables outside. Dishes have a pronounced North African influence (first courses €7–10, mains €10–14). Daily lunch & dinner; closed Mon Oct–May.

Scopello

SCOPELLO, 10km northwest of Castellammare, is a tiny inland hamlet perched on a ridge a couple of hundred metres above the coastline where stands the old tuna fishery (*tonnara*) that the village once serviced. The village consists of little more than **Piazza Fontana** – a paved square and a fountain – and a couple of alleys running off it. On one side of the square sits the gateway and enclosed courtyard of the village's eighteenth-century **baglio**, or manor house, now the focus of local life. In here – centred on a huge eucalyptus tree – the courtyard buildings harbour a ceramicist's workshop, artist's studio, craft shop, a couple of bars and a pizzeria-restaurant. With the lights on and the wind rustling the leaves, it's a magical place at night, though in July and August – when every bar table is full and queues develop – you could be forgiven for wishing for more solitude. Outside high summer, traditional village life is more to the fore: men playing cards at the tables, people gossiping around the fountain and neighbours helping out in each other's fields.

Three kilometres south of Scopello, the lovely bay of **Cala Bianca** offers some great swimming; the bus from Castellammare stops here.

9

Tonnara di Scopello

Always open • Free

Just before Scopello on the road from Castellammare, a right-hand fork will bring you after a few hundred metres down to the coast and the **Tonnara di Scopello**, set in its own tiny cove. This old tuna fishery and its associated outhouses was where the writer Gavin Maxwell lived and worked in the 1950s, basing his *Ten Pains of Death* on his experiences there. It's almost too picturesque to be true – not least the row of abandoned buildings on the quayside, fronted by lines of rusting anchors, and the ruined old watchtowers tottering on knobbly columns of rock above the sea. From the shore, it's still precisely as Maxwell described it more than fifty years ago: "a sea of purple and blue and peacock green, with a jagged cliff coastline and great *faraglioni* (rock towers) thrusting up out of the water as pinnacle islands, pale green with the growth of cactus at their heads".

The *tonnara* remained in intermittent use until the 1980s. Although it's still privately owned, the gate is always open (beverage machines inside the building) to allow visitors to wander around the quayside – provided, according to the notice, they don't bring with them a whole host of proscribed items (dogs, radios, chairs, umbrellas). An injunction like this is usually as a red rag is to a bull for your average Sicilian, and the place is regularly engulfed with all of the above on summer weekends – though more strictly enforced regulations may yet come into effect. Most visitors come to swim in the crystal-clear waters off the tiny shingle **beach** here. Whether or not you indulge in a dip, it's a thoroughly photogenic spot (and scenes from the film *Ocean's Twelve* were shot here).

ARRIVAL AND INFORMATION

SCOPELLO

By bus The bus from Castellammare drops you in Scopello's square; out of season, four services a day (Mon–Sat) run back to Castellammare, the last at 4.45pm. In summer, there are four additional services on Sunday; the last returns to Castellammare at 7pm.

Services You won't have to look far to find everything – there's an *alimentari*, a bakery, a butcher's shop and a post office, and an ATM inside the *baglio* courtyard.

ACCOMMODATION

Scopello can be rather an exclusive retreat, given the building restrictions that limit the **accommodation** choices. Book well in advance if you want to stay here in summer, and be prepared to accept **half-board** terms in the *pensioni*. Out of season you'll be able to pick and choose, and the prices drop a little too. All the official places to stay are within a thirty-second walk of the square – if everything is booked up, you might find **rooms to rent** by asking around in the bars and shops.

Angelo Via Marco Polo 4 ☎ 338 697 4276. This small B&B has two rooms with a/c, and a terrace overlooking Piazza Fontana. There's also a little kitchen where guests can prepare simple food. **€60**

Baia di Guidaloca ☎ 0924 541 262, ⓦ camping uidaloca.com. A lovely campsite, a stone's throw from a beach which bears a tempting resemblance to the one where Nausicaa met Odysseus in the *Odyssey*. It's some 3km south of Scopello; the bus from Castellammare passes right by. Closed mid-Sept to Easter. **€9** per person, plus **€8** for a pitch

La Tavernetta Via A Diaz 3 ☎ 0924 541 129,

ⓦ albergolatavernetta.it. Twelve very pleasant, freshly refurbished rooms, all with balconies, sea views and pretty stencilled furniture, and a restaurant in a huge garden of olives, prickly pears and citrus trees. Friendly accommodating owners and a restaurant specializing in local dishes like couscous (€10) and *spaghetti con sarde* (€8). Half board in Aug. **€85**

La Tranchina Via A. Diaz 7 ☎ 0924 541 099, ⓦ pensionetranchina.com. Simple en-suite rooms with a/c, and a friendly English-speaking owner: you'll eat well here, too, on fresh fish, and interesting pasta dishes. **€86**

EATING AND DRINKING

Il Baglio Baglio Isonzo 4 ☎ 0924 541 200. Extremely popular place for pizzas (€5–9), pastas (€10–16) and seafood dishes (€12–16), with attractive outdoor seating in the *baglio* courtyard. Eat early to avoid queues at weekends and in summer. Daily lunch & dinner; closed Nov–Feb.

La Tavernetta Via A. Diaz 3 ☎ 0924 541 129. Reliable pasta and fish dishes made with local ingredients, doled out either inside or out on the terrace. A hearty three-course meal with local wine runs to around €35, though you could eat for less. Daily lunch & dinner; closed Nov–April.

Riserva Naturale dello Zingaro

9

Reserve Daily: April–Oct 7am–8pm; Nov–March 8am–4pm • €3, includes entrance to the museums • **Museums** Daily, usually 10am–4pm • ☎ 800 116 616 or ☎ 0924 35 108, ⓦ riservazingaro.it

Accessible from both Scopello and San Vito Lo Capo (see p.331), the **Riserva Naturale dello Zingaro** was the first nature reserve to be established in Sicily. It comprises a completely unspoiled 7km stretch of coastline backed by steep mountains, and received protected status in 1980 following a successful protest to prevent a coast road being constructed from Scopello to San Vito Lo Capo. Around forty different bird species nest and mate here, including the rare Bonelli's Eagle, and there are some six hundred species of **plant**. Apart from the wide variety of fauna and flora, there's great archeological interest in an area that supported some of Sicily's earliest prehistoric settlements.

If you are approaching the reserve from San Vito, via the **northern entrance** (**Ingresso Nord**), note that there are no shops, bars or restaurants along the road from town. There are none in the park itself either (just seasonal refreshments at the two entrances), and in summer there is little shade, so come prepared. Coming from the other direction, the road from Scopello ends at **Ingresso Sud**, the **southern entrance** to the reserve, from where you can proceed on foot through pristine country and past some extremely beautiful coves and beaches. This is not exactly unknown territory, since hundreds of Palermitani descend on Scopello and its surroundings on summer weekends, but at other times – and especially out of season – it's one of the most tranquil places in Sicily. In addition, since the whole area is regulated by building restrictions that actually seem to be enforced, the water quality – and hence the swimming – is excellent. The easiest and best-maintained of the network of **paths** through the reserve keep close to the coast. Of the two main routes, the **Sentiero Alto** is best in spring for the vegetation and natural life, while the **Sentiero Basso**, hugging the shore, is best in summer if you want to stop for swims. The mid- and high-mountain routes are favoured by well-prepared walkers and ornithologists; refuges here can be used at night, so long as you book ahead through the park authority.

The Sentiero Basso

Following the **Sentiero Basso**, it takes less than twenty minutes to reach the first beach, **Cala Capreria**, which can as a result be crowded at weekends and in July and August. When it's not, it's perfect: a tiny cove of white pebbles, azure water, shoals of little fish nibbling at the edge and baby squid darting in and out. A small **Museo Naturalistico** and visitor centre stand just above the beach. Further up the coast, another twenty minutes or so onward, there's a museum above **Cala del Varo** dedicated to manna and the flowering manna-ash, examples of which grow hereabouts.

Sticking with the coastal path, it's 3km from the southern entrance to the successive coves of **Disa**, **Berretta** and **Marinella**, which should be a little more secluded. The next cove, **Cala dell'Uzzo**, holds a museum of rural life, while the **Cala Tonnarella dell'Uzzo**, 7km from the southern entrance, has a museum of fishing and other marine activity.

WALKING IN THE RISERVA ZINGARO

If you're heading off on Riserva Zingaro's coastal path, make sure you carry plenty of **water** – any water you see along the way may not be fit for drinking. There's a water fountain at the Ingresso Sud information hut and, in summer, a van selling ices and drinks. At the Ingresso Nord – the northern, San Vito Lo Capo, park entrance – you'll find another information hut, water and, in summer, refreshments. Before you decide to walk on to San Vito, 11km away, make sure you have water, as there are no facilities en route.

9

The northern entrance

The **northern entrance** to the reserve (**Ingresso Nord**) is 11km southeast of San Vito Lo Capo. Accessible by your own transport or on a boat trip from San Vito, it's also a fine walk from the town, initially following the road along the lungomare from San Vito and across the flat headland, before winding up into the mountains. In the higher reaches, the views are exhilarating, with the surrounding scenery almost alpine in character – fir trees, flowers edging the road, and the clank of bells from goats roaming the hillsides. Sadly, though, the road through this secluded and dramatic landscape offers few opportunities to descend to the alluringly deserted coves below.

The **access road** to the reserve is signposted just before the ruined Torre dell'Impiso, around a three-hour walk from San Vito. From the sign to the park entrance itself is about another 1km, following a gravel track and then a path, which runs down into the reserve, past the Tonnara dell'Uzzo. The beautiful little **cove-beach** below the entrance offers translucent water, with glorious peace and quiet all around – at least, whenever the first few little creeks here aren't inundated with bathers. Travel on for less crowded spots, or else take one of the higher paths for greater isolation. Scopello is a 10km walk south from the San Vito entrance.

ARRIVAL AND INFORMATION

RISERVA NATURALE DELLO ZINGARO

By bus Russo buses have a summer-only service from Castellammare del Golfo to the southern entrance.

Tourist information There are information huts at the Ingresso Sud and Ingresso Nord entrances. You can pick up a simple map showing the trails through the reserve – though as it's not entirely accurate it should be treated with some scepticism.

Boat tours and diving The waters offshore of the reserve have some excellent dive sites, with wrecks and grottoes to explore; Cetaria, Via Marco Polo 3, Scopello (☏ 368 386 4808, ⊛ cetaria.it), offer dives, boat excursions and equipment rental.

ACCOMMODATION

★ **Baglio La Luna** Via del Secco 11 ☏ 335 836 2856, ⊛ bagliolaluna.com. Seven kilometres out of San Vito on the Zingaro road, so ideal for forays into the reserve, this rural B&B boasts lofty views from its terrace and complete tranquillity. The airy whitewashed interior with tiled floors has five simple rooms – those with sea views cost €10 extra. You'll need your own transport to stay here, and there's a two-night minimum

stay in Aug. No credit cards. Closed Nov–March. **€110**

Casale Corcella Contrada Scardina ☏ 368 365 4482, ⊛ scopelloonline.com. Ideal for walkers, this is located 1km north of Scopello, within the Zingaro reserve. Five simple, cheerful and spotlessly clean rooms and five mini apartments. No credit cards. Closed Nov–March. Rooms and apartments **€80**

Segesta

Set amid deserted green countryside around 15km south of Castellammare del Golfo (and 30km east of Trapani), the remains of the ancient city of **Segesta** are among the most inspiring on the island. All that still stands is a Doric temple and a brilliantly sited **theatre**, relics of a city whose roots – like Erice's – lie back in the twelfth century BC. Unlike Erice, though, ancient Segesta was eventually Hellenized and spent most of the later period disputing its border with Selinus. The temple dates from a time of prosperous alliance with Athens, but it was never finished – work on it was abandoned when a new dispute broke out with Selinus in 416 BC.

Apart from the small café and shop at the site, the café-restaurant near the signposted turn-off is the only nearby place for **refreshments**, and the only **accommodation** hereabouts is in the nearby town of Calatafimi (see opposite). **Concerts and plays** are staged at Segesta's theatre between mid-July and early September. Ask at the tourist offices in Palermo (see p.70) and Trapani (see p.324) for details, or call ☏ 800 904 60. Special excursion buses leave from both cities to coincide with the performances, and tickets for the various productions cost around €15.

The site

Daily 9am–1hr before sunset; last entry 1hr before closing • €6, or €9 including the ruins at Selinunte • Half-hourly buses (€1.50) run from the site entrance to the theatre

The site is best seen early or late in the day, when visitors are fewer and the light less blanching in its effect. The **temple** itself, started in 424 BC, crowns a low hill beyond the café and car park. From a distance you could be forgiven for thinking that it's complete: the 36 regular stone columns, entablature and pediment are all intact, and all it lacks is a roof. However, get closer (and for once you're allowed to roam right inside) and you see just how unfinished the building really is: stone studs, always removed on completion, still line the stylobate, the tall columns are unfluted, and the cella walls are missing. In a way, this only adds to the natural grandeur of the site, and it's not too fanciful to imagine that the pitted and sun-bleached temple simply grew here – a feeling bolstered by the birds nesting in the unfinished capitals, the lizards scampering over the pale yellow stone, and, in spring, the riot of flowers underfoot.

From the main entrance, a road winds up through slopes of wild fennel to a small **theatre** on a higher hill beyond; if you don't relish the twenty-minute climb you can use the bus service. The view from the top is terrific, across green slopes and the plain to the sea, the deep blue of the bay a lovely contrast to the theatre's white stone – the panorama not much damaged by the motorway snaking away below.

Behind the theatre, **excavations** (explained by information boards) have revealed the foundations of a mosque and Arab-style houses. These were pulled down in the thirteenth century when a Norman castle was erected on the high ground – though this itself lasted less than a hundred years, as political forces on the island waxed and waned. There are also the remains of a late medieval church, built for local shepherds and landholders and used, in one form or another, until the nineteenth century. Thus it is a site of enormous significance and utility, spanning generations.

ARRIVAL AND DEPARTURE	SEGESTA

By bus Tarantola buses run direct to Segesta from Piazza Malta in Trapani, leaving at 8am, 10am, noon and 2pm (Sun 10am only), returning at 12.50pm, 1.05pm, 4.05pm and 6.30pm (Sun 1.05pm only). There are also bus services from Castellammare del Golfo and Palermo.

By train There are four trains daily from Trapani to Segesta-Calatafimi, from where it's a 20min uphill walk to the site.

By car If you're driving, it's easiest to see the site en route between Palermo and Trapani, since it lies just off the motorway.

Calatafimi

Defended by a castle (hence the Arabic *kalat* of its name) whose remnants top a wooded hill, **CALATAFIMI** gained fame as the site of the first of Garibaldi's victories against the Bourbon forces in 1860, which opened the way to Palermo and hence the rest of Sicily. The battle took place on the Salemi road, around 1km south of Calatafimi and then 3km up a hill, the summit marked by a white obelisk. It's signposted "Ossario di Pianto Romana", and named as such because the bones of the fallen from the battle are collected here. They used to be on display in cases for the edification of the local population; now they're hidden behind commemorative tablets underneath an Italian flag. The custodian might attempt an explanation of the history if your Italian is up to it – a tip wouldn't go amiss. The views outside, to Calatafimi itself, Erice and the Castellammare gulf, are magnificent.

ARRIVAL AND DEPARTURE	CALATAFIMI

By bus Calatafimi lies 4km south of its train station, so it's better to come by bus – there are four services daily from Trapani.

ACCOMMODATION AND EATING

Mille Pini Piazza F. Vivona 2 ☎0924 951 260, ⓦhotelmillepini.com. A fittingly old-fashioned hotel which has ten simple rooms with balconies and valley views, and a restaurant where you can eat well for around €15 – overall, it's a very nice place for a quiet night in the sticks. **€50**

Trapani

Although predominantly modern, **TRAPANI**, the first of three major towns on Sicily's western edge, has an elegant old centre that's squeezed into a narrow arm of land pointing out to sea. Lent an end-of-the-line feel by its port, the town's inconspicuous monuments give no great impression of its long history. Nonetheless, Trapani flourished as a Phoenician **trading centre** and as the port for Eryx (modern Erice), profiting from its position looking out towards Africa. As an important stopover on the sea routes linking Tunis, Naples and Aragon, the town played an enduring role throughout the Middle Ages, when Europe's crowned heads virtually passed each other on the quayside. The Navarrese king Theobald died here of typhoid in 1270; two years later Edward I of England touched down after a Crusade to learn he'd inherited the throne, while Peter of Aragon arrived in 1282 to claim the Sicilian throne, following the expulsion of the Angevin French. The city's growth over the last century has been founded on the development of salt, fishing and wine industries, though severe bombardment during World War II has given rise to an excess of dull postwar building around the outskirts.

Still, as a **base** for the rest of the west, Trapani can't be beaten. It offers a good few accommodation possibilities, mostly in the old-town area; regular trains south to nearby Marsala and Mazara del Vallo; buses to Erice, the resort of San Vito Lo Capo and the more distant site of Segesta; and the nearest of the Egadi Islands is only twenty minutes away by hydrofoil. The only time when you might find a room hard to come by is during the procession of the **Misteri** at Easter (see box, p.322).

The old town

Almost everything of interest in Trapani is found in the **old town**, west of the Villa Margherita gardens. Churches and palaces have been renovated in recent years, and a plethora of bars and restaurants has opened along stylish pedestrianized streets – notably Corso Vittorio Emanuele, Via Torrearsa and Via Garibaldi – and the northern seafront, above a long beach, has been considerably smartened up. However, away from here, there's still a scruffy, salty-old-port air to much of Trapani, its stark cubic houses, dusty streets and wind- and sun-thrashed palms more redolent of North Africa than Italy.

Corso Vittorio Emanuele

The old town is most elegant along **Corso Vittorio Emanuele**, the pedestrianized main street, dominated at its eastern end by the pinkish marble front of the **Palazzo Senatorio**, the seventeenth-century town hall. With its twin clocks separated by an imperious eagle, it adds a touch of grandeur to the thin promenading strip, otherwise hemmed in by balconied *palazzi*, a couple of Baroque churches, and the **Cattedrale** on the right, with its Baroque portico, cupolas and vast interior. Dedicated to San Lorenzo, it has a *Crucifixion* inside, in the fourth chapel on the right, attributed to Van Dyck.

Changing its name along the way, the Corso runs almost to the end of the curving promontory from which the town took its Phoenician name of Drepanon (sickle). At its very tip is the **Torre di Ligny**, a squat Spanish fortification dating from 1671, now privately owned, but a good spot for a sit-down with a sandwich. On the way back into town, a walk down the north side of the promontory will show you what's left of the medieval city wall, the *bastione*, breached by the thirteenth-century **Porta Botteghelle**.

TRAPANI

N

TYRRHENIAN SEA

Torre di Ligny

Villino Nasi

Lazzaretto

▲ **1** , **2** , Museo Regionale Pepoli, Santuario dell'Annunziata & cable-car

Egadi Islands, Pantelleria, Ustica, Naples & Civitavecchia ▶

Egadi Islands, Pantelleria, Cagliari & Tunis ▶

Egadi Islands, Pantelleria, Cagliari & Tunis ▶

0 — 200 metres

● RESTAURANTS

Angelino	10
Le Baccante	2
La Bettolaccia	8
Calvino	7
Cantina Siciliana	6
I Grilli	5
Le Mura	3
P&G	1
Tavernetta ai Lumi	4
Trattoria del Porto	9

■ ACCOMMODATION

Ai Lumi	5
Almaran	8
Casatrapani	1
Maccotta	7
Messina	5
Moderno	4
Nuovo Russo	6
Residence La Gancia	2
Villa Maria	9

■ BARS & CAFÉS

Bar Il Salotto	1
Gelateria Gino	3
Nuovo Caffè Ra' Nova	2
Torrepali Webcafé	4

● SHOP

Supermarket	1

9

TRAPANI'S MISTERI

One of Sicily's most evocative religious processions, held since the seventeenth century, takes place in Trapani at Easter, when the **Misteri**, extraordinary life-sized wooden statues depicting scenes from the Passion, are carried shoulder-high through the streets on Good Friday. The procession through the town takes ten hours, starting at 2pm and finishing back at the **Chiesa del Purgatorio** at midnight. Sculpted from cypress wood and cork in the eighteenth century, each of the twenty groups of chocolate-brown figures is associated with one of the town's trades – fishermen, metalworkers, saltworkers, and so on – whose representatives undertake to maintain them and, draped in cowls and purple robes, annually parade them. The rest of the time the statues are kept in the **Chiesa del Purgatorio**, on Via Francesco d'Assisi, south of the main Corso. The church is usually locked, but when it's open, there should be a priest around to explain which of the trades is responsible for each of the sculpted groups, and what the particular figures represent – though most of the scenes are familiar enough. When it's closed, you can arrange admission at the Cattedrale office.

Note that this is a very popular time to visit Trapani, so be sure to **book accommodation** well in advance.

Via Torrearsa

Back at the eastern end of Corso Vittorio Emanuele, Via Torrearsa is one of the old town's main shopping streets. At its southern end, the church of Sant'Agostino on Piazzetta Saturno boasts a pretty fourteenth-century rose window of interlocking stone bands; the church is occasionally used as a concert hall (details of performances from the tourist office). Architecturally more appealing is the sixteenth-century church of Santa Maria di Gesù, just to the east of Via Torrearsa, on Via San Pietro, whose two doors display a diversity characteristic of the town, the right-hand one Gothic, the other defiantly Renaissance.

The Jewish quarter

There's little more to see in this part of town apart from a few unusual facades, one of them buried in the wedge of hairline streets and alleys north of Corso Italia, at Via della Giudecca 43, where the sixteenth-century **Palazzo della Giudecca** sports a plaque-studded front and some Spanish-style Plateresque windows. The building lies at the heart of Trapani's old **Jewish quarter**, an area dating from Trapani's medieval heyday at the centre of Mediterranean trade. From here, it's not far to the **Villa Margherita**, the shady town gardens (daily dawn to dusk); concerts are staged here in summer (information available from the tourist office).

Santuario dell'Annunziata

Via Conte Agostino Pepoli 180 · **Santuario** Daily 8am–noon & 4–8pm, closes 7pm in winter · Free · ☎ 0923 55 3269

The main point of interest in Trapani's somewhat dull modern city is the lavishly decorated Santuario dell'Annunziata, a fourteenth-century convent and church whose cloisters incorporate the town's main museum. The sanctuary was rebuilt in 1760 and only the facade, with its Gothic portal and magnificent rose window, is original. Inside you'll find a series of sumptuous chapels, two dedicated to Trapani's fishermen and seamen – one echoes the facade's shell motif around the sides of the room – and, best of all, the Cappella della Madonna, containing Trapani's sacred idol: the beautiful, smiling Madonna and Child, attributed to Nino Pisano in the fourteenth century. Responsible for a host of miracles, the statue is housed beneath a grandiose marble canopy sculpted by Antonello Gagini and surrounded by polychrome marble – as well, generally, as a crowd of hushed worshippers.

Museo Regionale Pepoli

9

Mon–Sat 9am–1.30pm, Sun 9am–12.30pm • €6

Adjacent to the Santuario dell'Annunziata, and entered through the Villa Pepoli park, the wide-ranging collection at the **Museo Regionale Pepoli** takes in everything from exemplary Gagini statuary to seventeenth-century coral craftwork. Highlights downstairs include a little bronze **horse and rider** by Giacomo Serpotta and a sixteenth-century marble **doorway** by Berrettaro Bartolomeu, taken from the old church of San Giuliano, which, though badly worn in parts, displays a lively series of tableaux. Downstairs, too, bizarrely, is a grim wooden guillotine from 1789, with a basket for the head and a coffin at the ready. The museum houses a good **medieval art** section – including a powerful *Pietà* by Roberto Oderisio, and a couple of fine fifteenth-century triptychs by the anonymous *Maestro del Polittico di Trapani*. Other displays include a **coin collection**, with Greek, Roman, Arab and Italian examples; an eighteenth-century majolica-tiled scene of **La Mattanza** (tuna slaughter), with the fishermen depicted corralling the fish in their boats; a small **archeological section** with a few finds from Selinunte and Mozia, though nothing outstanding, and some intricate **coral work**, including crib scenes with alabaster and shell decoration.

ARRIVAL AND DEPARTURE

TRAPANI

By plane Trapani's airport, 15km south of the centre at Birgi, has flights to and from several Italian cities, and Lampedusa and Pantelleria (1–3 daily; 40min), as well as Ryanair services from mainland Europe, Britain and Ireland. Buses (run by Terravision, but usually with Segesta written on the side) call at Trapani port, Trapani station and Palermo's Piazza Politeama and Stazione Centrale and are timed to coincide with Ryanair flights: seats are available only to Ryanair customers (you have to show your boarding card to buy a ticket; the fare is €8). Journey time to Palermo is about two hours. AST also has a regular (hourly) service to Trapani port and station. If picking up the bus at the port, tickets need to be bought before boarding from the Egatour agency, across the road from the bus stop at Via Amm. Stati 13 (daily 5.30am–8pm; ☏ 0923 21 754, ⌨ www.egatourviaggi.it). Top Transfer (☏ 0923 27 899 or ☏ 337 896 010, ⌨ toptransfer .it) offers airport shuttles as well as longer-distance transfers.

By train Trains stop at the Stazione Centrale, just around the corner from the bus station and a short walk along Via Garibaldi from the old town.

Destinations Castelvetrano (13 daily Mon–Sat, 6 daily Sun; 1hr 10min); Marsala (12 daily Mon–Sat, 5 daily Sun; 30min); Mazara del Vallo (12 daily Mon–Sat, 5 daily Sun; 40min–1hr); Palermo (6 daily Mon–Sat, 4 daily Sun; 2hr 15min–4hr); Segesta-Tempio (3–4 daily; 25min).

By bus Most buses (including those to and from Erice) pull up at the terminal in Piazza Malta. If you're heading straight off to the Egadi Islands, note that the fast buses from the airport, Palermo, Palermo airport and Agrigento stop at the ferry and hydrofoil terminals as well as the bus station.

Destinations from Trapani Agrigento (3 daily Mon–Sat, 1 daily Sun; 3hr 10min–3hr 40min); Alcamo (2–3 daily Mon–Sat; 1hr); Bonagia (8 daily Mon–Sat, 3 daily Sun in summer; 25min); Castellammare del Golfo (5 daily; 1hr–1hr 20min); Castelvetrano (5 daily Mon–Sat; 2hr 15min); Erice (7–8 daily Mon–Sat, 4 daily Sun; 45min); Marsala (3 daily Mon–Sat; 45min); Mazara del Vallo (3 daily Mon–Sat; 1hr 30min); Palermo (1–2 hourly Mon–Sat, 14 daily Sun; 2hr); Palermo airport (4 daily; 1hr); San Vito Lo Capo (8–9 daily Mon–Sat, 4 daily Sun in summer; 1hr 20min); Segesta (2 daily Mon–Sat, 1 daily Sun; 50min); Trapani airport (1–2 hourly; 20–40min).

Destinations from Trapani airport Agrigento (3 daily Mon–Sat, 1 daily Sun; 2hr 45min–3hr 20min); Marsala (1–4 daily Mon–Sat, 2 daily Sun; 15min); Palermo (6–8 daily; 2hr 10min); Trapani (1–2 hourly; 20–40min).

BUS COMPANIES IN TRAPANI

S. Lumia ☏ 0922 20 414, ⌨ autolineelumia.it. Departures from Piazza Malta and Trapani airport for Agrigento and Sciacca.

Segesta ☏ 091 342 525, ⌨ segesta.it. Departures from Piazza Garibaldi for Alcamo, Palermo and Palermo airport.

Salemi ☏ 0923 981 120, ⌨ autoservizisalemi.it.

Departures from Trapani airport for Marsala and Palermo.

Tarantola ☏ 0924 31 020. Departures from Piazza Malta for Segesta.

Terravision ☏ 0923 981.120, ⌨ terravision.eu. Departures from the port, bus station and airport for Palermo.

9

By ferry and hydrofoil Ferries for the Egadi Islands, Pantelleria, Cagliari and Tunis dock at the Molo di Sanità, while hydrofoils for the Egadi Islands and Ustica dock to the east of the Molo, on Via A. Stati. The frequencies given below are year-round. Services usually increase between June 10 and September 10.

Ferry and hydrofoil companies All the companies have offices at the Stazione Marittima, Molo di Sanità, Via Ammiraglio Staiti. Grimaldi (☎0923 593 673, ⦿www .grimaldi-lines.com) sails to Civitavecchia and Tunis; Siremar (☎0923 24 968 or ☎892 123, ⦿siremar.it) to the

Egadi Islands and Pantelleria; Tirrenia (☎892 123, ⦿tirrenia.it) to Cagliari; and Ustica Lines (☎0923 873 813, ⦿usticalines.it) to the Egadi Islands and Ustica.

Ferry destinations Cagliari (1 weekly; 10hr); Civitavecchia (1 weekly; 13hr 30min); Favignana (1–2 daily; 1hr–1hr 25min); Lévanzo (1–2 daily; 50min–1hr 40min); Marettimo (1 daily; 2hr 35min–2hr 50min); Pantelleria (6 weekly; 5hr 45min).

Hydrofoil destinations Favignana (hourly; 15–40min); Lévanzo (11 daily; 20–40min); Marettimo (4 daily; 1hr); Ustica (3–4 weekly; 2hr 30min).

GETTING AROUND

By bus Everything in the old town is easily reachable on foot, though you'll need to catch a city bus to visit Trapani's museum, in the new part of the city: most routes depart from Piazza Vittorio Emanuele. Tickets are available from *tabacchi*, and are valid for one hour.

By taxi During the day, taxis usually wait outside the train station – just make sure they switch on the meter, or you could be in for a surprise. If you need to call a taxi, try ☎0923 30 0051, ☎337 896 010 or ☎368 734 0893 (24hr).

INFORMATION AND TOURS

Tourist office The main office is at Via Torrearsa 46 (summer Mon–Sat 9am–1pm & 4–7pm, Sun 9am–1pm; winter hours are changeable; ☎339 599 8645, ⦿stradadelvinoericedoc.it), and has bike rental as well as info on B&Bs and *agriturismi*. There's also a little kiosk at the foot of Via Torrearsa, near the port (same hours).

Tours Egatour, Via Amm. Stati 13 (daily 5.30am–8pm; ☎0923 21 754, ⦿www.egatourviaggi.it), run boat tours to Favignana and Lévanzo (€39) and to Favignana and Marettimo (€45), as well as a fascinating bus tour of the nearby salt flats (€15).

ACCOMMODATION

HOTELS AND B&BS

Ai Lumi Corso Vittorio Emanuele 71 ☎0923 540 922, ⦿ailumi.it. Five small but pristine rooms entered through a flower-filled courtyard. In summer, street-facing rooms can be noisy. **€90**

Almaran Via San Cristoforo 8 ☎0923 549 847 or ☎349 611 0211, ⦿almaran.it. Clean and pretty B&B close to the hydrofoil port; rooms have private bathrooms and a/c. The English-speaking owner is friendly and helpful, but breakfasts are basic. **€65**

Casatrapani Via Livio Bassi 196 ☎333 532 2010, ⦿casatrapani.it. In the modern town, but just a 10min walk from the station, this friendly B&B offers great rates, a pick-up from the airport or station, clean, colour-themed en-suite rooms with a/c, and the use of a kitchen with a washing machine. No credit cards. **€85**

Maccotta Via degli Argentieri 4 ☎0923 28 418, ⦿albergomaccotta.it. Smart and friendly place behind the Palazzo Senatorio. The spacious modern rooms have comfortable beds and a/c, but bathrooms are small, and it can be noisy. No breakfast. **€75**

Messina Corso Vittorio Emanuele 71 ☎0923 21 198. The city's cheapest option occupies the first floor of the eighteenth-century Palazzo Bernardo Ferro, and is entered through the same courtyard as *Ai Lumi*. Something of an endangered species these days, it's an unrepentant, basic

one-star hotel with shared bathrooms. It can be noisy, especially in summer, when the street- and bar-life of Corso Vittorio Emanuele is in full swing. **€40**

Moderno Via Ten. Genovese 20 ☎0923 21 247, ⦿hotelmoderno.trapani.it. As you might imagine, the *Moderno* is no such thing, though it does have more character than some, housed in an old *palazzo* with a courtyard where limited parking is available. The simple rooms have a/c and some have little balconies over the street. No breakfast. **€55**

Nuovo Russo Via Tintori 4 ☎0923 22 163, ✉nuovoalbergorusso@gmail.com. Trapani's oldest hotel has a great position on the main Corso, just a few minutes' walk from the port. There are 36 rooms, all of them different, and corridors sprinkled with a random assortment of family heirlooms. Rooms have been recently restored, mighty shutters cut out most of the street noise, and there are plans afoot to create a roof terrace. **€90**

Residence La Gancia Piazza Mercato del Pesce ☎0923 438 060, ⦿lagancia.com. Smart, if slightly sterile, contemporary rooms and mini-apartments (with and without cooking facilities), a great roof terrace (where breakfast is served) and a superb position on the northern seafront right above the town beach at the head of Via Torrearsa. Rooms **€130**; apartments **€115**

9

CAMPSITE

Villa Maria Via Torre di Mezzo, Lido Marausa ☎0923 841 363 or ☎340 556 4225, ⓦvillamaria.marausa.it. With a basic but clean and shady campsite and six apartments to rent, this rural spot may be in the middle of nowhere but it's the nearest accommodation to the airport, and one of the two closest campsites to Trapani (12km away), and 200m from the sea. Facilities are clean and reliable, and the lovely old couple running it are tops. You'll need your own transport though – it's off the SP21. Camping €12 per person including tent and car; apartments €50

EATING AND DRINKING

Eating out in Trapani is a real treat – you can get fresh fish and couscous almost everywhere, while the local pasta speciality, *alla trapanese*, is terrific – either spaghetti or home-made *busiate* served with a pesto of fresh tomato, basil, garlic and almonds. There are quite a few lively **bars** around, too, good for breakfast and snacks, and bustling at night with people stopping off from the clamorous *passeggiata* that fills Via Torrearsa and the bottom end of Corso Vittorio Emanuele.

RESTAURANTS

★ **Angelino** Via Ammiraglio Staiti 87 ☎0923 26 922. Examine the mouthwatering displays in this fashionable *pasticceria/tavola calda*, take a ticket, order at the bar and grab a table in the conservatory. You're spoiled for choice – *involtini* of aubergine rolled around *spaghettini*, stuffed sardines, rosemary-roast potatoes, lasagne and *focaccia*, all at extremely reasonable prices. Wine by the glass and coffee and delicious *dolci* to follow, if you can manage it. Aug daily lunch & dinner; rest of the year closed Mon.

Le Baccante Via Garibaldi 56 (no phone). This recently opened little restaurant/bar has appealing candlelit tables on atmospheric Via Garibaldi and in the stepped alleyway above. It's especially good in summer, as the cooking is light and fresh, with inventive salads, along with tasty pasta (from €7) and fish (from €10). Summer daily lunch & dinner.

★ **La Bettolaccia** Via Gen. Enrico Fardella 25 ☎0923 21 695. Popular with locals, this informal but sophisticated *osteria* is known for its excellent risotto and *busiate* dishes (mainly seafood, though *alla trapanese* is recommended). Expect to pay €30–40 per head, including good local wine. Delicious desserts include *parfait al pistacchio*. Book, or arrive early. Mon–Fri lunch & dinner, Sat lunch only.

★ **Calvino** Via N. Nasi 72 ☎0923 21 464. This backstreet pizzeria, with Moorish-style cubbyhole rooms, is a bit rough-and-ready but well worth a visit. The tasty pizzas come in four sizes, from *Piccola* (€5–6) to *Tripla* (€14–17), cut into bite-sized pieces and served on squares of greaseproof paper. Try the *Rianata*, a local speciality made with fresh oregano, tomato, garlic, anchovies and pecorino cheese; or a hearty plate of sausages and potatoes roasted with onions in the pizza oven, best washed down with cold beer. Book for a table, or be prepared to take away or queue. No credit cards. Mon & Wed–Sun 9am–1pm & 5–8pm.

Cantina Siciliana Via della Giudecca 32 ☎0923 28 673. In the old Jewish quarter, this cosy restaurant with blue-tiled walls is a great spot for a romantic dinner, though service can be poor. The menu features traditional Sicilian dishes as well as fish couscous, and desserts include a sublime lemon ice cream with limoncello. Pastas and meat or fish mains are all €8–12. Daily lunch & dinner.

★ **I Grilli** Corso Vittorio Emanuele 69 ☎0923 20 663, ⓦigrillibraceria.it. Several cuts above your average Trapani eatery, *I Grilli* focuses on simple, carefully sourced, high-quality grilled meats, along with an eclectic menu of French and Italian cheeses and hams, and over 150 wines. Even the mixed bruschetta (€3.50) is a gastronomic experience. Cheese and ham plates from €9, grilled meats €8–18, salads and grilled veg from €6. April–Oct Mon–Sat lunch & dinner, Sun dinner only; Nov–March Mon–Tues & Thurs–Sun dinner only.

Le Mura Viale delle Sirene 15/19 ☎ 0923 872 622. On the seafront below the Bastione della Conca, this is a lovely seafood restaurant– there's no better place to try the famed prawns of Mazara del Vallo. It serves exquisite fish dishes, with plenty of simple options as well as more elaborate dishes. A full meal will set you back €35–40. Tues–Sat lunch & dinner.

P&G Via Spalti 1 ☎0923 547 701. This long-established restaurant in the modern town has seen better days, but it still lays on a fine selection of *antipasti*, seafood and grilled meats. Among the pastas (€7–12), try the fresh *busiate casarecce*, with a pesto of anchovy, garlic, pine nuts and tomato. There are a few tables outdoors, and pizzas in the evening. Tues–Sun lunch & dinner.

★ **Tavernetta ai Lumi** Corso Vittorio Emanuele 71–77 ☎0923 872 418. The best restaurant in the old town occupies the brick-vaulted stables of an old palace – and there's a shady outdoor terrace for summer dining. A typical meal from the regional menu might be home-made pasta with zucchini and shrimp, followed by a seafood stew or braised rabbit, and the wine list features good Sicilian wines. It's not cheap, with most dishes €10–20. Mon & Wed–Sun lunch & dinner.

Trattoria del Porto Via Ammiraglio Staiti 45 ☎0923 547 822. Friendly, family-run trattoria (also known locally as *Da Felice*) opposite the port, with occasionally slow service but good food and outdoor tables under the arches.

9

Top choices are the *spaghetti marinara*, fish couscous, roast squid or, in season, *involtini di spada* (swordfish roulades). Good-value tourist menus are €20 and €30, otherwise there are plenty of dishes priced from €9–12. July & Aug lunch & dinner; rest of the year closed Mon.

BARS AND CAFÉS

Bar Il Salotto Via Garibaldi 1, corner Via Torrearsa ☎ 349 456 3480. A ravishing selection of cakes and puddings, fresh fruit salad for breakfast in summer, and *cornetti* with unusual fillings such as pear. Seats outside on Via Garibaldi, too. Daily 7am–4am; closes earlier in summer.

Gelateria Gino Piazza dalla Chiesa ☎ 0923 21 104.

Make a beeline here for excellent ice cream and *frullati*, from kiwi to coconut, and grab a table in the piazza. Daily 9am–2.30pm & 3.30pm–late.

Nuovo Caffè Ra' Nova Via Garibaldi ☎ 0923 23 311. Busy café with a range of hot snacks and pastas, and a large outdoor area on a traffic-free road. There's also a huge array of ice creams and cocktails. Daily 8am–9pm; opens later in summer.

Torrepali Webcafé Via Ammiraglio Staiti 73 ☎ 0923 25 532. Chic, contemporary bar opposite the hydrofoil port, good for beers, cocktails and snacks. With numerous terminals on hand and free wi-fi, it's a relaxed spot to catch up with your emails. Daily 6.30pm–2am.

DIRECTORY

Banks There are banks with ATMs on Piazza Umberto I, Corso Italia, Via Garibaldi and at the Stazione Marittima.

Hospital Ospedale S. Antonio Abate, Via Cosenza (☎ 0923 809 111).

Pharmacies Marini, Corso Vittorio Emanuele 117; Occhipinti, Corso Italia 67 (both usually Mon–Sat 8.30am–1.30pm & 4.30–8pm).

Police Questura at Piazza Vittorio Véneto (☎ 0923 598 111); Carabinieri, Via Orlandini (☎ 0923 330 000).

Post office At Piazza Vittorio Véneto, at the bottom of Via Garibaldi. Mon–Fri 8am–6.30pm, Sat 8.30am–1pm, but Aug Mon–Fri 8am–1.30pm, Sat 8.30am–1pm.

Supermarket Margherita Conad, Corso Italia 35 (Mon–Sat 8am–1.30pm & 5–8.15pm), is a central supermarket for food.

Erice

Despite being just a brief hop from Trapani and the coast, **ERICE** couldn't be further away in spirit. It's a walled mountain town – around 750m above sea level – thoroughly medieval, with its creeping hillside alleys, grey stone buildings and silent charm, but boasting a truly ancient lineage. Nowadays it's a centre for scientific conferences, and you're likely to see numbers of foreigners with labels on their lapels among the milling tourists.

Though there are enough cobbled alleys and quiet spots to enable you to avoid the tour groups, the constant tourist presence in this small town can be wearisome

---

THE FUNIERICE CABLE CAR TO ERICE

Even if it weren't the quickest means to reach Erice – far more convenient than driving or catching a bus – the **Funierice cable car** (*funivia*) ride from Trapani would be worth the excursion. In fact the ascent, which takes about twelve minutes, constitutes one of the region's most memorable experiences, revealing a gradually expanding panorama that extends over the flat saltpans to the south, the mountainous coast north, and out over the narrow limb that holds the old city to the Egadi Islands and the blue sea beyond. By night, the scene is very different, with Trapani's lights sparkling under a starry sky.

From the Trapani terminal on Via Caserta, **departures** are continuous (Mon 1–8pm, Tues–Fri 8.10am–8pm, Sat 10am–10pm, Sun 10am–8pm; ⊕funiviaerice.it), with tickets costing €5.50 one-way, €9 return. Note that the service may be cancelled if it's windy, in which case you'll have to take the AST bus from the stop on Via G.B. Fardella. Check whether the service is operating on ☎ 0923 869 720.

Driving to the cable-car station on Via Caserta, at the extreme eastern end of the modern city, is not straightforward: from the old centre, follow Via G.B. Fardella east, bear left at Corso Mattarella, keep straight along this and its continuation Via Manzoni (following signs for Erice), and turn left at the end into Via Fratelli Aiuto, from which it's a right turn into Via Caserta and the large car park. It's simpler **by bus**: take #21 or #23 from Piazza Vittorio Emanuele (direction Ospedale S. Antonio Abbate) and get off at the stop before the hospital, from where it's a short walk.

– especially in August, when the streets are busy until late at night as trippers and sojourners negotiate the polished cobblestones. **Easter** is another popular time to visit Erice, when the **Misteri** sculptures representing the Stations of the Cross are paraded through the streets on Good Friday. But the greatest pleasure here is simply to wander around. You'll soon get lost in the town's winding alleys, but the most convoluted of routes is only going to take a couple of hours, and every aspect is delightful. Square and solid from the outside, the houses hide pretty courtyards, and while most of the churches are locked, there's usually something to admire – a carved door, a cupola or a belltower. The only modern blots in the town's otherwise homogeneous aspect are the pylons that tower above the grey walls. Beyond these, the views from Erice's terraces are superb, taking in Trapani, the Egadi Islands and even (allegedly) distant Cap Bon in Tunisia.

Brief history

Founded by Elymians, who claimed descent from the Trojans, the city was known to the ancient world as **Eryx**. A magnificent temple, dedicated to Aphrodite Erycina, Mediterranean goddess of fertility, once topped the mountain and was big enough to act as a landmark to sailors. According to legend, it was here that **Daedalus** landed, unlike his son Icarus who flew too near the sun, after fleeing from Minos; he presented the temple with a honeycomb made of gold as his gift to the goddess. Even though the city was considered impregnable, Carthaginian, Roman, Arab and Norman armies all forced entry over the centuries, but all respected the town's sanctity, the Romans rebuilding the temple and setting two hundred soldiers to serve as guardians of the shrine. Later, the Arabs renamed the town Gebel-Hamed, "Mohammed's mountain", while Count Roger called it **Monte San Giuliano**, a name that stuck until Mussolini returned its ancient moniker in 1934.

9

Chiesa Madre

Daily: March 10am–4pm; April–June & Oct 10am–6pm; July & Aug 10am–8pm; Sept 10am–7pm; Nov–Feb 10am–12.30pm • €2.50

Just inside the Norman **Porta Trapani**, at the southwestern edge of town, is the battered stone **Chiesa Madre**. It dates from around 1314, though the massive Gothic entrance was added a century later and much of the structure was rebuilt in the nineteenth century. The neo-Gothic interior preserves some exceptional lace-like **carving**.

The church's stout, battlemented campanile owes its name, **Torre di Re Federico II**, to its original role as a lookout tower for Frederick III of Aragon (Frederick II of Sicily), who made Erice his base during the Wars of the Vespers. Climb to the top for sublime views over village, mountains and sea.

Piazza Umberto I

Museo Cordici Mon & Thurs 8.30am–1.30pm & 3–5pm, Tues, Wed & Fri 8.30am–1.30pm, plus Sat 9am–1pm in summer • Free

From Porta Trapani, the main Via Vittorio Emanuele climbs steeply past houses, shops and *pasticcerie* to the pretty **Piazza Umberto I**, where café tables are strewn adventurously across the sloping cobbles. The small **Museo Cordici** here boasts a good *Annunciation* by Antonello Gagini and the pick of the local archeological finds. Further north, the medieval **Porta Carmine** marks the other end of town, from where the line of ancient **city walls** leads back to the Chiesa Madre.

Castello di Vénere

April–Oct daily 10am–1hr before sunset; Nov–March Sat & Sun 10am–4pm • €3.50

A natural start or finish to an exploration of Erice is the ivy-clad **Castello di Vénere** at the far end of town; the Norman castle was built on the site of the famed ancient temple, chunks of which are incorporated in the walls. When it's fine, the **views** from the terraces of Erice are phenomenal – over Trapani and the slumbering whales of the Egadi Islands.

Giardini del Balio and around

Below the Castello di Vénere are the **Giardini del Balio** public gardens, in the middle of which sits a restored fifteenth-century tower, the **Torretta Pépoli**. From here, you can wind towards Piazza Umberto I, perhaps passing clifftop **San Giovanni Battista** and its distinctive dome before eventually negotiating the minuscule **Piazza San Domenico**, whose church and palace facade are among the town's most harmonious sights.

ARRIVAL AND INFORMATION ERICE

By cable car The easiest way to get to Erice fom Trapani is the cable car (see p.326).

By bus Buses from Trapani (7–8 daily Mon–Sat, 4 daily Sun; 45min) stop outside the Porta Trapani by the cable-car terminal.

By car From Trapani, it's a twisty half-hour's drive. Leave your car in the car park outside the Porta Trapani – don't even think of driving into the old town.

Tourist information The helpful tourist office (Mon–Fri 8am–2pm; ☎ 0923 869 388, ⓦ prolocovalderice.it) is just off Piazza Umberto I on Via Tommaso Guarrasi.

ACCOMMODATION

Staying the night in Erice is relatively expensive, and in summer, or at Easter and Christmas, you'd do well to book in advance. If you stay in the old town it's best to park outside Porta Trapani and carry your luggage up. The other option is to stay in Valderice (see p.330), a 20min drive back down the mountain.

Il Carmine Piazza del Carmine 23 ☎ 0923 869 089 or ☎ 0923 194 1532, ⓦ ilcarmine.com. Spacious, bright rooms, with separate private bathrooms, in a former Carmelite convent in the heart of town. €80

Elimo Via Vittorio Emanuele 75 ☎ 0923 869 377, ⓦ hotelelimo.it. Luxurious rooms in a beautifully restored

9

hotel with a small courtyard garden – this is *the* place to stay if you feel like treating yourself (though without breaking the bank). **€130**

San Domenico Via Tommaso Guerrasi 26 ☎ 0923 860 128, ⊕ hotel-sandomenico.it. Engaging family-run hotel in a medieval house in the heart of Erice – with the owners' children's toys in evidence in the sitting room along with some robust rustic antiques. Two sets of connecting rooms, and a triple. Breakfast is in a tiny courtyard. **€115**

Ulisse Camere Via S. Lucia 2 ☎ 0923 860 155 or ☎ 389 985 6089, ⊕ sitodiulisse.it. Nicely furnished rooms dispersed over two buildings, with private bathrooms. The most evocative are grouped around a tranquil central courtyard. **€65**

EATING AND DRINKING

Though **restaurant** prices are a good bit higher in Erice than elsewhere in the region, you can still eat out fairly reasonably if you stick to the set-price menus. Bring a picnic and you can sit in the shady Giardini del Balio, or there's a *panineria* on Via Vittorio Emanuele.

★ **Monte San Giuliano** Vicolo San Rocco 7 ☎ 0923 869 595. Entering this backstreet restaurant is like visiting a castle, through a stone archway and up steps. There's a sort of courtyard too, where tables are spread out amid plants with seaward views. Try the *ravioli védova allegra* ("happy widow"), with ricotta and squid ink. First courses are €8–10, mains are €10–18. Tues–Sun lunch & dinner; closed three weeks in Nov & Jan.

Pasticceria di Maria Grammatico Via Vittorio Emanuele 14 (no phone). Famous speciality cake shop and café selling marzipan fruits, *amaretti* and the like, a popular tourist stop. Maria Grammatico learned her trade as a girl in a convent, and has co-written a recipe book with writer Mary Taylor Simeti. You can admire the view from a minuscule balcony, and there's a more spacious garden with tables. Open daily in summer;

closed Tues in winter.

La Pentolaccia Via G.F. Guarnotti 17 ☎ 0923 869 099. Atmospherically housed in an old monastery, this moderately priced place serves excellent home-made pasta and couscous. Try the ravioli stuffed with *cernia* in a sauce of cherry tomato, swordfish, mint and prawns (€10), or the *pasta nostromo*, dressed with the roe of a John Dory, Mazzara prawns, tomatoes and garlic (€15). Mon & Wed–Sun lunch & dinner.

★ **Ulisse** Via Chiaramonte 45 ☎ 0923 869 333. Reached down the stepped Vico San Rocco, just off the main square, and with a pretty courtyard garden. The pizzas here (€5–9) are the best in town (and Sun sees a queue form early), while the regular menu is good too, if on the pricey side. Gluten-free dishes are offered. Daily lunch & dinner; closed Thurs in winter.

North of Trapani

North of Trapani, the main attraction is the resort town of **San Vito Lo Capo**, though with a car you could explore the rugged **coastline** en route, the road weaving under some of the gigantic outcrops of rock that characterize Sicily's west. The most spectacular, **Monte Cofano** (659m), is protected as a nature reserve. Although none of the settlements is particularly beautiful, a couple of outstanding hotels might make you decide to base yourself near **Valderice** or **Bonagia**.

Valderice and Bonagia

Between Trapani and San Vito Lo Capo, 40km away, two wide gulfs – Bonagia and Cofano – are backed by holiday homes and small plantations, overlooked both by the heights of Erice and by its lower neighbour **VALDERICE**, a ribbon development occupying a prominent ridge. From Valderice, a minor road winds 5km down to the coast at **BONAGIA**, where the old tuna fishery has been converted into a hotel that's well worth considering for anyone travelling with children.

ACCOMMODATION

VALDERICE AND BONAGIA

★ **Baglio Santa Croce** SS187, Km 12.3 ☎ 0923 891 111, ⊕ bagliosantacroce.it. A glorious renovation of a seventeenth-century stone-built estate, some 1km outside Valderice, whose rooms have beamed ceilings, exposed

walls, tiled floors and iron bedsteads (other rooms are in the modern annexe). There's a pool, a renowned restaurant and superb views to the coast. **€130**

Lido ValdErice ☎ 0923 573 477 or ☎ 349 854 2190,

Ⓦcampinglidovalderice.it. Located close to the sea and a couple of good bars, this is a small but clean and friendly campsite. It's connected by up to six buses a day from Trapani's bus terminal, a 30min ride, then a 5min walk from the bus stop. Closed Nov–Feb. Camping **€4.90** per person, plus **€7.90** per tent

Tonnara di Bonagia Piazza Tonnara di Bonagia,

Valderice Ⓣ0923 431 111, Ⓦtonnaradibonagia.it. Occupying the mellow buildings of an old tuna fishery, this is a perfect base for a pool-and-beach summer holiday. There is an excellent pool, and activities for children in summer. Paths lead to miniature rocky coves for those who prefer to swim in the sea. Accommodation is in either hotel rooms or self-catering apartments. Rooms **€140**

San Vito Lo Capo

With its dense ranks of trattorias, hotels and bars, **SAN VITO LO CAPO** is certainly geared to holiday consumers, but its comparative remoteness has helped to stave off the worst pressures of the tourist industry, even in high season. All the same, you'll have a lot more elbowroom outside the peak months – the best time to appreciate the town's beach, one of Sicily's finest.

Running down to the beach, San Vito's long shop- and restaurant-lined main strip, the pedestrianized **Via Savoia**, is the focus of the evening *passeggiata*, with its shops staying open late in summer. It holds one sight worth a glance: the curious, square and fortified-looking **Santuario** (concerts are held outside in summer; check posters around town). A pleasant promenade backs the **beach**, which stretches east of town. Framed by the looming cliffs behind and overlooked by jagged slabs of rock, the wide, curving stretch of white sand is ideal for swimming and sunbathing, though it gets pretty congested in August. Deckchairs and parasols are available to rent (€10–12/day).

West of the main beaches, an old watchtower at the small harbour is destined to hold the **Museo del Mare**, holding sundry marine exhibits, though don't hold your breath – it could take years. A ten-minute walk past the harbour brings you to the point of **Capo San Vito** itself – a rocky and windswept plain on which a fenced-off lighthouse is perched. For views you need to climb above the town (bear left on the way out to the lighthouse), up a steep road leading to the top of the high cliffs and looking down over the Golfo di Castellammare. The other local walk is east to the Riserva Naturale dello Zingaro, a nature reserve (see p.317).

SAN VITO LO CAPO

CAFÉS & RESTAURANTS	
Agorà	5
Caffè Pino	2
Delfino	3
Pocho	6
La Sirenetta	1
Thaam	4

ACCOMMODATION	
Baglio La Luna	5
El Bahira	9
Bougainville	7
Capo San Vito	1
Halimeda	6
La Pineta	4
Pocho	8
Poseidon	2
Sigiuma	3

ARRIVAL AND DEPARTURE

SAN VITO LO CAPO

By bus Regular daily AST buses run to San Vito from Trapani's bus terminal and Russo buses from Palermo's Piazza Marina; all stop on Via P.S. Mattarella, close to the seafront and three blocks up from Via Savoia.

Destinations Palermo (3–4 daily summer; 1–2 daily winter; 2–3hr); Trapani (8–9 Mon–Sat, 4 daily Sun in summer; 1hr 20min).

Bus companies AST, for Trapani and Bonagia (☎0923 23 222, ☻aziendasicilianatrasporti.it); Russo, for Castellammare del Golfo and Palermo (☎0924 31 364,

☻russoautoservizi.it).

By car Parking is highly restricted during the summer months: your best bet is to search out one of the car parks on the edge of town; some are free, others cost €5–6 per day. From the biggest of these, the free Parcheggio Comunale Sud (Villaggio Azzurro) shuttle – for which take an early right turn onto Via La Piana as you enter town – runs to the centre in the summer months. Alternatively, you can park between the blue lines in a few more central areas (€1/hr; buy a scratch-card from *tabacchi*).

GETTING AROUND

Car, bike and scooter rental Auto Vesco, Via Orazio di Bella 20 (☎388 140 8305, ☻autovesco.it), and Serse, Via Dogana 3 (☎0923 974 434, ☻autonoleggioserse.com),

have cars, motorbikes and scooters. Bikes can be rented May–Sept from various stalls behind the beach (usually €2.50/hr or €5–10/day).

INFORMATION AND TOURS

Tourist information The tourist office is at Via Venza 12 (June–Sept daily 9am–1pm & 5–11pm; Oct–May Mon–Fri 9am–1pm & 4–8pm; ☎0923 974 300, ☻sanvitoweb.com).

Festivals San Vito gets impossibly busy in August and during the Cous Cous Fest (☻couscousfest.it), which takes place over six days in late September and includes free samplings of dozens of versions of the dish, as well as nightly concerts in Piazza Santuario and a fireworks extravaganza on the last night at midnight. In recent years, a Cous Cous Preview, a sort of mini-version of the main event, has been staged over three days in early June;

and there are free concerts and more festivities around San Vito's day in mid-June.

Boat excursions Between May and September, boats operated by several companies run daily to Zingaro, Scopello and Monte Cofano. Hippocampus (☎338 612 5140; ☻hippocampus-sanvito.it) is well organized, with space for just twelve people in its boats, and has both morning and afternoon departures.

Services There's a pharmacy at Via Regina Margherita 26 (Mon–Sat 9.30am–12.30pm & 4.30–8.30pm, reduced hours in winter), and a Post office at Via Savoia 58 (Mon–Fri 8am–1.30pm, Sat 8am–12.30pm).

ACCOMMODATION

Accommodation in San Vito is plentiful and mostly central – as with all resorts, the nearer the sea, the more expensive the room. It's worth noting that in July and August and during the Cous Cous Fest of late September (see above), many places virtually double their prices and demand a minimum stay of three days or a week. Furthermore, you'll almost always have to agree to half-board terms, and you're unlikely to find anything suitable without an advance reservation. In winter, you won't find many places open; ask around the bars in the centre if you get stuck. There are several **campsites** in the area and the "No camping" signs on the town beach should be heeded.

HOTELS AND B&BS

Bougainville Via Mulino 61 ☎0923 972 207, ☻sanvitoweb.com/bougainville. Quite a walk from the beach, this family-run place features climbing plants, five decent rooms and a spiral staircase leading to a roof terrace. Fridge available for guests. Closed Oct–March. **€90**

Capo San Vito Via San Vito 1 ☎0923 972 122, ☻www .caposanvito.it. Right on the seafront, this top-of-the-range hotel has smart, modern rooms, those at the front (costing more) with balconies and sea views; those at the back can be noisy. There's a spa (not included in the price), meals are taken in the terrace restaurant, and a small garden gives on to the beach. Minimum stay six nights in high season. **€250**

Halimeda Via Generale Arimondi 100 ☎0923 972 399,

☻hotelhalimeda.com. This small, modern hotel away from the sea has spacious, themed rooms – Arabic, Nordic, Oriental, etc – each with minibar, a/c and internet access, and there's a lovely Art Nouveau staircase. Breakfast on the terrace includes fresh *cornetti*, biscuits and local *dolci*. There's free parking too – a useful bonus in San Vito. Normally a one-week minimum stay in Aug. Closed Nov–Feb. **€135**

Pocho Contrada Macari ☎0923 972 525, ☻pocho.it. Making the most of its coastal location, 4km south of town, this cliffside hotel-restaurant provides a stylish and soothing base for anyone with transport, with twelve quiet and elegant rooms with fridges and wi-fi (those sea views cost extra). The food is terrific too (see opposite), and there's access to the small rocky beach below. Closed Oct–March. **€150**

Poseidon Via P.S. Mattarella 28 ☎0923 972 444, ⓦ poseidonresidence.com. Good for families, these stylish one- and two-room apartments have a/c, kitchenette and shower, plus parking. Ground-floor apartments have garden access but no views; you get more light and a balcony higher up. Low-season rates are negotiable. Closed Dec–Feb. Two-person apartments from €400 weekly

Sigiuma Via Santuario 39 ☎0923 972 952 or ☎347 863 8967, ⓦ sigiuma.it. Very central B&B with ample rooms in bright, summery colours with fridges and a/c, and there's a patio (where breakfast is served) and a tranquil garden. The welcoming hosts – two brothers – are ready with local info and good advice. Closed Nov–March. €120

CAMPSITES

El Bahira Contrada Macari ☎0923 972 577, ⓦ elbahira.it. The largest and classiest of San Vito's sites, this "camping village" has a range of facilities as well as a private beach, but it's some way out of town, 4km south, and pricey. Caravans (€600 per week) and apartments (€1000 per week) are available. Closed Oct–March. Camping €8.90 per person, plus tent pitch €15.50

★ **La Pineta** Via del Secco ☎0923 972 818, ⓦ campinglapineta.it. With a bar, pizzeria, a pool and bungalows to rent, this is the best of San Vito's campsites, shady and efficiently run, located a 10min walk from town east along the seafront. Camping €10.30 per person, plus tent pitch €8.80

EATING AND DRINKING

Via Savoia and the lungomare are lined with **bars**, ice-cream parlours and pizzerias, and there's no shortage of fish **restaurants** either, most on the pricey side. It's always worth booking during San Vito's festivals (see opposite), when restaurant queues are common.

Agorà Piazza Marinella 5 ☎0923 974 442. Always busy, this smart trattoria near the seafront has tables in the piazza, and serves pastas for €8–15, mains for €12–15, or fresh fish at €5.50/kg. The house speciality is *cassatelle Agorà*, fresh pasta stuffed with zucchini, pistachio and basil, served with mussels and shrimps (€12). Mon–Tues & Thurs–Sun lunch & dinner, Wed dinner only; closed Wed in winter.

Caffè Pino Via Savoia 24 ☎392 358 0791. A nice choice for breakfast, with friendly service and delicious cakes and pastries. Try the *torrone* ice cream and the *cannoli*, but preferably not at the same time. Closed Thurs Oct–June.

Delfino Via Savoia 15 ☎0923 972 711. A pizzeria-trattoria on the main street and near the beach, with smoked-fish *antipasti*, fresh pasta, fish couscous and a short list of decent pizzas to eat in or take away. One of the cheaper places in town, it offers tourist menus for €15.50 including wine. Daily lunch & dinner.

★ **Pocho** Contrada Macari ☎0923 972 525. Small and casually chic, and with an unparalleled location overlooking the rocky coast 4km south of town, this place has tables inside – where there's a collection of Sicilian puppets – and on a lovely panoramic terrace. Inventive dishes are available on a six-course set menu (€38 including water and an aperitivo). The owner, Marilù, occasionally ends the evening with Sicilian songs. On Sunday there is a special couscous lunch (€38 per person). Mon–Sat dinner, Sun lunch.

La Sirenetta Via Savoia, corner of Via Faro (no phone). *Gelateria* overlooking the beach, with a summer shaded terrace and a choice of twenty ice creams. Specialities are *gelsomino* (jasmine flower, summer only), *torrone* and *caldofreddo* (ice cream with hot chocolate sauce). Daily 9am–late; closed Tues Nov–March.

Thaam Via Duca degli Abruzzi 32–36 ☎0923 972 836. Elaborately decorated restaurant with a marked Tunisian influence, with *merguez*, kebabs and couscous (all €12–13) featuring alongside more mainstream Italian dishes. The outdoor tables beneath a tent-like canopy fill fast, so book or arrive early. Daily lunch & dinner.

The Egadi Islands

Moored off the western coast, the three **Egadi Islands** (Isole Egadi) are the easiest of Sicily's offshore islands to visit – which accounts for the summer crowds that swarm over Favignana. The other islands are much less affected, however, and if you come out of season things are noticeably quieter everywhere.

The largest of the Egadis and the nearest to the Sicilian mainland, **Favignana** is also the site of the main fishery. The Genovese link is most apparent in the island of **Lévanzo**, across the strait, which is named after a quarter in Genova and shelters the **Grotta del Genovese**, a cave in which a rich bounty of prehistoric cave paintings was discovered. These days, with the annual tourist influx, the greatest hope for peace and quiet lies in the furthest island, **Marettimo**, whose rugged coasts are indented with a

9

succession of coves, ideal for clean and secluded swimming. The island also offers a choice of **hikes** across its interior and along the rocky coasts.

You could easily see any of the islands as a **day-trip** from Trapani; seeing two on the same day is also feasible. If you want to stay longer, be warned that **accommodation** is extremely limited, and in summer you should phone ahead to reserve a room. It's certainly worth staying over, though you should also bear in mind that, in general, **prices** for rooms and food are higher than on the mainland.

Brief history

Before the advent of tourism, the economic success of the Egadi Islands was largely based on a historical relationship with the northern Italian city of Genova, whose sailors plied the **trading routes** on which the Egadis stood throughout the Middle Ages. The link was formalized in the middle of the seventeenth century, when the Bourbon king Philip IV sold all the islands, in lieu of a debt, to Genoan businessmen. Then, as now, a major element in the local economy was the **tuna fish**, which congregate here to breed at the end of spring. Channelled through the straits between the two main islands during their migrations around the Sicilian coast, they have traditionally been systematically slaughtered in an age-old rite known as **La Mattanza** – though in recent years the practice has been discontinued due to falling stocks and the efficiency of the offshore "factory ships".

Favignana

Fifteen to forty minutes from Trapani by hydrofoil, **FAVIGNANA** has progressed over the years from tuna centre to prison and now tourist resort. Shaped like a lopsided butterfly, the island is almost split in two, its narrow "waist" holding the port, **Favignana town**, and most of the population. To the east lie the best swimming spots, accessible from a succession of rocks and inlets, while the western half of the island is only reachable along the southern coastal road, which tunnels through **Monte Santa Caterina** (300m).

Favignana town

FAVIGNANA TOWN is the focus of most of the tourist traffic. As the archipelago's only town, it holds the island's main services and best choice of accommodation and restaurants, but otherwise there's no particular reason to hang around. From the port, you can see the dome of the church: aim for that and you'll reach the main square, Piazza Madrice. Everything else is contained in the short streets between here and the nearby Piazza Europa.

GETTING TO THE EGADI ISLANDS

Ferries operated by Siremar (☏0923 24 968, ⊕siremar.it) and **hydrofoils** operated by Siremar and Ustica Lines (☏0923 873 813, ⊕usticalines.it) depart several times daily **from Trapani**. They're more frequent between June and September, and most frequent in July and August. They generally call at Favignana, Lévanzo and Marettimo, in that order, though Lévanzo is sometimes the first stop, and some services don't run as far as Marettimo.

Ferries depart from the Stazione Marittima in Trapani, and hydrofoils from further east along Via A. Staiti; you can buy **tickets** at booths on the dockside. Ferries are less frequent than hydrofoils and take at least twice as long, but they're cheaper. One-way ferry tickets from Trapani to Favignana and Lévanzo cost around €10, and to Marettimo around €15; one-way hydrofoil tickets are around €12 and €20 respectively; all return tickets cost double. In summer, Siremar also runs fast ferries (*navi veloci*) to Favignana and Lévanzo, which may take half the time of a normal ferry, depending on the route.

Ustica Lines also operate a year-round hydrofoil service three times daily to Favignana **from Marsala** (30min; €8.60).

The town's only distinctive feature is the imposing building near the port, the **Palazzo Florio**. Now part of the town hall, it was built by Ignazio Florio, an entrepreneur who took over the islands in 1874 and revitalized the fisheries; there's a statue of him in nearby Piazza Europa. His tuna fishery, **Stabilimento Florio**, is similarly impressive, its vaulted nineteenth-century buildings a solid counterpoint across the bay. It is currently open for visits (with a flexible timetable), and plans are afoot to open a marine and fishing museum here at some future date. Otherwise, all there is to do is window-shop in the many places selling *"prodotti tipici"* – traditional tuna products, of course, as well as *bottarga* (fish roe), oil, local dried herbs, wine and bloody postcards of *la Mattanza*.

Monte Santa Caterina

The island's sole hill, **Monte Santa Caterina** is topped by an abandoned Norman **castello**, floodlit at night, and reached by a crazy-paved stairway from the west side of Favignana town. Alternatively, follow the lower path over the mountain to a crest with views to Marettimo. The path down the other side, however, is hard to follow and you may end up scrambling over walls and through fields to reach the road.

The rest of the island

Away from the town, Favignana is tidily cultivated, pitted with square white houses built from **tufa** quarried from curious pits all over the island – an export that has historically provided the island with a second source of cash (after fishing). One of the old quarries, on the fringe of town by the decrepit chapel of Santa Anna, has been landscaped and turned into a quirky **sunken garden**.

You can swim at the beach near the town, but the sandy beach at **Lido Burrone**, on the island's south side, is better, with a friendly pizzeria-restaurant-bar that rents out parasols and sun-loungers. Otherwise, just follow the coast roads and plunge in off the rocks, or settle down on one of the tiny handkerchiefs of sand. Call in at **Cala Azzurra**, below the lighthouse at the island's eastern end, where there's a beautiful blue bay but little sand; or, just north, the spectacular **Cala Rossa**, where you can swim off rocks at the base of towering tufa cliffs. Its name – Red Cove – is said to derive from the blood washed ashore after the Roman defeat of the Carthaginians in a fierce sea battle in 241 BC. The road to Cala Rossa in particular is noted for its tufa quarries – just before the cove itself is a huge quarry where stacks of tufa and unexcavated pillars rise high from the gloomy depths. On the other side of the mountain, the best beach is at **Cala Rotonda**, where, local legend would have it, Odysseus washed up before being attacked by the Cyclops.

ARRIVAL AND DEPARTURE　　　　　　　　　　　　　　　　FAVIGNANA

By ferry and hydrofoil Siremar (☎0923 921 368, ⓦsiremar.it) and Ustica Lines (☎0923 921 277, ⓦusticalines.it) both have offices at the port in Favignana town. They operate services throughout the year between Trapani, Marsala and the other Egadi Islands. The services detailed below are year-round; schedules are increased from June 10 to September 10.
Ferry departures Lévanzo (2–3 daily; 35min); Marettimo (1 daily; 40min); Trapani (2–3 daily; 1hr 10min).
Hydrofoil departures Lévanzo (5 daily; 10–15 min); Marettimo (4 daily; 45min); Marsala (3 daily; 30min); Trapani (hourly; 20–40min).
By airport transfer Siciltransfert (☎348 262 0089) arranges transport direct to Favignana from Palermo (€45 per person) and Trapani (€30) airports (and vice versa), including hydrofoil crossing and taxi.

GETTING AROUND

By bike The best way to get around the island is by bike, since the flat terrain and good road surfaces enable you to see the whole of Favignana in an afternoon. There are bike rental shops all over town, including down at the port – look for the words *"noleggio bici"*, or try Isidoro, at Via Mazzini 40 (☎347 323 3058), which rents bikes for €3.50 a day (€6 in high season), and scooters for €25–30 a day (€35–45 in Aug).
By bus A bus service leaves from down by the port on three routes: #1 to Cala Azzurra, #2 to Punta Sottile, #3 to the turn-off for Cala Rossa. Departures are roughly hourly during the summer, much less frequent in winter; buy tickets on board (€1).
By taxi Call ☎347 479 6745 or ☎333 318 3112.

9

INFORMATION AND TOURS

Tourist information The tourist office is at no. 25 Piazza Madrice, Favignana town (Mon–Sat 10am–12.30pm, usually closed Jan & Feb; ☏0923 921 647). A useful website for Favignana and the whole archipelago is ⊕ egadi.com.

Boat tours Trips to the island's offshore grottoes are offered down at the port, costing around €35 per person

including lunch for a full day (less for a 2hr or 3hr excursion) – there's always someone around in summer, but you may have to ask in town at other times.

Diving Progetto Atlantide (☏ 347 517 8338 or ☏ 347 050 4492, ⊕ progettoatlantide.com) offers courses and equipment rental.

ACCOMMODATION

HOTELS AND B&BS

Albergo Aegusa Via Garibaldi 11, Favignana town ☏0923 922 430, ⊕ aegusahotel.it. Central, clean and quiet three-star hotel just off Via Roma. Rooms have a/c, minibar and safe; some are in an annexe, 100m away. It's worth taking half board here, as there's a rated garden restaurant. Closed Nov–March. **€90**

B&B Favignana Via Roma 10, Favignana town ☏392 725 2398, ⊕ bbfavignana.com. One of the cheapest choices on the island, this place has simple, colour-themed rooms with private bathrooms and a/c. It's a good choice if you want to stay centrally, just minutes away from the port. Prices almost halve in low season. No credit cards. Closed mid-Jan to mid-March. **€110**

Bouganville Via Cimabue 10, Favignana town ☏0923 922 033, ⊕ albergobouganville.it. This small, reasonably priced hotel has spacious rooms and a restaurant in the garden. It's near the beach on the southwestern edge of town: follow Via Diaz and Via Battisti from the centre, a 10min walk. Closed Dec–Easter. Half board obligatory in summer; prices are much reduced for the rest of the year. Half-board from **€110**

Cave Bianche Cala Azzurra ☏0923 925 451, ⊕ cave bianchehotel.it. Boutique hotel within an abandoned quarry, with chic and minimalist rooms. There's a pool, hydro-massage and a great restaurant, and scooters and bikes are available to rent. It's about 10min from town by bike. Closed Nov–March. **€305**

Hotel delle Cave Contrada Torretta Strada, Vic. della Madonna ☏0923 925 423, ⊕ hoteldellecave.it. This boutique hotel is built on the lip of an abandoned quarry a couple of kilometres east of town, in an area known locally as Zona Cavallo, with gardens, a hydro-massage pool and a restaurant inside the quarry itself. The structure is severely functional, but the rooms are full of designer features, and come with minibar, a/c and wi-fi. Excellent deals in low season. Closed Nov–Easter. **€230**

Villa Antonella Via Punta Marsala, Favignana town ☏0923 921 073, ⊕ egadi.com/villaantonella. A family-run B&B a couple of kilometres outside town which also has self-catering mini-apartments sleeping 2–4 people. A good choice for families or those on a budget who want to be able to cook for themselves. It is walkable from town, but you might prefer to have your own transport. **€50**

CAMPSITE

Camping Egad Contrada Arena ☏0923 921 555, ⊕ campingegad.com. A little over 1km east of town, and 500m from the beach at Lido Burrone, this has a range of accommodation, including rooms in wooden cabins, and igloo-type apartments with cooking facilities sleeping two–four. Facilities include bar, restaurant, store and scooter and bike-rental, and there's transport to and from the port. Closed Nov–Easter. Camping **€7.30** per person, plus pitches **€7.50**; cabins **€65**; igloos **€130**

EATING AND DRINKING

Piazza Madrice, Piazza Europa and the surrounding streets are where you'll find Favignana's **bars** and **restaurants**, but be warned: restaurant prices on the island tend to be high. Excellent slices of pizza, *schiacciata* and the like are sold at the bakery Costanza on Via Roma, just up from Piazza Madrice, or you may prefer to **picnic** on the town beach. For picnic provisions, carry on past Costanza to the Egadi **supermarket**, where the deli counter has local ricotta and a good range of cheeses and hams.

La Bettola Via Nicotera 47 ☏0923 921 988. With a terrace for eating *al fresco*, this popular spot serves up a memorable *couscous di pesce* (€19). As an *antipasto*, the *fritelle di gamberi* (prawn fritters) are also worth sampling. Prices are reasonable, with starters at €7–9, mains €10–15. Daily lunch & dinner; sometimes closed Mon in winter.

Pizza Pazza Via Mazzini 16, off Piazza Madrice (no phone). You can pick up excellent and inexpensive pizzas

here, cooked in a wood-fired oven. Don't miss the local speciality, *rianata*, made with pecorino instead of mozzarella, and oregano instead of the usual basil, and picnic on them in the piazza. Daily 7–10.30pm; closed Tues in winter.

Pizzeria Salvador Via Nicotera 7 ☏0923 921 271. This family-run place serves great pizza (from €5) and other dishes too, including local specialities like couscous. In summer there are tables outside. Daily lunch & dinner.

DIRECTORY

Banks The banks in Piazza Europa and Piazza Madrice both have ATMs.

Internet Elyos, Piazza Madrice 37 (April–Oct Mon–Sat 9am–1pm & 3–7.30pm, Sun 9am–1pm).

Pharmacy Abramo, Piazza Europa (English-speaking);

Barone, Piazza Madrice (both Mon–Fri 8.30am–1pm & 5–8.30pm). At other times see rota on the door.

Post office Via Marconi 2 (Mon–Fri 8am–1.30pm, Sat 8am–12.30pm).

Lévanzo

LÉVANZO, 4km north of Favignana, is the smallest of the three main Egadi Islands. Most of it is used to pasture sheep and goats, and, with its turquoise seas and white houses, it has very much the feel of a Greek island. Its population is concentrated in **LÉVANZO TOWN**, little more than a cluster of square houses and holiday homes around a tiny port, where you'll find the island's two hotel-restaurants and a couple of bars.

The **coastline** is rocky and largely inaccessible, but you can get around on foot by following the dirt paths along the shore and over the hills. Following the only road twenty minutes west of the port, you'll come to a rocky spire sticking out of the sea – the **Faraglione** – beyond which a rocky path leads north up the coast. This becomes a stone and dirt track once it reaches the upper part of the valley. If you stick to it, it takes around an hour to reach the lighthouse at **Capo Grosso** at the northeastern point of the island.

On your way to the cape, you can swim at the lovely white **Tramontana bay**: just before you reach an old metal gate, a track leads down the red-earth mountainside, ending in an acute concrete slope, which you can just about slither down, though scrambling back up is hard work. Tracing the coast eastwards from Lévanzo Town, you can reach **Cala Minnola** in about fifteen minutes – a lovely rocky cove ideal for swimming.

Grotta del Genovese

On the island's northwest coast, on a slope overlooking the sea, the **Grotta del Genovese** is the main attraction for most visitors. The cave walls display some remarkable Paleolithic **incized drawings**, discovered in 1949, as well as later Neolithic pictures; they're mostly of animals, and are between six thousand and ten thousand years old. Despite their age, the evocative drawings retain their impact, drawn by prehistoric man in an attempt to harness and influence the power of nature: one lovely picture of a deer near the entrance dates from when the island was still connected to the Sicilian mainland. The later Neolithic sketches are easy to pick out too; less well drawn, more stylized representations of men and even of tuna fish and a dolphin.

GETTING TO THE GROTTA DEL GENOVESE

All visits to the **Grotta del Genovese** (ⓦ grottadelgenovese.it) have to be arranged at least a day in advance through the official custodian, Signor Natale Castiglione: either telephone ☎ 0923 924 032 or ☎ 339 741 8800, or pass by at Via Calvario 11, above the quay. Tickets cost €22.50 each, either by jeep or by boat. **By boat**, the round-trip will take nearly two hours, usually departing at 10.30am and (if there's enough demand) 3pm. Note that the smallest swell may be enough to make it impossible for the boat to pull into the narrow rocky disembarkation point. You can also extend the tour by opting for the round-island trip (€5 supplement), taking up to three hours including a swimming stop.

By jeep, the two-hour round trip is roughly 10km, following an inland route through the valley in the centre of the island. The fairly difficult descent on foot to the grotto from where the jeep stops is not recommended for anyone infirm. You might negotiate a discount jeep fare if you feel like walking back. Booking for either route is essential. Winter tours only take place when the conditions are right – again, always telephone ahead.

9

By ferry and hydrofoil The port is just below the island's only road, Via Calvario. In summer both Siremar and Ustica Lines have ticket booths at the port; in winter, they move into the town, out of reach of stormy waves (precise locations vary from year to year). Services are good enough throughout the year to make day-trips from Trapani and Favignana an easy prospect.

ACCOMMODATION

In summer, the island's hotel will usually require a week's minimum stay and only accept guests on half-board terms, though as the only other options for food on Lévanzo are two bars, an *alimentari* and a bakery, this is no hardship. In any case, the food is good at both places. If you're self-catering at the *Lisola Residence*, you may want to bring supplies from the mainland, as the choice of food at the *alimentary* is a bit limited.

Lisola Residence ☎ 0923 194 1530 or ☎ 320 180 9090, ⓦ lisola.eu. Seven apartments 400m outside the port sleeping between two and four, occupying simple tufa cottages originally built by nineteenth-century tuna-canning magnate Florio for his workers. Extras include a large pool with parasols and sun-loungers, and free transport to the port whenever you need it. Closed Nov–March. Two-person apartments €500

Paradiso ☎ 0923 924 080, ⓦ albergoparadiso.eu. Close to the port, next to the bar, this has a terrace-restaurant and marvellous sea views from the en-suite, air-conditioned rooms, some of which are a bit cramped. Half-board doubles €170

Marettimo

Wildest and furthest out from Trapani, **MARETTIMO** was claimed by Samuel Butler, in his *The Authoress of the Odyssey*, as the original Ithaca, home of Odysseus. Even more far-fetched, Butler also thought that Homer himself was the princess Nausicaa of ancient Trapani. These theories aside, there are compelling reasons to come to Marettimo. Its spectacular fragmented coastline is pitted with rocky coves sheltering hideaway beaches, several of which – such as those at **Cala Sarde** and **Cala Nera** on the south coast, or at the **Saracen castle** at the northeastern point of the island – can be reached by footpath. Even in high season, you're likely to have much of Marettimo to yourself, as few tourists can be bothered to visit a place with limited accommodation and no more than half a dozen trattorias. That said, there are signs of heightened interest these days in the shape of a sprinkling of new holiday homes, while EU money has gone towards paving a couple of sections of track. However, such "improvements" are still fairly low-key and, at least for now, the island retains its air of being far off the beaten track.

Marettimo town

As you pull into port and explore its few streets, **MARETTIMO TOWN** appears almost North African in character, with its flat-roofed cube houses with blue shutters and painted tiles, and alleys full of tumbling bougainvillea. There's one main street, a little square and church, and a second harbour, the **fishing port**, just along from the main harbour. Two of the island's most popular **bathing** spots are conveniently close, one near the main harbour, one near the fishing harbour.

By ferry and hydrofoil Both Siremar (ferries and hydrofoils) and Ustica Lines (hydrofoils) run year-round from Trapani and Favignana to Marettimo, but there are far fewer services than to Favignana and Lévanzo. There is a skeleton low-season service, and boats are often cancelled due to bad weather.

Tourist information There's no information office on Marettimo, but plenty of useful stuff online at ⓦ marettimoweb.com.

Boat trips Various options are available via *Rosa dei Venti* (see opposite): around the island to Cala Bianca for swimming costs €15 per person; the same with a picnic (including home-cured fish and local cheeses and wines) is around €30 per person. On either, you can be left at a cove to swim and be collected an hour or so later. Alternatively, you could take a three-hour boat tour of the island (a "*giro dell'isola*"), available from operators at the main harbour, which allows you to see Marettimo's entire rocky coastline

MARETTIMO HIKES

None of the walks detailed below is particularly onerous, though you might have to scramble at times. Always make sure you're carrying enough water with you.

TO THE CASE ROMANE

Marettimo's simplest walk takes you to some old Roman defensive works, the **Case Romane**, which are still in pretty good condition. Climb up the road to the side of *Caffè Tramontana* and, at the top, scout around to the left and then right to find the signpost for the start of the walk. The remains are half an hour on, sitting next to a small and dilapidated church that shows marked Arab characteristics but is thought to have been built by Byzantine monks in the twelfth century.

TO CALA SARDE AND CALA NERA

Follow the road south of Marettimo port, turning inland after about 1km where the path divides. There's a steep climb, with the town's cemetery below you, rising to about 300m. After about half an hour, you'll pass a pine forest and a small outhouse, looking out on views towards Tunisia; below is the **Cala Sarde**, a small bay reachable along a smaller path to the left in another half an hour.

Instead of descending to the bay, continue for about an hour on the main path along the island's rocky west coast. You'll pass a lighthouse and a route down to **Cala Nera**, where you can swim off the rocks in perfect isolation.

TO THE CASTLE AT PUNTA TROIA

This walk follows the footpath all the way to the **northeastern tip** of the island, a hike that should take you around three hours; you'll need a head for heights in certain stretches. Go past the fishing harbour with the sea on your right, and keep to the coast along the path for about ten minutes, until the terrace wall on your left stops. When a sign here ("Castello Punta Troia") points to the left, cut up to find the main path on a small spur above you. This stretches along the whole length of the island about 100m above the sea, ending at some concrete steps that descend to a lovely secluded beach and the foot of the **castle**, perched on an impregnable rocky crag. This precipitous fortification was originally built by the Saracens, enlarged by Roger II, and further extended by the Spanish in the seventeenth century, when it became a prison, and acquired a dire reputation for cruelty.

and dive into otherwise inaccessible waters that are clean and clear and a joy for snorkellers.

Services Marettimo's main street, Corso Umberto, is about a minute's walk from the harbour where the ferries and hydrofoils dock. It holds a bank with an ATM, a Siremar ticket agency and an Ustica Lines agency in a little shop just up from Piazza Umberto.

ACCOMMODATION

Marettimo offers a better choice of **accommodation** than Lévanzo, with a couple of B&Bs and a few apartments and holiday residences for weekly rents. If these are full, ask around in the bars and restaurants for **rented rooms**, but it's always best to book before you come.

I Delfini Corso Umberto 34 ☎0923 923 137 or ☎339 239 9867, ⊛idelfinimarettimo.it. Central B&B with great sea views on one side. Rooms are simple but clean and comfortable, with private bathrooms, and there's a roof terrace on which delicious breakfasts are served. No credit cards. Closed Nov–March. €90

Marettimo Residence Via Telégrafo 3 ☎0923 923 202, ⊛marettimoresidence.it. Small resort-like cluster of cottages above a stony beach south of the main port, available for B&B or weekly rental (€1050 per week in high season). Demand is high, but you'll find greater availability and much lower prices outside the summer period. B&B rooms €165

Rosa dei Venti Punta Simone 4 ☎0923 923 249 or ☎333 675 8893, ⊛isoladimarettimo.it. As well as operating various other tourist activities, this outfit has rooms and self-catering apartments dispersed around the island, also available for short stays. €60

Sealife Corso Umberto and Via Tedesco ☎0923 923 288 or ☎347 542 9713, ⊛sealifesnc.com. The two apartments are centrally located, accommodating two to five people usually by the week, though they'll let you have them for shorter periods if there are vacancies. One has a terrace, the other a small courtyard, and both are equipped with barbecues. €550 per week

9

★ **La Terrazza** Via G. Pepe 24 ☎ 0923 923 252 or ☎ 368 768 1571, ⓦ bedandbreakfastmarettimo.it. The best feature here is the wide, semi-shaded terrace, with terrific views over the castle and sea, where breakfast is served and which guests can use all day. The four rooms are simply and tastefully decorated. No credit cards. Closed mid-Oct to March. **€80**

EATING AND DRINKING

Marettimo offers a reasonable range of **eating** options, though prices are a little higher than on the mainland, given the cost of shipping in ingredients. Not all the places listed below stay open throughout the year, but there's always something open. There are two *alimentari* on Via Garibaldi, off the main drag, one of which has takeaway items.

Baia del Sole Piazza Umberto. Next to the Siremar office on the main road, this bar has a few tables and excellent ice cream and *granitas*. Daily 8am–8pm.

Caffè Tramontana Via Campi. On the road above the fishing harbour, people gather here all day for the superb sea views. It's *the* place to come for breakfast, or for an aperitif with snacks at sunset. Summer daily 8am–late.

Il Pirata Via Scalo Vecchio ☎ 0923 923 027. *Pesce spada all'arancia* (swordfish with orange) and *pasta con le sarde* (with sardines, fennel seeds, pine nuts and raisins) are among the specialities in this pleasant trattoria by the fishing harbour. First courses are around €10, mains €10–18. For a real feast, splash out on the *zuppa di aragosta* – first you eat the flavoursome broth with pasta, then the lobster, at €55 per head. Daily lunch & dinner.

Il Veliero Corso Umberto ☎ 0923 923 274. Owned by a fisherman, this trattoria has excellent fresh seafood and a summer cane-and-fishing-trap-bedecked terrace by the harbour. First courses, such as pasta with squid ink or *bottarga* (tuna roe), cost around €12; mains aren't much more. Daily lunch & dinner; closed Nov–Feb.

Mozia and the saltpans

Fifteen kilometres down the coast from Trapani, the uninhabited **Stagnone Islands** (Isole dello Stagnone) have been mostly given over to salt extraction since the fifteenth century. On the mainland opposite, several windmills still stand near the surviving **saltpans**, which form a crystalline patchwork between Trapani and Marsala. Offshore, the long, thin Isola Grande shelters the only one of the Stagnone group that you can visit, **San Pantaleo**, set in the middle of a shallow lagoon that's now the year-round scene of **windsurfing**, **kitesurfing** and **sailing**. You can rent the equipment from shacks strung along the coast road; some outlets also rent out **canoes** (around €6 per half-day), allowing you to weave around the saltpans. San Pantaleo also holds the site of the ancient Phoenician settlement of Motya (**Mozia** in Italian); this is the the big cultural attraction hereabouts, and the whole island is usually referred to as Mozia rather than San Pantaleo.

Mozia

Daily 9.15am–6.30pm • €9

Flat, cultivated and only 2.5km in circumference, **Mozia** is one of the most manageable of Sicily's ancient sites, with the unique Phoenician ruins spread across the whole island. You could circle the perimeter in an hour or so, but it's more enjoyable to make a day of it and bring a picnic (and there's a bar with basic snacks on the island).

Along with Palermo and Solus (Solunto), Mozia was one of the three main Phoenician bases in Sicily, settled some time during the eighth century BC and completely razed to the ground by Dionysius I in 397 BC. It's the only one of the three

THE VIA DEL SALE BUS

Local bus company Salemi (☎ 0923 951 522, ⓦ viadelsaleinbus.it) run a hop-on, hop-off **bus** connecting all the main sites between Marsala and Trapani, including Mozia, the Saline Ettore e Infersa/Museo del Sale and several other windmills with small museums devoted to the history of **salt**. A day-ticket costs €12.50 for adults, €7.50 for children.

sites that wasn't subsequently built over, though it remained undiscovered until the seventeenth century, and wasn't properly excavated until **Joseph "Pip" Whitaker** (amateur archeologist and member of one of the marsala wine dynasties) bought the island in the late nineteenth century and started to dig it up.

You reach the island site and its archeological museum by a short **ferry** ride from the mainland. Although the linguistic link between the archipelago's name (Stagnone) and our "stagnant" is not entirely coincidental, that doesn't deter some visitors from wading into the lagoon on the mainland side and crossing to Mozia in beachwear – the island museum, at least, has had enough and won't allow entry to anyone who's not properly clothed.

Museo Whitaker

Daily 9.15am–6.30pm • Included in Mozia entry ticket

Joseph Whitaker's house – once incongruously furnished in Edwardian style – now holds the **Museo Whitaker**, which holds finds from the site. Its cool rooms are packed with a beautiful collection of jewellery, arrowheads, terracotta figurines and domestic artefacts, with the earliest pieces dating from the eighth century BC. Pride of place goes to the magnificent fifth-century BC marble **sculpture** of a youth, *Il Giovinetto di Mozia*, sensual and self-assured in his pose. The identity of the subject is unknown, but he was likely to have been a high-ranking official, suggested by the subtle indentations round his head, indicating some kind of crown or elaborate headwear.

Outside stands an aristocratic bust of "Giuseppe" Whitaker, and there's a shaded picnic area under the trees nearby.

Casa dei Mosaici and the cothon

The remains of ancient Mozia start immediately outside the Museo Whitaker. In front and 100m to the left is the **Casa dei Mosaici**, two houses containing some faded black-and-white mosaics made from sea pebbles. One, probably belonging to a patrician, shows animal scenes; the other, thought to be a craftsman's, yielded numerous shards of pottery. Further along the path you come to the **cothon**, a small artificial boat dock built within the ancient town's walls and similar in style to a much larger one at Carthage itself.

The north gate

To the right of the Museo Whitaker, rough tracks that were once the city's main thoroughfares cut through flowering cacti and vine plantations. Most of the tracks end at the once-impenetrable north gate, now a ragged collection of steps and ruined walls, which stands at the head of a causeway built by the Phoenicians in the sixth century BC to connect the island with the mainland (and a necropolis) at Birgi, 7km to the north. The road is still there, although these days it's submerged under the water.

Tophet burial ground

Left along the shore from the north gate is the Tophet burial ground. Most of the information about day-to-day life in Motya has come from here, the sanctuary revealing a number of urns containing the ashes of animals sacrificed to the Phoenician gods (chiefly Baal Hammon) and of children, probably stillborn or who died of natural causes. A remarkable series of inscribed votive stele from the Tophet is on display in the museum.

Cappiddazzu

Just inland of the north gate, the **Cappiddazzu** site shows the foundations of a large building, probably a temple, while between gate and Cappiddazzu is a Punic **industrial zone** that was dedicated to the production of pottery and ceramics. This was where the famous marble sculpture was found, probably hidden by the city's inhabitants as the Greeks stormed the island.

9

By bus From Marsala, take the local Linea D bus from Piazza del Popolo to the Mozia ferry landing. Return buses are on a similar schedule; a reduced service in either direction operates on a Sunday. From Trapani, you'll have to take the bus or the train to Marsala and connect from there.

By ferry Ferries out to the island are run by Arini & Pugliese (☎347 779 0218) and Mozia Line (☎329 476

0294) from two separate spots. Arini & Pugliese boats leave from the ferry landing near the bus stop, Mozia Line from a dock about 1km away. A steady flow of visitors ensures that there's usually a ferry waiting during the hours when the museum is open; tickets for the 10mn crossing cost €5 return. Parking is available near the two embarkation points.

ACCOMMODATION AND EATING

Baglio Vajarassa Contrada Spagnola 176 ☎0923 968 628, ⓦbagliovajarassa.com. This peaceful *agriturismo* lies a couple of kilometres south of the Arini & Pugliese ferry landing, and has rooms furnished with antiques, and typical local dishes for dinner around a communal table. Half board only. **€60**

Mamma Caura Mozia Lines Ferry Landing ☎0923 966 036. You can eat well here – try the fish couscous – but try to arrive early enough to watch the sun setting over the sea (they serve wine and nibbles as well). There are also canoes to rent. Daily dinner only.

The saltpans

The series of **saltpans** glistening in the shallows between Trapani and Marsala has been worked since Phoenician times. Bare-chested men toil with shovels, carting full wheelbarrows across from the pans to a rising conveyor belt that dumps 2m-high mounds of white salt along the banks. At different times of the day, as the light changes, there's a pink tint to the saltpans, while Marettimo rises in the distance through the haze.

Saline Ettore e Infersa and the Museo del Sale

April–Sept 9.30am–7pm; call ahead in winter as hours vary • Museo del Sale €6, audioguide €2 • ☎0923 733 003

On the mainland, just opposite Mozia, one of three windmills has been turned into a showroom and museum, the Saline Ettore e Infersa, dedicated to the whole salt-making process. It's free to enter if you just want to browse the locally produced foods and crafts in the showroom, but the **Museo del Sale** is fascinating, especially if you take the instructive audioguided tour.

Marsala

When the island-city of Motya had been put to the sword by the Syracusans, the survivors founded Lilybaeum (modern **MARSALA**), 10km to the south. The main city of the Phoenicians in Sicily, and the only one to resist the Greek push westwards, Lilybaeum finally succumbed to Rome in 241 BC, and not long after was used as a springboard for an attack against the Carthaginian heartland itself. The town's position at Sicily's western tip later made it the main Saracenic base on the island, and it was renamed Marsah Ali, Arabic for the "port of Ali", son-in-law of the Prophet, from which its modern name derives.

The town scored a place in modern Italian history for its role in the saga of the **Risorgimento**, the struggle for Italian unity in the nineteenth century. It was here that Garibaldi kicked off his campaign to drive out the Bourbons, in the company of his red-shirted "Thousand". Until a planned Garibaldi museum on Marsala's southwestern seafront (on Via Scipione l'Africano) gets round to opening, memorials to the swashbuckling freedom-fighter are confined to a few statues and street names, and the nearby Porta Garibaldi, at the end of Via Garibaldi, which recalls the hero's entry into the town. Local enthusiasts clad in red shirts parade through the gate each year on May 11, in commemoration of the exploits of the "Thousand".

Piazza della Repubblica

Marsala's town centre is a predominantly Baroque assortment of buildings, though there are hints of the older town's layout in the narrow, largely traffic-free streets around the central **Piazza della Repubblica**. The elegance of the square is due to its two eighteenth-century buildings: the arcaded **Palazzo Comunale**, and the **Chiesa Madre** – dedicated to San Tommaso di Canterbury, patron saint of Marsala – from which four statues peer loftily down. The church's large but rather disappointing interior has a few Gagini sculptures.

Museo degli Arazzi

Via Garraffa 57 • Tues–Sun 9am–1pm & 4–6pm • €4 • ☎ 0923 711 327

Behind the Chiesa Madre, the sole display at the **Museo degli Arazzi** is a series of eight enormous hand-stitched wool and silk **tapestries** depicting the capture of Jerusalem. Made in Brussels in the sixteenth century, they were the gift of the Spanish ambassador, who doubled as the archbishop of Messina, and are beautifully rich, in burnished red, gold and green.

Pinacoteca Comunale

Summer Tues–Sun 10am–1pm & 6–8pm; winter Tues–Sun 10am–1pm & 5–7pm in winter • Free

Past the Museo degli Arazzi, you can view the remains of **Punic walls** and pavements from the Greco-Roman period in Piazza San Girolamo. Still further, a left turn off Via Garraffa leads into Piazza del Carmine, where a fourteenth-century convent has been stylishly renovated to hold the **Pinacoteca Comunale**. Visitors can enjoy a good collection of art and regular exhibitions – mostly contemporary and with local connections.

9

Complesso San Pietro and the Museo Civico

Via Ludovico Anselmi Correale • Tues–Sun 9am–1pm & 4–8pm • Free • ☎ 0923 718 741

The **Complesso San Pietro** is a fifteenth-century monastery, now fully restored as a cultural centre that incorporates the **Museo Civico**, where you can see a selection of archeological items from the Punic, Greek and Roman eras and, more compellingly, rooms dedicated to Garibaldi's triumphant campaign in western Sicily, including letters, photos, arms and uniforms. The complex also contains the town library and a courtyard for occasional open-air performances.

Porta Nuova and Capo Boeo

At the far end of Via XI Maggio, through the eighteenth-century **Porta Nuova**, Piazza della Vittoria has a gate into the municipal gardens and a bar where you can sit and admire the austere Art Deco front of the Cine Impero, so out of keeping with the Baroque arch opposite. Beyond the piazza lies **Capo Boeo**, the westernmost point of Sicily that was the first settlement of the survivors of annihilated Motya. All the town's major antiquities are concentrated here, including the old **Insula Romana**, closed to the public at present, but normally accessible from Via Vittorio Véneto. The site contains all that's been excavated so far of the city of Lilybaeum, though most of it is third-century BC Roman, as you might guess from the presence of a vomitorium, lodged in the most complete section of the site – the **edificio termale**, or bathhouse. There's some good mosaic-work here: a chained dog at the entrance and, much better, a richly coloured **hunting scene** in the atrium, showing a stag being savaged by a wild beast.

San Giovanni a Marsala

Viale N Sauro • Usually daily 9am–noon & 3–6pm

From Piazza della Vittoria, Viale N. Sauro leads to the church of **San Giovanni**, under which is a grotto reputed to have been inhabited by the sibyl Lilibetana, endowed with paranormal gifts. There's another slice of mosaic here, and a well whose water is meant to impart second sight. A pilgrimage takes place every June 24, the feast day of San Giovanni.

THE MAKING OF MARSALA WINE

The Baglio Anselmi, which houses Marsala's archeological museum, is one of a number of old **bagli**, or warehouses, conspicuous throughout this wine-making region. Many are still used in the making of the famous dessert wine that carries the town's name. It was an Englishman, John Woodhouse, who first exploited the commercial potential of **marsala wine**, when he visited the town in 1770. Woodhouse soon realized that, like port, the local wine could travel for long periods without going off, when fortified with alcohol. Others followed: Ingham, Whitaker, Hopps and many more whose names can still be seen on some of the warehouse doors. Interestingly, it was the English presence in Marsala that persuaded Garibaldi to launch his campaign here rather than in Sciacca (his first choice), judging that the Bourbon fleet wouldn't dare to interfere so close to Her Majesty's commercial concerns.

Marsala owes much of its current prosperity to the marketing of its wine, which is still a thriving industry, though no longer in British hands. You can visit some of the *bagli* and sample the stuff for free: try the **Cantine Montalto** (Mon–Fri 9am–1pm & 3–6pm, Sat 9am–1pm, other times can be booked at ☎0923 969.667) at Contrada Bérbaro, 3km along the road south towards Mazara del Vallo, reached along Lungomare Mediterraneo. Free guided tours and samplings are offered, and there's an **Enomuseum** where you can look over the old apparatus and techniques for wine-making. Otherwise, you'll find marsala or the sweeter *marsala all'uovo* (mixed with egg yolks) in every bar, enoteca and restaurant in town.

9

Museo Archeologico

Lungomare Boeo • Tues–Sun 9am–7.30pm • €4 • ☎ 0923 952 535

One of the stone-vaulted warehouses that line the lungomare contains the **Museo Archeologico**, mostly dedicated to a very skeletal but still surprisingly well-preserved warship from the classical period. Displayed in a heat- and humidity-regulated environment, it ranks as the only extant *liburnian*, a specifically Phoenician or **Punic warship**, probably sunk during the First Punic War in the great sea battle off the Egadi Islands that ended Carthage's rule of the waves. It was discovered in 1971 and brought here after eight years of underwater surveying by a British team working under the archeologist Honor Frost. Originally 35m long, nearly 5m wide and rowed by 68 oarsmen, the vessel has been the source of much detailed information on the period, including what the crew ate and the stimulants they chewed to keep awake. Scattered about lie ranks of amphorae and anchors, and other items found in or around the ship, plus photographs and explanations (in Italian and English) of the ship's retrieval from the sea.

On the left-hand side of the building is displayed a medley of archeological finds from various sites hereabouts, both on land and sea. Prize exhibit is a marble torso dredged up from the sea in 2005, the **Venus of Lilybaeum**: comparable in style to the more famous Venus Landolina in Siracusa, it's probably a Roman copy of a Hellenistic statue of the second century BC. Other items include more mundane ceramics from the Punic tophet ("sacrificial grounds") on Motya and other ancient necropolises in the neighbourhood, a good Roman mosaic and some colourful examples of Italian and North African pottery.

ARRIVAL AND INFORMATION   MARSALA

By train Trains to Marsala, from Trapani in particular, are quicker and more frequent than buses. The train station is at the southeastern edge of town on Viale A. Fazio, a 15min walk from the centre.

Destinations Castelvetrano (10 daily Mon–Sat, 4 daily Sun; 45min); Mazara del Vallo (10 daily Mon–Sat, 4 daily Sun; 20min); Palermo (6 daily Mon–Sat, 3 daily Sun; 3hr 10min; may involve change); Trapani (12 daily Mon–Sat, 5 daily Sun; 30min).

By bus Buses arrive centrally at Piazza del Popolo (also known as Piazza Marconi), near Porta Garibaldi.

Destinations Agrigento (3 daily Mon–Sat, 1 daily Sun; 2hr 25min–3hr); Campobello (4 daily Mon–Sat; 55min); Castelvetrano (7 daily Mon–Sat; 1hr 15min); Mazara del Vallo (1–2 hourly Mon–Sat, 4 daily Sun; 30min); Palermo

(1–2 hourly Mon–Sat, 7–9 daily Sun; 2hr 30min); Salemi (2 daily Mon–Sat, 1 daily Sun; 35min); Sciacca (3 daily Mon–Sat, 1 daily Sun; 1hr–1hr 30min); Trapani (4 daily Mon–Sat; 55min–1hr 15min); Trapani airport (1–4 daily Mon–Sat, 2 daily Sun; 15min).

By hydrofoil Hydrofoil services to and from the Egadi Islands are operated by Ustica Lines (☎ 348 357 9863) at the harbour, a 15min walk from the centre – you can buy tickets on the dockside. There is year-round service to Favignana (30min) and in recent years there has also been a summer-only service to Marettimo (1hr 10min–2hr 15min).

Tourist information There's a tourist office at Via XI Maggio 100, off Piazza della Repubblica near the Chiesa Madre (Mon–Sat 8am–1.30pm & 3–8pm; ☎ 0923 714 097).

ACCOMMODATION

Centrale Via Salinisti 19 ☎ 0923 951 777, ⓦ hotelcentralemarsala.it. Plain but spacious and comfortable en-suite rooms with a/c and minibar, arranged around a courtyard. The hotel has a quiet location in the old town, and there's off-street parking. Breakfast is in a nearby bar. **€75**

★ **Hotel Carmine** Piazza del Carmine 16 ☎ 0923 711 907, ⓦ hotelcarmine.it. Very central, Marsala's most stylish hotel combines modernity with domed rooms, antique trimmings and fabulous breakfasts. The spacious rooms have exposed brickwork and wood or tiled floors, some with balconies, some overlooking the internal garden. **€125**

Palazzo Diaz Via Salinisti 22 ☎ 348 019 0662 or ☎ 329 216 3780, ⓦ palazzodiaz.com. This B&B in a converted nineteenth-century *palazzo* has large, airy rooms with a/c and en-suite bathrooms, and there's a grand roof terrace where breakfast is served. **€90**

Villa Favorita Via Favorita 27 ☎ 0923 989 100, ⓦ villafavorita.com. This beautiful, secluded villa on the outskirts of town is set in its own gardens and has a pool, a tennis court and a restaurant, where the food and service alternate between superb and dire. Regular wedding receptions can disrupt the overall serenity of the place. It's signposted 2km northeast of the centre, off Via Trapani. **€125**

EATING AND DRINKING

In the centre of Marsala at least, which empties of life after 9pm, **restaurants** can be hard to come by, but you'll eat well and relatively cheaply at the ones listed below. The couple of **bars** in Piazza della Repubblica are good for a *tè freddo alla pesca* (cold peach tea), accompanied by earnest discussion of lottery numbers – otherwise try the places listed below. For general groceries, there's a lively daily **market** around the Porta Garibaldi, selling fresh fish as well as fruit and vegetables.

Al Capo Via Lungomare Boeo 40 ☎ 328 862 8586. In a restored warehouse near the Museo Archeologico, this makes a handy pre- or post-museum lunch stop. There are several "*piatti unici*" (which means you get a pasta dish and a *secondo* combined) such as the fresh *busiate* with a sauce of tuna and aubergine, which comes accompanied by a slice of tuna (€15). There's also pizzas (from €5) in the evenings and fish couscous at weekends. Set-price menus at €15, €20 and €25. Daily lunch & dinner; closed Wed in winter.

★ **Divino Rosso** Largo di Girolamo ☎ 0923 711 770. Congenial pizzeria and wine bar where you can sit outside opposite a seventeenth-century *palazzo*. Snack on cheeses, cold meats, panini and salads, or go for a range of tasty pizzas (around €7). There are also some meat and fish dishes (€8–15), and a fantastic range of wines. Daily dinner only.

E&N Via XI Maggio 130 ☎ 0923 951 969. This classy *pasticceria* and *gelateria* has a small courtyard which makes for a nice place to sit and savour a pistachio ice cream or decadent pastry. There are savouries, too, at lunchtime. Mon–Tues & Thurs–Sun 8am–8pm.

Il Gallo e l'Innamorata Via S. Bilardello 18 ☎ 0923 195 4446. Small and friendly *osteria* with great food, including bruschetta with tuna, salami and tomato (€6), grilled fish (€5 per 100g) and, in season, *busiate con ragù di tonno* (pasta with tuna sauce; €12). Prices are very reasonable – you can eat abundantly for €30 per head including drinks. Mon & Wed–Sun lunch & dinner.

Mazara del Vallo

The North African element in Sicily's cultural melange is at its strongest in the major fishing port of **MAZARA DEL VALLO**, 22km down the coast from Marsala. Under the Muslims, Mazara was one of Sicily's most prosperous towns and capital of the biggest of the three administrative districts, or *walis*, into which the island was divided – hence the "del Vallo" tag. The first Sicilian city to be taken by the Arabs, and the last they surrendered, Mazara's prosperity lasted for 250 years, coinciding with the height of Arab power in the Mediterranean. Count Roger's anxiety to establish a strong Norman presence in this Muslim powerbase ensured that Mazara's importance lasted long after his conquest of the city in 1087, and it didn't give up its rank as provincial capital until Trapani took over in 1817.

The Arab links have revived since the port became the prime Sicilian destination for **Tunisian immigrants** flocking across the sea to work in the vast fishing fleet – one of Italy's biggest. Indeed, wandering through Mazara's casbah-like backstreets, there are moments when you could imagine yourself to be in North Africa, passing Tunisian shops and a café plastered with pictures of the Tunisian president, and Arab music percolating through small doorways. For the visitor, the attraction of Mazara is its profusion of fine churches in a slowly reviving – though far from genteel – old town. The tree-shaded lungomare and seafront gardens add another facet to its character, and with a row of sea-view restaurants, Mazara is one of the few towns in the west to make the most of its coastal location.

The old town

Mazara's **old town** is where all the interest lies, bordered by the River Mazaro and sea on two sides and the main corsos – Umberto I and Vittorio Véneto – on the other two. At the southern end of Corso Umberto I, Piazza Mokarta holds the scant ruins of Count Roger's **castello**, magnificently floodlit at night, when the square is the focus of promenading crowds.

From Piazza Mokarta, Via Garibaldi leads up to Santa Veneranda, perhaps the most beautiful of Mazara's Baroque churches, its twin belltowers styled with a jaunty twist.

9

Further west at the edge of the old town on a platform overlooking the Mazaro River, the church of **San Nicolò Regale** has a more restrained air. A restored Norman church, it has strong Arab elements, with a honey-toned, battlemented exterior and a simple interior rising to a single cupola.

The Duomo

Piazza della Repubblica • Usually daily 9am–noon & 4–7pm

Mazara's **Duomo** was originally Norman but completely remodelled in the late seventeenth century – though the relief over the main door showing a mounted Count Roger trampling a Saracen underfoot was carved in 1584. The light and airy **interior** reveals an almost indigestible profusion of stuccoed and sculptured ornamentation, including, behind the altar, a group of seven marble statues depicting the *Transfiguration*, carved by Antonello Gagini. To the right, a niche reveals a fragment of Byzantine fresco, dating from the end of the thirteenth century, while, through the marble doorway on the right side of the nave, you'll find some excellently chiselled Roman sarcophagi, with reliefs of a lively hunting scene and a battle, rich with confusion. Outside the Duomo, **Piazza della Repubblica** heralds a harmonious set of Baroque buildings: the square itself is flanked by the elegant, double-storey porticoed facade of the **Seminario** and the **Palazzo Vescovile**, both eighteenth century.

Museo del Satiro

Piazza del Plebiscito • Daily 9am–6pm • €6

The fifteenth-century church of Sant'Egido now houses the **Museo del Satiro**, whose centrepiece is a rather risqué fourth-century BC bronze satyr captured in the ecstatic throes of an orgiastic Dionysian dance. It was, quite literally, caught by a Mazara fishing boat in the waters between Pantelleria and Cap Bon, Tunisia, in 1998. Sadly, as the fishermen hauled the catch aboard, one of the arms broke off and has yet to be recovered. A 25-minute video with English subtitles relates the story.

The Tunisian quarter

Most of what remains of the old town was built after Mazara's teeming Arab population had dwindled to nothing – but it's here, especially in the Pilazza neighbourhood, that their descendants have returned, making up a low-key **Tunisian quarter** centred on Via Porta Palermo and nearby Via Bagno. Stroll around the quiet alleys here and you'll pass authentic Tunisian cafés and shops, and the occasional social club resounding with Arab music and the clack of backgammon tables.

The port

West of the Tunisian quarter, the waters of the Mazaro River are hidden by the hulls of the two hundred-odd trawlers that clog Mazara's **port**. Heavy overfishing and the use of illegal explosives (dropped into the sea to stun the fish) have greatly decreased the catch in recent years, but the rich waters above the continental shelf have ensured that there are enough fish left to make it worthwhile for the fishermen to pursue their trade – at least, given the reduced wages that the Tunisians are prepared to accept.

ARRIVAL AND INFORMATION

MAZARA DEL VALLO

By bus Buses stop at Via Salemi, either outside the train station or 200m up at Piazza Matteotti.
Destinations Agrigento (3 daily Mon–Sat, 1 daily Sun; 2hr–2hr 40min); Campobello (3 daily Mon–Sat; 20min); Castelvetrano (3 daily Mon–Sat; 40min); Marsala (1–2 hourly Mon–Sat, 4 daily Sun; 30min); Palermo (8–12 daily Mon–Sat, 2–6 daily Sun; 2hr–2hr 35min); Trapani (4 daily Mon–Sat; 1hr 30min–1hr 45min).
By train Mazara's train station is centrally located off Corso Vittorio Veneto.

Destinations Campobello di Mazara (11 daily Mon–Sat, 6 daily Sun; 10min); Castelvetrano (10 daily Mon–Sat, 5 daily Sun; 20min); Marsala (10 daily Mon–Sat, 5 daily Sun; 20min); Palermo (5 daily Mon–Sat, 3 daily Sun; 2hr 40min–3hr; may involve change); Trapani (10 daily Mon–Sat, 5 daily Sun; 50min).
Tourist office Mazara's tourist office is on Piazza Mokarta (Tues–Sat 8am–1pm & 3–7pm, Sun 8.30am–1pm; ☎0923 942 776).

ACCOMMODATION

Foresteria Monastica ☎0923 906 565 or ☎347 722 5069, ⓦforesteriasanmichele.com. Very plain but clean and quiet rooms in this old-town convent annexed to San Michele church. You probably won't see any sign of the seven Benedictine nuns who are resident here, and who make the local pastries served at breakfast, which costs €5. Closed Nov–Feb. €50
Hopps Hotel Via G. Hopps 29 ☎0923 946 133, ⓦhoppshotel.it. Large resort-style three-star centred on a palm-fringed pool, a 5min walk down the lungomare from the public gardens. Rooms are spacious if a bit dated, and breakfast is by the pool. All in all good value for what you get, though poolside entertainments in summer can be noisy. €75

Nosteon Via Plebiscito 9 ☎0923 651 619 or ☎347 571 8904, ⓦnosteon.it. Great-value B&B off Piazza Plebiscito, with a double room and an apartment consisting of a double in the loft and a bunk downstairs, with a kitchen and bathroom. Breakfast is taken at the nearby *Bar Garden* (see p.350). No credit cards. €40
★ **Villa Altair** Via Salemi 9 ☎0923 944 088 or ☎347 666 2963, ⓦvillaaltair.com. A couple of kilometres southeast of town (call for directions), this peaceful B&B occupies an old *baglio*, or farmhouse, in the middle of vineyards and olive groves. The five rooms have a/c and wi-fi connections, and the owners can arrange airport transfers, excursions and vehicle rental. €80

EATING AND DRINKING

RESTAURANTS

Alla Kasbah Via Itria 10 ☎0923 906 126. Don't be fooled by the name: apart from a very acceptable fish couscous, the food here is modern Sicilian rather than North African. You can just have *antipasto*, couscous and wine for €15; other fixed-price menus are €20–25. The ambience is relaxed and friendly. Daily lunch & dinner; closed Mon Sept–June.

La Béttola Via Maccagnone 32 ☎0923 946 422. Near the train station, this simple, old-fashioned place is recommended for regional fish and seafood specialities. Try the catch of the day, sliced thin and marinated, and the fish couscous (€12). Mon–Tues & Thurs–Sun lunch & dinner.
★ **Eyem Zemen** Via Porta Palermo 36 ☎347 386 9921. Tiny place, with three or four tables outside and

9

authentic and cheap Tunisian snacks – *brik* (fried pastry parcels), oily aubergine salads and couscous. You can eat well for €15. Daily lunch & dinner; closed Tues in winter.
Lo Scoiattolo Via N. Tortorici 9 ☎ 0923 946 313. With tables outside, "The Squirrel" has a fine *antipasto* buffet and daily fish specials, though many locals come here at night for the huge choice of pizzas (€4–6). All other dishes cost €7–12. Mon–Wed & Fri–Sun lunch & dinner.

BARS

Bar Garden Piazza della Repubblica 7 ☎ 0923 941 909. Facing the town's most harmonious buildings, this is a nice place for a breakfast or sit-down by day, and to soak up the weird green illuminations in the evening. Tues–Sun 8am–8pm, opens later in summer.
Villa delle Rose Via Conte Ruggero ☎ 0923 945 565. With tables under shady trees in the public gardens, this makes a pleasant retreat for a quiet evening drink. Daily 6pm–late.

Selinunte and Marinella di Selinunte

SELINUNTE, the site of the Greek city of Selinus, lies around 30km east of Mazara del Vallo, stranded on a remote corner of the coast in splendid isolation, just west of the modern village of **Marinella di Selinunte**. Selinunte is a crucial sight if you're travelling through the west of Sicily, its series of mighty temples lying in great heaps, where they were felled by earthquakes.

Most westerly of the Hellenic colonies, **Selinus** reached its peak during the fifth century BC. A bitter rival of Segesta, whose lands lay adjacent to the north, the powerful city and its fertile plain attracted enemies hand over fist, and it was only a matter of time before Selinus caught the eye of Segesta's ally, Carthage. Geographically vulnerable, the city was sacked by Carthaginians, any attempts at recovery forestalled by earthquakes, which later razed it altogether. However, people continued to live here until 250 BC, when the population was finally transferred to Marsala before the Roman invasion. The Arabs did occupy the site briefly, but the last recorded settlement at Selinunte was in the thirteenth century, after which time it remained forgotten until rediscovered in the sixteenth century. Despite the destruction, the city ruins have exerted a romantic hold over people ever since.

Marinella di Selinunte

Although it can get a bit hectic in summer, **MARINELLA DI SELINUNTE** is an atmospheric place to spend a few hours. Its most appealing parts lie on and around the long, narrow road that winds down to the small **harbour**, where fishing boats are hauled up onto the sands by pulleys.

Marinella is no longer the isolated place it used to be, with new buildings and streets in evidence everywhere, while the seafront has become top-heavy with trattorias, and shops selling Tunisian carpets, souvenirs and beachwear. But it remains an attractive place, of particular appeal if you're planning to use the fine sand **beach** that stretches west from the village to the ruins. The water isn't great to swim in, since it's often clogged with seaweed at the sand's edge, though this doesn't deter the kids. However, the **surfing** here can be good, and you can rent equipment in the summer, as well as pedalos, chairs, shades and all the usual beach paraphernalia. Another beach, **Mare Pineta**, is located east of the village, backed by pine trees stretching into the distance; follow the road east of the port for ten minutes.

ARRIVAL AND INFORMATION   MARINELLA DI SELINUNTE

By bus Buses from Castelvetrano (4–8 daily; 30min) to Selinunte pass through Marinella, and continue to the site.
Tourist information The small but obliging tourist office (Mon–Sat: summer 9am–7pm; winter 9am–1.30pm & 2–6pm; ☎ 0924 46 251), which is often thronged with

visitors in summer, is on the roundabout near the entrance to the site.
Services Costa del Sole, Via Castore e Polluce 17 (☎ 0924 46 712 or ☎ 389 698 1058) rents out bikes (€10/half-day, €13/day).

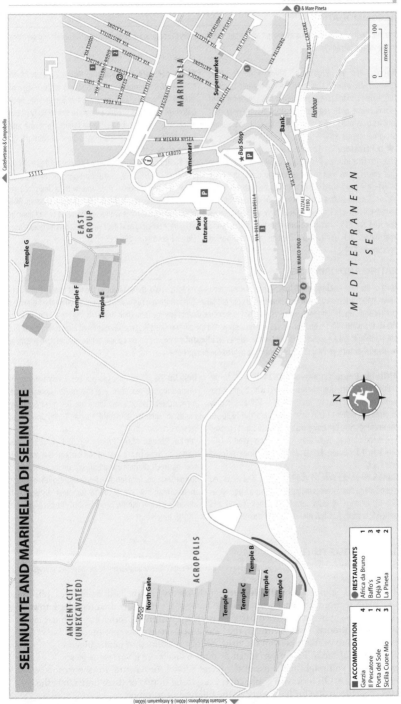

SELINUNTE AND MARINELLA DI SELINUNTE

ANCIENT CITY
(UNEXCAVATED)

ACROPOLIS

North Gate

Temple D
Temple C
Temple A
Temple O
Temple B

EAST
GROUP

Temple G

Temple F

Temple E

MARINELLA

Supermarket

Bank

Harbour

Alimentari

Park
Entrance

★ Bus Stop

VIA MEGARA NYSEA

VIA CABOTO

VIA DELLA CHIARELLA

VIA MARCO POLO

VIA CABOTO

VIA PIGAFETTA

PIAZZALE
EFEBO

M E D I T E R R A N E A N

S E A

VIA NICELTE

VIA MAGOLA

VIA ANTIGONE

VIA ALCESTE

VIA CALIPPO

VIA PALINURO

VIA DEL CAMENE

VIA PERICLE

VIA PERICLE

VIA SIRIO

VIA VEGA

VIA REGINALTI

CASTORE E POLLUCE

ORION E POLLUCE

CASSIOPEA

VIA ARISTOTELE

VIA PLATONE

GIOSUE VIA CARDO

SS115

N

Castelvetrano & Campobello ▲

▲ ② & Mare Pineta

▼ Santuario Malophoros (400m) & Antiquarium (600m)

0   100
metres

■ ACCOMMODATION	
Garzia	4
Il Pescatore	2
Porta del Sole	1
Sicilia Cuore Mio	3

● RESTAURANTS	
Africa da Bruno	1
Baffo's	3
Déjà Vu	4
La Pineta	2

9

ACCOMMODATION

You may well be offered **rooms** as you get off the bus, which are worth accepting in summer when the hotels and pensions in the village fill rapidly.

Garzia Via A. Pigafetta 2 ☏0924 46 024, ⓦhotelgarzia.com. This large, Arabic-themed hotel on the seafront road lacks charm, but it has a wide range of rooms (some with sea-facing balconies), friendly staff and its own patch of beach. The restaurant offers good set-price menus. **€89**

★ **Il Pescatore** Via Castore e Polluce 31 ☏0924 46 303, ⓦaffittacamereilpescatore.it. With a roof terrace that enjoys views over to the temples and sea, this place offers eight good-sized rooms with private bathrooms and a/c or fans, breakfast (that includes fresh fruit) on the terrace plus use of a kitchen. Alternatively, you can sleep on the roof for €15, and there are also four self-catering apartments. No credit cards. Doubles and two-person apartments **€80**

Porta del Sole Via Apollonio Rodio 32 ☏0924 46 035. A B&B offering four basic rooms with private or shared bathrooms, and there are five larger ones with balconies (not that there's a view) in the *Holiday House* across the road, run by the same family. Furniture and beds are from the visit-grandma school of comfort. No credit cards. **€40**

★ **Sicilia Cuore Mio** Via della Cittadella 44 ☏0924 46 077 or ☏336 612 769, ⓦsiciliacuoremio.it. Right across from the archeological site, and with a long terrace overlooking the sea in front, this friendly, modern B&B offers five rooms, three with a sea view and two of them in a separate building next door with a kitchen for guests' use. Closed Dec–March. **€80**

EATING AND DRINKING

Most of the best **eating** and **drinking** places are located on Via Marco Polo, the road above the west beach. That starts down at the little harbour where a couple of bars put out tables from which you can watch the sun set, while the fishermen chatter and dispute among themselves. At night in summer, visitors emerge from their holiday homes to join locals from the surrounding villages on foot, in cars and on Vespas, and the party chugs along merrily until well after midnight. If you are wanting to take a picnic up to the temple, there's an **alimentari** nearby on Via Caboto, while beyond it, in the main residential district, you'll find a **supermarket** behind the *Alceste* hotel.

Africa da Bruno Via Alceste ☏0924 46 456. In the residential district, this cheerful trattoria with bright white walls offers superlative *antipasti* (€4–10) and locally inspired fish dishes such as pasta with seafood (€10.50). In the evenings, you can enjoy crispy pizzas (from €5) cooked in a wood-burning oven. March–July Mon–Wed & Fri–Sun lunch & dinner; Aug daily lunch & dinner; closed Nov–Feb.

Baffo's Via Marco Polo 51 ☏0924 46 211. Sea views and a good menu that includes magnificent *forno a legna* pizzas (€6–8), a range of tasty fettuccine dishes (€8–9) and grilled fish. Daily lunch & dinner; closed Nov–March.

Déjà Vu Via Marco Polo (no phone). Lively bar/*birreria* overlooking the sea, open late, that makes a great venue for watching the sun set. There are DJs most Saturday nights in summer, and cold snacks. Daily 6pm–late; closed Oct–March.

★ **La Pineta** Mare Pineta ☏0924 46 820. This trattoria on the beach east of the harbour is a real find, serving fresh seafood including sea urchins (*ricci*). It's the perfect spot for a lunch or leisurely evening meal just metres from the sea (€10–18 for most dishes). Call ahead to book in winter. Summer daily lunch & dinner; winter lunch only.

The Selinus ruins

Daily 9am–1hr before sunset; last entry 1hr before closing • €9 including Segesta • Navetta buggies cost €6 for the nearer temples, €12 for the complete circuit

The **ruins** of Selinus are back behind the main part of Marinella di Selinunte, split into two main sections, the **east group** and the **acropolis**, with individual temples known simply as "A", "B" etc. The two parts are enclosed within the same site, with the car park and **entrance** – lying through the landscaped earthbanks that preclude views of the east group of temples from the road. Selinus is claimed to be the biggest archeological site in Europe, so it can be quite a challenge if you want to see everything; you might make use of the buggy service, or **navetta**, for the remoter sites, or rent a bike. On foot, you could cover everything in two or three hours, but the total lack of shade makes for hard work in the full heat of summer.

9

CAVE DI CUSA

If you have your own transport, it's well worth calling in at the quarries where the stone for the building of Selinus was extracted in the fifth century BC. They lie 3.5km south of the scruffy town of **Campobello di Mazara**, deep in olive country. From Selinunte, a lovely 20km drive takes you along country roads lined with olive groves and vines. When you reach Campobello, take the road to Tre Fontane and follow the signs ("Cave di Cusa"), keeping your eyes peeled and fingers crossed.

At the site of the **Cave di Cusa** (daily 9am–1hr before sunset; free), a path leads into a bucolic setting that is more reminiscent of English Romanticism than of ancient Greece. In early summer, workers fork hay into piles in between the rock ledges and tended shrubs, while behind them stretch shaded groves of olives. Everywhere, you can see the massive column drums and stumps lying randomly about, quarried and chiselled into shape here before being dragged to the ancient city on wooden carts, where they formed part of the great temple complex. There are examples of all the various stages of the process, with unfinished pieces poignantly abandoned, the work interrupted when Selinus was devastated in 409 BC. The most impressive pieces are those stone drums and column sections that remain in place where they were being excavated. A couple are 6m high and 2m across, with a narrow groove dug all the way around in which the stonemasons had to work – the reflected heat must have been appalling. Other rock sections indicate clearly where drums have already been cut – parts of the site look as though someone has been through with a giant pastry-cutter.

The east group

Shrouded in the wild celery that gave the ancient city its name, the **east group** temples are in various stages of reconstructed ruin. The most complete is the one nearest the sea (**Temple E**), probably dedicated to Hera (Aphrodite) and re-erected in 1958. A Doric construction, almost 70m by 25m, it remains a gloriously impressive sight, its soaring columns gleaming bright against the sky, its ledges and capitals the resting place for flitting birds. **Temple F**, behind, is the oldest in this group, from around 550 BC, while the northernmost temple (**Temple G**) is an immense tangle of columned wreckage, 6m high in places and crisscrossed by rough footpaths. In Sicily, the only temple larger than this is the Tempio di Giove at Agrigento.

The acropolis

The road leads down from the East Group, across the (now buried) site of the old harbour, to the second part of excavated Selinus, the **acropolis**, containing what remains of the other temples (five in all), as well as the well-preserved city streets and massive stepped **walls** that rise above the duned beach below. These huge walls were all constructed after 409 BC – when the city was sacked by the Carthaginians – in an attempt to protect a limited and easily defensible area of the old city.

Temple C stands on the highest point of the acropolis, giving glorious views out over the sparkling sea. Built early in the sixth century BC (and probably dedicated to Apollo), it originally held the finest of the metopes (decorative panels) that are now in Palermo's archeological museum. Its fourteen standing columns were re-erected in the 1920s: other fallen columns here, and at the surrounding temples, show how they were originally constructed – the drums lying in a line, with slots and protrusions on either side that fitted into each other. The buildings immediately behind **temples C and D** were shops, split into two rooms and with a courtyard each.

The rest of the site

At the end of the main street beyond stands the **north gate** to the city – the tall blocks of stone marking a gateway that was 7m high. Behind the north gate stood the rest of the ancient city, still largely unexcavated, though crisscrossed by little paths through the undergrowth. The **agora** was sited just north of here, and a necropolis further up, while to the west, across the Modione River, stood the

9

Santuario Malophoros, part of a complex that marked the western boundary of the city. Animal sacrifices were performed at the small well in front of the structure. Beyond it, on the edge of the archeological zone, the **Antiquarium** holds statuettes and terracotta fragments, mostly excavated in the 1980s from a temple dedicated to Hera Matronale, south of the Malophoros.

Castelvetrano

It's hard to recommend a visit to **CASTELVETRANO**, for any reason other than to get the bus straight out again. A depressed town, it's lightened only marginally by an elegant if traffic-choked centre, where the **Teatro Selinus** – looking rather like a copy of a Greek temple – boasts a proud plaque commemorating Goethe's visit in 1787. Just around the corner stands a good-looking **Chiesa Madre** from the sixteenth century. The church's finely engraved doorway leads into an interior warmly illuminated by stained-glass windows – a rare thing in Sicily – and ornamented by a number of stuccoes by Serpotta and Ferraro. Off the adjacent square, Piazza Garibaldi, it's a short walk down to Via Garibaldi 50 and the **Museo Civico** (Mon–Sat 9am–1pm & 3–7pm, Sun 9am–1pm; €2.50), home of the bronze *Éfebo di Selinunte*, a statue of a young man from the fifth century BC.

From behind the church, Via Vittorio Emanuele leads down towards Piazza Matteotti and the train station. Piazza Matteotti marks the end of Via Serafino Mannone, where aficionados of banditry can visit the courtyard in which the body of the island's most notorious outlaw, **Salvatore Giuliano** (see p.81), was found on July 5, 1950. The courtyard is between Via Mannone 92 and 100, though it's a rather less appealing spot than its legend might suggest.

Santissima Trinità di Delia

Three and a half kilometres west of Castelvetrano, the **Santissima Trinità di Delia** makes a pleasant rural excursion for anyone not in a blazing hurry. Head down Via Ruggero Séttimo from Piazza Umberto, along a country lane fringed by vineyards, keeping left where the road forks. A domed twelfth-century Norman construction, the church is signposted before you arrive at the artificial lake of Lago Trinità: ring the bell to the right of the church for the key. The small, square building, its four slender columns and triple apse reminiscent of Saracenic styles, was meticulously restored by two brothers, whose mausoleum the church has become. Their tombs, dominating the small interior, rival those of the Norman kings in Palermo for splendour.

ARRIVAL AND INFORMATION   CASTELVETRANO

By train To reach the town centre from the train station in Piazza Améndola, walk up to the main road and turn left: it's just a few minutes to Piazza Matteotti, from where Via Vittorio Emanuele leads all the way to the rear of the Chiesa Madre church.

Destinations Marsala (10 daily Mon–Sat, 5 daily Sun; 40min); Mazara del Vallo (10 daily Mon–Sat, 5 daily Sun; 20min); Palermo (6 daily Mon–Sat, 3 daily Sun; 2hr 30min–3hr; may involve change); Trapani (10 daily Mon–Sat, 5 daily Sun; 1hr 15min).

By bus Buses from Marsala and Trapani stop in Piazza Matteotti. To get to Selinunte from Castelvetrano, take the bus for Marinella from outside the train station – a timetable is posted inside the station – or from piazzas

Matteotti, Dante or Regina Margherita in town.

Destinations Agrigento (3 daily Mon–Sat, 1 daily Sun; 1hr 40min–2hr 25min); Campobello (7–11 daily Mon–Sat, 4–6 daily Sun; 25min); Gibellina (1 daily Mon–Sat; 1hr); Marinella (for Selinunte, 5–8 daily; 25min); Marsala (9 daily Mon–Sat; 1hr–1hr 15min); Mazara del Vallo (9 daily Mon–Sat; 30–40min); Palermo (10 daily Mon–Sat, 2–3 daily Sun; 1hr 45min); Salemi (1 daily Mon–Sat; 1hr 15min); Sciacca (3 daily Mon–Sat, 1 daily Sun; 30–50min); Trapani (4 daily Mon–Sat; 2hr 15min).

Tourist information There's a tourist office at Piazza Carlo d'Aragona, below Piazza Garibaldi (Mon–Sat 9am–1pm & 4–7pm, plus Sun in summer 9am–1pm; ☎0924 902 004).

The interior

9

North of Castelvetrano and east of Marsala, the **interior** of Trapani province is intensely rural, its few small towns little changed by the coming of the A29 autostrada, which cuts across the region. The whole area is green and highly fertile, mainly given over to vine-growing; indeed, the wine around the **Salemi** district is among Sicily's best. But, hard though it is to believe, the entire region still hasn't recovered from the **earthquake** of January 15, 1968, which briefly spotlighted western Sicily, sadly more for the authorities' inadequate response to it than for the actual loss of life. Four hundred died and a thousand were injured, no great number by Sicilian standards, but it was the 50,000 left homeless that had the most lingering impact on this already depressed part of the island, and the effects of the earthquake are still evident everywhere. Ruined buildings and ugly temporary dwellings still being used more than four decades later testify to the chronically dilatory response to the disaster, aggravated by private interests and particularly by the Mafia contractors who capitalized on the catastrophe. Even where rebuilding went ahead, such as in the new town of **Gibellina**, it's still possible to see the dread hand of inertia.

It goes without saying that this is a little-visited area of Sicily, but it's intriguing nonetheless. This is, after all, the part of the world known best to Giuseppe Tomasi di Lampedusa, whose classic novel, *The Leopard*, is partly set in the little town of **Santa Margherita di Belice** – also badly damaged in 1968 but emerging slowly from the doldrums, and an essential stop for anyone who's read the book.

GETTING AROUND   THE INTERIOR

By car Local buses run to all the towns in the region, but it's impossible to construct any kind of sightseeing itinerary using them – you have to have your own car, not least to avoid the possibility of getting stuck in backwaters with no accommodation.

Salemi

The town of **SALEMI**, 20km north of Castelvetrano and 30km east of Marsala, oddly enjoyed the privilege of being the first capital of a united Italy in 1860, albeit for only three days, as recorded by a plaque in front of its heavily restored thirteenth-century **castello** on Piazza Alicia, at the top of the town. Another plaque marks Garibaldi's declaration of a dictatorship, asserting that "in times of war, it's necessary for the civilian powers to be concentrated in the hands of one man" – namely Garibaldi himself, though King Vittorio Emanuele still gets a mention.

The Collegio dei Gesuiti museums

Via d'Aguirre • All Tues–Sat 10am–1pm & 4–7pm • Combined ticket for all museums €5

On Via d'Aguirre, the former Collegio dei Gesuiti houses a quintet of museums. The **Museo del Risorgimento** holds assorted pieces of "Garibaldini" – letters, documents and arms connected with the town's finest hour; the **Museo Archeologico** contains finds from local excavations including Monte Polizzo; the **Museo dell'Arte Sacra** gathers treasures from various local churches, including the cathedral destroyed in the earthquake; and the **Museo del Paesaggio** explores aspects of the Sicilian landscape by means of videos. The **Museo della Mafia** brings together films, photographs, recordings of interviews, and paintings and sculptures by local artists of prominent figures in the Mafia's history – including representations of the two assassinated anti-Mafia judges Falcone and Borsellino, plus work by a *pentito*, or informer. It's a pretty disparate mix, and fairly indigestible if you attempt to take them all in, but the collections are definitely worth putting aside a couple of hours for.

Tourist information There's a tourist office at the bottom of the hill on Piazza Libertà (daily: summer 9am–1pm & 4–8pm; winter 9am–1pm & 3–7pm; ☎ 0924 981 426), where buses stop.

Gibellina Nuova

Salemi escaped the earthquake lightly, even though a third of the population had to abandon their shattered homes. Other towns, like Gibellina, were completely flattened, and the population moved en masse to a site close to Santa Ninfa, reached from Salemi along the SS188. This is **GIBELLINA NUOVA**, a modern town that was once a symbol of progress in the region, its wide, empty streets adorned with numerous weird constructions and abstract **sculptures** designed by a handful of iconoclastic architects with big budgets. A vast stainless-steel star straddles the motorway where you exit for Gibellina, while elsewhere the town holds huge white spheres, giant ploughs, snails and much besides – some fifty constructions in all, though many of them are crumbling already (one church collapsed in 1994), and many of the designs themselves are embarrassingly frozen in the image of what appeared futuristic in the 1970s. The town, meanwhile, bakes in the summer sun, since all the modern piazzas are vast concrete spaces with little shade.

You can get a taste of what Gibellina is all about by driving to the main square – **Piazza XV Gennaio 1968**, in case there was any doubt about what's to blame for all this – where the arcaded City Hall is fronted by some particularly abstract examples, and the tall **Torre Belice** clocktower chimes four times a day with taped human voices instead of bells, a reminder of the earthquake victims.

Baglio di Stéfano

Museums Tues–Sun 9am–1pm & 3–6pm • €5 combined ticket • ☎ 0924 67 844, ⊛ orestiadi.it

The cultural centre, **Baglio di Stéfano**, to the east of the centre, is home to a couple of good museums, one containing **contemporary art** – mainly works by Italian painters, but the sculptor Arnaldo Pomodoro is also represented – the other, more gripping, dedicated to **Mediterranean culture**, from Spain to Turkey and from Corsica to Africa, taking in costumes, jewellery, ceramics, tapestries, calligraphy and carpets, all beautifully presented. A separate space here, the **Atelier**, holds pieces donated by the various sculptors and designers who contributed to Gibellina Nuova's townscape.

The Baglio di Stéfano complex also holds a **theatre**, which is the main venue for the **Orestiadi**, a series of classical and modern dramas, concerts and events performed almost nightly every July and August. As well as works by Euripides, Sophocles and others, there are modern interpretations by the likes of Jean Cocteau, Stravinsky and John Cage, plus a full programme of exhibitions, cinema and music.

La Massara Viale dei Vespri Siciliani 41 ☎ 0924 67 601. Inexpensive trattoria, a 10min walk from the central piazza, where the very filling house pasta, *busiate* *napoleonica* (€6), is made with aubergines, tomato and sausage. Tues–Sun lunch & dinner.

Ruderi di Gibellina

Eighteen kilometres east of Gibellina Nuova, overlooked by ranks of wind turbines, the old town of **RUDERI DI GIBELLINA** complements the new: a mountain of rubble from which smashed and mutilated houses poke out, strewn over a green hillside. On the way into town, you'll pass what is ironically its best-preserved fragment: a shady **cemetery** stretching down the side of the valley, where the inhabitants of the new town return every year to remember the catastrophe. Further down, modernism has left its mark here too, in the form of a wide, grey-white mantle of concrete, **Il Cretto**, poured

9

over one slope, and carved through by channels that recall the previous layout of streets. It's an arresting spectacle, not least for its sheer scale.

Everything else remains as it was after the earthquake struck: only a church has since been restored. Nearby, a jumble of scaffolding on a hummock cradles a stage that makes up one of the two venues for the **Orestiadi**, though it's only infrequently used.

Santa Margherita di Belice

Often ranked among the finest of all historical novels, Giuseppe Tomasi di Lampedusa's *The Leopard* ("Il Gattopardo" in Italian) is a masterpiece of manners and morals, written by a Sicilian prince who only ever completed this one work. Set in 1860s Sicily, it draws heavily on Lampedusa's own experiences, not least the summers he used to spend in his grandmother's palace in **SANTA MARGHERITA DI BELICE**, a small village 35km east of Castelvetrano. This is the Donnafugata of the book – the fictional prince's summer home, a place cherished for the "sense it gave him of everlasting childhood". The 1968 earthquake, unfortunately, completely wrecked the seventeenth-century palace and church described so intently in the novel, though fragments of the palace have been incorporated in a gleaming new **Municipio**. This, with its cool internal courtyards and lovely garden to the side, at least echoes the spirit of the original. More poignant is all that's left of the adjacent **Chiesa Madre** – a two-storey corner open to the elements, displaying its elegant marble tracery and painted medallions to the birds. Having paid your literary dues, it's a quick matter to look around the rest of Santa Margherita, which shows a few signs of revival these days – there's a thoroughly modern church with a space-rocket spire, new extensions grafted onto older, damaged buildings, and a traffic-free stretch of street with a café where you can grab a cold drink.

Pantelleria

With an area of 83 square kilometres, **PANTELLERIA** is the largest of Sicily's offshore islands. Forty kilometres closer to Tunisia than to Sicily, it has been occupied since early times by whichever power controlled the central Mediterranean. By the time of the Phoenicians, who colonized it in the seventh century BC, it was called Hiranin, "island of the birds", after the birds that still stop over here on their migratory routes; for the Greeks, it was Kossyra, or "small". Its present name probably derives from the Arabic *bint ar-riah* ("daughter of the winds"), after the restless breezes that blow around the island's rugged shores. Despite its remote, rocky appearance, however, Pantelleria is not as unsophisticated as some of Sicily's other offshore islands – it's long been on the African shipping route and

---

MAKING A LIVING ON PANTELLERIA

Surprisingly, most of Pantelleria's population of 8500 are **farmers** rather than fishermen. With a soil nourished by frequent past eruptions (the last in 1831), the islanders traditionally preferred tilling to risking life and limb in a sea swarming with pirates on the prowl. Farming on Pantelleria does have its problems, however, not least the numerous chunks of lava and basalt in the earth that preclude mechanical ploughing, not to mention the incessant wind, scorching sun and almost complete lack of water. The islanders have come up with methods of minimizing these disadvantages by some ingenious devices that would bring a gleam to an ecologist's eye. The prolific *zibbibo* vines are individually planted in little ridges designed to capture the precious rainwater; and the famous **giardini arabi** – high walls of stone built round orange trees and other plants – afford protection from the wind and the salt it carries with it. All over the island, various **cooperatives** (often signposted from the road) sell homegrown produce to visitors and locals – capers, wine, jojoba oil, honey and candles. If you want to buy, look for the words "*azienda agricola*".

has proved a popular destination for celebs: former aficionados like Truman Capote and Aldous Huxley have been succeeded more recently by such A-listers as Madonna, Giorgio Armani and Sting, and parts of *Il Postino* (*The Postman*) were filmed here, too.

Pantelleria is a dramatic, black island, thick with volcanic debris and dotted with dazzling white houses known as **dammusi**. Unembellished, these sombre cubic dwellings, unique to the island, blend in perfectly with their environment. These, too, are examples of technological adaptation, the thick walls and shallow-domed roofs designed to maintain a cool internal temperature, while ridges in the roofs catch the rain.

There are no **beaches** of any kind on Pantelleria, its rough black coastline consisting mainly of jagged rocks, but the swimming is still pretty good in some exceptionally scenic spots. Inland, the largely mountainous country offers plenty of **rambling** opportunities, all an easy moped or bus ride from the port, which holds most of the accommodation options. If you're spending any length of time on Pantelleria, a novel option is to rent one of the local *dammuso* houses: their strong walls and domed roofs keep the temperature down indoors.

The main drawback to spending time on Pantelleria is the cost of living: the few hotels are pricey, while food (and water) is mostly imported and therefore relatively expensive. However, a few days spent here will probably leave you wanting more. Best times to visit are May/June or September/October, before and after the crowds and scorching heat of summer.

GETTING TO AND AROUND PANTELLERIA

You can **reach Pantelleria** by ferry (year-round) or hydrofoil (summer only) from Trapani. Flights from Trapani or Palermo take under an hour and are convenient if more extravagant alternatives – however, taking the overnight ferry on the way out effectively negates the longer journey time while saving a night's accommodation expense.

Siremar **ferries** do the journey in around six hours (June–Sept daily; Oct–May daily except Sat), leaving Trapani at midnight, for a deck-class fare of €34 one-way (slightly less in low season). The summer-only **hydrofoil** service is equally frequent and a lot quicker (daily in summer; 2hr 30min). For €5.50 you can reserve a reclining chair (*poltrona*), an expense worth considering since the regular seats are difficult to sleep in and uncomfortably close to the TVs; or there are couchette-cabins for around €15 (without WC) or €21 (with WC) per person. **Tickets** are on sale in the Siremar office at the Stazione Marittima in Trapani (☎0923 24 968, Ⓦsiremar.it), right up until departure.

Pantelleria is just a forty-minute **flight** from Trapani (3 flights daily) or a fifty-minute flight from Palermo (2–3 flights daily). One-way tickets are €40–85, depending on availability and flexibility (try Ⓦexpedia.it, Ⓦskyscanner.com and Ⓦedreams.it); it's worth booking some time in advance in summer. Between April and September, there are also direct flights from Milan, Bologna, Rome, Verona and Venice.

GETTING AROUND

It's easy enough to get around the island by **bus**, and there are plenty of places offering **bike rental**.

To visit the isolated coves of the southeastern Dietro Isola, and other good swimming spots, you'll need to rent a **boat**. There are notices in the agencies along the harbour, in every hotel, and on the boats themselves. If you don't want to navigate yourself, you'll find **boat tours** from the port.

Pantelleria town

If you arrive off the ferry at dawn, **PANTELLERIA TOWN**, the only settlement of any size on the island, presents an undeniably romantic aura, revealing a spread of serene, white-painted cubes. Only close up do these emerge as modern rather than medieval, as most of the town was flattened during the last war when Allied bombers pulverized what had become one of the main German bases in the Mediterranean. Consequently, much of the town has a homogeneous appearance, its low-rise concrete buildings spreading back two or three streets deep from the harbour.

While it may not fit the stereotype of the idyllic island port, Pantelleria town has a certain appeal, and there's much to be said for simply observing the regular to-and-fro of delivery vessels and fishing smacks from one of the seafront café-bars, while the marina sees the manoeuvrings of some uncommonly flash yachts and even the odd schooner. Things get a bit livelier in the evening, when the harbourside fills with perambulating locals.

Castello Barbacane

Via Castello • Aug daily 6pm–midnight; call to arrange a tour at other times • Free • ☎ 327 363 9284

The only building that predates the war is the morose, black **Castello Barbacane**, a legacy of the Spaniards. Its partly restored interior is destined to hold an archeological museum, but in the meantime it's the venue for changing exhibitions and has photos and videos showing aspects of island history and culture, from World War II bombing to carnival celebrations.

ARRIVAL AND DEPARTURE

PANTELLERIA TOWN

By plane The airport (☎0923 911 172, Ⓦpantelleriairport.it) is 5km southeast of town. A bus service makes the 12min run into town four times daily from a stop outside. Taxis into town charge €15, though you might be able to haggle them down to €10 if you are lucky; alternatively, it's a 45min downhill walk. For airline tickets, try the La Cossira travel agency, Via Borgo Italia 77 (☎0923 911 078).

Destinations Palermo (2–3 daily in summer; 50min); Trapani (3 daily in summer; 40min).

By ferry and hydrofoil Arriving by sea, you'll disembark right in the centre of town, close to most of the bars, restaurants and hotels. In bad weather, you may be deposited instead at Scauri, a smaller port on the island's southwestern side, from where a bus takes foot passengers into town (remember to disembark promptly or it will leave without you). Siremar operates a ferry service to Trapani leaving at noon (June–Sept daily and Oct–May Fri & Sat) or at 10am (Oct–May Mon–Thurs); buy tickets from Agenzia Rizzo, Via Borgo Italia 22 (📞0923 911 120, 🌐siremar.it). Ustica Lines operates hydrofoils to Trapani from June to Sept only; buy tickets from Agenzia Minardi, Via Borgo Italia 15 (📞0923 911 502, 🌐usticalines.it).

GETTING AROUND

By bus Local buses make regular departures from Piazza Cavour to all the main villages on the island, with reduced or no services on Sundays. Buy tickets in advance from any *tabacchi* for €1, or on the bus for €1.20.

Destinations Bugeber (3 daily; 20min); Khamma (9 daily Mon–Sat; 25min); Rekale (9 daily Mon–Sat; 20min); Scauri (9 daily Mon–Sat; 20min); Siba (4 daily Mon–Sat; 30min); Tracino (9 daily Mon–Sat; 30min).

By taxi Consolo, Piazza Castello (📞0923 912 716 or 📞339 715 7586).

Bike rental Viva Pantelleria, Vicolo Leopardi 5 (📞0923 911 078 or 📞349 619 9210), charges €12 for up to 2hr, €15 for half a day. Escorted bike tours and kayak rental are also available.

Car and scooter rental Autonoleggio Policardo is at Via Messina 31 (📞0923 912 844, 🌐policardo.it) and at the airport. Expect to pay up to €65 per day for a Fiat 600, €60 per day for a scooter, less in low season.

INFORMATION AND TOURS

Tourist information There's no longer any tourist office on Pantelleria, but the Italian-language websites 🌐prolocopantelleria.it, 🌐pantelleria.it and 🌐tutto pantelleria.it are all useful.

Guided tours Excursions by jeep, on foot and on horseback are organized by the Gira l'Isola agency at Vicolo Messina 21 (📞0923 913 254), from about €30 per person. Cooperativa Uros (📞327 363 9284) conducts tours all over the island, including archeological and gastronomic tours, from €15 per person.

Boat tours Trips depart daily from the port in summer; a *giro dell'isola* (round-island tour) costs around €30 per person for a full day (leaving around 10am, returning at 4.30pm), including a spaghetti lunch. Call Franco Cosano (📞339 204 7757, 🌐francofutura.it) for details.

Diving Viva Pantelleria, Vicolo Leopardi 5 (📞0923 911 078 or 📞349 619 9210), offers diving excursions and equipment rental.

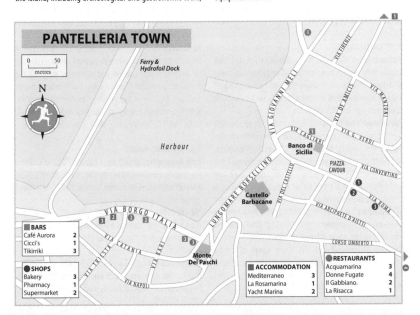

PANTELLERIA TOWN

BARS	
Café Aurora	2
Cicci's	1
Tikirriki	3

SHOPS	
Bakery	3
Pharmacy	1
Supermarket	2

ACCOMMODATION	
Mediterraneo	3
La Rosamarina	1
Yacht Marina	2

RESTAURANTS	
Acquamarina	3
Donne Fugate	4
Il Gabbiano.	2
La Risacca	1

9

PANTELLERIA ACCOMMODATION

Accommodation on Pantelleria is generally expensive, with options in the town usually cheaper than those in more remote and romantically located places. During July and August, many places impose a **minimum stay** of three days or even a week, but at other times of the year, there are no such constraints (indeed islanders are only too happy to have some out-of-season business), and prices drop considerably: be prepared to bargain. There's no campsite on the island, and camping rough is impractical given the terrain and lack of water.

The most alluring option is to rent one of the idiosyncratic **dammuso** houses dotted around the island. Ask at the tourist office or contact one of the agencies in Pantelleria town; try La Cossira, Via Borgo Italia 77 (☎0923 911 078, ⓦlacossira.it); Dammusi di Rukia (☎335 120 6226, ⓦpantelleria.com); or Pantelleria Travel (☎199 440 862, ⓦpantelleriatravel.com). Most *dammusi* are €300–1000 per week according to size and season (you may be able to book less than a week's rental in low season), and you'll usually need a car to get to and from them.

ACCOMMODATION

Mediterraneo Via Borgo Italia ☎0923 911 299. Immediately at the end of the dock, on the harbourfront, this three-star offers comfortable rooms and a pool. The restaurant at the top has great views (meals €20); a buffet breakfast is also served here. Free pick-up from the airport. **€130**

★ **La Rosamarina** Via Sicania 10, off Via Villa ☎328 924 0159, ⓔlarosamarina@hotmail.it. You'll find the lowest prices on the island in this friendly B&B, a

remodelled *dammuso* that's a 10min walk from the port and 300m from the sea. The two rooms have warm colours and a/c, and one has cooking facilities. There's a terrace, a garden and sea views. No credit cards. **€110**

Yacht Marina Via Borgo Italia ☎0923 913.649, ⓦmarinahotelpantelleria.com. Full of designer touches, this hotel has 37 rooms with a/c, satellite TV and internet access; the best, costing €20 extra, have a harbour-view balcony. **€120**

EATING AND DRINKING

There are several **restaurants** and **trattorias** in town – mostly rather flash, though not unaffordable. Many double as pizzerias – and good ones too – so you don't need to spend a fortune every night. As for drinking, the **bars** on the harbourfront are where all the action is, starting at 6am (when they open their doors for the arriving ferry passengers) and finishing any time between midnight and 2am depending on season and the manager's inclination. All have tables by the water, where prices are higher.

RESTAURANTS

Acquamarina Via Borgo Italia 1 ☎0923 911 422. This trendy little joint is the best-placed restaurant in town, with large windows overlooking the harbour. There's a long menu, including fish couscous (€15). Daily lunch & dinner; closed Sun Oct–May.

★ **Donne Fugate** Corso Umberto I 10 ☎334 760 3261. Small, rather unprepossessing place where you can nevertheless indulge in an excellent selection of *antipasti*, spaghetti *alla menta e gamberi* (with mint and prawns) and an unforgettable fish couscous (Thurs only). You'll pay around €40 for a full meal, drinks excluded. Mon–Tues & Thurs–Sat dinner only.

Il Gabbiano Via Trieste 5 ☎0923 911 909. Just off the seafront, this modest, white-walled and vaulted trattoria offers some of the cheapest food in town: nothing exceptional but the usual range of island specialities and a calm atmosphere. Pastas are around €6–8, *secondi* €6–10. Daily lunch & dinner; closed Wed in winter.

La Risacca Via Errera 18 ☎0923 912 975. At the end of the harbour, this busy *ristorante*-pizzeria with a terrace has an array of grilled seafood and outdoor seating. Try the ravioli *con pomodoro, burro e salvia* (with tomato, butter and sage €12), or, in the evening, *couscous alla pantesca*, with fish, aubergine, peppers, courgette and tomato (€16). Daily lunch & dinner; closed Mon in winter.

CAFÉS AND BARS

Café Aurora Via Borgo Italia 43 ☎0923 911 313. With a fine seating area overlooking the port, this bar serves classy aperitifs with olives and other nibbles. Daily 10am–late; closed winter.

★ **Cicci's** Via Cagliari 7 ☎0923 913 696. Just off the main piazza, this place has a lively evening crowd, musical accompaniment and snacks. Daily 6am–late; closed Sun in winter.

Tikirriki Via Borgo Italia 3 ☎0923 911604. Good snacks, pastries and ice cream, which you can eat by the harbour. Daily 8am–late; closed Sun in winter.

DIRECTORY

Banks ATMs at Banco di Sicilia, Piazza Cavour, Monte dei Paschi, Via Napoli 2, and Banco Nuova, Via Catania 5.

Hospital For first-aid and medical matters, go to the Ospedale B. Nagar, Piazzale Almanza (☎ 0923 910 234).

Pharmacy Farmacia Greco on Piazza Cavour (Mon–Fri 8.30am–1pm & 5–8.30pm; ☎ 0923 911 310). Pharmacies operate on a rota outside normal opening hours, noted on the door.

Police Carabinieri, Via Trieste 29 (☎ 0923 911 109).

Post office The island's main post office is off Piazza Cavour on Via de Amicis (Mon–Fri 8am–1.30pm, Sat 8am–12.30pm).

The southwest coast

The route south of Pantelleria town is initially very unpromising, through an industrial wasteland of noisome and noisy factories, abandoned farmhouses and past a military barracks. Things pick up after a couple of kilometres at the **Cuddie Rosse**, volcanic red rocks that mark the site of a prehistoric cave settlement. Fifteen minutes' walk further on, a signposted track on the left leads up 300m to the first of the island's strange **Sesi**, massive black Neolithic funeral mounds of piled rock, with low passages leading inside; a second one lies further up to the left. They're thought to be products of Pantelleria's first settlers, possibly from Tunisia. The main one here is 6m high, a striking sight, completely at one with its lunar-like environment. Scores of these must once have dotted the island, satisfying some primeval fears and beliefs. That so few survive is not so hard to understand when you take a look around at the regular-shaped stones from which the *dammuso* houses are built – centuries of plunder have taken their toll.

Beyond the Sesi, at **Punta Fram**, there's public access to the coast; look for a footpath, marked "*Discesa a mare*", opposite a side road to a little tower.

Sataria

On foot, it's just over an hour all told from the Sesi to **Sataria**, where concrete steps lead down to a tiny square-cut **sea-pool**, ideal for splashing around in. In the cave behind are more pools where warm water bubbles through, reputed to be good for curing rheumatism and skin diseases: a handful of people can usually be found jumping from pools to sea. There's room on the concrete apron around the pool to lay out a towel, and it's the only place for kilometres around with any shade – a nice place to eat your picnic.

EATING AND DRINKING ON PANTELLERIA

With its mix of Sicilian and North African elements, Pantelleria offers some unique gastronomic experiences. At some point, you ought to sample the locally produced ricotta-type cheese known as **tumma**, which is one of the ingredients of ravioli *con menta e ricotta*, a slightly bitter but fresh-tasting dish for which Pantelleria is famous. Pasta often comes served with **pesto pantesco**, a rough sauce of tomatoes, garlic and basil; while an *insalata pantesca* utilizes tomatoes, onions, cubes of boiled potato, herbs and local capers – the local capers are touted as the best in the Mediterranean.

The island's **wine** is well thought of too, made from the *zibbibo* grapes that grow well in this volcanic soil. The day-to-day drinking stuff – *vino pantesco* – is mostly white, with a nice fruity fragrance, while for something considerably stronger try the fortified **Moscato**, a sweet, amber-coloured dessert wine. Even better is the raisin wine, known generically as *passito*, which has a rich golden colour and a dry and heady flavour – the best-known variety is Tanit.

If you're **self-catering**, you'll find all you need in the town's supermarkets, bakery and fruit and veg shops, though for a taste of traditional island life, buy fresh fish from the stalls on the road to the hospital and the lighthouse, on the far side of the harbour from the dock, and fruit and veg from the morning market (Tues & Fri) on Via San Leonardo. Most shops are open daily in summer, and close Wednesday afternoons and Sunday at other times.

9

Scauri Porto and around

From the port at **Scauri**, on the west coast, you can see Cape Mustafa in Tunisia on a clear day. The village itself is a steep twenty-minute walk above its harbour, and consists of no more than a minuscule church perched on a shelf of land, surrounded by a cluster of houses; it does at least hold a bakery, as well as an *alimentari* that does decent panini, if you don't feel like splashing out in one of the restaurants.

Beyond here is **Rekale**, an even smaller and more remote hamlet, beyond which the extensive southeastern segment of the island, the **Dietro Isola**, curves round. Further hot springs at **Punto Nikà** are most easily reached by boat, though you can get there on foot.

ACCOMMODATION AND EATING   **SOUTHWEST COAST**

La Nicchia Scauri ☎ 0923 916 342. This is one of the island's most renowned eateries, and is worth dressing up for. You can dine inside or in the garden beneath the shade of an old orange tree, on such dishes as shrimps in a *zibbibo* sauce (see box, p.363) and the island speciality, mint- and *tumma*-stuffed ravioli bathed in sage butter (both €13). *Antipasti* run at €9–13, and *secondi* are around €15. Daily dinner only; closed Wed in low season.

La Vela Scauri Porto ☎ 0923 916 566. A very nice bar-restaurant, with a terrace right on the portside, where you can eat ravioli with ricotta and mint (€10), grilled fish and sweet, ricotta-filled *baci*. Open daily all day in summer; closed Nov–Easter.

Villaggio Punta Fram Contrada Camilla ☎ 0923 917 000, ⊕ aurumhotels.it. Posh hotel with a tennis court, a fine outdoor swimming pool and steps leading down to its own little rocky cove, where guests can swim happily. Full board is obligatory. Closed mid-Sept to mid-May. Doubles **€252**

The northeast coast

Although not the most striking part of the northeast coast, **Bue Marino**, some 1km east of town, has reasonable swimming from the rocks, though a little further on, there is better swimming from the flat rocks below the road junction to Bugeber.

East of here lies the **Cala dei Cinque Denti**, where fantastically shaped rocks jut out of the sea like monstrous black teeth – hence its name, "Bay of the Five Teeth" (though the rocks are really best seen from the sea). Just beyond, a minor road cuts away to the lighthouse at **Punta Spadillo**, where the cliff edges are covered with a carpet of surprising greenery that's somehow taken hold in the volcanic rocks.

The Specchio di Venere and Bugeber

From the first road junction on the northwest coast, it's a ten-minute walk up and around before you get the initial stunning views of the small **Specchio di Venere** (Venus's Mirror), shimmering below in a former crater. Though it glistens aquamarine in the middle, the lake has a muddy-brown edge, deposits of which you're supposed to apply to your body and allow to bake hard in the sun. Then you dive in and swim, washing all the mud off in the pleasantly warm water. A path skirts the edge of the lake, around which horse races take place as part of the August *ferragosto* celebrations.

Beyond the lake, the road climbs up for another 2km to the hamlet of **Bugeber**, set amid tumbling fields of vines and craggy boulders. The bus back to town runs past here three times a day; alternatively, walk the 3km past the lake back to the main road, where you can pick up any of the buses from Tracino.

Gadir

At a fork in the road past Punta Spadillo, the bus can drop you at the top of the smartly engineered route down into **Gadir**, one of the most perfect spots on Pantelleria. It's a small anchorage, with just a few houses hemmed in by volcanic pricks of rock, which – when the wind is up – can be battered and lashed by violent waves. At other times, people lie about on the flat concrete harbourside, and splash in the small thermal pools hereabouts.

Cala Levante and around

The lower road from Gadir toward Tracino is one of the loveliest on the island, following slopes that are terraced and corralled behind a patchwork of stone walls. Vines grow in profusion, with capers and blackberry bushes in the hedgerows. It's an easy, fairly flat hour's stroll to the charming **Cala Levante**, a huddle of houses around another tiny fishing harbour. There's good swimming from the rocks – provided the sea's not too rough – and a bar-restaurant above, with a terrace overlooking the sea. Where the road peters out, bear right along the path at the second anchorage and keep along the coast for another five minutes to view the **Arco dell'Elefante**, or "Elephant Arch", named after the lovely hooped formation of rock that resembles an elephant stooping to drink. Again there's no beach, but it's a good place to swim anyway.

Tracino and Khamma

From Cala Levante, a stupendously steep road climbs all the way up to **Tracino** in around twenty minutes, passing old *dammusi*, newer holiday homes, and striking gardens of vines and flowers. The top of the road marks the centre of Tracino, where there's a small square and a bar-restaurant. It's difficult to see where Tracino ends and adjacent **Khamma** starts, though this matters little once you're on the bus back to town.

Keen **hikers** make Tracino the start of their route into the pretty **Piano Ghirlandia**. The road runs out the other side of Tracino and soon becomes a track, which continues all the way down to meet the road on the south coast near Rekale.

Siba and the Montagna Grande

The summit of Pantelleria's main volcano, the **Montagna Grande** (836m) is the island's most distinctive feature when seen from out at sea. The walk up to the top begins in the crumbly old village of **SIBA**, perched on a ridge below the volcano, with views over the terraced slopes and cultivated plains to the sea. Few of the ancient *dammusi* here are so much as whitewashed, let alone bristling with mod cons. Outside, large wooden water barrels sit on the mildewed dry-stone volcanic walls, while the hamlet's only services are an *alimentari* and a *tabacchino*. If time hasn't exactly stood still here, it's in no great hurry to get on with things either. To find the trailhead, keep left at the telephone sign by the *tabacchino* here, and strike off the main road. The mountain's slopes afford the best views on the island, and are pitted by numerous volcanic vents, the **Stufe de Khazen**, marked by escaping threads of vapour.

Sauna Naturale

From Siba, another (signposted) path – on the left as you follow the road through the village – brings you in around twenty minutes to a natural sauna, **Sauna Naturale** (or Bagno Asciutto), where you can sweat it out for as long as you can stand. It's little more than a slit in the rock-face, where you can crouch in absolute darkness, breaking out into a heavy sweat as soon as you enter. It's coolest at floor-level; raising yourself up is like putting yourself into a pizza oven, while the ceiling is so hot it's impossible to keep the palm of your hand pressed flat against it. Ten minutes is the most you should attempt the first time – emerging into the midday sun is like being wafted by a cool breeze. Bring a towel.

Valle Monastero

From the road that descends from Siba to Scauri and the coast, you can take a track off to the left that runs through the so-called **Valle Monastero**. This lovely route leads past the abandoned monastery which gives the valley its name. Make sure you carry enough water if you tackle this hike, which is best accomplished early in the day. The path meets the road midway between Scauri and Rekale.

CAPPELLA PALATINA, PALERMO

Contexts

History

Sicily has a richer and more eventful past than any other Mediterranean island. Its strategic importance made it the constant prey of conquerors, many of whom, while contributing a rich artistic heritage, also turned Sicily into one of the most desolate war zones in Europe, their greed utterly transforming its ecology and heaping misery onto the vast majority of its inhabitants.

Prehistoric Sicily

Numerous remains survive of the earliest human settlements in Sicily. The most interesting of these are the cave paintings in the Grotta del Genovese, on Lévanzo in the Egadi Islands, which give a graphic insight into late Ice Age **Paleolithic** culture between 20,000 and 10,000 BC.

During the later **Neolithic period**, between 4000 and 3000 BC, a wave of settlers arrived from the eastern Mediterranean, landing on Sicily's east coast and in the Aeolian Islands. Examples of their relatively advanced culture – incised and patterned pottery and simple tools – are displayed in the museum on the Aeolian island of Lipari. Agricultural advances, the use of ceramics and the domestication of animals, as well as the new techniques of metalworking imported by later waves of Aegean immigrants in the **Copper Age** (3000–2000 BC), permitted the establishment of fixed farms and villages. In turn, this caused an expansion of trade, and promoted greater contact with far-flung Mediterranean cultures. The presence of Mycenaean ware from the Greek mainland became more noticeable during the **Bronze Age** (2000–1000 BC), an era to which the sites of Capo Graziano and Punta Milazzese on the Aeolian Islands belong. In about 1250 BC, further population movements took place, this time originating from the Italian mainland: the **Ausonians** settled in the Aeolians and the **Sikels** in eastern Sicily, pushing the indigenous tribes inland. It was the Sikels, from whom Sicily takes its name, who are thought to have first dug the vast necropolis of Pantalica, near Siracusa. At about the same time, the **Sicans**, a people believed to have originated in North Africa, occupied the western half of the island, as did the **Elymians**, who claimed descent from Trojan refugees: their chief city, Segesta, was alleged to have been founded by Aeneas' companion, Acestes.

The Carthaginians and the Greeks

After about 900 BC, Mycenaean and Aegean trading contacts began to be replaced by **Carthaginian** ones from North Africa, particularly in the west of the island. The Carthaginians – originally Phoenicians from the eastern Mediterranean – first settled at Panormus (modern Palermo), Solus (Solunto) and Motya (Mozia) during the eighth and seventh centuries BC. Their arrival coincided with the establishment of Aegean

20,000–10,000 BC	4000–3000 BC	2000–1000 BC
Paleolithic Sicilians paint caves on the island of Lévanzo	Neolithic adventurers from the Eastern Mediterranean settle on the Aeolian Islands and Sicily's east coast	Trade between eastern Sicily and Mycenaean Greece flourishes. Ausonians and Sikels from mainland Italy settle in the east, and Sicans and Elymians from North Africa in the west

Greek colonies in the east of Sicily, driven by a shortage of cultivable land back home and beginning with the colonization of **Naxos** in 734 BC. The Chalcidinians and Naxians who founded this colony were quickly followed by Megarians at **Megara Hyblaea**, Corinthians at **Ortigia** (Siracusa), and Rhodians, Cnidians and Cretans in **Gela**. While continuing to keep close links with their original homes, these cities became independent city-states and founded sub-colonies of their own, most important of which were **Selinus** (Selinunte) and **Akragas** (Agrigento). Along with the Greek colonies on the Italian mainland, these scattered communities came to be known as Magna Graecia, "Greater Greece".

The settlers found themselves with huge resources at their disposal, not least the island's **fertility**, which they quickly exploited through the widespread cultivation of corn – so much so that Demeter, the Greek goddess of grain and fecundity, became the chief deity on the island (the lake at Pergusa, near Enna, was claimed to be the site of the abduction of her daughter, Persephone). The olive and the vine were introduced from Greece, commercial activity across the Ionian Sea was intense and profitable, and the magnificence of the temples at Syracuse and Akragas often surpassed that of the major shrines in Greece. But the settlers also imported their native **rivalries**, and the history of Hellenic Sicily is one of almost uninterrupted warfare between the cities, even if they did generally join forces in the face of common foes such as the Carthaginians.

The Rise of Syracuse

It was the alliance against Carthage of Gela, Akragas and Syracuse, and the resulting Greek victory at **Himera** in 480 BC, that determined the ascendancy of **Syracuse** in Sicily for the next 270 years. The defeat, in about 450 BC, of a rebellion led by **Ducetius**, a Hellenized Sikel, extinguished the remnants of any native resistance to Greek hegemony, and the century which followed has been hailed as the "Golden Age" of Greek Sicily.

The accumulation of power by Syracusan **tyrants** attracted the attention of the mainland Greek states; Athens in particular was worried by the rapid spread of Corinthian influence in Sicily. In 415 BC, Athens dispatched the greatest armada ever to have sailed from its port. Later known as the **Great Expedition**, the effort was in response to a call for help from its ally, Segesta, while at war with Syracuse-supported Selinus. By 413 BC Syracuse itself was under siege, but the disorganization of the attacking forces, who were further hampered by disease, led to their total defeat, the execution of their generals and the imprisonment of 7000 soldiers in Syracuse's limestone quarries. This victory represented the apogee of Syracusan power. Civil wars continued throughout the rest of the island, attracting the attention of the Carthaginians, who responded to attacks on their territory by sacking in turn Selinus, Himera, Akragas and Gela. A massive counterattack was launched by the Syracusan tyrant **Dionysius I**, or "the Elder" (405–367 BC). That culminated in the complete destruction of the Phoenician base at **Motya**; its survivors founded a new centre at Lilybaeum, modern Marsala, on the western tip of the island.

The general devastation in Sicily caused by these wars was to some extent reversed by **Timoleon** (345–336 BC), who rebuilt many of the cities and re-established democratic institutions. But the carnage continued under the tyrant **Agathocles** (315–289 BC),

700–800 BC	734 BC	480 BC	450 BC
The Carthaginians arrive in Sicily and found Palermo	The Greeks establish their first Sicilian colony at Giardini Naxos	The battle of Himera sees the Greeks triumph over the Carthaginians	A Sikel rebellion led by Ducetius is defeated. Syracuse becomes the most important power in the Mediterranean

---

LIFE IN ROMAN SICILY

Much of Sicily's present appearance was determined during the Roman period. Forests were cut down to make way for grain cultivation, and the land was apportioned into large units, or **latifondia**, which became the basis for the vast agricultural estates into which the island is still to a certain extent divided. Conditions on these estates were so harsh that the second century BC saw two **slave revolts**, in 135–132 BC and 104–101 BC, involving tens of thousands of men, women and children, most of whom had been Greek-speaking citizens from all over Rome's newly won Mediterranean and Asian empire. These were isolated incidents, however, and on the whole Sicily benefited from the relative calm bestowed by the Romans. But little of the heavy tribute exacted by Rome was expended on the island itself and, though a degree of local **administration** existed, all important decisions were taken by the Roman Senate. That was represented on the island by two tax collectors, or **quaestors**, stationed in Syracuse and Lilybaeum, and a governor (**praetor**), who normally spent his year-long term extracting as much personal profit from the island as he could. The praetor **Verres** used his three terms of office, from 73 to 71 BC, to strip the countryside and despoil a large part of the treasure still held in the island's lavish temples. **Cicero's** prosecution of Verres, though undoubtedly exaggerated, constitutes our main source of information on Sicily under the Roman Republic: "When I arrived in Sicily after an absence of four years, it seemed to me a land in which there had been fought a prolonged and cruel war. Those fields and hills which I had seen bright and green I now saw devastated and deserted, and it seemed as if the land itself wept for its ancient farmers."

---

who was unrivalled in his sheer brutality. Battles were fought on the Italian mainland and North Africa, and the strife he engendered back in Sicily didn't end until **Hieron II** (265–215 BC) opted for a policy of peacekeeping, and even alliance, with the new power of the day, Rome.

The **First Punic War** – which broke out in 264 BC after the mercenary army in control of Messina, the **Mamertines**, appealed to Rome for help against their erstwhile Carthaginian protectors – left Syracuse itself untouched. It did however once again lead to the ruin of much of the island, before the final surrender of the Carthaginian base at Lilybaeum in 241. For Syracuse and its territories, though, this was a period of relative peace, and Hieron used the breathing space to construct some of the city's most impressive monuments.

Roman Sicily

Roman rule in Sicily can be said to have begun with **the fall of Syracuse**. That momentous event became inevitable when the city, whose territory was by now the only part of Sicily still independent of Rome, chose to side with Carthage in the **Second Punic War**, provoking a two-year siege that ended with the sacking of Syracuse in 211 BC. For the next seven hundred years, Sicily was a province of Rome, though in effect a subject colony, since few Sicilians were granted citizenship until the third century AD, when all inhabitants of the empire were classified as Romans. The island became Rome's granary or, as Cato had it, "the nurse at whose breast the Roman people is fed". As a key strategic province, Sicily suddenly became susceptible to age-old Roman political intrigue, notably during the **civil war** between Octavian, the

397 BC	265–215 BC	264 BC	212 BC
A force of 80,000 men from Syracuse destroys the Carthaginian base of Motya	Syracusan ruler Hieron II allies the city with Rome	The first Punic War between Rome and Carthage breaks out in Messina	In the Second Punic War, Syracuse sides with Carthage and is eventually sacked by Rome

future Emperor Augustus, and Sextus Pompey, who seized Sicily in 44 BC. For eight years the island's crucial grain exports were interrupted, and the final defeat of Sextus – in a sea battle off Mylae, or Milazzo – was followed by harsh retribution.

Once Octavian was installed as emperor, in 27 BC, Sicily entered a more peaceful period of Roman rule, with isolated instances of imperial splendour, notably the extravagant villa at Casale near Piazza Armerina. The island benefited especially from its important role in Mediterranean trade, and Syracuse, which handled much of the passing traffic, became a prominent centre of **early Christianity**, supposedly visited by Sts Peter and Paul on their way to Rome. Here, and further inland at Akrai, catacombs were burrowed from the third century AD onwards – and in caves throughout Sicily, Christian sanctuaries took their place alongside the shrines of the dozens of other cults prevalent on the island.

Barbarians, Byzantines and the arrival of the Arabs

Though Rome fell to the Visigoths in 410 AD, Sicily became prey to another Germanic tribe, the **Vandals**, who launched their invasion from the North African coast. The island was soon reunited with Italy under the Ostrogoth Theodoric, but the barbarian presence in Sicily was only a brief interlude, terminated in 535 AD when the **Byzantine** general Belisarius occupied the island. Although a part of the population had been Latinized, Greek remained the dominant culture and language of the majority, and the island willingly joined the Byzantine fold.

Constantinople was never able to give much attention to Sicily, however. The island was perpetually harried by piratical attacks, particularly from North Africa, where the Moors had become the most dynamic force in the Mediterranean. In around 700, the island of **Pantelleria** was taken, and only discord among the Arabs prevented Sicily itself from being next. In the event, trading agreements were signed, Arab merchants settled in Sicilian ports, and a fully fledged **Arab invasion** did not take place until 827, when a Byzantine admiral rebelled against the emperor and invited in the Aghlabid Emir of Tunisia. Ten thousand Arabs, Berbers and Spanish Muslims (known collectively as **Saracens**) landed at Mazara del Vallo, and Palermo fell four years later, though the invading forces only reached the Straits of Messina in 965. As with the Roman invasion, however, the turning point came with the fall of Syracuse in 878, when its population was massacred and the city plundered of its legendary wealth.

Arab Sicily

Palermo became the capital of the **Arabs in Sicily**, under whom it grew to become one of the world's greatest cities, wholly cosmopolitan in outlook, furnished with gardens, mosques (more than anywhere the traveller Ibn Hauqal had seen, barring Cordoba) and luxurious palaces. The Arabs brought great **benefits** to the rest of the island, too, renovating and extending irrigation works, breaking down many of the unwieldy *latifondia* and introducing new crops, including citrus trees, sugar cane, flax, cotton, silk, melons and date palms. Mining was developed, the salt industry greatly expanded and commerce improved, with Sicily once more at the centre of a flourishing trade network. Many Sicilian place names testify to the extent of the Arab settlement of the island. Prefixes such as *calta* (castle) and *gibil* (mountain) are plentiful, while other

38 BC	59 AD	410 AD	535 AD
Sextus Pompey is defeated by the future Emperor Augustus at the Battle of Mylae (modern-day Milazzo)	St Paul allegedly visits Syracuse. Christianity begins to gain followers	Rome falls to the Visigoths, and Sicily is attacked by tribes of Vandals	Sicily is occupied by Byzantines under General Belisarius

terms still in use indicate their impact on fishing, such as the name of the swordfish boats prowling the Straits of Messina (*felucca*), or the tuna-fishing terminology of the Egadi Islands. Taxation was rationalized and reduced, and **religious tolerance** was greater than under the Byzantines (though non-Muslims were subject to a degree of social discrimination).

The Arabs were prone to divisive feuding, however, and when in the tenth century the Aghlabid dynasty was toppled in Tunisia and their Fatimid successors shifted their capital to Egypt, Sicily lost its central position in the Arab Mediterranean empire and was left vulnerable to external attack. In 1038, the Byzantine general **George Maniakes** attempted to draw the island back under Byzantine sway, but he was unable to extend his occupation much beyond Syracuse. The real threat came from western Europe, particularly from the **Normans**, some of whom had accompanied Maniakes and seen for themselves the rewards to be gained. One of these, William "Bras de Fer" ("Iron Arm"), who had earned his nickname by his slaying of the Emir of Syracuse with one blow, was the eldest of the Hauteville brothers, whose exploits were soon to change the map of southern Europe.

The Normans

The **Hauteville brothers** had long been active in southern Italy by the time the youngest of them, **Roger**, seized Messina in 1061 in response to a call for help by one of the warring Arab factions. It took another thirty years to take control of the whole island, in a series of bloody and destructive campaigns that often involved the enlistment of Arabs on the Norman side. In 1072 Palermo was captured and adopted as the capital of **Norman Sicily**, and was subsequently adorned with palaces and churches that count among the most brilliant achievements of the era.

The most striking thing about the Norman period in Sicily is its brief span. In little more than a century, five kings bequeathed an enormous legacy of art and architecture that is still one of the most conspicuous features of the island. When compared with the surviving remains of the Byzantines, who reigned for three centuries, or the Arabs, whose occupation lasted roughly two, the Norman contribution stands out, principally due to its absorption of previous styles: the finest examples of Arab art to be seen in Sicily are elements incorporated into the great Norman churches. It was this fusion of talent that accounted for the great success of Norman Sicily, not just in the arts but in administration, justice and religious tolerance. The policy of **integration** was largely determined by force of circumstances: the Normans could not count on having adequate numbers of their own settlers, or bureaucrats to form a governmental class, and instead were compelled to rely on the existing framework. They did, however, gradually introduce a Latinized aristocracy and clerical hierarchy from northern Italy and France, so that the Arabic language was largely superseded by Italian and French by 1200.

The Hauteville dynasty

The first of the great Sicilian-Norman dynasty was **Count Roger**, or Roger I. He was a resolute and successful ruler, marrying his daughters into two of the most powerful European dynasties, one of them to the son of the western (or Holy Roman) emperor Henry IV. Roger's death in 1101, followed soon after by the death of his eldest son, left

827 AD	902 AD	1038	1061
A North African army of 10,000 lands at Mazara del Vallo	Tauromenium (Taormina) is the last Sicilian city to fall to the Arabs, who then make Palermo their capital	Byzantine General Maniakes occupies Syracuse; and William Hauteville slays the Emir of Syracuse	Roger Hauteville seizes Messina

Sicily governed by his widow Adelaide as regent for his younger son, who in 1130 was crowned **Roger II**. This first Norman king of Sicily was also one of medieval Europe's most gifted and charismatic rulers, who made the island a great melting pot of the most vigorous and creative elements in the Mediterranean world. He spoke Greek, kept a harem and surrounded himself with a medley of advisers, notably **George of Antioch**, his chief minister, or Emir of Emirs. Roger extended his kingdom to encompass all of southern Italy, Malta and parts of North Africa, and more enduringly drew up the first written code of law in the island.

His son, William I (1154–66) – "**William the Bad**" – dissipated these achievements by his enthusiasm for pleasure-seeking and his failure to control the barons, who exploited racial tensions to undermine the king's authority. During the regency that followed, the Englishman Walter of the Mill had himself elected archbishop of Palermo and dominated the scene for some twenty years, along with two other Englishmen, his brother Bartholomew and Bishop Palmer. This triumvirate preserved a degree of stability, but also encouraged the new king William II (1166–89), "**William the Good**", to establish a second archbishopric and construct a cathedral at **Monreale** to rival that of Palermo, just 10km away. The period saw a shift away from Muslim influence, though Arabs still constituted the bulk of the rural population and William himself resembled an oriental sultan in his style and habits, building a number of Arab-style palaces.

The death of William, aged only 36 and with no obvious successor, signalled a crisis in Norman Sicily. The barons were divided between **Tancred**, William's illegitimate nephew, and **Constance**, Roger II's aunt, who had married the Hohenstaufen (or Swabian) Henry, later to become the Holy Roman Emperor Henry VI. Tancred's election by an assembly was the first sign of a serious erosion of the king's authority: others followed, notably a campaign in 1189 against Muslims living on the island, which caused many of them to flee; and a year later the sacking of **Messina** by the English Richard I, on his way to join the Third Crusade. Tancred's death in 1194 and the succession of his young son, **William III**, coincided with the arrival in the Straits of Messina of the Hohenstaufen fleet. Opposition was minimal, and on Christmas Day of the same year Henry crowned himself king of Sicily. William and his mother were imprisoned in the castle at Caltabellotta, never to be seen again.

Hohenstaufen and the Angevins

Inevitably, Henry's imperial concerns led him away from Sicily, which represented only a source of revenue for him on the very outer limits of his domain. A revolt broke out against his authoritarian rule, which he repressed with extreme severity, but in the middle of it he went down with dysentery, died, and the throne passed to his three-and-a-half-year-old son, who became the emperor Frederick II, **Frederick I** of Sicily.

At first the running of the kingdom was entrusted to Frederick's mother Constance, but there was little stability, with the barons in revolt and a rash of race riots in 1197. Frederick's assumption of the government in 1220 marked a return to decisive leadership, with an immediate campaign to bring the barons to heel and eliminate a Muslim rebellion in Sicily's interior. The twin aims of his rule in Sicily were to restore the broad framework of the Norman state, and to impose a more imperial stamp on

1072	1166	1190	1194
The Normans capture Palermo and make it their capital	William Hauteville dies. Norman barons elect his illegitimate nephew Tancred to replace him	English King Richard I sacks Messina on his way to join the Third Crusade	Tancred dies. His son William III succeeds him but is defeated by Henry Hohenstaufen, who crowns himself King of Sicily

society, indicated by his fondness for classical Roman allusions in his promulgations and coinage. He allowed himself rights and privileges in Sicily that were impossible in his other possessions, emphasizing his own authority at the expense of the independence of the clergy and the autonomy of the cities. As elsewhere in southern Italy, strong **castles** were built, such as those at Milazzo, Catania, Siracusa and Augusta, to keep the municipalities in check.

A unified **legal system** was drawn up, embodied in his *Liber Augustales*, while his attempts to homogenize Sicilian society involved the harsh treatment of what had now become minority communities, such as the Muslims. He encouraged the arts, too, championing Sicilian vernacular poetry, whose pre-eminence was admitted by Petrarch and Dante. Frederick acquired the name "**Stupor Mundi**" ("Wonder of the World"), reflecting his promotion of science, law and medicine, and the peace that Sicily enjoyed during the half-century of his rule.

However, the balance of power Frederick achieved within Sicily laid the foundations for many of the island's future woes – for example, the weakening of the municipalities at a time when most European towns were increasing their autonomy. His centralized government worked so long as there was a powerful hand to guide it, but when Frederick died in 1255, decline set in, despite the efforts of his son **Manfred**, who strove to defend his crown from the encroachments of the barons and the acquisitiveness of foreign monarchs. New claimants to the throne were egged on by Sicily's nominal suzerain, the pope, anxious to deprive the Hohenstaufen of their southern possession, and he eventually auctioned it, selling it to the king of England, who accepted it on behalf of his 8-year-old son, Edmund of Lancaster. For ten years Edmund was styled "King of Sicily" despite the fact that the bill was never paid.

Charles of Anjou

French pope Urban IV deposed Edmund, who had never set foot in Sicily, and gave the title instead to **Charles of Anjou**, brother of the French king, on condition that he took over England's debt and paid the papacy a huge annual tribute. Backed by the papacy, Charles of Anjou embarked on a punitive campaign against the majority of the Sicilian population, who had supported the Hohenstaufen. He plundered land to give to his followers, and imposed a high level of taxation, though in the end it was a grassroots revolt that sparked off the **Sicilian Vespers**, an uprising against the French that began on Easter Monday 1282; it is traditionally held to have started after the bell for evening services, or Vespers, had rung at Palermo's church of Santo Spirito. The incident that sparked it all off was an insult to a woman by a French soldier, which led to a general slaughter in Palermo, soon growing into an island-wide rebellion against the French. This was the one moment in Sicilian history when the people rose up as one against foreign oppression – though in reality it was more an opportunity for horrific butchery and the settlement of old scores than a glorious expression of patriotic fervour.

The movement was given some direction when a group of nobles enlisted the support of **Peter of Aragon**, who landed at Trapani five months after the initial outbreak of hostilities and was acclaimed king at Palermo a few days later. The ensuing **Wars of the Vespers**, fought between Aragon and the Angevin forces based in Naples, lasted for another 21 years, mainly waged in Spain and at sea, while, in Aragonese Sicily, people settled down to over five centuries of Spanish domination.

1198	1220	1255
Henry Hohenstaufen's son Frederick becomes King of Sicily and Holy Roman Emperor at the age of three and a half. Sicily is ruled by his mother, Constance	Frederick takes the reins of power, initiating a period of strong rule	Frederick dies and his son Manfred is crowned king

The Spanish in Sicily

Sicily's new orientation towards **Spain**, and its severance from mainland Italy, meant that the island was largely excluded from all the great European developments of the fourteenth and fifteenth centuries. Large parts of Sicily were granted to the Spanish aristocracy, meaning a continuation of suffocating feudalism, and little impact was made by the Renaissance, while intellectual life on the island was stifled by the strictures of the Spanish Inquisition.

Although Peter of Aragon insisted that the two kingdoms of Aragon and Sicily should be ruled by separate kings after his death, his successor James reopened negotiations with the Angevins to sell the island back to them. His younger brother Frederick, appointed by James as Lieutenant of Palermo, convened a "parliament", which elected him king of an independent Sicily as **Frederick II** (1296–1337). Factions arose, growing out of the friction between Angevin and Aragonese supporters, and open warfare followed until 1372, when the independence of Sicily was guaranteed by Naples. Under the terms of the subsequent treaty the island became known as **Trinacria** ("three-cornered"), an ancient name revived to distinguish the island from the mainland Regnum Siciliae, ruled by the kingdom of Naples.

The constant feuding had laid waste to the countryside and the interior of Sicily became depopulated and unproductive, exacerbated by the effects of the Black Death. The feudal nobility lived mainly in the towns, building wealthy mansions in the **Chiaramonte** or the later, richly ornate Catalan-Gothic styles. A tradition of artistic patronage grew up, though most of the artists operating in Sicily came from elsewhere – for example, Francesco Laurana and the Gagini family were originally from northern Italy. A notable exception was **Antonello da Messina** (1430–79), who soaked up the latest Flemish techniques on his continental travels. Following the closing off of the eastern Mediterranean by the Ottoman Turks in the fifteenth century, Sicily was isolated from everywhere except Spain – from which, after 1410, it was ruled directly. Sicily found itself on the very fringes of Europe, and the unification of Castile and Aragon in 1479, followed soon after by the reconquest of the whole Spanish peninsula from the Moors, meant that Sicily's importance to its Spanish monarchs declined even further. The island came under the rule of a succession of **viceroys**, who were to wield power for the next four hundred years. Few of these were Sicilian (none at all after the first fifty years), while the only Spanish king to visit the island during the entire viceregal period was Charles V, on his way back from a Tunisian crusade in 1535.

The island's political bond to Spain meant that its degeneration deepened in tandem with Spain's decline in the seventeenth and eighteenth centuries. There were occasional revolts against the excesses of the zealous Inquisition, but on the whole discontent manifested itself in a resort to **brigandage**, for which the forest and wild maquis of Sicily's interior provided an ideal environment. The mixed fear and respect that the brigand bands generated played a large part in the future formation of an organized criminal class in Sicily.

Already burdened by the ever-increasing taxes demanded by Spain to finance its remote religious conflicts (principally, the 1618–48 Thirty Years' War), the misery of the Sicilians was compounded at the end of the seventeenth century by two appalling natural disasters. The **eruption of Etna** in 1669 devastated a large part of the area around Catania, while the **earthquake** of 1693 – also in the east of the island

1261	1282	1410	1693
French Pope Urban IV gives Sicily's throne to Charles of Anjou	The Sicilian Vespers uprising. Peter of Aragon is declared king, and the War of the Vespers begins	Spain wins the War of the Vespers, and Sicily falls under direct Spanish rule	An earthquake devastates southeast Sicily and kills around five percent of the population

– flattened whole cities, and killed around five percent of the island's population. With the death of Charles II of Spain in 1700 and the subsequent Wars of the Spanish Succession, the island once more took a back seat to mainland European interests. It was bartered in the **Treaty of Utrecht** that negotiated the peace, and given to the northern Italian House of Savoy, only to be swapped for Sardinia and given to Austria seven years later.

The Bourbons

The **Austrian government** of the island lasted only four years, cut short by the arrival of another Spaniard, **Charles of Bourbon**, who claimed the throne for himself. Although he never visited Sicily again after his first landing, **Charles III** (1734–59) brought a refreshingly constructive air to the island's administration, showing a more benevolent attitude towards his new subjects. But, with his succession to the Spanish throne in 1759 and the inheritance of the Neapolitan crown by his son, **Ferdinand IV**, it was back to the bad old days. Any meagre attempts at reform made by his viceroys were opposed at every turn by the reactionary local aristocracy, who were closing ranks in response to the progress of the Enlightenment and the ideas unleashed by the French Revolution. When the ensuing **Napoleonic Wars** wracked Europe, Sicily, along with Sardinia, was the only part of Italy not conquered by Napoleon, while the Neapolitan *ancien régime* was further buttressed by the decision of Ferdinand (brother-in-law of Marie Antoinette) to wage war against the revolutionary French. He was supported in this by the British, who sustained the Bourbon state, so that when Ferdinand and his court were forced to flee Naples in 1799, it was **Nelson's** flagship they sailed in, accompanied by the British ambassador to Naples, Sir William Hamilton, and his wife Lady Emma. Nelson was rewarded for his services by the endowment of a large estate at Bronte, just west of Etna.

The arrival of the British

Four years later, Ferdinand was able to return to Naples, though he had to escape again in 1806 when Napoleon gave the Neapolitan crown to his brother Joseph. This time he had to stay longer, remaining in Palermo until after the defeat of Napoleon in 1815 – a stay that was accompanied by a larger contingent of British troops and a heavy involvement of British capital and commerce. **Liberalism** became a banner of revolt against the king's continuing tax demands, and Ferdinand's autocratic reaction provoked the British commander **William Bentinck** to intervene. Manoeuvring himself into a position where he was the virtual governor of Sicily, Bentinck persuaded the king to summon a new parliament and adopt a **constitution** whereby the independence of Sicily was guaranteed and feudalism abolished.

Although this represented a drastic break with the past, the reforms had little direct effect on the peasantry, and, following the departure of the British, the constitution was dropped and Ferdinand (now styling himself Ferdinand I, King of the Two Sicilies) repealed all the reforms previously introduced. Renewed talk of independence in Sicily spilled over into action in 1820, when a rebellion was put down with the help of Austrian mercenaries. The **repression** intensified after Ferdinand I's death in 1825, and the island's fortunes reached a new low under Ferdinand II (1830–59), nicknamed "Re

1700	1713	1735
Charles II dies childless, prompting the War of the Spanish Succession	Sicily is handed to the royal Italian House of Savoy at the Treaty of Utrecht	The Spanish King Charles of Bourbon claims the throne of Sicily, initiating a brief period of enlightened rule

Bomba" for his five-day **bombardment of Messina** following major insurrections there and in Palermo in 1848–49. Another uprising in Palermo in 1860 proved a spur for Giuseppe Garibaldi to pick Sicily as the starting point for his unification of Italy.

Unification

On May 11, 1860, **Giuseppe Garibaldi** landed at Marsala with a thousand men. A professional soldier and one of the leading lights of **Il Risorgimento**, the movement for Italian unification, Garibaldi intended to liberate the island from Bourbon rule, in the name of the Piedmont House of Savoy. His skill in guerrilla warfare, backed by an increasingly cooperative peasantry, ensured that the campaign progressed with astonishing speed. Four days after disembarking, he defeated 15,000 Bourbon troops at **Calatafimi**, closely followed by an almost effortless occupation of Palermo. A battle at **Milazzo** in July decided the issue: apart from Messina (which held out for another year), Sicily was free of Spain for the first time since Peter of Aragon acquired the crown in 1282.

A **plebiscite** was held in October, which returned a 99.5 percent majority in favour of union with the new **kingdom of Italy** under Vittorio Emanuele II. The result, greeted by general euphoria, marked the official **annexation** of the island to the Kingdom of Savoy. Later, however, many began to question whether anything had been achieved by this change of ruler. The new **parliamentary system**, in which only one percent of the island's population was eligible to vote, made few improvements for the majority of people. Attempts at opposition were met with ruthless force, sanctioned by a distant and misinformed government convinced that the island's problems were fundamentally those of law and order. Sicilians responded with their traditional defence of *omertà*, or silent non-cooperation, along with a growing **resentment** of the new Turin government (transferred to Rome in 1870) that was even stronger than their distrust of the more familiar Spanish Bourbons.

The "southern problem"

A series of reports made in response to criticism of the Italian government's failure to solve what was becoming known as the "**southern problem**" found that the lot of the Sicilian peasant was, if anything, worse after Unification than it had been under the Bourbons. Power had shifted away from the landed gentry to the *gabellotti*, the middlemen to whom they leased the land. These men became increasingly linked with the **Mafia**, a shadowy, loose-knit criminal association that found it easy to manipulate voting procedures, while simultaneously posing as defenders of the people. At the end of the nineteenth century a new, more organized opposition appeared on the scene in the form of **fasci** – embryonic trade-union groups demanding legislation to protect peasants' interests. Violence erupted and the Italian prime minister, **Francesco Crispi** – a native Sicilian who had been one of the pioneers of the Risorgimento – dispatched a fleet and 30,000 soldiers to put down the "revolt", while also closing newspapers, censoring postal services and detaining suspects without trial.

Although there were later signs of progress, in the formation of worker cooperatives and in the enlightened land-reform programmes of individuals such as **Don Sturzo**, mayor of Caltagirone, the overwhelming despair of the peasantry was expressed in

1848	May 1860	October 1860
Insurrections against Bourbon autocracy are put down at Messina and Palermo	Garibaldi and his 1000 followers land at Marsala, and defeat 15,000 Bourbon troops at Calatafimi. Sicily is freed from Spanish rule	Sicilians vote to join the Kingdom of Italy

mass emigration. One and a half million Sicilians decided to leave in the years leading up to 1914, most going to North and South America. Many had been left homeless in the wake of the great **Messina earthquake** of 1908, in which upwards of 80,000 lost their lives. Though the high rate of emigration was a crushing indictment of the state of affairs on the island, it had many positive effects for those left behind, who benefited not only from huge remittances sent back from abroad but from the wage increases that resulted from labour shortages.

The world wars

The Italian **conquest of Libya** in 1912 was closely followed by **World War I**, and both were heavy blows to the Sicilian economy. In 1922 **Mussolini** gained power in Rome and dispatched **Cesare Mori** to solve "the southern problem" by putting an end to the Mafia. Free of constitutional and legal restrictions, Mori was able to imprison thousands of suspected *mafiosi*. The effect was merely to drive the criminal class deeper underground, while the alliance he forged with the landed classes to help bring this about dissolved all the gains that had been made against the ruling elite, setting back the cause of agrarian reform. In the **1930s** Mussolini's African concerns and his drive for economic and agricultural self-sufficiency gave Sicily a new importance for Fascist Italy, the island now vaunted as "the geographic centre of the empire". In the much publicized "**Battle for Grain**", wheat production increased, though at the cost of the diversity of crops that Sicily required, resulting in soil exhaustion and erosion. Mussolini's popularity on the island is best illustrated by his order, in 1941, that all Sicilian-born officials be transferred to the mainland, on account of their possible disloyalty.

During **World War II**, Sicily became the first part of Europe to be **invaded** by the Allies when, in July 1943, Patton's American Seventh Army landed at Gela, and Montgomery's British Eighth Army came ashore between Pachino and Pozzallo further east. This combined army of 160,000 men was the largest ever seen in Sicily, but the campaign was longer and harder than had been anticipated, with the Germans mainly concerned with delaying the advance until they had moved most of their men and equipment across the Straits of Messina. Few Sicilian towns escaped **aerial bombardment**, and Messina itself was the most heavily bombed of all Italian cities before it was taken on August 18.

Post-war Sicily

The aftermath of the war saw the most radical changes in Sicily since Unification. With anarchy and hunger widespread, a wave of banditry and crime was unleashed, while the Mafia were reinstated in their behind-the-scenes role as adjudicators and powerbrokers, now allied to the landowners in the face of large-scale land occupations by a desperate peasantry. **Separatism** became a potent rallying cry for protesters of all persuasions, who believed that Sicily's ills could best be solved by cutting its links with the mainland. A Separatist army was formed, financed by some of the gentry, but it lacked the organization or resources to make any great impact. It was largely in response to this call for independence that, in 1946, Sicily was granted **regional autonomy**, with its

1893	1908	1908–1915
Italian Prime Minister Francesco Crispi sends an army of 30,000 into rural Sicily to quash those demanding rights for peasants	An earthquake devastates Messina, killing 80,000	With the island racked by poverty, one and a half million Sicilians emigrate

own assembly and president. The same year saw the declaration of a republic in Italy, the result of a popular mandate.

Autonomy failed to heal the island's divisions, however, and brute force was used by the Mafia and the old gentry against what they perceived as the major threat to their position – **communism**. The most famous bandit of the time, **Salvatore Giuliano**, who had previously been associated with the Separatists, was enlisted in the anti-communist cause. He organized a campaign of bombings and assassinations, most notoriously at the 1947 May Day celebrations at Portella della Ginestra. Giuliano's betrayal and murder in 1950 was widely rumoured to have been carried out to prevent him revealing who his paymasters were, though it all helped to glorify his reputation in the popular imagination.

By the 1950s, many saw the **Christian Democrat** party, Democrazia Cristiana, as the best hope to defend their interests. Along with the emotional hold it exerted by virtue of its close association with the Church, the DC could draw on many of the Sicilians' deepest fears of change; the party was also too closely involved with business and the land-owning classes to have any real enthusiasm for genuine reform. All attempts at enterprise were channelled through the DC's offices, and favours were bought or bartered. Cutting across party lines, political patronage, or **clientelismo**, grew to be stronger than ever. It still affects people's lives on every level today, especially in the field of work – from finding a job to landing a contract. The favours system was also evident in the workings of Sicily's sluggish **bureaucracy**, so that the smallest reforms often took years to effect. The essential problem is unchanged today, with the elaborate machinery of the civil service often exploited to accumulate and dispense personal power.

One area that managed to avoid bureaucratic control or planning of any sort was **construction** – one of Sicily's greatest growth industries, the physical evidence of which is among the visitor's most enduring impressions of the island. The building boom was inextricably connected with the Mafia's involvement in land speculation, and boosted by the phenomenal rate of urban growth all over Sicily. But in both the towns and rural areas, minimum safety standards were rarely met, as highlighted by the **1968 earthquake**, in which 50,000 were made homeless along the Valle di Belice in the west of the island. **Industry**, too, has been subject to mismanagement and, apart from isolated cases, has rarely fulfilled the potential it promised after the discovery of oil near Ragusa and Gela in the 1950s, and the development of refineries and petrochemical plants along the Golfo di Augusta.

Substantial subsidies have been channelled into many ventures, largely from the **European Union**, which Italy joined in 1958. However, it's still the great urban centres in the north that flaunt their prosperity, while the south of Italy, known as Il Mezzogiorno, is left far behind. Conversely, the huge financial concessions made to Sicily have provoked resentment from Italy's more self-sufficient regions, who point to massive corruption and incompetence on the island. Few Sicilians would wholly deny this; a longer view, however, argues that Sicily's disadvantages are derived principally from the past misuse of resources, coupled with a culture and mentality that have never given much credence to collectivist ideals. There is more awareness, too, on the part of the state that the fight against **organized crime** requires more than moralistic speeches. Indeed, in 1992, following the murders of anti-Mafia investigators Falcone and

1914	1943	1946
World War I breaks out, severely damaging the Sicilian economy	160,000 English and American troops land in Sicily. Messina becomes the most heavily bombed city in Italy	Sicily is granted regional autonomy

Borsellino, the chief of police of Palermo was sacked, while 7000 troops were sent to the island to patrol prisons and search towns with a known Mafia presence. There have been significant breakthroughs, though these are mostly connected with a change in the public attitude towards criminality, resulting in part from a campaign to reform Sicily's dilapidated **education** system. In the 1990s, a campaign of anti-Mafia education began in Sicilian schools, aiming to cut the secondary-school drop-out rate by encouraging children away from the traditional path of corruption and crime.

Sicily today

Despite superficial improvements, the deep problems that have always bedevilled Sicily remain in some form. Unemployment is still high, and not helped by the diminishing opportunities for **emigration**, though a million still managed to escape the island between 1951 and 1971, along with the majority of Sicily's most outstanding artists and writers. Ironically, the late 1990s saw the problem of **immigration** hitting the agenda for the first time, as political and economic refugees from North Africa started to arrive by regular boatloads, particularly on the two southernmost islands of Lampedusa and Pantelleria. These *extracomunitari* (literally, "those from non-EU countries") are routinely rounded up and sent to crowded processing centres, where they languish for months, before almost all are eventually returned to their countries of origin. Others slip through and join the already strained jobs market. Despite harsh anti-immigration legislation introduced by the Italian government, illegal immigration continues to be a contentious issue that has affected Italy more than most EU countries.

In the long run, perhaps the greatest hope for Sicily lies in **tourism** and related services. Visitor numbers are growing (helped by budget airline routes to fast-growing Trapani airport and the new airport at Comiso), and there's an increasing emphasis on boutique and eco-tourism, in the shape of hundreds of new B&Bs, rural tourism ventures and outdoor activity operators. Many towns and resorts (particularly on the outlying islands) have a positively fashionable air, while more and more Italians are throwing off their distrust of the south and discovering the island's potential, especially its outdoor attractions, wildlife and crystal-clear seas. The creation of **regional parks** in Etna and the Nébrodi and Madonie ranges, and the **marine reserves** around Ustica and the Egadi and Pelagie islands, are a reflection of this, and an encouraging pointer for the future.

1950	1968	late 1990s–present day
The conservative (and Mafia-backed) Christian Democrat party dominates Sicilian politics	An earthquake at Belice leaves 50,000 people homeless	Political and economic immigrants – mostly from North Africa – arrive in Sicily

The Mafia in Sicily

In Sicily, there is "*mafiosità*" and there is "the Mafia". *Mafiosità* refers to a criminal mentality, the Mafia to a specific criminal organization. In Italy's deep south, a man can look *mafioso*, or talk like a *mafioso*, meaning he has the aura – or stench – of criminality about him, even though he has no explicit connection to the crime syndicate. And, while notions of family solidarity and the moral stature of the outlaw mean that *mafiosità* can never be completely extirpated from Sicilian society, the Mafia is an entity whose members can be eliminated and its power emasculated.

What has always prevented this is the shadowy nature of the organization, protected by the longstanding **code of silence**, or *omertà*, that invariably led to accusations being retracted at the last moment, or to crucial witnesses being found dead with a stone, cork or a wad of banknotes stuffed into their mouths, or else simply disappearing off the face of the earth. As a result, many have doubted the very existence of the Mafia, claiming that it's nothing more than the creation of pulp-thriller writers, the invention of a sensationalist press and the fabrication of an Italian government embarrassed by its inability to control an unusually high level of crime in Sicily.

The background

In 1982, however, proof of the innermost workings of the Mafia's organization emerged when a high-ranking member, **Tommaso Buscetta**, was arrested in Brazil, and – after a failed suicide attempt – agreed to prise open the can of worms. His reason for daring this sacrilege, he claimed, was to destroy the Mafia. In its stampede to grab huge drug profits, the "Honoured Society" (La Società Onorata) had abandoned its original ideals: "It's necessary to destroy this band of criminals", he declared, "who have perverted the principles of Cosa Nostra and dragged them through the mud." He was doubtlessly motivated by revenge: all of those he incriminated – Michele Greco, Pippo Calò, Benedetto Santapaola, Salvatore Riina and many others – were leaders of, or allied to, the powerful Corleone family who had recently embarked on a campaign of terror to monopolize the drugs industry, in the process eliminating seven of Buscetta's closest relatives in the space of four months, including his two sons.

Buscetta's statements to Giovanni Falcone, head of Sicily's anti-Mafia "pool" of judges, and later to the Federal Court in Manhattan, provided crucial revelations about the structure of Cosa Nostra. Mafia "families" are centred on areas, he revealed: villages or quarters of cities from which they take their name. The boss (*capo*) of each group is chosen by election, and appoints a lieutenant (*sottocapo*) and one or more *consiglieri*, or counsellors. Above the families is the *cupola*, or **Commission**, a governing body that includes representatives from all the major groupings. Democracy and collective interest, Buscetta claimed, had been replaced in the Commission by the greed and self-interest of the individuals who had gained control. Trials of strength alone now decided the leadership, often in the form of bitter feuds between rival factions – or *cosche* (literally, "artichokes", their form symbolizing solidarity).

The existence of the Commission sets the Mafia apart from the normal run of underworld gangs, for without a high level of organization the international trafficking in heroin in which they engage would be inconceivable. The route is circuitous, starting in the Middle and Far East, moving on to the processing plants in Sicily, and ending up in New York, where American Mafia channels are said to control sixty percent of the heroin market. This multimillion-dollar racket – known in the US as the "**Pizza Connection**", because Sicilian pizza parlours were used as covers for the operation – was blown apart chiefly as a result of Buscetta's evidence, and led to the trial and conviction of the leading members of New York's Mafia Commission in September 1986.

The history

The Mafia has certainly come a long way since its rustic beginnings in **feudal Sicily**. Although Buscetta denied that the word "Mafia" is used to describe the organization – the term preferred by its members is "Cosa Nostra" – the word has been in currency for centuries, and is thought to derive from the Arabic, **mu'afah**, meaning "protection". In 1863, a play entitled *Mafiusi della Vicaria*, based on life in a Palermo prison, was a roaring success among the high society of the island's capital, and gave the word its first extensive usage. When the city rose against its new Italian rulers three years later, the British consul described a situation where secret societies were all-powerful: "*Camorre and maffie*, self-elected juntas, share the earnings of the workmen, keep up intercourse with outcasts, and take malefactors under their wing and protection." Until then, *mafiosi* had been able to pose as defenders of the poor against the tyranny of Sicily's rulers, but in the years immediately following the toppling of the Bourbon state in Italy *mafiosi* were able to entrench themselves in Sicily's new power structure, acting as intermediaries in the gradual redistribution of land and establishing a modus vivendi with the new democratic representatives.

There is little documentary proof of the rise to power of the "Honoured Society", but most writers agree that between the 1890s and the 1920s its undisputed boss was **Don Vito Cascio Ferro**, who had close links with the American "Black Hand", a Mafia-type association of southern Italian emigrants. Ferro's career ended with Mussolini's anti-Mafia purges, instigated to clear the ground for the establishment of a vigorous Fascist structure in Sicily. **Cesare Mori**, the Duce's newly appointed Prefect of Palermo, arrived in the city in 1925 with the declared aim of "clearing the ground of the nightmares, threats and dangers which are paralyzing, perverting and corrupting every kind of social activity". This might have worked, but the clean sweep that Mori made of the Mafia leaders (in all, 11,000 cattle rustlers, thieves and "conspirators" were jailed during this period, often on the basis of flimsy hearsay) was annulled after World War II when the prisons were opened and Mafia leaders, seen as unjustly jailed by the Fascist regime, returned to their regular operations. In the confusion that reigned during Italy's reconstruction, crime flourished throughout the south, and criminal leagues regrouped in Naples (the Camorra) and Calabria ('ndrangheta). In Sicily, men such as **Don Calogero Vizzini** were the new leaders, confirmed in their power by the brief Anglo-American postwar administration, in return for their contribution towards the smooth progress of the Allied landings. One of them, **Lucky Luciano**, a founder member of the American Commission, was even flown out from prison in America to facilitate the invasion. Later he was alleged to be responsible for setting up the Sicilian-American narcotics empire, which was taken over at his death in 1962 by **Luciano Leggio**, who subsequently manoeuvred himself into the leadership of the Corleone family.

The new Mafia

The cycle was by now complete: the Mafia had lost its original role as a predominantly rural organization, and had transferred its operations to the cities, moving into entrepreneurial activities such as construction, real estate and, ultimately, drug smuggling. The growth of the heroin industry raised the stakes immensely, as shown by the vicious feuds fought over the division of the spoils, and the struggle for control of narcotics trafficking played a key role in the consolidation of power within the Mafia.

The Italian state responded with an **anti-Mafia Parliamentary Commission** that sat from 1963 to 1976, and posed enough of a threat to provoke a change of tactics by the Mafia, who began to target important state officials in a sustained campaign of terror. In 1971, Palermo's chief public prosecutor, Pietro Scaglione, became the first in a long line of "**illustrious corpses**" – *cadaveri eccellenti* – which have included journalists, judges, lawyers, police chiefs and left-wing politicians. A new peak of violence was reached in 1982 with the murder in Palermo's city centre of **Pio La Torre**, regional secretary of the Communist Party in Sicily, who had proposed a special government dispensation to allow lawyers access to private bank accounts.

Among the mourners at La Torre's funeral was the new Sicilian prefect of police, **General Dalla Chiesa**, a veteran in the state's fight against the anarchist/terrorist Red Brigades. The prefect began to investigate Sicily's lucrative construction industry, and his scrutiny of public records and business dealings threatened to expose one of the most enigmatic issues in the Mafia's organization: the extent of corruption and protection in high-ranking political circles, the so-called "**Third Level**". However, exactly 100 days after La Torre's death, Dalla Chiesa himself was gunned down, together with his wife, in Palermo's Via Carini. The whole country was shocked, and the murder revived questions about the depth of government commitment to the fight. In his engagement with the Mafia, Dalla Chiesa had received next to no support from Rome, to the extent that Dalla Chiesa's son had accused the mandarins of the Christian Democrat party – former prime minister Andreotti among them – of isolating his father. Nando Dalla Chiesa refused to allow many local officials to his father's funeral, including Vito Ciancimino, former mayor of Palermo and a Christian Democrat. Later, Ciancimino was accused, not just of handling huge sums of drug money, but of actually being a sworn-in member of the Corleone family. Those who were present at the funeral included the Italian president and senior cabinet ministers, all of them jeered at by an angry Sicilian crowd.

To ward off accusations of government inertia or complicity, the law that La Torre had demanded was rushed through Parliament soon afterwards, and was used in the **super-trials**, or *maxiprocessi*, that arose from the confessions of Buscetta and the other *pentiti* (penitents) who had followed his lead. The biggest of these trials, lasting eighteen months, started in February 1986, when five hundred *mafiosi* appeared in a specially built maximum-security bunker adjoining Palermo's Ucciardone prison. The insecurity felt by the Mafia was reflected in continuing bloodshed in Sicily throughout the proceedings, but the worst was to come after the trial closed in December 1986, starting right on the steps of the courthouse with the murder of one of the accused *mafiosi* – many of whom were freed after they had squealed on their accomplices. Of those who were convicted, 19 received life sentences, and 338 others sentences totalling 2065 years.

The fightback in the 1990s

The violence reached a new level of ferocity during the 1990s, starting in 1992 with a wave of assassinations of high-profile figures. In March, **Salvatore Lima**, a former mayor of Palermo who later became a Euro MP, was shot dead outside his villa in Mondello. Lima didn't have police bodyguards because he didn't believe he needed them; he had, in fact, been in the Mafia's pocket throughout his political career. His "crime" was his failure to fix the Supreme Court, which had gone ahead and confirmed the convictions of scores of *mafiosi* who had been incriminated in the super-trials of the 1980s.

This murder was followed by two more atrocities in quick succession: in May, the best-known of Sicily's anti-Mafia crusaders, **Giovanni Falcone**, was blown up by half a tonne of TNT on his way into Palermo from the airport, together with his wife and three bodyguards, while two months later his colleague, **Paolo Borsellino** (with five of his police guards), was the victim of a car bomb outside his mother's house, also in Palermo. As ever, public opinion was divided over what it all meant. There were those who claimed that these murders were public gestures, while others saw in them increasing evidence of the panic percolating through the Mafia's ranks in the face of the growing number of defections of former members who were turning *pentiti*.

The carnage certainly propelled the state into action, and a dramatic breakthrough came shortly afterwards. In January 1993, **Salvatore Riina**, the so-called "Boss of all the Bosses", and the man held ultimately responsible for the murder of the anti-Mafia judges, was arrested. **Leoluca Bagarella**, Riina's successor and brother-in-law, and the convicted killer of the chief of the Palermo Flying Squad in 1979, was captured in 1995 (Bagarella's hideout turned out to be a luxury apartment overlooking the heavily guarded home of two of the judges who had helped catch him). Another of the Corleone clan, **Giovanni Brusca**, was arrested in 1996 – a particularly gratifying coup for the anti-Mafia forces, as Brusca was one of the organization's most ruthless hitmen, the mastermind behind Falcone's assassination and believed to have been responsible for the strangling of an informant's 11-year-old son, whose body was then disposed of in a vat of acid. Elsewhere, **Natale D'Emanuele**, alleged to be the financial wizard behind the Mafia in Catania, was arrested and charged with trafficking arms throughout Italy, using hearses and coffins to transport them in a throwback to 1930s Chicago.

On the political front, **Leoluca Orlando**, the mayor of Palermo who was forced out of office by his own Christian Democrat party in 1990, established an independent power base on an anti-Mafia ticket, at the head of his Rete (Network) party. Meanwhile, the confessions of Tommaso Buscetta began to provide evidence for the first time of the postwar alliance between Italy's former leading party and organized crime. Allegations inexorably focused on the very highest levels of government, and specifically on the relationship of Mafia stooge Salvatore Lima to his protector, **Giulio Andreotti**, the Christian Democrat leader and Italy's most successful postwar politician. Formerly considered untouchable, Andreotti finally bowed to increasing pressure to relinquish his parliamentary immunity and, in September 1995, aged 75, went on trial in Palermo for complicity and criminal association. Much fuss was made of the famous *bacio*, a kiss he was reported to have symbolically exchanged with Riina, according to *pentiti* revelations in 1994. However, the fact that most of the charges levelled against Andreotti were based on the testimony of Mafia informers (and therefore unreliable witnesses) led to Andreotti's complete acquittal in 1999. Many saw the result as simply further evidence of the famous cunning and survival skills of this political stalwart, which have given him the nickname *la volpe* ("the fox").

Statements by *pentiti* and others accused of Mafia associations were also at the bottom of investigations into the business dealings of the then-prime minister **Silvio Berlusconi**. This time they were considered serious enough to warrant a raid on Berlusconi's Milan headquarters by an elite anti-Mafia police unit in July 1998, and a hasty dash to Sicily by Berlusconi to defend himself against charges of money-laundering for Cosa Nostra. Despite these high-profile events, though, the very concept of Mafia involvement was becoming increasingly irrelevant to most Italians, as reports of political and business corruption began to dominate public life throughout the 1990s. As the mayor of Venice remarked, in response to whispers of Mafia involvement in the fire that destroyed La Fenice opera house in 1996, "claiming it was burnt by the Mafia is about as useful as saying it was attacked by alien spacecraft."

Contemporary events

Since the turn of the millennium, the violence has for the most part calmed down. While killings still occur, few political figureheads are targeted these days, perhaps because fewer are willing to take the visible risks that sealed the fate of crusaders like Falcone and Borsellino. More Mafia bosses have been jailed – **Bernardo Provenzano**, for thirteen years *capo dei capi*, was captured in 2006, quickly followed by 52 arrest warrants against the top echelons of Cosa Nostra in Palermo, while the man thought to be Provenzano's successor, **Salvatore Lo Piccolo**, was arrested in 2007. Perhaps more significantly, the last decade has seen the repossession by Palermo's anti-Mafia magistrate of billions of euros in assets held by *mafiosi*, largely from the real estate and construction industries.

The most important development, however, has been the growth of a new open attitude towards the Mafia, in contrast to the previous denial and *omertà*. One of the most watched TV programmes in Italy in recent years has been *La Piovra* ("The Octopus"), a drama series along the lines of *The Sopranos*, while in Corleone, an anti-Mafia centre has opened to educate both foreigners and Sicilians alike. Sicilians themselves are now bolder than ever in their public demonstrations of disgust at the killings and intimidation, and a new movement against paying **pizzo**, or protection money, has gathered force throughout the island. An increasing number of brave individuals are willing to make a stand: people such as Rita Borsellino, sister of murdered judge Paolo Borsellino and now an anti-Mafia figurehead, or Giovanna Terranova, widow of another "illustrious" victim, Judge Cesare Terranova (killed in 1979), who launched a women's movement against the Mafia with the words, "If you manage to change the mentality, to change the consent, to change the fear in which the Mafia can live – if you can change that, you can beat them."

It is precisely that element of "consent" among ordinary Sicilians that has always been the strongest weapon in the Mafia's armoury, indeed the very foundation of the Mafia's existence, bolstered by an attitude that has traditionally regarded the *mafioso* stance as a revolt against the State, justified by centuries of oppression by foreign regimes. This historical dichotomy is perhaps best expressed by one of Sicily's greatest writers, Leonardo Sciascia, who proclaimed, "It hurts when I denounce the Mafia because a residue of Mafia feeling stays with me, as it does in any Sicilian. So in struggling against the Mafia I struggle against myself. It is like a split, a laceration."

At least the problem is being confronted, and few Sicilians now hold any illusions about the true nature of the Mafia, shorn of its one-time altruistic ideals – if they ever existed. And crucially, the myth of the Mafia's invincibility has been irreparably dented.

Sicilian Baroque

Most of the church and civic architecture that you'll come across in Sicily, certainly in the east of the island, is Baroque in style. More particularly, it's of a type known as Sicilian Baroque. What follows is a brief introduction to the subject, designed to serve as a handy reference for some of the more important aspects of the style mentioned in the Guide.

Origins

To some extent, the qualities that attract art historians to the Sicilian Baroque – its "warmth and ebullience", "gaiety", "energy", "freedom and fantasy"– typify all **Baroque** architecture. The style grew out of the excesses of Mannerism, a distorted sixteenth-century mode of painting and architecture that had flourished in Italy in reaction to the restraint of the Renaissance. The development of a full-blown, ornate Baroque style followed in the late sixteenth century, again originating in Italy, and it quickly found a niche in other countries touched by the Counter-Reformation. The Jesuits saw in Baroque art and architecture an expression of a revitalized Catholicism, its theatrical forms involving the congregation by portraying spiritual ecstasy in terms of physical passion. The origin of the word "Baroque" itself is uncertain: the two most popular theories are that it comes either from the seventeenth-century Portuguese *barroco*, meaning a misshapen pearl, or the term *barocco*, used by philosophers in the Middle Ages to mean a contorted idea. Whatever its origins, it was used by contemporary critics in a derogatory sense, implying odd or extravagant shapes, as opposed to the much-vaunted Classical forms of the Renaissance.

Although Baroque was born in Rome, the vogue quickly spread throughout Europe. Everywhere, the emphasis was firmly on elaborate **ornamentation** and **spectacle**, something that reflected the growing power of the aristocracy, who had begun to challenge the established wealth and tradition of the Church. The primary motivating force behind the decoration of the buildings was the need to impress the neighbouring gentry; building to the glory of God came a poor second.

Some of the finest examples of Baroque architecture are to be found in Sicily, although there's some debate as to the specific origins of the **Sicilian Baroque** style. During the eighteenth century alone, Sicily was conquered and ruled in turn by the Spanish Habsburgs, the Spanish Bourbons, the House of Savoy, the Austrian Habsburgs and the Bourbons from Naples, lending a particularly exuberant flavour to its Baroque creations – which some say was borrowed from Spain. Others argue that the dominant influence was Italian: Sicilian architects tended to train and to travel in Italy, rather than Spain, and brought home what they learned on the mainland, adapting prevalent Roman Baroque ideas to complement peculiarly Sicilian architectural traditions. Both theories contain an element of the truth, though perhaps more pertinent is Sicily's unique long-term history: two and a half millennia of invasion and domination have produced a very distinct culture and society – one that is bound to have influenced, or even produced, an equally distinct architectural form.

Baroque towns

Sicily's seismic instability has profoundly affected its architectural history. The huge **earthquake of 1693** that almost flattened Catania, and completely destroyed Noto, Ragusa, Avola and Modica, provided a fantastic opportunity for local architects, who began massive rebuilding programmes in the southeast corner of Sicily. To them, a **Baroque town** aspired to be, and should be seen to be, a centre of taste and sophistication, They designed their new towns to delight their citizens, to encourage the participation of passers-by and to impress outsiders, with long vistas contriving to focus on the facade of a church or a palace, or an unexpected view of the sea. To enhance the visual effect even more, a building was designed to offer multiple, changing views from different angles of approach. This way, a completed plan might include all the buildings in a square or series of squares, and the experience of walking from place to place through varied but harmonious spaces was considered as important as the need to arrive at a destination. Moreover, as much of eighteenth-century Sicilian town-life took place outside, the **facade** of a building became synonymous with the wealth and standing of its occupant. External features became increasingly elaborate and specialized, and some parts of buildings – windows and staircases, for example – were often merely there for show. Invariably, what seem to be regular stone facades have been cosmetically touched up with plaster to conceal an asymmetry or an angle of less than ninety degrees: a self-conscious approach to town planning that can sometimes give the impression of walking around a stage set. Interestingly, this approach remained confined to the south and east of Sicily; outside the earthquake zone, in the west of the island, local architectural traditions continued to dominate in towns that hadn't had the dubious benefit of being levelled and left for the planners.

The "ideal city"

Ideally, where there was scope for large-scale planning, an entire city could be constructed as an aesthetic whole. As early as 1615 the Venetian architect and theorist **Vincenzo Scamozzi** published a treatise, *Dell'Idea dell'architettura universale*, in which he stated that the architectural harmony of the "**ideal city**" should reflect the perfect relationship between the prince, the judiciary, the Church, the marketplace and the populace.

Noto is an almost perfect example of Scamozzi's ideal. After the 1693 earthquake, the old town was so devastated that it was decided to move its site and rebuild from scratch, and the plan that was eventually accepted was almost an exact replica of Scamozzi's. Noto is constructed on a grid plan, traversed from east to west by a wide corso crossing a main piazza, which is itself balanced by four smaller piazzas. The buildings along the corso show remarkable balance and grace, while the attention of the Baroque planners to every harmonious detail is illustrated by the use of a warm, golden stone for the churches and *palazzi*.

Neighbouring towns in the southeast were also destroyed by the earthquake and rebuilt along similar lines. Both **Avola** and **Grammichele** were moved from their hill-top positions to the coastal plain, and their polygonal plans were similarly influenced by Scamozzi. Grammichele, particularly, retains an extraordinary hexagonal layout, unique in Sicily. **Ragusa** is more complex, surviving today as two towns: the medieval Ragusa Ibla, which the inhabitants rebuilt after the earthquake, and the Baroque upper town of Ragusa, which is built on a sloping grid plan, rather similar to Noto. Although Ibla isn't built to any kind of Baroque pattern, it does lay claim to one of the most spectacular of Sicilian Baroque churches.

Catania was not completely destroyed by the earthquake, but was instead rebuilt over its old site. Broad streets were built to link existing monuments and to facilitate rescue operations in case of another earthquake. The city is divided into four quarters by wide streets that meet in Piazza del Duomo, and wherever possible these spaces are used to maximize the visual impact of a facade or monument. The main Piazza del Duomo was conceived as a uniform set piece, while the main street, Via Etnea, cuts a swath due north from here, always drawing the eyes to Mount Etna, smoking in the distance.

On the other side of the island, Baroque **Palermo** evolved without the impetus of natural disaster. There's no comparable city plan, Palermo's intricate central layout owing more to the Arabs than to seventeenth- and eighteenth-century designers; what Baroque character the city possesses has almost entirely to do with its highly individual churches and palaces. These were constructed in a climate of apparent opulence but encroaching bankruptcy; as the Sicilian aristocrats were attracted to Palermo to pay court to the Spanish viceroy, they left the management of their lands to pragmatic agents, whose short-sighted policies allowed the estates to fall into neglect. This ate away at the wealth of the gentry, who responded by mortgaging their lands in order to maintain their living standards. The grandiose palaces and churches they built in the city still stand, but following the damage caused during World War II many are in a state of terrible neglect and near collapse; wild flowers grow out of the facades, and chunks of masonry frequently fall into the street below.

Specific features

Eighteenth-century aristocrats in Palermo escaped the heat to **summer villas** outside the city, and many of these still survive around **Bagheria**. The villas tend to be simply designed, but are bedecked with balconies and terraces for afternoon strolling, and were approached by long, impressive driveways. Above all, they are notable for their **external staircases**, leading to the main entrance on the first floor (the ground floor usually contained the kitchen and servants' quarters). It's typical of the Baroque era that an external feature should take on such significance in a building – and that they should show such a remarkable diversity, each reflecting the wealth of the individual owners. Beyond the fact that they were nearly always double staircases, symmetrical to the middle axis of the facade, each was completely different.

While **balconies** had always been a prominent feature of Sicilian domestic architecture, during the eighteenth century they became prolific. The balcony supports, or buttresses, were elaborately carved: manic heads, griffins, horses, monsters and mythical figures all featured as decoration, fine examples of which survive at Noto's **Palazzo Villadorata**, as well as in Modica and Scicli. The wrought-iron balustrades curved outwards, almost like theatre boxes, to allow room for women's billowing skirts.

Church building, too, flourished during this period. Baroque architects could let their imaginations run wild: the facade of the **Duomo** at Siracusa was begun in 1728, based on designs by Andrea Palma of Palermo, and the result is highly sophisticated and exciting. Other designs adapted and modified accepted forms for church architecture, as well as inventing new ones. In Palermo especially, typically Sicilian elements – like central circular windows – were used to great effect.

It was in the **church interiors**, however, that Sicilian Baroque came into its own, with tomb sculpture ever more ostentatious and stucco decoration abundant. Inlaid marble, a technique introduced from Naples at the start of the seventeenth century, became *de rigueur* and reached its prime during the second half of the century, when entire walls or chapels would be decorated in this way. Palermo fields some of the best examples of all these techniques, at their most impressive in the church of **San Giuseppe dei Teatini**, designed by Giacomo Besio, a Genovese who lived most of his life in Sicily. For real over-the-top detail, though, the churches of **Santa Caterina** and **Il Gesù**, also in Palermo, conceal a riot of inlaid marble decoration.

Architects and sculptors

Rosario Gagliardi was responsible for much of the rebuilding of Noto and Ragusa, and became known as one of the most important architects in southeast Sicily. Born in Siracusa in 1698, he worked in Noto as a carpenter from the age of 10, and was first acknowledged as an architect in 1726. Between 1760 and 1784 he was chief architect for the city of Noto, and during this time also worked on many different projects in Ragusa and Modica. As far as is known, he never travelled outside Sicily, let alone to

Rome, yet he absorbed contemporary architectural trends from the study of books and treatises, and reproduced the ideas with some flair.

Gagliardi's prime interest was in facades, and his work achieved a sophisticated fusion of Renaissance poise, Baroque grandeur and local Sicilian ornamentation. He had no interest, however, in spatial relationships or structural innovation, and the interiors of his buildings are disappointing when compared to the elaborate nature of their exteriors. Perhaps his most significant contribution was his development of the **belfry** as a feature. Sicilian churches traditionally didn't have a separate belltower, but incorporated the bells into the main facade, revealed through a series of two or three arches – an idea handed down from Byzantine building. Gagliardi extended the central bay of the facade into a tower, a highly original compromise satisfying both the local style and the more conventional notions of design from the mainland. The belfry on the church of **San Giorgio** in Ragusa Ibla, Gagliardi's masterpiece, is an excellent example of this.

The principal architect on the design and rebuilding of Catania after the 1693 earthquake, **Giovanni Battista Vaccarini**, was born in Palermo in 1702. He trained in Rome and embraced the current idiom, working with such illustrious figures as Alessandro Specchi (who built the papal stables) and Francesco de Sanctis (designer of the Spanish Steps). In 1730 he arrived in Catania, having been appointed as city architect by the Senate, and at once began work on finishing the Municipio. Outside he placed a fountain, whose main feature is an obelisk supported by an elephant, the symbol of Catania – reminiscent of Bernini's elephant fountain in Rome.

Giacomo Serpotta, master of the Palermitan oratories, was born in Palermo in 1656. He cashed in on the opulence of the Church and specialized in decorating oratories with moulded plasterwork in ornamental frames. He would include life-sized figures of Saints and Virtues, surrounded by plaster draperies, trophies, swags of fruit, bouquets of flowers and other extravagances much beloved of the Baroque. Among his most remarkable works is the Oratory of the Rosary in the church of **Santa Zita**, where the end wall is a reconstruction of the Battle of Lépanto. Three-dimensional representation is taken to an extreme here, and actual wires are used as rigging.

Other Baroque architects are less well known, but are influential in Sicily all the same. **Giacomo Amato** (1643–1732) was a monk, sent to Rome in 1671 to represent his Order, where he came into contact with the works of Bernini and Borromini. Dazzled by what he'd seen, he neglected his religious duties after his return to Palermo in order to design some of the city's most characteristic churches, **Sant'Ignazio all'Olivell** and **San Domenico** among them. **Vincenzo Sinatra** had a more traditional career, starting as a stonecutter before working with Gagliardi in the 1730s as his foreman. In 1745 he married Gagliardi's niece, a move which did him no harm at all, since by 1761, when Gagliardi had a stroke, Sinatra was managing all his affairs. For ten years he directed the construction of Noto's Municipio, and during the rest of his life Sinatra worked in collaboration with the other city architects on a variety of projects. More important was **Giovanni Vermexio**, who was active in Siracusa at around the same time. His work graces the city's Piazza del Duomo, notably the **Palazzo Arcivescovile**, while he gets a couple of ornate-interior credits, too, in the shape of one of the Duomo's chapels, and the octagonal **Cappella di San Sepolcro** in the church of Santa Lucia in the Achradina quarter of Siracusa.

Books

Although only a few modern writers have travelled in and written about Sicily, the island has provided the inspiration for some great literature, by both Sicilians and foreign visitors. Translations of Italian and Sicilian classics are also often available at bookshops in major towns and resorts in Sicily. The best books in this selection are marked by a ★ symbol.

TRAVEL AND GENERAL

★ **Vincent Cronin** *The Golden Honeycomb*. Disguised as a quest for the mythical golden honeycomb of Daedalus, this classic, erudite travelogue is a searching account of a sojourn in Sicily in the 1950s.

Duncan Fallowell *To Noto*. Follows the author's trip from London to Baroque Noto in an old Ford – a witty tale, complete with pithy observations on Sicily and the Sicilians.

Matthew Fort *Sweet Honey, Bitter Lemons*. Cheery food-writer Fort returns to the island he first visited in the 1970s, only this time he comes on a Vespa and eats his way around, from ice cream to anchovies.

★ **Norman Lewis** *In Sicily*. A sweeping portrait of the island which Lewis came to know well through his wife and her family. Subjects range from reflections on Palermo's ruined *palazzi* to the impact of immigration, and there's plenty on the Mafia.

Daphne Phelps *A House in Sicily*. An Englishwoman inherits a grand *palazzo* in Taormina in the late 1940s, and turns it into a guesthouse to make ends meet. Cue the usual cultural misunderstandings while she learns to love the locals, leavened by vignettes of her eminent guests – including Bertrand Russell, Tennessee Williams and Roald Dahl.

Gaia Servadio *Motya*. On one level, an account of Phoenician history and culture as they relate to the excavated ruins of Motya – but in truth, so much more than that, as Servadio explores the fabric of Sicily and its people in uncompromising, enlightening detail.

★ **Mary Taylor Simeti** *On Persephone's Island: A Sicilian Journal*. Sympathetic record of a typical year in Sicily by an American who married a Sicilian professor and has lived in the west of the island since the early 1960s. It's full of keenly observed detail about flora and fauna, customs, the harvests, festivals and – above all – the Sicilians themselves.

Elio Vittorini *Conversations in Sicily*. A Sicilian emigrant returns from the north of Italy after fifteen years to see his mother on her birthday. The conversations of the title are with the people he meets on the way, and reveal a prewar Sicily that, while affectionately drawn, is ridden with poverty and disease.

HISTORY, POLITICS AND ARCHEOLOGY

David Abulafia *Frederick II: A Medieval Emperor*. Definitive account of the Hohenstaufen king, greatest of the medieval European rulers, with much on his reign in Sicily. It's a reinterpretation of the received view of Frederick, revealing a less formidable king than the omnipotent and supreme ruler usually portrayed. Also see the same author's *Italy, Sicily and the Mediterranean, 1100–1400*.

★ **Sandra Benjamin** *Sicily: Three Thousand Years of Human History*. An instantly engaging, intelligently researched book that brings the history of Sicily vividly to life. If you buy only one book on Sicily, make it this one.

Samuel Butler *The Authoress of the Odyssey*. Eccentric book by the author of dystopian novel *Erewhon* which presents the argument that the *Odyssey* was written by a Sicilian woman, and was set around Trapani and in the Egadi Islands.

Brian Caven *Dionysius I: Warlord of Sicily*. The life of Dionysius I, by a historian who sees him not as a vicious tyrant but as a valiant crusader against the Carthaginians.

Christopher Hibbert *Garibaldi and His Enemies*. A popular treatment of the life and revolutionary works of Giuseppe Garibaldi, thrillingly detailing the exploits of "The Thousand" in their lightning campaign from Marsala to Milazzo.

R. Ross Holloway *The Archaeology of Ancient Sicily*. The standard work on the ancient monuments and archeological discoveries of Sicily, from the Paleolithic to the later Roman period.

★ **John Julius Norwich** *The Normans in Sicily*. Published together under one title, J.J. Norwich's *The Normans in the South* and *Kingdom in the Sun* tell the story of the Normans' explosive entry into the south of Italy, and their creation in Sicily of one of the most brilliant medieval European civilizations.

Steven Runciman *The Sicilian Vespers*. The classic account of Sicily's large-scale popular uprising in the thirteenth century. Runciman's *A History of the Crusades: 1, 2 & 3*, meanwhile, covers the Norman kings of Sicily, as well as the crusading Frederick II.

CRIME AND SOCIETY

John Dickie *Cosa Nostra*. Dickie, an Italian professor at University College London, is an expert on the Mafia and its role in Sicilian society, and offers an in-depth look at the secret workings of the Mafia, from its early days in the mid-1800s to its current manifestation.

David Lane *Into the Heart of the Mafia*. This look at life in the Italian south offers a contemporary journey through corruption from Naples to Sicily, an essential counterpoint to any number of expat-life-in-a-vineyard experiences.

Norman Lewis *The Honoured Society*. Originally written in the 1960s, this is the most famous account of the Mafia, its origins, personalities and customs, and is still the most accessible introduction available to the subject.

Clare Longrigg *Boss of Bosses*. One of the Mafia's most notorious *capo dei capi* (Boss of Bosses), Bernardo Provenzano, was arrested in Sicily in 2006 after four decades spent evading the law. Longrigg's careful unravelling of his successful shifting of criminal enterprise into mainstream business explains the subtitle: *How One Man Saved the Sicilian Mafia*.

★ **Gavin Maxwell** *The Ten Pains of Death*. Maxwell lived in Scopello during the 1950s, and recorded the lives of his neighbours in their own words. There's much on Sicilian small-town life and poverty, and sympathetic portraits of traditional festivals and characters. His *God Protect Me from My Friends* is a sympathetic biography of the notorious bandit Salvatore Giuliano, ripe with intrigue and double-dealing.

★ **Peter Robb** *Midnight in Sicily*. The Australian Robb spent fifteen years in the Italian south tracing the contorted relations between organized crime and politics. Here, he focuses on the structure of the Mafia, the trials of the bosses in the 1980s, the high-profile assassinations that ensued, and the trial of Andreotti, providing deep insights into the dynamics of Sicilian society.

Alexander Stille *Excellent Cadavers*. An important book tracing the modern fight against the Mafia as led by Giovanni Falcone and Paolo Borsellino, whose assassinations in 1992 finally sparked the Italian state into action.

NOVELS ABOUT SICILY

Allen Andrews *Impossible Loyalties*. Fast-moving narrative of an Anglo-Sicilian family caught up in the turmoil of World War II, containing an authentic portrait of prewar Messina society.

Michael Dibdin *Blood Rain*. Dibdin's Venetian detective, Aurelio Zen, is an idiosyncratic loner, always up against the Italian state and society in an unequalled series of crime novels. Here, Dibdin sends him to Sicily, with dark consequences for all concerned, and offers the only glimpse you are ever likely to have of Catania's long-closed Museo Civico.

Simonetta Agnello Hornby *The Marchesa; The Almond Picker*. From aristocratic nineteenth-century Palermo to 1960s' village life, Hornby's bestselling Sicily novels are full of subtle intrigue, voluptuous imagery and period detail.

Norman Lewis *The March of the Long Shadows*. An affectionate novel set in postwar Sicily, dealing with the Separatist movement, the bandit Giuliano and a whole cast

of endearing characters. *The Sicilian Specialist* is Lewis's Mafia thriller, which flits from Sicily to the US to Cuba on the trail of a Mob assassin.

★ **Dacia Maraini** *The Silent Duchess*. The tale of a noble eighteenth-century family seen through the eyes of a young duchess – beautifully written and dripping with authentic detail. *Bagheria*, meanwhile, is a delightfully engaging memoir of Maraini's childhood in the town of the title.

Lily Prior *La Cucina*. Subtitled a "novel of rapture", this chronicles the romance between a spinster librarian from Castiglione and an enigmatic English chef. Drawn into the plot are the Mafia, copious recipes and the convolutions of Sicilian family life.

★ **Mario Puzo** *The Godfather*. The New York Godfather – Don Corleone – was born in Sicily and the majestic book (a great read, even if you've seen the films) touches on all things Sicilian.

SICILIAN LITERATURE

Gesualdo Bufalino *The Plague Spreader's Tale, Blind Argus, The Keeper of Ruins* and *Night's Lies*. Bufalino arrived late on the literary scene, publishing his first novel, *The Plague Sower*, in his 60s. Subsequent publications enhanced the reputation made by this remarkable debut, notably *Night's Lies*, which won Italy's most respected literary award, the Strega Prize, in 1988. Bufalino himself – seeking to explain the Sicilian character – commented, "Don't forget that even our most obscene vices nearly always bear the seal of sullen greatness".

★ **Andrea Camilleri** *Inspector Montalbano Mysteries*.

Born in Agrigento, Camilleri is one of Italy's favourite modern authors, though he writes in Sicilian dialect that not all Italians can understand. His intelligent – and often vulgar and graphic – crime novels have subsequently become hugely popular all over Europe, masterfully translated into English by the New York poet, Stephen Sartorelli. Inspector Montalbano delves deep into the folds of Sicilian culture in an ongoing series, starting with *The Shape of Water*. More than a dozen of the books have been translated into English, including *The Terracotta Dog*, *The Voice of the Violin* and *August Heat*.

SICILIAN CUISINE AND COOKBOOKS

There are Sicilian recipes in all the major Italian cookbooks, starting with **Elizabeth David**'s classic *Italian Food* (published 1954), the book that introduced Mediterranean flavours and ingredients to Britain. (Olive oil, famously, was previously something you could only buy in chemists.) **Antonio Carluccio**, Britain's avuncular Italian master, is good on Sicilian fish and snacks in his *Southern Italian Feast* – his *arancini* recipe is definitive – while *Southern Italian Cooking* by **Valentina Harris** has an excellent chapter on Sicilian cooking. However, there are also plenty of specifically Sicilian books on the market, notably ★ *Sicilian Food* by **Mary Taylor Simeti**, which combines recipes with fascinating detail about life and traditions on the island. Simeti also co-authored *Bitter Almonds: Recollections and Recipes from a Sicilian Girlhood*, alongside **Maria Grammatico**, who was raised in a convent where she learned the pastry-cooking skills that she employs in her outlets in Erice. For an anecdotal trawl through the classics and the lesser-known dishes, including several from out-of-the-way places like Pantelleria and Stromboli, consult *The Flavors of Sicily* by **Anna Tasca Lanza**, the respected owner of a cooking school established at her family estate on the island – hence also her *Heart of Sicily: Recipes and Reminiscences of Regaleali, a Country Estate*. At the other end of the social scale, *Pani Caliatu*, by Susan Lord and Danilo Baroncino, explores the austere cuisine of the Aeolian Islands in a fascinating and beautifully designed book that combines social history, interviews, recipes and photographs.

★ **Giuseppe Tomasi di Lampedusa** *The Leopard*. The most famous Sicilian novel, written after World War II but recounting the dramatic nineteenth-century years of transition from Bourbon to Piedmontese rule from an aristocrat's point of view. David Gilmour's *The Last Leopard: A Life of Giuseppe Tomasi di Lampedusa*, is the first biography in English of Lampedusa, a readable account of the life of an otherwise rather dull man.

Luigi Pirandello *Six Characters in Search of an Author, Henry IV, The Late Mattia Pascal, Short Stories*. His most famous and accomplished work, *Six Characters...*, written in 1921, and his *Henry IV*, written a year later, contain many of the themes that dogged Pirandello throughout his writing career – the idea of a multiple personality and the quality of reality. *The Late Mattia Pascal* is an entertaining early novel (1904), though the collection of abrasive short stories is perhaps the best introduction to Pirandello's work.

★ **Leonardo Sciascia** *Sicilian Uncles, The Wine-Dark Sea, Candido, The Knight and Death, Death of an Inquisitor, The Day of the Owl, Equal Danger*. Sciascia's short stories and novellas are packed with incisive insights into the island's quirky ways, and infused with the author's humane and sympathetic view of its people. The first to describe the Mafia in Italian literature, he wrote metaphysical thrillers in which the detectives often turn out to be the hunted; the best known is *The Day of the Owl*.

Giovanni Verga *Short Sicilian Novels, Cavalleria Rusticana, Maestro Don Gesualdo, I Malavoglia* or *The House by the Medlar Tree, A Mortal Sin, La Lupa* and *Sparrow*. Born in the nineteenth century in Catania, Verga spent several years in various European salons before coming home to write his best work. Much of it is a reaction against the pseudo-sophistication of society circles, stressing the simple lives of ordinary people, with much emotion, wounded honour and feuds to the death. D.H. Lawrence's translations are suitably vibrant, with excellent introductions.

Films

Though Sicily doesn't have its own motion picture industry, the island's stunning scenery has served as a backdrop to a number of very successful films. The Aeolian and Pelagie islands, in particular, have proved popular settings for some interesting films, a few of them now classics of Italian cinema.

Michelangelo Antonioni *L'Avventura* (1960). Shot on the barren rocks of Panarea's Lisca Bianca, this film notes the beginning of a marked change in postwar Italian social mores. When a group of friends get together for a day out in the islands, one gets lost, and the relationships between those remaining begin to fracture. Here, Antonioni focuses ingeniously on the internal responses of those affected.

Emanuele Crispalese *Il Respiro* (2002). Filmed on the southern island of Lampedusa, this is a timeless, well-constructed look at how an eccentric mother is misunderstood by other islanders. Crispalese's second film, it addresses the overwhelming patriarchy of Italian families and the sexual tension latent between family members.

Francis Ford Coppola *The Godfather* (1971). Mario Puzo's brilliant screenplay tells the story of how Don Vito Corleone, *capo* of the New York Sicilian Mafia, tries to maintain his hold on the family business and his old-world values, despite his renegade son Michael. Since the town of Corleone itself was far too developed for the period filming, much of it was shot in Savoca and Forza d'Agro, outside Taormina.

Pietro Giermi *Divorzio alla Siciliana* (1961). Proof that not all Sicilian films need be deep or cinematic, this is a hilarious and pointed satire of Italian marital conventions. Marcello Mastroianni plays a Sicilian nobleman trying to prove his wife unfaithful so he can kill her and marry his younger cousin. Known as *Divorce Italian Style* in English, it was filmed in Ispica near Ragusa, and got Giermi nominated for a Best Director Oscar.

Nanni Moretti *Dear Diary* (1994). Moretti plays himself as he tours Italy on a Vespa, visiting all the Aeolian Islands, showing how the inhabitants of each differ in mentality and lifestyle. Mostly comic, but a real downer at the end.

Michael Radford *Il Postino* (1994). An international favourite, featuring a postman on a small island who learns to love poetry after befriending the exiled poet Pablo Neruda. The film was shot in the town of Pollara on Salina, leading to a dramatic increase in tourism to the island.

Roberto Rossellini *Stromboli: Terra di Dio* (1949). Starring Ingrid Bergman as a tormented young refugee who marries an Italian to escape the war, this is a sad story of solitude and cynicism, which received little praise in its home country. The real star, however, is the volcano itself, whose brooding presence undermines the illusion of an idyllic, happy island.

Giuseppe Tornatore *Cinema Paradiso* (1988). Though derided by critics for its saccharine storyline, this Oscar-winning film by Sicilian director Tornatore received popular acclaim the world over. Shot around Cefalù, it follows the friendship between a young boy and the local cinema projectionist, and is in many ways a homage to cinema itself.

Italian

The ability to speak English confers enormous prestige in Sicily, and plenty of locals – particularly returned emigrati – are willing to show off their knowledge. Few outside the tourist resorts, however, actually know more than a few simple words and phrases, more often than not culled from pop songs or films. To get the most from your visit, therefore, you'd do well to master at least a little Italian.

Some tips

Attempting to speak Italian brings instant rewards; your halting efforts will often be greeted with smiles and genuine surprise that an English-speaker should stoop to learn the language. In any case, Italian is one of the easiest European languages to learn, especially if you already have a smattering of French or Spanish, both of which are extremely similar grammatically. The best **phrasebook** is Rough Guides' own *Italian Phrasebook* (Penguin), while Collins publishes a comprehensive series of **dictionaries**.

Easiest of all is the **pronunciation**, since every word is spoken exactly as it's written, and usually enunciated with exaggerated, open-mouthed clarity. The only difficulties you're likely to encounter are the few **consonants** that are different from English:

c before **e** or **i** is pronounced as in **ch**urch, while **ch** before the same vowels is hard, as in **c**at.

g is soft before **e** and **i**, as in **g**entle; hard when followed by **h**, as in **g**arlic.

gn has the **ni** sound of our on**i**on.

gl in Italian is softened to something like **li** in English, as in vermi**li**on.

h is not aspirated, as in **h**our.

sci or **sce** are pronounced as in **sh**eet and **sh**elter respectively.

When **speaking** to strangers, the third person is the polite form (ie *Lei* instead of *Tu* for "you"); using the second person is a mark of disrespect or stupidity. It's also worth remembering that Italians don't use "please" and "thank you" half as much as we do: it's all implied in the tone, though if you're in doubt, err on the polite side.

All Italian words are **stressed** on the penultimate syllable unless an **accent** denotes otherwise, although accents are often left out in practice. Note that the ending -**ia** or -**ie** counts as two syllables, hence *trattoria* is stressed on the i. We've put accents in, throughout the text and below, wherever it isn't immediately obvious how a word should be pronounced: for example, in *Marittima*, the accent is on the first **i**; conversely *Catania* should theoretically have an accent on the second **a**. Other words where we've omitted accents are common ones (like *Isola*, stressed on the I), some names (*Domenico, Vittorio/-a*), and words that are stressed similarly in English, such as *Repubblica* and *archeologico*.

None of this will help very much if you're confronted with a particularly harsh specimen of the **Sicilian dialect**, which virtually qualifies as a separate language (see p.394). However, television has made a huge difference, and almost every Sicilian can now communicate in something approximating standard Italian.

USEFUL WORDS AND PHRASES

BASICS			
Good morning	Buongiorno	Goodnight	Buonanotte
Good afternoon/ evening	Buonasera	Hello/goodbye	Ciao (informal; when speaking to strangers use the phrase above)

Goodbye	Arrivederci (formal)	**Excuse me**	Permesso (in a crowd)
Goodbye	Arrivederla (more formal)	**I'm sorry**	Mi dispiace
		I'm here on holiday	Sono qui in vacanza
Yes	Sì	**I live in…**	Abito a…
No	No	**I'm English**	Sono inglese
Please	Per favore	**I'm Welsh**	Sono gallese
Thank you (very much)	Grazie (molte/mille grazie)	**I'm Scottish**	Sono scozzese
		I'm Irish	Sono irlandese
You're welcome/ after you	Prego	**I'm American**	Sono americano/a (masculine/feminine)
Alright/that's OK	Va bene	**I'm Australian**	Sono australiano/a (masculine/feminine)
How are you?	Come stai/sta? (informal/formal)	**I'm Canadian**	Sono canadese
I'm fine	Bene	**I'm from New Zealand**	Sono neozelandese
Do you speak English?	Parla inglese?	**I'm South African**	Sono sudafricano/a (masculine/feminine)
I don't speak Italian	Non parlo italiano		
I don't understand	Non capisco	**Today**	Oggi
I haven't understood	Non ho capito	**Tomorrow**	Domani
I don't know	Non lo so	**Day after tomorrow**	Dopodomani
Excuse me/sorry	Scusa (informal)	**Yesterday**	Ieri
Excuse me/sorry	Mi scusi (formal)	**Now**	Adesso

THE SICILIAN LANGUAGE

For political reasons, all regional languages in Italy are considered **dialects** of Italian. In reality, however, each has its own history and influences, and the majority of them are, linguistically speaking, separate languages. During the 600-year-long Roman occupation of Sicily, Vulgar Latin became the lingua franca for the entire island, though it was highly influenced by close contacts with Arabic, Norman and Spanish languages. The grammar, lexicon and phonology of Sicilian thus differs immensely from modern standard Italian – so much so that during the American Mafia trials of the 1980s, the FBI had to enlist special agents fluent in Sicilian to translate the conversations of *mafiosi* based in New York. The **Sicilian language** even has its own regional dialects (*parrati*), though in general these are understood by all Sicilians.

Today nearly all Sicilians speak and understand standard Italian, though, unlike numerous other dialects spoken throughout Europe, the language is in no danger of extinction: in most towns, the younger generation prefers Sicilian to Italian, and almost everyone speaks Sicilian at home. While Sicilians are well known for using their hands and arms as much as their vocal cords to communicate, their language is rich in idioms and sayings. Below are some favourite

SICILIAN PROVERBS

Si vo' passari la vita cuntenti, statti luntanu di li parenti.
If you want a quiet life, stay away from relatives.

Sciarri di maritu e mugghieri duranu finu a lu lettu.
Quarrels between wives and husbands always end in the bed.

Cu'arrobba pri manciari nun fa piccatu.
He who steals to eat is no sinner.

Cu'asini caccia e fimmini cridi, faccia di paradisu nun ni vidi.
He who seeks girls and asses will never reach heaven.

Camina chi pantofuli finnu a quannu non hai i scarpi.
Walk with your slippers until you find your shoes (ie make the best of a bad situation).

Cu' va a Palermu e nun va a Murriali, si nni parti sceccu e torna maiali.
He who visits Palermo and not Monreale arrives an ass and returns a pig.

Later	Più tardi	Quickly/slowly	Velocemente/lentamente
Wait a minute!	Aspetta!	Slowly/quietly	Piano
In the morning	Di mattina	With/without	Con/senza
In the afternoon	Nel pomeriggio	More/less	Più/meno
In the evening	Di sera	Enough/no more	Basta
Tonight	Stasera	Mr...	Signor...
Here/there	Qui/là	Mrs...	Signora...
Good/bad	Buono/cattivo	Miss...	Signorina...
Big/small	Grande/piccolo		(il signore, la signora,
Cheap/expensive	Economico/caro		la signorina when
Early/late	Presto/ritardo		speaking about
Hot/cold	Caldo/freddo		someone else)
Near/far	Vicino/lontano	First name	Primo nome
Vacant/occupied	Libero/occupato	Surname	Cognome

ACCOMMODATION

Hotel	Albergo	Do you have anything	Ha niente che costa
Is there a hotel	C'è un albergo qui	cheaper?	di meno?
nearby?	vicino?	Full/half board	Pensione completa/
Do you have a room...	Ha una camera...		mezza pensione
for one/two/	per una persona,	Can I see the room?	Posso vedere la
three people	due/tre persone		camera?
for one/two/	per una notte,	I'll take it	La prendo
three nights	due/tre notti	I'd like to book	Vorrei prenotare
for one/two weeks	per una settimana,	a room	una camera
	due settimane	I have a booking	Ho una prenotazione
with a double bed	con letto matrimoniale	Can we camp here?	Possiamo fare il
with a shower/bath	con doccia/		campeggio qui?
	bagno	Is there a campsite	C'è un camping qui?
with a balcony	con terrazza	nearby?	
hot/cold water	acqua calda/	Tent	Tenda
	fredda	Cabin	Cabina
How much is it?	Quanto costa?	Hostel	Ostello
It's expensive	È caro	Youth hostel	Ostello per la
Is breakfast	È compresa la prima		gioventù
included?	colazione?		

QUESTIONS AND DIRECTIONS

Where? (Where is/	Dove? (Dov'è/	Can you tell me	Può dirmi quando
are...?)	Dove sono?)	when to get off?	devo scendere?
When?	Quando?	What time does	A che ora apre?
What? (What is it?)	Cosa? (Cos'è?)	it open?	
How much/many?	Quanto/Quanti?	What time does	A che ora chiude?
Why?	Perché?	it close?	
It is/There is	È/C'è (È/C'è...?)	How much does	Quanto costa?/
(Is it/Is there...?)		it cost?/do they cost?	Quanto costano?
What time is it?	Che ora è?/	What's it called	Come si chiama
	Che ore sono?	in Italian?	in italiano?
How do I get to...?	Come arrivo a...?	Left/right	Sinistra/destra
How far is it to...?	Quant'è lontano a...?	Go straight ahead	Sempre diritto
Can you give me	Mi può dare un	Turn to the right/left	Gira a destra/
a lift to...?	passaggio a...?		sinistra

GETTING AROUND

Aeroplane	Aereo	What time does it leave?	A che ora parte?
Bus	Autobus/Pullman		
Train	Treno	When is the next bus/train/ferry to…?	Quando parte il prossimo pullman/treno/traghetto per…?
Car	Macchina		
Taxi	Taxi		
Bicycle	Bicicletta		
Ferry	Traghetto	Where does it leave from?	Da dove parte?
Ship	Nave		
Hydrofoil	Aliscafo	Which platform does it leave from?	Da quale binario parte?
Hitch-hiking	Autostop		
On foot	A piedi	Do I have to change?	Devo cambiare?
Bus terminal	Capolinea	How many kilometres is it?	Quanti chilometri sono?
Bus station	Autostazione		
Train station	Stazione ferroviaria	How long does it take?	Quanto ci vuole?
Ferry terminal	Stazione marittima		
Port	Porto	What number bus is it to…?	Che numero di autobus per…?
A ticket to…	Un biglietto a…		
One way/return	Solo andata/andata e ritorno	Where's the road to…?	Dov'è la strada a…?
		Next stop, please	La prossima fermata, per favore
Can I book a seat?	Posso prenotare un posto?		

SIGNS

Entrance/exit	Entrata/uscita	To let	Affitasi
Free entrance	Ingresso libero	Platform	Binario
Gentlemen/ladies	Signori/signore	Cash desk	Cassa
WC/bathroom	Gabinetto/bagno	Go/walk	Avanti
Vacant/engaged	Libero/occupato	Stop/halt	Alt
Open/closed	Aperto/chiuso	Customs	Dogana
Arrivals/departures	Arrivi/partenze	Do not touch	Non toccare
Closed for restoration	Chiuso per restauro	Danger	Pericolo
Closed for holidays	Chiuso per ferie	Beware	Attenzione
Pull/push	Tirare/spingere	First aid	Pronto soccorso
Out of order	Guasto	Ring the bell	Suonare il campanello
Drinking water	Acqua potabile	No smoking	Vietato fumare
Not for drinking	Non potabile		

DRIVING

Parking	Parcheggio	Slow down	Rallentare
No parking	Divieto di sosta/Sosta vietata	Road closed	Strada chiusa
		No through road	Vietato il transito
One-way street	Senso unico	No overtaking	Vietato il sorpasso
Both sides of the street	Ambo i lati	Crossroads	Incrocio
		Speed limit	Limite di velocità
No entry	Senso vietato	Traffic light	Semaforo

NUMBERS AND DAYS OF THE WEEK

1	Uno	7	Sette
2	Due	8	Otto
3	Tre	9	Nove
4	Quattro	10	Dieci
5	Cinque	11	Undici
6	Sei	12	Dodici

13	Trédici	70	Settanta
14	Quattordici	80	Ottanta
15	Quindici	90	Novanta
16	Sédici	100	Cento
17	Diciassette	1000	Mille
18	Diciotto	Monday	Lunedì
19	Diciannove	Tuesday	Martedì
20	Venti	Wednesday	Mercoledì
25	Venticinque	Thursday	Giovedì
30	Trenta	Friday	Venerdì
40	Quaranta	Saturday	Sabato
50	Cinquanta	Sunday	Domenica
60	Sessanta		

FOOD AND DRINK

BASICS AND SNACKS

Aceto	Vinegar
Aglio	Garlic
Biscotti	Biscuits
Burro	Butter
Caramelle	Sweets
Cioccolato	Chocolate
Formaggio	Cheese
Frittata	Omelette
Gelato	Ice cream
Grissini	Bread sticks
Maionese	Mayonnaise
Marmellata	Jam
Olio	Oil
Olive	Olives
Pane	Bread
Pane integrale	Wholemeal bread
Panino	Bread roll
Patatine	Crisps/potato chips
Patatine fritte	Chips/French fries
Pepe	Pepper
Pizzetta	Small pizza
Riso	Rice
Sale	Salt
Uova	Eggs
Yogurt	Yoghurt
Zucchero	Sugar
Zuppa	Soup

ANTIPASTI AND STARTERS

Antipasto misto	Usually mixed cold cuts, salamis and cheese (sometimes accompanied by olives, sundried tomatoes or tasters of other dishes in this list)
Caponata	Mixed aubergine, olives and tomatoes
Caprese	Tomato and mozzarella cheese salad
Insalata di mare	Seafood salad
Insalata di riso	Rice salad
Insalata russa	"Russian salad": diced vegetables in mayonnaise
Melanzane alla parmigiana	Fried aubergine baked in tomato sauce with parmesan cheese
Mortadella	Salami-type cured meat with nuggets of fat, often with pistachios
Pancetta	Italian bacon
Peperonata	Grilled green, red or yellow peppers stewed in olive oil
Pomodori ripieni	Stuffed tomatoes
Prosciutto cotto	Ham (cooked, usually boiled, sometimes roast)
Prosciutto crudo	Parma ham
Salame	Salami
Salmone/tonno/ pesce spada/affumicato	Smoked salmon/tuna/ swordfish

PIZZAS

Biancaneve	"Snow white": mozzarella only, popular with kids
Calzone	Folded pizza with cheese, ham and tomato
Capricciosa	"Capricious": topped with whatever they've got in the kitchen, usually including baby artichoke, ham and egg
Cardinale	Ham and olives
Diavolo	"Devil": spicy, with hot salami or Italian sausage

Funghi	Mushroom: tinned, sliced button mushrooms unless it specifies fresh mushrooms, either funghi freschi or porcini
Frutti di mare	Seafood: usually mussels, prawns, squid and clams
Margherita	Cheese and tomato
Marinara	Tomato and garlic
Napoli/Napoletana	Tomato, anchovy and olive oil (often mozzarella too)
Norma	Tomato, grilled or fried aubergine and grated ricotta (either salted, *salata*, or baked, *infornata*)
Quattro formaggi	"Four cheeses": usually mozzarella, fontina, Gorgonzola and Gruyère
Quattro stagioni	"Four seasons": the toppings split into four separate sections, usually including ham, peppers, onion, mushrooms, artichokes, olives, egg etc
Palermitana	Tomato, anchovies, breadcrumbs
Rianata	Fresh tomato, pecorino, oregano, garlic and anchovy; a western Sicilian speciality
Romana	Anchovy and olives

THE FIRST COURSE (IL PRIMO)

PASTA

Cannelloni	Large tubes of pasta, stuffed
Farfalle	Literally "bow"-shaped pasta; the word also means "butterflies"
Fettuccine	Narrow pasta ribbons
Gnocchi	Small potato and dough dumplings
Lasagne	Lasagne
Maccheroni	Macaroni (tubular pasta)
Pappardelle	Pasta ribbons
Pasta al forno	Oven-baked pasta, usually with minced meat, eggs, tomato and cheese
Penne	Smaller version of rigatoni
Ravioli	Ravioli (stuffed, square-shaped pasta)
Rigatoni	Large, grooved, tubular pasta
Risotto	Cooked rice dish, with sauce
Spaccatelle	Long, open pasta curls
Spaghetti	Spaghetti
Spaghettini	Thin spaghetti
Tagliatelle	Pasta ribbons, another word for fettuccine
Tortellini	Small rings of pasta, stuffed with meat or cheese
Vermicelli	Very thin spaghetti (literally "little worms")

PASTA SAUCES (SALSA)

Aglio e olio (e peperoncino)	Tossed in garlic and olive oil (and hot chillies)
Amatriciana	Cubed pork and tomato sauce, with onions and hot chillies (originally from Rome)
Arrabbiata	Spicy tomato sauce, with chillies
Bolognese	Meat sauce
Burro e salvia	Butter and sage
Carbonara	Cream, ham and beaten egg
Frutta di mare	Seafood
Funghi	Mushroom
Panna	Cream
Parmigiano	Parmesan cheese
Pesto	Ground basil, pine nut, garlic and pecorino
Pomodoro	Tomato sauce
Puttanesca	Tomato, anchovy, olive oil and oregano sauce (literally "whorish")
Ragù	Meat sauce
Trapanese	Cold puréed tomato, garlic and basil
Vongole (veraci)	Clam and tomato sauce (fresh clams in shells, usually served with oil and herbs)

THE SECOND COURSE (IL SECONDO)
MEAT (CARNE)

Agnello	Lamb
Bistecca	Steak
Cervello	Brain
Cinghiale	Wild boar
Coniglio	Rabbit
Costolette/cotolette	Cutlets/chops
Fegatini	Chicken livers
Fégato	Liver
Involtini	Steak slices, rolled and stuffed
Lepre	Hare
Lingua	Tongue
Maiale	Pork
Manzo	Beef
Ossobuco	Shin of veal
Pollo	Chicken
Polpette	Meatballs
Rognoni	Kidneys
Salsiccia	Sausage
Saltimbocca	Veal with ham
Scaloppina	Escalope (of veal)
Spezzatino	Stew
Tacchino	Turkey
Trippa	Tripe
Vitello	Veal

FISH (PESCE) AND SHELLFISH (CROSTACEI)

Note that *surgelato* or *congelato* written on the menu next to a dish means "frozen" – it often applies to squid and prawns.

Acciughe	Anchovies
Anguilla	Eel
Aragosta	Lobster
Baccalà	Dried salted cod
Bottarga	Fish roe
Calamari	Squid
Céfalo	Grey mullet
Cernia	Grouper
Cozze	Mussels
Dattile	Razor clams
Déntice	Dentex (like sea bass)
Gamberetti	Shrimps
Gamberi	Prawns
Granchio	Crab
Merluzzo	Cod
Nasello	Hake
Orata	Gilthead bream
Ostriche	Oysters
Pesce spada	Swordfish
Polpo/polipo	Octopus
Ricci di mare	Sea urchins
Ricciola	Amberjack
Rospo	Monkfish
Sampiero	John Dory
Sarago	White bream
Sarde	Sardines
Séppie	Cuttlefish
Sgombro	Mackerel
Sogliola	Sole
Spigola	Sea bass
Tonno	Tuna
Totani	Species of squid
Triglie	Red mullet
Trota	Trout
Vongole	Clams

VEGETABLES (CONTORNI) AND SALAD (INSALATA)

Asparagi	Asparagus
Basilico	Basil
Broccoli	Broccoli
Capperi	Capers
Carciofi	Artichokes
Carciofini	Artichoke hearts
Carote	Carrots
Cavolfiori	Cauliflower
Cavolo	Cabbage
Ceci	Chickpeas
Cetriolo	Cucumber
Cipolla	Onion
Fagioli	Beans
Fagiolini	Green beans
Finocchio	Fennel
Funghi	Mushrooms
Insalata verde/ mista	Green salad/mixed salad
Melanzane	Aubergine/ eggplant
Origano	Oregano
Patate	Potatoes
Peperoni	Peppers
Piselli	Peas
Pomodori	Tomatoes
Radicchio	Red chicory
Spinaci	Spinach
Zucca	Pumpkin
Zucchini	Courgettes

DESSERTS (DOLCI)

Amaretti	Macaroons
Cassata	Ice-cream cake with candied fruit
Gelato	Ice cream
Macedonia	Fruit salad
Torta	Cake, tart

Zabaglione	Dessert made with eggs, sugar and marsala wine
Zuppa Inglese	Trifle

CHEESE

Caciocavallo	A type of dried, mature mozzarella
Fontina	Northern Italian cheese used in cooking
Gorgonzola	Soft, strong, blue-veined cheese
Mozzarella	Soft white cheese, traditionally made from buffalo's milk
Parmigiano	Parmesan cheese
Pecorino	Strong-tasting, hard sheep's cheese
Provolone	Cheese with grooved rind, either mild or slightly piquant
Ricotta	Soft white cheese made from ewe's milk, used in sweet or savoury dishes
Ricotta Salata	Ricotta which has been salted to preserve it; can be grated
Ricotta Infornata	Oven-baked ricotta, with a sweet caramelized crust
Vastedda	Similar to Caciocavallo, but tastes slightly more acidic

FRUIT AND NUTS

Albicocca	Apricot
Ananas	Pineapple
Anguria/coccomero	Watermelon
Arancia	Orange
Banana	Banana
Cacco	Persimmon
Chicco d'uva/uva	A grape/grapes
Ciliegia	Cherry
Fico	Fig
Fico d'India	Prickly pear
Fragola	Strawberry
Lemone	Lemon
Mandorla	Almond
Mela	Apple
Melone	Melon
Néspola	Medlar
Pera	Pear
Pesca	Peach

Pinolo	Pine nut
Pistacchio	Pistachio nut
Smerge/Sberge	Cross between a plum and a peach with a hint of vanilla

COOKING TERMS

Affumicato	Smoked
Arrosto	Roast
Ben cotto	Well done
Bollito/lesso	Boiled
Alla brace	Barbecued
Brasato	Cooked in wine
Cotto	Cooked (not raw)
Crudo	Raw
Al dente	Firm, not overcooked
Ferri	Grilled without oil
Al forno	Baked
Fritto	Fried
Grattugiato	Grated
Alla griglia	Grilled
Al marsala	Cooked with marsala wine
Milanese	Fried in egg and breadcrumbs
Pizzaiola	Cooked with tomato sauce
Ripieno	Stuffed
Sangue	Rare
Allo spiedo	On the spit
Stracotto	Braised, stewed
Surgelati	Frozen
In umido	Stewed
Al vapore	Steamed

SICILIAN SPECIALITIES
STARTERS AND PASTA

Arancini	"Little oranges": deep-fried rice balls with minced meat, cheese and peas (*al ragù*) or cheese, ham and bechamal (*al burro*). Also made with spinach, pistachio, or aubergine
Caponata	Sautéed aubergine, with olives, peppers, almonds and tomatoes; served cold
Cozze alla marinara	Mussels in a rich wine-based soup
Cozze pepata	Mussels in spicy tomato stock
Crocchè di patate	Potato croquettes

		MAIN COURSES	
Insalata di arance	Orange salad, dressed with oil and parsley, and sometimes with fennel	Cuscus	Couscous, usually served with fish and vegetable sauce, sometimes meat; a common dish in western Sicily and on the islands of Lampedusa and Pantelleria
Maccu	Fava-bean soup flavoured with wild fennel		
Panelle	Chickpea fritters		
Pasta con i broccoli arriminati	Pasta cooked with broccoli, anchovy paste, pine nuts and saffron	Fritto misto	A standard seafood dish; deep-fried prawns and squid rings in batter
Pasta con la mollica	Pasta with oil and toasted breadcrumbs	Fritto di pesce	As above but also with other fried fish, like sardines and whitebait
Pasta con le sarde	Macaroni with fresh sardines, fennel, raisins and pine kernels; a speciality of Palermo		
Penne all'arrabbiata	Short tubular pasta with spicy tomato sauce made with chillies (*arrabbiata* means "angry")	Involtini di pesce spada	Slices of swordfish, stuffed, rolled and fried
		Pesce spada alla Ghiotta	Swordfish cooked in spicy tomato sauce with capers and olives; from Messina province
Peperonata	Peppers (capsicum) sautéed in olive oil until soft and sweet, either served as antipasto or as a vegetable	Sarde a beccafico	Sardines stuffed with breadcrumbs, nuts, dried fruit and anchovies; a Palermitan speciality
Spaghetti alla carrettiera	"Carter's spaghetti", cooked with garlic, oil, pecorino and salt and pepper; common in Catania province	Scaloppine di maiale al Marsala	Escalopes of pork cooked in marsala wine; the most common way of cooking meat with this Sicilian wine
Spaghetti alla Norma	Spaghetti with tomato sauce topped with fried aubergine and parmesan or pecorino cheese; a speciality of Catania, named after one of Bellini's operas	Stocca alla Messinese	Dried cod stewed with potatoes, olives, tomatoes, capers and celery; a speciality of Messina, although there are other regional variations
Spaghetti alla Trapanese	Spaghetti tossed with cold puréed tomatoes, basil and garlic; a pungent dish from Trapani		
Uova/funghi in tegame	Eggs/mushrooms fried in olive oil, served at the table in a little metal pan	Zuppa di cozze/ vongole	A big dish of mussels/ clams in rich wine-based soup
Zuppa di San Giuseppe	A kind of *maccu* made pulses and a mixture of short or broken pasta, usually spiked with chilli and wild fennel.	Zuppa di pesce	As above but usually with pieces of cod, squid and prawns, and served with fried bread

DESSERTS AND FESTIVAL FOOD

Cannoli	Fried pastry stuffed with sweet ricotta and candied peel; a Carnevale speciality
Cassata	Ice-cream cake with candied fruit
Crispelle di riso	Sweet rice fritters
Frutti di Martorana	Marzipan-based confection shaped and coloured to look like fruit, vegetables, and even fish
Ossa dei morti	Literally "dead men's bones", a clove-flavoured, sugared pastry handed out to children on All Hallows' Eve (October 31), and almost identical to *Agnellini pasquali* (Easter lambs)
Sfinci	Fried pastry stuffed with ricotta; served at the festival of St Joseph (San Giuseppe)
Torrone di mandorle	Crystallized almonds and sugar, sold at markets around All Saints' Day
Zeppole	Deep-fried bread dough, stuffed with ricotta and anchovies, or nutella

DRINKS

Acqua minerale	Mineral water
Aranciata	Orangeade
Bicchiere	Glass
Birra	Beer
Bottiglia	Bottle
Caffè	Coffee
Cioccolata calda	Hot chocolate
Ghiaccio	Ice
Granita	Iced coffee/ fruit drink
Latte	Milk
Limonata	Lemonade
Selz	Soda water
Spremuta	Fresh fruit juice
Spumante	Sparkling wine
Succo di frutta	Concentrated fruit juice with sugar
Tè	Tea
Tonico	Tonic water
Vino	Wine
Rosso	Red
Bianco	White
Rosato	Rosé
Secco	Dry
Dolce	Sweet
Litro	Litre
Mezzo	Half-litre
Quarto	Quarter-litre
Salute!	Cheers!

GLOSSARIES

ARTISTIC AND ARCHITECTURAL TERMS

Agora Square or marketplace in an ancient Greek city

Apse Domed recess at the altar-end of a church

Architrave The lowest part of the entablature

Atrium Forecourt, usually of a Roman house

Bothros A pit that contains votive offerings

Campanile Belltower

Capital Top of a column

Catalan-Gothic Hybrid form of architecture, mixing elements from fifteenth-century Spanish and northern European building styles

Cavea The seating section in a theatre

Cella Sanctuary of a temple

Cupola A dome

Decumanus The main street in a Roman town

Entablature The part of the building above the capital on a classical building

Ex-voto A thanksgiving or offering to a saint – sometimes a plaque, often a silver or pewter body part

Hellenistic period 323–30 BC (Alexander the Great to Augustus)

Hypogeum Underground vault, often used as an early Christian church

Kouros Standing male figure of the Archaic period (700 BC to early fifth century BC)

Krater Ancient conical bowl with round base

Loggia Roofed gallery or balcony

Metope A panel on the frieze of a temple

Naumachia Mock naval combat, or the deep trench in a theatre in which it took place

Nave Central space in a church, usually flanked by aisles

Odeon Small theatre, usually roofed, for recitals

Orchestra Section of the main floor of a theatre, where the chorus danced

Pantocrator Usually refers to Christ, portrayed with outstretched arms

Pediment The triangular front part of a building, usually surmounting a portico of columns

Polyptych Painting or carving on several joined wooden panels

Portico The covered entrance to a building

Punic Carthaginian/Phoenician

Scene-building Structure holding scenery in Greek/ Roman theatre

Stelae Inscribed stone slabs

Stereobate Visible base of any building, usually a temple

Stoa A detached roofed porch, or portico

Stylobate Raised base of a columned building, usually a temple

Telamon A supporting column in the shape of a male figure

Thermae Baths, usually elaborate buildings in Roman villas

Triptych Painting or carving on three joined wooden panels

ITALIAN WORDS

Aliscafo Hydrofoil

Anfiteatro Amphitheatre

Autostazione Bus station

Autostrada Motorway

Belvedere A lookout point

Cappella Chapel

Castello Castle

Cattedrale Cathedral

Centro Centre

Chiesa Church (main "mother" church, Chiesa Matrice/ Madre)

Comune An administrative area; also, the local council or the town hall

Corso Avenue/boulevard

Duomo Cathedral

Entrata Entrance

Faraglione Obelisk-shaped deposits of volcanic rock rising out of the sea

Festa Festival, carnival

Fiume River

Fumarola Volcanic vapour emission from the ground

Golfo Gulf

Lago Lake

Largo Place (like piazza)

Lungomare Seafront promenade or road

Mare Sea

Mercato Market

Mongibello Sicilian name for Mount Etna

Municipio Town hall

Palazzo Palace, mansion or block (of flats)

Parco Park

Passeggiata The customary early-evening walk

Pedaggio Toll

Piano Plain (also "slowly", "gently")

Piazza Square

Pineta Pinewood

Pro Loco Local office, usually funded by the Comune, overseeing cultural events and providing tourist information

Santuario Sanctuary

Sottopassaggio Subway

Spiaggia Beach

Stazione Station (train station is *stazione ferroviaria*; bus station is *autostazione*; ferry terminal is *stazione marittima*)

Strada Road/street

Teatro Theatre

Tempio Temple

Torre Tower

Traghetto Ferry

Uscita Exit

Vicolo/Vico Alley

Via Road (always used with name, as in Via Roma)

X Quick way of writing per, or for, and often found on timetables, which means the opposite of the English "ex". So, for example "aliscafo x Salina" refers to a hydrofoil to Salina.

Zona Zone

ACRONYMS

ACI Italian Automobile Club

FS Ferrovie Statali (Italian State Railways)

IVA Imposta Valore Aggiunto (VAT)

RAI The Italian state TV and radio network

SP Strada Provinciale; a minor road, eg SP116

SC Strada Comunale, a road maintained by the local council

SS Strada Statale; a main highway, eg SS120

ZTL Zona di Trafico Limitato – limited access area (eg for residents only)

Small print and index

A ROUGH GUIDE TO ROUGH GUIDES

Published in 1982, the first Rough Guide – to Greece – was a student scheme that became a publishing phenomenon. Mark Ellingham, a recent graduate in English from Bristol University, had been travelling in Greece the previous summer and couldn't find the right guidebook. With a small group of friends he wrote his own guide, combining a highly contemporary, journalistic style with a thoroughly practical approach to travellers' needs.

The immediate success of the book spawned a series that rapidly covered dozens of destinations. And, in addition to impecunious backpackers, Rough Guides soon acquired a much broader readership that relished the guides' wit and inquisitiveness as much as their enthusiastic, critical approach and value-for-money ethos.

These days, Rough Guides include recommendations from budget to luxury and cover more than 120 destinations around the globe, as well as producing an ever-growing range of eBooks.

Visit **roughguides.com** to find all our latest books, read articles, get inspired and share travel tips with the Rough Guides community.

Rough Guide credits

Editor: Polly Thomas
Layout: Pradeep Thapliyal
Cartography: Ashutosh Bharti
Picture editor: Rhiannon Furbear-Williams
Proofreader: Jan McCann
Managing editor: Monica Woods
Assistant editor: Dipika Dasgupta
Production: Charlotte Cade

Cover design: Nicole Newman, Rhiannon Furbear-Williams, Pradeep Thapliyal
Editorial assistants: Olivia Rawes and Rebecca Hallett
Senior pre-press designer: Dan May
Programme manager: Helen Blount
Publisher: Joanna Kirby

Publishing information

This ninth edition published May 2014 by
Rough Guides Ltd,
80 Strand, London WC2R 0RL
11, Community Centre, Panchsheel Park,
New Delhi 110017, India
Distributed by Penguin Random House
Penguin Books Ltd,
80 Strand, London WC2R 0RL
Penguin Group (USA)
345 Hudson Street, NY 10014, USA
Penguin Group (Australia)
250 Camberwell Road, Camberwell,
Victoria 3124, Australia
Penguin Group (NZ)
67 Apollo Drive, Mairangi Bay, Auckland 1310,
New Zealand
Penguin Group (South Africa)
Block D, Rosebank Office Park, 181 Jan Smuts Avenue,
Parktown North, Gauteng, South Africa 2193
Rough Guides is represented in Canada by Tourmaline
Editions Inc. 662 King Street West, Suite 304, Toronto,
Ontario M5V 1M7
Printed in Malaysia by Vivar Printing Sdn.Bhd

416pp includes index
A catalogue record for this book is available from the
British Library
ISBN: 978-1-40934-199-4
The publishers and authors have done their best to
ensure the accuracy and currency of all the information
in **The Rough Guide to Sicily**, however, they can accept
no responsibility for any loss, injury, or inconvenience
sustained by any traveller as a result of information or
advice contained in the guide.
3 5 7 9 8 6 4

MIX
Paper from
responsible sources
FSC™ C018179
www.fsc.org

Help us update

We've gone to a lot of effort to ensure that the ninth
edition of **The Rough Guide to Sicily** is accurate and up-
to-date. However, things change – places get "discovered",
opening hours are notoriously fickle, restaurants and
rooms raise prices or lower standards. If you feel we've got
it wrong or left something out, we'd like to know, and if
you can remember the address, the price, the hours, the
phone number, so much the better.

Please send your comments with the subject line
"**Rough Guide Sicily Update**" to ✆ mail@uk.roughguides
.com. We'll credit all contributions and send a copy of the
next edition (or any other Rough Guide if you prefer) for
the very best emails.
Find more travel information, connect with fellow
travellers and plan your trip on ⓦ roughguides.com

Acknowledgements

Ros Belford: On Salina, thanks to Emma, Gaetano, Max,
Ilana, Chiara, Alex, Corallina and Ondina Zangari; to Giulia
Profeti for a summer retreat in Valdichiesa; to Franco the
bus driver for being the "anima di Salina" and making
every day start well; to Pela for extraordinary insights; to
Annamaria and Nico for a magical night on the mountain;
and to the Costa family for letting Paolo Noce exist. To
Melo, Liviana, Silvana and Alessandra for letting me
make *Il Gambero* my office the week the internet died; to
Giorgia, Katerina, Elena and Cristiana for nine summers in
the piazza; and to Pina for moral support, sunset chasing
and making silicone jellyfish. Elsewhere in Sicily, thanks to
Franco Masera for showing me the footpaths of Filicudi; to
Michele Gallo for an amazing tour of Porto Empedocle; to
Antonio Sarnari and the artists of Il Gruppo di Scicli for an
unforgettable weekend; to the Missione Amici dei Santi
Angeli for an extraordinary opportunity; and to Sarah
Milthorpe, Hannah Milthorpe and Seby and Silvia at *Blu* in
Ortigia for aperitivi, moral support and trips to the beach
and Lidl. Most of all to Ismene, Juno and Giovanni.

ABOUT THE AUTHOR

Ros Belford co-authored the first edition of this guide, and has since written and broadcasted extensively about Italy and the Mediterranean. She has two daughters and spends as much time as she can on the Aoelian island of Salina.

Readers' updates

Thanks to all the readers who have taken the time to write in with comments and suggestions (and apologies if we've inadvertently omitted or misspelt anyone's name):

Richard Andrews; Amanda Brown; Angela Butler; Tim and Maggie Cawkwell; Vittorio LaCerva; Mark Dyer; Agnes and Paschal O'Flaherty; Gary French; Bernice Garlick; Gija Gee; Ian House; David Humphreys; Kyrie James; Carrie and Tim Johnson; Julia Keddie; Elizabeth Kelly; Andrew Kemp; Jan Ksienzyk; Sian Lerwill; Laura Maldonado; Ian and Mo Nelson; Didier Pico; Susan Plowden; Pedro Polla; Michael Brian Readhead; Louise Restell; Sofie Reynders; Michael Riding; Bonnie and Rick Salsman; Anna Searle; Doug Simpson; Jennifer Speake; Katie and Stever Tabor; Kevin Tierney; John Townend; Ian Valentine; Sue Watson; John White; Mikael Zacho.

Photo credits

Index

Maps are marked in grey

Map symbols

The symbols below are used on maps throughout the book

✈	Airport	⁘	Ruins	Gorge		🛕	Monastery
★	Bus stop	Ṫ	Gardens	Viewpoint		✝	Church (regional maps)
P	Parking	⊠-⊠	Gate	Cave			Church (town maps)
♦	Point of interest	⤚	Bridge	Campsite			Building
@	Internet access	≈	Pass	Lighthouse			Market
ⓘ	Tourist information	Mountain range		Tower			Stadium
✉	Post office	▲	Mountain peak	Wall			Cemetery
✚	Hospital	Cliff		Cable car			Park
♟	Museum	Rocks		Ferry route			Beach

Listings key

- ■ Accommodation
- ● Eating
- ■ Drinking and nightlife
- ● Shop/market

A ROUGH GUIDE TO
ROUGH GUIDES

Published in 1982, the first Rough Guide – to Greece – was a student scheme that became a publishing phenomenon. Mark Ellingham, a recent graduate in English from Bristol University, had been travelling in Greece the previous summer and couldn't find the right guidebook. With a small group of friends he wrote his own guide, combining a highly contemporary, journalistic style with a thoroughly practical approach to travellers' needs.

The immediate success of the book spawned a series that rapidly covered dozens of destinations. And, in addition to impecunious backpackers, Rough Guides soon acquired a much broader readership that relished the guides' wit and inquisitiveness as much as their enthusiastic, critical approach and value-for-money ethos.

These days, Rough Guides include recommendations from budget to luxury and cover more than 120 destinations around the globe. We also as produce an ever-growing range of eBooks. Visit Ⓦ roughguides.com to see our latest publications.

ROUGH GUIDES

WE GET AROUND

ONLINE start your journey at roughguides.com

EBOOKS & MOBILE APPS

GUIDEBOOKS from Amsterdam to Zanzibar

PHRASEBOOKS learn the lingo

MAPS so you don't get lost

GIFTBOOKS inspiration is our middle name

LIFESTYLE from iPads to climate change

...SO YOU CAN TOO

BOOKS | EBOOKS | APPS

Start your journey at **roughguides.com**
MAKE THE MOST OF YOUR TIME ON EARTH™